Encyclopedia of
Themes in Literature

MONTGOMERY COLLEGE
ROCKVILLE CAMPUS LIBRARY
ROCKVILLE, MARYLAND

Encyclopedia of Themes in Literature

VOLUME II

PART II: Authors F–M

Jennifer McClinton-Temple, Editor

✓ Facts On File

An imprint of Infobase Publishing

1348556

JUN 1 3 2011

Encyclopedia of Themes in Literature

Copyright © 2011 by Jennifer McClinton-Temple

All rights reserved. No part of this book may be reproduced or utilized in any form or by any means, electronic or mechanical, including photocopying, recording, or by any information storage or retrieval systems, without permission in writing from the publisher. For information contact:

Facts On File, Inc.
An imprint of Infobase Publishing
132 West 31st Street
New York NY 10001

Library of Congress Cataloging-in-Publication Data

McClinton-Temple, Jennifer.
  Encyclopedia of themes in literature / Jennifer McClinton-Temple.
     p. cm.
  Includes bibliographical references and index.
  ISBN 978-0-8160-7161-6 (hc : alk. paper) 1. English literature—Themes, motives—Encyclopedias.
2. American literature—Themes, motives—Encyclopedias. I. Title.
  PR19.M35 2010
  820.9'303—dc22   2009047605

Facts On File books are available at special discounts when purchased in bulk quantities for businesses, associations, institutions, or sales promotions. Please call our Special Sales Department in New York at (212) 967-8800 or (800) 322-8755.

You can find Facts On File on the World Wide Web at http://www.factsonfile.com

Text design by Kerry Casey
Composition by Hermitage Publishing Services
Cover printed by Sheridan Books, Ann Arbor, Mich.
Book printed and bound by Sheridan Books, Ann Arbor, Mich.
Date printed: December 2010
Printed in the United States of America

10 9 8 7 6 5 4 3 2 1

This book is printed on acid-free paper.

CONTENTS

PART II

Authors and Works F–M

FAULKNER, WILLIAM *As I Lay Dying* (1930)

As I Lay Dying, one of the finest examples of William Faulkner's distinctive writing style, was first published in 1930. The novel is the first to introduce Faulkner's fictional Yoknapatawpha County, which serves as the setting for many of his novels and short stories. As in his other works, *As I Lay Dying* showcases Faulkner's ability to reveal the intricacy of the human psyche.

Told from multiple perspectives, the novel has 59 sections written mostly in stream-of-consciousness—a literary style marked by a character's uninterrupted flow of thoughts. Also, Faulkner uniquely employs symbols throughout his work. For example, he substitutes a coffin symbol in place of the actual word and uses a blank space when one of his characters is unable to express her thoughts.

As I Lay Dying tells the story of the Bundrens—a poor family from the Deep South—that faces trials and tragedy on their journey to bury their dead wife and mother in the town of Jefferson. Throughout the story, the reader is introduced to the family members and discovers that each has his or her own reason for traveling to Jefferson. For instance, Anse Bundren, husband and father, sets off for Jefferson to buy a new set of teeth and to remarry, while his daughter, Dewey Dell, goes to town to get an abortion. Each character shares his or her perspective on the journey, with the exception of Jewel Bundren, the only character who does not have his own section. Through the Bundrens' expedition, Faulkner discusses such themes as FAMILY, DEATH, INDIVIDUAL AND SOCIETY, RELIGION, and SUFFERING.

As I Lay Dying is a complex story that causes the reader to question the characters' motives in their actions and interpretations of events. Most of all, it is a story that explores the complexities of human nature.

HanaRae Dudek

FAMILY in *As I Lay Dying*

William Faulkner's *As I Lay Dying* centers on the Bundrens—a poor southern family that embarks on a journey to the town of Jefferson to bury the dead wife and mother. Throughout the novel, the Bundrens exhibit their dysfunctional relationships with one another as each family member offers his or her own perspective on the other characters and their actions. In *As I Lay Dying*, Faulkner demonstrates how a group of people can band together in times of adversity and tragedy yet can criticize and even abandon each other in pursuit of their own selfish exploits—all in the name of "family."

From the beginning of the novel, members of the Bundren family display their complex relationships with one another. While Addie Bundren lies dying, her son Cash builds a coffin outside of her window.

He insists on finishing the coffin because he values his carpentry work more than spending time with his ailing mother. However, Cash also believes that he is helping her more by building her coffin than he could if he were sitting with her inside of the house. Surprisingly, Addie does not seem offended by her son building the coffin right in front of her.

When Addie dies, her husband, Anse, insists upon the family traveling to Jefferson to bury his wife, at any cost. He maintains that she must be buried in Jefferson because that had been Addie's only request. Seemingly, all of the children agree to travel to Jefferson in order to fulfill their mother's wish. However, each family member—with the exception of Jewel—reveals his or her own reasons for going into town. For example, Anse admits that he wants a new set of teeth. Cash wants to display his carpentry work and look for a gramophone. Although not directly, Dewey Dell reveals that she is pregnant and wants an abortion, and the youngest, Vardaman, wants a toy train. While he does not have a materialistic desire, Darl travels to Jefferson in order to keep track of his family's actions and to make sure his mother gets her burial.

Throughout their journey, the Bundrens face multiple obstacles. For example, Vardaman, who does not fully comprehend his mother's death, drills into Addie's face while trying to create air holes in the coffin so that the corpse can "breathe." Also, when the family discovers that a bridge has collapsed, they ford a river, dragging Addie's coffin under water. Cash breaks his leg while trying to rescue the coffin. Then, when the family stops at Gillespie's, a local farm, the barn burns down—almost destroying the coffin.

Although the family seems to work together in its struggle to get Addie to Jefferson, each family member works to fulfill his or her own desires. For instance, the Bundrens could have spent the evening at a neighbor's home instead of dragging Addie's coffin through the river. Also, Cash reveals that he jumps into the river not only to rescue the coffin, but also to retrieve his carpentry tools. Later, Anse sells Jewel's beloved horse in order to buy a new team of mules. Even Addie speaks from the coffin to reveal her selfishness. She admits to having an extramarital affair with the local preacher, who is Jewel's biologi-

cal father. Further, Addie admits that she wants to be buried in Jefferson because she wants to spend eternity as far away from the Bundrens as possible.

Throughout the expedition, Darl—the son whom most people refer to as "queer" because of his alleged telepathic ability—is the only Bundren who questions the family's motives. After eight days, Darl tires of the spectacle of dragging his mother's corpse through the county and sets fire to Gillespie's barn in an attempt to burn the coffin and Addie's putrefied body. Out of respect for his mother and a belief that she should have been buried earlier, Darl tries to burn the coffin in one of the most selfless acts in the novel. Ironically, the rest of the Bundren family deems Darl insane and has workers from a sanitarium take him away from the middle of town shortly after Addie's burial.

After facing the difficulties of the journey to Jefferson, the Bundrens remain unified at the end of the novel. When Anse gets his new teeth, he immediately remarries and introduces his children to the new Mrs. Bundren. Perhaps from their own understanding of selfishness, the children are able to accept their father's actions. Through the Bundrens in *As I Lay Dying,* Faulkner explores the complexities of human beings and their relationships with one another and demonstrates that each member of a family is, after all, only human.

HanaRae Dudek

GRIEF in *As I Lay Dying*

Within the confines of the narrative in *As I Lay Dying*, grief clouds the day to day existence at the Bundren household. While Addie Bundren lies on her deathbed, her children and husband negotiate their way through her imminent but uncertain death, the urgency to prepare a coffin for her, arranging for her burial far away in another town, as Addie so desires, and the need for the FAMILY to not let go of the opportunity to earn a few more dollars. Life among the southern American poor must be lived on a daily basis.

Faulkner accords grief a palpable presence in the novella. We share the burden of grief that envelops the Bundrens as well as those it touches incidentally, such as the neighbors. Faulkner also allows us a glimpse into the minds of characters through a series of monologues, which is the narrative strategy of the novella. The Bundrens articulate their anguish, which arises from a death in the family as much as from life's larger context in which death is only one of life's many preoccupations. Faulkner's remarkable plotting lets us discover their secret sorrows—as opposed to their public distress couched in the death of a mother and wife—after we have fully absorbed their settled grief resulting from Addie's death and the family's struggle to reach Jefferson for her burial in extremely inclement weather that thwarts their intentions in more ways than one. As seen in Cash's painful injuries, his father's thoughtless handling of his son's predicament, Dewey Dell's unwanted pregnancy, her seduction, her struggle to secure an abortion and Jewel's sense of betrayal when his father deprives him of his beloved horse he had bought with money earned through hard labor, Darl's descent into insanity and his incarceration for arson, the local minister Whitfield's battle with his conscience to confess his adulterous relationship with Addie and the fact of Jewel being their bastard son—grief is a factor in their lives, generally and individually.

As they confront their grief and deal with their grief-stricken lives, the Bundrens may appear passive and helpless. But they establish an inescapable truth of the human condition when they accept that life must go on. If their grief appears to have no sting, that is how it appears on the surface. Their sorrows are, much like uninvited guests, both a distressing burden as well as an unavoidable component of existence.

However sharply and richly drawn they strike the readers, the characters in *As I Lay Dying* draw their vivid fashioning from belonging to a group. Even though Anse and his children form a family, they act more like Thomas Hardy's rustics, motivated by common desires and a common code of life and living. Often reminiscent of the humorous dimensions in Hardy's rustics, the Bundrens' tragic drama is played out in comic terms. Addie had been laid in her coffin "head to foot so it won't crush her dress. It was her wedding dress and it had a flare-out bottom, and they had laid her head to foot in it so the dress could be spread out, . . ." No conflicts mar their homogeneity as a family and a group. They seem bound to stay committed to each other. The neighbors and others who are close to them must participate, as members of the community, in such common occurrences of life as Addie's death and Sunday rituals.

Such being the case, Faulkner's treatment of grief takes the form of a living rendering of the fate of a community rather than a scrutiny of the grief-stricken heart of an individual. "Doom" and "defeat" are words often used to describe Faulkner's characters. As Ralph Waldo Emerson said in another context, "There are people who have an appetite for grief." But the Bundrens counter grief with strategies of survival as well as their ability to withstand pressure. Above all, they endure.

Addie's monologue points to deeper meanings in human existence and suggests a pragmatic view of life. Life is important. Living is important. Whether one lives in joy or in sorrow is of little consequence. Addie breaks open the cocoon of inherited familiarities when she says: "One day I was talking to Cora. She prayed for me because she believed I was blind to sin, wanting me to kneel and pray too, because to people to whom sin is just a matter of words, to them salvation is words too." She thus offers testimony to the truth of her father's words—". . . the reason for living was to get ready to stay dead for a long time" —as well as to the inevitability of grief and anguish as the defining values of human existence.

Gulshan Taneja

FAULKNER, WILLIAM *Light in August* (1932)

At the center of William Faulkner's novel *Light in August* is the story of Joe Christmas. He is a loner who knows he is part-black and part-white, but cannot identify with either of the racially divided communities. The novel traces Christmas's life, from his time as a young child in an orphanage to when he is adopted by a cold, Christian man and his feeble-minded wife, to his arrival in Jefferson, Mississippi. He works in a sawmill there before quitting to sell moonshine. Eventually he is accused by the town of murdering a white woman, Joanna Burden.

Intertwined with Christmas's story is Lena Grove's story. The two characters never meet, but are connected by their relationship with other characters in the book, including Byron Bunch, Joe Brown, and the Reverend Gail Hightower. Lena is a poor young girl who is pregnant and intent on finding the father of her child—a man whom she calls Lucas Burch but everyone else knows as Joe Brown. Lena, who has nothing but her baby, serves as a foil to Christmas's repudiation of the community. She is repudiated by some members in the community for being an unwed mother, but embraced by others because of her needy situation. Faulkner explains that Lena represents "the basic possibility for happiness and goodness."

Light in August can be read as a powerful commentary on RACE and racial matters in the United States, particularly in the Deep South in the 1930s. RELIGION functions in the book as an elitist set of principles, meant to exclude people like Christmas. Christmas and Lena are each examples of the INDIVIDUAL who moves through a SOCIETY that judges and spurns them. Society, in *Light in August*, functions as a gossiping mob, rejecting those who do not conform to its standards of propriety or respectability.

Elizabeth Cornell

INDIVIDUAL AND SOCIETY in *Light in August*

"Man knows so little about his fellows" observes the unnamed narrator in William Faulkner's *Light in August*. This line seems to summarize what is true throughout the novel: Neither the community of Jefferson nor the book's major characters who move on the community's margins know much about each other. Everyone depends upon gossip to speculate why anyone acts or speaks in a particular way. Unless individuals conform to certain norms and values, they may be judged or condemned by society, rather than supported and empowered by it. The lack of open, honest communication between the INDIVIDUAL AND SOCIETY often has negative results.

Perhaps the character in the book most condemned by society is Joe Christmas. His mother dies in childbirth and from that point he moves through the world as an individual without home, family, or community, living on the fringes of society. Faulkner describes Joe as "a phantom, a spirit, straight out of its own world, and lost." Although

Christmas passes as a white man, his mixed racial background causes him to feel disconnected from society. He lives on the outskirts of Jefferson and rarely interacts with the community; the townspeople can only speculate about his private life. His repudiation of society works against him most clearly when Joanna Burden is murdered. Although they have no concrete evidence, the townspeople conjecture that only a black person could commit such a grisly crime. When Joe Brown comes forward and accuses Christmas of the murder and supports his accusation by revealing that Christmas is part-black, the town quickly convinces itself of Christmas's guilt: "He don't look any more like a nigger than I do," says one townsperson. "But it must have been the nigger blood in him" that made him commit such an awful crime. No one knows for sure if Christmas murdered Joanna, but they need a murderer. Christmas—a man who has shunned their society—perfectly fits their profile.

Like Christmas, Joanna Burden lives on the outskirts of Jefferson. She associates not with the respectable white folks in town, but with black families who live nearby. The town regards her with "astonishment and outrage," and will never "forgive her and let her be dead in peace and quiet." Further, her death provides the townspeople with "an emotional barbecue, a Roman holiday" in which they can gossip about her private life and speculate about the "Negro" they believe ravished her before killing her. The town thinks she deserved to die this way because of her sympathetic dealings with black people. Nonetheless, because she is a white woman, her murder must be avenged. It is an excuse for the town to form a posse and find a suitable black suspect.

The Reverend Gail Hightower is also shunned and gossiped about by Jefferson society. He is burdened and obsessed by his family's Confederate past, which contributes to his alienation from society. Hightower's single friend, Byron Bunch, manages to glean from the townspeople details about the minister's complex past. Hightower arrived in Jefferson with his wife years ago, but his wife started acting strangely and later killed herself at a Memphis hotel. The town blames Hightower for these events, even though no one knows the true story. The town believes he caused his wife to "go bad" and that he "was not a natural husband, a natural man." Byron recognizes the insidiousness of this small-town gossip, where an "idea, a single idle word blown from mind to mind" can be driven out of proportion. Hightower refuses to leave Jefferson after his wife's death because the family ghosts reside in Jefferson; the burden of the past is too strong. He lives alone, spurning the town just as the town spurns him. It is only when he delivers Lena Grove's baby, and tries to protect Joe Christmas from the angry mob, that he can heal his troubled relationship with the past and, in effect, feel comfortable about his place in society.

Lena Grove seems to be a counterbalance to all the loners who populate this novel. Lena is unwed, poor, pregnant, without family or permanent home. Gossip about her situation follows in her wake wherever she goes. But Lena carries tremendous faith that everything will work out. She accepts her situation without struggling against it, and can journey through southern towns thanks to the "folks taking good care of her." Society, as this novel shows, can be cruel and heartless, particularly toward individuals who do not conform. But, as seen with Lena, that is not entirely true. Ultimately, the human heart has enough compassion so that society will not destroy itself. Faulkner puts it best in his 1951 Nobel Prize speech: "I believe that man will not merely endure: he will prevail. He is immortal . . . because he has a soul, a spirit capable of compassion and sacrifice and endurance."

Elizabeth Cornell

RACE in *Light in August*

Perhaps no subject in American culture is more controversial than race. Throughout his work, William Faulkner examines how race divides individuals, families, and entire communities. *Light in August* is no exception. At the center of this story is the shadowy figure of Joe Christmas, whose mother was white and father most likely black. The dietitian at the orphanage where he lives until he is five years old makes him aware of how being part-black can be used against him by people in power. It is there that he learns the importance of concealing this part of himself. As an adult, Joe shifts between white and black worlds, failing to find comfort in either

one. When he briefly lives in a black community in Chicago, he shuns whites and attempts to become fully "Negro," "trying to breathe into himself" their essence, "the dark and inscrutable thinking and being" of black people, but fails. One of the tragedies about Joe Christmas is that it is impossible for him to be either all black or all white; he is both, in a society that refuses to accept someone who is not "pure."

Prejudice and racism against those who are different prevent people from accepting Joe. Part of the problem are the negative and untruthful stereotypes that white people perpetuate against blacks, such as laziness and dishonesty. Joe Brown insists that the only black people who work hard must be slaves. But Christmas disproves the stereotype: He works hard and solidly, first on his adoptive father's farm, then at the mill in Jefferson. Later, he develops a successful business selling moonshine. He is no more dishonest for selling the illegal liquor than the upright white fathers and brothers who buy it from him. In fact, Brown, who is white, more clearly fulfills the negative stereotypes about blacks than Christmas. When Brown quits the job at the mill for the easier and more lucrative job of selling moonshine for Christmas, he is seen around town "idle, destinationless, and constant . . . lolling behind the wheel" of a new car. Faulkner's intent here, which can be found throughout his body of work, is to confront the white hypocrisy embedded in negative stereotypes of blacks.

Joe Brown's repeated assertion of his whiteness after the murder of Joanna Burden is a good example of how important it is to be white in this southern community. The townspeople believe only a black man is capable of such a grisly murder; their sense of community is linked in part by this accusation and their shared racism and prejudice. Hightower puts the situation best when he learns Joe Christmas has "negro blood" and is accused of the crime: "Think Byron; what it will mean when the people—if they catch . . . Poor man. Poor mankind." Hightower knows that, if given the chance, some people would lynch Christmas.

Hightower's statement no doubt refers to white supremacists like Percy Grimm. Grimm, under the pretense of protecting America and the white race, organizes a group of men to be ready for action should such an opportunity occur to lynch Christmas. The opportunity does arise when Christmas escapes from prison and Grimm chases after him on a bicycle. Grimm tracks him to Hightower's house where Christmas takes refuge. In this grisly scene, Grimm castrates and then murders Christmas.

Faulkner's liberal use of the words "Negro" and "nigger" in his work has caused some readers to label him a racist, or at least consider the possibility. Most Faulkner scholars disagree with this assessment. These words were commonly used in the United States in the early 20th century. "Nigger" was used pejoratively by some whites to refer to blacks, and "Negro" was commonly used by blacks and whites. If Faulkner had written *Light in August* without using these words, some of the book's power might have been diminished. Moreover, it is important to separate the author from his work. In the 1950s, when the Civil Rights movement began, Faulkner was outspoken in his support of a move away from segregation and supported equal rights for black people. Although he received much criticism in the South for this position, even from his own family and friends, he maintained this position until his death in 1962. Works such as *Light in August* are a testament to his belief that racism and prejudice are not only wrong but also a detriment to society.

Elizabeth Cornell

RELIGION in *Light in August*

In William Faulkner's novel, *Light in August,* the use and abuse of the Christian religion is a significant theme. Simon McEachern and Joanna Burden are two characters who rely on biblical texts and Christian orthodoxy to justify their hypocritical views and destructive behavior. In various ways, they believe a God-given knowledge exists "out there," independent of human thought or invention. Only certain, chosen people are privy to this knowledge, a knowledge that often gives them the sense they are superior to everyone else. Joe Christmas is one whom the chosen consider to be among the unchosen.

Simon McEachern uses religion as an excuse for abusing another human being. When he adopts Christmas, he vows to raise him to "grow up to fear God and abhor idleness and vanity despite his ori-

gin." McEachern's disdain for Christmas's origin—that is, a child likely conceived in sin rather than in a marriage bed (he does not know about Christmas's racial background)—indicates his view that Christmas is not, unlike himself, among God's chosen. It is because of McEachern that Christmas's distaste for religion develops early on, and he refuses to learn the Presbyterian catechism that McEachern forces upon him. In response, McEachern whips Christmas and deprives him of food, using religion as justification for this abuse. Later, McEachern uses religion as his justification to condemn Christmas's act of dating the waitress, Bobbie. When McEachern discovers them together at a dance, he perceives himself as "just and rocklike" and as an "actual representative of the wrathful and retributive Throne" before he attacks Christmas. But Christmas sees only the "face of Satan" and kills McEachern with a chair.

Like McEachern, Joanna Burden believes she is among the chosen to interpret God's word and share it with others such as Joe Christmas. But long before the crucial moment when Joanna asks Christmas to kneel and pray with her, the two have carried on a passionate, animal-like love affair. Christmas has awakened the sexual appetite of a starved woman described as a "New England glacier exposed suddenly to the fire of the New England biblical hell." The pleasure she experiences with Christmas seems to be as much derived from her knowledge that he is a black man (miscegenation is taboo) as the idea of her living "not alone in sin but in filth" too. Joanna's gleeful rejection of religion exposes how deeply repressive religious beliefs can be on basic human desires.

The relationship, however, quickly becomes one in which Christmas feels Joanna is attempting to dominate him. She offers to send him to law school for blacks and insists on bearing his child; Christmas refuses to comply. He does not want her to determine the course of his life. Her sense of superiority over him is most concretely exposed when, after the passion in the relationship is nearly extinct, she asks Christmas to kneel with her and pray: "It is not I who ask it. Kneel with me.'" Her statement implies her belief that she has a direct connection with God and he does not. Christmas does not believe in this bond, and refuses to pray with her, even when she points an old revolver at him. Once again, because of an individual acting upon an elitist interpretation of Christian belief, Christmas believes he has no choice but to kill.

Joe Christmas has no use for the so-called God-given spiritual knowledge possessed by many characters in this book, in part because this is the religion of white people, and he does not feel a part of this group. The serious and troubled conflict about who he is and what he is aligns him with Christian martyrs, ascetics, and Christ himself. Indeed, contrary to what McEachern and Burden believe, understanding God and being a spiritual being is no easy task. The path to enlightenment is difficult and treacherous and the journey itself may be as important as the goal. This difficult journey makes us human. Christmas's struggle in a world bent on destroying him humanizes him in a way that Christ's struggles in a hostile world put a human face on Christianity. McEachern and Burden's elitist, inhuman brand of Christianity is the kind that hurts and destroys others as well as themselves—precisely not the kind taught by Christ.

Elizabeth Cornell

FAULKNER, WILLIAM   "A Rose for Emily" (1930, 1931)

"A Rose for Emily," first published in the April 1930 issue of *Forum* magazine, may be William Faulkner's most widely read short story. A slightly amended version was published in *These 13* (1931) and later in *Collected Stories* (1950). The story has received critical attention because of the ways in which it highlights several recurrent themes that appear in Faulkner's longer works (such as repressed sexuality, loss and GRIEF, and commentary on SOCIAL CLASS).

Faulkner presents the story in five non-linear sections and employs an unnamed, first-person plural narrator to relay the details of Miss Emily Grierson's life. The short story contrasts Miss Emily's early life of social privilege against her later life of ALIENATION and financial struggles following the death of her repressive father and the sudden loss of her romantic partner. Faulkner explores the standards of social customs through the telling of several different scenes, such as the town leaders' attempts

to save Miss Emily embarrassment over unpaid taxes or the stench of her property. Most important, the narration explores the consequences of Miss Emily's unorthodox relationship with the lower-class Homer Barron and the subsequent town gossip it incites. Despite the foreshadowing of a gothic ending, it is not until Miss Emily's death and the townspeople's exploration of her previously shut-up home that the gruesome facts of Miss Emily's life become apparent. Miss Emily poisoned Homer Barron years earlier and had since been sleeping next to the disintegrating corpse in what would have been their marriage bed. The narrative makes important comments about the literary themes of DEATH, ALIENATION, COMMUNITY, SOCIAL CLASS, AND GENDER.

Jennifer Smith

DEATH in "A Rose for Emily"

Within this short work, Faulkner presents compelling, but occasionally contradictory, views of death. In this tale, death functions as a process that not only can provide moments of clarity and revelation but also can yield more unresolved questions than answers. Faulkner bookends the tale of Miss Emily's life with a narration surrounding the scene of her death and, in doing so, suggests the very important role that this phenomenon plays in how we come to know and understand this character.

The tale starts with the narrative of the moments following Miss Emily's death. The town has remained fascinated by Miss Emily throughout her life, and only upon her death are the townspeople able to begin to satisfy some of their curiosity about the woman who held such a respected place in Jefferson County for the better half of a century. Miss Emily's death breaks the societal spell that she held over the town in her life, and permits the townspeople to begin to illuminate the puzzle of her later years. Death becomes a moment of revelation. Indeed, it is only upon Miss Emily's death and the subsequent exploration of her previously unseen living quarters that the townspeople are able to understand fully the truly grotesque nature of her later life. Yet despite this level of exposure that her passing engenders, Miss Emily's death also brings forth even greater questions about her life.

Faulkner marks the major milestones in Miss Emily's life by the death of men important to her—first the death of her father and then the death of Homer Barron. Many might herald the death of Miss Emily's father, a man who repressed Miss Emily for most of her CHILDHOOD and young adult life, as a welcome relief from the tyranny of her father's house. Yet this is not the case for Miss Emily. Miss Emily is instead in a perpetual state of delusion regarding the very real instances of death that surround her. The day after her father's death, Miss Emily does not register any signs of grief on her face, and, upon the arrival of townswomen bringing condolences to the house, Miss Emily denies the fact that her father has died at all. She continues this denial for three days until she finally allows the burial of the body—under the threat of legal actions. Miss Emily's actions upon this first major death in her life suggest the danger of remaining stuck in this first stage of GRIEF for an extended period, and foreshadow the irrational approach that Miss Emily takes toward her later relationship with Homer Barron. Miss Emily, denied so many of the human connections that life offers, is unwilling or unable to function in terms of everyday society.

Of course, the scene that most memorably presents the phenomenon of death and our varied reactions to it is the one centered on Homer Barron's gruesome disappearance. The moment of revelation comes when we find, along with the townspeople, the long-deceased body of Homer Barron that lies in Miss Emily's wedding bed, assembled in a posture of affection. The plot of the text finally comes together as we realize that Miss Emily likely poisoned Homer and has since lain with the dead body as though every night was their wedding night. Yet this instance of death brings forth so many more questions than it answers, not least of which is the question of why Miss Emily decided to kill Homer Barron at all. Why would Miss Emily, so unwilling to accept the death of her father, the only man previously in her life, prematurely take the life of a man she loved?

Death functions within this tale in several different ways. It iterates the human preoccupation we have with denying death at all costs, even in the face of inescapable evidence. The assembled scenes also highlight the many questions that we have about death, life, and the inner workings of an individual mind. Many readers find the gothic scene Faulkner creates here to be incomprehensible in several ways, especially concerning what it might suggest about human life and death. Yet Faulkner's tale also reveals much about the ways in which we are fascinated by the cycle of life and our responses to it, and makes interesting commentary about the complex role that death plays in how we understand life and each other.

Jennifer Smith

SOCIAL CLASS in "A Rose for Emily"

"A Rose for Emily" highlights the ways in which human beings function in socially stratified communities, commenting on the social mores that class depends upon as well as the psychological and sociological consequences such hierarchies inspire. Though many highlight the individual psychological dementia of Miss Emily as the generative force behind Faulkner's dismal ending, failure to consider the social implications of this ending leads only to a very flat understanding of the tale. The plural narrator establishes Miss Emily at the outset of the tale to be a figure of social esteem within the community of Jefferson. Indeed, in the first line, the narrator refers to the late Miss Emily as a "fallen monument"—a term that well describes the role that she fulfilled in this stratified society. Yet Faulkner does not just rest in establishing the different social classes that exist in Jefferson; he also makes artful commentary on the ways that such societal standards come into play through the hopes and feelings that inhabitants of a given COMMUNITY might have toward one another.

Miss Emily is one of the last holdouts of a gentrified society—and the narrator constantly remarks upon this fact through his characterizations of her. Upon Miss Emily's entrance into a room, men rise. The town leaders hold special tax meetings in order to discuss Miss Emily's unique case, and, ultimately, make an exception to customarily rigid tax laws for the sake of Miss Emily's honor. Honorable men of the town prowl about like burglars outside of her house, sprinkling lime rather than risking the embarrassment of having to suggest to Miss Emily that her property stinks. It is clear that Miss Emily holds a special standard in the town of Jefferson. Yet what responses does this situation invoke?

Social class comes into play frequently in the reactions that Miss Emily's misfortunes inspire in the community. As Miss Emily continues to age and does not settle down with a husband in her early adult life, the townsfolk express a general feeling of vindication; while they are not exactly happy, they are comforted in their belief that Miss Emily and her family had tried to hold themselves too far above the average man. One can imagine that, had Miss Emily been a poverty-stricken unfortunate when her father died, and had since remained unmarried, the town's general reaction to her situation might have included more empathetic responses.

As the narrative progresses, the townspeople come to regard Miss Emily with a seemingly deeper pity, and though they worry over her, they seem resigned to Miss Emily's fate as a lonely, unmarried woman. It may be a shock, for the reader to comprehend that when Miss Emily does seem to find happiness in her relationship with Homer Barron, the class differences between the two incite even more gossip among the townspeople. Because of the place that Miss Emily's family once held in the socially divided society, she seems forever relegated to the outskirts of that community, and purposefully excluded from the general society of her fellow townspeople.

Another aspect that one must consider when thinking about social class in this tale is that of the context in which Faulkner was writing. Faulkner comments on the ideals of a deeply stratified southern society throughout the tale, and points the reader to the potentially negative effects this degree of stratification inspires. The close of the tale reveals Miss Emily's necrophilia, and, at the same time, points an accusing finger at the townspeople for committing the same metaphorical crime. Unable to live in the present moment, the town, like Miss Emily, continually dallies with a past that is long over but still haunts the communal mind-set. Miss Emily's family dates back to a prior generation of community members who upheld much different standards about power structures in society—a generation well versed in the expectations of antebellum America. The community members of Jefferson County who remain fascinated with Miss Emily are also transfixed by an image of a society divided. Jefferson County may have long ago abolished slavery, but the habits and mentality that such a divisive practice instilled in its inhabitants remain very well entrenched.

To attempt to understand "A Rose for Emily" without accounting for the varied and significant ways in which social matters influence the text is to take an overly simplistic approach to the work. In this tale, Faulkner makes some not-so-subtle comments on the dangerously pervasive ways in which social roles can divide communities. Exploring representations of social standards in Jefferson County helps us to understand better Miss Emily's character, the reasons behind her questionable actions, and the responses that these events provoke.

Jennifer Smith

FAULKNER, WILLIAM   *The Sound and the Fury* (1929)

William Faulkner's *The Sound and the Fury* began as a short story centered around some children who are sent away from their grandmother's funeral to protect them from the sight of grieving adults. After Faulkner wrote the story, he became interested in the relationship of a "truly innocent" child to the world. That child became Benjy Compson, a mentally handicapped 33-year-old man who narrates the first section of the book. Faulkner recognized, however, that the erratic time shifts in Benjy's section made the story difficult to understand, so he wrote three more sections, each time retelling the story in an attempt to make it clearer. What emerged was a novel about the sibling love and lost innocence within the relationships between Caddy Compson and her three brothers, Quentin, Jason, and Benjy. The book is also about the slow decline of the Compsons, a family that has seen its reputation and finances fall upon hard times amid the dying traditions of the old South. Each of the three sections is narrated by a different brother, who provides his perspective of this story. In the last section, the story is told by an unidentified narrator and features a detailed portrait of the family's loyal black servant, Dilsey Gibson.

Faulkner, who won the 1949 Nobel Prize for his literary achievements, considered his masterpiece a "splendid failure" because he felt he never got the story right. Readers, however, know otherwise. Although *The Sound and the Fury* can be challenging, especially to first-time readers, its themes and style are quintessentially American and modern. The book's influence on writers has been far-reaching since it was first published in 1929.

Elizabeth Cornell

GRIEF in *The Sound and the Fury*

After Caddy Compson is exiled from the Compson household, the doomed family of William Faulkner's *The Sound and the Fury* must cope with the loss of their only daughter. The mentally handicapped Benjy has essentially lost the one family member (besides their servant, Dilsey) who expresses love for him. Although his vivid memories of his sister Caddy give him the impression that her loving presence still exists, whenever he is thrust back into the present his grief over her absence is painfully rehabilitated. His brother Jason's grief takes the form of bitterness and vengeance. Caddy's divorce prevented Jason from getting a job with her husband in a bank, and he is now responsible for her daughter. Jason's theft of the money she sends to support her daughter is a form of revenge against Caddy, but the money he takes may also be seen as compensation for the loss of his sister. Although Jason's pilfering may be partly to blame for the unruly behavior exhibited by Caddy's daughter, Quentin, her rebellion is also an angry response of grief over her mother's absence from her childhood. Finally, since Caddy never presents her side of the story, readers experience a kind of loss of her as well. Like Miss Quentin, we are mainly left to speculate about her, gathering what little we can from the subjective viewpoints of others.

One such viewpoint belongs to Caddy's brother, Quentin. He cannot believe that he will one day recover from the hurt he feels. That hurt is caused by Caddy's lost virginity and marriage, and Quentin knows the passage of time will make this pain fade. Thus, he is obsessed with time from the moment he awakens each day. Quentin breaks his pocket watch in an attempt to stop time, as if to prevent his cherished memories of Caddy from fading and thus leading to the diminishment of his grief and hurt. But Quentin's handless watch keeps ticking; the changing sunlight, his persistent shadow, and the hourly church bells are other reminders of passing time. He realizes time cannot be escaped, prevented from passing, or reversed. Quentin's loss is such that he cannot visualize a future in which he might be reunited with his sister or even transcend his deep grief. Taking his life is the only way Quentin can imagine stopping time and keeping his grief intact.

Although Caddy is certainly his greatest loss, Benjy undergoes other significant experiences of loss. He loses his field next door when the Compsons sell it to developers for a golf course so Quentin can go to Harvard. One consequence is that he must suffer the experience of hearing the word *caddy* throughout the day, reminding him anew of his grief over Caddy's absence. His testicles are another loss—removed after he chased a neighbor girl, who he believed was Caddy. Mrs. Compson changes his name from Maury to Benjamin, a name that means "son of my sorrow," because she considers his condition "a judgment" on her. Benjy's bellowing, which disturbs every character in the book, is a potent expression of grief for everything he and each Compson has lost.

No one feels more persecuted by those losses than Mrs. Compson. She wonders what she has done to deserve a mentally challenged son, a selfish daughter, a son who kills himself, an unruly granddaughter, and a husband who drinks himself to death. Only Jason, she claims, has never given her "one moment's sorrow," although Jason has done many things behind her back that would give her grief. When Miss Quentin disappears, Mrs. Compson leaps to the conclusion that her granddaughter has also committed suicide. She seems to thrive on these occurrences of loss, and blames them for her sickly, confined life. Rather than grieve for her losses and set an example of strength by moving forward in spite of everything, Mrs. Compson takes to her bed as if nothing more can be done but wait for the next round of loss and grief.

With such an oppressive atmosphere of loss and unresolved grief surrounding the Compson household, there seems little hope of anyone thriving there. No wonder Caddy and her daughter must each seek their escape, and as far from Jefferson as possible. No wonder Quentin must take his own life. Of all the characters, only Dilsey, the family's servant, seems to have coping tools. When she cries during the Easter service, her tears feel like a natural and much needed release. When Dilsey says "I seed de first and de last," she indicates her ability to hope, to have courage and love, and endure in a world filled with constant and pervasive loss.

Elizabeth Cornell

LOVE in *The Sound and the Fury*

Love is a powerful and destructive force that threads through William Faulkner's *The Sound and the Fury.* One focus of love in the novel is Caddy Compson. Her brother, Benjy, is frequently flooded with memories of his exiled sister. He remembers that, of all the Compsons, Caddy conveyed the most compassion, understanding, and love for him during his childhood. He depended on her gentle care and words: "You've got your Caddy" she often reassured him. Unlike the rest of the family, Caddy enjoyed playing with him and taking care of him. For example, she made sure he wore gloves on a cold day. Yet even with his limited mental faculties, Benjy could sense when Caddy's love for him was threatened. He cried at the sight of her muddy drawers, which may be read as representing her developing sexuality. Later, he became upset at the smell of her perfume, which can be understood as representing the loss of her virginity. At Caddy's wedding, he bellowed at the sight of her veil. In each instance, Caddy was there to comfort him. Following her exile, however, in the present time of the book, Benjy is left only with memories of her. Thus, whenever he hears the word "caddy" echoing from the golf course next door, it reminds him of her and causes him to bellow. Since Caddy is no longer there to soothe him, his consolation comes in substitute love objects, such as a slipper or a flower. Benjy's obsession over his absent sister's love becomes a destructive force in his life because he is unable to accept solace or love from anyone else, even from the family's compassionate and loving servant, Dilsey.

Quentin's love for his sister is no less deep than Benjy's, but more conflicted and complex. Quentin cannot bear that his sister might love anyone but him, and his chivalric attempts to defend her honor fail. Thus, the loss of her virginity, and her later marriage to Herbert, whom Quentin knows she marries only because she is pregnant by another man, affect him deeply. He loves Caddy so much that he wishes the "world would roar away" and leave them alone together. At one point, Quentin pretends he has committed incest with her, but his father knows he is lying. Quentin cannot bear, as his father points out, to think that someday his memories of Caddy will fade and that his love for her might ebb. The keen pain Quentin feels about his sister's circumstances keeps his love and memories fresh. But Quentin knows his father's words bear truth. Suicide is the only way Quentin can stop time and prevent his love for her from diminishing, as well as escape the guilt from his incestuous feelings toward her.

Jason, whom Faulkner considered his most evil character, is clearly not Caddy's most loving brother. Jason's bitterness over Caddy's absence is taken out on her teen-aged daughter, Quentin, for whom he is responsible. Each month, Jason brings his mother a fake copy of the check Caddy sends to support Quentin, which Mrs. Compson burns. Jason secretly cashes the check and keeps the money. Caddy's money functions as a substitute for the love she has withheld from him. Jason's actions also attempt to deprive Caddy of her daughter's love, just as Caddy deprived him. By leading his niece, Quentin, to think she is supported by him, Jason believes he is entitled to her loyalty and obedience, if not her love. But Jason's selfish, vindictive behavior ultimately backfires, causing Quentin to despise him and run away with the stolen money.

However, love is not an entirely destructive force in the novel. Dilsey, the Compson family's loving and tireless servant, offers unconditional love that functions like a glue that holds the fragmented family together. She makes sure Benjy receives a cake on his birthday. She defends Quentin from her Uncle Jason's anger. Although Dilsey is old, she runs up and down the stairs at Mrs. Compson's every whim. But even Dilsey's love has not prevented Caddy's downfall or exile, nor will it save the rest of the Compsons. In the book's final section, when Dilsey says she has seen the "beginnin" and that now she sees the "endin," she indicates, in part, that love, including the love she bears for her family as well as the Compsons, cannot keep things from growing worse.

Love is a word rarely mentioned in Faulkner's novel, perhaps because, like Caddy, it is often absent. Dilsey seems to be one of the few characters in the novel who knows how to give compassion and love. But eventually she will die, and mainly people like Jason, who are selfish and self-serving, will remain to carry on in a modern world that seems emptied of people who truly care for others.

Elizabeth Cornell

TRADITION in *The Sound and the Fury*

In William Faulkner's *The Sound and the Fury*, the Compsons have embodied genteel southern traditions since before the American Civil War. Yet these traditions are eroding in the early 20th century, and Quentin Compson is particularly sensitive to this. Like many southern families, the Compsons follow the tradition of sending their eldest son north to Harvard University. His mother's proud words, *"Harvard my Harvard boy Harvard,"* echo in Quentin's head, but he knows he will never feel like one of the "old sons of Harvard." In part because he understands that Harvard's reputation for cultivating moral young men is nearly a thing of the past. For example, Quentin knows that Herbert Head, who marries Caddy, cheated on examinations while at Harvard. Quentin is also invested in the traditional male role of defending female honor. When he encounters a lost little girl, Maria, during his ramble in Boston, he feels responsible for helping her find the way home. They eventually stumble upon her brother, but the man assumes Quentin means to harm Maria, so he punches Quentin in the face. This scene reinforces Quentin's larger failure in chivalry to defend the honor of his sister. He loves Caddy so much, he cannot stand to think of her being with any man. Quentin's love, however, cannot prevent her from shirking the tradition that she save her virginity until marriage. Nor can he prevent her out-of-wedlock pregnancy, which threatens her family's respected reputation as well as her own. Quentin commits suicide partly because he knows the standards for the traditions he values can no longer be upheld.

Jason, Quentin's brother, has a conflicted relationship with tradition. As the eldest male Compson, Jason feels entitled to the traditional role of household head but shows little sympathy for his family. He is offended by the tradition-bucking behavior of his niece and resents having to be responsible for her and his "slobbering" retarded brother. Money, not family, seems most important to Jason. He adheres to the New South's mentality that money "just belongs to the man that can get it and keep it." Yet Jason's embrace of the New South's values over traditional ones is his downfall. He no longer owns part of the hardware store where he works, and he gambles on cotton futures rather than following the tradition of saving or reinvesting in his business. Having spurned the traditional support network of family, Jason is impoverished both socially and financially.

Also possessing a strong sense of dying traditions is Luster, the young black man who takes care of Benjy. Southern society was traditionally composed of a patriarchal ruling class and a class of people who were ruled, such as slaves and later servants. Luster's grandfather, Roskus, was a servant (and possibly born a slave) for his entire life. Unlike his grandfather, Luster appears to have no interest in continuing his family's tradition of servitude. He desires his independence, and knows he can achieve this with money, which traditionally was rarely available to blacks. His ardent quest for his lost quarter represents an obsession with money that seems equaled only by Jason's. Luster's attempt to sell golf balls back to golfers suggests the industriousness he will need to move ahead in society and leave the old servant tradition behind. The "stiff new straw hat" Luster wears to church indicates his upwardly mobile aspirations in a world where old traditions no longer apply.

The novel's structure and style must also be considered in this discussion of tradition. The book's fractured plot and frequent time shifts, which make it difficult to understand during initial readings, distinguish the novel as modernist. Faulkner's narrative style represents a break with the traditional novel form: There is little linear story progression or even a clear beginning and ending. The novel is not told by a traditional, omniscient narrator or from the perspective of one or two characters. Rather, the reader must untangle a narrative presented by four narrators, each with a unique, limited viewpoint. Quentin's interior monologue, with its stream-of-consciousness ramblings and time shifts, reflects the chaos and uncertainty he encounters in a world where order and tradition, which gave life meaning and significance, seem to have evaporated.

The theme of the demise of tradition in the Old South undergirds Faulkner's novel. For Quentin and Jason, this loss means a disappearance of traditional family and community values. For Luster, it means the chance to lead a better life than his forebears, and perhaps the opportunity to establish new traditions. *The Sound and the Fury* illustrates, in plot and in its narrative style, that old practices are inevitably replaced—whether those changes are welcome or not.

Elizabeth Cornell

FIELDING, HENRY   *Tom Jones*   (1749)

Tom Jones, seldom called by its full name, *The History of Tom Jones, A Foundling*, is one of the earliest examples of the English novel. Its realistic style and foregrounding of specific times and places sets it, as well as contemporaneous novels such as Defoe's *ROBINSON CRUSOE* and *MOLL FLANDERS*, Behn's *OROONOKO*, and Richardson's *Clarissa*, apart from the romances and prose poems that came before them. The novel was a new way of looking at the world that emphasized realism and experience in an unprecedented way.

Divided into 18 smaller books, *Tom Jones* begins with the discovery of the orphaned infant Tom on the property of the wealthy and compassionate Squire Allworthy. Allworthy raises Tom as his ward, alongside the squire's nephew Blifil. Tom is a handsome, passionate, impulsive young man, who, although he is kind and means well toward those for whom he cares, has a hard time keeping his passions in check. He loves Sophia Western, the daughter of his neighbor, but they cannot marry because of his inauspicious birth. Ultimately, a marriage is planned between Sophia and Blifil, and as a result of Blifil's trickery, Tom is banished from the squire's home. He wanders around, attempting to make his own way in the world, but frequently falls prey to those less honest and kind than he is. In the end, it is discovered that Tom is actually the son of the squire's sister, and thus his rightful heir, so he and Sophia can, and do, marry after all. The novel highlights themes of SOCIAL CLASS, JUSTICE, and HEROISM.

Jennifer McClinton-Temple

HEROISM in *Tom Jones*

In the early chapters of *Tom Jones*, we are introduced to Tom as a child and we see all of his good and bad qualities. The narrator's description does not prepare the reader for a typical hero. He describes the boy as "having from his earliest years discovered a propensity to many vices." Also, "he was indeed a thoughtless, giddy youth, with little sobriety in his manners and less in his countenance." The narrator's view of Tom influences our own, of course, and we are prepared for Tom's mistakes and follies throughout the novel. The narrator continues reminding the readers that Tom is not someone from whom we should expect great things: "it was the universal opinion of all Mr. Allworthy's family, that he was certainly born to be hanged." This hero's story has an inauspicious start.

But Tom is a traditional hero in many ways. He is tall, well dressed, "one of the handsomest young fellows in the world." In action, he is strong, able-bodied, and brave, while also polite and gentle. As a child, he saves Sophia's bird, protects the gamekeeper from being fired, and does everything he can—even robbery—to support Black George's family. As an adult, he fights highwaymen and protects women. Tom has several exceptional qualities.

What makes Tom an interesting and contradictory hero is that his good qualities are offset by bad ones. Tom is reckless, impulsive, naïve, and lustful. He often acts without thinking, and sometimes his actions cause others harm. At 14, he sells his own possessions to help the Seagrims, though he hurts Squire Allworthy in doing so. In addition, he lacks a full respect for his masters, is careless with money, and is almost executed for murdering Mr. Fitzpatrick. But his most pronounced weakness is his fondness for women. Even though it is clear he truly loves Sophia, he has sex with three other women. Tom's questionable relations with women seem unsuitable to a hero, but it is interesting to note that the women are the aggressors in each of these scenarios. Molly Seagrim and Mrs. Waters very deliberately seduce him, and Mrs. Bellaston hounds him unmercifully. Tom's passionate, sentimental nature allows him to fall for these women, but he also feels sorry for each of them and is afraid to offend or hurt them.

These faults, while substantial, appear less so when presented in contrast to other characters' more serious faults. Tom comes by his impulsiveness and recklessness naturally. He almost cannot help himself, most often acting without thinking. This naturalness contrasts with characters like Blifil, whose faults are more studied. Blifil is cruelly ambitious. He sees opportunities to thwart Tom's efforts and purposely takes them. When Tom sells his Bible to Blifil to raise money for Black George's family, Blifil makes sure to stroll frequently through the house reading the Bible, showing it to his masters, pointing out passages in it. Naturally, people notice Tom's name in the book, and Tom is punished. Blifil's lowest act, keeping Tom's parentage secret, negatively affects everyone's lives around him. Blifil is a hypocrite and a dissembler. Another character who is contrasted with Tom is the companion on his travels, Partridge. Partridge, though a good man at heart and not a hypocrite, is fearful, suspicious, and he has an agenda: He hopes to benefit monetarily from reuniting Tom with Squire Allworthy. Though he often acts as a true friend to Tom, he also acts selfishly at times, keeping his hoped-for prize in sight. The constant scrapes the two get into show the contrast between the easy-going and courageous Tom versus the fretful and weak Partridge. One example is when a highwayman jumps them and demands their money. Tom wrestles him to the ground, while Partridge scrambles from his horse and cowers in the bushes, all the while crying out that he is dying. Heroism, in Tom's case, is relative.

Ultimately, Fielding suggests that a hero does not need to be perfect, that he can in fact be fallible. While never excused, Tom's weaknesses appear unimportant compared to the weaknesses of others and to his own virtues. He seems worthy of love because his heart is open and loving. The two most admirable and charitable characters, Squire Allwor-

thy and Sophia, end up accepting Tom's faults and embracing him. Here, the hero is not entirely exceptional, only relatively so.

Cynthia Henderson

JUSTICE in *Tom Jones*

The plot of *Tom Jones* is set in motion by an injustice. Tom Jones's housemate, Blifil, lies to Squire Allworthy about Tom's actions, causing Allworthy to reject his ward and banish him from his presence forever. Tom must therefore go out into the world and make his way with nothing. The injustice of his situation is clear to the reader during all Tom's adventures, and the question of how or when Allworthy will discover this injustice is felt throughout. The parallel situation of Sophia running away from her father because of his unjust treatment of her sets up the two lovers for the many challenges they must face before they can be reconciled.

One way the idea of justice is explored is through the character of Squire Allworthy. As a squire, he has the RESPONSIBILITY of determining how his dependents must be punished for their crimes. His word, literally, is law. We see early in the story how he punishes Jenny Jones for abandoning her child. Many around him tell him Jenny should be judged harshly; however, Allworthy decides to be kind to her. Indeed, he is grateful to have Tom in his life, and he lets that emotion guide his treatment. Therefore, he sends her away rather than putting her in prison. He deals similarly with the child's father, as well as showing mercy in his dealings with Tom, Blifil, Black George, and Dowling.

What constitutes justice is openly debated several times in the novel: When an offense or crime occurs, two characters debate what would be a just punishment. We see this when Square and Thwackum repeatedly quarrel about how to discipline Tom when he is a child: Thwackum always argues men should answer to religious law, and Square argues for guidance from the ancient philosophers. Another instance is when Tom and Partridge take positions on how to deal with the highwayman who jumps them near London. Partridge wants him executed, but Jones ultimately lets him go free because he sympathizes with the highwayman's sad circumstances. Finally, there is the ongoing debate over how to punish Sophia for refusing to marry Blifil. Her father believes he has the right to lock his daughter up, but her aunt thinks no woman deserves such harsh treatment.

At times during the narrator's frequent addresses to the readers he discusses how confusing justice may be to them. When Tom lets the highwayman go and gives him money to help his family, the narrator tell us, "Our readers will probably be divided in their opinions concerning this action; some may applaud it perhaps as an act of extraordinary humanity, while those of a more saturnine temper will consider it as a want of regard to that justice which every man owes his country." The narrator's occasional appeals make the readers question their own assumptions about justice.

Overall, however, it becomes clear that the world of *Tom Jones* is one where a merciful and personal justice is the best choice, one that considers the circumstances and the humanity of the wrongdoer over what RELIGION, philosophy, or the law may say. Several characters who commit a crime are shown mercy, and as a direct result, they improve themselves. George's crime of keeping the £500 he finds is forgiven, and he ends up trying to return the money. Though Allworthy tries to argue with Tom for being too sympathetic with George, saying "'[s]uch mistaken mercy is not only weakness, but borders on injustice,'" Tom still releases him. Another man who receives merciful justice, the highwayman, reforms himself and starts providing for his family. When Tom is told how well the highwayman's family is doing he can't help thinking of the "dreadful consequences which must have attended them, had he listened rather to the voice of strict justice than to that of mercy."

Finally, Tom's own crimes of imprudence and acting impulsively are completely excused by the two most noble and charitable characters, Allworthy and Sophia. Allworthy ultimately forgives Tom everything and bequeaths all his fortune to him. Similarly, Sophia, though upset at Tom's past indiscretions with other women, forgives him everything and marries him. Instead of concentrating on Tom's weaknesses and punishing him for his mistakes, both treat him with LOVE and charity. The happiness all three experience in the end—living together

in peace and comfort—reinforces this notion of a merciful justice. Ultimately, Fielding suggests that justice requires weighing the whole of a man's circumstances, character, and motives, not merely adhering to a prescribed system of justice.

Cynthia Henderson

NATIONALISM in *Tom Jones*

Henry Fielding's writing of *The History of Tom Jones* was interrupted by the 1745 Jacobite Rebellion, which pitted the supporters of the ruling Hanoverian royal family against supporters of the ousted Stuart family. The Jacobites, as they were known, were marshaled by Charles Edward Stuart, the grandson of James II, also called the "Young Pretender," who had been deposed in 1688 in the Glorious Revolution, which was as much about James's Catholicism as about the role of Parliament and hereditary right. The two major political parties fell within similar lines: the Whigs, who believed in the contractual role of Parliament with the Hanoverian throne, and the Tories, who supported the monarchial view and the Stuart claim. Following an aborted French invasion of England in 1744, Charles Edward landed in Scotland, raised an army of mostly Scottish Highlanders, and marched toward London, hoping to meet up with another French force coming from the south. The rebels achieved some military success and reached as far south as Derby before being routed at the Battle of Culloden in 1746, which ended the rebellion and any real hope for the return of a Stuart king. Although Jacobite influence declined precipitously following Culloden, their popularity remained in parts of the country and their questioning of the legitimacy of the Hanover family marked a significant moment in conflicting notions of nationalism in 18th-century England, asking who was the rightful ruler.

Most accounts characterize Fielding as a Whig, citing the anti-Stuart sentiments expressed in his political journalism, including *The True Patriot* and the satiric *Jacobite's Journal*. However, his novel *Tom Jones,* which is set during the '45 Rebellion, suggests a more complex engagement with the issue. Fielding populates his novel with both Tories and Whigs, Hanoverians and Jacobites. A Tory Jacobite supporter, Squire Western, for instance, toasts the "King over the water" and names his favorite horse *Chevalier,* the honorific given to Charles Edward's father, but his urban sister contemptuously cites the Tory *London Evening Post* to her brother, indicating her Hanoverian leanings. Likewise, the novel's cast of characters features a secret Jacobite sympathizer in Partridge, an avowed anti-Jacobite in the Man of the Hill, as well as a company of soldiers on their way to fight the rebels in the north, all of which combine to provide a panoramic vision of mid-18th-century politics.

Tom himself has been viewed in parallel terms with Charles Edward. Although in book 7, Tom, as "a hearty Well-wisher to the glorious Cause of Liberty, and of the Protestant Religion," decides to join the company of soldiers marching to meet the rebels, he shares with "Bonnie Prince Charlie" a reckless, romantic nature. Both are disinherited (as we later discover about Tom) and both are exiled, Charles Edward to France and Rome, Tom from Allworthy's estate. While Charles Edward never regains the throne, Tom finds himself restored as the heir to Squire Allworthy in the end. Whether or not this is some sort of wish fulfillment is unclear, but to simplify Fielding in conservative terms is unfair.

Similarly, in book 11, the innkeeper mistakes Sophia Western for Jenny Cameron, a fictionalized version of the real Jean Cameron, who reportedly raised and led 300 men in support of the Young Pretender. While there is no record of any type of intimate relationship between Jean Cameron and Prince Charles, Whig pamphleteers depicted her as his mistress and often pictured her armed and in highland attire. The romantic connection to Charles Edward ironically informs Mrs. Honour's defense of Sophia:

> Would you imagine that this impudent villain, the master of this house, hath had the impudence to tell me, nay, to stand it out to my face, that your ladyship is that nasty, stinking wh—re (Jenny Cameron they call her), that runs about the country with the Pretender? Nay, the lying, saucy villain had the assurance to tell me, that your ladyship had owned yourself to be so; but I have clawed the rascal; I have left the marks of my nails in his impudent face. My lady! says I, you saucy scoundrel; my lady is meat for no pretenders. [. . .] My lady to be called a nasty Scotch wh—re by such a varlet!—To be sure I wish I had knocked his brains out with the punch-bowl.

More concerned with her true identity being discovered as she has escaped from home, but finally understanding the landlord's behavior, Sophia do aught but smile at the accusation, which earns yet another reproof from Mrs. Honour. Sophia's reaction to the appellation, especially in contrast to that of the histrionic Mrs. Honour, is intriguing in terms of questions of nationalism. While she does not expressly follow her father's political inclinations, she is also not a secret Jacobite, like Partridge. Even more than the parallel between Tom and Charles Edward, conflating Jenny and Sophia conflates nation and home, and the political tensions in the air are partially allayed as Sophia, fearing her father has discovered her, is relieved that it is only "several hundred thousand" French supporters of Charles Edward come to murder and ravish, as feared by the innkeeper. By poking fun at the exaggerated fears, Fielding contributes to the political discourse of the day focused on nationalist questions.

Eric Leuschner

FITZGERALD, F. SCOTT   *The Great Gatsby* (1925)

F. Scott Fitzgerald's masterpiece of American literature, *The Great Gatsby,* holds a prominent place in both the secondary and the college classroom. While offering a portrait of the Roaring Twenties in America, Fitzgerald gives readers a story of love and intrigue and demonstrates the possibility of social class movement within the United States. Jay Gatsby, the story's central character, exemplifies the economic rise of a poor midwesterner to the heights of financial success. His life's goal is to recapture the love interest from his youth, Daisy Fay, a Kentucky native and former debutante, who is wealthy in her own right—and now married to Tom Buchanan. The novel concerns itself with the struggles of reinventing oneself to attain the dreams and pleasures of one's youth. In Gatsby's case, the effort goes terribly awry. Readers learn not only about the shaky prosperity of 1920s America, which ended in the economic devastation of the stock market crash and Great Depression of the 1930s, but also about the manner in which one man can similarly teeter on a fragile dream that shatters easily.

In addition to the main plot about Jay Gatsby's remaking himself, there are episodes that highlight racism, gender oppression, and the struggle of certain groups to achieve wealth and prosperity in the United States during the 1920s. Readers will gain an understanding of this fascinating decade of the 20th century while meeting characters who represent both its possibilities and limitations.

Carla Verderame

The AMERICAN DREAM in *The Great Gatsby*

Educators and lay readers alike often describe *The Great Gatsby* as a novel about the American dream—the opportunity for individuals to achieve economic independence and succeed in areas that are most important to them. Does the American dream exist in the 21st century? While opinions may vary as to whether America continues to offer those from beyond its shores the possibility of prosperity and a comfortable homeland, this novel, with its emphasis on reinventing oneself and its celebration of the Roaring Twenties, clearly focuses on themes of opportunity and possibility. While the story's end is a tragic one that gives readers pause about the American dream and alludes not only to its possibilities but also to its limitations, the title character, Jay Gatsby, embraces the American dream on his terms and throughout his life.

Born into a humble midwestern family, Jay Gatsby longs for all the material comforts given to a person of means. He works at various occupations—some of questionable integrity—to amass substantial wealth. Believing that money is necessary to attract the object of his desire, Daisy Fay Buchanan, he remakes himself into a corporate magnate who acquires a great fortune. He relives the years when he and Daisy dated, thinking that his new money will return him to the happiness of his youth and to the woman of his dreams.

Gatsby's ability to reinvent himself comes from his belief in the American dream: He embraces the economic opportunities afforded to him by a nation based on a free-enterprise system. Further, he welcomes the idea of a fluid society—one in which individuals enjoy the opportunity to succeed financially. However, the novel itself poses interesting questions about the American dream. It celebrates the American dream by emphasizing Gatsby's financial prowess, which he hopes will impress Daisy enough for her to return to him. He knows one of the reasons they were unable to marry years ago was that Daisy's FAMILY and SOCIAL CLASS frowned on an engagement between a wealthy woman and a young man of modest means. However, the novel portrays the great financial disparity between the upper and lower classes of New York City and its environs—a setting that serves as a microcosm of the socioeconomic class distinctions that can be found throughout the United States. For example, George Wilson, who owns a service station, represents America's working class. While George works diligently for his piece of the American dream, he will never achieve the status of Tom Buchanan (Daisy's husband) or the wealth of the title character, Jay Gatsby. George Wilson was not born into a prominent family, such as the Buchanans of Chicago, Illinois—nor did he follow the way of Jay Gatsby by remaking himself into someone else.

While F. Scott Fitzgerald draws on characters of various backgrounds who interact with one another in an attempt to show the spectrum of class dynamics in America, the author also uses various settings in the novel to highlight the complexity of the American dream. While some of the scenes are set in New York City, much of the novel takes place either in East Egg or West Egg, New York; the distinction between the two towns on the north shore of Long Island is made clear to readers early in the story. Nick Carraway, the novel's narrator, points out that his rented summer cottage is located next door to Gatsby's mansion, but is still located in less fashionable West Egg. Those with "old money," such as the Buchanans, live in East Egg. This not-so-subtle reminder of class distinction underscores Gatsby's humble background and suggests the challenges of moving beyond one's origins. Regardless of Gatsby's financial success, he is still considered "new money" and, therefore, not quite up-to-par by the established families in the area.

Another setting that calls the American dream into question is the Valley of Ashes. This is a desolate and abandoned strip of land that people travel through on their way to New York City. It functions to remind readers of the disparity between not only those with old and new money, but also those who enjoy a comfortable living in America and those who struggle to attain one. The Valley of Ashes juxtaposes the magnificence of Gatsby's lavish parties and the comfort of the Buchanans' lifestyle.

The Great Gatsby gives readers an opportunity to reconsider the American dream and whether it serves, or indeed could ever fulfill, its supposed purpose. Also, the novel investigates themes of social class and social justice through the prism of a single man who longs for the happiness of his youth.

Carla Verderame

IDENTITY in *The Great Gatsby*

At the end of *The Great Gatsby* the novel's narrator, Nick Carraway, suggests that the story of Jay Gatsby is a story of the West and that those who figure prominently in the book—Tom and Daisy Buchanan, Jordan Baker, Jay Gatsby, and Nick himself—are all westerners. The theme of identity looms large in Fitzgerald's text and the characters' birth places are not insignificant to their sense of self or to their role in the story. That is, one of the themes of the novel is that identity, for Fitzgerald's characters, is very closely linked with native region and that while New York City and its environs are central to the action of the novel, the characters' identities are drawn from and sustained by the area of their birth, although they are not literally "westerners."

At the beginning of the story, readers learn the social distinction between Tom Buchanan, a man of considerable means from Chicago, Illinois, his wife Daisy (Fay) Buchanan from Louisville, Kentucky, also of considerable means, and Jay Gatsby, a self-made man who hails from a small town in Minnesota. Newcomers to New York City and its surroundings, Tom and Daisy settle in fashionable East Egg, while Jay Gatsby, a millionaire in his own right but whose money has been earned under

suspicious circumstances, owns a mansion in the less fashionable West Egg, where Nick Carraway rents a small cottage for the summer. Nick, Daisy's second cousin and an acquaintance of Tom's in college, observes and relates the goings-on of the Buchanans and Jay Gatsby during the summer and early fall of 1922. He retells their story in the form of a flashback.

Jay Gatsby's determination to establish a new identity for himself sets him apart from the other characters in the text. Gatsby's focus on acquiring wealth is unnecessary for the rest of the ensemble who come from comfortable economic backgrounds. Gatsby's belief that wealth is an important aspect of his new identity and an equally important attribute to obtain Daisy's love turns out to be wrong-headed in the end. In fact, Gatsby's wealth gains him only superficial acquaintances who take advantage of his lavish parties and notable generosity.

The love story between Daisy Fay and James Gatz reinforces the great lengths to which the title character will go in order to change his identity. James Gatz renames himself Jay Gatsby and works hard to build, through questionable activities, a lifestyle to which Daisy is accustomed. Thinking that he can return to the past when he and Daisy dated, and marry her now despite her current marriage to Tom, Gatsby arranges a meeting with Daisy through Nick. The reunion is an emotional one; it demonstrates the "rags to riches" story of the protagonist who is temporarily attractive to the well-to-do Mrs. Buchanan. The two reminisce about their early life together when Daisy was a popular debutante and Gatsby a soldier in World War I. Gatsby and Daisy have a short affair while Tom Buchanan carries on an extramarital affair of his own with Myrtle Wilson.

The story ends badly for Gatsby. Mr. Wilson shoots Gatsby because he mistakenly believes that Gatsby was responsible for the car accident that killed his wife, Myrtle. Mr. Wilson was suspicious of his wife's recent behavior but he was unaware of the true identity of his wife's lover—Tom Buchanan. The case of mistaken identity turns out to be significant at the end of the novel.

While the role of Jordan Baker is a small one in the story compared to that of her friend, Daisy Buchanan, Jordan's character also focuses on the theme of identity in that she is a professional golfer who has gained a reputation for cheating—and is presented as somewhat careless and self-absorbed. A brief love interest of Nick's, he comes to see Jordan for who she really is, which reinforces not only the carelessness of the upper classes in the story but also the importance they assign to a specific identity. That is, Jordan admits to her carelessness and self-centeredness but enjoys both the status and the material possessions that wealth makes available.

Finally, as Nick concludes, the midwesterners in the novel who travel East find that they can neither abandon who they are, nor remake themselves into something new. Jay Gatsby, in particular, attempts to reinvent himself in order to return to a past that offered promise, only to pay the highest price, his life, for his discomfort with his humble beginnings and for attempting to manipulate his original identity.

Carla Verderame

SOCIAL CLASS in *The Great Gatsby*

F. Scott Fitzgerald's literary masterpiece, *The Great Gatsby,* provides a useful commentary on social class in America during the 1920s. The title character, Jay Gatsby, moves to a higher class from that into which he was born by amassing great wealth. He represents "new money" and is, therefore, looked upon with skepticism by Tom Buchanan, one of the most prominent and well-to-do characters in the novel. Tom's wife, Daisy (Fay) Buchanan, and her distant relative, Nick Carraway, have enjoyed a high social standing throughout their lives. While they acknowledge the inequities of class in America— Nick's opening narrative recalls his father's advice not to judge others who did not benefit from the same advantages as he—they begin a summer of splendor on the outskirts of New York City.

But the summer ends tragically: Both Jay Gatsby and Myrtle Wilson die in the prime of their lives, suggesting not only the fragility of life but also the complexity of social class and the problems that occur when desperate people hold fast to a social role that does not fit them. That is, straddling the divide among the classes comes at a great cost for both Jay Gatsby and Myrtle Wilson. Gatsby is killed by Myrtle's husband, George Wilson, who mistakenly thinks Gatsby was driving the car that ran over his wife. In fact, Daisy drove the car that killed Myrtle after a complicated series of events in New York City.

While America promises economic opportunities for everyone, the characters in the novel demonstrate the difficulty in moving among classes by doing so recklessly and without regard for people who may be hurt along the way. For example, Myrtle Wilson focuses on material possessions available to her from her lover, Tom Buchanan, but shows little regard for the lives disrupted by her extramarital affair with Tom. Myrtle's husband, George, is so devastated by the loss of his wife that he is driven to shoot Jay Gatsby in cold blood.

Conversely, Jay Gatsby strives to recapture his days as a young soldier who dated Daisy Faye with the hope of marriage and a life together. Gatsby's determination to achieve great wealth and to shift from lower to upper class is all done in an attempt to reclaim Daisy. He believes that wealth will impress her and she will divorce Tom and marry him. Gatsby wants to relive the time when he and Daisy dated, which he feels was the best time of their lives. Class status figures prominently in the episodes with Tom and Myrtle and Gatsby and Daisy because Myrtle and Gatsby believe that they are "moving up." That is, they take the idea of class status and what it can offer seriously. However, Tom and Daisy, comfortable with wealth and accustomed to getting what they want, act in a frivolous manner. While Tom may care for Myrtle on some level, and Daisy may feel some tenderness toward Gatsby, Tom and Daisy enter their affairs mostly for fun and as a distraction from their daily lives.

Nick Carraway, a faithful friend of Gatsby to the end, is disgusted at Tom and Daisy's behavior. He says, "They were careless people, Tom and Daisy— they smashed up things and creatures and then retreated back into their money or their vast carelessness or whatever it was that kept them together, and let other people clean up the mess they had made. . . ." Nick learns that Tom, Daisy, and others in their circle are not the least bit interested in the consequences of their actions.

Fitzgerald's text takes a hard look at the subject of social class in America not only through the exploits of the Buchanans and their friends but also through the story's various settings. The Valley of Ashes, in its state of decay, juxtaposes the lavish environs of East Egg and West Egg, New York. Readers are made aware of the idea of place in the novel and the manner in which it contributes to the author's commentary on social class. Further, Tom Buchanan's racist musings will also demonstrate the complicated link between race and social class and the way these categories of analysis play out in the novel. Finally, Fitzgerald suggests through the Buchanans' (and other characters') actions, that social class is not insignificant and the boundaries that distinguish social class categories are not easily overcome.

Carla Verderame

FITZGERALD, F. SCOTT   *Tender Is the Night*   (1934, 1951)

First published in four installments of *Scribner's Magazine* in early 1934, *Tender Is the Night* contains many autobiographical similarities to Fitzgerald's life. It follows the 1925 publication of *The Great Gatsby* as his final completed novel. In 1951, a second version was published posthumously; these two versions differ in terms of the novel's chronology. The more frequently studied 1934 version, which was revised 12 times by Fitzgerald without an altered time scheme, opens in the present and uses flashbacks, while the 1951 version begins with background information and proceeds chronologically. Both versions tell the story of a young psychiatrist who marries one of his patients and later experiences another relationship that pushes him to drunkenness, disillusion, infidelity, and violence.

The main characters of *Tender Is the Night* are Dr. Dick Diver, his wife and former patient Nicole, and Rosemary Hoyt, an idealistic young woman who marks a turning point in the doctor's life while vacationing on the French Riviera. Through this triangle, Fitzgerald presents complicated relationships and the effects of their blurred boundaries: relationships like those between doctor and patient, husband and wife, parent and child, and lover and beloved. ALIENATION, ETHICS, ILLNESS, LOVE, and SEX AND SEXUALITY are important themes explored

through these three individuals and their unique bonds.

Tender Is the Night shows how relationships with others may inspire stagnation or change. With Nicole, Dr. Diver stays unfulfilled and lonely, while with Rosemary, he becomes desirous and restless. Alone, he is his own man, albeit a bit lost.

Erica D. Galioto

ALIENATION in *Tender Is the Night*

The theme of alienation most potently summarizes *Tender Is the Night* in its entirety. Indeed, Fitzgerald's novel revolves around Dr. Dick Diver and his experience of alienation, or separation from himself and from others. This alienation can be divided into two main sections: before Dick meets Rosemary Hoyt and after he meets her. Before Dick meets Rosemary, he is certainly alienated from himself and from others, but he seems largely ignorant of this fact. After marrying his former psychiatric patient Nicole and for the six years of their marriage prior to his meeting Rosemary, Dick appears alienated from others and from his own personal and professional desires. This alienation stems from his unethical union with Nicole.

When Dick and Nicole marry, their relationship continues to resemble the relationship between doctor and patient. As such, Dick concerns himself primarily with Nicole and her thoughts and emotions, rather than his own. Because psychiatrists are supposed to remain neutral in their professional relationships, Dick maintains this neutrality with his wife. He purposely alienates himself from his own emotions to heal her, so there is a separation in their romantic relationship. Dick must always hold back his own emotions to protect his wife from unpredictability, and he must react to her behavior rather than initiating his own. Unable to be completely truthful, relaxed, and intimate, they are alienated from each other as husband and wife and know each other only as doctor and patient. This separation not only works a wedge in their marital relationship, but it also separates Dick from his own identity. By withholding his own emotions for the good of Nicole's continued treatment, he also sacrifices himself.

Nicole, as wife and patient, is at the center of Dick's world, and so he sidelines his own professional work to focus on her. While he once held promise as a young psychiatrist with several well-received publications, he abandons his treatise entitled *A Psychology for Psychiatrists*. As predicted in Zurich, his personal and professional life revolve around one person, and he finds himself alienated from her, himself, and his professional interests. Sadly, Dick does not even seem to realize his own alienation until he meets Rosemary six years into his marriage with Nicole. Punctuated by Nicole's occasional breakdowns and mindless conversations with other Americans abroad, Dick's life moves weakly in mindless repetition.

After meeting Rosemary, however, Dick appears to realize his own alienation. When Rosemary inserts herself into the reality of Dick and Nicole, she arouses Dick's desire but leaves it unfulfilled. Left with this unfulfilled desire, Dick, for the first time in six years, begins to acknowledge his own alienation from himself and others. "The turning point in his life" inspires him to feel his emotions, and, more important to change. When Rosemary abandons Dick, he is left wanting as he returns to his humdrum life. There he finds Nicole the same as before, but he feels different; he feels their disconnection, their alienation from one another. Once he acknowledges this separation, he turns away from her; he refuses his role of psychiatrist at home, turns his back on his domestic duties, and symbolically turns away from Nicole at night in bed. Confronting his own alienation and letting go of his past is a painful process; indeed, Dick engages in many negative and destructive behaviors during this time. He turns to alcohol, verbal and physical violence, and extreme disillusion. Perhaps his lowest point occurs after a night of debauchery when he is mistaken for the rapist of a five-year-old girl and becomes the object of public hatred.

Those acquainted with the positive "Lucky Dick" find his transformation painful as well; the "Black Death," his term for himself, destroys others as he metaphorically destroys himself. Through this painful destruction, Dick's metamorphosis strips him of everything, so he may experience a rebirth. His father dies, he loses his job, and he loses the respect of others. He loses himself, but he also loses his wife and his intense alienation. For Dick, hitting rock bottom moves him in new directions—but not Nicole. She quickly replaces Dick with another authoritarian male figure, Tommy Barban, with whom she is likely to continue yet another repetitive, alienated love in sickness and health. Dick, on the other hand, returns to private practice and moves deep into western New York after his painful transformation. Dick's life is now simple, quiet, solitary, and wandering, but more connected to his own desires.

Erica D. Galioto

ILLNESS in *Tender Is the Night*

Psychological illness, rather than physical illness, pervades F. Scott Fitzgerald's *Tender Is the Night*. Dick Diver is studying psychiatry at Johns Hopkins University during 1917 when America enters World War I. Grateful to escape actual combat after joining the army, he is instead sent to the Dohmler psychiatric clinic in Zurich, Switzerland, to finish his medical degree. While there, he makes a strong impression on a teenage patient, Nicole Warren, during a brief meeting when she is captivated by his uniform and he is unaware of her condition. When the army assigns Dick an executive director position at a neurological unit in France, Nicole writes him roughly 50 letters over the course of eight months. Through this emotional correspondence, Nicole's symptoms improve, and when Dick returns to the clinic in Zurich, he seeks her out immediately.

Upon his return, Dick learns the truth about Nicole's mental illness through case files recounted by his friend and colleague Dr. Franz Gregorovius. Nicole's early symptoms were characterized by paranoia, fear, and anxiety: all in relation to an illogical hysteria surrounding men who she feared would attack her. Her older sister, Baby, and father, Devereux, noted that these fantastical fits were first directed toward male figures she knew, but as time passed, her tantrums were more intense and included men who were strangers. Diagnosed with the divided personality of schizophrenia, Nicole leaves Chicago for the Zurich clinic, but the doctors insist on receiving more information from her father. He reveals, after much pushing and resistance, that he and Nicole developed a very close relationship when she was 11 after her mother died. On one occasion, their relationship turned physical and Devereux had sex with his young daughter. Both ignored the incest immediately following and it never happened again, but five years later, Nicole's bizarre symptoms point to her private mental torture. Once the source of her mental illness is uncovered, the doctors in Zurich agree to treat Nicole provided Devereux cuts off his contact with her.

Though her fear of men is understandable when viewed through the lens of her disturbing rape by her father, Nicole is still considered sick because she cannot control her emotions. Her doctors diagnose her mental illness as a self-defense against men; due to her perverted sexual experience, she comes to view all men as evil, which manifests in extreme fright toward males. Her cure, the doctors think, would come when she learns to trust men again, and, ultimately, when she falls in love. To this end, the doctors seek to encourage a healthy transference between Nicole and a psychiatrist; through this psychological relationship, Nicole would transfer, or direct, her negative emotions toward men onto her doctor, and he would simultaneously receive them and inspire her to trust men again with his comforting responses. This transference does occur for Nicole, not within the walls of the clinic, but within her letters to Dick. Not until her epistolary communication with Captain Diver, as she calls him, does Nicole's condition show any signs of improvement. Through the arc of these personal letters, Nicole's hatred of men lessens and her symptoms dissipate. She once again begins to desire life outside the clinic and away from her past emotions.

After learning of Nicole's background and recent improvement, Dick meets her in person in Zurich, where her transference and improvement continue though they see each other only sporadically. Soon he is instructed by the other doctors at the clinic to break off the transference because they have located a cure in her recent emotions; Nicole is sufficiently in love with Dick and ready to be redirected. In clinical practice, this would be the point in analysis when the doctor removes support and encourages the patient to experience real life with these new-found desires. As both a psychiatrist and love interest, Dick has made Nicole's transference strong, but their emotional tie works on him as well. Unable to maintain the professional and ethical neutrality necessary for such a practitioner, Dick falls in love himself. While he knows that continuing the transference outside the clinic would mean devoting his personal and professional life to one person, he fails to end it. He gives in to Nicole and to his romantic feelings for her, and she replaces her authoritarian father with him. Unwilling to stave off his own desire, Dick marries Nicole and concedes to a life of stagnation: He is the healer, and she is the sick.

Erica D. Galioto

LOVE in *Tender Is the Night*

Dr. Dick Diver has two relationships in *Tender Is the Night* that reflect love in different ways. First, he experiences a repetitive love with his wife, Nicole, and second, he experiences a transformative love with a young woman named Rosemary Hoyt. Before Nicole becomes Dick's wife, she is his psychiatric patient, and due to this prior relationship, their marriage mirrors that arrangement. They claim to love each other, but their love is one that depends on each playing a certain role. Despite six years of marriage and two young children, Dick and Nicole are stuck in a repetitive pattern: Nicole is the patient and Dick is the doctor, Nicole breaks down and Dick repairs, Dick wants to heal and Nicole is sick. In short, Dick has a savior-complex, and Nicole needs to be saved.

Their love exists only when each plays the appointed part, and those specific roles insist upon a denial of other personal characteristics. In their marriage, Dick and Nicole are not two people coming together with their unique differences, but they form a separate entity based on their relationship of dependence. The other vacationers on the French Riviera notice this coalescence as well and rarely refer to them individually, but rather as "the Divers" or even "Dicole." Both Dick and Nicole sacrifice individuality to participate in this fusion. Without individual identities and with only endless repetition, Dick and Nicole's love begins to wane. Nicole constantly feels as if Dick views her as the ignorant, tormented, weak girl of 16 she once was, and he knows how to relate to her only through the methods and practices of the psychiatrist he is. Governed by her moods and his diagnosis and cure, their love suffocates them both. In her own right, Nicole yearns for an emotional privacy she has never had, while Dick wants to put himself first. Once Dick and Nicole are named doctor and patient respectively, they cannot end their repetitive love until Rosemary Hoyt comes between them.

While Dick and Nicole's love is characterized by repetition and fusion, Dick and Rosemary's love can only be termed transformative. Through the six years of the Divers' marriage there have been other young women who needed saving and Dick's rescue mind-set certainly obliged. His relationship with Rosemary begins much the same way as it had with Nicole and with the others who succeeded her. Like his initial transference with Nicole, Rosemary quickly falls in love with Dick as she watches him on the beach. She idealizes him instantly and, unaware of his marital displeasure, sees him as perfect, omniscient, and perceptive. When she announces that she is in love with both him and Nicole, Dick dully mumbles that he has heard this admission many times before. Rosemary shares many similarities with Nicole. She is roughly the same age Nicole was when she met Dick, both of their fathers are doctors, and both seek men from whom to garner their own strength. Compelled by her idealization of him and similarity to Nicole, Dick begins to fall in love with Rosemary. Superficially, their relationship resembles his early bond with Nicole, but it soon becomes a transformative love instead.

While Dick and Nicole find themselves in a repetitive love dependent on the adherence to old roles, Rosemary represents something new altogether. Nicole allows herself to be saved by Dick over and over, but Rosemary does not and refuses Dick's plea to rescue her. This refusal represents a turning point in Dick's life because for once he does not have to doctor a romantic interest. Paradoxically, young Rosemary decides to "give up" Dick, despite her feelings of love. Sensing the impossibility of a sustained relationship, Rosemary pulls back and relinquishes her claims on him. When she pulls back, she pulls back with love, but she pulls back at a time when Dick has opened himself to love her back. This movement leaves him with his own pulsing desire. For once, it has no obvious outlet, either with Nicole and her sporadic moods or with another young female desperate for his rescue. The passionless solitary kiss between Dick and Rosemary is emblematic of this strong renunciation.

Rosemary walks away, despite Dick's desire, and in so doing, she opens his life to its greatest transformation. The metamorphosis first pulls him away from Nicole and then toward himself and his desires: personal, professional, and romantic.

Erica D. Galioto

FLAUBERT, GUSTAVE   *Madame Bovary* (1857)

Madame Bovary was controversial from the moment it was serialized in 1856. First published in book form in 1857 (and only after its author, Gustave Flaubert, was tried for obscenity), it remains one of the most important novels of all time. It is the story of a young French woman who quickly regrets her marriage to a provincial doctor and engages in two unsatisfying affairs before taking her own life.

The novel begins by depicting Charles Bovary, but shifts its focus to Emma once the two are married. Emma quickly decides he is hopelessly dull. Her first words in the novel are striking: "Oh, why, dear God, did I marry him?" Longing for the romantic fantasies that she has read of in literature, Emma Bovary dreads her daily life and fills her time buying various luxuries. She finds a kindred spirit in Léon Dupuis, a handsome young clerk. They flirt and fall in love, but they do not realize each other's feelings. Emma is seduced by Rodolphe Boulanger, a man who has had a number of affairs. When Rodolphe begins to tire of the affair, he dumps Emma in a contrived letter. She is heartbroken and nearly commits suicide; afterward she collapses into ILLNESS. After her recovery, a chance meeting with Léon leads to a second affair. When her debts overwhelm her and none of her lovers can save her, she commits suicide. The novel ends with the DEATH of Charles, and their child Berthe consigned to labor in a cotton-mill. Through these depressing (but often comic) twists, Flaubert explores a number of important themes, particularly LOVE, FATE, FREEDOM, GENDER, and COMMERCE.

James Ford

FATE in *Madame Bovary*
Fate plays a curious role in *Madame Bovary*. The characters often speak of fate and bemoan the role

of destiny, but ultimately the events of the novel are driven more by the characters' free choices than by any fate or destiny. Emma blames fate for her unhappiness, consistently refusing to see the role her own choices have played in determining the course of her life. Early in her marriage she feels destined for a blank, empty life. She contrasts the "endless twists of fate" that chance might bring in everyone else's lives with her life, in which it is "the will of God" that "nothing was going to happen." Of course, a great many things will happen in Emma's life as the result of the choices she makes, but she is unable to see her freedom. Instead "she cursed God for his injustice," for dooming her to a life of boring domesticity instead of the exciting romances she imagines. Soon she realizes that Léon loves her, and she wishes fate would allow her happiness—"If only heaven had willed it!" Thrilled at the possibility, Emma becomes consumed with love for Léon, but fails to act on it. Those around her see her suffering and dedication as "the pale mark of a sublime destiny," and praise her devotion to her familial duties, while the reader knows that her devotion just masks her real passion for Léon. Completely oblivious to her unspoken feelings, Léon grows tired of waiting in vain and leaves for Paris. Emma is left even more depressed than before, until Rodolphe Boulanger arrives to exploit her ennui.

Rodolphe uses the idea of fate to seduce Emma, playing on her romantic naïveté. He tells her that society is organized to prevent true happiness, but that ultimately two souls "will be together, will be lovers, because Fate ordains it, because they were born for each other." He says that some "decree of Fate" has caused him and Emma to meet, that their "unique inclinations have been pushing us toward one another." All of this talk of fate appeals directly to her literary ideas of love and destiny, not to mention her vanity. She is soon swept off her feet. He clinches his "scheme" when he tells her how futile it is to resist her destiny: "why struggle against Fate . . . why resist the angels smiling!" Unfortunately he soon grows tired of their affair, and when she urges him to rescue her from her life, he turns to fate for his escape. In his farewell letter, he explains that their love would have quickly faded, "for such is the fate of things human," and tells her to "blame only fate!" for their meeting. Rodolphe's self-conscious use of fate as a cover for his desires only highlights the emptiness of grand ideas in the novel. As he says to himself while composing the letter, fate is "a word that always makes an impression." Upon reading the letter, Emma is crushed. She decides she is "free" to commit suicide, but at the last minute she is called back from the edge. When she recovers from the illness that follows, she still blames fate (rather than Rodolphe or herself) for her troubles. She dreams of "the life that could have been hers, if only fate had willed it so."

Charles Bovary rarely considers grand ideas, but when he does, he too blames his suffering on fate. When his operation on the clubfooted Hippolyte fails miserably, Charles decides that "Fate must have had something to do with it." What Charles sees as fate, other characters consider "the will of the Lord"; the end result is the same. In the end Charles speaks once more of fate, but the encounter only highlights how empty the idea of fate is in the novel. After Emma's death, finally confronted with the overwhelming evidence of her infidelity and having just sold the last of his possessions to pay her debts, Charles runs into Rodolphe, who invites him to have a beer. The narrator notes that Charles says the only "grand phrase" of his life: "Fate is to blame!" (209). Rodolphe knows that he "controlled this particular fate," and he realizes how hollow Charles's words truly are. In the world of *Madame Bovary*, fate is just another rationalization for the choices individuals make.

James Ford

FREEDOM in *Madame Bovary*

The idea of freedom is bound up with considerations of wealth, gender, and power in *Madame Bovary*. Emma complains that only men are free, while she sees herself constrained by a variety of forces—fate, lack of wealth, her marriage, her sex, and even her child. Emma's attitude is clearest during her pregnancy, when she longs for a son. A man, she thinks, is free, free to "explore each passion and every kingdom, conquer obstacles, feast upon the most exotic pleasures." In her mind a man is free to act upon his desires, to follow his will wherever it leads, while a woman's desire is always bound by "the convention restraining." At other times, she equates freedom with wealth, as when she says to Rodolphe that he cannot be "wretched," because he is free, he is rich. Long after their affair fades, she still describes Rodolphe as "rich and happy and free." In Emma's imagination, these are synonymous. Men are rich, happy, and free, while women are poor, miserable, and subservient to the men around them.

Emma is not deluded in seeing the world this way—her possibilities *are* limited in comparison to the men of the novel. Rodolphe is free to seduce whomever he wishes and to end the affair at a time of his choosing. But Emma herself freely embraces the affair, fulfilling her own desires despite the weight of convention. Léon is free to leave Yonville for Paris when he tires of provincial life (and his unfulfilled longing for Emma), a choice that she lacks. But Emma and Léon seem to be relative equals at the beginning of their affair, and ultimately he becomes her mistress as she comes to dominate their relationship. She has more freedom than she realizes, although not as much as her male companions. But even they are less free than she imagines.

For Charles as a young man, playing dominoes is "a precious act of liberty," an entrée into a forbidden adult world. He begins to enjoy life, memorizing poetry and hanging out in taverns; all of which leads him to fail his medical exams the first time out. Successful the second time, he begins his practice and his mother finds him a wife. Foolishly, Charles thinks this will be his chance to escape his mother's rule, to be truly free; he "had pictured marriage as the advent of a better life, thinking he would be more free, and able to dispose of his own person and his own money." But just as his mother dominated his youth, Charles's first wife is master during their marriage. Freedom comes with her death, and Charles is briefly happy living alone, until he begins to long for Emma. After their marriage, Charles is happy and free again, because he is "the master of this lovely woman whom he adored." Given that she feels trapped and miserable in the marriage, his own freedom is short-lived.

After Rodolphe breaks off his affair with Emma, she recognizes a different kind of freedom, the freedom to end her life. "Why not have done

with it? Who was to stop her? She was free." At the last minute Charles's shouts of "Wife! Wife!" call her back, and she does not commit suicide—yet. Later she pursues an affair with Léon, and throughout it all she continues to spend more than she can afford on an endless supply of material goods. When her debts overcome her, and her lovers refuse to help her, she sees no other way out; she swallows arsenic.

The novel's last word on the complex relations among freedom, gender, and wealth is the plight of Berthe, Emma's daughter. When Charles dies not long after Emma, poor Berthe is sent from relative to relative until she is taken in by a poor aunt, who sends young Berthe "to earn her living in a cotton-mill."

James Ford

LOVE in *Madame Bovary*
Love is a fickle sentiment in *Madame Bovary,* flaring brightly, dying quickly, and rarely producing any happiness. The first hint of this is the account of Charles Bovary's parents. The narrator explains that Charles's mother was initially "mad about" his father, but the "servility" of her love only turned him against her. Her affection for her husband quickly turns to rage at his carousing. She focuses her attention on her son Charles, who will himself be doomed to unhappy marriages. Madame Bovary chooses a wife for her son, an ugly, older widow, desired by many for her money. Charles expects to be free and happy in marriage, but is soon disappointed. His wife is his master, and his life is a boring routine until he falls in love with Emma, the daughter of one of his patients. Meanwhile, the manager of his wife's money runs away with it all, much to the chagrin of Charles's parents. Only a week after a confrontation in which Charles tries to defend his wife from his parents, she dies. He mourns her briefly ("she had loved him, after all"), but then is free to pursue a new life. He is happy for a time, living alone, until he begins to think again of Emma. Soon they marry, and all seems well. Charles loves his wife, but it is a one-sided love; he is blissfully happy to be "master of this lovely woman whom he adored."

For Emma, love is a "lightning flash" and a "tempest." She longs for the kind of passionate love found in "the pages of the books." She thought that she was in love with Charles before the wedding, but she decides she was mistaken when she does not feel "the happiness of which she used to dream." Crushed by the gap between the happiness of her imagination and the plain dullness of her married life, Emma's first words highlight her anguish: "'Oh, why, dear God, did I marry him?'" She spends the rest of the novel (and her life) searching for the passion of which she dreams.

Emma's second chance at love comes when she realizes Monsieur Léon loves her. Outwardly she becomes the perfect wife, but inside she is "in turmoil." The more she realizes her love for Léon, the more she hides it. She blames Charles for her unhappiness, while Léon becomes convinced that she is unattainable. Once again the ideal of love is detached from the reality of love, and Emma becomes an angel in Léon's mind. He grows "tired of loving for nothing," and so leaves Yonville for Paris. Emma's regret at failing to act only intensifies her desires and her depression, though her love for Léon soon fades. She is easy prey for Rodolphe Boulanger, an expert with women, who takes advantage of Emma's unhappiness. Rodolphe tells her their love is destined, and appeals to all her fantasies about love. She rejoices at the thought of "a lover," and she is certain that at last she will know the passion of her "own imaginings." Rodolphe, the great seducer, marvels at the newness of "undebauched love," but he soon falls into his old habits. The more affectionate Emma is to him, the more indifferent he becomes. She longs for the happiness of her youth, and tries even to love Charles, repenting of her affair, but she is unable to follow through. She looks to Rodolphe to save her, to free her from her life; but he also longs to be free. Ultimately he agrees to take her away, only to stand her up on the appointed day. She nearly commits suicide, collapsing into illness.

During her illness Emma has a vision of "a further love above all loves . . . a love that would blossom eternally." She wants to be a saint, but her passion for God cools as quickly as her earlier loves. If only she could have loved purely, she thinks, "before the blight of marriage and the disillusion of adultery," she would have been perfectly happy.

Meeting Léon again, she begins an affair with him. At first he is enraptured, because his imagination is fulfilled: "she was the lover in every novel." But their love for each other fades, as she wonders again why reality falls short of her books. Emma is "immersed in her passions," completely neglecting her increasing debts. When none of her lovers can pay her bills, she commits suicide, professing real love for her husband with her dying breath.

James Ford

FORSTER, E. M.   *A Passage to India* (1924)

Forster began *A Passage to India* (1924) before World War I and completed it after travel to India; it illustrates his belief that British imperialism devastated colonized countries, their people, and the relationship between the colonized and the imperial power. The novel is divided into three parts: "Mosque" and "Caves" are set near Chandrapore, India, and the final section, "Temple," is set two years after the events of the first two sections, at the temple of Mau. The story follows Mrs. Moore, Adela Quested, Ronny Heaslop, Cyril Fielding, and Dr. Aziz. The first two sections detail the complicated relationships formed between the British and the Indians. Mrs. Moore and Adela journey to India so Adela can meet English barrister Ronny Heaslop, her potential fiancé, son of Mrs. Moore. Mrs. Moore and Adela do not comprehend the Britons' hatred of the Indians and often meet with Dr. Aziz. The climax, a trip to the Marabar Caves organized by Dr. Aziz for Adela and Mrs. Moore, outlines Adela's attack in the caves. The novel is not explicit as to whether it is physical; the attack can also be understood as psychological panic. Adela, however, testifies that Dr. Aziz did not attack her and leaves India. The novel ends after Fielding and Aziz have reunited in a Hindu community with the declaration that the two cannot cultivate a friendship as long as India remains colonized.

Danielle Nielsen

COMMUNITY in *A Passage to India*

In *A Passage to India*, E. M. Forster draws a complicated picture of India and Britain's colonial relationship through the depiction of their religious and ethnic communities and the borders they transcend. The communities' desires to maintain autonomy emphasize the colonial repression suffered by the Indians. To highlight the struggles, Forster illustrates failed interpersonal relationships and inter-community relationships, and through the narrative, readers see that while members of each community strive to keep others out, seclusion is not only impossible but also may not be desirable. Three communities make up the core of the novel: the Anglo-Indians like Ronny Heaslop, Cyril Fielding, the Turtons and Burtons, and Adela Quested; Muslims, such as Dr. Aziz, Mahmoud Ali, and Hamadullah; and the Hindus, Professor Godbole and his followers at Mau. While the Indian community is culturally and religiously diverse, many of the same struggles for freedom from colonialism are fought by the myriad Indian communities. This camaraderie is vital during the trial scene when the Hindu sweepers strike, Muslim women go on hunger strikes, the streets fill with riots, and little distinction is made between the religious groups and the desire for judicial fairness.

The novel is fraught with failed interpersonal relationships between members of disparate communities, and Forster shows the distance between the diverse Indian community and the Anglo-Indian rulers at a "bridge party." At the party, Adela meets some "real Indians" that she desires to see; it also facilitates political maneuvering between the Anglo-Indians and the upper-class Hindu, Muslim, and Parsee leaders. Though the men talk to one another, the interactions between Adela and the Indian wives highlight the differences between the British and Indian communities and the strain that colonialism places on interpersonal communications. Miss Quested attempts to talk to the "friendly Indians," but they are too polite to cross this social boundary. Adela sees the bridge party as an opportunity to close the gap between the Britons and the Indians, and she wants to befriend the Indian women. Even though many of these upper-class women have traveled to England, Paris, and Italy, and speak English, Adela cannot make them speak to her because she is English. The Indian women's civility, their colonial oppression, and their regard for colonial rulers

prevent them from seeing Adela as one who understands and relates to their community. The Indian women see themselves in a much different social and cultural community than the British women, and they treat the cultural and social differences as boundaries to communication and sympathy. They see Adela as a woman who must be esteemed as a ruler, even though she does not see herself that way. Adela's inability to communicate with the Indian women as a friend strengthens Forster's assertion at the end of the novel that "No, not yet . . No, not there" could Aziz and Fielding become friends. The strain that colonialism places on friendships and the inequality between communities prohibits friendship between Adela and the Indian women, between Aziz and Fielding, and ultimately between the Anglo-Indian and Indian communities.

The community boundaries are rarely crossed for friendship but often for necessity. Forster demonstrates that colonial communities work against one another through dichotomies such as ruler/ruled, outsider/native, and dominant/subordinate. The court scene in which Aziz is tried and released for the assault on Adela demonstrates an overlapping of the communities. When Mahmoud Ali defends Aziz, he wishes to call upon Mrs. Moore; he tells the court that Mrs. Moore is a friend to the Indians. Her name is immediately Indianized; she is deemed "Esmiss Esmoor," a "Hindu goddess." The groups in the street chant her name; Adela draws strength from her dead friend and the chanting around her, and she renounces the charges. When the Indians make Mrs. Moore a deity, they draw from the colonial culture to challenge it, for they saw in Mrs. Moore a freedom and stubbornness that few other Britons displayed. The Indians embrace Mrs. Moore and Adela as allies. Without these *British* women, Aziz may have been found guilty. The Indians learn that seclusion from other communities is impossible; within colonialism, the oppressed must use all of the tools available to them, even if they are shared with the colonizers.

Danielle Nielsen

GENDER in *A Passage to India*
Gender plays a significant role in *A Passage to India*, for it allows us to consider the novel's purpose and

the racial interactions from a different perspective than the normal anti-colonial stance. Forster portrays two types of gender relations between the Britons and the Indians: a stereotypical fear of Indian men and their sexual advances toward British women and a moderate view that demonstrates Indian men's attempts to befriend British women without threatening them.

In the novel, many British women maintain Victorian standards of femininity and gender roles, specifically the "angel in the house" attitude that asserted women were the moral exemplar of the British home. Auxiliary activities like acting, however, permitted women to portray different roles, yet the women required protection from the peering eyes of the Indians. Early in the narrative, the narrator alerts the reader to the social and racial "propriety" of the memsahibs (the British women in India) when he explains that the "windows [of the playhouse] were barred, lest the servants should see their mem-sahibs acting." Women like Mrs. Callendar, Mrs. Burton, and Mrs. Turton (all wives of longstanding civil servants in the colony) demonstrate a stereotypical fear of and repulsion from the Indian people. The attitudes and actions of the Anglo-Indians promote a strict separation between the colonized and the colonizers, and they go to great lengths to protect their women from being seen by the servants. To remain hidden from servants while acting allows the women to act "improperly" without losing status in the colonial hierarchy, for the women are of a "superior" race (British) but not of a "superior" gender (female). It is obvious that gender identity is not as simple as being male or female, for the narrator indicates that the gender of the British actors (female) is just as important as the racial status of the performer and the potential viewer. This intricate and delicate relationship between "superior" race and "inferior" gender drives many of the interactions in Forster's novel. Moreover, gender relations are rarely separated from other aspects of the novel like social class or race, and in *A Passage to India* it is often impossible to separate gender from other attributes that determine the characters' social status in the colony.

Not only are the memsahibs afraid that their servants (who are Indian) may watch them act, but they also maintain that their husbands should avoid befriending any Indian man. The British schoolmaster, Cyril Fielding, "had discovered that it is possible to keep in with Indians and Englishmen, but that he who would also keep in with Englishwomen must drop the Indians." While the husbands attempt to maintain that status quo of Victorian gender relations in the colony, the women in the novel, specifically those like Mrs. Callendar, Mrs. Burton, and Mrs. Turton, dictate the relationships that they will have, or more fairly, will not have with the Indian men. These women's insistence that Indian men are troublesome and dangerous determines much of the colonial strife between the colonizers and the colonized and leads to the panic after Adela's experiences in the caves.

Forster portrays the memsahibs as stereotypical Anglo-Indians who are afraid of Indian men and believe that they must be protected. Forster, however, demonstrates that women need not fear Indians because, during much of the novel, Adela Quested attempts to befriend the Indians. Instead of treating the Indians as inferior people, she disregards the gender roles placed on her. Soon after her arrival in the colony, Miss Quested visits the college with Professor Godbole, Dr. Aziz, Cyril Fielding, and Mrs. Moore. As Fielding shows Mrs. Moore around the college, Adela remains with Godbole and Aziz. Adela does not show any discomfort with the two Indian men. It is only when Ronny Heaslop, Adela's fiancé, confronts Fielding, explaining that he "oughtn't to have left Miss Quested alone" because he doesn't "like to see an English girl left smoking with two Indians," that Adela's actions cause concern. While Adela demonstrates that Indians and British women can try to befriend one another, Ronny the bureaucrat attempts to maintain the strict gender boundaries devised by the memsahibs. The relationship Adela forges with the Indians cannot withstand the pressure of the other British women. She experiences discrimination from them, and her challenge to the stereotype eventually debilitates her and forces her to return to England. Thus, not only are relationships between different genders challenged and challenging, but the expectations held by those of the same gender generate stress.

Danielle Nielsen

NATIONALISM in *A Passage to India*

An understanding of nationalism allows us to analyze the relationship between the Indian residents and the British rulers in Chandrapore, gain a better understanding of the Indian desire for freedom, and see who the proponents for freedom are in the novel. The complicated relationships expose the complicated sense of nationalism in a country yearning for freedom. Forster's portrayal of nationalism illuminates the relationships and ideologies between two opposing groups and their concepts of political control in India.

For much of the novel, the British espouse the most nationalistic beliefs to avoid the Indian subjects who surround them, while the Indians quietly go along. After Adela Quested and Mrs. Moore intimate the desire to meet some Indian subjects, the memsahibs reluctantly throw a bridge party and invite some of the middle-class Indians. This gathering, however, is not successful. As Mrs. Moore and Adela observe the uncomfortable tension between the Indians and the British, Ronny Heaslop explains to them that "The educated Indians will be no good to us if there's a row, it's simply not worth while conciliating them, that's why they don't matter. Most of the people you see are seditious at heart. Ronny's remarks illustrate both the Indians' and the Britons' nationalist beliefs. Few of the Indians invited "mattered," and many were not of the highest caste in Chandrapore. Rather, those invited dressed in a manner similar to the Britons, and they were more likely to be loyal to the British than other Indians. The Indians who would "be no good" to the British are instead loyal to the Indian cause as Indian nationalists. As with the bridge party, the British exert their control over the middle-class Pathans in India by inviting them to gatherings and by placating them to increase the possibility that these Pathans will relinquish any nationalist tendencies and support the British regardless of the Indian nationalism surrounding them.

Furthermore, Ronny's anxiety regarding a "row" relates to the growing tensions between the Indians and their British colonizers and exposes the different ways that nationalism plays a role in the Britons' use of the Indians. Because so many of the educated, high-caste Hindus favor freedom, they are perceived not only as nationalist but also as dangerous to the empire. In essence, Ronny's sense of nationalism—his pride in Britain, his pride in colonialism's role, and his pride in his job—encourage him to see the real Indians as only those people who would support the Britons. Furthermore, Ronny's pride indicates a British nationalism that bolsters the imperial power and prestige of Britain.

While Ronny's comments at the bridge party demonstrate his beliefs about nationalism—or lack of nationalism—in the Indian mind, the atmosphere at Aziz's trial reveals the power of Indian passion and Cyril Fielding's sedition. Aziz's imprisonment causes Chandrapore workers to strike, specifically the sweepers, and even Muslim women declare a hunger strike. These actions demonstrate both support of Aziz and anti-British sentiments. Though the women's hunger strike has no effect because they are concealed in harems, the sweepers' strike is detrimental to the health of the city. By striking, the Indians demonstrate their desire to control the atmosphere and the judicial system—in essence, the desire to control their country. The Indians, who "did not matter" at the bridge party, suddenly do. The narrator describes the Britons' anger at Fielding: "he [Fielding] encouraged the Boy Scout movement for seditious reasons; he received letters with foreign stamps on them, and was probably a Japanese spy. This morning's verdict would break the renegade, but he had done his country and the Empire incalculable disservice" (238). Just as Ronny suspects the Indians' ability to be "seditious" to the Indian cause, the Britons feel that Fielding shows the same sedition to the Empire. Forster illuminates the different ways in which nationalism can play out between different ethnic and social hierarchies.

For Forster, the nationalism lies either with the British Empire or with free India, and it is revealed not only by those who ethnically belong to the group, but also by those who support it. Thus, middle-class Indians who thrive under the raj support the British, while Britons who oppose the raj can align themselves with the Indian populace. Nationalism, however, is not simply between the Indians and Britons, as indicated by the role that middle-class Indians and Fielding play, but also between the Hindu and Muslim populations, and this relationship is played out more extensively in the novel's final section.

Danielle Nielsen

FORSTER, E. M.   *A Room with a View* (1908)

A Room with a View follows Lucy Honeychurch and her cousin, Charlotte Bartlett, to a small English-run hotel in Florence, Italy. Lucy, who was used to having more FREEDOM, finds her every step watched and protected by her cousin. Themes of NATURE, INNOCENCE AND EXPERIENCE, and TRADITION emerge through the novel's many conflicts. Lucy and Charlotte meet a father and son, Mr. Emerson and the younger George Emerson, when they trade rooms to get a better view. The radical, open-minded Emersons invite scorn from other travelers who disapprove of their outspoken manner. Lucy becomes very bored in Italy until suddenly she witnesses a stabbing. After she faints from shock, George comforts her and admits to an interest in her.

Shortly after an unexpected kiss from George on a day outing, Lucy and her cousin return to England. Lucy finally accepts the third marriage proposal of Cecil Vyse, an uptight, snobbish suitor. But scandal keeps threatening her placid life. Lucy largely remains submissive to her relatives and fiancé. She finds her confidence shaken when the Emersons move into a nearby neighborhood. After much personal turmoil and some counseling from the elder Emerson, Lucy breaks off her engagement with Cecil and turns to George instead. She embraces a more passionate life free from many of the senseless expectations her family and society have of her. The exaggerated characterization adds a comical approach to *A Room with a View,* and mocks the grave importance the characters attach to ordinary social situations.

Elizabeth Walpole

INNOCENCE AND EXPERIENCE in *A Room with a View*

A Room with a View follows several young characters whose actions reveal their innocence. Lacking experience in their social circles, they try following older adults or rebelling against them to test the limits of their actions. While the story focuses on the theme of finding one's own view of the world, it also shows the obstacles and mistakes the young characters must face as they mature.

Lucy and George romanticize the idea of being young. In their relationship, any contact they have holds monumental importance for each of them. Although Charlotte suggests that George is using Lucy, George's eagerness to be with Lucy is actually a sort of innocent first love. He takes life very gravely and struggles with youthful questions about the purpose of his existence, as when he leaves "an enormous note of interrogation" scrawled on paper in his room. He sees Lucy not just as an attractive girl but as a savior. Before he is able to comprehend or recognize his love for her, he remarks, "I shall want to live." In his youthful inexperience with love, he swings quickly from one drastic emotion to another.

Lucy fears adulthood because she thinks it is completely stifling. She much prefers playing tennis with 19-year-old Freddy and 13-year-old Minnie. Enjoying the exercise, she concludes, "how much better to run about in comfortable clothes than to sit at the piano." She believes that to grow up is to step into society's mold for her. Her fatalistic attitude blinds her from seeing her ability to make her adult life enjoyable. Lucy sees marrying Cecil as her only option. She dreads living with Cecil, who refuses even to join a game of tennis. From a city upbringing and a good education, Cecil despises "the physical violence of the young," even in sports. Lucy does not realize other types of men might be more compatible with her personality. Her lively spirit delights in more rowdy, imaginative games such as "bumble-puppy" in which each tennis ball has a name, and one hits "tennis-balls high into the air, so that they . . immoderately bounce." She willingly makes up her own rules for tennis, but her fear of failure prevents her from taking such charge of her own life.

Many of the "ridiculous child" characters find opportunities to rebel. Although Charlotte's attempts to shelter Lucy are often exaggerated, Charlotte understands how easily Lucy might tarnish her reputation. Lucy does not see the scandal in switching to George's room or exploring Italy on her own. Charlotte, while not being a very loyal friend, certainly has more experience with matters of gossip than Lucy does. As Charlotte predicted, the story of George kissing Lucy finds its way into Miss Lavish's novel. Lucy is horrified when she realizes the romance in the novel mimics her own encounter in the Italian field of violets. The scene, filled with language such as, "he simply enfolded her in his manly arms," sounds even more risqué than Lucy's actual experience. Suddenly, Charlotte's warnings seem more meaningful.

Other characters are less thoughtful than Lucy when it comes to rebellion. Their brutal honesty reveals innocent ambivalence to etiquette. When Cecil asks Freddy if he is happy about Lucy's engagement, Freddy admits, "I had to say no. He ought never to have asked me." Minnie, the rector's niece, likewise blatantly refuses to attend church. In her "church protesting" Minnie questions, "why shouldn't she sit in the sun with young men?" The nature of Minnie's protest is not on religious grounds, but instead shows her opposition to following the rest of the women in a dull activity. By asking the reason for going to church, she points out how it is more of a social than religious obligation. She also inadvertently reveals that there is a wider range of freedoms allowed for men than women.

Although George asserts that "love and youth matter intellectually," the end of the novel raises doubts as to whether these virtues will flourish for long. Lucy and George try to escape English society to avoid conflict. The novel's end treats the situation as though the couple has found a haven away from social connections. They act as though in a foreign country social codes are nonexistent. While Lucy and George have found freedom to grow up as they please, they remain largely inexperienced and their idyllic views show a lot of naiveté.

Elizabeth Walpole

NATURE in *A Room with a View*

Many of the most significant events in *A Room with a View* occur outdoors. Forster seems to suggest that when the characters are in nature, they can behave more naturally. In a novel where manners and social standing carry great importance, being in nature gives characters moments away from judgmental eyes. Nature affords them privacy and extended space for expression.

For example, the characters enjoy Italy's countryside by planning a group picnic. While Charlotte fusses about catching a draft from the damp ground, Lucy treks through the woods. She follows the Italian driver through dense undergrowth and brush to see George. During this walk, Lucy feels that "for the first time she felt the influence of Spring." When she sees George it is as though nature has set him up as a suitor, since he is surrounded by "violets [that] ran down in rivulets and streams and cataracts, irrigating the hillside with blue." The overwhelming beauty of her surroundings heightens her surprise and intensifies her reaction to George's presence.

George and his father express a special appreciation for nature. Their last name, "Emerson," refers to Ralph Waldo Emerson, a 19th-century American author. He was part of the Transcendentalist movement, which valued nature and individualism. His writings, similar to the Emerson characters' behavior, rebelled against society's usual philosophical and spiritual beliefs. The Emersons in *A Room with a View* display their love of nature when they "picked violets and filled all the vases in the room of . . . the Miss Alans." The Miss Alans react to the gesture by calling it, "so ungentlemanly and yet so beautiful." The Emersons appreciate the flowers' potential to bring great happiness. In a very natural way, they behave according to their instinct of goodwill and do not pause to consider the strangeness of such a gift.

Cecil, in contrast, pretends to be an expert on nature, which he calls the "simplest of topics." His confidence, however, is unfounded and seems even more false in the presence of Lucy, who grew up in the country. Cecil points out to Lucy, "I had got an idea—I dare say wrongly—that you feel more at home with me in a room . . . Never in the real country like this." Cecil's comment is accurate, as it relates to Lucy demanding to leave Florence immediately after George kissed her at the field of violets. The discomfort that Cecil recognizes applies to his own feelings as well. He feels equally nervous being alone with Lucy on the path through the woods. Before kissing Lucy, Cecil "became self conscious and kept glancing round to see if they were being observed." Cecil seems unable to act naturally, even if it means growing closer to Lucy.

Lucy suddenly realizes that she is not content with Cecil, who loves only the part of her personality he feels is secure and predictable, instead of admiring the Lucy who "dreamily" recalls bathing in the Sacred Lake. Although religion is often mocked in this novel, the hidden pond in the woods is called "holy." It has a sense of magic that harkens back to Lucy and Freddie's childhoods. When Freddie feels uncomfortable meeting the Emersons, his immediate reaction is to ask them to "have a bathe." Although his suggestion sounds like a joke, Mr. Beebe, Freddie, and George jump in the tiny pond for a swim. When Cecil, Lucy, and her mother accidentally stumble across this rowdy gathering, they are shocked and speechless. George and Cecil each use the opportunity to make an impression on Lucy. George, a complete mess and without clothes, walks up to the crowd and says hello. Cecil, who felt uncomfortable knowing that Lucy herself used to play in this pond, tries to usher her aside to prevent her from becoming upset. These telling moments help Lucy realize that she does not want to be sheltered by others, especially when she is not even frightened or in danger.

A Room with a View reveals two important elements of nature. Nature is the outdoors, where fickle weather and inviting landscapes disrupt the characters' carefully made plans. But nature is also human nature, and characters must learn to rely on their instincts when their emotions are stirred for better or worse. For Lucy, the time spent outdoors provides her with an opportunity for private and honest communication. She feels free to act "naturally." From learning to interpret and appreciate nature, the characters form closer connections with each other.

Elizabeth Walpole

TRADITION in *A Room with a View*

Mr. Emerson's first words in the novel are "I have a view!" Although he is speaking about good scenery outside his window, his words also introduce the prevalence of traditions in the novel. Each charac-ter's view, or perspective on life, has been shaped by the habits of his or her society. Either by seeing their cultural and familial traditions as essential or tossing them aside for more radical behavior, the characters are all affected by the framework of tradition.

In Italy, the English characters' mix of confusion, fascination, and disgust toward native Italians begins the novel with a great clash of cultural tradition. When led by the young Italian driver to George Emerson, Lucy swings back and forth in her generalizations about Italians, from "Italians are born knowing the way" to "an Italian's ignorance is sometimes more remarkable than his knowledge." Even being unable to speak Italian, Lucy is eager to observe a different culture and assess it in relation to her own.

Aspects of Italy's ancient traditions appear when Forster refers to Roman gods and goddesses or great painters. The superhuman nature of the myths contrasts with the English characters' trivial worries. Specifically, after the carriage ride, the characters feel as though the god Pan has played tricks on them. Their idea of Pan has already lost some of this god's grandeur, as he only "presides over . . . unsuc-cessful picnics." Instead of recalling epic battles and LOVE affairs described in Roman mythology, the English tourists are preoccupied with their guide-books and the rain ruining a drive. The English obsession with mundane drawing-room chatter obscures the excitement of Italy's rich, imaginative heritage surrounding them.

Back in England, Lucy and her family have strong social ties to the neighborhood based on the false presupposition that they are part of the aristocracy. In fact, Lucy's father was a lawyer who bought the country home to fix it up and then ended up moving into it. Their family is not old nobility at all. Lucy's mother finds this mistake "extremely fortunate for the children" and accepts the opportunities it presents for her to easily make friends. Even the illusion of representing a traditional, well-off country family is enough to grant SUCCESS in Lucy's neighborhood.

Cecil, Lucy's fiancé, is as confused as the neighbors concerning what to expect from Lucy's neighborhood. His intensely proper behavior comes from his lack of understanding of country traditions.

Cecil grew up in London with more cosmopolitan traditions and so becomes very impatient and frustrated when he has to make trips to all the country homes to meet many friends of the family. He cannot abide how his "engagement is rendered as public property." Cecil and Lucy cannot decide whether country or city traditions are superior. Lucy finds herself bored with her neighbors' "kindly affluence, their inexplosive religion, their dislike of paper bags, orange-peel, and broken bottles." At the same time, Cecil doubts his own environment and instead wants to "bring [his children] up among honest country folks for freshness, send them to Italy for subtlety, and then—not till then—let them come to London." Regardless of any final decision on the matter, Lucy and Cecil are curious about each other's traditions and use their different backgrounds to explain why they have trouble understanding one another.

Mr. Emerson and his son, George, represent a rejection of typical English traditions and ways of thinking. Mr. Emerson brags that he gave his son a childhood "free from all superstition and ignorance that lead men to hate one another in the name of God." He startles fellow tourists in Italy when he complains loudly in a church about unfair treatment for laborers and the ugliness of religious art. Whereas Lucy comments on her admiration for Giotto's paintings because she remembers reading about them, Mr. Emerson ignores traditional opinions. Mr. Emerson teaches Lucy to care less about other opinions and instead encourages her to continue on her tour even after she loses her guidebook and her chaperone.

By the end of the novel, Lucy becomes more open-minded and realizes that a break from tradition is sometimes necessary for personal happiness. At first, Lucy had thought that "life . . was a circle of rich, pleasant people, with identical interests and identical foes." Her experience in Italy opens her mind, as when she observes, "social barriers were irremovable, doubtless, but not particularly high." She takes a risk and breaks off her engagement with Cecil. Lucy causes her mother great shock when she moves to Italy with George. A letter from home reminds Lucy that "she had alienated Windy Corner, perhaps for ever." By abandoning her family traditions and defying their expectations, Lucy learns to trust her own conscience and explore more unconventional views as well.

Elizabeth Walpole

FRANK, ANNE   *Anne Frank: The Diary of a Young Girl*   (1950)

Like many girls before and after her, Anne Frank began to write her deepest secrets, greatest fears, and strongest desires in the confines of her adolescent diary. Unlike most girls, Anne's diary became known throughout the world. *Anne Frank: The Diary of a Young Girl* is one of our most profound insights into the lives of Jews in hiding during World War II.

Anne's initial revelations of schoolyard crushes and birthday party plans change drastically when she is forced to go into hiding in 1942, following the 1940 Nazi occupation of Holland and the institution of strict policies against Jews in that country. Although cloistered in the annex of her father's warehouse, Anne's life is a rich one as she navigates the throes of adolescence. Although often in despair over the atrocities committed against Jews outside of her little world, the constant battle of identities with her mother, and the sheer dreariness of a life spent entirely indoors, Anne manages to take comfort in her writing, a crush on her roommate, Peter Van Daan, the warm relationship she shares with her father, and her tireless studies.

Although Anne died at the Bergen-Belsen concentration camp in Lower Saxony in March 1945, her words and thoughts have lived on. Following Anne's removal from the annex, Miep Gies, one of the Dutch women who helped care for the Franks and their companions, collected the scattered pages of Anne's diary and saw them published in 1947 with the help of Anne's father, Otto Frank. Since then Anne's diary has become one of the most widely read and widely published books in history.

Jeana Hrepich

CRUELTY in *Anne Frank: The Diary of a Young Girl*

Although readers know nothing of Anne Frank's life in Bergen-Belsen, the concentration camp where her life was taken, they can assume that her story would have been one laden with the cruel existence of such a treacherous place. Before Anne, along with her family and friends, was found in the secret annex that concealed them from Nazi forces for just over two years, she speculated about the lives of Jews who were not as lucky as she perceived herself to be. Anne's frequent reveries about the atrocities being committed outside of her cloistered world and the extreme deprivations that she and her companions in the annex faced make *Anne Frank: The Diary of a Young Girl* one of the most important chronicles of the cruelty committed against Jews during World War II.

Even before Anne made her home in the annex of her father's warehouse she experienced some of the restrictions imposed on Jews. In 1940 Germany occupied Holland, where Anne made her home, and like all Jews she was forced to wear the yellow Star of David, which came to symbolize captive Judaism. Jews were also commanded to yield to a curfew, deliver up their bicycles, and shop within a limited frame of time in designated Jewish shops. Jews were forbidden to drive, ride in trams, partake in public sports, go to the cinema and other arts arenas, and visit Christians. Anne's friend from school, Jopie, said to her, "You're scared to do anything, because it may be forbidden." Yet Anne felt that "things were still bearable" in spite of the ever-increasing restraints against Jews. Like so many Jews at the time, Anne did not appreciate the fact that these restraints were incremental nails in the proverbial coffin.

Circumstances were no longer bearable for the Franks when Anne's sister, Margot, was "called-up" by German forces. Intending to escape one cruel fate, Margot and her family trade in their lives for another. On one hand the Franks are lucky to have an alternative life available to them. On the other hand the ISOLATION and destitution they would endure for just over two years was a hardship deeply felt by all. Anne explains that "silence fell on the house; not one of us felt like eating anything" the night before they were to begin their new life. On their arrival at the annex Margot and Mrs. Frank are too miserable to help unpack their belongings. Yet their lives in the annex develop into a state of sustainability, though misery abounds. After about a year in hiding Anne writes: "We miss so much here, so very much and for so long now." She goes on to say, "I long for freedom and fresh air."

Anne's SUFFERING pales in comparison to the suffering of others in the annex, though. Perhaps because she retains steadfast HOPE, or maybe because of her youth, Anne is able to rebound more easily than her mother, who seems to feel the cruelty of her situation more acutely than anyone in the annex. Anne says of her mother, "Her counsel when one feels melancholy is: 'Think of all the misery in the world and be thankful that you are not sharing in it.'" Anne rarely depicts her mother out of her usual malaise. Readers might assume she habitually follows her own advice. As Anne very astutely notices, however, Mrs. Frank's means of surviving her own cruel fate is flawed. If Mrs. Frank should ever "experience the misery herself," how is she supposed to live? Like all of the women in the annex, Mrs. Frank died in a concentration camp after being discovered by the Gestapo.

Anne, too, cannot stop herself from comparing her life to the lives of other Jews. "If I just think of how we live here," Anne writes, "I usually come to the conclusion that it is a paradise compared with how other Jews who are not in hiding must be living." Indeed, Anne's perception of the barbarism committed against Jews outside of her walls was on point. Anne saw other people face the same cruelties she would endure later. "Day and night more of those poor miserable people are being dragged off, with nothing but a rucksack and a little money. On the way they are deprived even of these possessions. Families are torn apart, the men, women, and children all being separated." Like so many before her, Anne was stripped of all of her belongings, including her diary. She had to endure being separated from her father, her mother, and eventually her sister. Families were sent to concentration camps where many faced a certain death. Anne Frank, who felt the suffering of others, died of typhoid disease just a few months before she would have been liberated. Her voice carries the resounding story of the cruel fate of the 6 million Jews who died at the hands of the Nazi regime.

Jeana Hrepich

HOPE in *Anne Frank: The Diary of a Young Girl*

In the classic picture of Anne Frank, a set of dark, penetrating eyes peer out of a radiant face. Across her lips lurks a contented smile, a sign of a happier time than her famous record, *Anne Frank: The Diary of a Young Girl,* chronicles. Yet despite the tragedies and grave ordeals Anne confided in her diary, she still maintained a sense of hope that her photographs often exude.

Perhaps not surprisingly, Anne's first entry, written on her birthday, is permeated with the kind of hope familiar to most 13-year-old girls. She is eager about birthday gifts: books, flowers, and food. What puzzles the mind is that the later entries, written in Anne's second and third years in hiding in a secret annex, are still hopeful, still seeking light amid so much darkness.

Anne acknowledges that while most people can find happiness while surrounded by nature, she can no longer afford that luxury. Once she could ride her bike down Amsterdam streets. Later her only access to nature is a view of it out of a window in the secret annex, in the attic of her father's business. Sitting in front of that window Anne contemplates the freedom she once had, and her desire to breath fresh air again. Rather than bemoan her fate, Anne concludes that what she does have, a pureness of heart and happiness that can only be temporarily smote, is plenty of restitution for what she has suffered, and she hopes that God will bring her comfort. "As long as this exists," Anne says, "I cannot be unhappy."

At the same time, Anne believes that God is to blame for the torment she and other Jews have suffered, but she also believes that he will redeem the many fallen at the hands of Hitler and the Nazi Party. Like most adolescents, she wavers between extremes, at times preoccupied by an impassioned frustration and later dominated by a zealous faith in God and mankind. In comparing herself to her mother, Anne cannot comprehend how Mrs. Frank can focus on the misery that exists in the world when Anne is so preoccupied by the love and beauty that persists around her. "On the contrary, I've found that there is always some beauty left," confides Anne. While Mrs. Frank would cheer one up by comparing their plight with those who are worse off, Anne prefers to revel in the existence of a benevolent God, the beauty and sunshine in nature, and the loveliness that abides within every human spirit. In effect, Anne's position is one that she must take in order to survive: Losing hope would be capitulation to misery.

Anne's ability to hope amid despair, to see beauty and love in one of the darkest periods of history, has much to do with her budding relationship with Peter Van Daan, the teenage son of the family that shares the annex with the Franks. Her tender relationship with Peter, which includes the first throes of romance and physical titillation, marks a new phase for her sexually and developmentally. Anne's emotional attachment to Peter and her burgeoning sexuality are fresh and exciting in an environment where all else is stagnant. Anne blooms with hope and breathless anticipation as the intimacy of her encounters with Peter deepen.

Even when Anne ponders more sober matters, such as the crisis of the Jewish people, she hopes against all odds that when the war is over, her suffering and the suffering of those worse off than she will precipitate a universal education about the atrocities committed against them. She hopes that the people of the world will learn goodness by this vulgar scar on history. Instead of forsaking her religion, Anne reminds Kitty, the name she gives her diary's persona, that God has never deserted her people, and that "a solution will come." Although her faith and history were all that she had to encourage such beliefs at the time, she insists that the strong will not only survive but prevail.

Anne is not irrationally hopeful throughout the whole of her diary, however. In fact, she frequently writes in despair. Nevertheless, given the loneliness, the isolation, and the privations Anne endured, one might expect her diary would be a tome of anguish. In the true spirit of her character, Anne was hopeful despite tremendous adversity. Anne assures Kitty, "we still hope, hope about everything." The soulful eyes that stare back from her photos reflect her withstanding spirit and a reservoir of something essential to her constitution: hope.

Jeana Hrepich

SURVIVAL in *Anne Frank: The Diary of a Young Girl*

Few readers who pick up a copy of *Anne Frank: The Diary of a Young Girl* are unaware of the demise of its titular heroine. Like 6 million other Jews, Anne Frank died in a concentration camp during World War II at the hands of Adolf Hitler's Nazi regime. It may seem strange, then, to identify survival as a guiding theme in her work. However, Anne Frank's diary chronicles a succession of days in which the only task at hand for the eight people living in the annex of Otto Frank's warehouse was to survive. The fact that Anne's diary also survived extinction is a happy miracle.

The greatest stress for the denizens of the secret hiding place was the constant fear of being found. Burglars nearly found their way to the annex on more than one occasion, causing great trepidation among its inhabitants. In fact, any unusual noise or unexpected visitor below was cause for alarm. When the bell rings one evening without reason Anne "turned white at once, got a tummy-ache and heart palpitations, all from fear." Anne suffers terrible dreams on the heels of such events. In one recurring dream, she says, "they come and take us away at night." Anne sees the annex as an island in the midst of so much chaos, but her dreams foreshadow a darker time when danger will engulf their safe refuge. For over two years Anne and her seven companions survive the perils of exposure, but the fate Anne believed was inevitable came to pass when they were finally discovered, arrested, and sent to concentration camps.

Those two years spent in hiding were filled with hardship and suffering. Anne and her family endured deprivations from food to light to fresh air. Frequent illnesses made captivity even more stifling. Food especially preoccupied their minds since faltering rations and decaying stores of fruit, meat, and vegetables confronted them three times a day. Anne and her cohort obtain food through coupons and ration cards, and purchases made on the black market. The economic effects of the war on the Dutch trickle down to affect the secret annex, too. What may seem like small losses such as diseased potatoes or days without butter are enough to turn the whole annex into a "tedious existence." Light was used at a bare minimum. When Anne begs her father to light the candle during a particularly treacherous air raid, the usually doting father refuses until Anne's mother intervenes. Coal runs out quickly, leaving the annex colder than before. Illness, too, plagues Anne, as she must contort herself uncomfortably to avoid being heard. "It's wretched to be ill here," she said, "When I wanted to cough—one, two, three—I crawled under the blankets and tried to stifle the noise." Yet everyone did survive the lack of proper food, lack of light and heat, and sickness.

Perhaps for Anne, especially, the deprivation of fresh air and sunlight was almost insurmountable. The youngest member of the annex, Anne had to survive the same fears and privations as her roommates while also going through puberty under their watchful eyes. Had Anne not been required to escape into anonymity with her family, her tense relationship with her mother, which brought out in Anne a caustic, sometimes cruel reaction, may not have been so severe. While Anne felt spring blooming inside of her, she was captive to the endless winter of the secret annex.

Anne writes in her diary that she can hardly remember the girl she once was before she met her fate in the secret annex. The girl she was would not have survived what Anne endures in hiding. Anne says, "I hear nothing but this sort of talk the whole day long, invasion and nothing but invasion, arguments about suffering from hunger, dying, bombs, fire extinguishers, sleeping bags, Jewish vouchers, poisonous gases, etc. etc." The constant chatter in the annex revolves around these issues of life and death. Gone are the days of schoolboy crushes and bantering with teachers. In hiding, Anne grapples with the serious business of survival on a daily basis.

Anne's diary is one of the most widely read first-person accounts of the Holocaust. For decades her voice has been a resounding reminder of the cruelties inflicted on Jewish people during World War II. Miep Gies, one of Otto Frank's devoted employees who aided their survival while they hid, collected Anne's diary after she and her family were removed to concentration camps. Anne's voice has endured even her own death, and the millions of people who continue to read her words are a testament to her survival.

Jeana Hrepich

FRANKLIN, BENJAMIN   *The Autobiography of Benjamin Franklin* (1791, 1818, 1868)

The Autobiography of Benjamin Franklin, one of the most famous autobiographies in literature, was first published in French in 1791, the year after Franklin's death. This version was incomplete. Franklin's grandson published a more complete version in 1818. In 1868 John Bigelow purchased the original manuscript and published the entire work. Bigelow's edition is the one usually used for later reprints.

The *Autobiography* is divided into four parts. The first part, which was written for Franklin's son William, was composed in 1771. The second part is introduced by a memo from Franklin and was written in the early 1780s. Here he says that the first section contained family stories and that the second was written for public consumption. In this section Franklin details his plan to achieve moral perfection. The third part begins with a note from Franklin saying that he has lost many of his papers in the Revolutionary War, but some were saved. Among these are his observations on history and yearly comments on his life. This section was written in 1778. The 1818 edition ends here. Franklin wrote part 4 the year of his death and it describes his efforts in England on behalf of the colonies in 1757.

While Franklin's autobiography does not cover the Revolutionary War period, it does provide perspectives that have survived Franklin himself and are just as relevant today as they were when he wrote them. The book, with its development of Franklin's thoughts on WORK, FAMILY, SUCCESS, EDUCATION, RELIGION, and other themes, is a delightful read.

Suanna H. Davis

FAMILY in *The Autobiography of Benjamin Franklin*

The Autobiography of Benjamin Franklin begins with a clear emphasis on family; the first words in the book are "Dear Son." In the letter, Benjamin Franklin proposes to acquaint his son William with the particulars of his life, offering it as an example for others to emulate. He begins by detailing anecdotes of his ancestors, thus establishing the theme of family in the work.

Franklin reminds his son of the search made for their remaining family in Ecton, Northamptonshire. Here the Franklin family had lived since at least 1555, according to the church registers, which began then. In his readings, Franklin, who was the youngest son of 17 children, discovered that he was the youngest son of the youngest son for five generations.

Franklin continues, examining other common family traits. He writes that Josiah, his father, apprenticed under his brother John, just as Franklin later apprenticed under his brother. Thomas, the eldest uncle, becoming a scrivener and a political power in the county; Franklin notes the similarities between Thomas's life and his own.

The family tie-ins continue. Franklin was named after his uncle Benjamin, who was "an ingenious man" (8) and when Franklin was young his uncle lived in their home in Boston for several years. Franklin shows his regard for his uncle by mentioning that when pamphlets Benjamin had purchased and subsequently sold were brought to his notice after his uncle's death, Franklin bought them.

Franklin develops his discussion of family with his father who married young and had three children when he moved to New England. There Josiah had another four children. After his first wife died, Josiah married Franklin's mother, Abiah Folger, who Franklin introduces as the daughter of one of New England's first settlers. His parents had another 10 children together.

While family is a positive theme in the book, Franklin does not attempt to minimize problems within his family. Franklin recounts that he was sent to work for his brother James, a printer. This did not work out well and Franklin is blunt in saying that his brother often beat him. When Franklin was able to leave his apprenticeship, he did so. After several years he came home and showed off, which made his brother angry. Despite their mother's pleadings, the two did not reconcile. But 10 years later they re-established relations as James was dying, and he requested that Franklin raise his son and establish him in printing, which Franklin did.

As part of his development of the theme of family within his autobiography, Franklin writes of his courtship of Miss Read, who later became his wife.

When Franklin first arrived in Philadelphia he met and stayed with the Read family. He and Miss Read courted, but Franklin left on a business trip. Gone for months he wrote only one letter, telling her he did not know when he would return. In response to this, and at the urging of her mother, Miss Read married someone else. Franklin makes it clear that Miss Read was right to not wait for him, mentioning among other things that he made advances to another woman while in England. Upon the death of Miss Read's husband, Franklin and Miss Read were married. Franklin says she was cheerful, industrious, and frugal and that they were happy together.

Even though Franklin begins the autobiography with a letter to his son and it is purportedly written to him, Franklin discusses William's experiences throughout the book, describing his trip with Franklin researching ancestors, replacing Franklin as a clerk for the assembly, serving in the war against Canada, procuring for Braddock's army, and touring England with Franklin. This is part of the development of the family theme, incorporating his son's history into that of the rest of the relations.

Franklin ends the third section of his autobiography by describing his tour of London with his son. Thus the theme of family, focused as it is on his son, comes full circle. In the 1818 version, published by his grandson, this is the end of the book. Franklin offered his autobiography as an example for others to follow, and his emphasis on family within the book says that family should be valued.

Suanna H. Davis

SUCCESS in *The Autobiography of Benjamin Franklin*

On the very first page of his autobiography, Benjamin Franklin begins to develop the theme of success when he writes that, since he has gone from being poor and unknown to being well off and famous, since he has had a happy life, he can offer himself as an example of success for others to imitate. Franklin does not limit his discussion of success to business, but also develops the theme of success through a description of his marriage, civic projects, and political career.

Franklin was successful in his career. Though he was originally slated to enter the church and then worked with his father as a tallow-chandler, he was eventually apprenticed to his brother to be a printer. Franklin worked hard and learned the trade of printer well. He also used his time with the educated men of Boston to learn to discuss and to write persuasively. This served him well later in life when he wanted to make changes and found that he could make them happen through his writing. Franklin makes clear that his success as an apprentice was not limited simply to his learning a trade.

When Franklin left his brother, he ended up in Philadelphia working for another printer. Franklin left the printer's employ and worked in England for a while as a printer. He then returned to Philadelphia as a store clerk. He was happy in the work and had financial success until the death of the owner, at which time he went back to work for the printer as a manager in his printing shop, teaching the trade to the workers who had been hired. It was clear that he would soon work himself out of a job, and Franklin determined once again to set up his own printing house. Eventually Franklin was able to start his business through the generosity of two friends. He was so successful in his business that he was able to form partnerships in which junior partners took his printing apparatus and set up shops in other cities throughout the colonies and then bought out his majority interest from their earnings. The theme of success in the work is clearly developed through Franklin's success in business.

Franklin also describes his success in marriage. He courted Miss Read of Philadelphia successfully, but when he left for England and did not return soon, she married someone else. Her first marriage was unhappy, and when her husband died, she married Franklin. She was, he writes, a "good and faithful helpmate," who helped him in the business and ran the household. They worked to make each other happy and succeeded in that, too.

Franklin then discusses his successes in civic projects. He helped create a subscription library that was so successful it eventually became Philadelphia's first public library. Also he helped form the Union Fire Company, Philadelphia's first fire company. He used his persuasive skills as a writer to bring about a change in the constabulary and helped obtain public and private funding for a hospital. He made

Philadelphia more livable by persuading the government to pave and light the streets. In all these civic projects he was a success, and his success was a boon to his adopted city as well.

Another success that Franklin mentions is as a political figure. He became a clerk of the General Assembly, writing a paper arguing for the creation of a militia, making him a key figure in its establishment. Then he decided an academy was needed and encouraged his friends and the public to participate and set one up. He became so financially successful that he thought to retire, but the public "laid hold" of him and he was immersed in the civil government. He became an alderman and a burgess and tried being a justice of the peace. He was chosen to be a member of the Royal Society on account of his scientific experiments. By that time, Franklin says, he no longer had need of governors' favors because he was a success on his own.

Franklin wrote *The Autobiography of Benjamin Franklin* partially because friends recommended that he share his story in order to influence youth so that they might be as successful as he was. Thus the impetus behind the presentation of the autobiography makes clear the theme of success that Franklin developed throughout the book.

Suanna H. Davis

WORK in *The Autobiography of Benjamin Franklin*

One of the main themes in *The Autobiography of Benjamin Franklin* is work, which can be evidenced by the fact that Franklin uses the words "work" and "business" more than 100 times each within the text.

In introducing people in his narrative, Franklin focuses often on their occupation. Of his own FAMILY, Franklin says that a smith's business was their source of sustenance. He mentions that his grandfather and his three younger sons were all dyers and that the older one was a smith who became a scrivener. Franklin presents these men to posterity by the business each was engaged in.

The theme of work is also apparent when Franklin discusses his own evolving work situation in great detail. While his family initially expected him to serve in the church, Franklin was soon at home working with his father. Since Franklin did not wish to follow in his father's occupational footsteps, he was introduced to various trades. Franklin says that he found his trade through his love for reading and he was then apprenticed to his brother as a printer. He became a printer, worked as a store clerk for a time, returned to printing, and eventually became a business owner of a printing house and a stationer's store.

Franklin develops his theme of work through discussion of its difficulties and rewards. His apprenticeship was unpleasant because James was a harsh master. It was also pleasant, because Franklin liked the work, met other readers, and was able to advance his EDUCATION. His work in Watt's printing house in England brought difficulties, when the composers insisted that he contribute to their alcohol purchases. He resisted and all his work was undone whenever he was not looking. When he gave in and paid, his experience and his clear head—he did not indulge in drinking—brought him a better position in the company.

In developing the positive and negative aspects of work, Franklin describes some of his employers. Franklin spends a few paragraphs on the character of one whom he admired as a good businessman. Denham was a store owner and Franklin worked as his clerk. They roomed together and, until Denham died, he served as Franklin's adviser. Franklin enjoyed his work with Denham and it was financially renumerative, even after Denham's death, because Denham included Franklin in his will. Franklin then gives a negative example of an employer in his next boss, Keimer. Keimer had hired several people, promising to teach them the trade of printer, but Keimer did not know the printing trade. Eventually he hired Franklin to manage his printing house. Franklin quickly realized that if he taught Keimer's employees how to do their work, he would be out of a job, but he taught them and further straightened out the business. Keimer forced a public quarrel with Franklin, and Franklin's work for him ended after little more than six months.

The positive and negative aspects of work continue to be detailed through Franklin's discussions of partners. At one point, a man Franklin had taught proposed that they go into business together. This turned out to be a bad idea, because the man drank and Franklin was the only one caring for the business. Franklin eventually bought him out. Another potential partner rejected Franklin's proposal with scorn, which was good, because he lived above his means and soon ran his business into the ground.

Another example of the negative aspects of work is developed through Franklin's descriptions of other printers. He described his former boss Keimer as a compositor, not a pressman. Eventually Keimer sold his printing house to pay his debtors. Franklin labels Bradford, another printer, illiterate and not bred to the work. Bradford, who was also the postmaster for a time, refused to send Franklin's papers by the post and Franklin had to resort to bribing the carriers.

Franklin details the positive aspects of work by describing his own experience as an employer. Franklin was not only industrious, but he rewarded his employees who showed industry as well. He promoted these workers, sending them throughout the colonies in joint ventures. Due to their own diligence, they were often able to buy Franklin out, thus becoming the sole proprietors of their own printing houses.

In a clear development of the theme of work, Franklin says that not only was he a hard worker, but he also made this obvious to those around him by not engaging in leisure pursuits other than reading, which was a part of his business. He states that since industry, together with frugality, enabled him to pay off his debts and acquire his fortune, anyone who wants to be a businessman should follow his model.

Suanna H. Davis

FROST, ROBERT   poems   (1874–1963)

Robert Frost is one of the most important American poets of the 20th century. His poems, many of which chronicle the day-to-day tasks related to country living, are reminiscent of a quieter, simpler time in history. Though he wrote poetry the average man could relate to and understand, Frost's work cannot be considered simplistic. In fact, many readers have discovered profound, symbolic meanings deep within his words.

Portraying both the joys and hardships of rural life, Frost paid careful attention to rhyming patterns and diction. Not only could the average reader understand his works, but also they were especially appreciated when read aloud. His poems are full of imagery, as he paints vivid pictures of STAGES OF LIFE, NATURE, ISOLATION, and WORK.

Frost was no stranger to hardship. Born in 1874, he studied at Harvard and Dartmouth but never earned a degree, and worked a number of odd jobs before becoming an unsuccessful farmer and eventually a teacher. His later years were marked by tragedy. Three of his children passed away, including one son who committed suicide. Additionally, one of his daughters suffered from mental illness. In spite or perhaps because of these tragedies, he remained a productive poet, receiving honorary degrees and accolades during his lifetime, including the honor of reading one of his poems at the inauguration of President John F. Kennedy. He died in 1963.

Though he composed poems throughout his adult life, it is his earlier works which are most familiar. Ultimately, it is the accessibility of Frost's poetry—that he wrote with the common man in mind—that will continue to keep him one of the best-loved poets of his generation.

Erin Brescia

ISOLATION in the poetry of Robert Frost

Isolation is frequently alluded to in many of Robert Frost's poems. In some, it is something to be enjoyed, or even savored, while in others it is considered unnatural and unnecessary.

In his poem, "Mending Wall," two neighbors make their yearly trip to the wall that joins their property in order to make improvements. Between the elements and hunters, the wall becomes damaged over each year. The narrator gives no indication that he and his neighbor spend time together aside from this project, but every year they "meet to walk the line and set the wall between us once again" (l. 13–14).

The narrator is not entirely sure that this wall is necessary. They have no animals between them to wander in each other's yards; however, his neighbor merely replies: "good fences make good neighbors" (l. 27). The message he sends here is that as long as each individual keeps to himself, they will remain friends. The narrator questions his neighbor's philosophy. As long as no harm will come to their property, why would they want to keep the other out? He goes so far as to suggest that this theory is antiquated, calling it "his father's saying." Because the narrator's neighbor was raised on the idea that fences are important, he will never stray from his father's counsel.

The narrator notes that even nature does not promote fences—that the "frozen ground" adjusts the boulders so that they shift from one another and are no longer effective. Symbolically, Frost is saying that men are not always meant to be isolated from one another; interaction with others is a vital part of living. The irony is that they will continue to keep the wall between them as they work together to mend it.

In another poem, however, Frost praises the idea of isolation as it relates to hard work. In "Stopping by Woods on a Snowy Evening," he speaks of a man on an assignment. He is traveling alone in the woods with his horse. In this case, the owner of the property is not nearby but lives in town. The man pauses for a moment to enjoy his surroundings as the woods around him fill with snow.

Again, nature asserts the idea that isolation is unnatural when the horse shakes his harness "to ask if there is some mistake" (l. 10). The horse realizes it is more customary to stop when they reach a farmhouse and other people, rather than in the middle of the forest while it is snowing. The man, however, enjoys this moment of solitude. He refers to the woods as "lovely, dark and deep" (l. 13). They seem an eternal abyss; a place he is content to stay awhile if not for his impending task. Despite the fact that he enjoys the isolation and the quiet forest, he has "promises to keep" (l. 14). These promises will undoubtedly return him to civilization. His surroundings could also reflect that he is in the "winter," or the final stages, of his life and that he is ready to rest and enjoy the isolation.

"The Road Not Taken," full of symbolism concerning the choices one must make in life, also quietly alludes to one key idea concerning isolation: One must make these choices alone. The narrator is in the forest with two paths before him. He knows he must choose one road to take, and that this choice will alter the course of his life. There is no one available to offer an opinion; no one to ask. The decision is entirely his own.

Nature may not promote the idea of isolation, but when faced with important choices, Frost suggests, it is absolutely necessary. It is the individual who is responsible for his decisions; he should never rely on those around him to choose the path he is to take, as this could potentially lead to disaster. Isolation might be unnatural, but it is required by thinking people so that they may think for themselves.

The idea of isolation in Frost's poems has a threefold purpose: to remind readers to savor the quiet moments, to find solace in the company of others, and to remember that, in the end, one is entirely responsible for making his own existence worthwhile.

Erin Brescia

STAGES OF LIFE in the poetry of Robert Frost

Robert Frost's most famous poem, "The Road Not Taken," has been used as the theme of many commencement addresses. It is most relevant for graduation exercises because of the idea of "choices." Like the subject of the poem, students are often faced with important decisions after completing their degree. Frost eloquently notes these decisions by comparing them to paths in the wood.

First, in making this decision, the subject is sorry that he "could not travel both" paths. Knowing what lay at the end of each road would undoubtedly help him make his choice, but this is impossible, just as it is impossible to predict the future. The narrator understands that the choice he is about to make regarding which path he travels will alter the course of his life. There are two roads: two paths that will lead to two entirely different outcomes.

According to the narrator, the paths are "equal." One path is not good and the other evil, one is not treacherous and the other easy; they are simply paths. Each path has been chosen by someone before him—someone with a choice to make. Though both paths are worn "about the same," the narrator notices that one is less worn, and this becomes the "road less traveled." As he looks back on his life, the narrator realizes that when it was time to make the choice, the path he chose "made all the difference."

This poem is about decisions and the passage of time. A true "coming of age" poem, "The Road Not Taken" symbolically highlights the freedom one has to create his own destiny. Given the narrator's "sigh," the reader is unsure if the narrator is pleased with the road he traveled, or if he has made a mistake. While some take the right path, not everyone makes the appropriate choice. When reminiscing, there are those who wish their life had taken a different course. By then, however, it is too late. The choices made early in life have permanent outcomes, which is why symbolically, readers are encouraged to "choose wisely."

Like "The Road Not Taken," Frost's "Birches" presents an older narrator looking back on life. Here, the focus is on life's hardships and their effects. The narrator is looking at the bent branches of a birch tree. He wishes to believe that they are bent because young boys have been swinging on them, but knows that this does not bend the branches "down to stay." It is more probable that the branches are bent because of the ice storms they have weathered.

Frost describes the icy winter morning and its picturesque beauty, though it is destroying the shape of the branches. When the storm is over, the sunlight causes the ice to melt and break. He describes their shattering as "such heaps of broken glass to sweep away" (l. 12). This is reminiscent of the pieces that are left to be picked up after a tragedy has occurred: the aftermath. What is important to note is that, though the branches are altered, they are not broken.

What the narrator would prefer, however, is that the boy—left to his own entertaining devices—bent the branches by swinging on them. Frost describes how perfectly the boy would swing, learning the technique so as not to break them, until "not one was left for him to conquer" (l. 33).

The narrator confesses that he, too, was once a swinger of birches, "and so I dream of going back to be" (l. 43). By admitting this, there seems to be a correlation between the ice storms that affect the branches and the hardships he has seen. Ultimately, he would like to return to a simpler time in life where he had the freedom to play in the woods as a boy. Even now, he wishes to climb the trunk and have the branches set him down again. He con-cludes that there are worse things in life than being "a swinger of birches" (l. 70).

In each of these poems, Frost discusses the various stages of life and the challenges they bring. First, there is the young boy without a care, one who can spend his days climbing trunks and swinging from trees. As he grows, he becomes the young man who must choose his course in life—knowing that his decision will alter him forever. Then, looking back, there is the old man who has endured the trials and hardships of living—who may or may not regret the path he has traveled, but would rather be a young boy with the freedom to swing on the branches from heaven and back to earth again.

Erin Brescia

WORK in the poetry of Robert Frost

One of the reasons Robert Frost's poetry is enjoyed is his ability to capture the reality of everyday living in language that is accessible to the average reader. In essence, the subjects of Frost's poems are everyday men and women doing ordinary, common things. The idea of work is mentioned in many ways throughout his various poems. Many times he speaks of specific chores and tools, while elsewhere he alludes to the effect work has on the common man.

For instance, in his poem "Putting in the Seed," he writes of the narrator's passion for planting apple seeds in the spring. Though he knows that someone will stop by soon to fetch him for dinner, he almost dares them to try to pull him away from his work. In fact, he realizes that more than likely he who comes to fetch him will become caught up in his work as well: the "slave to a springtime passion for the earth" (l. 9). In this case, the work is pleasurable; the narrator enjoys planting seeds and watching them grow.

Frost also refers to the satisfaction of work. In "The Pasture," the narrator has a list of chores that must be accomplished. He plans to rake the leaves out of the pasture spring and check on a young calf. He encourages others to come with him because once the work is done, there are benefits to reap. For instance, after cleaning the pasture spring he may stay for a while "and wait to watch the water clear" (l. 3).

In "The Tuft of Flowers," Frost writes of how well it is that men work together. Whether or not it makes the job easier, or allows them to finish faster, the narrator has found a "spirit kindred" in the man who works alongside him. They work hard together, and, when they become weary, rest in the shade together. In the final stanza, the narrator tells his comrade that "men work together . . . whether they work together or apart" (l. 10). This alludes to the idea that everyone works together for the common good of man. Though they may not work on the same task, people who work are connected to one another, laboring toward a tangible goal. This satisfaction is what makes work bearable.

In other poems, however, work is merely to be tolerated, something that must be done. In these poems, men are tired and overworked. Many times they find solace in nature and their surroundings. In "Stopping by Woods on a Snowy Evening," the narrator is a weary traveler, working his way toward his destination. Frost never mentions the purpose for this man's journey, only that he has made a promise he must keep. At this point, he still has miles to go before he is able to rest, so he stops for a moment to enjoy the woods around him as they fill with snow. Here, the narrator knows that the task must be accomplished no matter his physical or mental state. The idea here is that there is time to rest when the job is finished.

In Frost's poetry, work is seen as having a profound effect on the common man. For many, work becomes a death sentence. Others are physically and mentally altered by the work they have done over the years. In "Birches" the narrator describes life as a "pathless wood" (l. 44), where one is required to make his own way through the cobwebs and the trees. The way is long and difficult and painful, and he is altered by it in the same way the birch trees are altered by the ice storm. In the winter, the branches are heavy with ice that bend the tree down to stay, just as the narrator, in the winter of his life, is bent from the work and hardships he endured. Because of this, he dreams of a simpler time and the ability to again be a "swinger of birches" (l. 41); a young man who, while he is out tending to the cows, still has the time and energy to play in the trees.

Work is a complicated theme throughout Frost's poetry, and his attitude toward it may never be fully understood. His poems, though, speak of the realities of work: that sometimes it can be enjoyed, sometimes it is meant to be tolerated, that the physical proof of the accomplished task is something of which to be proud, and finally, if one is not careful, work can lead to an early grave.

Erin Brescia

GAINES, ERNEST J. *The Autobiography of Miss Jane Pittman* (1971)

Ernest J. Gaines, a powerful contemporary African-American writer from Louisiana, is best known for exploring the theme of heroism among disenfranchised and emasculated African-American men. His work has been compared to the work of William Faulkner, like Faulkner; Gaines created a mythical town, Bayonne, set in his birth state of Louisiana, where his characters face the trials and tribulations of being black. In their heroic quest for dignity and meaning, strong black women teach them the importance of small acts of heroism. In this fictional autobiography, Gaines represents the profound struggles of just such an indomitable black woman. This novel, remarkable for its innovations in form, established Gaines as a brilliant writer whose apparently simple, folk style of writing holds profound messages.

In *The Autobiography of Miss Jane Pittman*, Gaines, without abandoning his mission of exploring African-American male heroism, creates a remarkable female protagonist who transcends the traditional representations of black womanhood. Additionally, he explores the difficult and mine-ridden task of negotiating the contradictions inherent in the tensions between progress and regress that every person encounters as she charts out new paths in unfamiliar territories. A fictional autobiography narrated by the reclusive and reluctant 110-year-old Miss Jane Pittman, the autobiographical material is gleaned and edited by a persistent history teacher who does so in order to compile a folk history of black Americans between the years of emancipation and civil rights. The different voices of the community that Gaines heard, growing up on the porch of his paraplegic great aunt, Augusteen Jefferson, are brilliantly captured in a communal voice. This communal voice is perfect for telling the individual story that is the life of the brave and ethical Miss Jane Pittman who, at the tender age of 10, has the profound insight that we cannot "let what happened yesterday stop us today." Renamed Jane by a Union soldier from Ohio, after his own daughter Jane Brown, Miss Jane searches for the meaning of freedom as she carves out a life for herself as a free individual, a difficult task given the soul-depleting ideology of slavery that continues to enslave people's minds. However, forced to rely at a very young age on only herself, Miss Jane constructs a belief system that grows out of her 110 years of life experience.

Su Senapati

COMMUNITY in *The Autobiography of Miss Jane Pittman*

Ernest P. Gaines in *The Autobiography of Miss Jane Pittman* reveals the strong communal bond of fellow responsibility that exists in the black community as he explores the problems of engendering African-American leaders and the need for understanding between blacks and whites during important junctures in time. After the Emancipation Proclamation, the newly freed slaves charted out new paths and constructed new paradigms to improve their lives. However, the deep divide between blacks and whites and traditional and progressive ideas unleashed uncertainty and violence, making the reconstruction of the South a harrowing process. Progress was slow since racist ideology first had to be erased from both white and black consciousness for equitable laws to be created and transformed into social reality. To achieve this end, Gaines deems education, time, and community to be essential.

Furthermore, Gaines's unwavering belief in the black community's ability to rise like the proverbial phoenix is revealed through the creation of his protagonist, Miss Jane Pittman, who from the age of 10 willingly abandons the security of the familiar to courageously tread uncharted territories. When Jimmy the chosen "One" is frustrated by his failure to inspire ex-slaves to join the Civil Rights movement, Miss Pittman reminds him that downtrodden and enslaved people need time to develop fortitude to recognize and fight their wretchedness and that it is not the individual leader that fails but rather the

community that succeeds. She tells Jimmy, "People and time bring forth leaders . . . leaders don't bring forth people." Moreover, so strong is Gaines's faith in the community that he narrates the autobiography of the remarkable Miss Jane Pittman through the communal voice of African Americans.

Miss Pittman's belief that leaders evolve naturally from within the community over a period of time is validated by the examples of Big Laura, Ned Douglas, Jimmy Aaron, and finally Miss Jane Pittman herself. However, since community leaders seek radical change by teaching the disenfranchised to think for themselves, they are perceived as threats and killed by the powerful, only to be replaced by others who take on their roles or continue their progressive work. Big Laura, because of her size, strength, and quiet fortitude, innocuously slips into the role of leading two dozen freed slaves away from servitude, but while she succeeds in maintaining order within the traveling group she fails to stave off attacks by Confederate soldiers. Her orphaned, infant son, Ned, also grows up to be a leader, but he too is assassinated for daring to educate poor blacks. Nonetheless, when Ned is killed the work of educating blacks is continued: A school is built and children educated through the collective effort of the community. Yet his death creates such a vacuum and the community is so in need of a leader that when Jimmy is born, he is nominated as the "One." But instead of spiritually leading the people, he leads them politically. But he too is assassinated and the 110–year-old Miss Pittman, who has shied away from leadership roles, openly defies Robert Samson and leads the protest march Jimmy had planned, becoming the wise icon of African-American solidarity that Jimmy had envisioned. Thus the 10-year-old child Jane, who without any qualms took on the responsibility of protecting the infant Ned, bringing him to safety and mothering and raising him to be a leader, embodies not only the solidarity of the black community but also the heroic qualities of a new kind of leader for the community.

However, while the bonds within the black community are strong and people nonchalantly and without fanfare take on responsibilities of caring for and nurturing those in need, the bonds with whites are nonexistent. The powerful white community is not only ignorant of the need to establish human bonds with former slaves but is also oblivious to the suffering it incurs for adopting and participating in racist ideology. For example, Robert Samson uses Verda sexually and denies the existence of his "half-nigger" son Timmy, even though Timmy is more like Robert than Robert's legitimate son Tee Bob is. Although Tee Bob adores Timmy and the two are inseparable, Robert has no qualms about sending Timmy off the plantation even after the overseer Tom Joe has beaten Timmy cruelly and unjustly. The contradictions inherent in this ideology finally unravel in the fractured consciousness of Tee Bob who, unable to reconcile the apparent acceptability of being allowed to have a sexual relationship with the mulatto Mary Agnes LeFebre but not to love her or marry her, commits suicide. After Tee Bob's suicide, all Robert is concerned about is taking revenge on the equally innocent Mary Agnes. Only Jules Reynard's calm control and threat of exposure prevents Robert from taking vengeance. As Reynard and Miss Jane Pittman discuss the tragedy of Tee Bob's suicide they realize that "he was bound to kill himself one day for our sins." When Miss Pittman feels sorry for Tee Bob and says "Poor Tee Bob," Reynard reminds her, "No, poor us," exposing how everyone is a loser in a divided community.

The fact that bonds of friendship do exist and can exist among people divided artificially along color lines is brought home by the hit man Albert Cluveau's feeble attempts to protect Ned. Lacking the courage, wherewithal, and initiative needed to defy the orders of his powerful white employers, he feels compelled to reveal to Jane his orders to kill Ned. That communal bonds of friendship do exist among blacks and whites who live together and that such bonds are short-circuited by racist ideology that reduces communal bonds to the lowest common denominator of survival is also revealed by Cluveau's clinical execution of unethical orders. Finally, the fact that economic wealth is not what determines the strength and health of an individual and her/his community is revealed when, at the end of the novel, the reader realizes that the childless, penniless orphan Miss Jane Pittman has more fam-

ily, love, and respect than the powerful plantation owner, Robert Samson, with all his wealth, progeny, and financially dependent ex-slaves.

Su Senapati

STAGES OF LIFE in *The Autobiography of Miss Jane Pittman*

The Autobiography of Miss Jane Pittman is divided into four discrete sections, War Years, Reconstruction, Plantation, and Quarter. These correspond with the stages of African-American history. Miss Jane Pittman's life can be divided into five sections that may be explained using psychologist Abraham Maslow's theory of hierarchy of needs and ethical development, a movement from a preoccupation with the self to the community. These stages of Miss Jane Pittman's life are (1) Freedom March, (2) Raising Ned and Losing Ned, (3) Finding Love and Losing Love, (4) Recovery, (5) Community. During all the stages of her life, Miss Jane is preoccupied with responsibilities of survival and safety, but her self-respect, tenacity, ethical acumen, pragmatism, and ability to overcome challenges and solve problems, even linked to her sworn enemies, make her an unparalleled leader.

During the first stage of her life, Miss Jane has no name, lineage, or history that defines her as a person, but she has a commodity value that translates into endless work. Once emancipated, her service value is removed and the market economy tries to destroy and dump the devalued commodity that was once a slave. Hunting and killing of freed slaves traveling north thus becomes a common phenomenon during Reconstruction.

While the older slaves on the Bryant plantation prefer the familiarity of known hardships, and choose to stay behind, the younger ones, including Miss Jane, choose to leave and venture into unknown geographies. But every one of them, even the strong leader, Big Laura, is hunted down and brutally murdered; only child Jane and baby Ned survive.

However, Jane's recognizable life as a human begins before she is freed, when a Yankee soldier, Colonel Brown, names her Jane after his own daughter. Colonel Brown may be seen as an adoptive parent; although he does not provide any of the necessities an adoptive parent provides, he gives Jane her name, thereby giving her social legitimacy. Her goal in journeying to Ohio is to locate her adoptive father, but when she does find him he does not recognize her, just as at birth the parent who has abandoned a child would not. Unfazed by the disappointment, she sets up a life where she is a parent and not a child and gives to Ned what she has never received, love, care, and respect. So the second stage of Miss Jane's life as a freed slave is one of creating an instant family for the vulnerable, which includes herself.

Miss Jane's role as a mother to Ned gives her life immediate meaning and agency until Ned becomes an adult and carves out his life's mission to empower his people and improve their living conditions. But he is forced to abandon his mission. After a brief sojourn to escape being killed, Ned returns, having transformed himself from Ned Brown to Ned Douglass after Frederick Douglass. Because of Jane's nurturing Ned is able to quickly move to Maslow's highest stage of ethical development, giving service to his community. But his empowering mission threatens the white-black social hierarchy in the South; like most noble leaders who initiate ethical change, he is brutally murdered. When hired killer Albert Cluveau kills Ned, Jane is furious and curses Cluveau, but soon after, she helps Cluveau's daughters, refusing to withhold compassion even from her enemies.

Having quelled her childhood and erotic stages of life to raise Ned, Jane has an opportunity to participate in the stage of erotic love after Ned's departure. She falls in love with Joe Pittman, a highly independent, spirited horse breaker, who through sheer hard work has earned his release from economic bondage and taken to breaking wild horses, never to be beholden to another master because during slavery, while slaves were kept in literal and metaphorical chains, after slavery they were kept in social and economic chains.

During this stage of finding love and losing love, which spans a decade, Jane is happy and content, but she has to surrender to the gender hierarchy of marriage. Joe Pittman's age and wildness further exacerbate this hierarchy. When Joe meets Jane, he already has a family of two girls and is interested in Jane to some extent to find a surrogate mother for his children. Insecure in her role as a spouse, Jane is afraid, a fear that manifests itself as an unexplainable paranoia of losing Joe. What she fears at this stage is separation anxiety, a fear felt by children and associated with the first stage of life. Being loved and being in love makes Jane vulnerable, much more so because she has not gone through the traditional first stage of life development, so her vulnerability leads her to bizarre acts that culminate in Joe's death.

Devastated though she is by Joe and Ned's deaths, she keeps faith by keeping her hands busy as she enters the recovery stage of her life. She travels from one work establishment to another, preferring to work outside in the fields doing heavy labor rather than domestic chores, forming a philosophy that steady work, not too much work, and eating fish does a body good. She does not take sides, but works and rests and consoles those in need; but she can trust no one and nothing. Though old and wise and most suited to give the young direction, she does not lead, refusing even to speak of her long and eventful life to the history teacher who reconstructs her autobiography. A leader imposes a larger collective will on others and Jane is dead set against it, having chaffed under the heavy authority of slavery. She shies away from such a role, afraid it brings in the same master-slave paradigm of willful domination. When the young workers talk about the Civil Rights movement Dr. King has started she is skeptical, but when news of Jimmy's death arrives she cannot stay uninvolved.

Miss Jane's biggest challenge has been finding out what to believe in, since familiarity and ubiquity make even the wrong appear right. So for Miss Pittman whose life is steeped in and shaped by injustices, believing in any kind of ideological movement is difficult. Experience has taught her to trust only the individual and make no generalizations about either race.

Having lost so many black pioneers and potential leaders in her community, she cannot bear losing any more. She decides to lead. Because the people so badly want a messiah she becomes the messiah, but an earthly one, not a heavenly one. Her wisdom comes when she believes and relies on the validity of something outside of herself, something she has not learned to trust, for all she could ever trust or rely on was herself. Though frail and old, she leads the freedom march, although she knows the social rules and consequences: death. A former illiterate slave girl who has managed to live for 110 years by the sweat of her brow is not afraid of death, for she has not been afraid of life. Though she has not gone through the traditional stages of life development, she has lived her life through principles of work, ethics, courage, and compassion, which have made her life meaningful and important. Her journey from self to community is complete.

Su Senapati

WORK in *The Autobiography of Miss Jane Pittman*

Since identity is intricately tied to the work a person does and since slaves had historically been separated from the product of their labor, Gaines pays particular attention to the theme of work. The protagonist of this story, Miss Jane Pittman, starts her work life at the age of 10 as a caretaker of children and later in life works as a field hand, a cook, and a laundress, but no matter what she does and no matter how menial the task, she does it well and this gives her the strength and courage to face all challenges in life.

Born into slavery, all Jane knows is work; however, although her masters appropriate the product of her labor, they cannot appropriate the sense of self that she derives from her work. Ironically, when she is a child slave at the Bryant plantation, the added work of supplying water to exhausted soldiers passing by brings her in contact with Colonel Brown and the outside world, which in turn propels her on a journey of growth and enlightenment. A child herself, she without hesitation shoulders the responsibility of protecting, nurturing, and educating baby Ned, working endlessly to give what has been denied to her, an education. Her hard work pays off, for Ned grows up to be a marvelous human being who works to uplift the lives of the poor and the persecuted.

Jane takes pride in her ability to work hard and earn adult wages on the Boone plantation. The foolishness of such pride, though excusable in a child, has disastrous consequences in adults as is revealed by the Katie Nelson and Black Harriet incident on the Colonel Dye plantation. Such events where pride and competition at work cause havoc shape Jane's work mantra for life, for as a former slave she must define the parameters of work, since excessive work has been the cause of injury and death for many a slave. She concludes, "Hard work can kill you, but plain, steady work killed nobody. Steady work and eating plenty of fish killed nobody."

Although work is empowering to the individual, not all work is empowering. Albert Cluveau, the hit man who kills Ned, spends the last 10 years of his life cowering in bed with his daughters, frightened of the "Chariots of Hell" that he is convinced are pursuing him. He has killed over a dozen men and for him killing is work, a way of making a living; but it is dirty work where the exercise of free will and ethical choice are willingly suspended, reducing the worker to subhuman levels and denying her/him any sense of self-worth.

Furthermore, work is a concrete manifestation of the African-American contribution to the building of America; so, when newly freed slaves are riddled with confusion and have no place to go and rumblings of "go back to Africa" slogans are heard, Ned urges ex-slaves to question the validity of such statements, reminding them of the back-breaking work they have rendered: "This earth is yours . . . your people's bones lays in it; it's yours because their sweat and their blood done drenched this earth." However, just physical labor is not enough as Ned reminds his students: "Working with your hands while the white man writes all the rules and laws will not better your lot," for until the products of African–American labor are appropriated by African-American laborers, they will be exploited and their sense of self-worth crippled.

But Joe Pittman's work ideology best summarizes the reason and importance of work. When Jane, frightened by dreams of Joe's death, asks him to quit breaking horses for a living, he says that man is contracted to die but until he does, "he should do what he is good at doing" so that when he dies people can say, "He did good as he could." Joe and Ned and Jimmy and many others like them know and recognize their calling in life, but for many others such callings in life are closed because of mind-numbing work that disallows their participation in the full spectrum of meaningful work. Thus Gaines in *The Autobiography of Miss Jane Pittman,* while showing the importance of work in the formation of identity, also advocates the need for better correspondence between the work one does and the product of that work for more holistic and human identities.

Su Senapati

GAINES, ERNEST J.   *A Lesson before Dying*   (1993)

A Lesson before Dying depicts rural Louisiana in the 1940s. A young African American named Jefferson has been accused of killing a shop owner during a robbery and is confined in prison. In fact, he was in the shop, accompanying two of his friends, when a violent argument between the two and the proprietor erupted, as a result of which the three fighting men shot each other to death. Jefferson's court-appointed attorney compares him to an animal and calls him a "hog," indicating that the defendant's racial inferiority incapacitates him from acting with premeditation. These words do not influence the jury's verdict, which is a death sentence, but they have a powerful effect on the black people in Jefferson's community. The convict's elderly godmother, Miss Emma, asks the teacher from the plantation school, Grant Wiggins, to talk to Jefferson and help him recover his sense of dignity. Initially, Grant's visits to the prison are fruitless; he is reluctant to carry out his task, while Jefferson reacts to him with anger, impatience, or indifference. However, in the course of time, the young convict begins to appreciate the gestures of goodwill from the teacher and finds reassurance in the "lessons." He discovers the meaning of his SUFFERING.

One of the central concerns in Gaines's novel is the attachment to place and the extent to which the place and the time of a person's birth determine the entire course of his or her later life. The narrator is Grant Wiggins; from his point of view, the necessity to live on the plantation where he had grown up and where he returned after his studies is literally a curse. In his native region, racism is the overwhelming historical legacy that underlies the existing social relations. Racial segregation is a law, therefore it sustains, if not aggravates, the inequalities between white and black people. It is not surprising that Wiggins's narrative is permeated by a sense of hopelessness mixed with anxiety. He is acutely aware there is no force that would change the present state of things. However, even if the external conditions cannot be improved, people's consciousness can still be transformed. The death sentence for Jefferson provides an impetus for the entire community to acknowledge the value of sacrifice for the sake of others. It is not only Jefferson who learns an essential lesson, but also his kinsfolk from the plantation. This is primarily a lesson in dignity. On the one hand, *A Lesson* is a story of disillusionment and desperation, on the other, a tale of endurance and transformation. The narrative and thematic aspects of the novel combine the issues of ALIENATION and COMMUNITY. The historical context highlights the problems of RACE and IDENTITY.

Marek Paryz

ALIENATION in *A Lesson before Dying*

Grant Wiggins is a very ambivalent narrator because, on the one hand, he has been virtually forced by his aunt to become involved with Jefferson as a distinguished member of the black COMMUNITY, but on the other, he feels alienated from his kinfolk and even tries his best to minimize his affinity with them. His alienation is primarily caused by the determination to remain loyal to himself rather than to the group; furthermore, he considers his commitment to the community to be a possible threat to his personal integrity. He is an educated man, has been to other places, and has a chance to go to California; however, his unusual EDUCATION and unique prospects make him even more vulnerable to the misery and hopelessness of the local existence. Unlike Wiggins, most community members do not think about alternatives for their lives for the simple reason that they do not have any.

Grant's alienation seems to be inseparable from his sense of entrapment. The fact that he returned to the plantation after his studies makes him feel as if he were caught in a vicious circle. The prospect of leaving Louisiana is delayed until Vivian has received a formal divorce. With the passing days,

Wiggins experiences his estrangement more and more painfully. He tends to think rather than act and, paradoxically, his incessant musings about a better life elsewhere possibly attest to his strong attachment to the native region, much stronger than he would wish to admit. The more actively he engages in the "lessons" with Jefferson, the more visibly he follows the community's imperatives, but this does not alleviate his alienation. The point is that his acceptance of a RESPONSIBILITY imposed on him by the community is accompanied by a further separation from the community through a close acquaintance with another man on strictly personal terms.

An important aspect of Grant's alienation is his break with the church. He abandoned religious practice much earlier than the novel's time of action, and his aunt has held a grudge against him because of that ever since. His detachment from religion is so severe that he gets irritated at the sound of songs and prayers reverberating in the church. His religious indifference is not only an expression of his personal choice, but also a manifestation of his distinction from others. He refuses to identify with the people who delude themselves that God will save them and that better times will come after death. A crucial episode in *A Lesson* is Wiggins's confrontation with Reverend Ambrose. Grant suspects that the preacher, whom Tante Lou and Miss Emma trust unconditionally, wants to use him instrumentally. Indeed, Ambrose wants to persuade him that Jefferson should express his religious feelings before the execution so as to give his godmother a final consolation and to convince the community that his sacrifice will not be made in vain. Grant, who cares about Jefferson's personal transformation and ignores the collective wishes or expectations, challenges Ambrose on the grounds that he does not respect the convict's individual feelings and talks only about empty gestures.

Whereas the theme of alienation evidently revolves around the dilemmas faced by Grant Wiggins, it is further developed in the presentation of Matthew Antoine, the local schoolteacher from the time of Grant's youth. In the portrayal of this character, Gaines directly points to RACE as a factor behind individual alienation. Basically, Antoine is a Creole and as such he does not belong to the black community, even though he devoted most of his life to African Americans. Antoine feels that he wasted his life, and now that he is an old man it is much too late to improve his situation. When he looks at Grant, he recognizes himself from his younger years, recognizes his own dreams and illusions. However, despite the odds, Grant still has a chance for a radical change in his life, which makes Antoine even more bitter and hateful.

The theme of alienation plays a central role in Gaines's novel as it facilitates the exploration of the problems arising at the intersections of individual and collective experience. Individual alienation results from, as much as it leads to, a variety of tensions between a person and a group. The analysis of such tensions provides a key to the understanding of social phenomena and historical circumstances.

Marek Paryz

COMMUNITY in *A Lesson before Dying*

In *A Lesson before Dying*, Ernest J. Gaines portrays two communities, black and white, and while he looks closely at the life of the former, he also explores the relations between both racial groups and pays special attention to important contrasts between them. The presentation of any community usually has a double focus: the place and the people. In Gaines's novel, the people in the black community live in a special quarter of the plantation that has been allocated to them. Such an organization of the plantation area suggests that the situation of African Americans in the rural South has not changed visibly since the time of slavery, when black people occupied run-down buildings located at a distance from the plantation house. Although the black Americans described in the novel are obviously free, the place where they live imposes drastic limitations on them and reduces their possibilities to the minimum. They live with the awareness that they belong to an inferior social category.

The central building in the quarter used by the black community is the church, which on weekdays houses a school. The school exists thanks to the dubious generosity of whites and possesses little means. There is only one qualified teacher, and the children of different ages have classes at the same time; therefore Wiggins, the teacher, relies on the assistance of older students when he organizes the teaching of the youngest. The miserable school conditions make the children realize their low personal value to their society and deprive them of their aspirations. Despite this, the children at school not only acquire the basic skills, but they also learn to help one another and to act collectively. An important episode that shows the strengthening of bonds between the youngest members of the African-American community is their preparation of a nativity play for Christmas festivities.

The centrality of the church in the black quarter points to the significance of RELIGION in the community's life. African Americans are poor people who bear humiliation on a daily basis; that is why they need spiritual support and religious consolation so much. The HOPE that there is a loving God makes their lives tolerable and saves them from utter resignation. Thus it is understandable that Reverend Ambrose, who is in charge of the church, is a figure of authority in the black people's eyes and a natural leader of their community. He allows them to believe that the salvation of souls will be a compensation for the privations and humiliations of earthly life. Although he has doubts about his methods, and even about his calling, he realizes that he would fail his people completely if they knew about his incertitude; therefore he remains firm in his public role.

It is important to notice that women play a crucial role in the African-American community. The main female characters in *A Lesson* are Miss Emma, Jefferson's godmother, Tante Lou, Wiggins's aunt, and Vivian, his beloved. Miss Emma and Tante Lou are both women of faith; in particular, they believe that Jefferson will regain his dignity and religious consciousness before the execution. The two women cooperate closely with Reverend Ambrose, who not only confirms them in their faith, but also suggests to them ways of influencing Grant and Jefferson. Although Miss Emma and Tante Lou are elderly and therefore delicate women, they know how to exert pressure on men and they instigate actions undertaken by men. This is particularly true of Grant who unwillingly yields to his aunt's persuasion after she has blackmailed him. Miss Emma and Tante Lou function as mother figures for Jefferson and Grant, respectively. Even Vivian, though she is

Grant's lover, offers him almost motherly support. It can be said that the black community in Gaines's novel has certain matriarchal features.

The significance of women in the black community accounts for the contrast with the strictly patriarchal white community. In general, in patriarchal societies all power resides in the hands of men. In *A Lesson* the white community is represented almost exclusively by male characters. Moreover, the white men portrayed by Gaines belong to the local elite, as they are landowners and entrepreneurs, or they hold various public offices. For example, Henri Pichot owns the plantation, Louis Rougnon runs a bank in a nearby town, and Sam Guidry is the sheriff. They stand for economic privilege and institutional power.

Marek Paryz

RACE in *A Lesson before Dying*

The relations between the communities of whites and blacks are determined by the difference in race and the resulting prejudices. The context evoked in the novel is characterized by a long history of racism, which has become a social norm. Even though *A Lesson's* racism does not portray brutal or violent forms of racism, it inevitably highlights a variety of situations where white people have been involved with blacks. The best illustration of how whites assert their superiority and remind African Americans that they are seen as an inferior category of human is the episode when Grant comes to Mr. Pichot's house and has to wait in the kitchen for more than two hours before the host kindly meets him. In general, when a black person wants to be treated favorably by whites, he should speak humbly and avoid looking white people straight in the eyes.

White people control African Americans by means of certain oppressive measures, sanctioned by the law; indeed, Jefferson's punishment for a crime he did not commit is the most striking example of racial oppression. Gaines presents the young convict as a scapegoat, in other words, a man who is punished mercilessly, even though he does not bear any GUILT. The mechanism of scapegoating manifests itself in relations between individuals as well as between groups, such as national or ethnic communities; Gaines is interested in the latter case.

The identification and punishment of a scapegoat is a symbolic reminder of who exercises power and who yields to it. The sentence for Jefferson serves as a warning for his kinfolk that it is white people who make the laws and that anyone who tries to undermine such an order will be punished most relentlessly. The sacrifice of a scapegoat has symbolic significance for the oppressed group. It not only forces them to admit their powerlessness, but also strengthens their solidarity in the face of external hostility.

The inability to think outside racial stereotypes has a dehumanizing effect on both blacks and whites. African Americans tend to look at themselves through the prism of white people's contemptuous view of them; this is why Jefferson begins to think of himself as an animal-like being after he has been called a "hog." When Grant resumes the "lessons" with Jefferson, the young prisoner, in the beginning, keeps saying that he behaves in certain ways because this is how animals behave. In a sense, albeit profoundly disturbed by having been compared to an animal, Jefferson apparently tries to confirm that the white man in court was right. While the dehumanization of blacks is caused by the overwhelming impact of white people's negative perceptions of them, the whites also become dehumanized as a consequence of their inability to renounce racial prejudices. Essentially, they cease to experience certain human emotions, most of all empathy. They become inconsiderate and heartless; for instance, several prominent white men, who talk to Wiggins at Pichot's place, make bets whether the teacher will manage to elicit any positive change in Jefferson.

The fact that African Americans assess their personal value and collective potential in the light of white people's prejudices accounts for the psychological mechanism of self-hatred. Individual self-hatred is inseparable from the hatred a person feels for his ethnic group. In *A Lesson,* Jefferson experiences powerful negative emotions toward himself, because he has been deprived of his personal dignity. With Wiggins's support, he eventually recovers his sense of selfhood and accepts his ethnic IDENTITY. However, Wiggins himself is not completely free from the feeling of self-hatred, as he lives with a painful awareness of how little he will ever achieve as a black man in spite of his education. There is also Matthew Antoine, Grant's former Creole teacher, a very embittered man, for whom the very sight of black people on the plantation exacerbates his sense of downright failure.

White people and black people are neighbors, but in fact they inhabit separate worlds. However, although the racial divide runs deep, goodwill helps to overcome it. During his visits to the prison, Wiggins becomes acquainted with a young deputy named Paul, who supports the African-American cause. Paul sympathizes with Jefferson and offers assistance to Grant. Individuals may discover in themselves the power to remove racial barriers, but in the universe of Gaines's novel it is a rather uncommon gift.

Marek Paryz

GARCÍA MÁRQUEZ, GABRIEL *One Hundred Years of Solitude* (1967)

One Hundred Years of Solitude, published in Spanish in 1967 and written by Colombian Nobel Prize winner Gabriel García Márquez, recounts the history of the Buendías who establish an imaginary Latin American community, Macondo. While Macondo is initially a utopia, it devolves until its annihilation, just as the last of the Buendía line is discovering the true nature of his origins. In between, generations of Buendías experience challenges that offer a pessimistic critique of Latin American civilization.

The plot's circular structure is complicated by the recycling of characters' names, the confusion of incestuous relationships, and the blending of magic and reality, which portray Latin America as self-destructive and insular. The tale also references historical events affecting the region. From the questionable influence of technology, seen in the inventions introduced by Melquíades and the Gypsies, to the arrival of the banana company, which mimics the scandal of the United Fruit Company, it is clear that contact with the outside world contributes to Macondo's problems and, by extension, those of Latin America.

This masterpiece shares themes of other *boom* novels, avant-garde works written during Latin

America's 20th-century literary explosion. Among these themes are FAMILY and COMMUNITY, MEMORY and HISTORY, REALITY and MAGIC. Its complex structure parallels the complexity of Latin American civilization. Its many layers—family, community, nation, region—provide insight into a culture colored by contrasts and conflicts and one that seems eternally doomed to repeat its mistakes.

Anne Massey

COMMUNITY in *One Hundred Years of Solitude*

Communities define themselves through shared interests, goals, or values and by the manner in which the group distinguishes itself from outside influences. Macondo, although a fictional village, serves as a model for examining the processes whereby Latin American communities define themselves. To accomplish this, the narrative traces Macondo's history from its founding by the Buendías to its destruction by the apparently unavoidable winds of eternal return, a concept in which events, although appearing to move forward, destructively revert to their origins. Macondo represents a community sharing an interest in progress but ultimately doomed to fail in the face of internal and external forces.

At first, Macondo's progress appears to be deterred primarily by outside influences. The village begins as an apparent utopia with founder José Arcadio Buendía arranging the homes so that all have equal sun and river access, but this spirit of social initiative ends with the fever of invention. The fever, spawned by interactions with the Gypsies, outsiders who thrill to technological marvels—such as magnets and ice—instills in José Arcadio a desire to move Macondo to a place more accessible to science. Only intervention by his wife, Ursula, prevents the move.

Another outside threat seems linked with the arrivals of Visitación and Rebecca. Shortly after their appearance in the community, Macondo begins to suffer from a plague of insomnia, an illness in which its sleepless victims forget everything, including the memories of their own identities. Unable to fall asleep, the villagers tell stories and plan strategies to compensate for their failing memories. This threat would have destroyed the community except for a magical potion provided by the wise Melquíades.

Two final outside entities influence Macondo: the federal government and the banana exporters. Government interference includes tampering with ballot boxes and involvement in the war between Liberals and Conservatives. The corruption and the futility of the violence threaten Macondo. Even Colonel Aureliano Buendía, an active military leader, eventually becomes "weary of the uncertainty of the vicious cycle of the eternal war that always found him in the same place but always older, wearier, even more in the position of not knowing why, or how, or even when." The banana company brings its own changes of order, entering Macondo in a "tumultuous and intemperate invasion." Eventually, the government and the banana company conspire against the village, massacring thousands when banana company workers strike.

However, outside influences are not entirely to blame for Macondo's demise; issues within the community create havoc as well. Key among these is the incestuous relationship of its founding family, symbolized by the confusing and repetitive use of proper names for the Buendía offspring and predicted from Macondo's inception as the cause of future problems. Throughout, various characters fear that such relationships will produce children with pigs' tails, an indication of the inappropriate nature of these unions.

Jealousy and disputes over behavior divide the community as well. For instance, when both Amaranta and Rebecca fall in love with Pietro Crespi, the girls enter a complex cat-and-mouse game that ends only when Rebecca marries the son of Macondo's founder and his wife Ursula. However, Ursula, considering the marriage disrespectful, as the adopted Rebecca and her new husband have been raised as siblings, forbids the couple from entering her home again. Fernanda, who has married into the Buendía family, considers Macondo's citizens beneath her social standing and separates herself and her family from the community at large. Representative of this posture are the closed windows of her home and the gold chamber pots bearing her family crest.

Despite Macondo's auspicious beginnings, in the end both community and outside influences erode the utopia envisioned by the founders. The community is abandoned by its inhabitants; following the banana company massacre Macondo decays under the persistent, drenching rains; the last of the Buendía line is born with a pig's tail, suggesting a return to more primitive beginnings; and finally the annihilating winds begin to blow and the alpha and omega of Macondo's existence collide. To the extent that Macondo mimics 20th-century Latin American communities, the novel describes internal and external forces that create or exacerbate a myriad of problems in the region, including: failure to understand and to utilize technology effectively, a regional identity crisis, government-sponsored violence, corruption in international business dealings, an inability to cope with social issues and class disparities, and an isolationist perspective that prevents Latin America from proactively seeking and engaging in solutions.

Anne Massey

FATE in *One Hundred Years of Solitude*

Eternal return is a view of events in which history and time are perceived as repetitive processes that doom society to revert back to its origins without ever progressing. This concept is pervasive throughout *One Hundred Years of Solitude* as the novel recounts the history of Macondo from its founding to its annihilation, a destruction that coincides with a potential rebirth as the last of the Buendías seeks to uncover the secrets of his personal and communal past. However, at the exact moment that these origins are to be revealed, destructive forces prevail, the town is swept away in a windstorm, and the opportunity to revitalize the community through a new beginning is lost. Instead, Macondo, and by implication Latin America, is fated to repeat its past, unaware that it is merely participating in a new destructive cycle. With the recollection of past mistakes erased by the storm, the missteps of history will inevitably lead yet again to the community's complete eradication.

Specific details and scenes support this pessimistic view. The repetition of identical or similar names—Aureliano, Arcadio, Aureliano José, Aureliano Segundo, José Arcadio Segundo, etc.—over the course of generations reflects the repetition of

eternal return. Moreover, such repetition creates confusion as characters and events overlap. This repetition and confusion, a destruction of logical order, are microcosms of the larger pattern; each generation, a cycle unto itself, mirrors the creation, decay, and destruction seen in the history of Macondo as a whole.

Melquíades's character undergoes a similar cycle. The Gypsy initially appears able to evade aging and death. In fact, José Arcadio Buendía believes that Melquíades has brought eternal life to the entire community with the daguerreotype. The community's patriarch observes that the people of Macondo begin to wear away, but their images are forever preserved. Although Melquíades may symbolize eternal life and even declares that he has discovered immortality, shortly after this declaration, he is discovered drowned. José Arcadio Buendía resists burying his friend but is forced to do so as the body begins to decompose in the inevitable cycle of creation-decay-death.

Macondo's founder, José Arcadio Buendía, has numerous experiences related to the cyclical nature of time. He believes Monday continuously repeats itself and grows violent trying to escape the cycle. He laments the breaking of the time machine, a mechanism that might have permitted escape from the eternal repetition and spends time trying to find concrete evidence of the passage of time. His family, overwhelmed by his violent behavior, decides to tie him to a tree, where he is all but forgotten. The life of this community patriarch, a would-be inventor himself, mimics the process of eternal return.

At the start of his imprisonment, Colonel Aureliano Buendía has a moment of *déjà vu,* and later he expresses his weariness over the eternal war in which nothing changes except his own aging. He even creates his own symbolic cycle, molding golden fishes only to melt them down again. When Ursula, the community matriarch, sees that the Gypsies no longer bring their inventions to Macondo, she fears the end of the world. Later, she observes that time seems to be working in reverse, and when she goes blind, she realizes that every day the family repeats the same words and actions. Finally, she dies after devolving into fetal form. Fernanda, who takes over the family's care in the midst of Ursula's decline, imposes her parents' norms on the household, returning to the past. And, despite her efforts at cleanliness and order, the house is overtaken by lizards, rodents, ants, and moss; the structure itself begins to revert back to a primeval state. When Amaranta Ursula, great-great-granddaughter of Macondo's founders, herself attempts to reorganize the house, her efforts fail. The destructive circle of time continues as she and her nephew make love amid the sounds of Macondo's ghosts trying to stave off creation's inevitable entropy. Indeed, their love ends when Amaranta dies, having repeated family history by giving birth to a child with a pig's tail.

Shortly after Amaranta's death, Macondo is blown away by the winds of fate. This ending, foretold by the history of prior Buendía generations, depicts both the futility and fatality faced by an insular Latin America. Any community unable to recognize and to break the constraints of its own historical cycle and intrinsic patterns of behavior is doomed not only to repeat the past but also to be eternally destroyed by it.

Anne Massey

MEMORY in *One Hundred Years of Solitude*

Memory in *One Hundred Years of Solitude* functions, or malfunctions, simultaneously on two planes—individual and collective recall. From beginning to end, recollection and its opposition, forgetting, point to the insufficiency of familial ties and societal connection in the face of Latin American political corruption and the economic reality of poverty.

The novel's opening—Colonel Aureliano Buendía's standing before a firing squad and remembering his father's taking him to discover ice—segues into a description of the idyllic beginnings of Macondo and the Buendía family. This connection between pleasant memory and DEATH demonstrates the inadequacy of familial and societal bonds in the face of unjust political manipulations. The utopia of the colonel's youth will not withstand the decay brought about by political contamination.

Indeed, early in the novel all efforts to manipulate memory for individual or community benefit fail. The Gypsies, who introduce a machine to make people forget bad memories, so confuse the COMMUNITY that the citizens of Macondo become lost in their own streets. When faced with the ILLNESS of insomnia that destroys memory, both José Arcadio Buendía and his son unsuccessfully attempt to fend off complete erasure of past events with various inventions, including a machine designed to aid in recall. In the end, only through the magic of Melquíades is the community rescued and memory restored.

Eventually, memory fades, dominated by the slow invasion of forgetting. Perhaps the most extreme example of forgetting is the massacre engineered by the government and the banana company during a strike by the company's workers. Three thousand people are gunned down in the town square, but afterward no one recalls the event except José Aureliano Segundo and the boy he rescued from the mob. In fact, José Aureliano Segundo can find no evidence of the massacre, and when the boy attempts to force the people of Macondo to recall the gruesome day, he is written off as insane. Here, the failure of collective memory serves as a metaphor for the community's inability to confront the political abuse found in much of Latin American history as well as its failure to address economic manipulation by nations outside of Latin America, in particular the United States.

Over time, memory in the novel evolves into nostalgia, recollection colored by a longing for the unattainable. Nostalgia heightens the sense that Latin America's societal bonds are insufficient mechanisms for resolving conflicts. For instance, upon returning from the war, Colonel Aureliano Buendía, feeling trapped by nostalgia, destroys all evidence of his past and attempts suicide. Afterward, lauded as a martyr for his suicide attempt by fickle followers who accuse him of selling out the war effort for personal gain while honoring him for rejecting the Presidential Order of Merit, the colonel considers starting a new war simply to please his supporters. This is an odd position for a man who once advocated working with the opposition to bring an end to conflict. Seen through the lens of nostalgia, societal bonds are not only insufficient buffers against political corruption, but also have become destructive forces in and of themselves.

The novel's conclusion joins memory and forgetting as final proof that societal structures fail to meet the challenges posed by political and economic realities. Aureliano, the last survivor in Macondo, opens Melquíades's papers, which magically relate the history of Macondo 100 years before it occurred. Aureliano begins to read, turning each page, advancing toward the past, seeking his origin. As he finds his beginning, and that of Macondo, a strong wind begins to blow, sweeping away the town. Such destruction implies that memory, presented here as a memoir of a people written before the fact, cannot offer salvation from the fatalistic forces that have consistently eaten away at the fabric of Latin American community. Moreover, it is in the exact moment before Aureliano discovers the answer he has been seeking—the true nature of his origins—that the destructive winds prevail. That is to say, just as Aureliano, society's sole survivor, is about to have revealed to him not only his beginning but also the origin of his community as a whole, this moment of revelation and its power to rescue an entire people from a repetitive cycle of destruction are ripped away. Memory fails to rescue a society from its inevitable fate. In broader terms, Latin American history, doomed to repeat itself, cannot save a people who fail to remember the pitfalls of the past.

Anne Massey

GASKELL, ELIZABETH *North and South* (1854)

Elizabeth Gaskell's *North and South* contrasts life in the agrarian south of England with the livelier, more energetic way of life afforded in the manufacturing center of Milton-Northern, undoubtedly a pseudonym for Manchester, the industrial capital of 19th-century England.

With this backdrop of regional and cultural transition Gaskell introduces questions about society and authority. She contrasts the typical "marriage of convenience"—matches made for economic advantage—with Margaret Hale's dismissal of two successful prospects without consulting her parents.

The Hales also question "justice" when hearing from their son Frederick of the horrid treatment of fellow sailors at the hands of their captain. Because of Frederick's intervening for the men, the captain places Frederick adrift. Authorities label the incident a "mutiny"; Frederick would be hanged if he were to return to English soil. How can justice prevail when loyal subjects cannot receive a fair hearing?

Similarly, Gaskell raises questions about the justice of the factory system and its operation under the principles of "supply and demand." Wages are kept low, and workers can barely survive. Again, Margaret Hale raises difficult questions about what owners owe workers and how the two groups might cooperate for the benefit of all. Gaskell advocates a greater sense of community between these groups, which had traditionally been economically and socially separated.

A revolutionary look at the elements of society, *North and South* demonstrates the need for mutual understanding to break the barriers of class and economic disparity. Through the presence of a strong female protagonist, Gaskell ultimately seeks to prevent the kind of systemic abuses with which most people of her day were all too familiar.

Anthony Grasso

GENDER in *North and South*

Readers first encounter Margaret Hale in London at the Hawley Street home of her Aunt Shaw and cousin Edith as the family is preparing for the latter's marriage to Captain Lennox. One is led to assume that only the traditional Victorian plot complications will arise. However, once back home in Helstone, a small agricultural community in the south, Margaret is wooed by Henry Lennox, brother of the captain and a successful attorney who has come expressly to propose. She rejects him politely but abruptly. Margaret's action is surprising on at least two counts: First, a young woman of 18 rejects an excellent proposal; and, second, she does so without parental consent or involvement and this notion is anything but Victorian. Later the Hale family is required to move to the industrial city of Milton-Northern when Mr. Hale, a minister, struggles with conscience over the autonomy of the church and gives up his living. Once settled there Margaret is placed in a similar situation when John Thornton, a successful mill owner, proposes. Although she and the Hales are considered economic and social inferiors, and this offer would have been prized by Victorian standards as an excellent match for her,

Margaret rejects him outright, again without the knowledge or consent of her parents.

Elizabeth Gaskell, the daughter and wife of Unitarian ministers, really shares the fundamental belief of Mary Wollstonecraft, author of *A Vindication of the Rights of Woman,* that women must be treated as rational and responsible because subordination is contrary to Christianity and because only rational beings can be capable mothers. Throughout the course of the novel, one senses Margaret—and Gaskell—bristling at any sense of power or entitlement over women that men may have been taught or raised to think was their right by social position. Margaret will not be stereotyped, even to the point of engaging the businessmen and mill owners, factory workers and others in a debate about their lives and responsibilities.

Women in the novel are strong, except for those who represent typical domestic types: Margaret's cousin, Edith, and Fanny Thornton, the mill owner's sister, seen also preparing to wed a much older husband who is wealthy and successful. Both of these women are portrayed as dependent and concerned with frivolous matters, such as purchasing clothing and having dinner parties, knowing French, embroidery, piano, and social customs, but not having much purpose in life. Mrs. Hale, in contrast, feels she has made a bad marriage since her husband has not amounted to much, but she is a strong figure who stands by his decisions, survives the loss through exile of her son Frederick owing to his role in the mutiny against an unjust naval captain, and becomes ill with cancer, dealing stoically with her painful illness. Mrs. Thornton, John's mother, lost her husband to suicide because he had made bad investments and lost his fortune. She stood behind her son's climb back to becoming a mill owner and restoring the family fortune. She also spent time on the mill floor, helping her son to supervise workers—not the common role for a middle-class woman of means. Ironically, both women have been strengthened by the hardships in their lives, benefiting from adversity rather than being shielded from it as middle-class Victorian domestic hierarchy would have tended to do.

Part of the gender theme surrounds and is intertwined with the working world of the industrial north, which offers few roles and opportunities, changing customs and behaviors for women and also for both genders. Early in the novel, as Margaret wanders the streets of her new urban home, she is taken by what she perceives as the "forwardness" of men and women who actually touch her garments as they pass, commenting on their quality and on her fresh, natural beauty, which they admire without being lewd or untoward. One would never encounter such behavior in the strict social setting of London, or the more traditional and deferential agrarian south where Margaret was raised.

Margaret is open to the change and discusses it with Betsy Higgins, the factory girl whom she befriends, and her father Nicholas, the union organizer and factory hand whom she tries to get John Thornton to hire after the strike. In fact, Margaret has been raised and educated by her father on a par with her brother Frederick. She is versed in the classics, in biblical themes, and in political economy as is seen in discussions at the Thorntons' dinner party, where her opinions about the need for mill owners to care more for the welfare of their workers is quite controversial. Again, Gaskell departs from traditional gender roles by showing Margaret as a woman who is able to hold intelligent conversation about that matter of industry and the national economy, not restricted to conversations about trends in fashion or who is available for marriage.

Through the death of her parents and the unfortunate turn of events of John Thornton's mill, Margaret ends up as owner (from the behest of Mr. Bell, her guardian after her father's sudden death). She is ready to assume not only legal ownership, but also a rightful place as an enlightened owner who knows the workers, their situation, and the realities of the industrial world at Milton-Northern. Only then, as an equal, can she and Thornton consider feelings for one another. Gaskell's *North and South* offers an expanded and enlightened view of gender that serves as a model by which other 19th-century heroines and readers can judge women as rational, capable, and strong individuals with minds and lives of their own.

Anthony Grasso

JUSTICE in *North and South*

Gaskell's concerns over law and justice are squarely placed within a context of practice: How are laws and judgments made, and how ethical or moral are they really? Questions are raised on all social and religious fronts about how prejudice, custom, and erroneous human judgments affect the interpretation of laws and the carriage of justice throughout society.

Early in the novel we are faced with Mr. Hale's scrupulous examination of "The Thirty-Nine Articles" doctrine, stating tenets of faith to which all followers in the Church of England must adhere. When he has difficulty accepting some points of church authority, recently reinterpreted, Mr. Hale questions his own integrity and the justice of continuing in the ministry. Conscious of the great changes and possible hardships such a choice will mean for his family, he concludes as a matter of conscience that, since he can't obey all the beliefs, he cannot remain as a practicing minister. This decision sets in motion the Hales' move from Helstone in the south of England to Milton-Northern, a large industrial city in the north. While it may seem a small matter by today's standards, Mr. Hale's principle and adherence to the justice of earning a living falsely leads him to sacrifice a livelihood no one would have questioned.

Frederick, whom readers discover only when Mrs. Hale becomes terminally ill, has been forced to live in Spain owing to his role in a professed mutiny aboard an English naval vessel on which he had served. The captain, obviously unbalanced, took beatings and punishments of the men and boys aboard to awful degrees. When the pleading of Frederick and other officers was not heard, they arranged a boat and decided to remove the captain with provisions, so as not to cause him harm but to correct what was a horrible situation. For that action, since the captain was eventually rescued, Frederick would return to England under pain of death if caught, because this action was treated as a "mutiny." Gaskell questions the justice of laws in the naval code that clearly protect an incompetent leader who continually abuses power, over those who seek to redress the wrong and ensure the protection of lives essential to the safety of the entire vessel and crew.

Frederick's clandestine return to visit his dying mother, precipitated by Margaret's letter to him, causes another crisis and issue. Needing to spirit

Fred out of the country after he spends some time with his mother, Margaret is seen with him at night at the railway station by John Thornton, whom she had earlier rejected as a suitor, complicating the social stigma. Fred is also recognized there by a former acquaintance, Leonards; in the ensuing struggle to escape and board the awaiting train, Fred inadvertently causes the drunken Leonards to fall, causing his ultimate death. Margaret, questioned by the police as a witness in the hearing, must lie to protect her brother's life until she is certain that he is safely out of England. Two issues emerge: (1) the justice of the law that condemned Frederick for doing what was right to protect younger men and those under his care; and (2) the right of people to judge Margaret to be a "loose" woman, which John Thornton and his mother did, because she was seen walking at night in public with a man who was not her husband. Again, Gaskell questions how our flawed and often prejudicial human judgment affects the way in which laws are carried out, the role of conscience, and the importance of civil disobedience in opposing unjust laws.

Throughout this interesting novel, Gaskell examines how people live and how society's institutions function through a lens of justice, pointing out how fragile even the law is, let alone the weight of "tradition" that many social customs have accumulated, owing to the limitations of human knowledge and judgment. Ultimately, Gaskell promotes mutual human respect and interaction between and among all groups, rather than reliance upon hastily formed judgments, to ensure the understanding of the other as the way to realize the ideal of just treatment for every member of the society. One key example occurs after the strike. One of the main organizers, Nicholas Higgins, who has two daughters to support, also assumes responsibility for a widow and her five children, orphaned by their father who died by his own hand, despairing of being able to support his family. When no one will hire Higgins, because of his union connections, Margaret encourages John Thornton to overcome his lofty principles, to sacrifice "face" or honor, as Higgins himself had done by waiting for five hours in the damp, cold weather to ask Thornton for the job. There is real justice in sacrificing abstract "principles" to help the pressing needs of those around you in society, for whom a person of some authority or means may have or can accept increased responsibility.

Gaskell reviews "authority" and its uses at every level of society to tackle the increasingly complicated question of "law and order" in her time and culture, a relevant question for us today as well. As the upward mobility of social groups was growing and the basic foundations of a strict society began to undergo rapid change during the Industrial Revolution, Gaskell is thinking about the implications for the betterment of community and of all people so that they will be treated fairly under the law and daily practices of the society. Throughout *North and South* she asks her readers to do the same.

Anthony Grasso

PRIDE in North and South

As in Jane Austen's *Pride and Prejudice,* characters in *North and South* suffer from and create problems for others owing to extreme pride. Early in the novel Margaret Hale, coming from modest means, is contrasted with her cousin Edith Shaw, with whom her parents have sent her to live so that she might gain the social advantages of meeting well-to-do young men. After Edith's marriage to Captain Lennox, Margaret returns to rural Helstone and Henry Lennox, the captain's brother and a lawyer, proposes to her. Her response—"I have never thought of you, but as a friend—I am sure I could never think of you as anything else"—is abrupt and stings Lennox's pride. Lennox disappears from Helstone immediately, leaving the Hale family in a quandary as to his abrupt departure.

With the family's removal to Milton-Northern, Margaret meets John Thornton, the new mill owner whose mother is fiercely proud and overly protective of her son who has single-handedly brought the family back from financial ruin. Their pride comes from fierce determination and hard work, but the struggle to be regarded well in society's eyes comes at a cost: Both are stern and suspicious of others' intentions. As he was leaving for his lesson at the Hales' house, Mrs. Thornton says to John "Take care you don't get caught by a penniless girl, John."

Pride that comes from the attempt to "cover" perceived economic or social wants and setbacks

leads to mistaken judgments of others' actions and motives. When John eventually proposes to Margaret, smitten as he is with her difference in background and demeanor, as well as her fiery spirit, she rejects him even more strongly than she had done to Henry Lennox, saying "Your way of speaking shocks me. It is blasphemous." She'd disagreed with him on matters of political economy about the responsibilities of mill owners toward workers.

Major misunderstanding comes when Margaret is caught at the Thorntons' during a riot, since a strike is on at the mills. She has gone to the house to borrow a water bed, offered by Mrs. Thornton for her ailing mother to use. John Thornton has brought in Irish workers to keep his mill going, and has housed them on the premises. When the striking laborers hear about it and congregate outside, Margaret urges him to go down to talk with them, then runs outside herself, eventually taking a stone to the head thrown by a rabble-rouser, which was meant for Thornton. While being cared for in the Thornton household, she hears servant gossip indicating that she had "thrown herself" at him. Concern over her own reputation and behavior prevents Margaret from seeing that the normally stoic John has been so affected by her strength, forwardness, and independence, that he drops his normal fierceness of demeanor to reveal his true heart. Her abrupt dismissal is more a defensive maneuver out of pride, yet causes greater pain to him than she had meant or even understood.

Margaret also is the recipient of similar treatment at the hands of the Higgins family, fiercely proud workers whom she encounters on a walk. Set in her southern ways Margaret assumes, as the minister's daughter and the economic superior of the workers, that she can "call" on them anytime for a visit as she did in the rural parish at Helstone. When she asks where they live and what their names are, Nicholas responds: "Whatter yo' asking for?" Higgins is defensive of having his "betters" visit his home, not wanting to be dependent on anyone's charity.

Interestingly, Higgins the "uneducated" laborer provides the key to overcoming natural pride and shattering the accepted boundaries of social class. When he assumes financial responsibility for a family whose father died during the strike, he seeks employment from Thornton's mill. As a union organizer, he is "persona non grata" at any of the mills, and he knows that Thornton is a hard man to bargain with. After some prompting, Thornton hears about Higgins's situation, follows him to where he lives in order to verify the story, and calls him to his office to apologize for misjudging his character. Higgins's ability to place others first overcomes any reticence or aloofness that pride sets up.

Once Higgins begins employment, he and Thornton devise a "lunchroom" scheme to provide workers and their families with employment and a means to have healthy food. The willingness to see beyond one's prejudgments, and Higgins's ability to act out of humility and concern for others' needs, leads to deeper understanding of shared humanity, and levels of cooperation and friendship that bring social and economic barriers down.

Anthony Grasso

GAY, JOHN   *The Beggar's Opera*   (1712)

John Gay's operatic play dramatizes the story of Peachum and his partners in crime, whose lives become complicated when Macheath falls in love with Polly, Peachum's daughter. The play begins with the Peachums extolling the virtues of single women to Polly, who responds that she has already married Macheath. Distraught over Polly's marriage, Peachum laments the loss of his daughter's contributions to his gang's coffers, then seeks retaliation against Macheath. Peachum attempts to ruin Macheath by having him imprisoned, but intercessions by Polly and Lucy (Macheath's other wife) ensure that Macheath escapes hanging. The play then concludes with the Player and Beggar determining that Macheath may avoid the gallows "to comply with the taste of the town."

Gay satirizes the exploits of the aristocracy through the shenanigans of Macheath and the other criminals in *The Beggar's Opera* much as he satirizes foreign opera via the play's numerous ballads: by sarcasm juxtaposed with action. Lockit the jailor, for instance, demands a cash bribe before granting Macheath light manacles, and Macheath while in prison sings an aria that blames women—not his

life of crime—for his incarceration. Polly, likewise, sings an aria that accuses Lucy of "ruining" their marriage to Macheath, but Polly's tone—like that of the other characters—is serious, though her words jest. The satiric action coupled with the humorous depiction of married life in the early 18th century leaves modern audiences with little wonder as to why *The Beggar's Opera* has maintained its popularity over the years.

James N. Ortego II

INDIVIDUAL AND SOCIETY in *The Beggar's Opera*

The one character who emerges as a solitary figure in Gay's *The Beggar's Opera* is known simply as "Macheath," a degenerate gambler and polygamist who escapes punishment from the law at the play's end. Macheath is a part of the criminal element satirized by Gay, but is constantly at odds with his fellow law-breakers. In a society filled with prostitutes, thieves, and all sorts of other criminals, Macheath manages to excel at the art of law-breaking, yet the society that suffers from his crimes refuses to punish him. Gay's dramatic satire consequently laments not London's criminal types such as Macheath, but the society that allows the Macheaths of the world to prey on its citizens.

Macheath is introduced early in the play as a "gamester and highwayman," which interestingly enough is acceptable to the Peachums, until Mr. Peachum learns that his daughter Polly thinks Macheath "a very pretty man." But Mr. Peachum's subsequent denunciation of Macheath centers on married couples and spousal abuse; Peachum is not concerned with Macheath's harsh character, his gambling problem, or his life as a thief, but with Polly's regulation to secondary status once she marries Macheath. As the play's primary representative of the criminal underworld, Peachum holds much influence over those around him; when he approves of Macheath's lifestyle but denounces Polly's desire to marry, spectators typically laugh, but the joke is centered squarely on a society that allows criminals such as Macheath to prosper, not necessarily on Peachum's marital views.

The opening scenes that feature the Peachums discussing Polly and Macheath's future as a married couple establish Macheath as an outsider who breaks an unspoken code of conduct when he attempts to marry and abandon his criminal lifestyle. Now that Macheath has considered marriage, he has become a terrible criminal whom his fellow thieves do not tolerate. By isolating Macheath via a proposed marriage with Polly, Gay cleverly establishes Macheath for his audience as an example of one whose faults lie not in willingly breaking the law, but in consorting with young women in the hopes of marrying them. Macheath emerges as a lone individual looking into a society that rejects his marital views but not his criminal lifestyle. Gay's view, however, is consistently tempered with satire, as Macheath exclaims, "What a fool is a fond wench!" (3.3.71); and Polly may be thought of as "foolish" for pursuing Macheath, who is certainly not an exemplary suitor, but this is Gay's satirical point.

As punishment for his "crime" of consorting with Polly and hindering Peachum's criminal efforts, Macheath is soon imprisoned at Newgate during a scene that isolates him as an exemplary criminal of the heart. As Lockit chains Macheath, the guard takes notice of Macheath's crimes, and then marvels as the prisoner blames his misfortune on women. But Gay's construction of the jail scene distinguishes Macheath from a society of criminals who seek to punish him for crimes against marriage instead of crimes against humanity. Macheath is guilty of stealing, gambling, beating and robbing travelers, and cheating at cards and dice, but these offenses are seldom mentioned as faults of Macheath. The focus appears to be on marriage, especially when Lucy visits Macheath to scold him, then accepts his promise because she wants to be made an "honest" woman. The audience, however, cannot help but remember that Macheath's crimes against society go unpunished, which for Gay's satire seems to be the real crime.

For the duration of the play, Macheath remains in jail, subject to harsh verbal reproaches from Polly and Lucy (two of his six wives) for his deceitful marital practices, but at the end of the play, Macheath faces execution for a crime against society: "having broke prison." The execution does not happen, however, due to the interference by the Player and Beggar, long thought by scholars to represent the voice of English society and John Gay the playwright,

respectively. Once the Beggar orders the guards to release Macheath, the Player concedes that "All this must we do, to comply with the taste of the town" (3.16.15). And thus Macheath escapes punishment for his crimes against society, but not for his crimes against marriage, for he is forced to live with his six wives. The play's conclusion suggests that Macheath's most terrible crimes involve marriage, not society, yet the subtle change to force an "opera to end happily" implies that Gay was not laughing at Macheath's womanizing, but at those who allow criminals such as Macheath to escape justice for crimes against society.

James N. Ortego II

JUSTICE in *The Beggar's Opera*

The Beggar's Opera begins with an aria that imposes a moral judgment on the play to follow, yet from beginning to end, none of the main characters serves justice for their crimes. The Peachum gang regularly escapes punishment from the laws they break (although Macheath is incarcerated for a short time), but with good reason: to satirize the ineffectualness of 18th-century law enforcement and the penetration of crime throughout English society. Gay's satire suggests not only that 18th-century laws were widely broken and seldom enforced, but also that the criminal element included persons from all social classes, any of whom might easily escape the law simply by bribing officials. Justice in *The Beggar's Opera* is essentially nonexistent, and this is part of the play's thematic concern with crime and justice.

Soon after the play's introductory aria, Peachum and Filch discuss the forthcoming trial of Black Moll, a common thief, who sardonically does not suffer for her crimes but instead receives a pardon via Peachum's friendship with the prison officials at Newgate. After Peachum instructs Filch to hasten to Newgate to "let my friends know what I intend," Filch responds that "'tis a pleasure to be the messenger of comfort to friends in affliction" (1. 2). This early dialogue between Peachum and Filch establishes Peachum as a manipulator who easily evades the law and justice. Black Moll is by all accounts a drain upon society; her crimes cost the citizens their money and peace of mind, yet she, like every other criminal in the play, escapes punishment. The world of the Peachums and the Black Molls is corrupt and unjust, but their corruption permeates all of society. Peachum's ability to free Black Moll derives from his symbiotic relationship with the guards at Newgate, for as long as criminals such as Peachum and his gang control the prison officials, society will not see justice served. *The Beggar's Opera* satirizes the ineffectiveness of justice, which is a thematic concern that seems ironic when spectators remember that a criminal during Gay's time could face hanging for more than 500 offenses.

Not even the threat of hanging can deter Peachum's gang, who in act 2 discuss their various misdeeds, but in a manner that satirizes 18th-century English society and its inability to dole out justice to the criminal element. Beginning with the rhetorical question, "Why are the laws levelled at us?" Crook-fingered Jack and his companions satirically validate their crimes by comparing themselves to the nobility, who, according to the gang, are no better than common criminals. After reaffirming that each gang member would die for his friends and keep their secrets safe, Matt of the Mint says, "Show me a gang of courtiers that can say as much," a response that suggests that the nobility of Gay's England does not have the same "decency" as the common criminal. Gay implies through Matt of the Mint's sarcasm that class is the only distinction among thieves; while theft was certainly forbidden by 18th-century laws, the play's thematic concern with justice suggests that only the poor suffer from the laws, yet the play punishes no one. When Jemmy Twitcher wonders, "Are we more dishonest than the rest of mankind?" spectators must silently answer "no" and muse about a society that attempts to punish its lower-class criminals but ignores similar offenses among the nobility.

While the play features characters who consistently worry about escaping the law, no one except Macheath suffers any punishment that may be considered "just," and that for only a short period of time. Once Peachum realizes that Macheath's marriage threatens the Peachum gang, Peachum frames Macheath and has him imprisoned, but Polly manages to help Macheath escape from prison in much the same manner that her father helps Black Moll

escape the law. Ironically, Peachum has trained his daughter too well, for she thwarts his attempts to ruin Macheath and "aid[s] him in his escape," yet neither Polly, Peachum, nor Macheath suffer justice for their crimes.

Before Macheath is led away to be hung, the Beggar and the Player interrupt and free Macheath "to comply with the taste of the town." This final allusion to an inadequate justice system marks for Gay a concluding commentary that demonstrates that not only do criminals mock the courts and their officials, but such instances also are commonplace among all members of society. The upper, middle, and lower classes all suffer the pangs of injustice, and in the end, only the audience is laughing.

James N. Ortego II

LOVE in *The Beggar's Opera*

The Beggar's Opera owes its resounding success in part to the play's thematic concerns with love and marriage. Polly, the oft-simplistic daughter of Mr. and Mrs. Peachum, finds herself at the center of a love triangle involving herself, Macheath, and Lucy, a prostitute. Additional problems arise for the young lovers when Polly's parents decidedly forbid her to marry Macheath. Polly's conflict stems from her filial duty to her parents and her love for Macheath, but her arguments that dismiss "honor or money" in favor of "love for him" fall on the deaf ears of her father, Peachum. Polly wants simply to become like the "gentle town ladies" she admires, but her marriage would cause her parents great financial loss. Early 18th-century women who married became literally the property of their husbands, which is what the Peachums fear might happen to Polly. Her entreaties to her parents (often expressed in song) for a union with Macheath frequently elicit from her father threats of violence and misery, which in turn prompt Polly to pursue Macheath in secret. Polly and Macheath determine that—for his own safety—"we must part" until she can devise some way to convince Peachum that marriage would best suit her interests. The two lovers then part with a kiss and a song as the play's focus then shifts to the criminal lifestyle of the Peachums.

Macheath, upon his departure from Polly, visits a group of his fellow criminals to discuss the hazards of criminal activity while he ponders his "foolish wench," Polly. Macheath confesses that Polly's affections sway him to consider marriage seriously, but his thoughts are soon interrupted by the entrance of Mrs. Coaxer and her stable of prostitutes. After much banter concerning the "kind service" provided by Mrs. Coaxer's women, Macheath is shortly arrested by Peachum, the culmination of his plot to remove Macheath from Polly's life. Macheath then curses women as "decoy ducks" who seek only to destroy men, a sentiment that soon sours his attitude toward Polly.

Macheath is first visited in Newgate Prison by Lucy, a former lover, who immediately rebukes him for his relationship to Polly. Macheath has a way with words, however, and he is soon able to calm Lucy's trepidations. Peachum, meanwhile, has presented his case against Macheath to Lockit the prison guard, who confirms Macheath's guilt and threatens him with execution. Polly then visits Macheath as he broods in prison, and she meets Lucy for the first time, and the two women learn of Macheath's polygamy. The rival women first focus their anger toward Macheath, then turn their rage upon each other. Each jilted women takes little comfort in Macheath's assurance of love as a "joke." Soon Lucy begins to soften her stance toward Macheath, but Polly remains in turmoil.

Lockit meanwhile finds himself trying to keep track not only of Macheath, Polly, and Lucy, but also of Peachum's plot to have Macheath executed for his crimes. The multiple subplots prove too much for Lockit, however, and Macheath manages to escape with Lucy's aid, only "to go to her" (Polly), as Lucy fears. To calm her worries, Lucy then decides to confront Polly and settle the argument between them once and for all, and the two women carry on numerous arguments and discussions about love, men, marriage, and women. Neither woman reaches a satisfactory conclusion regarding themselves and Macheath, and the play then hastens to a conclusion that leaves the love triangle involving Lucy, Polly, and Macheath unresolved.

After finally being confronted by both women in prison near the end of the play, the Jailor introduces "four women more," each one "bearing a child" to Macheath. Six women now appear on stage and each claims an amorous association with Macheath, but rather than pick one of the six, the Beggar and Player suddenly appear and release Macheath from prison to appease the audience, and there the play ends. The audience never knows which woman Macheath ultimately chooses, if he chooses any woman at all, nor whether or not he is legally married to Polly, Lucy, or both. Instead, *The Beggar's Opera* ends on a humorous note that leaves the spectators to draw their own conclusions regarding love.

James N. Ortego II

GILMAN, CHARLOTTE PERKINS
The Yellow Wallpaper (1892)

The Yellow Wallpaper was first published in *New England Magazine* as "The Yellow Wall-Paper" in 1892. Although now seen as Gilman's most important work, during her lifetime she was most known for *Women and Economics* (1898), a nonfiction work that explored the place of women in late-19th-century America. *The Yellow Wallpaper* was largely critically ignored until it was reissued by the Feminist Press in 1973.

The Yellow Wallpaper is the first-person account of a woman undergoing a "rest cure." She has been diagnosed with a "hysterical tendency" by her physician husband because she has been unable to care for her newborn baby. As part of her "rest cure," she has been confined to an attic room and forbidden to have any physical, emotional, or intellectual stimulation. This includes the instruction that she is not to write. The story, her journal account of her experience, becomes evidence of her disagreement and defiance of this prescription.

Shortly after being confined, the narrator decides that there is something strange about the wallpaper that covers the walls of this attic room. As the story progresses, she becomes convinced that there are women trapped inside the strange pattern of the wallpaper. The story ends with the narrator's attempt at freeing the women in the wallpaper. Three major themes explored by Gilman in *The Yellow Wallpaper* are ILLNESS, GENDER, and FREEDOM.

Since its republication, *The Yellow Wallpaper* has been considered an important work, not only of feminist literature but also of American literature.

Almost all major anthologies of American literature include *The Yellow Wallpaper*.

Carmine Esposito

FREEDOM in *The Yellow Wallpaper*

The main character's fight for freedom is a major theme of *The Yellow Wallpaper*. At the start of *The Yellow Wallpaper*, we are told that the narrator is being treated by her physician husband for a nervous condition. As part of her treatment, the narrator is confined to an attic room and "absolutely forbidden to 'work.'" Even though the narrator disagrees with this treatment, she is powerless to fight it, "Personally, I believe that congenial work, with excitement and change, would do me good. But what is one to do?" The narrator finds herself at the start of the story both physically and psychologically confined. As the story progresses, we witness the narrator free herself from the psychological strictures that bind her.

Undergoing the "rest cure," the narrator is not free to make decisions about her life as even trips and visitors are carefully regulated by her husband, "I tried to have a real earnest reasonable talk with him the other day, and tell him how I wish he would let me go and make a visit to Cousin Henry and Julia. But he said I wasn't able to go, nor able to stand it after I got there." Unable to communicate with her husband, the narrator finds strength in writing her thoughts in her journal, "And I know John would think it absurd. But I *must* say what I feel and think in some way—it is such a relief!" Writing becomes the vehicle through which the narrator begins the process of freeing herself.

In the first half of the story, the room in which the narrator is confined becomes, for her, a symbol of her lack of freedom, "I don't like our room a bit. I wanted one downstairs that opened on the piazza." The garden that she can see from the windows of her attic room becomes a symbol of freedom, "There is a *delicious* garden! I never saw such a garden—large and shady, full of box-bordered paths, and lined with long grape-covered arbors with seats under them." As the story progresses she begins to see a woman in the wallpaper that covers the walls of her attic room, "Behind that outside pattern the dim shapes get clearer every day. It is always the same

shape, only very numerous. And it is like a woman stooping down and creeping about behind the pattern." The narrator realizes that the woman in the wallpaper is trapped by the pattern of the wallpaper much in the same way as she is trapped in the attic room: "The faint figure behind seemed to shake the pattern, just as if she wanted to get out."

In the second half of *The Yellow Wallpaper*, the narrator struggles to free the woman in the wallpaper as she fights to free herself from her life of servility as a mother and wife. She begins by tearing down the wallpaper that confines the woman; "I pulled and she shook, I shook and she pulled, and before morning we had peeled off yards of that paper." As the narrator fights for her freedom, her attitude toward the room changes; "I quite enjoy the room, now it is bare again." What earlier was a symbol of her servility, the room, becomes a source for her freedom. In the attic room, she is free to act as she chooses; "It is so pleasant to be out in this great room and creep around as I please." The garden, which had earlier represented freedom for her, now promises only confinement. In the garden, the narrator would not be free to act as she chooses, "I don't want to go outside. I won't, even if Jennie asks me to. For outside you have to creep on the ground, and everything is green instead of yellow."

In this way, *The Yellow Wallpaper* can be read as a story of liberation. At the end, the narrator is able to free herself from the life of servility that patriarchal culture would have her accept as normal. But what is also clear is that this liberation is limited and her freedom comes with a price. Ironically, the narrator can be free only when she decides to confine herself to her attic room. Through this, *The Yellow Wallpaper* shows us that all struggles for liberation and freedom are limited by the culture that surrounds them.

Carmine Esposito

GENDER in *The Yellow Wallpaper*

One way to read *The Yellow Wallpaper* is as a story that explores the relationship between gender and power in the United States in the 19th century. At the start of the story the narrator tells us about the nature of her relationship with her husband: "John laughs at me, of course, but one expects that in marriage." The attitude John has toward the narrator reflects the general attitude of men toward women at this time. More important, at the beginning of the story, the narrator agrees with and accepts this attitude as "natural."

At the start of the story, we see that this attitude leads the narrator to be treated as if she were a child. She is put in an attic room even though she wanted a room that opened onto the garden. She believes that this attic room was used as a nursery in the past, which reflects her suspicion that she is being treated as a child. In addition, the narrator is never named by the author. The story is written in the first person, being made up of her journal entries. However, her husband never refers to her by her name, always referring to her by a pet name, such as "blessed goose" or "little girl," which reduces her to a child.

Throughout the first half of the story, the narrator compares herself to her sister-in-law Jenny and the housekeeper Mary. She feels very badly that she cannot perform her "duties" as a wife and mother: "It does weigh on me so not to do my duty in any way!" We find out that the reason they have hired Mary and that the narrator is considered "sick" is that the narrator is unable to take care of her child: "It is fortunate Mary is so good with the baby. Such a dear baby! And yet I *cannot* be with him, it makes me so nervous." For the narrator, her sister-in-law comes to represent the ideal wife and mother, the woman who finds fulfillment in putting her husband and children's well-being and desires above her own: "She is a perfect and enthusiastic housekeeper, and hopes for no better profession." Part of the narrator's "problem" is that she doesn't want to put her "duties" as a mother and wife above her own desire to write, a choice her husband is not forced to make. When she tells her husband that she feels better when he is at home and asks him to stay with her, he answers, "Why, how can I, dear?" meaning his responsibility to his profession and patients comes before his wife's needs. As a woman, the narrator could never put her professional responsibilities above the needs of her husband or child.

In the second half of the story, the narrator begins to see women trapped behind the wallpaper that covers the walls of her attic room. These women can be read as psychological projections of the narrator's predicament: As they are trapped behind the wallpaper, she is trapped in this attic room. They can also be read as a metaphor for the position of women in the United States in the 19th century. The women trapped behind the wallpaper represent the lack of power and freedom women had at this time.

After encountering these women, the narrator notices that they "creep," saying "And it is like a woman stooping down and creeping about behind the pattern." Creeping becomes a metaphor for any unacceptable behavior by women, "It must be very humiliating to be caught creeping by daylight! I always lock the door when I creep by daylight." It is at this point that the narrator decides to free the women by tearing down all the wallpaper in the room. In tearing down the wallpaper, the narrator not only frees the women in the wallpaper but also starts the process of her own questioning of the "naturalness" of gender roles.

This questioning leads to the reversals in gender roles that signal the shift in power at the end of the story. While in the first half of the story, the narrator was treated as a child, silenced by her husband, and locked in her attic room, at the end of the story, she turns her husband into a child by calling him "young man," she locks everyone out of *her* room by tossing the key out the window, and silences her husband when she informs him, "'the key is down by the front steps, under a plantain leaf!'"

The final reversal of power takes place in the last two lines of the story, "Now why should that man have fainted? But he did, and right across my path by the wall, so that I had to creep over him every time!" At the time this story was written, melodrama was very popular, and in traditional melodrama, women faint. John's fainting at the end of the story signals to us a reversal in gender roles. And the narrator's continuing to "creep," even after her husband has "blocked" her path, signals to us a reversal of power. The narrator is no longer "under" her husband, but "over him."

Carmine Esposito

ILLNESS in *The Yellow Wallpaper*

The Yellow Wallpaper is an autobiographical short story based on Charlotte Perkins Gilman's own experience with illness and the "rest cure." At the beginning of *The Yellow Wallpaper,* we learn that the narrator, like Gilman, has been diagnosed as suffering from a "temporary nervous depression—a slight hysterical tendency," following the birth of her child. The narrator's husband, John is a physician. The treatment they have prescribed for the narrator is the "rest cure."

At the end of the 19th century, the "rest cure" was a common treatment for upper-class women deemed to be suffering from "women's diseases" such as "hysteria." The "rest cure" required that patients have no physical or intellectual stimulation. Part of what this means for the narrator is that she has been forbidden to write. The narrator does not agree with this prescription, and *The Yellow Wallpaper* itself becomes evidence of her resistance to her treatment, since it is made up of the journal entries she has been secretly recording. The narrator is threatened that if she doesn't get well and follow her husband's instructions, she will be sent to Dr. S. Weir Mitchell, whom the narrator describes as, "like John and my brother, only more so." Mitchell was the physician who treated Gilman for "hysteria" and who was famous for his "rest cure" for "hysterics."

In the late 19th century, "women's diseases" such as "hysteria" were often associated with actions or emotional responses that were seen as inappropriate for women. In the narrator's case, she is diagnosed with "hysteria" because she has not "properly" bonded with her baby—"It is fortunate Mary is good with the baby. Such a dear baby! And yet I *cannot* be with him, it makes me so nervous"—and because of her heightened imagination, "He says that with my imaginative power and habit of story-making, a nervous weakness like mine is sure to lead to all manner of excited fancies, and that I ought to use my will and good sense to check the tendency." It is important to note that in the late 19th century neither of these traits would be seen as an illness in men.

The narrator's imaginative tendency is contrasted to John's scientific approach to life: "John is practical in the extreme. He has no patience with faith, an intense horror of superstition, and he scoffs openly at any talk of things not being felt and seen and put down in figures." Even in judging if his wife's con-

dition is improving, John uses quantifiable criteria: "You are gaining flesh and color, your appetite is better, I feel really much easier about you." When the narrator suggests that her "problem" may be other than physical, she is quickly silenced, "Better in body perhaps—." In the world the narrator lives in, reason equals health and imagination equals illness. But ironically, it is only when the narrator indulges her imagination in contemplating the mystery of the wallpaper that she begins to feel better. "John is so pleased to see me improve! He laughed a little the other day, and said I seemed to be flourishing in spite of my wall-paper. I turned it off with a laugh. I had no intention of telling him it was *because* of the wall-paper—he would make fun of me."

Illness can be read in two ways in *The Yellow Wallpaper,* one literal and one metaphorical. On one level, the story can be read as a protest against the treatment that Gilman herself received under Dr. Weir Mitchell's care. Gilman believed that her condition worsened while undergoing the "rest cure" and that she improved only when she took control of her own treatment and indulged her creative impulses. Gilman's experience with the "rest cure" is reflected in the experience of the narrator of *The Yellow Wallpaper.* In fact, Weir Mitchell acknowledged the role the *The Yellow Wallpaper* played in his abandoning the "rest cure" as a treatment. Metaphorically, illness can be read as a device used by patriarchal culture to control the behavior of women. When the narrator of *The Yellow Wallpaper* behaves in ways that are seen as inappropriate for a woman to act, she is deemed ill and is locked in a room until the inappropriate behavior can be controlled. In this way, the story employs illness as a metaphor for the control patriarchal culture has over the lives of women.

Carmine Esposito

GLASPELL, SUSAN   *Trifles*   (1916)

In *Trifles,* Susan Glaspell depicts the murder case of John Wright. Based on a trial that Glaspell covered as a journalist, the play takes place in the Wright home on the morning after John's wife, Minnie, was arrested for strangling her husband. Men enter the house on official business: The county attorney, the sheriff, and Mr. Hale are there to secure evidence and find clues that might aid them in solving the crime. In their search, they concentrate on the bedroom, where the body was found, and the entrance ways to the house to see if an intruder might have killed John Wright.

On the other hand, Mrs. Peters and Mrs. Hale, while packing some things together for the incarcerated Minnie, find evidence among Minnie's things that not only prove Minnie's guilt, but also bear witness to her lonely and isolated life with a husband who did not care much about her. Minnie's quilt, a nice and carefully done piece for the most part, was sewn together haphazardly in other places—a sign to the women that told them of Minnie's distress and preoccupation. Furthermore, Mrs. Hale and Mrs. Peters stumble over the body of a dead canary. They conclude that it must have been John Wright who had wrung its neck, and Minnie put it away lovingly in a box because the bird had been the only thing to ever bring some joy into her life. Full of sympathy and understanding for Minnie, the women conceal the evidence from the returning men who consider the kitchen as too unimportant to contain anything of value for their investigation.

Elke Brown

GENDER in *Trifles*

Gender is probably the central theme of *Trifles*. Indeed, it pervades all other aspects and themes of the play, such as ISOLATION and JUSTICE.

In *Trifles*, we are confronted with very clear gender definitions: Men and women have their own spheres, and they each follow their own ethical and moral standards. In the setting of the play, men stand for the rational, objective, professional world. Thus, the men's idea of justice follows the interpretation of the law without much consideration of emotional or psychological circumstances. For example, the attorney is looking for a suspect, but he does not stop to consider the question of motive for John Wright's murder. Consequently, in his complete dismissal of the female sphere, he fails to recognize clues as such. This male arrogance, born of century-old feelings of superiority over women, precludes any success in his investigation.

The same kind of arrogance also led to John Wright's death. Admittedly, being a man who loves his quiet and dislikes singing may just be a personality issue. However, nothing gave Wright the right to dominate and terrorize his wife, Minnie. According to Mrs. Hale, the Wrights' neighbor, Wright was a harsh man, and his moods and possible violence caused Minnie's spirit to be subdued. Finally, when Wright killed Minnie's canary in an outburst of rage, he also destroyed the last bit of beauty that had been in her life. This act seals his fate: Without anything to care for other than a husband who does not seem to care much for her, Minnie strangles her husband.

The clues that might explain her motive are all found in and around the kitchen—traditionally, the very symbol of the woman's place. In fact, Mrs. Hale and Mrs. Peters are the ones who find these clues and interpret them correctly. As women, they know about life as a farmer's wife. They share the experience of living a fairly isolated life of hard work. Even if their marriages are happier than Minnie's was, life in this midwestern community for women is similar enough to draw the correct conclusions about Minnie's motive.

While women and men clearly have different attitudes and their spheres seem separate enough, they are not entirely separate from each other. The play clearly demonstrates how, whenever a relationship exists between men and women, the women are supposed to convert to the male point of view. When the attorney addresses Mrs. Peters, he fully expects her to act in the spirit of her husband's official orders. As a sheriff's wife, she is married not only to Mr. Peters, the person, but also to his profession. Hence, her idea of justice is supposed to be submission to the official (male) interpretation of the law.

Mrs. Peters is governed by this dogma, until she remembers the silence in her own house after the death of one of her children. This memory produces a powerful bond between her and Minnie's experience of isolation and loneliness, so powerful, indeed, that Mrs. Peters herself attempts to hide the box with the dead canary in it—fully aware that this action goes against everything society and her husband expect her to do, not only on legal grounds but also because, as a wife, Mrs. Peters is not supposed to act against her husband. Both Mrs. Peters and Mrs. Hale consciously defy the laws laid down by the patriarchal order and thus declare their rights as individuals and women.

In our so-called enlightened time, we occasionally overlook the truth that, even today, inequalities between men and women exist—be they employment opportunities or the question of equal pay. When *Trifles* was written, the woman as the "angel in the house" was an idea as popular as it had been in the late 19th century. However, it would be wrong to assume that *Trifles* has no significance beyond the 1920s. What the drama depicts, most of all, is a psychological study of power structures in a patriarchy where men and women are on opposing sides and what can happen if the angel in the house is married to a devil.

Elke Brown

ISOLATION in *Trifles*

In her play *Trifles,* Susan Glaspell alerts us to the harsh life of the midwestern farmer's wife. Through the sheer vastness of the land, people in a farming community live relatively far apart, but spatial isolation does not necessarily lead to murder. Minnie Wright's case illustrates that it is her social and emotional isolation from the community that drive her to her desperate act.

Certainly, the logistical and geographical conditions of a farming community preclude proximity. Yet communal activities exist: Mrs. Hale laments the fact that Minnie stopped singing in the church choir and being a member of the Ladies Aid. She assumes that Minnie felt she could not attend anymore because she could not contribute enough. Thus, her financial circumstances preclude Minnie from perceiving herself as being on equal social footing with the other women. She feels uncomfortable in their company and gives up on joint projects.

While it is not clear from the play whether John Wright had anything to do with Minnie's decision to stop any of these activities, Mrs. Hale's description of him makes it seem very likely that he did. According to her, Wright was a harsh man, who liked to have his quiet and disapproved of conversation and singing. For that reason, he wrung the canary's neck. Likewise, he killed his wife's creative and musical spirit, turning a happy, cheerful Minnie Foster into a lonely, desperate Minnie Wright.

This lack of cheerfulness in the Wright household isolated Minnie only further. While all farmers' wives lead a busy life with everything there is to do around a farm and to keep up a household, Mrs. Hale admits that this had not been the reason why she stopped visiting her neighbor Minnie. Indeed, it was the lack of cheerfulness, the tangible coldness of the place that kept her away. Now that Minnie is in jail and John Wright dead, Mrs. Hale feels guilty about not coming more often, thinking that, if Minnie had had one thing to look forward to—the visit of a friend—she might not have killed her husband.

Minnie's loneliness and isolation are symbolized in the quilt that she had been working on. Ironically, it is this quilt that "speaks" to Mrs. Hale and Mrs. Peters in Minnie's stead. The quilt she had been working on is a log cabin pattern and, as the women explain to the men, Minnie was going to knot it. The first clue about Minnie's real state of mind lies in the fact that parts of the quilt have been sewn together haphazardly—Mrs. Hale at once sets to correcting the stitches, probably fully aware of the fact that she is destroying evidence. Apparently, Minnie was too distracted and preoccupied after her husband killed the canary to pay attention to her sewing.

Traditionally, quilting is a communal activity. That Minnie was working on this quilt by herself is another indication of her isolated state. Yet, quilting provided her with a creative outlet that would also produce something useful. It would, thus, have been an acceptable activity to her husband. The fact that Minnie was going to knot the quilt—a method of joining the layers of a quilt—illustrates the fact that her emphasis was on getting the job done quickly rather than producing a fine piece of art, certainly reflective of John Wright's attitude toward household items.

Furthermore, the quilt is a log cabin pattern. In this pattern, each square begins with a small middle square around which rectangular strips are sewn until the block is complete. The quilt and its overall pattern are revealed only when all the blocks are joined. The single block contributes to the pattern but has no significance on its own. Minnie's position equals that of the innermost, smallest square that, although the center of the block, is the tiniest and least remarkable one.

This position is supported by Minnie's sleeping arrangements. As she tells the sheriff, she did not notice John Wright's death because she was lying on the inside of the bed. Thus, she was boxed in by walls and her husband. To break free, she had to break one or the other.

Trifles shows us that, while spatial conditions can contribute to isolation, they are not the deciding factor. In fact, Minnie's unbearable isolation was caused by her husband's complete lack of understanding or tolerance of her personality. These gender relations, the complete dominance of the patriarchal authority that does not leave Minnie any space to be herself in a place and time that does not allow for divorce without making Minnie a complete outcast, force her to the desperate final act of killing her husband.

Elke Brown

JUSTICE in *Trifles*

Although we like to think of justice as a completely objective, impartial force, *Trifles* nicely demonstrates that this is not the case. In fact, we are confronted with various interpretations of what justice entails.

At first glance, there appears to be only the kind of justice illustrated by its official representatives, namely Sheriff Peters and the county attorney. These two represent the law and have to make sure that the investigation of the crime scene, John Wright's house, follows due procedure. They are there to secure evidence and discourage any tampering with the crime scene.

However, as the play progresses, the simple, clear-cut definition of justice becomes increasingly complicated. It soon becomes evident that there is a distinction between insiders and outsiders of the community. The county attorney, as outsider, demands the following of protocol. He knew neither John nor Minnie Wright or anything about their history, and he cuts off the others every time they begin to explain the nature of their neighbors' relationships. What he is looking for is hard, tangible evidence; he is not interested in any psychological implications.

The people who knew the Wrights, however, place some importance on their knowledge of the couple. Repeatedly, they attempt to inform the county attorney of little facts that reveal the fabric of the community. While both the men and women try to interest the attorney in the Wrights as people and not just as murder victim and suspect, it is the women who have the clearest insight into their relationship. Although they are constantly dismissed by the lawyer, they ironically uncover all the evidence that points to Minnie as her husband's murderer.

In the exchange between Mrs. Hale and Mrs. Peters, the complicated nature of justice becomes evident. Mrs. Hale has known Minnie for a long time but stopped visiting her because the joyless atmosphere in the Wright house made her feel uncomfortable. Now she feels guilty for having abandoned Minnie and partially responsible for Wright's murder. Her idea of justice is guided by the knowledge of what life is like for a farmer's wife and her acquaintance with the Wrights. Knowing that John Wright was a hard man who did not allow for singing or even much talking around him, she senses that he destroyed Minnie's happy spirit. After their marriage, Minnie stopped attending any social functions and did not sing anymore, although she had always enjoyed being in the church choir. When Mrs. Hale finds the canary with its broken neck, she immediately realizes that this bird symbolizes Minnie's spirit broken by her husband just as he broke the canary's neck. Mrs. Hale understands that the bird provided Minnie with song and joy in her lonely, childless marriage. Mrs. Hale surmises that, after Wright killed the bird, his wife's despair over the loss of the one thing that brightened her life drove her to strangle her husband with a rope. Mrs. Hale questions the institution of justice as it is pursued by its officials; to her, Minnie's crime—though gruesome—is justified and the people who should be on trial are John Wright and her as a representative of the community that abandoned Minnie.

On the other hand, Mrs. Peters at first tries to share the official stance of her husband and attempts to keep any personal knowledge from interfering with the investigation. However, as a fellow woman and insider of the community, she is well aware of the harshness and isolation of the midwestern farmer's wife. She eventually completely connects with Minnie's plight when Mrs. Hale tells her about the oppressing stillness of the house. Having lost a child and reflecting on how quiet it got after its death, Mrs. Peters fully comprehends Minnie's loneliness. It is this shared experience that convinces her of the righteousness of Mrs. Hale's manipulation of the evidence. At first shocked when Mrs. Hale sits down to undo a piece of Minnie's quilt that the latter had been working on but that had been sewn badly and haphazardly due to Minnie's state of mind, Mrs. Peters tries to stuff the box that contains the dead bird into her bag. Since she cannot fit it in there, Mrs. Hale hides it in her coat pocket, so that the men will not be able to find it and use it against Minnie. The women thus decide that their humanistic idea of justice outweighs the men's dogmatic reading of the law.

Elke Brown

GOLDING, WILLIAM *Lord of the Flies* (1954)

William Golding's first novel, *Lord of the Flies,* was originally published in 1954, and it has been required reading in most schools and colleges since the early 1960s. The novel centers around a group of English schoolboys whose plane crashes onto a deserted island during World War II. They subsequently try to form a mini-civilization only to reach a horrific outcome. The book's views on human NATURE and its relationship to civilization, illustrated through the boys' behavior, has caused it to be one of the most challenged books of the late 20th century.

The main characters consist of Ralph, Piggy, and Jack. Ralph, one of the older boys, becomes the impromptu leader of the group. He, with the help of the socially inept Piggy, sets about creating a society on the island through building shelters, constructing a signal fire, and organizing the collection of food. Jack is the leader of the hunters and Ralph's rival for power over the group. Eventually most of the boys follow Jack's example and become swept up in the thrill of the hunt, leaving Ralph and the island society behind, with disastrous results. Golding uses these children to explore themes such as INDIVIDUAL AND SOCIETY, CRUELTY, SURVIVAL, COMMUNITY, ETHICS, ISOLATION, and SPIRITUALITY.

Lord of the Flies is meant to be an allegory. Its characters represent abstract principles such as reason, societal rules, spirituality, and savagery. Golding

seems to think that all of these influence human behavior and have a part in human nature. However, he appears to view savagery as the core of human nature, based on the behavior of most of the boys by the end of the book.

Ryan Neighbors

CRUELTY in *Lord of the Flies*

Lord of the Flies by William Golding centers on a group of schoolboys who are marooned on a deserted island after their plane crashes. Initially, the boys try to set up life on the island much as it was in civilization—they create an island democracy, choose a "biggun," Ralph, as their leader, and set about building shelter and finding food. However, as the boys spend more time on the island, they become increasingly cruel.

This tendency toward cruelty can be seen very early in the novel. For instance, in one scene, Henry, one of the "littluns," plays with plankton on the beach, trapping them in his footprint when the tide comes in. He enjoys this cruel control over other living things. Little does he know that one of the bigguns, Roger, is exerting the same control over him. As Henry plays, Roger watches from the jungle, throwing rocks in a circle around the little boy. The implication is that Roger not only longs for that control but also actually wishes to do harm to Henry. All that stops him are cultural values he has learned from his parents and from his society.

The cruelty in the novel continues through the boys' desire to hunt. This hunting begins innocently enough—Jack, one of the older children, dubs the choirboys the hunters and himself their leader, intending to help provide food for all of the boys. However, hunting soon becomes an obsession. In fact, the hunters eventually shun all of their other responsibilities in favor of the hunt. This even causes the group to miss a chance at rescue, because the hunters fail to keep the signal fire lit as a ship passes by the island.

Their obsession with hunting eventually leads them to bloodlust, frenzy, and murder. This descent begins when the hunters kill a sow. They stick its head on a pike and begin to dance in a ritualistic, tribal celebration. In the midst of this commotion, Simon, one of the older boys, wanders into the group, and the other boys kill him, thinking him a monster. Ralph and his friend Piggy feel remorse over Simon's death and try to get Jack and his hunters to see reason. However, Jack will not listen. Roger rolls a boulder over Piggy, killing him, and the hunters chase Ralph into the jungle. He hides for nearly a day as he is hunted like an animal. The only thing that saves him is the boys' rescue by the British navy.

The main symbol for cruelty in the novel is the beast. From the beginning, the "littluns" have nightmares, and many believe a monster lurks on the island. One night when a dead pilot drops from the sky in a parachute, the boys believe they have actually seen the monster. As they become more enthralled in the hunt and its bloodlust, they even begin to worship this beast, leaving it sacrifices, such as the sow's head on a pike, as if it were a tribal god. Only Simon is able to realize the truth. He sees the dead pilot for what he really is and also realizes the truth of the beast through a vision in which the sow's head talks to him as "Lord of the Flies." Simon realizes there is no external beast. There is only the cruelty that exists in each of the boys. They fear it because it is in them. It is this knowledge and Simon's innate morality that necessitates his death. In a sense, he is too good for the island, and the world.

This seems to be the central point of the story—cruelty is a basic aspect of human nature. The island does not make the boys barbaric. They are naturally that way. The island only provides an environment, away from societal norms and values, for their true nature to manifest itself. That is why the descent into cruelty progresses as it does in the novel. It takes time for the societal values to wear away, leaving behind the boys' true selves, ending with terrible consequences.

Ryan Neighbors

INDIVIDUAL AND SOCIETY in *Lord of the Flies*

In William Golding's *Lord of the Flies,* a group of English schoolboys are stranded on a deserted island when their plane is shot down as they flee Britain. In the beginning of the novel, the boys have a meeting and form a mini-civilization, electing an older boy named Ralph as their leader. As the novel progresses, however, more and more of the boys begin to live as hunters, led by self-proclaimed warrior-dictator Jack, turning their backs on the society they have created on the island. This tug-of-war between individual impulses and the rules and welfare of their society is apparent in nearly all of the schoolboys and through several symbols in the novel.

This struggle is seen most clearly in the novel's protagonist Ralph. Ralph represents society and order in Golding's narrative. He uses the conch shell to call the meeting and is named as the boys' leader, initiating their island democracy. He immediately urges the boys to construct huts on the beach and build a signal fire on the mountain, so they will hopefully be returned to the society of the adults. During the course of the novel, however, Ralph, like the other boys, begins to feel the bloodlust within himself. On his first hunt, he experiences the thrill of violence and even gets swept up in the dancing frenzy after the killing of a sow. It is the murder of Simon at this celebration, though, that returns Ralph to his senses. He again becomes a civilizing influence to the boys, even though most of them have already turned their backs on society to indulge their individual urges.

This indulgence of impulses centers around the character of Jack. He is the boy who suggests the children hunt in the beginning of the novel. In fact, he becomes obsessed with the activity, and his enthusiasm spreads to many of the other boys. He leads the group in the killing of the sow, the resulting tribe-like celebration, and the murder of Simon. Later in the novel, he even breaks away from Ralph's newly formed society, forming his own tribe of hunters. Jack comes to represent the barbaric, self-indulgent turning from society that most of the boys embrace.

Perhaps the most disturbing example of the conflict between the individual and society in the novel is Jack's friend, Roger. In the early pages of the novel, Roger seems like a perfectly normal boy. In the book's fourth chapter, however, a scene foreshadows the character's turn from society. It is in this chapter that we see Henry, one of the "littluns," playing with plankton on the beach. As the tide comes in, the plankton become trapped in the depression of Henry's footprint. The little boy feels exhilarated at being in control of other living things. Unbeknownst to him, Roger watches from the jungle. The older boy begins to throw rocks at the younger, intentionally missing and forming a circle of rocks around him. Roger is, in essence, exerting the same control over Henry that Henry exerts over the plankton. He does not injure the smaller boy because his arm has been conditioned by the society they have been separated from. These societal rules soon fade from Roger's mind, though. Toward the end of the novel, the earlier scene is mirrored when Roger murders Piggy with a boulder. Society's rules no longer hinder his individual nature.

Finally, a few symbols represent this interplay between the individual and society. The conch shell that first appears in the opening chapter symbolizes civilization. The boys use it to conduct their meetings, and only the boy holding the conch can speak. As the novel progresses, the boys' journey away from society is shown in their disregard for the conch and its rules. This culminates in the destruction of the shell at Piggy's death. Likewise, the signal fire points to the boys' desire for the society they have left behind. As the hunters become more engrossed in killing, they forget to keep the fire ablaze and actually miss a chance at rescue. By this point, their desire for violence outweighs their desire for rules and peaceful coexistence.

It appears that Golding is making the statement that humans are not innately moral beings; they naturally hunger for barbarism, violence, and power. In Golding's novel, morality is imposed on the children by their society, and when the society is no longer there to police them, they revert to a more primitive state. It is only at the end of the novel, when faced with the prospect of returning to civilization, that they see where disregarding societal rules has taken them.

Ryan Neighbors

SURVIVAL in *Lord of the Flies*

In *Lord of the Flies* by William Golding, a group of schoolboys of various ages must survive on a deserted island after their plane is shot down as they try to escape Britain during World War II. The book centers around the attempts they make to survive, beginning with forming an island democracy and including the eventual turning from that democracy and its rules. In all, the boys take several steps to guarantee their survival. These steps are taken to ensure their safety and to meet their basic needs. They include creating an island society, building shelter, starting a signal fire, and hunting.

The boys create an island society to establish order on the island and to mirror the society they have left where they felt secure. They elect a leader, Ralph, and define the rules of their society, such as allowing only the person holding the conch shell to speak at meetings. Eventually, however, the boys turn their backs on the societal rules they have created, instead relying on their barbaric natures to ensure their survival. This turning from society begins with their disregarding the rule of the conch shell. It reaches its symbolic peak in the destruction of the conch shell toward the end of the novel.

The first task the boys set about after creating their island society is to build shelters and gather food. Though all of the boys seem excited about the plan to build huts, only Ralph and Simon work to build them while the others play in the lagoon. This implies that while all of the boys want their basic needs met, only a couple of the older ones are willing to do what it takes to ensure their survival. Likewise, the boys set about gathering fruit to eat, though it is mainly just a few of the older ones who are willing to do this, as well. In addition to gathering fruit, many of the boys, led by Jack, opt to hunt for their food. This desire to hunt arises after Jack sees a sow, though it is several days before the sow will provide sustenance for them. Nevertheless, the hunt soon consumes many of the boys, leading to the fall of the island society.

Early in the novel, Piggy, the voice of reason in the group, brings it to the others' attention that it will likely be some time before they are rescued. This revelation frightens many of the children but eventually prompts them to create a signal fire on the mountain. In their first attempt at building the fire, the boys spend more time playing than actually attending to it. The fire begins to burn out of control, burning a large path through the forest and presumably killing one of the "littluns." Eventually, the group, led by the hunters, is able to safely control the fire and let it continue to burn. However, much like their turning from their island society, the boys become so focused on hunting that they ultimately quit keeping up the signal fire, causing them to actually miss a chance at rescue. Once again, the boys turn their backs on all other aspects of survival in favor of the hunt.

It is this avenue of survival—the hunt—that eventually engrosses most of the boys. The thrill they get from hunting intoxicates them, leading to a sort of bloodlust. It is exemplified in the frenzied, tribal dance that occurs after the killing of the sow. However, the bloodlust and barbarism they feel becomes generalized, not being focused solely on the island wildlife. The irony is that this method of surviving actually leads to the death of several boys, including Simon and Piggy. The savage nature of the hunters even makes Ralph run for his life as they try to kill him.

This leads to the central point that Golding is trying to make: Human nature is inherently corrupt. In essence, he is saying that our natures are so corrupt that even the boys' attempts at survival become twisted and lead to death, particularly in the case of hunting. What at one time was used for the benefit of all of the group actually results in the death of some of its members and forces the group's former leader Ralph to escape his former followers. Because of this corrupt nature, no one is safe, and it is every man for himself.

Ryan Neighbors

GORDIMER, NADINE   *Burger's Daughter*   (1979)

South African-born Nadine Gordimer's 1979 novel, *Burger's Daughter*, deals with the three themes of JUSTICE, RACE, and SURVIVAL cyclically and extensively. Taking place within the sociopolitical climate of the massacres at Sharpeville in 1960 and Soweto in 1976, the dramatic events of *Burger's Daughter* are recounted through the perspective of young Rosa Burger, daughter of Lionel and Cathy Burger. Descendants of white Dutch settlers who came to be known as Afrikaners, the Burgers become martyrs for the cause of racial equality and social justice for all South Africans. Lionel, a medical doctor, sees in communism what he believes is the solution to the problems plaguing South Africa, and he becomes an active member of the South African Communist

Party. Rosa's parents are imprisoned and eventually die for their cause, and the young girl is left to carry on their legacy while crafting some semblance of a life for herself. Because of her family's history of radical involvement in activist causes, she remains "Burger's daughter" long after Lionel's death and is placed under government surveillance for the rest of her life. The novel challenges readers with its stream of consciousness narrative threads, which simultaneously reflect the horrifying realities of time and place while representing Rosa's innermost thoughts and perspectives.

Walter Collins III

JUSTICE in *Burger's Daughter*

Tied closely to the issue of race, the notion of justice, or lack thereof, permeates *Burger's Daughter*. Through the mind and eyes of Rosa Burger, readers learn of the ubiquitous injustices black South Africans confront due to lives lived in a prejudiced society. Rosa's parents, Lionel and Cathy, are the agents through whom many of the issues of justice are exposed in the novel and their stances against inequality and discrimination based on race and economic situation leave them subject to recrimination by fellow Afrikaners who fail to view certain sociopolitical practices in South Africa as problematic.

Early on, Rosa recalls her father's speech, given in defense of fighting for black South Africans, during the course of one of his trials. For more than an hour, Lionel testifies to the injustices that abound in society. During his lifetime, he has witnessed bigotry in the schools, in religious organizations that proclaim to "worship the God of Justice [yet] practice discrimination on the grounds of the colour of skin," and later, as a doctor, he observed unfair treatment of blacks in hospitals where he practiced. It is because of these situations that Lionel subscribes to Marxism. At one point in his speech, he asserts: "This contradiction that split the very foundation of my life, . . . in Marxism I found it analysed in another way: as forces in conflict through economic laws. I saw that white Marxists worked side by side with blacks in an equality that meant taking on the meanest of tasks . . . I saw whites prepared to work under blacks. Here was a possible solution to injustice to be sought outside the awful fallibility in any self-professed morality I knew." Lionel risks everything, including his own life, as he holds to his personal convictions and his conception of justice while fighting against ever-present injustice.

Gordimer's story suggests that nothing short of a sweeping change of the ways in which things have always been handled will cause a change in Afrikaners' minds concerning notions of societal justice and injustice. Marxism, with its attendant shift in personal viewpoints of perceived racial and social hierarchies, clearly evokes the idea of revolution. And while the Burger family stands strongly for such radical change to help the down and out of any race, Rosa is dubious that well-off whites will ever willingly espouse any such transformation. She realizes that "children the white couple would make in their whites' suburb would [no longer] inherit the house bought on the municipal loan available only to whites, or slot safely into jobs reserved for whites against black competition." Likewise, Rosa continues to be haunted by the sight of a white man dead on a park bench, seen one day during her lunch break, and she wants to believe that "when we had changed the world, . . . the 'elimination of private conflicts set up by the competitive nature of capitalist society' would help people to live, even people like this [dead man], who, although white and privileged under the law of the country, couldn't make a place for himself." The oppositions of life and death, privilege and disadvantage, justice and injustice cause Rosa to reflect on life's inherent challenges, which seem to be overly magnified in the society she knows. Rosa even wrestles with the seeming meaninglessness of a life—a universal preoccupation—as depicted in the scene of the dead man in the park. She reckons: "Justice, equality, the brotherhood of man, human dignity—but *[death] will still be there* . . . ." Any semblance of justice—simply having a few things, working hard, or living life according to one's desires—remains elusive in *Burger's Daughter.*

The Burgers' collective fight for justice becomes all-consuming as details of their personal lives are slowly and almost completely erased by deeds done on behalf of those who are less fortunate. Even traditional celebrations hardly take place in their home as they fete instead "the occasions . . . when some-body got off, not guilty, in a political trial. Leaders came out of prison. A bunch of blacks made a success of a boycott or defied a law. There was a mass protest or a march, a strike. . . ." Such "celebrations of justice" dot their lives as they continue to work toward comprehensive social change, understanding that complete justice lies somewhere in the days ahead: "There is nothing but failure, until the day the Future is achieved. It is the only success. Others—in specific campaigns with specific objectives, against the pass laws, against forced dispossession of land—would lead to piecemeal reforms . . . Failure is the accumulated heritage of resistance without which there is no revolution." By the end of the text, it is clear that "No one knows where the end of suffering will begin." While small victories are celebrated along the way, the novel's concluding pages suggest that real South African justice remains uncertain.

Walter Collins III

RACE in *Burger's Daughter*

Burger's Daughter is a story of racial struggle. Because of their belief in racial equality, Lionel and Cathy Burger and daughter Rosa stand in stark contrast to the majority of whites, the Afrikaners, who populate South Africa. Their activism is the cause of frequent encounters with government officials. Indeed, as the novel opens, readers join Rosa in line, arms full of clothing and other provisions, outside a prison where detainees, including her mother, are held. The Burgers constantly expect prison detention, unfair court proceedings, and eventual martyrdom. Traitors, by most Afrikaners' assessments, the family members reject what for them would be easy "[positive] reputation, success and personal liberty." Instead they live and die for a revolution that "would change the lives of the blacks who left their hovels and compounds at four in the morning to swing picks, hold down jack-hammers and chant under the weight of girders, building shopping malls and office towers in which whites .. moved in an 'environment' without sweat or dust." Filtered through Rosa's stream-of-consciousness reflections, the novel illustrates the hardships of blacks during apartheid.

In stores, blacks are routinely treated as second-class citizens. In one scene, Dhladhla recounts his experience: "When I go into the café to buy bread they give the kaffir yesterday's stale. When he goes for fruit, the kaffir gets the half-rotten stuff the white won't buy. That is black." Additionally, unlike whites, blacks are required to carry passbooks when in public. One of Lionel's early realizations regarding the passbooks catalyzes his enduring mission for racial equality. Rosa recounts this moment of her father's recognition: "Lionel once told me how when he was about fourteen and had just come to boarding-school in Johannesburg he saw torn-up passbooks in the street . . . and curiosity led him to realize for the first time that the 'natives' were people who had to carry these things while white people like himself didn't." Later, when a black father, Fats, contends that his son should be allowed to participate in sports and be seen as the equal to any big name international boxer, he receives this response: "Your boy can negotiate to go to Germany and America and hell. He's still a 'boy' that's been let out like a monkey on a string. . . . You'll make a lot of money and he can show his medal with his pass when he gets back." Not only does the future look bleak for this player, but also Gordimer demonstrates that South African blacks know that sports cannot solve national issues of racial inequality: "And if next year or the year after white soccer clubs play blacks, and take in black members, the soccer players will shout there's no more racism in sport. But everywhere else in this country the black will still be a black. Whatever else he does he'll still get black jobs, black education, black houses—." Ubiquitous racism never deters the Burger family from attempts to mollify its effects.

Their involvement with Baasie exemplifies the extent to which theirs is a personal cause. In a place where segregation and inequality rule, the Burgers take Baasie in and treat him like family. Baasie and Rosa fall asleep together in her bed at night, Baasie is educated illegally in Rosa's private school and he is taught to swim and more. Baasie "fought for the anchorage of wet hair on Lionel Burger's warm breast in the cold swimming-pool" as he is taught not only to swim but to claim freedom from what would be incapacitating fears even if his was a desegregated society. In adulthood, when Rosa again meets Baasie, she becomes aware of his bit-

terness over treatment of blacks by whites. With his own perspectives concerning South African racism and without gratitude to Rosa for her family's earlier concerns, he rejects any white aid, sincere or otherwise: "I'm not your Baasie, just don't go on thinking about that little kid who lived with you, don't think of that black 'brother', that's all—." Baasie's attitude reflects the attitudes of other blacks who feel that whites, no matter how pure their motives, can never really help blacks. Instead, for truly untainted lives, blacks must establish their own equality.

In the end, readers realize that "All collaboration with whites has always ended in exploitation of blacks." In Dhladhla's words: "We must liberate ourselves as blacks, what has a white got to do with that?" Implicit in this notion is that South Africa's hope and future lie with black citizens. Ancient black spirits interweave with contemporary black spirits working for freedoms today to convey that "Through blackness is revealed the way to the future." And once blacks and whites escape wholly the oppression of apartheid everyone will find the way "to the only rendezvous that matters, the victory where there will be room for all." Racially speaking, *Burger's Daughter* ends on a guardedly hopeful note.

Walter Collins III

SURVIVAL in *Burger's Daughter*

Along with issues of RACE and JUSTICE, the issue of survival permeates Gordimer's *Burger's Daughter*. Lionel Burger dies in prison of nephritis in the third year of his life sentence for fighting for the equality of black South Africans. Cathy and Tony, Rosa's mother and brother, face untimely deaths. But the complex notion of survival is embodied in Rosa's life. The text makes it clear throughout that in her personal and professional dealings she will always be Burger's daughter—eternally connected to her father's ideals, principles, and controversial ideological stances. Rosa continues her father's WORK, and in that very real existence she ensures the survival of the family's cause. Considered from another angle, actual human survival becomes complicated as well, due to the promotion of divisive racial equality and social justice causes.

At the beginning of the novel, Rosa is waiting in line in front of a prison to visit her mother. Within the first few pages, readers also learn that Rosa's father is serving a life sentence in prison. The stability of the family might easily be compromised given the activist roles that Lionel and Cathy play. However, security and protection of their family are important to the Burgers even as fighting for racial and social equality is highly valued. Rosa recollects the strategies her parents purposely employed to ensure the survival of their family. She recalls:

I think that while my mother was alive and my brother was a baby my parents arranged their activities so that one of them was in the clear, always, one would always have a good chance of being left behind to carry on the household if the other were arrested . . Then when my brother and mother were gone, there was me. If my father were to be arrested, there would always be me.

Lionel and Cathy negotiated their activist roles in order to ensure the survival of their family members and the survival of their message.

A card Rosa receives from her Auntie Velma and Uncle Coen Nels crystallizes the degree to which the influence of Lionel's work to bring about equality will survive within the family. Velma and Coen, who had been strictly against Lionel's efforts, offer for Rosa to come and stay at their farm whenever she would like or whenever she needs rest. Rosa states that

[Velma] does not ask from what activity [I might seek rest,] she does not want to know in case it is, as her brother's always was, something she fears and disapproves to the point of inconceivability . . . The Nels have never had any difficulty in reconciling pride in belonging to a remarkable family with the certainty that the member who made it so followed wicked and horrifying ideals . . . Whatever my father was to them, it still stalks their consciousness.

In very apparent ways, the work of the Burger family survives and affects lives. In the end, one only hopes that the Burgers' struggle for equality will be realized for all.

Survival in *Burger's Daughter* encompasses the complexities of both RACE and SOCIAL CLASS. When Rosa observes a dead man in a park one day during her lunch break, she ponders the depths of inequality and divisiveness in South Africa. Rosa is astonished to learn in the newspaper the identity of this man who is "white and privileged under the law of the country." Out of work, on hard times, and with no hope of securing gainful employment, this man finds it difficult to survive even as a white person:

The paper said the man's name was Ronald Ferguson, 46, an ex-miner, no fixed abode. He drank methylated spirits and slept in bus shelters. There is an element of human wastage in all societies. But—in [the Burgers'] house—it was believed that when we had changed the world . . .—the 'elimination of private conflicts set up by the competitive nature of capitalist society' would help people to live, even people like this one, who . . . couldn't make a place for himself.

If survival is difficult for this white, middle-aged man, then it becomes all the more difficult for black South Africans.

Perhaps the incident in *Burger's Daughter* that most distinctly demonstrates the difficulty of survival is the Soweto Uprising of June 1976. Near the end of the text, the narrator tells of the loss of life and the struggle to survive that many youth in Soweto faced following the riots: "The school riots filled the hospital; the police who answered stones with machine-guns and patrolled Soweto firing revolvers at any street-corner group of people encountered, who raided high schools and picked off the targets of youngsters escaping in the stampede, also wounded anyone else who happened to be within the random of their fire." After a long catalogue of gruesome images of destruction, *Burger's Daughter* closes on a note of measured hope that the noble objectives of the Burger family will live on to ensure not only the physical survival of the disenfranchised but also the betterment of life for all South Africans.

Walter Collins III

GRASS, GUNTER *The Tin Drum* (1959)

Oskar Matzerath is undoubtedly one of the most remarkable characters in modern fiction. Both first-person narrator and main character of *The Tin Drum* (1959), Oskar, a 30-year-old inmate of an asylum, relates his life story. Born, he claims, with fully developed intellectual abilities, he decides at the age of three, the age at which he acquires his first tin drum, to reject the adult world and to stop growing. In order to provide an explanation for his stunted growth, he says, he throws himself down the cellar stairs. Thus able to view the world from the perspective of a perpetual three-year-old, Oskar witnesses the rise and fall of Nazi Germany and the brutal events of World War II. As the war draws to a close, Oskar begins to grow again. In the final chapters of the book, Oskar recounts his family's move from Danzig to West Germany and his experience from the postwar years up until his confinement in the mental institution.

Grass employs a complex narrative structure for the novel, moving between first- and third-person narration. Oskar refers to himself as "I" but also as "Oskar," as if he is speaking about another person. Oskar's self-alienation, his status as a mental patient, and his often contradictory accounts of the past, make Oskar a very unreliable narrator. The reader must therefore question the truthfulness of his account, an autobiography that links the events of Oskar's life to the catastrophes of the first half of 20th-century German history.

Christina Kraenzle

GUILT in *The Tin Drum*

One of the novel's central themes is the question of guilt. Oskar begins his account from the confines of a mental institution, where he has been incarcerated for the murder of Sister Dorothea Köngetter. Oskar denies the charge, but admits to an obsession with the nurse, giving considerable support to the case against him. However, on his 30th birthday there is a new development in the case. Oskar reports that fresh evidence suggests the murder was committed by a jealous, fellow nurse; the courts have recognized his innocence and he will soon be released. But as the reader by this point is keenly aware, Oskar is an unreliable narrator, often changing his story to either admit or deny his complicity in past events. We cannot take this final claim of innocence at face value.

Moreover, this is not the first death in which Oskar has been involved. Throughout the novel, Oskar claims responsibility for the deaths of his mother and his two "presumptive" fathers, Alfred Matzerath and Jan Bronski. The first to die is Oskar's mother Agnes, who gorges herself on fish after discovering the pregnancy that may well be the result of her affair with Jan Bronski. While Oskar initially displays no signs of guilt, he later tells Roswitha Raguna that others hold him responsible. Later, Oskar suggests that he was exaggerating his account in an attempt to impress Roswitha. Still later, however, Oskar reports that he indeed overheard his grandmother blaming him, claiming that Agnes died because she could no longer stand Oskar's drumming. Several chapters later, Oskar claims responsibility for both his mother's and Jan Bronski's death.

Oskar offers a similarly contradictory account of Jan Bronski's death. In the first version of the story, Oskar describes how Jan is driven away by the Germans and waves a last goodbye to Oskar. In the next chapter, however, Oskar declares that he must correct an omission, namely that when the Germans arrived, Oskar pretended to the soldiers that Jan Bronski had forced him into the post office in order to use him as a human shield. Subsequently, Bronski is beaten, taken away, and later executed. Oskar allegedly commits the act of treachery out of concern for his own comfort and safety and to protect his precious tin drums.

In the case of Alfred Matzerath's death, Oskar initially maintains that he takes the Nazi Party pin, which Matzerath has discarded, only to protect young Kurt. He ostensibly hands it back to Matzerath because he wishes to pick a louse from a Russian soldier's collar. Matzerath panics, attempts to swallow the incriminating object, and chokes, prompting one of the soldiers to kill him. In the next chapter, however, Oskar changes his story and claims he deliberately exposed Matzerath's party membership, and even opened the pin so that his father might choke on it.

The amount of incriminating evidence that Oskar discloses at the very least suggests a guilty conscience. However, in each case, it is impossible to determine unequivocally the degree of Oskar's guilt. Oskar changes his stories repeatedly; moreover, it is his version of events, and therefore subjective and possibly entirely of his own invention. He also freely admits to being a liar, as in the case of the Dusters' trial, where he plays the role of innocent victim to avoid punishment. Furthermore, as a mental patient, all of Oskar's recollections become highly questionable.

Less compelling perhaps than Oskar's individual guilt is the greater and more complex issue of collective guilt for the crimes of National Socialism. Oskar connects the two in his account of Jan Bronski's death when he describes how he tries to assuage his guilty conscience. Here Oskar equates his personal feelings of guilt with the collective guilt of the nation. Like everyone else, he says, he soothes his guilty conscience by making excuses for past misdeeds. Later, he describes how he participates in discussions at the British Centre, where individuals talk about collective guilt so that later their consciences will be clear. Here, the novel casts doubt on the process of *Vergangenheitsbewältigung* (a German term meaning "coming to terms with the past"), suggesting that national debates about collective guilt have not effectively tackled questions of complicity, but simply help individuals to distance themselves from the past. Oskar's autobiography, which oscillates between confession and denial of guilt, must be seen in this broader context. It thus offers a reflection on the complicated process of dealing with national responsibility for the crimes of Nazi Germany.

Christina Kraenzle

IDENTITY in *The Tin Drum*

One of the most striking features of *The Tin Drum* is the complexity of its main character, Oskar, a highly ambivalent figure who portrays himself alternately as naïve child and knowing adult, unwitting participant in events and active shaper of his own destiny, innocent bystander and complicit villain. He is also quite likely a madman, a possibility supported by a narrative structure that moves between first- and third-person narration. Oskar's tendency to refer to himself not as "I" but as "Oskar" suggests self-alienation and identity crisis. But the challenge of *The Tin Drum* is not to try to determine what constitutes the "real" Oskar, but rather to consider how these multiple identities coexist.

The multiplicity of identities is introduced at the beginning of the novel when Oskar recalls his many outings to the cinema with Klepp, after which they have their passport photos taken. Oskar describes how he and Klepp manipulate the photos, folding or cutting them to combine old and new photographs or to merge the features of both men into new images of themselves. As a metaphor for identity, the montages that Oskar and Klepp create point to the multifaceted influences and self-identifications that make up Oskar's character. They also suggest the constructedness of the images Oskar offers: Just as Oskar and Klepp fashion their own photographic images, Oskar, the autobiographer, creates multiple, and often conflicting, self-images in his written account.

Oskar's identity crisis is reflected in his obsessions about his parentage, in particular his uncertainty about which of his two "presumptive fathers" is in fact the biological one. While he at first suggests that Jan Bronski is his true father, he later suggests that it is most likely Alfred Matzerath. This uncertainty leads Oskar to refer to himself both as Oskar Matzerath and Oskar Bronski. He also takes the name Koljaiczek, after his maternal grandfather, with whom he also identifies.

Oskar's education under the tutelage of Gretchen Scheffler, who introduces him to both Goethe and Rasputin, also shapes his self-image. Oskar takes pages from the two books and shuffles them randomly to create a new volume that he reads throughout his life. Oskar alternately identifies with Goethe, who represents enlightenment and rationality, and with Rasputin, who represents darkness and irrationality. Oskar later asks Bruno to fashion a string figure that will combine the features of Oskar, Goethe, and Rasputin, symbolizing the two poles that constitute Oskar's identity.

His mother's frequent visits to church introduce Oskar to religion, and he subsequently identifies with both Jesus and Satan. Oskar believes he resembles the figure of Jesus in the Church of the Sacred

Heart; he later introduces himself to the Dusters as Jesus and becomes their leader. When the Dusters break into the church, Oskar has the Jesus figure removed and takes its place while mass is read. Later, the painter Raskolnikov will depict Oskar as Jesus. In his alleged sexual encounter with Sister Dorothea, however, Oskar claims to be Satan.

Questions of identity are important also for a number of minor characters. Oskar's maternal grandfather, Joe Koljaiczek, assumes the identity of Joe Wranka in order to escape the authorities. Haunted by his memories of Lucy Rennwand, Oskar believes he recognizes her in the person of Regina Raeck, a fellow refugee from Danzig. He continues to confuse their identities throughout the trip. He also confuses Leo Schugger and Willem Slobber, believing them to be the same person. Oskar's neighbor, Mr. Münzer, calls himself Klepp because, like Oskar, he does not want to take his father's last name. Oskar's landlord exhibits a split personality, violently breaking liquor glasses and then carefully sweeping up the shards. In one passage, Oskar refers to these sides of his landlord's personality with two different names: Oskar uses the nickname Hedgehog to refer to the landlord's violent personality and his real name, Zeidler, to refer to his more orderly side.

The theme of identity is also significant on a larger, national scale. As many commentators have noted, Oskar can be seen as an embodiment of the German nation. At one point Oskar notes that the two poles of his identity, represented by Goethe and Rasputin, always exist in tandem. This idea can also be applied to Germany, a nation that spawned numerous intellectuals and artists, but also Hitler and the Nazis. With its complicated main character and its depiction of how ordinary citizens support the rise of National Socialism, Grass's *The Tin Drum* insists that polar opposites such as good and evil or rational and irrational cannot be easily separated. Instead, the potential for both enlightenment and brutality coexist in unsettling ways.

Christina Kraenzle

VIOLENCE in *The Tin Drum*

Throughout his life, Oskar witnesses countless acts of violence and brutality. Oskar encounters many violent individuals, and also observes the organized violence of the Nazi regime and the war. Grass's novel thus connects the personal and the political, showing how ordinary citizens commit acts of brutality, both in the private and public sphere.

As a child, Oskar is subjected to the cruelty of the neighborhood children who force him to eat a noxious soup made with live frogs, saliva, and urine. At his kindergarten, Stephan Bronski is viciously beaten by a boy named Lothar who refers to Stephan as "Polack," thus alluding to the Polish-German tensions leading up to the war. After the war, Oskar encounters Zeidler, the rooming house landlord who flies into violent and seemingly unprovoked rages and shatters liquor glasses to vent his anger.

Oskar also recounts how Meyn, irritated by the smell from his four tomcats, brutally attacks the animals with a fire poker and stuffs them, mortally wounded but still alive, into a garbage can. Meyn is later expelled from the SA for inhumane cruelty to animals, despite his involvement, Oskar says, in the events of *Kristallnacht*. Oskar then goes on to describe, in the final chapter of Book One, the *Kristallnacht*—known in English as *Crystal Night* or *The Night of Broken Glass*—the organized and systematic terrorizing of Jews that occurred throughout Germany and parts of Austria on November 9 and 10, 1938. Oskar recounts how his father, Alfred Matzerath, watches the events with approval, how men in uniform and civilian clothes participate in the destruction, and how firemen look on while the local synagogue burns. Oskar further describes how businesses, including Sigismund Markus's toyshop, are vandalized, and recounts how Markus commits suicide before SA officers descend on his store. Oskar's comment that Meyn is condemned for the violence against the cats, but celebrated for his participation in the violence against the Jewish population, illustrates the extent to which Nazis devalued and dehumanized the Jewish people. The participation of ordinary citizens in the events of *Kristallnacht* also show how anti-Semitic Nazi violence was condoned and even, in many cases, supported.

As Oskar notes early in the novel, "where there is politics, there is violence." As political tensions turn to war, Oskar witnesses countless acts of brutality. He is present during the bloody battle at the

Polish post office; he stands by as Russian soldiers kill Alfred Matzerath; he watches Corporal Lankes senselessly murder a group of nuns, and he looks on as Roswitha Raguna is hit by a stray shell during an Allied attack.

Oskar also relates numerous cases of violence against women. Herbert Truczinski is killed in his attempt to sexually assault the figure of Niobe in the Danzig Maritime Museum. Oskar witnesses the rape of Lina Greff by Russian soldiers, attesting to the prevalence of sexual violence in situations of war. In the postwar years, Lankes repeatedly beats his girlfriend, Ulla, and later, on his trip with Oskar to Normandy, sexually assaults a nun. Oskar's alleged sexual encounter with Sister Dorothea, who is later found murdered, can also be interpreted as an assault.

While Oskar is often a witness to violent events, he is more than simply an innocent bystander. Although he insists on his innocence in the case of Sister Dorothea, he may well be her murderer. Spurned by Maria, he physically assaults her after he learns of her affair with Alfred Matzerath and subsequently tries to abort her pregnancy by causing her to fall from a ladder. Later, he plans to stab her in the belly with a pair of scissors, but is prevented when Maria notices his intentions. During the war, Oskar becomes the leader of the Dusters and although he claims not to participate in their attacks on their rivals, he accepts their activities. As a child, Oskar exhibits a violent temper, especially when anyone threatens to take away his tin drum. He responds by shattering glass with his voice, an act that is reminiscent of landlord Zeidler's violent fits of rage or the violence and destruction of *Kristallnacht*.

Toward the end of the novel, Oskar witnesses an attack on Victor Weluhn, carried out by three men who claim to be fulfilling an execution order issued in 1939 for Victor's involvement in the defense of the Polish post office. Although the war is long over, the men insist on carrying out this former obligation. Here Grass satirizes misplaced notions of duty and order. Throughout the novel, countless acts of private and public violence attest to the potential for savagery that underlies apparently well-ordered society.

Christina Kraenzle

GREENE, GRAHAM *The Heart of the Matter* (1948)

The Heart of the Matter is one of 20th-century British Catholic writer Graham Greene's most widely considered to be masterpieces. It concerns the efforts of police officer Henry Scobie to lead a just life amid suffering, corruption, and temptation at an unidentified British colony in Africa during World War II. Over the course of the novel, Scobie suffers a gradual descent from justice, a descent motivated by pity and pride. Because he pities a Portuguese ship captain, Scobie destroys a letter that he should have reported to the commissioner; because he pities his emotionally crippled wife, Louise, he sends her to South Africa with the proceeds of a compromising loan from a black marketeer named Yusef; and because he pities shipwreck survivor Helen Rolt, he begins an affair with her. In an effort to maintain the reputation his devotion to justice has earned him, he hides his affair and his connection with Yusef, to the point that he allows the murder of possibly the only person he truly loves, his young servant Ali. Unable to bear his fall from grace, he commits suicide by overdosing on a heart medicine.

Though Greene himself considered it a failure, the novel has been admired for its rich evocation of the self-defeating conflicts that attend the human search for a code to live by.

Scott Daniel

FUTILITY in *The Heart of the Matter*

The sense of the futility of all human endeavor pervades Graham Greene's *The Heart of the Matter*. The novel's closing implies a static future as effectively as its opening conveys the sense of an unchanging past, so that the story itself, chronicling Scobie's misguidedly heroic efforts to help others, is the story of change imploding, collapsing upon itself, quashed by the very forces it sets in motion.

The stability of Henry Scobie's situation—epitomized by his being passed over for a position that he is, by all appearances, eminently qualified for: commissioner—rests upon a distorted stoicism that is in a sense inaction or indifference disguised as JUSTICE. While faultlessly performing his duties as public servant, Scobie wallows in futility, gluttonously savoring his lack of advancement, Louise's desperation, and the moral, human squalor of his environment. It is not until the incident on a ship called the *Esperança*—that is, HOPE—that Scobie becomes unmoored from this stability. Hiding the captain's infraction of the maritime code gives him the opportunity to act on his frozen GRIEF for his daughter, who died at school in England several years before the novel begins, and this sets in motion his hopeless battle with FATE. He borrows money to send his wife to South Africa; he begins an affair with shipwreck survivor Helen Rolt.

Through these actions Scobie puts himself at the mercy of the Syrian trader Yusef. Like Iago in Shakespeare's *OTHELLO*, Yusef has an almost preternatural knowledge of Scobie's personality and his actions, so that every attempt Scobie makes to improve his life or that of those around him—most particularly, his wife Louise and mistress Helen Rolt, but even that of the *Esperança*'s captain—further enmeshes him in a trap. Yusef's blackmailing and double dealing is but a visible correlative of the psychological and spiritual futility of Scobie's actions, most tellingly revealed in how quickly his relationship with Helen becomes a carbon copy of his relationship with Louise. A criminal by profession, Yusef is a sort of guarantor of permanent stasis, and just so, he becomes more powerful the more Scobie attempts change.

Until he is moved to act, Scobie has a certain empty acceptance, if not contentment, that belies the term futility, which carries a heavy psychic burden. That burden is upon Louise, whose exasperation with their lack of advancement borders on the hysterical. In some sense, Louise is Scobie's pain, is where Scobie hurts, and his sending her away is a logical means of freeing them both of that burden. The boy Ali is where Scobie feels peace, and Scobie dreams of happy calm times with him in the future. It is a measure of the futility of human affairs that instead of settling into the peace of a narrowed life with his loyal and innocent servant, Scobie immediately falls in love with Helen Rolt, who has already become the new locus of his pain, and begins an affair that will result in Ali's death. From the novel's perspective, it is futility and not justice that governs human events. Indeed, this point is made early in the novel. Approaching first

the courts and then the police station, Scobie sees this system as being full of grandiloquence but ultimately lacking strength. Justice, then, is futility. Henry Scobie governs his life with a rigorous Stoic philosophy, but he leaves one of the central tenets of that philosophy unexamined. The Stoic does his duty, but he also accepts that it is only his justice, and not the justice of the universe, that is within his control. Once moved to action, Scobie cannot accept his lack of power.

In the end, human futility is but a foil for the glacial but certain movement of the church toward the fulfillment of God's promise, and Greene's intent, as we see with other themes the novel addresses, is to create a picture of a Christianity that is meaningful and convincing, if not compelling, to his existentialist contemporaries. In *The Heart of the Matter*, the only efficacious action is sacramental, and its power is LOVE, such that, having avoided it for as long as he could in life, Henry Scobie may not even be able to escape it in death, as the priest suggests to Louise that even a suicide may not be beyond God's mercy and grace.

Scott Daniel

RELIGION in *The Heart of the Matter*

The Heart of the Matter is, of course, a novel about religion. Graham Greene foregrounds Catholic concerns; indeed, much of the dramatic tension of the plot depends on the characters' belief in the Catholic vision of human life. Scobie believes his immortal soul is imperiled in that he will not repent his affair with Helen Rolt; Louise returns from her rest in South Africa because she believes her husband's immortal soul is at risk; the tension is to a degree resolved, the tragedy of the protagonist's suicide diffused, by the priest's closing words to Louise about the unfathomable mystery of God's grace.

The novel's closing scene is an informal theological dialogue between the confused and grieving widow and Father Rank. The conversation seems to match legalistic against mysterious Catholicism. Louise, fearing to hope for a man who has taken his own life, finds the comfort of despair in calling her husband a "bad Catholic" who must have known that he was sinning. Consistently, Rank removes religion from the institution of the church and from the doctrines and toward matters of the heart. He claims that both the human heart and God's mercy are unknowable. This scene illustrates the importance of religion in the novel, as our sense of a resolved plot depends upon our accepting the terms of the debate.

Thus, the Catholic faith exerts its influence not merely on the characters' minds but also on the text of the narrative. Greene artfully conveys a Christian view of evil in the scene in which Scobie and Helen first kiss. It is not a matter so much of him seducing her or her seducing him but of the two of them being seduced by a moment. As is so often true, the narrator's comment on this turn of events gives it a Catholic pall; he says that the apparent "safety" of their relationship was actually "the camouflage of an enemy." Here, temptation is revealed to be demonic and malevolent. It is one thing to say that Yusef and Wilson are devil figures in the novel, but Greene goes further, with a vision of a sentient, supernatural evil that works through seduction and deception. In a similar vein, it is one thing to say that Ali is a Christ figure, but Greene's character assumes a divine grace attendant upon the crucifixion and resurrection of the actual Christ.

The same Christian perspective is evident in Scobie's character flaw. In many respects, he is a typical tragic hero and can be read profitably as such: He is a man of high rank who is not entirely good or bad; he has a character flaw that leads him to an act of hubris, or excessive PRIDE that precipitates his downfall and has consequences that extend beyond the individual. Scobie lacks a clear moment of self-recognition, though a Christian recasting of such a moment might be implied by Father Rank's closing remarks. If self-recognition is the grace note of the Greek tragic hero, then the priest holds out the possibility that in God's grace Scobie will after death see his sin clearly enough to finally be able to repent it. Like his self-recognition, Scobie's hubris is colored by faith. What he seems most to be guilty of is a pride that masquerades as compassion and virtue. The text observes: "Virtue, the good life, tempted him in the dark like a sin." He believes that he is important, that he can make a sacrifice that in its way exceeds that of Christ, for he is risking eternal death to provide a little solace to others. Even worse,

Scobie understands the consequences of his actions, he even recognizes his own self-destructiveness, but he never seems to see the pride that taints his perspective. The pride of good works is a uniquely Christian vice, a moral trap that one finds along the path of virtue. The reader sees by the end of the novel that Scobie's heroic virtue is also his undoing, that his humility is partial and blind and does not prevent the inflation of ego that makes tragedy possible.

The very tenor of the novel's emotions, then, would not be possible without the Catholic faith of the author and his characters. In Greene it is always evident that, ultimately, it is only with defective vision that one sees a universe where, as for the existential hero, the absurd fact of our existence precludes any possible meaning. Scobie suffers because life does have a meaning, a religious dimension, that he can neither reject nor embrace.

Scott Daniel

SUFFERING in *The Heart of the Matter*

Suffering is a palpable atmospheric effect in Graham Greene's *The Heart of the Matter*. It is as geographic and meteorological as it is psychological. His title, perhaps a play on Conrad's *Heart of Darkness*, points to an understanding of this setting as a metaphor for a universal human condition. Indeed, if one thinks of the title as an implied riddle, and asks what lies at the heart of the matter, suffering might well be the answer.

Every character copes with suffering differently and, indeed, suffering treats each character differently, taking the measure of his or her soul. Harris's relatively shallow suffering is a function of idleness, and the solution is to turn killing cockroaches into a sport, a sort of poor man's lacrosse. While his suffering is all but alleviated by this game, his neighbor Wilson has a surplus of suffering that a mere pastime, however violent and competitive, will not assuage. His suffering has a shallowness of its own, though, as he pursues an emotional affair with Louise for largely egotistical reasons. For him, besting Scobie in a romantic rivalry is sufficient succor. His fulfillment hinges, then, on one person, on Louise. Not so Louise: Her loneliness is of epic proportions. Though in many ways crippled by her suffering, she is a remarkable judge of character, viscerally perceiving her husband's emotional dryness and intellectually unraveling Wilson's fundamental dishonesty. She imagines that only a whole nation can satisfy her want, and thus goads her husband to send her to South Africa.

Louise's case highlights the fact that, ultimately, each character's response to suffering is inadequate. Each seeks a superficial remedy, whereas suffering is a condition of existence. This discrepancy between the scope of the problem and the manner of coping is nowhere more evident than in the novel's protagonist, Henry Scobie. His stoic devotion to duty and justice above all else empowers him to repress his own hurt, but then his wife, Louise (and later, his mistress, Helen Rolt) becomes for him nothing more than the voice of his own inner pain. For this reason, he thinks he can get rid of his suffering by getting rid of her. His actions and his daydreams are both reflective of this mentality. In contrast to Louise, Scobie views emotional isolation as a solution to suffering. For him, the problem is larger than even a country. It is the world, before which he stands isolated and weary.

Since the heart that is the heart of the matter is geographical as well as psychological, the West African natives are also native to suffering. For them, suffering is just the medium in which they operate. It is not something to be coped with or striven against. Scobie sees this fundamental difference between the colonists and the natives, and for him it is the principal appeal of his assignment. He reflects: "Nobody here could talk about a heaven on earth . . . on this side flourished the injustices, the cruelties, the meanness that elsewhere people so cleverly hushed up. Here you could love human beings nearly as God loved them, knowing the worst." Succinctly and concisely, Greene's prose accomplishes a devastating critique of Western civilization, for here it appears to be nothing more than an accretion of inadequate and essentially self-deceptive coping mechanisms. The suffering abides, only in disguised form. Western man, then, is alienated from his own condition in a way that the native is not. Ironically, it is this alienation that enables his image of himself as a savior of the native, or even, more modestly, as a counselor. Though a detective, Scobie seems engaged in something more like social work, and it is telling in this regard that he is often slow to realize how shrewdly the natives deceive the colonial authorities.

However ideal the natives might appear to Scobie, the novel ultimately does not endorse their casual acceptance of suffering. Instead, it is Louise Scobie who finds the right balance. There is a world of difference between the Louise who returns from South Africa and the Louise who left, perhaps because upon learning of Henry's infidelity, she reorients herself from reliance on her husband to reliance on the Catholic Church. She returns, then, not as Scobie's savior but as his ally, encouraging him to attend mass and confession and showing a merciful tolerance of his human failings. Louise seems especially forgiving as contrasted to Scobie's self-damnation or to the lovesick accusations of the diabolical Wilson. Their loathing is part and parcel of their suffering, which comes from seeking to be God (as savior on Scobie's hand, and as judge on Wilson's) rather than submitting to Him.

Scott Daniel

HALEY, ALEX, AND MALCOLM X
The Autobiography of Malcolm X (1965)

Malcolm X's autobiography describes a life of multiple transformations, figurative DEATHS, and rebirths, which give his story a mythic quality. Born Malcolm Little in Nebraska, Malcolm and his family moved to Michigan after his birth. The murder of his father led to the dissolution of his family. After time in a detention home, Malcolm moved to Roxbury, Massachusetts with his half-sister, Ella, where the evolution of his IDENTITY was set in motion.

With Shorty as his mentor, Malcolm conked his hair, donned a ZOOT suit, and metamorphosed into Red. In Harlem, under the tutelage of West Indian Archie, Malcolm developed into Detroit Red, a prominent member of a criminal syndicate. His stint in prison led him to Elijah Muhammad's Nation of Islam, within which he became Minister Malcolm X. After his fallout with the Nation, Malcolm made his pilgrimage to Mecca and returned El-Hajj Malik El-Shabazz.

These name-changes represent fundamental shifts in Malcolm's worldview. Much of his story's power comes from the fact that he wrote it while internalizing facts about Elijah Muhammad and the Nation that he had been unable to let himself see. His pilgrimage solidified other suspicions he had harbored about Elijah Muhammad, and undermined sweeping indictments of whites that he had previously made. Thus, in addition to a testimony to the impact of racism, the power of EDUCATION, and the way an individual's life is defined by meaningful WORK, *The Autobiography of Malcolm X* documents an evolving consciousness and offers authenticity to the notion of "self-discovery."

Jeffrey Bickerstaff

EDUCATION in *The Autobiography of Malcolm X*

Malcolm X hoped his autobiography would be read as a testimony to how ghetto conditions shape the minds and lives of millions of black Americans. Malcolm refers to his life as "the life of only one ghetto-created Negro." Although Malcolm X was in many ways exceptional, readers should recognize how his early educational experiences mirror those of many blacks throughout America.

Malcolm describes how during junior high in Michigan his history textbook contained exactly one paragraph on Negro history. The paragraph told the story of slavery and emancipation while perpetuating such cruel stereotypes as shiftlessness and stupidity. His history teacher, Mr. Williams, laughed through the reading before adding his own note about the enormity of Negro feet.

Another teacher integral to Malcolm's educational experience was Mr. Ostrowski, a teacher Malcolm describes as a self-appointed adviser. Mr. Ostrowski advises seventh-grade class president Malcolm Little, whose grades are among the highest in the school, that it is unrealistic for him to aspire to be a lawyer. Mr. Ostrowski patronizingly encourages Malcolm to WORK with his hands and become a carpenter. He assures Malcolm that his popularity would garner him plenty of work. Malcolm X describes this interaction as the first major turning point in his life, and notes that afterward he drew away from white people, his job, and school.

As a teenager Malcolm moves to Boston and befriends a studious girl named Laura. Laura's interest in science elicits in Malcolm regret over turning away from the books he had enjoyed in Michigan. Laura insists that Malcolm could pick up where he was and become a lawyer. Instead, Malcolm embraces the life of a "hustler" and finds himself taking that path to Harlem.

In Harlem, Malcolm, now known as Red, runs numbers for the West Indian mobster, Archie. Remembering Archie's mathematical genius, Malcolm X asserts that Archie's talents were wasted by society because he was black. Malcolm describes his criminal friends as victims of the American social system. Crammed into ghettos, blacks could aspire to nothing beyond survival. Malcolm recalls his friends as individuals who might have cured cancer, built industries, or explored space (93). Malcolm's account of how his ambitions were dismissed invites the reader to speculate that Archie and the other so-called criminals each had a "Mr. Ostrowski" in their life stories.

Malcolm X describes this criminal version of himself as "mentally dead." He estimates that his working vocabulary then was less than 200 words, and after arriving in prison he begins to confront how street life had erased all he had learned in school. In prison, Malcolm admires a prisoner named Bimbi, the first man he had ever seen command total respect solely on the merits of his words. Bimbi encouraged Malcolm to take advantage of the library and correspondence courses, and influenced Malcolm to study word derivations.

Malcolm chronicles his transformation within the walls of the Norfolk Prison Colony. His sister, Ella, had worked to secure his transfer to the progressive jail with no bars and a library donated by a millionaire named Parkhurst, whose particular interests were history and religions. Malcolm X describes this phase of his reading as an attempt to obtain "some kind of homemade education." He transcribes the dictionary to build a foundation of knowledge and can soon read a book and understand its meaning. Malcolm X describes the new world then opening for him, and reflects that the ability to read stirred in him "some long dormant craving to be mentally alive."

His careful study of religion and history facilitates Malcolm's rebirth. Malcolm would draw on, as he would say, his "stock of knowledge" in his work as a human rights advocate. At the end of the story, Malcolm mourns his lack of a formal education. And here, at the end of his life, after several transformations, Malcolm knows he would have been a good lawyer. With his "homemade education," though, Malcolm X creates a model for young scholars to follow in order to realize the historical basis of social injustice and realistically confront it. Had Malcolm taken Mr. Ostrowski's advice, or had he taken Mr. Williams's mockery of Negro history to heart, he would never have undertaken his life's work. These two teachers worked to keep Malcolm ignorant and in his place. When Malcolm recognized the connection between knowledge and power and how it had been wielded against him and other "ghetto-created Negroes," his education began.

Jeffrey Bickerstaff

SUFFERING in *The Autobiography of Malcolm X*

In his autobiography, Malcolm X describes how periods of great suffering yielded personal transformations in his life. His world was first shattered at the age of six when his father's skull was crushed and his body nearly cut in half. Blacks in town whispered that Earl Little had been attacked and laid over streetcar tracks. The insurance company, however, claimed that he committed suicide and refused to pay on his policy. Malcolm's mother, Louise, devastated and alone with eight children and no money, struggled to maintain her family. Her condition deteriorated over the next six years, and she was eventually committed to the state mental hospital.

Malcolm recounts how even after their mother was gone, his family tried desperately to stay together, but the state prevailed and Malcolm and his siblings were separated from one another. They became "state children" under the authority of a judge in Lansing: "a white man in charge of a black man's children! Nothing but legal, modern slavery." Malcolm uses this comparison to emphasize the history of black families being controlled and undermined by the white power structure. Readers should recognize the similarity of his situation to the agony wrought by the practice of selling members of slave families to different masters throughout the country.

Malcolm's story shows that breaking up black families continued after emancipation, and he notes that "ours was not the only case of this kind." With his foundation gone, Malcolm slid into a world of drugs and crime until, just shy of his 21st birthday, he was sentenced to 10 years in prison for his role in a burglary ring. In prison, Malcolm became a serious reader and devoured books dealing with the history of slavery. He began to contextualize his personal suffering within the greater struggle of his people, and stresses in his autobiography that the factors leading to his incarceration were typical for many black Americans.

Reflecting on his time in prison, Malcolm explains why he and other prisoners embraced Elijah Muhammad's Nation of Islam with such fervor. Malcolm describes the typical convert as a man put into a cage by a white judge. He says, "Usually the convict comes from among those bottom-of-the-pile Negroes, the Negroes who through their entire lives have been kicked about, treated like children." Years of oppression through institutional racism make them "the most perfectly preconditioned to hear the words, 'the white man is the devil.'" The intensity with which Malcolm believed this doctrine is reflected by the turmoil he feels later when his faith in Elijah Muhammad is shattered.

Malcolm describes the myths that comprise Elijah Muhammad's racial cosmology. Years after he had first heard them in prison, he learns that these "tales" had infuriated eastern Muslims. Malcolm countered that their own failure to make "real Islam known in the West" created "a vacuum into which any religious faker could step and mislead our people." Malcolm's word choice, "faker," indicates how intensely he feels betrayed by Elijah Muhammad. Malcolm's faith was destroyed not by Mr. Muhammad's adultery, but his willingness "to hide, to cover up what he had done." Malcolm asserts that the Nation diverted members' attention from the scandal toward him. "Hating me was going to become the cause for people of shattered faith to rally around."

Malcolm's break with the Nation caused him torments beyond description. He wandered "in a state of emotional shock" until he began to recognize that he "had believed in Mr. Muhammad more than he believed in himself." This realization provided Malcolm with the strength to face the facts of his life and think autonomously. In Mecca, he grasped the danger of considering anyone "divinely guided" and "protected" and declared himself finished with "someone else's propaganda."

The suffering that preceded this intellectual emancipation exemplifies Malcolm's dictum that "it is only after the deepest darkness that the greatest joy can come; it is only after slavery and prison that the sweetest appreciation of freedom can come." His anguish also indicates that revolution "means the destroying of an old system, and its replacement with a new system." Malcolm recognizes that both the destruction that precedes creation, and the suffering that comes before renewal, are two distinct phases of the same process, which comprises life.

Jeffrey Bickerstaff

WORK in *The Autobiography of Malcolm X*

Malcolm describes his father as a Baptist minister committed to organizing for Marcus Garvey's Universal Negro Improvement Association. Although Malcolm rejected Christianity and embraced Islam, the winding path of his life led him back to his father's footsteps. After experiencing firsthand the limited range of choices available to young blacks, Malcolm's life came to be defined by his work as a minister dedicated to improving the lives of black people.

For Malcolm, honesty, dignity, and work were inextricably linked. As a youth in Roxbury, he scorned blacks who affected impressive job titles. Neighbors described a bank janitor as being "in banking" and a bond-house messenger as "in securities." Cooks and maids assumed a haughty tone when describing themselves as being "with an old family." Annoyed by such dishonesty, Malcolm would later work to puncture "the indignity of that kind of self-delusion."

However, Malcolm's early experiences with work necessarily involved affectation. Hooked up with a shoe-shining "slave" (a hipster term that meant job), Malcolm soon learned that whites tipped generously when he would "Uncle Tom a little," which included making the shine rag "pop like a firecracker." This sound was part of his hustle, "a jive noise" that gave the impression he was exerting more effort than he was.

Malcolm also applied this practice to his railroad waiter job. He quickly surmised that white people would buy anything if he gave them a show. Malcolm describes himself and his coworkers as "servants and psychologists." Cognizant of white people's delusions of self-importance, their work required them to compromise their dignity and "Uncle Tom" for whites eager to pay for a show of black inferiority.

Malcolm's route between Boston and New York led to his involvement with Harlem's underworld. Malcolm ran numbers, peddled drugs, and steered clients toward prostitutes. These clients, wealthy white men, used Harlem as "their sin-den, their fleshpot." Malcolm describes how they took off the "dignified masks they wore in their white world" to indulge their sexual perversities. Consequently, white talk about the Negro's "low morals" angered Malcolm. Malcolm came to see how America's racial system created Harlem, where, instead of finding meaningful work that benefited the COMMUNITY, almost everyone "needed some kind of hustle to survive." These hustles catered to whites' illicit appetites, which perpetuated the residents' need to "stay high" to forget all they had to do to survive. Thus, the racial structure created a cycle that coerced blacks into ghettoes and forced them to do whatever was necessary to endure. The white beneficiaries of this system could then indulge their appetites for drugs and flesh by exploiting blacks desperate to sustain themselves, while deriding them for having low morals.

Malcolm's criminal career culminated in his burglary conviction. He converted to Islam in prison, and upon his release he worked to spread a doctrine of black self-reliance. Malcolm saw firsthand how white merchants in ghettos drained money out of the black community. As a minister in the Nation of Islam, Malcolm recognized that Muslim-owned grocery stores exemplified how blacks could break their dependence on white money by hiring and trading among themselves. Malcolm stresses that the key to black self-respect is the building of their own businesses and decent homes.

After leaving the Nation, Malcolm still adhered to the philosophy of economic self-determination: "It's because black men don't own and control their own community's retail establishments that they can't stabilize their own community." He established the Muslim Mosque, Inc., to combine his economic outlook with the goal of ridding his community of the vices that undermine its moral fiber. Malcolm never forgot that economic subservience fosters a desperation that leaves people prone to lascivious exploitation. In his last chapter, Malcolm reminds us that he was raised with Marcus Garvey's Black Nationalist teachings. Like his father before him, Malcolm worked to instill in his community racial dignity and the confidence to stand for itself.

The concept of work permeates *The Autobiography of Malcolm X.* His dedication page acknowledges that the sacrifices and understanding of his wife and children made his work possible. His father's murder, his time as a criminal, and the enmity caused by his split with the Nation of Islam convinced Malcolm that he would die young and violently. Thus, he regarded his mission as urgent, and lived every day with the knowledge that "no man is given but so much time to accomplish whatever is his life's work."

Jeffrey Bickerstaff

HANSBERRY, LORRAINE *A Raisin in the Sun* (1959)

Lorraine Hansberry's *A Raisin in the Sun* debuted on Broadway on March 11, 1959. The title comes from the opening lines of "Harlem," a poem by Langston Hughes that catalogs what happens when dreams are deferred. Dreams figure largely in the play, as the Younger FAMILY struggles to achieve its dream of economic and social FREEDOM. The play takes place in Chicago's South Side sometime between World War II and 1959, and is staged completely within a small, dilapidated apartment over the course of a couple of weeks.

The play centers on the Younger family: Lena, a widow, her children, Walter, an ambitious chauffeur, Beneatha, a college student who wants to be a doctor, Walter's wife Ruth, and their son Travis.

When the play opens, the family is waiting for a $10,000 insurance check, and each family member has a different plan for the money. Walter dreams of investing the money in a liquor store. Lena wants to buy a house for the family. After Walter hounds his mother and tells her that he wants to be the man of the house, Lena gives him $6,500: $3,000 to put away for Beneatha's studies and $3,500 to start his business. However, on the day that the family is set to move into their new house, Walter learns that he was scammed out of $6,500. Their troubles increase when Karl Lindner, a representative of their new neighborhood, tells them that they are not wanted in all-white Clybourne Park. The play ends with the family deciding to move into their new home.

Courtney Marshall

The AMERICAN DREAM in *A Raisin in the Sun*

The Younger family, Ruth, Walter Lee, Travis, Beneatha, and Lena, are like any other American family: They want success, respect, and a home. Simply stated, they are in pursuit of the American dream. In Lorraine Hansberry's play *A Raisin in the Sun*, written in 1958, the Younger family struggles to realize the American dream by escaping from ghetto life on the South Side of Chicago. Every member of the Younger family has a separate, unfulfilled dream—Ruth, a home for her family; Beneatha to become a doctor; and Walter Lee simply wants enough money to provide for his wife and children. These dreams mostly involve money. In the 1950s when *A Raisin in the Sun* takes place, the stereotypical American dream was to have a house with a yard, a big car, and a happy family. The Youngers aspire to this dream, but their struggles are different from the struggles a non-African-American family living at the same time might have had, simply because being middle class for the Youngers is also a dream.

Symbolic of the American dream is the plant Mama lovingly cares for throughout the play. For Mama this plant symbolizes the garden she will tend after moving into her dream house. The last thing that happens on stage is that Mama opens the door, comes back in, grabs her plant, and goes out for the last time. This small potted plant is a temporary stand-in for Mama's much larger dream and her care for the plant represents not only her protection of her dream but also her care and protection of her family. She cares for the plant just as she cares for her family: just enough light and water to grow. The plant remains feeble and spindly in spite of Mama's love and care, simply because there is so little light. Likewise, Mama's dream of a house and better life for her family is tenuous simply because it is difficult for her to see beyond her family's day to day situation.

Beneatha's dream, to become a doctor, is different from Mama's in that it is more self-serving, more indulgent. Her desire to express herself sets Beneatha apart from the other women in *A Raisin in the Sun*. She is the least traditional of the women not only because she is the youngest, but also because she is more independent, career oriented, and does not want to rely entirely on George Murchison to provide for her. Beneatha believes in education as a means to success and understanding, and her version of the American dream is centered on this philosophy. It is her attitude toward her boyfriend, George Murchison, in contrast to her attitude toward Joseph Asagai, an African friend, where Beneatha's search for the American dream can be most clearly seen. Mama and Ruth are confused by her dislike of George Murchison, and Beneatha even indicates to them that she might not get married, something that runs counter to the more traditional, stay-at-home roles that most women fulfilled in the 1950s. Beneatha's version of the American dream is solitary, less traditional, and not as concerned with family; hers is a less conservative version of the American dream.

While the theme of the American dream is found throughout Hansberry's play, the central conflict of the play is found in Walter's idea of what the American dream entails. The concept of the "self-made man," who starts with nothing, works hard, and achieves great wealth, seems innocuous enough. However, the idea becomes destructive when it evolves into an idolization of wealth and power. A life insurance check from his father, Walter Sr., means Walter Jr. can buy his way into a business and out of a servile job. In the beginning of *A Raisin in the Sun* Hansberry shows how Walter Jr. envies Charlie Atkins's dry-cleaning business because it grosses $100,000 a year. Desperate to achieve success, Walter ignores his mother's moral objection to achieving his goals by running a liquor store. However, the liquor store is merely a means to an end for Walter. Walter's dream, like his mother's, is to escape the South Side ghetto, and to provide a better life for his wife and child. The Younger family's dreams and aspirations for a better life are not confined to their race, but are identified with by people of all backgrounds. Although the definition of the American dream is different for each character, the underlying motivation is universal: the opportunity for a better life.

Sharon Brubaker

FAMILY in *A Raisin in the Sun*

The Younger family is under a great deal of emotional and financial stress in the play. Hansberry highlights the claustrophobic nature of their lives by staging the play completely within their small, rundown apartment.

In the play, family roles break down along GENDER lines. The female characters in the play argue over the best ways to care for the male family members. Lena and Ruth bump heads about the best way to take care of Travis. Lena makes his bed for him and questions Ruth about what she's feeding him for breakfast. Early in the play, Ruth tells Walter to eat the eggs she's prepared, and he uses the phrase "eat your eggs" to symbolize the ways that he feels disrespected in the family. Walter imagines whenever a man gets excited about an opportunity that will change his and his family's life, the women in his life come along and tell him to settle down. They think they are nourishing him by feeding him, but what he really wants is an understanding ear. For him, family limits him and keeps him from fulfilling his individualistic dream to own a liquor store. This individual dream is in stark contrast to the women's communal dream of owning a home.

The most important symbol in the play, Lena's houseplant, also represents the resilience of family and the difficulties of caring for and nurturing living things. At the beginning of the play, Lena moves directly toward the plant to take care of it. Though the plant never gets enough light in their dark apartment, she is impressed with its tenacity. This quality runs through her family. Though she and her late husband, Big Walter, had to flee southern VIOLENCE and racism, she still manages to care for her children and grandson. The plant also symbolizes the dream she has to own a home. She wants to plant her family in richer soil in order to give them, especially Travis, the opportunities that she never had.

Lena becomes upset because she thinks that her children, particularly Walter, have lost the family values that she and her husband tried to give them. She doesn't want the insurance money to tear the family apart, and Ruth's desire for an abortion represents, to her, the destruction of the family.

After Walter loses the money, Beneatha tells her mother that he is no longer her brother. Lena tells her that she was taught to love her brother and that she should mourn for him. This speech makes the play end on a complicated note. Walter, in telling Karl Lindner that he and his family will move into their new house, had been allowed to be the patriarch. However, the fact remains that he has lost Beneatha's tuition money, a move that demonstrates his naïveté and self-centeredness. We are not sure whether Walter has truly understood the gender relations within his family. In addition, the family's breaking of the color line and moving to Clybourne Park poses a whole new set of challenges. However, Hansberry portrays a family that has its internal problems, but still strives and works together.

Courtney Marshall

RACE in *A Raisin in the Sun*

A Raisin in the Sun lies at the intersection of the integrationist Civil Rights movement of the 1950s and the emergent hostility of the Black Power movement of the 1960s. As such, it presents a complicated view of American race relations and a relatively new exploration of black culture. In the play, the Younger family decides to move from its run-down Chicago tenement into a home in an all-white neighborhood, Clybourne Park. The governing body of the Youngers' new neighborhood, the Clybourne Park Improvement Association, sends Karl Lindner to persuade them not to move into the neighborhood. Lindner says that the whites are not racist, but that everyone gets along better when they are segregated. He questions the FAMILY's insistence

on moving into a place where they are not wanted. Though he tries to bribe the family in order to keep them out, Walter tells him that they will move because his father would want them to. The speech's central claim is that black Americans should have right to enjoy the AMERICAN DREAM just like white Americans. Mr. Lindner and the people he represents can see only the color of the Younger family's skin, and Walter wants him to see them as just another family. He holds his son Travis and tells Lindner that he makes the sixth generation of the Younger family in America. Walter asserts their right to the American dream by portraying them as contributors, not strangers in the country.

In addition, the play explores issues of blackness, namely the relationships between black Americans and black Africans. The only picture of Africa that Lena gets is the one she receives from Christian missionaries. Her daughter, Beneatha, has a deeper appreciation for the continent. Beneatha is torn between two men, George Murchison, the son of a wealthy businessman, and Joseph Asagai, a Nigerian student. Her relationship with these two men symbolizes her struggle to understand her IDENTITY as an African-American woman. Beneatha explores her black identity through her hair. At the beginning of the play, Beneatha has chemically straightened hair. After Joseph Asagai visits her home and questions her choice, she decides to cut her hair in order to be more "black." To her, wearing an Afro means that she is in touch with her blackness and connection to Africa. When Walter and Fred see her Afro, they immediately tease her political views. The play is not completely sympathetic to Beneatha's transformation. At the beginning of act 2, when she wears the Nigerian clothes Asagai brought her, she models them in a way that Hansberry describes as being "more like Butterfly than any Nigerian." Beneatha mimics Oriental mannerisms and thinks they are African. This demonstrates her ignorance of Nigerian culture. To her, Africa is an idea, and though she is more interested in African culture, she is as ignorant as her mother on certain issues.

However, her final decision to practice medicine in Africa promises a more informed view of the continent.

Courtney Marshall

HARDY, THOMAS *Jude the Obscure* (1895)

The love and life story of Jude Fawley is Hardy's last novelistic achievement. Rural orphan boy Jude dreams of an academic career encouraged by his teacher and role model Phillotson. After a rash and failed marriage to Arabella, Jude pursues his career plans in Christminster (modeled on Oxford) where he meets and falls for his free-minded cousin Sue Bridehead. Instead of being accepted into college Jude becomes a stonemason, while Sue attends a training school to become a teacher and then (forced by social pressure) marries Phillotson. Jude tries to take up a clerical pathway. These plans become obsolete when Sue leaves Phillotson to live with Jude. They have several children, while a boy from Jude's first marriage to Arabella goes to live with them. Their libertine life is overshadowed by material hardships and anguish caused by public rejection. Social ostracism leads to homelessness, nomadic life, unemployment, poverty, and finally to catastrophe: Jude and Arabella's boy kills the other children and himself: "Done because we are to menny." Sue is thrown into existential crisis and has a miscarriage; convalescing, she returns to Phillotson, convinced of her own and Jude's guiltiness: She believes now that they have caused the disaster by living together in sin. Jude, existentially defeated and becoming seriously ill, is lured into remarrying Arabella. He pays a final visit to Sue, then on the voyage home completely loses his health. While Arabella is out with another man, he dies alone.

Thomas Schares

AMBITION in *Jude the Obscure*

Not all is love in Hardy's love story of Jude Fawley and Sue Bridehead. As a young boy, Jude decides to follow the example of his schoolmaster Phillotson and go to the city and to the university to become a scholar. This will be his lifelong obsession and ambition. As with many of his time's rural working class, Jude is attracted to the city. The city stands for the chance of social ascent. He pursues his destiny monomaniacally by teaching himself classical works in his childhood and youth, until his hasty marriage to Arabella ends his efforts prematurely. After the failure of this (forced) marriage, however, Jude leaves for Christminster (Oxford) and becomes a part of the rural migration to urban areas. He picks up the profession of stonemasonry in order to earn his living before admission to the university. Again, his plans are postponed, because he meets and falls in love with his cousin Sue. The assumed path to wisdom for Jude turns out to be stony; the answer to his letter of inquiry from one of the heads of a university college is a signpost of class barriers and social rank haughtiness in Victorian England: ". . . judging from your description of yourself as a working man, I venture to think that you will have a much better chance of success in life by remaining in your own sphere and sticking to your trade. . . ."

The blow of this rejection letter does not cause Jude to refrain from his ambitions. That Jude's ambitions are more than infatuation becomes unmistakably clear when, the same evening, he embarrasses students in a pub by quoting the latin Credo flawlessly from memory. This phase of his life being molded by the struggle for Sue, he reshapes his original plans for an academic career: He starts to consider applying for a position with the church (the only traditional alternative for the poor in which to pursue university studies). These plans also become obsolete when his life with Sue begins. They live together "in sin," which, of course, is not suitable for a post in the church.

Like Jude, the whole ensemble of *Jude the Obscure* reveals ambition as an elementary human impetus, aiming at varying objectives: Jude's first wife, Arabella, mainly represents the struggle for wealth and the urge to marry (materially) well; hers is the life-policy of immediate personal advantage. She leaves Jude the moment she finds out that he is not so promising after all in these terms. Sue, on the other hand, lives more for ideas than for aspirations. She is prone to compromise (marriage to Phillotson, religious turn in the end), since her ideals and ideas of new womanhood find little grounding in life as it is in Victorian England and to some extent cause her to act inconsistently. She is able and ambitious to become a teacher, but her lack of conformity renders this impossible. Jude's teacher and the later husband of Sue, Phillotson, is the model of young Jude's ambitions: The nobility of his character becomes apparent when he risks his career to consent to Sue's leaving him; this noble trait is revoked, however, when he takes back devastated Sue in the end. This, as a side-effect, amplifies his career again. Like all the other characters of the novel, he is a contradictory person.

Jude, in the end, will never see the interior of a college. For him, ambition has resulted in restless wandering. Consequently, Jude and Sue have the happiest time of their lives when they have given up their ambitions and live together as an unmarried couple with their children. Sue says "We gave up all ambition, and were never so happy in our lives. . . ." This kind of happiness is terminal; this time the reason is not social immobility as determined by class structure but Sue and Jude's offense against the rigidity of Victorian morality.

A fascinating aspect of these two social factors is that class structure and moral code are not solely affecting the protagonists from without, but they are rather a part of the collective subconscious within the individual. Sue's regression into devoutness, after the catastrophe has befallen her and Jude's shared life, demonstrates this. The pessimism of the novel pivots around the two issues apparent here. The longing for love is constrained by a repressive contemporary moral code, and the longing for cultural education (which equals social ascent) is blocked by impenetrable social barriers. Thus, the repressive Victorian society prevents individuals from achieving happiness.

Thomas Schares

LOVE in *Jude the Obscure*

Jude the Obscure is the tragic love story of Jude Fawley and his cousin Sue Bridehead. The whole plot of the novel is focused on and determined by their love, which is outlined as an elective affinity: Irrefutably, both are drawn to each other. Jude pursues Sue in Christminster, he even changes his plans and residence when she moves. Sue flees from the training school to Jude, and they always meet again in spite of all vows not to. The notion that the two are meant for each other is maintained throughout the novel, and even by antagonist characters: "They seem to be one person split in two!" This recurrent image of "two in one" alludes to the story of the separation of the two sexes by Aristophanes as given in Plato's

Symposium: As a punishment, the gods cut the original whole human creature in half. They then went about separated and in unquenchable longing for their lost other half—a primeval desire for fusion through love.

But the love of Sue and Jude in the whole course of events is not much more than a promise—a promise, maybe an ideal, never to be fulfilled, a tragic love that will end in catastrophe. They share only a brief period of living together happily. But during most of the novel's events, they have to bear being apart, and Jude also has to cope with the experience of being abandoned repeatedly. Although there seems to be nothing more desirable to both of them than being together, there are always events preventing this—up to the tragic ending. Why this has to be, the novel refuses a definite answer, but there is far more to it than foreshadowings of dark hereditary family pathology. The novel reaches deeply into the psychology of its protagonists and offers various explanations and hints. But one social fact in the novel is a prominent obstacle and a concept most contradictory to Sue and Jude's love: marriage. Discussed widely and repeatedly within the text and by the protagonists, Sue and Jude both believe it is the institution of marriage that destroys them. In fact, each marries another person: In his younger years, Jude is lured into marriage by the voluptuous Arabella, but she is disappointed and leaves him soon. Jude comes to consider this marriage "a permanent contract on a temporary feeling." Sue, while ambitious to become a teacher, marries her patron and Jude's former teacher Phillotson, because she feels like "a woman tossed about, all alone, with aberrant passions, . . ." although she certainly loves Jude. The strange magnetism between Jude and Sue soon brings this marriage to an end, too. Phillotson consents to divorce and Sue and Jude start living together. But their brief period of physical union, the joys of two children and a third on the way are marred by their different attitudes toward sexuality, as well as the reappearance of Arabella and miserable material circumstances. After their respective divorces, Jude and Sue attempt a couple of times to marry "to make their natural marriage a legal one" but always resolve "to go home without killing their dream."

The catastrophic death of their children marks the end of their union. It throws Sue's mental balance, causing her—once a New Woman with a free and bright intellect—to turn religious, thereby finally adopting the rules of late Victorian society she used to oppose so vehemently. She believes now that Jude and she living together in sin has caused the misery to the family and, repenting, returns to the detested Phillotson, having convinced herself that she is attached to him indissolubly by religious law. Arabella, by now widowed, also manages to trick Jude back to her. He subsequently falls ill with desperation and dies. Sue conforms and Jude gives in. It may be the bitterest irony of the novel that both protagonists conclude their lives by remarrying their unloved partners. There has been no hope for the love of Sue and Jude, the disappointments and delusions the situation has caused are too numerous. Jude sums up: "Perhaps the world is not illuminated enough for such experiments as ours."

Thomas Schares

SEX/SENSUALITY/EROTICISM in *Jude the Obscure*

When the novel appeared in 1895 it caused a scandal among its cleric critics, one of whom renamed it *Jude the Obscene*. These agitations are hardly comprehensible nowadays, as the reader will not find any openly described sexuality in the book. Contemporary critical rejection of the novel is understandable because marriage as well as religion are attacked heavily. The only (sexually) gross event depicted involves a butchered pig's "pizzle" (penis), which Arabella, Jude's first wife-to-be, throws playfully at Jude on the occasion of their first acquaintance. While sexual performance is banished behind the scenery (we know it is happening frequently because of the children emerging), the characters do not refrain from discussing their sexuality; this also was probably unsettling for the Victorian reader.

Mainly through her conversations with Jude it becomes apparent that Sue, Jude's great love, is not a sensual creature: Rejection of sexual intercourse (with men) is a stable disposition of her character. She tells Jude of a former relationship, a "friendly intimacy with an undergraduate at Christminster" . . . "he wanted me as a mistress, in fact, but I wasn't in love with him." Sue admits: "I have mixed with [men]—one or two of them particularly—almost as one of their own sex." Her attitude toward men is unconventional, as is her sexual nature. She has a hysterical breakdown when she assumes that her then-husband Phillotson is trying to persuade her into her matrimonial duties. In fact, as Sue believes toward the end, from the moment she gave in to Jude, their lives began to worsen and, in this later interpretation of events, to lead to catastrophe. But the constant rejective posture of Sue is a symptom of her whole disposition: She feels "that before a thing was done it might be right to do, but that being done it became wrong; or, in other words, that things which are right in theory became wrong in practice." Consequently, Sue prefers the mere possibility of a (sexual) relationship with Jude to its fulfillment. Her attitude toward sexuality reveals a very complex and much-debated character, which cannot be unfolded extensively here (gender perspective is be left out of this brief account). Many times, a kiss is the most intense token of love Jude can obtain from Sue, and it takes them a while of living together before their sexual relationship commences—in a moment of crisis when Sue feels threatened by Arabella's return. The fairy-like, asexual constitution of Sue marks a sharp contrast to Jude's less refined inclinations to "savage" sexuality (as with Arabella) and drinking. Jude's (occasionally fulfilled) desire to fully love Sue is an urge to possess the unpossessable (she being his cousin). The contrast is evident when Jude compares her to Arabella: In observing Sue's bosom, "the small, tight, apple-like convexities of her bodice, so different from Arabella's amplitudes." To Jude Sue is "the most ethereal, least sensual woman I ever knew to exist without inhuman sexlessness."

Jude's attachment to his first wife, Arabella, is of a completely different nature. They attract each other mutually, but this attraction is purely sexual. In all other aspects of matrimonial life and in terms of affection for each other, they fail; after a short while, Arabella flees from Jude to immigrate to Australia. To Jude, this marriage was "buying a month's pleasure with a life's discomfort." After her second husband has died, Arabella turns to Jude again, taking advantage of his miserable state. Two times Arabella lures Jude into marriage by employing sexual desire and alcohol as bait.

The overall impact of sexuality and eroticism is ambivalent in *Jude the Obscure,* the gender question being obscured by observations on society. There is no purely satisfying and blissful sexuality (neither sexual identity) to be found throughout the novel; in the end it always has sad consequences. It forces Jude into his first marriage, it keeps him from the city and his ambitions awhile, it kills his ambitions again when he has to feed the hungry mouths of his and Sue's family, he even betrays Sue with Arabella on one occasion. Concerning Jude, sexuality is one of the factors that have formed the tragedy of his life. "For each ecstatic instant / We must an anguish pay" as Emily Dickinson puts it. Yet Jude refrains from a clerical path to be no longer "the soldier and servant of a religion in which sexual love was regarded as at its best a frailty, and at its worst damnation." The negative powers are not inherent in sexuality itself but in what society makes of it. And maybe here lies one purely fatalistic strain of Hardy's thinking, as, at this point, his pessimism is projected onto society. For example, characters who behave progressively are punished by society; as Jude says, "I perceive there is something wrong somewhere in our social formulas," and Phillotson loses his teaching position as a consequence of letting his wife, Sue, go to live with Jude ("She is not [my wife]; she is another man's except in name and law." To sum up: A repressive society prevents both pure love and a satisfying sexuality by the instruments of religion and, indeed, marriage.

Thomas Schares

HARDY, THOMAS *Tess of the d'Urbervilles* (1891)

Thomas Hardy's *Tess of the d'Urbervilles,* set in rural southwestern England, was published serially in a periodical before appearing in book form in 1891. Hardy faced a great deal of criticism from his audience and from publishers who disapproved of the "infidelity" and the "obscenity" of this novel that narrates Tess's hardships following her unwilling loss of innocence. Hardy resented the changes editors expected him to make; after a similarly nega-

tive reaction to his next novel, *Jude the Obscure,* he announced that he would never write fiction again. However, the last novel sold well and was a financial success, though many readers found it depressing and shocking.

Tess of the d'Urbervilles takes place during a time of dramatic social and economic change in England, and, like many of Hardy's novels, illustrates a great awareness of the trials and hardships faced by the rural poor, especially the women. Here, Hardy presents a compassionate depiction of a young woman victimized by a morally rigid and often hypocritical society. Moreover, Hardy examines the nature and implications of the slow transition from an old-fashioned, community-centered agricultural society to a modern, industrial economy driven by money and in which individuals often must fend for themselves.

Erica Artiles

COMMUNITY in *Tess of the d'Urbervilles*

The first image readers get of Tess Durbeyfield is that of a young woman dressed, like her peers, in white, participating in a May Day dance. Despite her simple, natural beauty, Tess does not stand out, but rather fits well into this safe, comfortable community that she has known for her entire life. Following a series of events that jeopardize her family's livelihood, Tess leaves her native Blackmoor and its familiar community. While away, she encounters a new, rougher community and is sexually violated by her employer, Alec d'Urberville. As a result of her loss of virginity, Tess finds herself cut off from her native society and begins a futile search for a new community and a sense of belonging.

As a girl, Tess was popular. She had two particularly close friends with whom she spent a great deal of time. Moreover, she played a very important role in the community of her family, caring for and loving her younger siblings when her mother failed to do so. Despite her safe and comfortable position, Tess leaves her home behind in order to cultivate relations with the d'Urberville family in Tantridge, hoping to help out her family that has suffered the loss of their horse, their primary means for income. In Tantridge, Tess meets a rough, hard-drinking community of men and women. Though they are willing to accept Tess, she feels threatened and remains distant from them. Consequently, she leaves their company while on the way home from a dance late one night and finds herself alone with Alec d'Urberville, who seduces her against her will and leaves her pregnant.

Tess briefly returns home following the loss of her innocence, but no longer fits neatly into the community from which she came. Despite the fact that her friends come to see her, Tess can no longer take part in their chatter, laughter, and good-humored teasing of her. She feels lonely, guilt-ridden, and unable to relate either to her peers or to her family. Although she leaves her house periodically to work in the village, Tess spends most of her time hiding in her family's house and avoiding all company.

Eventually, Tess leaves her native Blackmoor again, this time to seek employment at Talbothay's Dairy. There, no one knows anything of her past. Farmer Crick and his wife, the milkmaids, and the apprentice Angel Clare eagerly welcome her into their warm and happy community. Tess revives during her time there, thrives in the natural environment, and strikes up a romance with Angel Clare. Tess initially resists engaging in a relationship with Clare because of her past actions, but eventually she succumbs to love and accepts his offer of marriage. Following their wedding ceremony, the couple leaves the dairy community behind. Though Tess tries repeatedly to tell Angel of her past, she does not succeed until their wedding night when they both reveal indiscretions. Furious with Tess, Angel rejects her, leaving the girl entirely alone and ashamed to return to Talbothay's dairy. She briefly returns home once more, but finds her bedroom occupied by siblings and her father questioning the validity of her marriage. Feeling more isolated and alone than ever, Tess again leaves.

Needing work, Tess accepts a series of temporary jobs that demand more and more from her physically. She suffers extreme poverty and has no real connections to anyone. While at Flintcomb-Ash, she reconnects with Marion, whom she knew at the dairy. Here, brutally hard field work and dire conditions prevent the development of any real community and Tess struggles alone, testing the limits of her physical ability. During a chance encounter, Tess meets Alec d'Urberville who has reformed his ways and become a traveling preacher. Tess rejects his advances initially, but familial hardship again leads her to accept his assistance. In exchange for helping her family, she agrees to live as his mistress. They take up residence in a fine house in a resort town on the English Channel. Despite her elegant lodging and her fine dress, Tess continues to feel isolated and disconnected from any larger community. When Angel returns, she abandons this life with Alec, whom she murders, and retreats to an abandoned mansion with her husband, forming a small but relatively happy community of just the two of them. Their happiness is short-lived, however. Pursued by the law, Tess leaves the mansion and heads for Stonehenge completely alone to await her fate.

Erica Artiles

GUILT in *Tess of the d'Urbervilles*

In *Tess of the d'Urbervilles*, Thomas Hardy explores both the origins and consequences of guilt through the story of the title character's fall from grace. Throughout the novel, Tess finds herself in difficult and complex situations that lead to her victimization and her inability to act in her own best interest. Only by overcoming the overwhelming sense of guilt that plagues her can Tess finally take responsibility for her own fate.

Tess's guilt arises from two primary sources: her overwhelming sense of responsibility to her family and her acceptance of the traditional Christian equation of virtue and purity with chastity. As the daughter of an alcoholic father and an incompetent mother, Tess takes responsibility for her younger siblings and helping to run the household. When she spends an afternoon dancing and reveling with other girls her age, Tess feels guilty for getting grass stains on the white dress that her mother washed and ironed. Later, when her father drinks too much and cannot take the family's beehives to the market, Tess offers to drive them despite the fact that she is exhausted and inexperienced. During the journey, Tess dozes off briefly, leading to the death of the family's horse. Guilt and responsibility lead Tess to submit, against her better judgment, to her mother's plan for her to make connections with the very wealthy d'Urberville family to whom, her mother and father believe, they are distantly related.

In an effort to aid her family, Tess accepts employment caring for Mrs. d'Urberville's pet fowl and encounters Alec d'Urberville, who is attracted to Tess and repeatedly tries to seduce her. Though dependent upon Alec for her livelihood and socially inferior to him, Tess stands her ground and repeatedly rejects his advances. One night, though, Tess impulsively accepts his offer for a ride home from a village dance in order to avoid a confrontation with some members of the Tantridge community. During the dark and foggy night, Alec loses his way, leaving him and Tess alone in the woods together. Alec again entreats her as a lover and informs her of the many gifts he has given her family, including a new horse for her father. In response to his request, perhaps motivated by a sense of guilt, Tess is indecisive when answering his request. Though she never explicitly agrees, Tess helplessly succumbs to his advances.

Shortly after losing her virginity, Tess returns to her family pregnant and riddled with guilt and shame. On the way home, she encounters a man painting religious messages about damnation and sin throughout the countryside. When she asks him about sin that one does not commit willingly, he ignores her question and instead talks about the ability of such messages to incite guilt. Though Tess says that she does not believe the validity of such messages, she leaves the company of the painter profoundly affected. Tess returns home only long enough to bear and bury her sickly child. Following her sexual experience, Tess senses a chasm that divides her from her former self as well as from her former companions.

This social chasm reflects society's linking of chastity with virtue, and Tess accepts the fact that her sin has made her an immoral woman and an outcast. She becomes overwhelmed with guilt at defying both social conventions and religious prohibitions. Consequently, she resists Angel Clare's love at Talbothay's dairy, despite her powerful feelings. Later, her guilt prompts her to accept Angel's unreasonably harsh rejection of her as a lover and a wife, despite his own past indiscretions. Later, following the unexpected death of her father, Tess returns home and again, out of a sense of guilt and

responsibility, defies her own judgment to help her family. Having recently encountered Alec again, Tess refuses his continuing advances until he offers assistance to her homeless and desperate family. She agrees to live as his mistress, taking on even greater guilt, in order to have her mother and siblings provided for.

Once Angel returns, however, Tess regrets conceding to Alec, kills her lover, and follows her husband to an abandoned mansion where, apart from society, they consummate their marriage and live as husband and wife until they are discovered. Though her action here is complex, one could argue that she has rejected her sense of responsibility to her family and her guilt over her past actions. About to be captured, Tess heads for Stonehenge by herself and sleeps on an altar, where victims were sacrificed to the gods, before being taken by the authorities.

Erica Artiles

SOCIAL CLASS in *Tess of the d'Urbervilles*

Thomas Hardy, in *Tess of the d'Urbervilles*, presents a cast of male characters that represent various social classes of late-19th-century England. Tess's involvement with each of the men illustrates some of the problems and inconsistencies inherent in each class. The story opens with Tess's father, John Durbeyfield, learning that he is the sole remaining member of the ancient d'Urberville line. He is lazy and poor, scraping together a living by doing odd jobs and peddling various wares. Once he learns of his lineage, Durbeyfield becomes proud and arrogant, taking on some of the worst traits of the aristocracy without the money or social standing that define the class. The meager living he does make becomes jeopardized when he is too intoxicated to take his beehives to the market in Casterbridge. Tess offers to go instead and inadvertently kills their horse, the primary means of the family's livelihood.

Hoping to establish a connection with and to profit from what he assumes to be another, wealthier branch of the d'Urberville family, John sends Tess to Tantridge where she encounters Alec d'Urberville. He is the son of a successful merchant, Simon Stokes, who changed his name to d'Urberville after he found records of what he believed to be an extinct family line in the British Museum. Following his father's death, Alec takes control of the fortune and makes the most of the new money and the new family name. Although Alec does assist the Durbeyfield family and offers Tess a job tending his invalid mother's fowl, his primary motives for hiring her are personal. He is attracted to Tess and relentlessly pursues her. Tess, however, has no feelings for Alec, firmly resisting his many advances until he takes advantage of her one night when they are traveling alone together on an abandoned road. After learning she is pregnant, Tess returns home and gives birth to a son, Sorrow, who represents the merging of an old name with new money. The child lives for only a short time.

After burying the child, Tess accepts employment as a dairy maid and encounters many honorable, hard-working country folk, including Farmer Crick. He is a master of his trade, treats his employees well, and works hard for his living. While there, Tess meets and falls in love with Angel Clare, a member of the ambitious middle class. He is the son of a minister, yet he has rejected the clergy, choosing instead to seek his fortune in agriculture. Angel has grand ambitions, which include buying a large plot of land and establishing a farm, but no genuine aptitude for farming or clear sense of direction. On their wedding night, he and Tess both confess their past indiscretions. Though Tess immediately forgives him for an affair he once had in London, he cannot accept her past. After giving her some money, he leaves Tess behind and boards a boat to Brazil.

Following her rejection by her husband, Tess sets out in search of a place in this stratified society. As one born into a poor country family, seduced by a member of the newly rich, and married to an ambitious middle-class gentleman, Tess does not fit anywhere. She tries returning to the fields, but nearly collapses under the cruel conditions and the strain of the labor. When she learns that her mother is ill, Tess returns home. Within a few weeks, her mother recovers and her father passes away, causing the family to be evicted from their cottage. In an effort to keep her mother and siblings fed and sheltered, Tess reluctantly agrees to live with a still smitten Alec, whom she meets during a chance encounter.

Alec provides for the family, and for a brief time Tess lives the life of a wealthy lady, dressing in fancy clothes and residing in a luxurious boardinghouse. Seeing the error of his ways, Angel returns from Brazil to reclaim his wife and finds Tess in her new life. He tells her that he has forgiven her and begs her to return to him, but Tess refuses, saying that he has come too late. Angel leaves heartbroken and Tess regrets her decision to stay with her lover. After stabbing Alec to death, she flees with Angel to an abandoned country mansion where they live in relative luxury for a week until they are discovered. Tess is captured at Stonehenge and put to death, bringing an end to her search for a place and social identity.

Erica Artiles

HARTE, BRET   "The Luck of Roaring Camp" (1868)

Bret Harte's 1868 short story "The Luck of Roaring Camp" depicts a fictional western COMMUNITY in the Sierra foothills of California, known as Roaring Camp. The small, male-dominated community of rowdy and at times uncivilized characters are faced with the challenges of accepting and raising a newborn child while at the same time upholding their belief in not welcoming newcomers into their community.

When Cherokee Sal, the only female at Roaring Camp, dies during childbirth, the inhabitants of Roaring Camp find themselves taking care of a newborn baby, whom they later name Tommy Luck or "The Luck." Stumpy, who helps deliver the child, is elected to take the lead in raising the child with the only other female entity in the camp, a mule named Jinny.

As the camp comes together to help raise the child, the men find themselves indulging in their "softer" sides, often exchanging their rowdy behavior for a quieter, more civilized way of life. The men at Roaring Camp, including Kentuck, a rough individual without much attention to his outward appearance who takes a particular liking to Tommy Luck, nurture the child in their own way by bringing flowers and gifts from nature to the young child. The birth of Tommy Luck introduces a range of unfamiliar concepts to the residents of Roaring Camp—the innocence of a newborn child and the realization of their own flaws.

Several months after the birth of the child a great flood washes Roaring Camp away, sending buildings and the camp's inhabitants into the river. Stumpy is the first known victim of the flood as his body is found washed on the shore. "The Luck" is found, barely alive, as is Kentuck. The story concludes with Kentuck and "The Luck" being washed into the river to meet their deaths.

Andrew Andermatt

COMMUNITY in "The Luck of Roaring Camp"

Bret Harte's short story, "The Luck of Roaring Camp" (1868), depicts a fictional western community in the foothills of the Sierra Mountains of California. Roaring Camp is a small, male-dominated community that seems, on the surface, to reject civilized behavior in favor of a rugged, violent society. The community that makes up this fictional setting is best analyzed through a reading of the camp's gender, sense of identity, and the way these elements, in conjunction with the characters' actions, lead to the overall changing of the community in which they find themselves.

Early in the story Harte gives his readers a glimpse at the community life that exists within the boundaries of Roaring Camp. First, we see the residents of Roaring Camp congregated at a cabin in the clearing where "Cherokee Sal," the only female in Roaring Camp, is ready to deliver a baby. With this detail, the reader assumes the "novelty" of the event that is ready to commence. While residents of the camp are regularly exposed to violence and death, a birth is fairly unknown. Here, Harte begins to paint this community as a stereotypical, anti-female, male entity. Roaring Camp itself is referred to as a male-gendered individual, rather than a group of people. After the residents elect one of their own residents, Stumpy, to help deliver the baby, the narrator states that "Roaring Camp sat down outside, smoked its pipe, and awaited the issue."

What continues to develop this community's stereotypical "maleness" is the camp's strict opposition to female inclusion, as illustrated by Harte's decision to "kill off" Cherokee Sal shortly after the delivery of her baby. Once "Tom Luck" or "The Luck" is born and in the care of the male camp, the narrator states that "The introduction of a female nurse in the camp also met with objection," and that the camp "didn't want any more of the other kind," a clear reference to the community's view of male superiority and female subordination.

To be fair to the residents of Roaring Camp, it is important to consider that the narrator makes a point of telling readers that the camp, in general, "looks suspiciously on all strangers," which suggests that while the members of the camp may not welcome women, they equally shut out anyone who is not part of their community. "They're mighty rough on strangers," the narrator asserts while reminding readers that encouragement to immigration of any kind was not given.

Another characteristic of the inhabitants' identity that leads to their overall sense of community is the descriptions of the men themselves. The narrator tells us that some of the men gathered around are fugitives from justice, criminals, and reckless individuals. Even though the term "roughs" is applied to them, the narrator makes a point to let us know that the term is one of "distinction" rather than definition, as the men hardly look the part of their reputation, with their soft voices, diminutive stature, and "Hamlet-like" appearance. The barbaric picture painted of these characters is more or less the way these characters want their community to be viewed rather than what really is the case.

Harte continues to explore this true identity of the community within Roaring Camp by showing how the arrival of "The Luck" brings out the sensitivity of the men. The mere gathering around Cherokee Sal invokes a "maternal" instinct within the men, who are anxious to see the orphan and bring gifts to the baby. Moreover, the men are enthusiastic about keeping the baby and raising it themselves and, with the baby's safety at heart, are concerned about what may happen if he were to be taken from the camp. The true sense of the nurturing community of the men at Roaring Camp is seen when everyone comes together for the child's christening and naming; and, while Stumpy takes charge of the baby's care, Roaring Camp as a community serves as both the baby's mother and father.

The arrival of "The Luck" clearly shifts the identity of this community from the stereotypical, rugged male-dominated society to one that clearly is capable of civilized behavior. The camp undergoes a complete transformation, illustrated through the characterization of Kentuck, one of the residents of the camp whose clothing changes only when "sloughed off through decay." During the transformation, or "subtle influence of innovation," as the narrator puts it, Kentuck appears regularly in a clean shirt and washed face. The camp's once boisterous and violent ways have subsided so as not to disturb the baby, and cursing becomes a thing of the past.

Andrew Andermatt

GENDER in "The Luck of Roaring Camp"

Bret Harte's short story, "The Luck of Roaring Camp," depicts a fictional western community in the foothills of the Sierra Mountains of California. Roaring Camp is a small, male-dominated community that seems, on the surface, to reject civilized behavior in favor of a rugged, violent society. The community that makes up this fictional setting is best analyzed through a reading of the camp's GENDER, sense of IDENTITY, and the way these elements, in conjunction with the characters' actions, lead to the overall changing community in which they find themselves.

Early in the story Harte gives his readers a glimpse at the community life that exists within the boundaries of Roaring Camp. First, we see the residents of Roaring Camp congregated at a cabin in the clearing where "Cherokee Sal," the only female in Roaring Camp, is ready to deliver a baby. With this detail, the reader assumes the "novelty" of this event. While residents of the camp are regularly exposed to VIOLENCE and DEATH, a birth is fairly unknown. Here, Harte begins to paint this community as a stereotypical, anti-female, male entity. Roaring Camp itself is referred to as a male-gendered individual, rather than a group of people. After the residents elect one of their own, Stumpy, to help deliver the baby, the narrator states that "Roaring Camp sat down outside, smoked its pipe, and awaited the issue."

What continues to develop this community's stereotypical "Maleness" is the camp's strict opposition to female inclusion, as illustrated by Harte's decision to "kill off" Cherokee Sal shortly after the delivery of her baby. Once "Tom Luck" or "The Luck" is born and in the care of the male camp, the narrator states that "The introduction of a female nurse in the camp also met with objection," and that the camp "didn't want any more of the other kind," a clear reference to the community's view of male superiority and female subordination.

To be fair to the residents of Roaring Camp, it is important to consider that the narrator makes a point of telling readers that the camp, in general, is suspicious of all outsiders, which suggests that while the members of the camp may not welcome women, they equally shut out anyone who is not part of their community. The narrator asserts that they are rough on strangers while reminding readers that encouragement was not given to immigration of any kind.

Another characteristic of the inhabitants' identity that leads to their overall sense of community is the descriptions of the men themselves. The narrator tells us that some of the men gathered around are fugitives from justice, criminals, and reckless individuals. Even though the term "roughs" is applied to them, the narrator makes a point of letting us know that the term is one of "distinction" rather than definition, as the men hardly look the part of their reputation, with their soft voices, diminutive stature, and "Hamlet-like" appearance. The barbaric picture painted of these characters is more or less the way these characters want their community to be viewed rather than what really is the case.

Harte continues to explore this true identity of the community within Roaring Camp by showing how the arrival of "The Luck" brings out the sensitivity of the men. The mere gathering around Cherokee Sal invokes a "maternal" instinct within the men, who are anxious to see the orphan and bring gifts to the baby. Moreover, the men are enthusiastic about keeping the baby and raising it themselves and, with the baby's safety at heart, are concerned about what may happen if he were to be taken from the camp. The true sense of the nurturing community of the men at Roaring Camp is seen when everyone comes together for the child's christening and naming, and the fact that, while Stumpy takes charge of the baby's care, Roaring Camp as a community serves as both the baby's mother and father.

The arrival of "The Luck" clearly shifts the identity of this community from the stereotypical, rugged male-dominated society to one that clearly is capable of civilized behavior. The camp undergoes a complete transformation, illustrated through the characterization of Kentuck, one of the residents of the camp whose clothing changes only when "sloughed off through decay." During the transformation, or "subtle influence of innovation," as the narrator puts it, Kentuck appears regularly in a clean shirt and washed face. The camp's once boisterous and violent ways subside so as to not disturb the baby, and cursing becomes a thing of the past.

Andrew Andermatt

ISOLATION in "The Luck of Roaring Camp"

Isolation as a literary theme may appear in a variety of forms. In some cases, isolation may present itself through a story's protagonist or antagonist—most commonly when the main character(s) experience loneliness because of a physical separation. Isolation may also occur much more figuratively—perhaps emotionally or psychologically as a symbol for a larger idea such as a generation gap between characters or inequality between the sexes. In Bret Harte's "The Luck of Roaring Camp," Harte presents the concept of isolation in three ways—as an entity that is in constant contrast with or perpetuated by the notion of "togetherness," as a commentary on the separation of the sexes, and as a voluntary act to avoid shortcomings.

The opening paragraph sets the story's tone and introduces the reader to two competing themes, loneliness and togetherness. First, readers are presented with the notion that the camp is a lonely and desolate place. The narrator describes not only the ditches and claims, but also "Tuttle's Grocery," as being deserted. The vacancy of the grocery, which seems to regularly entertain gamblers, suggests that the camp is unusually and eerily abandoned. The camp must be quite desolate, as the narrator reflects that not even a shootout between French Pete and Kanaka Joe could stop the patrons from playing a game. While the camp seems abandoned in some areas, there is a sense of camaraderie and togetherness as we learn that all residents are collected at a cabin at the outer edge of the clearing. The theme of isolation is in constant competition with togetherness, most obviously with the descriptions the narrator offers in the opening paragraph and later with Cherokee Sal, the only female character, and the male community that makes up Roaring Camp. Harte seems to want readers to understand that the community that constitutes the camp also engenders the camp's primary isolation.

The most obvious case of isolation in the story centers on the only female member of Roaring Camp, Cherokee Sal. When readers meet Cherokee Sal, she is ready to give birth, with the community of males surrounding her cabin waiting to hear news of what is taking place. The narrator tells us that Cherokee Sal feels loneliness particularly because she lacks the compassion of her own SEX. She is the only one at the camp who can experience the pain of childbirth, and her rough and tough male counterparts are the only people who can comfort her. In this case, Cherokee Sal is obviously an outsider at Roaring Camp—as unable to relate to the male population as the males are to her giving birth and nurturing a child.

While Harte may be commenting on the isolation of females in male-dominated 19th-century communities, he seems to view the males of Roaring Camp as equally isolated as females. The men are first and foremost isolated from their former lives. Readers do not get insight from the narrator as to what these previous lives were, but the narrator makes it clear that the men have left behind some part of their identities. The narrator states that only two of the roughly 100 men are fugitives, but all are reckless. With the exception of Stumpy and Kentuck, whom readers get to know only through their interaction with Tommy Luck, the residents of Roaring Camp all seem to take on one identity. There really is no individualization at the camp.

The camp itself is also isolated, secluded from the world and even its own shortcomings. Roaring Camp is unwelcoming to strangers. The narrator explains that the camp is not only physically isolated by the mountains, but also that it does not encourage visitors who stumble upon it to stay. It seems that the camp has somehow willfully secluded itself, striving to make its isolation from the rest of the world "perfect."

Andrew Andermatt

HARTE, BRET "The Outcasts of Poker Flat" (1869)

"The Outcasts of Poker Flat," one of Bret Harte's most successful and anthologized western frontier tales, was first published in the January 1869 issue of *Overland Monthly,* a magazine Harte edited. The story of individuals exiled from a hypocritical society who form a community of LOVE and compassion in the face of impending DEATH, it shows the goodness that exists in all humanity.

Four outcasts, shunned by the town of Poker Flat in a fit of moral cleansing, are being sent to Sandy Bar. They are led by the philosophical gambler, Mr. John Oakhurst, who appears in several other Harte stories, notably "THE LUCK OF ROARING CAMP" (1868). It is Oakhurst who prompts the town's outrage by winning several thousand dollars of their money in a card game. The other three—"The Duchess," a prostitute; "Mother Shipton," presumably her madam; and "Uncle Billy," a drunkard and thief—represent all the moral ills that Poker Flat deems worthy of exile. Before the four can reach Sandy Bar, however, they must take shelter at the foot of the Sierra Nevada of northern California. By fate or chance, they are met by Tom Simson, an "Innocent" from Sandy Bar, and his 15-year-old fiancée Piney Woods. They all struggle to accept their individual and collective fates. After Uncle Billy steals a horse and their mules, and a snowstorm leaves them no way out, we see illustrations of themes common to Harte's work, such as COMMUNITY, FATE, HEROISM, INNOCENCE AND EXPERIENCE, NATURE, SOCIAL CLASS, and SURVIVAL.

Though the story ends in tragedy (of the six, only the Innocent survives), its true message is that appearances are deceiving. The "outcasts," by their selfless love and sacrifice for one another, are shown to be morally superior to those who shunned them.

Gary Kerley

FATE in "The Outcasts of Poker Flat"

Because the events of the story revolve around the actions of Mr. John Oakhurst, a professional gambler from Roaring Camp, fate, chance, and circumstance play a major role. At the beginning of the narrative, Oakhurst senses an ominous change in the air of Poker Flat. On the morning of November 23, 1850, he is aware that the citizens of the town are experiencing a virtuous reaction to his winning several thousand dollars. He accepts the sentence because, as a gambler, he knows not to tempt Fate.

His gambler's experience tells him that the odds are always in favor of the house, in this case the town of Poker Flat. Though some in the town want to hang Oakhurst, he is escorted out of town at gunpoint, accompanied by three other undesirables: "The Duchess," a prostitute; "Mother Shipton," presumably her madam; and "Uncle Billy," a gold thief and drunkard. Because he accepts his fate, Oakhurst does not grumble or curse as do the others. In fact, he remains cheerful and philosophically calm; he even gives his best horse to the Duchess.

Halfway between Poker Flat and Sandy Bar, the next town, the outcasts camp in a wooded area in the foothills of the Sierra Nevada. Oakhurst believes that they do not have time to stop; he senses something fateful in the air, much as he did the morning of their exile. The sky is ominously clouded and, in his gambler's vernacular, they are throwing up their hands before the game is played out.

Fate again enters the story when the outcasts are joined by Tom Simson, the "Innocent" of Sandy Bar, and his 15-year-old fiancée, Piney Woods. Tom is on his way to Poker Flat to marry Piney and seek his fortune. Tom and Oakhurst had met a few months before when Oakhurst won all of Tom's fortune, $40, in a game of cards. Oakhurst, knowing Tom's naiveté and inexperience, returned the money and told Tom never to gamble again. Whether the meeting is coincidental or fated, the addition of Tom and Piney further complicates matters. There are now two more mouths to feed, and Oakhurst cannot persuade Tom and Piney to travel on toward Poker Flat.

As snow begins to fall, Oakhurst discovers that Uncle Billy has stolen a horse and the mules and deserted his fellow outcasts. Though none of the others are surprised, Oakhurst alone is truly aware of their predicament: They are too far away from either Poker Flat or Sandy Bar to make it on what provisions are left. They have food enough for only 10 days. As the others in the party amuse themselves with music and stories around a campfire, Oakhurst is more and more aware of their impending, dire circumstances. Always the gambler, Oakhurst likens the situation to a streak of bad luck. Their luck has changed since they left Poker Flat, he announces to the others. Their fate is sealed, but only he seems aware of how bad things are likely to get.

A week goes by, and the party becomes imprisoned by the snow in a small cabin; their provisions are running out. Oakhurst calls it a losing hand, though the others try to make the best of it. Ironically, Mother Shipton, the strongest of the party, is the first to die because she starved herself to give her food to the young Piney so she can live longer. Eventually, all of them realize that their situation is hopeless, but Oakhurst, in a last attempt to cheat fate, sends Tom back to Poker Flat on a pair of snowshoes fashioned out of an old horse saddle. It is a two-day journey on foot, but it is his only chance to save Piney. Though Oakhurst could save himself, he never once thinks of deserting the others.

The next morning, both Piney and the Duchess accept their fate, and when they are found by the men from Poker Flat, they are covered in snow, locked in each other's arms. It is Oakhurst's fate to be the last of the outcasts to die. His body is found under the snow beneath a tree on which he has left his own epitaph, written on a deuce of clubs, the lowest card in the deck. Oakhurst lived as a gambler and dies the same way. At the end he writes that he has "struck a streak of bad luck" and "cashed in his checks." His fate has finally caught up to him. The ominous sense he felt the morning of the exile has been realized.

Gary Kerley

INNOCENCE AND EXPERIENCE in "The Outcasts of Poker Flat"

Mr. John Oakhurst, an experienced gambler, the central character of the story and the impetus for the casting out of undesired elements in Poker Flat, is a natural foil for a young Tom Simson, the "Innocent" from Sandy Bar, another camp one day's journey away. The two characters represent opposites in both life experience and understanding. Oakhurst is described at the beginning of the story as a professional gambler who is not at all surprised by the townspeople's sudden moral indignation. He has been in situations like this before, and he takes

the sentence of exile with calmness and a bemused acceptance of Fate.

Tom Simson's inexperience and naiveté are evident when he is first introduced to the outcasts. He and Oakhurst had met a few months before when Oakhurst won Tom's entire fortune of $40. Because of Oakhurst's knowledge of human nature, he returns the youth's money and urges him never to gamble again. Though Tom is excited to see his old friend, he again shows his inexperience by telling Oakhurst that he is going to Poker Flat to make his fortune and to elope with Piney Woods, a waitress. Piney, on meeting the others, hides behind a tree, blushes, and acts even younger than her 15 years.

Oakhurst's fellow outcasts have diverse experiences in the ways of the world. The narrative clearly implies that both the Duchess and Mother Shipton are ladies of questionable character, and Uncle Billy is a gold thief and a drunkard. When they are exiled from Poker Flat, they are not surprised, only indignant. When Tom assumes the Duchess is Mrs. Oakhurst simply because she is traveling with him, Uncle Billy has to be restrained from laughing out loud. Oakhurst also has to keep Uncle Billy in check when he starts to tell Tom and Piney that their situation is getting desperate.

Even before a snowstorm traps the outcasts and their new acquaintances, it is Oakhurst who correctly sizes up the situation. When Uncle Billy leaves them stranded by taking off with a horse and mules, Oakhurst's years of gambling experience help him remain calm. He chooses not to tell Tom and Piney the truth about the defection, telling them that Uncle Billy accidentally stampeded the animals. Oakhurst remains cheerful and merely says they have had a run of bad luck. He even likens their situation to a week-long camping trip.

As the storm worsens and their provisions dwindle, Oakhurst continues to keep himself calm and to keep Tom and Piney in the dark, thereby leaving them content, even happy. The group builds a big fire, and Tom plays his accordion and regales the others by acting out stories from a copy of the *Iliad*.

Both the Duchess and Mother Shipton are aware of their predicament. They are not surprised to learn that Uncle Billy stole the mules, but neither dares to upset Tom or especially the young Piney.

Mother Shipton, in an act of selflessness that belies the town's moral judgment of her, starves herself in order to keep Piney alive. In the end, however, even Piney loses her innocence by accepting her dark fate and realizing there is no escape from death. When the townspeople of Poker Flat find her, she and the Duchess are both in the cabin, covered in snow, locked in each other's arms.

Oakhurst's experience and philosophical calm finally play themselves out. He gives his companions a few days' worth of fuel before he leaves the cabin in order to keep them alive a little longer. He could have saved himself earlier, but he sacrificed his own life, hoping that Tom could save Piney by returning to Poker Flat for help. Oakhurst read his own fate. At the end of the story, the townspeople find his cold dead body under a tree. On the tree is pinned a deuce of clubs, and written on it in his own hand is Oakhurst's epitaph: *"Beneath this tree lies the body of John Oakhurst, who struck a streak of bad luck on the 23rd of November, 1850 and handed in his checks on the 7th of December, 1850."*

It is ironic that, in the end, both innocence and experience are brought together by the characters' fateful exile from Poker Flat. The snow, pure but deadly, covers the morally questionable Duchess and the virginal Piney. Even the law of Poker Flat recognizes that sense of merged innocence and experience, and they turn away, not disturbing the bodies. Oakhurst, experienced in getting out of previous scrapes, cannot win this time, so he takes his own life in the face of certain DEATH.

Gary Kerley

SURVIVAL in "The Outcasts of Poker Flat"

Reading "The Outcasts of Poker Flat" when it was first published in 1869, contemporaries of Bret Harte were familiar with the struggle to survive in the rugged Sierra Nevada of northern California. They would have known of the tragedy of the Donner Party during the winter between November 1846 and February 1847. Of 87 migrants, 40 died and many of the survivors resorted to cannibalism. Survival challenges would continue to plague many immigrants on their westward rush to California in the years following the discovery of gold at Sutter's Mill in 1848.

On the morning of November 23, 1850, Mr. John Oakhurst, a professional gambler, is the center of controversy in the town of Poker Flat. Because he won several thousand dollars, he senses that he is in danger of being hanged or, at best, run out of town. His knack for survival is hard-won. A gambler from Roaring Camp, Oakhurst has been through similar scrapes before. He knows what to expect when the men of Poker Flat get a sudden urge to rid their town of him and three other undesirables: "The Duchess," a prostitute; "Mother Shipton," presumably a madam traveling with her; and "Uncle Billy," a gold thief and drunkard. All of these outcasts are experienced in the ways of the world and not surprised to be scapegoats of Poker Flat's need to rid itself of bad elements.

The story centers around Oakhurst's reactions, and it is mostly his ability to predict the outcome of any situation by weighing the odds that best illustrates the theme of survival. The outcasts are sent out of town at gunpoint and head toward the camp of Sandy Bar, one day's ride away. The road to Sandy Bar lies over the beautiful but precipitous mountain range. Because the road is both narrow and difficult, the Duchess refuses to go on, and the party halts in a wooded amphitheater surrounded on three sides by steep granite cliffs.

Oakhurst's gambler sense tells him that the outcasts are not equipped to stop; they lack the provisions to delay their journey. As he surveys the steep cliffs a thousand feet above them, he can also see that the sky is becoming overcast. However, he keeps his fears to himself and reacts as if nothing is wrong. In the past, survival has meant keeping his cards close to the vest and maintaining a poker face.

A new twist in their predicament comes in the form of Tom Simson, the "Innocent," who happens to be coming from Sandy Bar to seek his fortune. He is eloping with 15-year-old Piney Woods, a waitress from the Temperance House. Tom calls it a lucky break when he runs into Oakhurst, even though the gambler won all of Tom's fortune in a poker game a few months before. Oakhurst, however, sees the arrival of young Tom and Piney as two more mouths to feed while the weather grows more and more ominous. He cannot persuade Tom to keep moving to Poker Flat, but he does not tell him or the others about his ever-increasing feeling of dread.

After 10 days of dwindling provisions and 20-foot snow drifts making a prison of their small cabin, escape is no longer possible. Tom and Piney ignore the inevitable by turning to one another. Mother Shipton, the strongest of the party, is the first to die. She tells Oakhurst that she has starved herself to give her week's worth of food to Piney so she can live a little longer.

The only chance for survival is for someone to get back to Poker Flat. Oakhurst, though he could have survived earlier by deserting his fellow outcasts, tells Tom that Piney can be saved if Tom uses the snowshoes Oakhurst has fashioned from an old saddle. He sends him off to make the two-day walk back to Poker Flat. As night falls, Oakhurst gathers enough fuel to heat the cabin for several more days before leaving himself. By the next morning, both the Duchess and Piney realize their fate.

The storm is at its worst, and the snow has started to invade the cabin. The fire they had built dies way, and the two huddle together, dying in each other's arms. Tom does return with help, but it is too late. Not only are the Duchess, Piney Woods, and Mother Shipton dead, but also the men of Poker Flat find the body of John Oakhurst buried beneath the snow under a tree. On the tree he pinned the two of clubs with his epitaph. He chose to end his life rather than freeze to death or starve. His gambler philosophy and instincts for survival finally catch up with him.

Gary Kerley

HAWTHORNE, NATHANIEL "The Birth-mark" (1846)

Nathaniel Hawthorne's "The Birth-mark" tells the story of a scientist named Aylmer and his inability to see past a birthmark on his wife's face. The story charts the progress of Aylmer's obsession and its repercussions on his life. Aylmer is married to a beautiful woman, yet he is unable to look past a singular hand-shaped blemish on her cheek. Throughout the story he focuses on the mark until both he and his wife become miserable, she even more so than he. A man of SCIENCE, Aylmer wishes to experiment on the mark in an effort to remove it, to which his heartbroken wife agrees. When the day arrives on which the experiment is to take place, Hawthorne introduces Aylmer's assistant, the rough-looking Aminadab. Despite his haggard appearance, Aminadab does not share Aylmer's crude obsession with the mark and suggests another plan of action, which is quickly ignored. At this point Hawthorne shows the difference between husband and wife, when Georgiana finds a record of Aylmer's past, failed experiments and comes to LOVE him more for his flaws. As Aylmer is incapable of the same type of love, the experiment finally takes place. The mark is removed, but Georgiana dies in the process. The story ends with Hawthorne offering up a moral lesson to his readers: Blemishes and imperfections are what make us human, and to try to remove them is a sin in itself. Aylmer's flaws make him unable to understand, or even hear, this message.

Ronald Davis

LOVE in "The Birth-mark"

In "The Birth-mark," Nathaniel Hawthorne offers two contrasting views of love. The story centers around Aylmer, a renowned scientist, and his wife, Georgiana. Aylmer has based his life on experimentation, devoting himself primarily to the study of science. The only way Aylmer's love for his wife can exceed his love for science is "by intertwining itself with his love of science, and uniting the strength of the latter to its own." Georgiana, on the other hand, loves Aylmer unconditionally. Her happiness is dependent upon his. For this reason, when he begins to take issue with a birthmark on her cheek, her perception of the mark quickly changes. To this point she has looked at the mark as a charm, but when Aylmer tells her that it "shocks" him, she is irrevocably hurt.

Aylmer's discontent with the mark, and therefore his wife, grows by leaps and bounds until he becomes obsessive about the blemish. He begins to dream about it and verbalizes his discontent in his sleep, which Georgiana hears. This pains her even more. She finally asks if he is capable of removing the mark from her face, and Aylmer, in love not only with science but also with his belief in his own ability, tells Georgiana that he is capable. Georgiana insists that he try to remove it, stating that as long as her mark upsets her husband, she is willing to give up her life. Georgiana's love for him is so great that she is willing to give up her life in an attempt to make him content with her; further, her own hatred for the birthmark has now surpassed her husband's because of her love for him. Aylmer's behavior, on the other hand, indicates that his love for his wife is now even more secondary to his love for science, as he has already put a great deal of thought into the surgery that would remove the mark.

Aylmer's love/obsession with science causes the tale to build toward its climax—the attempted removal of the birthmark. Aylmer takes Georgiana into his laboratory and, with the help of Aminadab, his rough and dirty assistant, begins preparations for the experiment. As the two men prepare, Aminadab offers up a view of love much closer to that of Georgiana's, saying that if he were married to her, he'd never part with the mark. This comment is quickly forgotten, as Aylmer focuses on making Georgiana more comfortable. This suggests a certain degree of caring for his wife, although at this point it seems that Aylmer looks at her more as the subject of his experiment than his love.

While Georgiana waits for Aylmer, she begins to browse his collection of journals. One contains all of her husband's experiments; as she reads through it, she realizes that the majority of his successes were by-products of failed experiments. His failures make him more human, and cause her to "love him more profoundly than ever." His imperfections have made him more human and caused her love for him to grow. Aylmer, on the other hand, loves Georgiana less as a person and more as a potential experiment, because of her "imperfection." If he succeeds, his love for her will grow, but only because she will represent his own ability to change nature, to play God.

By tale's end, Aylmer succeeds in removing the mark. He gives Georgiana a liquid-filled goblet to drink, and she falls into a deep sleep. As she rests, the mark disappears, and Aylmer begins to rejoice. As Georgiana wakes, he praises both the success of his experiment as well as her perfection but still fails to mention his love for her. Georgiana, however, continues to put Aylmer's interests ahead of hers; the liquid given to her has poisoned her body and she is dying, yet her first words upon waking are of concern for her husband. His happiness now supersedes even her own desire to live.

Hawthorne aptly distinguishes between two opposing versions of love in "The Birth-mark." Aylmer's love of science and his own intellectual pursuits run just as deep as Georgiana's love for him, and both characters become obsessive in their love. Also, because Georgiana's love centers on a desire for the complete happiness of her beloved, she is in love with an entity that can never be satisfied. Aylmer's hubris can never be sated; there will always be more to learn and more experiments to attempt.

Ronald Davis

SCIENCE AND TECHNOLOGY in "The Birth-mark"

An unnatural obsession with science and technology is the catalyst for the major events within "The Birth-mark." One of the main characters, Aylmer, is a renowned scientist and recluse, having dedicated so much time to scientific pursuits that he has little time for anything else. Even Aylmer's LOVE for his wife, Georgiana, is second to his love of science. Through Aylmer and Georgiana's relationship, Hawthorne offers a warning against Aylmer's reckless experimentation, showing as he does in other works how things can go horribly awry when a desire for intellectual pursuits supersedes a desire for emotional sustenance. Through this relationship, he also explores the nature of obsession and objectification.

Early in the story, Aylmer begins to focus on a small blemish marking Georgiana's cheek. Georgiana is hurt by Aylmer's comment that he finds the mark shocking, and because she doesn't wish to cause her husband any distress, she asks him to rid her of the mark. Oblivious to his wife's sensitivity, Aylmer leaps at the opportunity to perfect her. Having already thought a great deal, and even dreamed, about the process of removing the mark, Aylmer immediately sets into motion a series of experiments designed to destroy it. The next day, the process begins. Aylmer takes Georgiana to his lab and shows her his various experiments. He is invigorated by her presence in his laboratory, most particularly by her attention to and admiration of his tales of scientific discoveries. Thoroughly obsessed with his own knowledge, he can enjoy her presence only when she reflects his love for science. As he explains the history of alchemy, he becomes more animated and lively than we have seen him before. Displaying his intellect for his wife reaffirms his priorities, as his pleasure is not derived from the interaction with her but from the opportunity to have his intellect admired. This is, in part, an effort to reassure her of his abilities. However, while Georgiana waits for him to be ready, she discovers a record of Aylmer's experiments and comes to find that the grand majority of his successes were actually the unexpected outcomes of failed experiments. Here, Hawthorne comments on the unstable nature of scientific progress: One cannot always predict accurately the outcome of one's experiments. He is also foreshadowing the tragic outcome of the tale; if Aylmer's experiments rarely work out the way he wants them to, Georgiana might be in more danger than she thinks. However, rather than grow concerned about Aylmer's ability and obsession with science, Georgiana grows to love her husband even more for his imperfections.

Shortly before conducting his final experiment with Georgiana, Aylmer shows her a container of elixir, which represents the power of science to destroy. It is at this point that Aylmer's obsession is revealed to be a god complex, and when Georgiana professes her worship of him, he tells her she may admire him more fully after he rids her of the birthmark. While it was clear before that Aylmer's concern with the mark was selfish, this comment shows that he wants to remove it not just for the pleasure he'd derive from seeing his wife as "flawless," but also for the twisted sense of importance he would gain from altering NATURE to please him.

As the tale comes to an end, Aylmer's last experiment completes his pattern of failure, and while the mark does disappear, Georgiana dies in the process. Aylmer's obsession with science made him dissatisfied with what he had, made him think he could improve it, and the story ends sadly.

This tale brings up a number of issues, including the nature of love as well as the morality, or lack thereof, behind human experimentation. Aylmer's ego has twisted his sense of his own scientific prowess to the point that his wife becomes a test subject and he becomes a god. Technology is no help to Aylmer and does nothing more than help him to kill his wife. In the end he is left with nothing to show for this latest experiment but another failure, not because he failed to remove the birthmark but because he failed to recognize the value of love over the value of science.

Ronald Davis

WORK in "The Birth-mark"

Work has the potential to become an all-consuming force in Nathaniel Hawthorne's "The Birth-mark." Two of the three main characters, Aylmer and Aminadab, both work in a laboratory. Aylmer is a scientist, and Aminadab is his assistant. While both men focus on furthering scientific knowledge, they do not share the same dedication to their work. Aylmer will risk anything for the sake of discovery, whereas Aminadab tempers his dedication to his work with common sense and human compassion.

The final main character, Aylmer's wife Georgiana, does not hold a traditional job. Instead, her work is to love and care for her husband unconditionally. In this way she is very similar to Aylmer; both characters hold their "work" above all else and cannot be persuaded to deviate from it for any reason. Throughout the story, the work of the two characters intertwines. Aylmer takes it upon himself to attempt to remove a birthmark from Georgiana's face via scientific means; Georgiana's attempts to be an ideal wife allow for this experimentation to happen, with no argument as to the safety, or the sanity, of the pursuit.

As the story progresses, Aylmer focuses more and more on the removal of the birthmark, sacrificing all other pursuits and allowing his job to invade even his dreams at night. He becomes haunted by the mark, which causes Georgiana to feel bad. In her mind, her birthmark has changed from a mark of her character to a symbol of how she displeases her husband and, in turn, how she is failing at her job. One night Georgiana hears Aylmer speaking of the mark in his sleep, and this provokes a conversation between husband and wife in which they both determine the best course of action to fulfill their respective duties. Aylmer must have the mark out; Georgiana must please her husband, therefore the two come to the conclusion that work must be done to get rid of it. It is clear at this point in the story that duty has blinded both of them to common sense. Neither will accept the mark for what it is; rather, they have both turned it into something hideous, something hindering their happiness, something it is their duty, as workers, to fix.

In preparation to remove the mark, Aylmer takes Georgiana into his laboratory. It is at this time that the reader is finally introduced to Aminadab. Hawthorne describes Aylmer's assistant in a rough manner, with a ragged appearance and low intelligence, yet it is Aminadab who expresses disapproval of Aylmer's pursuit. It is ironic that the man who appears so scruffy has the keener understanding. Aminadab is able to see Aylmer's overzealous dedication to his work, but as is often the case in Hawthorne's fiction, the wisest person is the one most easily ignored.

As Georgiana awaits the removal of the mark, she explores Aylmer's laboratory and happens upon a record of his prior experiments. In perusing them, she discovers that all of his successes were unexpected outcomes of larger failures. Rather than looking upon this revelation as a blemish on Aylmer's character, this knowledge compels Georgiana to LOVE him even more, thus further fulfilling her duty as a good wife. The realization of her husband as imperfect allows her to better complete her own work, just as Aylmer's creation of an imperfection within his wife has provided him with a way in which to further experiment and, if successful, to be a better worker as well.

Throughout the story, Aylmer has moved from seeing Georgiana as his wife to seeing her as his latest experiment. Ultimately, Aylmer's obsession with his work causes Georgiana's death. The mark disappears, but so does Georgiana's life force. In typical fashion, Hawthorne ends the story before his characters have any sort of revelation or experience any closure regarding their actions, but it is safe to assume that Aylmer looks upon the experience as an occupational failure rather than the loss of his beloved.

Work and work-obsession take on two forms in this story, the most obvious being Aylmer's blind focus on his experiments, although Georgiana's

dedication to and love for Aylmer come across as blind pursuits as well. Both are unable to separate existence from work, and this leads to their respective downfalls. In "The Birth-mark," Hawthorne juxtaposes two very different types of work, scientific and emotional, but shows that, in either one, obsession is capable of transcending boundaries, obliterating rational thought, and destroying happiness.

Ronald Davis

HAWTHORNE, NATHANIEL *The House of the Seven Gables* (1851)

Published in 1851, Nathaniel Hawthorne's novel *The House of the Seven Gables* mixes elements of the gothic tale, romance, and realism, while telling the story of the descendants of Matthew Maule, the original proprietor of the land on which the titular house would be built, and Colonel Pyncheon, the man who "asserted plausible claims" to the land. Colonel Pyncheon sees to it that Matthew Maule is tried and hanged for witchcraft, and on the scaffold, Maule points to the colonel and utters, "God will give him blood to drink!" The moral, as Hawthorne phrases it in the preface, is that "the wrongdoing of one generation lives into successive ones," but the novel also examines the tension between public and private, between COMMUNITY and social stratification, and between different perceptions of the past.

The main plot threads revolve around the descendants of Colonel Pyncheon: Hepzibah, Phoebe, Clifford, and Judge Jaffrey, as well as Mr. Holgrave, the photographer whom we later learn is a descendant of Matthew Maule. Judge Jaffrey believes his cousin Clifford knows where the deed to lands in the east is located and threatens to have him sent to a mental asylum if he does not cooperate in the search for the deed. Hepzibah later finds Clifford and the deceased judge in the house, and we learn later that Judge Jaffrey died due to medical problems. The remaining Pyncheons inherit the judge's country house and decide to move there, leaving behind the House of the Seven Gables. Phoebe and Holgrave pledge to marry.

Jeffrey Pettineo

COMMERCE in *The House of the Seven Gables*

Hawthorne's descriptions and characterizations provide a lens through which to examine 19th-century Americans' attitudes toward wealth and material possessions. The main points of concern are the greed of Colonel Pyncheon and Judge Jaffrey, the episodes related to Hepzibah's cent-shop, and the mystery surrounding the deed to the lands in the east.

Colonel Pyncheon's greed for Matthew Maule's land initiates the conflict—". . . after some thirty or forty years, the site covered by this rude hovel had become exceedingly desirable in the eyes of a prominent and powerful personage, who asserted plausible claims to the proprietorship of this, and a large adjacent tract of land. . . ." The land is the eventual site of the House of the Seven Gables, designed by one of Matthew's descendants, Thomas. Hawthorne describes the house—and possessions like it—as so impressive that it becomes its own excuse for existence. "There is something so massive, stable, and almost irresistibly imposing, in the exterior presentment of established rank and great possessions, that their very existence seems to give them a right to exist."

Once a seamstress, Hepzibah in her old age is forced to open a "cent-shop" in the house due to her nearsightedness and her "tremulous fingers." Hepzibah had imagined herself to have been part of the "aristocracy," but "after sixty years of narrowing means," she has to "step down from her pedestal of imaginary rank." This is the point at which Hepzibah is transformed from the "patrician lady" to the "plebian woman." At first, Hepzibah is reluctant to appear to society in a business capacity, having once considered becoming a teacher. After her first day at the shop, Hepzibah feels that "the shop would prove her ruin, in a moral and religious point of view, without contributing very essentially towards even her temporal welfare." Hepzibah's customers include Uncle Venner, who doles out advice such as "Give no credit!" and "Never take paper money!" One of the townspeople, Dixey, comments on Hepzibah's scowl as something that prevents her from retaining customers—"Why, her face—I've seen it . . her face is enough to frighten the Old Nick himself . . . People can't

stand it, I tell you! She scowls dreadfully, reason or none, out of pure ugliness of temper!" Another townsperson indicates that such shops are doomed to failure due to all the competition. "This business of keeping cent-shops is overdone, like all kinds of trade, handicraft and bodily labor," to which Dixey responds, "Poor business!" When Phoebe arrives at the house, she brings a new energy and spirit to the environment, even influencing the operations of the shop, exclaiming at one point, "We must renew our stock, Cousin Hepzibah!" The townsperson and Dixey once again consider the Pyncheons' good fortune at the end of the novel as Dixey reflects, in a reversal of her earlier sentiment, "Pretty good business!" The setting of the cent-shop provides Hawthorne with a vehicle through which to examine the personality of Hepzibah as well as the tension between social classes and Americans' attitudes toward wealth and commodities. In contrast to the cent-shop are settings such as the garden, which are described in more metaphysical terms.

Another commercial concern is the deed to a "vast, and as yet unexplored and unmeasured tract of eastern lands." The lands in Maine are "more extensive than many a dukedom, or even a reigning prince's territory, on European soil." The territory was eventually given over to "more favored individuals" and "partly cleared and occupied by actual settlers." Hawthorne describes the claim as something almost laughable and unsubstantial: "This impalpable claim, therefore resulted in nothing more solid than to cherish, from generation to generation, an absurd delusion of family importance, which all along characterized the Pyncheons." However, the claim turns out to be nothing more than a piece of worthless parchment for which Judge Jaffrey forces Clifford to suffer. Holgrave later discovers the deed hidden in the recess of a wall, covered by a portrait of Colonel Pyncheon. Thus, Judge Jaffrey's desire for the deed resulted in the false imprisonment of Clifford and the alienation of Hepzibah.

Commerce, therefore, operates on one hand as something necessary and even laudable, as it requires tremendous effort and a willingness to take risks. On the other hand, commercialism can become something destructive if pursued with unmitigated greed and avarice, as in the case of the colonel and Judge Jaffrey.

Jeffrey Pettineo

COMMUNITY in *The House of the Seven Gables*

How the Pyncheons deal with their declining social status despite generations of "aristocracy" is a major concern for Hawthorne. Hepzibah, in particular, becomes the "new plebian woman" and is forced to deal with the larger community after she establishes her cent-shop. Clifford must also learn to reintegrate into society after the debilitating effects, both mental and physical, of almost 30 years in prison. Phoebe helps both Hepzibah and Clifford recover some sense of each character's respective place as part of humankind in broader terms, rather than simply as part of a particular SOCIAL CLASS.

Hepzibah's initial contact with the larger community is manifest through her cent-shop business, with initial visits from Holgrave, the little boy (whom the narrator describes as an "urchin"), and townsfolk identified as Dixey and Dixey's friend. The townsfolk are initially skeptical about Hepzibah as well as the potential success of her shop, noticing her dreadful scowl born out of "ugliness of temper." Hepzibah worries about the disregard of the townsfolk: "She was absurdly hurt, moreover, by the slight and idle effect that her setting up shop—an event of such breathless interest to herself—appeared to have upon the public . . . they cared nothing for her dignity, and just as little for her degradation."

Like Hepzibah, Clifford also has a difficult time attempting to deal with society. The "Arched Window" chapter gives us glimpses into the longing of Clifford to "dive" into the "river of life" as he witnesses an entertainer stopping under an elm to play music on his organ. Clifford is at once scared and delighted by the sight: "With a shivering repugnance at the idea of personal contact with the world, a powerful impulse still seized on Clifford, whenever the rush and roar of the human tide grew strongly audible on him." Hawthorne describes the fascination as generating a human longing for connection: "It might so fascinate him, that he would

hardly be restrained from plunging into the surging stream of human sympathies." Clifford's desire manifests in an attempt to jump down from the window frame, but Hepzibah and Phoebe interpret this action as a possible suicide attempt. Clifford, however, believes that if he had survived the jump, he would have been a better man for it: "Fear nothing—it is over now—but had I taken that plunge, and survived it, methinks I would have made me another man!" Clifford sees this as an attempt not only to rejoin the community, but also to regain a sense of what it means to be human, to experience connections of filial love, what the narrator refers to as "the broken links of brotherhood." Moreover, as Clifford watches Phoebe walk to church, he muses to Hepzibah that he could possibly see himself in prayer once again, if he was surrounded by other people praying in a communal church setting: "'Were I to be there,' he rejoined, 'it seems to me that I could pray once more, when so many human souls were praying all around me!'" Later in the novel, when Clifford and Hepzibah are traveling in the railroad car, Hepzibah feels herself "apart from humankind," but Clifford is elated at the thought of being among other human beings: "Here we are, in the world, Hepzibah!—in the midst of life!—in the throng of our fellow beings!"

Compared to Clifford and Hepzibah, Phoebe is a much more personable and integrated member of the community, as she never has to face the hardships Clifford underwent, nor the shame that Hepzibah feels about her new status. "Phoebe, it must be understood, was that one little offshoot of the Pyncheon race to whom we have already referred, as a native of a rural part of New England, where the old fashions and feelings of relationship are still partially kept up." Moreover, Phoebe's experiences regarding the mingling of classes were not considered "improper": "In her own circle, it was regarded as by no means improper for kinsfolk to visit one another, without invitation, or preliminary and ceremonious warning." Phoebe, therefore, becomes an exemplar for social integration.

Hawthorne's own experiences in helping establish the utopian community at Brook Farm were probably responsible, at least in part, for his concern with community and brotherhood, themes represented most concretely by the thoughts, feelings, actions, and relationships of Hepzibah, Clifford, and Phoebe.

Jeffrey Pettineo

ILLNESS in *The House of the Seven Gables*

Many of the Pyncheons in *The House of the Seven Gables* appear to be suffering from mental illness or, as Holgrave calls it, "lunacy." Clifford, Hepzibah's brother, is initially described as suffering from a sort of psychosomatic illness as a result of having been incarcerated. Moreover, before Phoebe arrives, the House of the Seven Gables is personified as a diseased entity, beset by corruption and decay.

The primary sufferer from illness is Clifford, who was falsely tried and convicted of murdering Colonel Pyncheon, the patriarch of the Pyncheon family. He has been incarcerated for 27 years, an event that Hawthorne likens to a burial: ". . . this long-buried man was likely, for some reason or another, to be summoned forth from his living tomb." Hepzibah, Clifford's sister, and Phoebe, cousin of Hepzibah, Clifford, and Judge Jaffrey, first meet Clifford as he walks in halting fashion down a staircase, much like an old man. The narrator notes that ". . . there were no tokens that his physical strength might not have suffered for a free and determined gait. It was the spirit of the man, that could not walk." Clifford longs for happiness, but keeps reinforcing in his own mind the mental illness others have projected on him. "Alas, poor Clifford! You are old, and worn with troubles that ought never have befallen you. You are partly crazy. . . ." Judge Jaffrey even threatens at one point to send Clifford away to an asylum if he does not cooperate in helping Jaffrey find the deed to lands "in the east," but this reveals only Jaffrey's outward cruelty toward Clifford and his using of Clifford for the sake of material gain.

Hawthorne vividly describes the psychological effect that others may have on a sick person. "The sick in mind, and perhaps in body, are rendered more darkly and hopelessly so, by the manifold reflection of their disease, mirrored back from all quarters, in the deportment of those about them; they are compelled to inhale the poison of their own health, in infinite repetition." In "The Flight of Two Owls" chapter, Clifford begins to reclaim some of his youthful spirit and happiness as he gets a chance to converse with an intellectual traveling on the same train. It is partly Phoebe's concern for Clifford, though, that helps him regain some of his "spiritual health" by novel's end. Phoebe is careful to always maintain a cheery demeanor around Clifford for fear that the opposite will exacerbate Clifford's ill health. Hawthorne frequently contrasts Phoebe with Clifford, associating Phoebe with growth, vibrancy, and youth, and Clifford with darkness, shadows and old age.

The other main "character" that is afflicted with disease is the House of the Seven Gables itself. The spring that feeds the house's well begins to lose some of its nourishing qualities after Colonel Pyncheon occupies the mansion: ". . . it is certain that the water of Maule's Well, as it continued to be called, grew hard and brackish. Even such we find it now; and any old woman of the neighborhood will certify, that it is productive of intestinal mischief to those who quench their thirst there." Just as Phoebe's youth, spirit, and beauty help Clifford return to health, so too do these characteristics aid in the "rejuvenation" of the house. Phoebe's "genial spirit" and work ethic help to erase the "grime and sordidness" of the house. Holgrave, the daguerreotypist, descendant of Matthew Maule and later husband of Phoebe, also notes the impoverished state of the house, but refers to its purification as more a metaphorical destruction of all things old, including institutions. He claims the grime and sordidness of the house is the result of the "crystallization on its walls" of the breath of those who have lived there in "discontent and anguish." Thus, his attraction to Phoebe is also a metaphorical attraction to the regenerative power of youth and idealism. Holgrave also believes that the youth of Phoebe has shielded her from the effects of the "lunacy" that has infected the bloodlines of the Pyncheons.

The most common antidotes for the illnesses witnessed in the novel are brotherhood, companionship, and compassion, and these elements conspire to return both the house and Clifford to their former states. Hawthorne also employs health and illness metaphors in order to comment on and develop other themes. For example, Clifford's "illness of spirit" and the decay of the titular house are a direct result of the effects of greed, treachery, and corruption.

Jeffrey Pettineo

HAWTHORNE, NATHANIEL "Rappaccini's Daughter" (1844)

Nathaniel Hawthorne's "Rappaccini's Daughter" is one of his most widely read short stories. It was published in 1846 as part of the collection *Mosses from an Old Manse* in which other well-known stories such as "The BIRTH-MARK" and "The Artist of the Beautiful" were also included.

The tale is set in medieval Padua, in Italy. A young medical student, Giovanni Guasconti, arrives in the town and finds lodging in a building kept by Lisabetta, an elderly housekeeper. Giovanni's room directly oversees a beautiful garden that displays all kinds of strange plants. As he is gazing into the garden he sees an old man, Giacomo Rappaccini, and his young, beautiful daughter, Beatrice, who lives confined within the walls that surround the garden. Giovanni falls in love with Beatrice and trespasses the door of the garden in order to talk with her. He ignores the advice of Professor Pietro Baglioni, who warns him against the deathly nature of Rappaccini's experiments with plants. As the story progresses we learn that the plants that grow in the garden have a poisonous nature and only Beatrice is able to touch them without protection because her father has rendered her, like the plants he cultivates, poisonous to whoever touches her. Eventually, Beatrice dies after drinking an antidote that Giovanni has obtained from Baglioni in an effort to both free Beatrice from her poisonous nature and save himself from the same effects, since Rappaccini, in his desire to find a suitable companion for Beatrice, has rendered Giovanni poisonous.

"Rappaccini's Daughter" provides an insightful criticism of the dangers of scientific pride, which ultimately leads to isolation and death. The scientist's obsession to outwit nature and the consequences this obsession brings onto those that surround him is a theme that Hawthorne explored in other texts, such as "The Birth-mark."

Teresa Requena

DEATH in "Rappaccini's Daughter"

In "Rappaccini's Daughter," Nathaniel Hawthorne chooses a garden as the main setting for the action of the story. It apparently echoes the Garden of Eden in its bountiful presence of plants and herbs. Hawthorne, however, distorts the idyllic image to turn the garden into a walled space, separated from the outside world, whose inhabitants, Beatrice and Giacomo Rappaccini, also live isolated lives. Hawthorne's depiction of the mysterious garden in gothic terms—a ruined marble fountain, a wreathed plant around a statue—soon discloses the deathly trap it represents. Only the water that flows from the fountain seems to be an "immortal spirit" amongst deathly creatures.

Such an impression begins to take hold when Giovanni first sees Rappaccini, whose sickly look quickly puts him in clear opposition to the exuberance of the garden, in which plants seem to grow with no limit. Like the marble fountain or the marble vases, we are told that the scientist's heart is equally dead, with "a face singularly marked with intellect and cultivation, but which could never, even in his more youthful days, have expressed much warmth of heart."

The garden's malignant secret is revealed to Giovanni little by little. When he observes Rappaccini moving among the plants, he sees that the scientist is careful not to allow any portion of his skin to be in direct contact with them, not knowing that the plants' poisonous nature makes their touching impossible without protection. Such carefulness raises suspicions in Giovanni, who imagines a deadly malice of the garden. However, it is not only the scientist who seems to hide a secret. As he observes Beatrice from his window, Giovanni notices the easiness with which she moves among the plants, without any protection. Later, he observes the killing power of Beatrice's breath on lizards and insects, and the withering effect that Beatrice has on the bouquet that Giovanni gives her.

Giovanni's perception finds confirmation when he learns from his friend Professor Baglioni about Rappaccini's experiments. In his desire to outwit nature, the isolated scientist has been experimenting with plants and he has transformed them into extremely beautiful poisonous creatures that are also bringers of death. Thus, Rappaccini is presented as an egotistical character whose only design in life is to advance in his knowledge of science by what the scientific community considers to be unethical means. It is such forbidden procedures that have earned Rappaccini a bad reputation among the scientific community. Hawthorne's tale condemns that attitude when he describes the scientist as being willing to "sacrifice human life, his own among the rest, or whatever else was dearest to him, for the sake of adding so much as a grain of mustard seed to the great heap of his accumulated knowledge." That Rappaccini's efforts result in the addition of something as small as a grain of mustard clearly poses a criticism of the man's immoderate ambition, which brings not only isolation but also death to what he seems to love most, his daughter.

Although now aware that Beatrice's touch or breath is deadly to anything raised outside the garden, Giovanni falls in love with Beatrice. Soon he realizes that he, too, has become as poisonous as Beatrice. Like her, he can kill insects with his breath. When he realizes what has happened, Giovanni accuses Beatrice of infecting him despite Beatrice's claim that her father is the one to blame. In an effort to save them both, Giovanni produces an antidote that Professor Baglioni has given him with the hope that their deathly nature can be purified. Beatrice takes the drink first so that Giovanni can see the effects of the drink before he takes it. The effect of the antidote is contrary to that expected, and Beatrice dies. Thus, she becomes the final victim of Rappaccini's experiments and his desire to alter the natural course of nature through scientific means.

Beatrice's death at the end of the tale coincides with a tradition of female characters in Hawthorne's short fiction who suffer in their own flesh the effects of the male's obsessions and his actions taken in order to achieve a desired aim. As the writer explored in other tales such as "The Birth-mark," the death of the female character also symbolizes the negative consequences of pursuing an egotistical endeavor, in which the male character is unable to realize that his experiments or desires are incompatible with a social life.

Teresa Requena

ISOLATION in "Rappaccini's Daughter"

Many of Hawthorne's short stories are populated by isolated characters that, for different reasons, live their lives apart from the social world. "Rappaccini's Daughter" provides a neat example of such a theme in the characters of Rappaccini and, most poignantly, Beatrice.

The story opens when Giovanni travels north to study at the University of Padua. Once there, he rents a small, gloomy, and dark room in an old building. His initial sadness is somehow relieved when he peers through the window and discovers a beautiful and bountiful garden that holds a variety of strange and mysterious plants and herbs that grow all around. In the middle, there is a decayed fountain that supplies water to an exceedingly beautiful and fragrant flower.

As Giovanni continues to observe the garden, the housekeeper explains that it belongs to Doctor Giacomo Rappaccini, a reputed scientist in Italy who grows these plants to make medicines. A few minutes later, he spots Rappaccini walking around the garden wearing thick gloves and a mask so that he does not touch the poisonous plants and herbs nor inhale the fragrance they shed. As the story progresses we learn that Rappaccini has always been guided by an irrational passion for experimentation beyond what is seen as reasonable. His scientific ambition and experimentation with poisonous plants has led to his isolation from the scientific community, which questions his scientific methods and goals.

Rappaccini's loneliness in what seems to be his outdoor laboratory is apparently eased by the presence of his daughter Beatrice, who is described as a beautiful and lively girl. Mysteriously, she is the only one who is able to touch and approach the plants without any protective means. Upon seeing her, however, Giovanni affirms that Beatrice seems another of the plants that Rappaccini has in his garden and, like them, she has to be touched with gloves or approached with a mask.

Giovanni's curiosity toward the garden and the plants it nourishes soon leads to observation of the beautiful Beatrice; little by little, he feels deeply attracted toward her. His interest in the scientist's daughter impels him to trespass in the garden, and once inside, he meets Beatrice and talks with her. It is in the conversations between the two youngsters inside the garden that Giovanni, and the reader, realize the extent and pain of Beatrice's isolation in a life severed from any contact with other human beings. Her questions to Giovanni about the world outside the garden wall reveal her lifelong seclusion with the plants and herbs her father has grown.

Actually, Giovanni is right in his appreciation that Beatrice cannot be approached without danger since there is a secret behind Beatrice and Rappaccini. As Giovanni learns, the old scientist has fed his daughter on poison since the day she was born as part of an experiment to make her invulnerable to any danger. Later, Beatrice further explains to Giovanni that the very same day of her birth, Rappaccini also created a poisonous plant to grow up alongside Beatrice as a sister. The result is that everything that Beatrice touches inevitably dies, and therefore she has not been able to lead a life among human beings.

Her peculiar poisonous nature discloses Beatrice as the most dramatic case of isolation in the story, which is the direct result of her father's scientific experiments. Rappaccini's desire to outwit nature led him to experiment with his own daughter regardless of the possible effects on Beatrice's life. Like other characters such as Aylmer in "The Birth-mark," Rappaccini's obsessive pursuit of scientific achievements inevitably leads him and those around him to live a life apart from the social world and human warmth. Thus, Beatrice is the dramatic outcome of the father's pursuits, and after a life of seclusion in the garden she confesses her unhappiness and misery to Giovanni.

The story ends with still another turn of the screw on the theme of isolation when Giovanni realizes that he has also been turned into a poisonous creature. Initially blaming Beatrice, the last paragraphs reveal that it has been Rappaccini who, once more, has defied nature to create another being equal to his lonely daughter, and thus they both stand apart from common men and women. The scientist deems his deed a great victory over nature, while Beatrice and Giovanni realize the doomed future awaiting them. Eventually, Beatrice's death ends dramatically her lifelong isolation.

The story thus portrays isolation from the social world and human warmth in negative terms by clearly showing the effects it has on the characters and by arguing that isolation is the price to be paid for any obsession.

Teresa Requena

PRIDE in "Rappaccini's Daughter"

In Nathaniel Hawthorne's texts the examination of pride figures as a prominent theme. Stories such as "Young Goodman Brown" or "The Minister's Black Veil" explore the consequences of male characters' religious pride when these characters assume that their actions will have no effects on their religious principles. In "Rappaccini's Daughter," Hawthorne investigates intellectual pride in relation to scientific advancements.

The text focuses on Rappaccini and Giovanni's friend, the professor of medicine Pietro Baglioni. In the case of Rappaccini, his scientific pride leads him to the firm belief that he can outwit nature with his scientific discoveries. In the same way, Professor Baglioni represents another angle of scientific pride in his desire to prove Rappaccini's experiments wrong. For instance, upon Giovanni's first meeting with the professor, the sense of old rivalry between Rappaccini and Baglioni is made evident when Giovanni takes the opportunity to mention the scientist's name. It is then that Baglioni changes his attitude and does not "respond with so much cordiality as he had anticipated." The reasons for Baglioni's reluctance seem to be grounded on moral qualms, since he recognizes Rappaccini's contribution to scientific progress but disapproves of his unethical scientific goals. In this line, Baglioni assures young Giovanni that the main objection to Rappaccini's practices is that "he cares infinitely more for science than for mankind." As the conversation progresses, the rivalry between the two scientists surfaces again when Baglioni speculates that Beatrice, with all the instruction she has received from her father, may strip him of his professor's chair at the university. Baglioni's thoughts also betray his own scientific pride and ambition when at the end of his conversation with Giovanni he affirms that "it is too insufferable an impertinence in Rappaccini, thus to snatch the lad out of my own hands, as I may say, and make use of him for his infernal experiments" (988).

The consequences of the scientific pride that both characters exhibit become clear at the end of the story. It is then that both men see their opportunity to outwit each other. In the case of Baglioni, he discloses Beatrice's true poisonous nature to Giovanni when he visits the young student in his lodgings and deems Beatrice "the victim of his [Rappaccini's] zeal for science." Wishing to amend Rappaccini's deed, Baglioni offers Giovanni the chance to bring Beatrice back to social life by showing him a little silver vase that contains an effective antidote to the most devastating poison. It is this antidote that, according to the professor, will effectively cure Beatrice from her poisonous nature. However, rather than wishing to save Beatrice from an alienated existence, Baglioni secretly enjoys the opportunity to defeat Rappaccini. To that effect, Baglioni gives Giovanni the vase and the young student goes to meet Beatrice. Baglioni's revelation has already had a profound effect on Giovanni by inspiring wrath, despair, and doubt about Beatrice and her monstrous nature at the same time that he discovers his own poisonous condition. Upon that realization, Giovanni understands that the only option for him and Beatrice to live their love among society is to resort to Professor Baglioni's antidote, which Giovanni deems "almost divine in its efficacy." Thus, Giovanni proposes that both of them shall drink it in order to be purified from their monstrous condition. Beatrice, playing a traditional self-sacrificing female role, offers to drink it first so that Giovanni can examine the effects.

The final scene brings all the characters together and again reveals the two scientists' pride. When Beatrice openly blames her father for having brought the pain of rejection upon her, Rappaccini's answer betrays his pride in his science and in its capacity to surpass the natural laws of life. He calls his daughter "foolish" for not being able to understand the supposed benefits of his experiments, among which he lists the possibility to transcend weakness and defeat by being powerful enough to inflict evil upon anybody. Equally, Beatrice's death leads the proud professor Baglioni triumphantly to ask Rappaccini whether Beatrice's death was really the planned result of his experiment.

Teresa Requena

HAWTHORNE, NATHANIEL *The Scarlet Letter* (1850)

Set in Puritan Boston, *The Scarlet Letter* chronicles the life of Hester Prynne. The novel opens as Hester, with her infant Pearl in her arms, is led from the town prison to a scaffold that stands in the marketplace. Hester stands on the scaffold as part of her punishment for adultery; on her chest is a scarlet letter A that the magistrates decree that she must wear. Hester and Pearl live an isolated life on the outskirts of Boston, and Hester makes her living through her needlework skills. She has used these skills to embellish her "A" with flourishes of gold thread, and she dresses Pearl in red and gold as if to emphasize that both are symbols of her adultery. Throughout the novel, Hester keeps two secrets. The first is that her husband, who was to follow her from Europe to the new world, arrived in Boston as she stood upon the scaffold. Remaining anonymous, he lives under the name of Roger Chillingworth. Hester's second secret is the identity of her lover, the respected young minister Arthur Dimmesdale. Though Hester refuses to publicly name Dimmesdale as Pearl's father, Chillingworth suspects him. Acting as the minister's physician, Chillingworth takes up residence with Dimmesdale, all the while trying to ferret out his secret. In his dying moments, Dimmesdale publicly confesses that he is Pearl's father. Hester and Pearl later leave Boston, but at the novel's end Hester returns to her seaside cottage and again takes up her scarlet "A." Hawthorne uses Hester's story to explore the nature of symbolism and the themes of RELIGION, PARENTHOOD, and the INDIVIDUAL AND SOCIETY, among others.

Laurie A. Sterling

INDIVIDUAL AND SOCIETY in *The Scarlet Letter*
The second paragraph of *The Scarlet Letter* introduces the notion of the social contract when the narrator says, "The founders of a new colony . . . have invariably recognized it among their earli-

est practical necessities to allot a portion of the virgin soil . . . as the site of a prison." Once Hester Prynne is ushered through the prison door in the next chapter, the scarlet "A" upon her chest provides a symbolic focus for the novel's exploration of the relationship between the individual and society. The magistrates clearly intend for the scarlet letter to embody their judgment; they clearly mean to mark Hester as an adulteress through this "A." And yet Hester silently challenges their laws and their evaluation of her. Using her imagination and her skill with the needle, she embellishes the "A" with "flourishes of gold thread. . . . greatly beyond what was allowed by the sumptuary regulations of the colony." Like Pearl, the living reflection of the scarlet letter, the luxuriously decorated "A" expresses the "warfare of Hester's spirit." Through its exploration of the effects and the efficacy of the scarlet "A," *The Scarlet Letter* comments upon the rigid and inflexible social codes of Massachusetts Bay Colony.

The most obvious effect of Hester's punishment is isolation. While she makes a living with her needle, she "inhabited another sphere. . . . like a ghost that revisits the familiar fireside, and can no longer make itself seen or felt." As a result of the magistrates' punishment, Hester is transformed. She is robbed of her femininity and her passion, and in her isolation she recognizes that "the world's law was no law for her." Similarly, Pearl, who functions both as a character and a symbol in the novel, also suffers. Born an "outcast of the infantile world," Pearl instinctively knows that she has no place within Puritan society. Without playmates, she occupies herself through imaginary play but tellingly, "she never created a friend." Always outside of a social structure, Pearl cannot "be made amenable to rules" or to discipline.

Contemplating Hester's profound isolation and the transformation that it evokes, the narrator seems to challenge the efficacy of the "dismal severity of the Puritanic code of law" in a solitary sentence that forms a paragraph: "The scarlet letter had not done its office." Yet even before this, the novel hints at the shortcomings of Hester's punishment, for the community at large does not completely accept the rulings of the magistrates. As

Hester continues her life on the outskirts of Boston, the community's interpretation of her and her letter varies greatly from the magistrates' original meaning. Hester's "A," they claim, stands for "Able" or for "Angel." By the novel's end, "the scarlet letter ceased to be a stigma which attracted the world's scorn and bitterness, and became a type of something to be sorrowed over, and looked upon with awe, yet with reverence too."

While Hester undergoes public punishment, Dimmesdale grapples with his sin privately. He longs to confess his sin publicly but cannot manage to do so until the novel's end. His relationship to society and social codes best explains his inability. The narrator describes the minister saying, "it would always be essential to his peace to feel the pressure of a faith about him, supporting, while it confined him within its iron framework." Hester's experience has forced her outside of her community, but Dimmesdale's experience has not afforded him this latitude of speculation. He is a prisoner of societal codes: "At the head of the social system . . . he was only the more trammeled by its regulations, its principles, and even its prejudices." Thus, even when he and Hester resolve to flee Boston, Dimmesdale finds it impossible to leave his socially constructed identity. He is anxious to stay until he preaches the Election Sermon, and he thinks to himself, "At least, they shall say of me . . . that I leave no public duty unperformed, nor ill performed!"

While Dimmesdale finally manages confession but not escape, Hester eventually leaves Boston with Pearl. But Hawthorne complicates the relationship between Hester and her Puritan society further at the novel's end. Despite the freedom of her earlier views, Hester returns to Boston and takes up the scarlet "A" of her own accord, perhaps affirming society's role in shaping an individual's identity.

Laurie A. Sterling

PARENTHOOD in *The Scarlet Letter*

Hawthorne modeled the character of Pearl in *The Scarlet Letter* after his own first born, Una, and while the novel is clearly about sin and retribution, it is also a FAMILY drama that emphasizes the import and the power of familial ties. While

Hester and Dimmesdale must grapple with their sin, Pearl reminds readers that both Hester and Dimmesdale are parents who bear an obligation to their child. From the second chapter, the novel links Pearl and the scarlet "A" that Hester wears; both are "token[s] of [Hester's] shame." Hester emphasizes this connection by dressing Pearl in scarlet and gold, and the novel frequently reminds readers that Pearl is the scarlet letter in human form. Like her dress, Pearl's behavior also sets her apart. Pearl is impish and capricious; she is the "wild infant," the "elf-child." Many in Puritan Boston attribute Pearl's wild and uncivil behavior to her parentage. Hester remembered "talk of the neighbouring townspeople; who, seeking vainly elsewhere for the child's paternity, and observing some of her odd attributes, had given out that poor little Pearl was a demon offspring." Because of such fears, the Puritan magistrates of Boston propose to take the child from Hester.

In the face of this challenge to "a mother's rights," Hester mounts an argument to maintain custody of her child. She claims that her punishment has made her a better mother: "This badge hath taught me . . . lessons whereof my child may be the wiser and better, albeit they can profit nothing to myself." Perhaps a stronger argument for Hester's custody of Pearl can be found in the benefits that motherhood holds for Hester. Pearl becomes a kind of savior for her mother. Pearl's name tells something of Hester's feelings for her daughter and her thoughts about motherhood: "she had named the infant 'Pearl,' as being of great price,—purchased with all she had,—her mother's only treasure!" As she grows, Pearl is Hester's "sole treasure" and "all her world." As Hester faces the magistrates, she emphasizes the connection between Pearl and the scarlet letter, arguing that while humanity had marked her with the scarlet "A" as a result of her sin, God had given Pearl to her. Pearl, she argues, is her salvation:

> God gave me the child! . . . He gave her, in requital of all things else, which ye had taken from me. She is my happiness!—she is my torture, none the less! Pearl keeps me here in life! Pearl punishes me too! See ye not, she is

the scarlet letter, only capable of being loved, and so endowed with a million-fold the power of retribution for my sin?

Hester's "unquiet elements" were "soothed away by the softening influences of maternity," and Pearl keeps Hester connected to the world around her. As Hester leaves Governor Bellingham's mansion, his sister, a reputed witch, asks Hester to travel with her to the forest to meet with the devil. Hester replies, "I must tarry at home, and keep watch over my little Pearl. Had they taken her from me, I would willingly have gone with thee into the forest," to which the narrator replies, "Even thus early had the child saved her from Satan's snare."

Once the magistrates decide that Pearl should remain with Hester, Mr. Wilson asserts that "every good Christian man hath a title to show a father's kindness to the poor, deserted babe." It seems, though, that the elf-child cannot be made fully human without paternal influence. In her meetings with Reverend Dimmesdale, Pearl seems instinctively to understand their familial ties, and she challenges the minister to acknowledge their relationship publicly. As Dimmesdale, Hester, and Pearl stand together on the scaffold under the cover of night, Pearl asks, "Wilt thou stand here with mother and me, to-morrow noontide?" It is not until the novel's second-to-last chapter that Dimmesdale publicly acknowledges his relationship with Hester and Pearl. As he once again stands on the scaffold, the minister asks Pearl to kiss him, and with that kiss, the narrator says, "A spell was broken. . . . and as her tears fell upon her father's cheek, they were the pledge that she would grow up amid human joy and sorrow, nor forever do battle with the world, but be a woman in it." The novel's conclusion gives evidence that Pearl marries, becomes a mother herself, and remains mindful of her mother even after Hester returns to her seaside cottage in Boston.

Laurie A. Sterling

RELIGION in *The Scarlet Letter*

The Scarlet Letter examines and critiques the theocratic society of Puritan Boston, in which "religion and law were almost identical." Hawthorne begins this examination with the novel's first chapter, "The Prison Door," which opens with a "throng of bearded men, in sad-colored garments and steeple-crowned hats . . . assembled in front of a wooden edifice, the door of which was heavily timbered with oak, and studded with iron spikes." Both the prison and the people tell readers a great deal about the Puritans and their laws—both are hard, stern, and unyielding. The imagery Hawthorne uses in this opening chapter remains consistent throughout the novel. He repeatedly describes the Puritans and their society though imagery of darkness and hardness. The novel's first sentence also links the Puritans of Boston with Hawthorne's own Puritan ancestors, whom he describes in the novel's introductory sketch, "The Custom-House." Like his heroine, Hester Prynne, Hawthorne also feels the disapproval and the "scorn" of the "stern and black-browed Puritans," and like Hester, Hawthorne uses his *Scarlet Letter* to challenge the Puritan beliefs, attitudes, and laws.

Early in the novel the narrator emphasizes that in this period when "the forms of authority were felt to possess the sacredness of divine institutions," these Puritan leaders, though "doubtless good men," were incapable of "sitting in judgment on an erring woman's heart, and disentangling its mesh of good and evil." Not only are these men stern and unsympathetic, the novel soon reveals their hypocrisy. Puritan hypocrisy is a theme that surfaces frequently in Hawthorne's work, and it is particularly apparent in the community's use of Hester's needlework. The narrator says that "Deep ruffs, painfully wrought bands, and gorgeously embroidered gloves . . . were readily allowed to individuals dignified by rank or wealth, even while sumptuary laws forbade these and similar extravagances to the plebeian order."

It is hypocrisy that finally dooms Dimmesdale. The minister recognizes the value of publicly confessing his sin. When they meet in the forest, he tells Hester, "Happy are you, Hester, that wear the scarlet letter openly upon your bosom! Mine burns in secret!" and he later exclaims, "We are not, Hester, the worst sinners in the world." Chillingworth, he realizes, has "violated . . . the sanctity of a human heart," a transgression that Hawthorne believed

was an unpardonable sin. Despite this revelation, the minister remains unable to publicly confess his own sin until the end of the novel. Earlier, when Dimmesdale tells his congregants that he is "utterly pollution and a lie," the narrator says, "The minister well knew—subtle, but remorseful hypocrite that he was!—the light in which his vague confession would be viewed. . . . He had spoken the very truth, and transformed it into the veriest falsehood." Weakness dooms Dimmesdale to hypocrisy; he finds it impossible to live outside of the "iron framework" of Puritan society, and he confesses only in his dying moments.

In contrast to Dimmesdale, Hester's sin is clearly manifest in both the "A" and in her daughter Pearl. As the beadle leads Hester from the prison to the scaffold in chapter 2, he calls Massachusetts Bay Colony a place "where iniquity is dragged out into the sunshine." Another townsman describes it as "a land where iniquity is searched out, and punished in the sight of rulers and people." The magistrates, in placing the "A" on Hester's chest, mean to make her "a living sermon against sin." Despite this, Hester remains a constant challenge to Puritan laws and beliefs, as Hawthorne's numerous comparisons between Hester and Anne Hutchinson emphasize. A Puritan woman, Hutchinson gained a following when she began to hold weekly meetings to discuss sermons in her home. In defiance of Puritan beliefs, she began to preach salvation through faith and God's revelation to the individual through inner experience. Her popularity and her perceived heresy brought about a political crisis, and she was eventually banished from Massachusetts Bay Colony for antinomianism (being opposed to religious authority). If it were not for Pearl, the narrator says, Hester "might have come down to us in history, hand in hand with Anne Hutchinson, as the foundress of a religious sect." Like Hutchinson, Hester finds that "the world's law was no law for her." While Hester and her beliefs do not bring about the political upheaval that Hutchinson did, even at the novel's end she comforts other outcasts with "her firm belief, that, at some brighter period, when the world should have grown ripe for it, in Heaven's own time, a new truth would be revealed." And by the novel's end she seems to have brought about some change in Puritan attitudes and beliefs, for the townspeople, and even the magistrates themselves read the "A" as representing "able" and "angel."

Laurie A. Sterling

HAWTHORNE, NATHANIEL
"Young Goodman Brown" (1835, 1851)

Nathaniel Hawthorne first published the short story "Young Goodman Brown" in 1835 and it was later collected in *The Snow Image and Other Twice-Told Tales* (1852). In this story Hawthorne reveals his preoccupation with history, particularly that of Puritan New England, and issues of guilt, sin, individual conscience, and social morality. Many of these themes resurface in Hawthorne's best-known work, *The Scarlet Letter*, which is also set in Puritan New England.

In the story, the young Puritan, Goodman Brown, takes leave of his wife Faith one evening for a solitary expedition into the forest. As he ventures deeper into the wilderness, Brown encounters many of his neighbors, including the religious and political leaders of his community. All seem eager to participate in a sinister ritual in the dark woods. At an altar in the midst of the congregation, Brown sees his young wife. At the last moment, he calls upon Faith to resist temptation. Suddenly, the whole scene vanishes and the young man is left alone. But forever after that night, Brown is gloomy and distrustful, even of members of his own family.

Human nature is put to the test in this disturbing story, as Brown's perception of his experience challenges the notion that people are basically good. The story raises issues concerning INNOCENCE AND EXPERIENCE, INDIVIDUAL AND SOCIETY, RELIGION, ALIENATION, and the AMERICAN DREAM. The cost of following one's conscience is also a prominent theme here, as it is in many important works of American literature in the 19th century.

Mary Goodwin

INDIVIDUAL AND SOCIETY in "Young Goodman Brown"

A complex and problematic relationship unfolds between the individual and his society in Nathaniel Hawthorne's "Young Goodman Brown" (1835,

1851). The young Puritan Brown is confronted with troubling issues concerning his place in society. As his faith in human nature is tested in the course of an evening, Brown must decide if he is better off alone or in company. Does society offer solace and support to the individual, or only mutual guilt and fatal temptation?

The story begins as Brown embarks on what seems a solitary journey of self-discovery, taking leave of his wife Faith one night to venture into the woods on a mysterious errand. Brown soon encounters other townspeople in the forest, but the company they offer is not comforting. Brown meets a sinister older man who carries a walking stick shaped like a snake. Amiable at first, the man later tells Brown his ancestors were guilty of injustice and cruel persecution. Brown then sees Goody Cloyse, a townswoman who had taught him his catechism. In the woods, however, the old woman expresses great enthusiasm for witchcraft and dark rituals. As Brown reaches a clearing, he sees many other townspeople gathered for a mysterious ceremony. Standing at the altar, Brown discovers his young wife is also beside him. At the last minute, he calls out to Faith to resist the temptation of evil. Suddenly everything vanishes and he is left alone. The narrator raises the possibility that Brown has dreamed it all; nevertheless, ever after this night, the young man holds himself apart from other townspeople, suspecting all of secret sin. He is a stranger even to his wife, and maintains a gloomy solitude for the rest of his life. The effect of his experience is to make society hateful to him.

The plot seems to follow a typical rite of passage, in which a young person leaves his community and undergoes experiences that help him mature. Upon his return, he takes his place as an adult in the community. But in Hawthorne's tale, society seems to offer the individual not comfort, stability, or salvation but rather guilt, complicity, and moral ruin. Early in his journey Brown expresses fears of the "Indians" in the forest. Soon, however, he learns that the real threat is from his own townspeople, even the most apparently respectable among them. Brown's experience may help him to "grow up," but it makes him unsuited for his community.

Issues of religion and social interaction intersect in the story. As the Puritan church is based on the

Calvinist conviction of the total depravity of human-kind, so Brown, after witnessing the secret evil of the townspeople, ends convinced that "evil is the nature of mankind." In this story, the good and the wicked are mixed together in an abased version of democracy, and the wicked inevitably corrupt the good, as seems the case with Brown's wife Faith. The community is prone to violence and mass hysteria, as demonstrated in the witch-hunts in which Brown's ancestors participated. These themes are also central to Hawthorne's most famous novel, *The Scarlet Letter*.

The story seems to mock American political ideals as well. Community bonds in early America were described in terms like "covenant," "communion," and "congregation," but this lexicon is perverted in Hawthorne's story, and "congregation" becomes coven or den of evil. The challenge of American civil life has always been in how to balance the needs of the individual against the good of the group. The new democracy had to be forged by common consent, by people working together. But it is very difficult to achieve social cohesion if, as Hawthorne's story suggests, you cannot trust your neighbor.

The story seems to offer the possibility of individual salvation, even in the face of a corrupt society. Brown's ability to resist the ominous ritual seems to save him; the dark vision disappears and he is left alone. Brown makes his own decision regarding his fate in rejecting what he perceives as evil in society. However, the result is that Brown becomes estranged from the townspeople, even from his own family. This suggests that the cost of the individual's decision to follow his or her conscience is social ostracism.

Much American literature, especially in the 19th century, is concerned with the issue of individual conscience and its cost. In essays and fiction, writers like Emerson, Thoreau, Hawthorne, Melville, and Twain exhorted readers to follow their own sense of right, even if it meant acting counter to the interests and wishes of the majority.

Mary Goodwin

Innocence and Experience in "Young Goodman Brown"

As Hawthorne's tale begins, young Goodman Brown sets off on a solitary expedition into a dark, forbidding forest. Brown is a Puritan "everyman," and his journey can be seen as an initiation into knowledge and experience of the world along the road of life. In tracing the chronological progress of Brown's life from young adulthood to old age and the grave, the story charts the effects of his experience on his character and convictions.

But Brown's journey does not proceed as the reader might expect. In the first place, the young man sets forth at sunset, a time of day associated with the onset of old age and death rather than new beginnings. It is also strange that the newlywed Brown leaves his young wife, Faith, behind, rebuffing her when she tries to persuade him to stay the night with her. And although he seems willing to make the trip, Brown at times expresses reluctance to proceed on what he refers to as his "evil" mission. His journey is thus a solitary and troubling undertaking in which he moves further and further away from "faith."

As Brown travels deeper into the forest, he encounters other travelers who unsettle rather than comfort him with their company. His first companion is an older man who carries a staff in the shape of a snake. This sinister person says that he had known Brown's ancestors, shocking the young man by revealing that his forebears had not been good Christians at all but oppressive and cruel. The man also claims that he is on intimate terms with many others in Brown's community who are respected for their high position and apparently unimpeachable character. An old woman who had taught Brown his catechism appears in the forest, and the young man is disturbed by her eagerness to join the sinister occasion of the night. The stranger with the staff warns Brown that everyone, no matter how pure or venerable in appearance, harbors secrets of evil deeds. The final blow to Brown's innocent, naïve faith in the goodness of human nature comes with the evidence that his wife is among the nighttime congregation. Spying a pink ribbon of the sort that Faith wears on her cap, Brown declares that the world is an evil place and belongs to the devil. He rushes into what appears to be a witches' mass in the forest, and sees his wife there. They stand together to be joined in an unholy marriage attended by those townsfolk he had once respected.

Brown loses the innocence of his youthful convictions at this altar. Later, after he returns to the village, he suspects everyone he meets of secret vice, coldly rejecting even the tender touch of his young wife. His mood darkens over the course of his life and he dies a gloomy old man.

In the span of a night, Brown learns that youth is not necessarily innocent, nor age venerable and wise. He goes to his grave convinced that human nature is evil and human beings are easy prey to temptation, even those whose hearts are as pure as his wife's. Hawthorne's tale thus seems to accord with the Puritan view of human nature as corrupt and innately depraved, stained by the original sin of Adam and Eve. With Brown the reader may suspect that "sin is but a name" and innocence merely an illusion.

However, this interpretation is twisted by hints in the last paragraphs that Goodman Brown has dreamed the whole episode. Beside Faith at the fateful altar, Brown had exhorted her to look to heaven. At that moment, the entire sinister congregation had vanished and Brown was left alone in the forest. In suggesting that Brown dreamed it all, the narrator implies that the young man made up his own mind to distrust others, possibly projecting his own sense of guilt onto those around him.

The ambiguous ending thus allows a variety of interpretations of the tale. Perhaps we are meant to understand that the world is not an innocent place, a somber lesson taught through hard experience of evil. Or the tale may teach that the experience of life is what one makes of it, with innocence and guilt only matters of perspective shaped by temperament and circumstance. Another possibility is that the loss of faith leads to a loss of innocence. Hawthorne seems to entertain all of these possibilities in this and other important works.

Mary Goodwin

RELIGION in "Young Goodman Brown"

A major theme in Nathaniel Hawthorne's story "Young Goodman Brown" is the place of religion in American life. Although it was written in the 19th century, the story is set 200 years earlier, in a Puritan community in colonial Massachusetts. The Puritans' Massachusetts Bay Colony was a theocracy, meaning a community in which the state is dominated by a church, and civil law has its basis in religious law (in the Puritans' case, biblical law). In such a place, religion naturally plays a dominant role in many aspects of life.

"Young Goodman Brown" reflects the importance of matters of faith in daily life in that period, with key plot events stressing in particular the social aspects of religion. Goodman Brown, a young member of a Puritan community, leaves his wife Faith one night to embark on a mysterious mission into the forest near his village. On his way out of town he passes the meetinghouse, which is the Puritan place of worship and the center of social life for the community. This landmark serves to remind the reader of the deeply communal nature of the Puritan religion. The matter of social interaction in church activities takes on deeper meaning as Brown travels into the woods: He starts out alone but soon encounters other townspeople, all of whom he identifies as members of his church. There is Goody Cloyse, an old woman who had taught Brown his catechism. The young man also spies the town's minister and deacon in the woods. Brown has always thought of his neighbors as pious, upstanding members of the community. Now he is shocked to find them all in the woods on the same dark mission, apparently bound for a witches' mass.

The social aspects of religion in the story encompass history, including that of Brown's family. On his way into the forest, Brown is met by a sinister old man, a devil-like figure holding a staff that resembles a snake. The man tells Brown that he knew his ancestors to be cruel persecutors, not the good Christians Brown had thought them to be. He also tells Brown that many pious-seeming townspeople are stained with secret sin. Brown's conversation with the old man points to the hypocrisy at the heart of Puritan religious practice.

Hawthorne's story explores the deeply personal as well as social aspects of religion. Although shocked to discover that his townspeople are hypocritical sinners, Brown is himself in the forest bent on some dark purpose, which raises questions about his own moral credibility. Brown's mission is a kind of religious parody: In order to pursue his "quest," he must leave behind Faith—his wife—and, apparently, his beliefs and moral convictions. His destination is a sinister altar, a parody of a church gathering. For Brown the experience in the woods has a pernicious influence on his own spiritual development; after that night, his faith in religion and in other people, including his wife, is destroyed. Concluding that the world is evil, Brown goes to his grave a bitter old man.

Personal choice in matters of faith seems an important issue in the story, with the individual urged to follow his conscience even if it means standing in opposition to his community. Brown has a choice of whether or not to enter the forest and take part in the ritual. At the dark altar, when he thinks he sees the shade of his mother urging him to resist evil, he cries out to his wife. At that moment, the scene vanishes and Brown is left to wonder whether he only dreamed it.

However, following his conscience and making the "right" decision doesn't guarantee Brown a happy life; rather, the experience causes him to lose faith in humanity. Saved from one evil, he is, as a consequence, poisoned to life and human society. The story hints at the insufficiency of moral religious life, either as a means to root evil out of the human heart, or as a comfort to the righteous individual who turns away from corrupt human society.

In "Young Goodman Brown," issues of religion and faith touch all aspects of a person's life, as an individual, in the family, and as a member of society. In this story religion is trailed by its shadow, the sinister secret desires of the heart. As in Hawthorne's famous novel *The Scarlet Letter,* which is also set in Puritan New England, the quest for meaning in life is woven into issues of religion and faith, with the individual faced with the difficult decision of standing alone against his community.

Mary Goodwin

HELLER, JOSEPH   *Catch-22*   (1961)

Catch-22 is a brilliant satire of the military that illustrates the darkly humorous side of the insanity that is warfare. No organization or institution is safe from the ire of Heller's pen. He sends up the military bureaucracy, free-market enterprise, organized RELIGION, and SOCIAL CLASS.

Catch-22 is the story of John Yossarian and his quest to survive World War II. He has only one problem: Catch-22. Catch-22 is the military bureaucratic rule that states that any soldier must be removed from combat duty if he is deemed insane; however, removing oneself from an endless continuation of suicidal missions is an act that proves a soldier is sane enough to continue to fly and fight. This institutional catch traps Yossarian on the island of Pianosa in perpetual danger, as the war rages on and thousands of people whom he has never met are trying to kill him.

Catch-22 is a landmark of American fiction, one of the rare works of literature that defined a century and introduced a new term into the lexicon of the English language. Heller's masterful and humorous condemnation of warfare continues to entertain, inspire, and educate readers from the high school senior to the retiree.

Heller's comedic portrayal of men seeking only to survive and those who seek only to profit from the iniquities of humanity destroys the fallacy that war is romantic and for all time defines SURVIVAL as the one true heroic act of war.

Drew McLaughlin

HEROISM in *Catch-22*

Catch-22 is a story of heroes and cowards. The island of Pianosa, the fictional setting of the novel, is populated by a motley crew of cowardly heroes and heroic cowards. Such is the maddening, paradoxical world of *Catch-22.*

John Yossarian is an unlikely protagonist, a bombardier by trade, a coward by nature. He is heroic through his cowardice. Yossarian is driven by one thing: SURVIVAL. He is described as having given up his soldierly mission in favor of saving himself. "Yossarian was a lead bombardier who had been demoted because he no longer gave a damn whether he missed or not. He had decided to live forever or die in the attempt, and his only mission each time he went up was to come down alive" (29). Yossarian lies and schemes his way out of combat duty and into the hospital, always searching and exhausting every opportunity to escape the clutches of Catch-22. He thinks,

There was only one catch and that was Catch-22, which specified that a concern for one's own safety in the face of dangers that were real and immediate was the process of a rational mind. Orr was crazy and could be grounded. All he had to do was ask; and as soon as he did, he would no longer be crazy and would have to fly more missions . . . Yossarian was moved very deeply by the absolute simplicity of this clause of Catch-22.

Catch-22 imprisons Yossarian through his own rationality. Yossarian's recognition of the insanity of his predicament proves his sanity.

Yossarian battles not only Catch-22, but also Colonel Cathcart, his commanding officer. Cathcart is a cowardly hero. An officer devoted to duty, country, and winning the war would not normally invite admonition; however, whereas Yossarian is driven by self-preservation, Cathcart is driven by self-promotion. He wants to receive a promotion to general. He is unconcerned with the mental or physical welfare of his men, and seeks only fame and glory in his petulant drive for career advancement. To achieve his goal, he volunteers his squadron for only the most dangerous missions, increasing the unit's medals and citations; he cares little about completing a successful mission and more about collecting great aerial photographs of bombing runs, and continually raises the number of missions required of the squadron before any member is permitted an honorable discharge.

Whenever Yossarian nears the magic number, Cathcart raises the mission total and Yossarian's subsequent refusal to fly into danger in perpetuity keeps him in the air. Every mission Yossarian flies increases the likelihood of his death, and he soon realizes Cathcart will never allow him to achieve his discharge through the bureaucratic system, which forces Yossarian to become inventive in order to skirt the letter of Catch-22 in order to survive.

Yossarian's refusal to fly any more missions affects the unit's morale: "Morale was deteriorating and it was all Yossarian's fault. The country was in peril; he was jeopardizing his traditional rights of freedom and democracy by daring to exercise them." Cathcart attempts to bribe Yossarian, promising to send him home if he agrees to "like" the colonel and not tell the squadron that he is being sent home

as a result of his defiance. Also, Yossarian will be promoted, given another medal for valor, and hailed as a "hero" back in the States. Cathcart hopes that Yossarian's "heroics" will inspire the men to fly more missions, amplifying the colonel's chances for promotion.

Yossarian flirts with the idea, but ultimately rejects the colonel's offer. To surrender his beliefs would be a capitulation to Cathcart, and a victory for the proprietors of the army bureaucracy and the creators and enforcers of Catch-22. He says,

> I've flown over seventy goddam combat missions. Don't talk to me about fighting to save my country. I've been fighting all along to save my country. Now I'm going to fight a little to save myself. The country's not in danger anymore, but I am, . . .
>
> . . . The Germans will be beaten in a few months. And Japan will be beaten a few months after that. If I were to give up my life now, it wouldn't be for my country. It would be for Cathcart. So I'm turning my bombsight in for the duration.

Cornered, unable to outwit the system, Yossarian comes to understand that his only true option is to run away. Yossarian displays the courage necessary to defy his commander, his army, and his country in order to save his own life. Yossarian flees Pianosa to Sweden. His most heroic action is this desertion.

Catch-22 finds heroism in cowardice. The insanity of war compels men and women to act to achieve contradictory ends and relinquish individuality to preserve independence. They must kill in order to save. Yossarian's desertion is justified because in the end there are no heroes or cowards, nor saints or sinners, there are only men, fighting for the most fundamental of human values, not for any idealistic notions of independence and patriotism, but for life itself. After all, survival is the one true heroic act of war.

Drew McLaughlin

RELIGION in *Catch-22*

In times of war, soldiers may turn to their faith to cope with the horrors they see and the deaths of their closest brothers-in-arms. *Catch-22* examines this source of solace and also explores its limits. Not only do combat soldiers question their own faith, but they also doubt the proprietors of the faith sent to minister to the men.

There's an old saying, "There are no atheists in foxholes." Atheists and the devout populate the island of Pianosa equally in *Catch-22*. *Catch-22*'s treatment of religion and faith is both comical and tragic. Yossarian is a devout atheist who believes in an incompetent creator. He attacks an entity he does not believe exists for allowing such CRUELTY and inhumanity in His finest creation, which is supposed to be reflective of Himself. Yossarian says to Lieutenant Scheisskopf's wife, an unbeliever as well, "What a colossal immortal blunderer! When you consider the opportunity and power He had to really do a job, and then look at the stupid, ugly little mess He made of it instead. His sheer incompetence is almost staggering." She retorts that the God that she doesn't believe in is merciful and kind. Faith and God provide no consolation to Yossarian, but rather an outlet to vent his frustration at the war, Cathcart, and Catch-22. He views God as part of the problem, not the solution, and his atheistic views are not altered by the end of the novel.

The chaplain, of course, begins the novel as a believer. His spiritual decline begins as he sees the military bureaucracy led by Colonel Cathcart corrupt faith and exploit it for their personal advancement. At one point, Cathcart summons the chaplain and tells him he wants to start a prayer session before every mission not for any altruistic goal of consoling the men before they fly off to fight and perhaps die, but so they will bomb more effectively.

> Now, I want you to give a lot of thought to the kind of prayers we're going to say. I don't want anything heavy or sad. I'd like you to keep it light and snappy, something that will send the boys out feeling pretty good . . . Your job is to lead us in prayer, and from now on you're going to lead us in prayer for a tighter bomb pattern before every mission. Is that clear?

Cathcart seizes religion and faith as a weapon of war and manipulates the chaplain, a man of God and peace, to support and direct the killing of men and women with divine consent. The chaplain's faith begins to unravel as he sees how even pure faith can be corrupted, and he struggles to understand the inverted values of war, where killing is considered a virtue.

The chaplain begins to questions if there is even a God, as Yossarian does, and if so, how could he ever be sure of His existence. He thinks, "*Was* there a true faith, or a life after death? With what matters *did* God occupy Himself in all the infinite aeons before the Creation."

The chaplain resents the ALIENATION that accompanies his calling and his commission. The soldiers act and speak differently around him because he is the "chaplain," and that ISOLATION furthers his doubts. He begins to wonder if he wouldn't have been better off enlisting in the infantry and taking his chances. He begins to doubt the foundations of the Christian faith, thinking,

> There was the Bible, of course, but the Bible was a book and so were *Bleak House, Treasure Island, Ethan Frome,* and *The Last of the Mohicans.* Did it indeed seem probable, as he had once overheard Dunbar ask, that the answers to the riddles of creation would be supplied by people too ignorant to understand the mechanics of rainfall? There were no miracles; prayers went unanswered, and misfortune tramped with equal brutality on the virtuous and the corrupt.

The joy with which people like Milo and Cathcart inflict suffering with impunity and the way they exploit the war for profit and career ascent, pushes the chaplain to question everything he has come to believe and to serve.

The destructive nature of war knows no boundaries. Human life, human sanity, a foundational faith in the kindness of humanity, and even institutionalized religion are not beyond the domain of the carnage—they are just casualties of war.

Drew McLaughlin

SUFFERING in *Catch-22*

DEATH and suffering are constant and inescapable realities of war. Their specters haunt all soldiers and break many psychologically. It is common to all theaters of war in all times, from the jungles of Vietnam, the sands of Iraq, the mountains of Afghanistan, or 30,000 feet above Earth where John Yossarian, the hero of *Catch-22,* encounters death and suffering on a daily basis as a bombardier on a B-24.

Yossarian and his squadron are stationed and imprisoned on the island of Pianosa, off the coast of Greece, by their certifiable commander and the simplistic lunacy of Catch-22. The catch is that any person who continues to fly bombing missions in the face of certain death is insane and as such entitled to be relieved of duty; however, any person who recognizes the truth of the situation and requests to be removed from flight status for that reason must be sane enough to fly. Catch-22 traps Yossarian and his squadron on interminable flight duty, unable to go home until they fly the requisite number of missions or they die trying. Yossarian comes to realize that the only avenue of escape is death because the squadron commander, Colonel Cathcart, always raises the total number of missions one has to fly as soon as someone nears the mark.

Throughout the novel, Yossarian hatches a series of schemes to escape the brutal realities of war, but the suffering and death surround him, whether he is in the air, in the hospital, or in his bunk. Mudd, referred to throughout the novel as "the dead guy in Yossarian's tent," is killed on a mission before the military bureaucracy actually processed him as a member of the squadron, and he is never listed as having arrived. Mudd becomes an invisible man who is dead, but not declared dead, and no one in the unit retains the authority to remove his personal belongings from Yossarian's tent. This is one of the constant reminders of death that Yossarian deals with in *Catch-22.*

Yossarian constantly evades active duty by claiming to be ill. He spends days on end in the hospital with mysterious ILLNESSes that the doctors cannot diagnose or treat. While lying in the hospital, Yossarian encounters the soldier in white, a man with no name and bandaged from head to toe. "The soldier in white was encased from head to toe in plaster and gauze. He had two useless legs and two useless arms." The soldier in white dies and is replaced by another, although everyone in the hospital assumes it is the same person, which signifies the perpetual, anonymous casualties that war inflicts.

Yossarian witnesses other tragic events more directly in *Catch-22.* McWatt, a daredevil pilot who seldom follows orders, buzzes the beach as a stunt but accidentally flies too close and slices Kid Sampson in half with the propeller of his B-24. McWatt, consumed by guilt and regret, crashes his plane into the side of a mountain. Nately is a patriotic 19-year-old in love with a prostitute in Rome. He completes his required 70 missions but will not return home until he can bring his lover with him. Yossarian pleads with him in vain, but Nately volunteers to fly Milo Minderbender's missions for him. Nately is killed on a bombing mission along with 12 other men.

These tragic deaths contribute to Yossarian's suffering, but Snowden's death, by far, makes a more devastating imprint. Snowden's death is a marker in the novel. Unable to forget and incapable of moving on, Yossarian recalls his death continually. The gory circumstances of Snowden's death are gradually revealed as the story progresses.

On a bombing raid against Avignon, Snowden is wounded by artillery flak, and Yossarian crawls into the tail of the plane to tend to his wounds. Yossarian consoles Snowden, who repeatedly cries out that he's cold, as Yossarian dresses the gaping wound in Snowden's leg. Yossarian assures Snowden that he will live until he notices blood trickling out from under Snowden's bomber jacket. The narrator describes Snowden's death:

Yossarian ripped open the snaps of Snowden's flak suit and heard himself scream wildly as Snowden's insides slithered down to the floor in a soggy pile and just kept dripping out. A chunk of flak more than three inches big had shot into the other side just underneath the arm and blasted all the way through, drawing whole mottled quarts of Snowden along with it through the gigantic hole in his ribs it made as it blasted out. Yossarian screamed a second time and squeezed both hands over his eyes. His teeth were chattering in horror . . . Here was God's plenty, all right, he thought bitterly as he stared—liver, lungs, kidneys, ribs, stomach, and bits of the stewed tomatoes Snowden had eaten that day for lunch.

Snowden dies in Yossarian's arms as he helplessly consoles Snowden in his final moments with the words, "there, there," because that is all he can think to say.

This grisly scene robs Yossarian of his courage, nearly captures his sanity, and finally forces him to see the fragility of life and the utter insanity of war. Snowden's death propels Yossarian on his crusade of self-preservation at all costs. He ultimately escapes the clutches of Catch-22 by essentially quitting the war. He flees to neutral Sweden, because he will not sponsor Colonels Cathcart and Corn's plan to saddle the squadron with 80 missions in exchange for his discharge. To save his life, his honor, and the respect of the squadron, he deserts.

Suffering and death in war is often meaningless despite its great consequences; however, sometimes death can be redemptive. Snowden's death galvanizes Yossarian and empowers him to save his own life.

Drew McLaughlin

HEMINGWAY, ERNEST *A Farewell to Arms* (1929)

Written in 1929, *A Farewell to Arms* is the semi-autobiographical story of an American, Lieutenant Frederic Henry, and his love affair with his British nurse, Catherine Barkley. Lieutenant Henry (often referred to in the novel as *tenente*, Italian for "lieutenant") is an ambulance driver near the Italian-Austrian Front in World War I. He is injured in an Austrian mortar attack, and during his convalescence in Milan, he woos and becomes lovers with Catherine, a nurse transferred to Milan from the previous town where the two met. He returns to the front, where a retreat is sounded; due to a series of missteps and dangerous double-crossings, he deserts the Italian army. Surreptitiously collecting Catherine from her new post, they go to Switzerland together. Escaping the war, they wait out Catherine's pregnancy; in childbirth, both she and the baby die. But the book is far more than just the elements of this plot.

Hemingway took his real-life experience as a 19-year-old ambulance driver in World War I, the injuries he sustained in a mortar attack, along with the extended hospitalization and physical therapy that followed, and a brief love affair with an older nurse, and turned these events into one of the great novels of the 20th century. *A Farewell to Arms* is, in part, about the adventures of Lieutenant Henry and his affairs in war-torn Europe, but it is also a personal exploration of the soldier, wanting to see action, adventure, and life but stuck in the violent, depressing, immoral, unanticipated realities of wartime. Hemingway captures the relationship between the man and the war in intimate, and often profound, ways as he risks the rejection of the glories of war for the more human, and possibly more tragic, intimacies of husband and father.

Aaron Drucker

NATIONALISM in *A Farewell to Arms*

In *A Farewell to Arms,* Hemingway evokes a running commentary on nationalism through ridicule and omission. This may best be described as an anti-nationalistic impulse in the book, but one that never quite reaches the sense that nationalism is negative so much as it is not held in particularly high esteem. Lieutenant Henry represents, almost by definition, a problematic position. He is an American in the Italian army. Rather than defending his country, the rights of his men, the land of his birth, he is saving strangers as a kind of adventure and romance. His compatriots are Italian, and they fight to hold the line against Austrian incursion. Of one fellow soldier, Lieutenant Henry notes, "Gino was born a patriot, so he said things that separated us sometimes, but he was also a fine boy and I understood his being a patriot. He was born one." Neither adhering to Americanism nor evolving an expatriate's sense of Eurocentrism, Lieutenant Henry's presence in the Italian army explicitly questions the value and ethics of nationalism.

There is no compelling explanation for why Lieutenant Henry is in Italy fighting for the Allies. At the outset of the novel, the Americans have yet to enter World War I. It is not that Lieutenant Henry feels particularly obliged by conscience to fight against the Austrians and Germans. To be sure, he chose the side that opposed military expansion, but it all seems a grand adventure. Catherine Barkley asks him, "Why did you do it?" He claims not to know. Ms. Barkley, like his readers, should be skeptical. Nonetheless, his response is notable for its lack of rationale. He places himself in mortal danger, driving from the front lines of active battle back to hospitals and stations, through difficult (and sometimes impassable) terrain, under fire and exposed to the constant threat of injury or DEATH. And yet he offers no reason for it. There is no history to dictate his dedication to this cause. His family is not recently immigrated. His home is neither affected nor in danger due to the war. There is no apparent need for his presence at the front. Yet he comes to Italy to seek out a position in the Italian army.

Although nationalism can be hard to define, some would call it the (often) extreme dedication to patriotic feeling, principles, or efforts. Putting one's life on the line for a national cause is the textbook instance. Austria and Germany are invading Italy, and Gino, Rinaldi, the priest, and the other officers are fighting for their homes. Their cause is personal and patriotic. They are passionate in their nationalism. Even nurse Barkley joined the war effort because her life and home are threatened (Britain is also at war with Germany). In the end, however, it is Lieutenant Henry's story, and Hemingway's choice of narrator dictates the polemic of the novel's perspective. While Lieutenant Henry never explicitly takes a position on nationalism, it is clear from his attitude that he is not nationalistic but believes himself motivated by a higher calling.

For Lieutenant Henry, nationalism, and its personal counterpoint of "patriotism," is at best an excuse and at worst a compulsion. He finds the label useful only to withdraw funds against his grandfather's goodwill. He poses the rhetorical question of whether or not his grandfather can morally send him to jail rather than give him the money. Clearly, however, such "sight drafts" are a manipulation of the nationalistic impulse of his grandfather. Though Lieutenant Henry may be doing the right thing in engaging in the war, his motive for using the patriotic sympathies of his family and friends is manipulative. Beyond the simple utility of nationalistic rhetoric, it holds little value for the lieutenant.

If nationalism is not used to better his own situation, it is the force by which otherwise peaceful men are conscripted and condemned. In a short conversation with an orderly at the convalescent hospital, Lieutenant Henry offers a compelling rationale for those who would make war versus those who would otherwise be peaceful: "But [those who make war] make them do it . . . And the ones who would not make war? Can they stop it?" The orderly responds, "They are not organized to stop things and when they get organized their leaders sell them out." Nationalism leads to conscription, then. Perhaps there are better reasons than nationalism to fight and defend one's home (family, heroism, masculinity to name a few), but invoking love of the land upon which you happen to be born is only rhetoric and propaganda.

Aaron Drucker

PARENTHOOD in *A Farewell to Arms*

At its end, World War I was the deadliest international conflict in history. It was called "The War to End All Wars." The second half of the novel *A Farewell to Arms* chronicles the romance of Lieutenant Frederic Henry and nurse Catherine Barkley. The affair begins as such wartime romances do: a friendly meeting, growing closer, an injury, the recovery, and finally the passionate exchange. Catherine becomes pregnant with Lieutenant Henry's child; after a series of unfortunate events, they decide to desert their posts in Italy, have their child, and move to America. Their son, the product of their passion in a time of fear and VIOLENCE, is meant to grow and thrive in the aftermath of the decimation of Europe. But in the face of destruction, desertion, and ISOLATION, life proves too difficult to sustain. In war, all life is stillborn.

Joking as they make their escape, Lieutenant Henry assures Catherine, "Rowing in moderation is very good for the pregnant lady." They cross into Switzerland to escape the war and begin their life as a family. At the onset of book 5, the reader rejoins the couple settling into a routine of lazy ease near Montreux. They have thwarted the deadly insanity of war. "We had a fine life," Lieutenant Henry extols. "We lived through the months of January and February and the winter was very fine and we were very happy." Throughout the last few chapters of the novel, however, there is an insistent insecurity about the promise of new life. Once labor begins, Lieutenant Henry is gripped by foreboding. "People don't die in childbirth nowadays. That was what all husbands thought. Yes, but what if she should die? She won't die. She's just having a bad time." Birth is the beginning, the first moment of life; the world is new and full of wonder. But for Lieutenant Henry, it is "the byproduct of good nights in Milan," the last vestiges of a life marked by violence and pain. The nights themselves were aberrances, punctuated notes of joy and pleasure breaking the monotony, agony, and omnipresent fear. What was meant to be harmless fun becomes a lifetime commitment, no matter how much of a blessing it might be, and Lieutenant Henry is left powerless. Birth, for Lieutenant Henry, represents all that is outside of his control: Catherine, marriage, children, the future, life, and DEATH. The relentless back and forth in his mind, the agitation that cannot be satisfied by simple satiation, and the separation between self and situation each manifest as a commentary on Lieutenant Henry's inability to cope with a future that is entirely beyond his control. The story happens around him, is described by him, but never happens to him. Unlike the war, this is Catherine's story as much as Lieutenant Henry's, and this frustrates him. His anxiety is relieved after certain tragedy: The baby is stillborn, Catherine dies, and only Lieutenant Frederic Henry remains. Birth is the tragic reminder that happiness is beyond control. It is outside the self, coming from loved ones and bright futures and goodly promises. In the stillborn birth of his son, Lieutenant Henry recaptures his own life, his own days, and his own, solitary destiny.

The reader should be reminded that the novel itself is a fictionalized account of Hemingway's wartime adventures, including a romance with a mysterious nurse. The real-life drama ended rather prosaically, but in the reimagined world of the heroic Lieutenant Henry, Hemingway builds to a climax both tragic and philosophical. Both his son and Catherine die in childbirth, victims of circumstance (and possibly medical malpractice). But there is a definite ambivalence in Hemingway's portrayal of birth. The closer to reality it comes, the further the prose seems to separate from the characters. Lieu-

tenant Henry's descriptions become more abstracted from the moment. There is a palpable sense of distance between the narrator and his story. The first three-quarters of the novel show a very present Lieutenant Henry: aware, engaged, sporting. He is always in the moment. But as the lieutenant and his consort escape the wartime drama, it becomes a tale of minutiae. He spends a full chapter on the quality of his beard. The pacing is uneven. Time snaps forward in fits and starts, until the protracted birth sequence, during which Hemingway attempts to capture the anxiety of being in the other room. Life goes on behind closed doors. Drama and tragedy occur off-stage, as the reader waits with the audience for the action to unfold. This gives the anticipation of birth a quality of distance and paranoia that produces the sense of relief when Lieutenant Henry is informed that his child is stillborn and his lover will soon die. Instead of the shock of tragedy, Lieutenant Henry's narration is saddened but distant; he is a victim unburdened of responsibility. He leaves the war with nothing but a gentle limp. The war promised him heroism, valor, machismo, a wife, and a child but delivered nothing. Its promise is stillborn.

Aaron Drucker

SURVIVAL in *A Farewell to Arms*

"Survival" is the only word in a time of war. Hollywood has spent the past century glamorizing war: the challenges, the heroism, the victories. While recent renditions of war have made the effort to make the terror, demoralization, and VIOLENCE more visceral to the modern audience, the narrative of the war hero-protagonist victorious against overwhelming obstacles is still the standard. *A Farewell to Arms* makes a different claim. For Lieutenant Henry and his fellow soldiers in the Italian army, World War I is neither heroic nor valorous. Men sit together and try to pass the time, with their world punctuated by violent, senseless attacks and counterattacks in order to gain, and then lose, a few hundred meters of hillside. These men might be fighting for country, honor, duty, or idealism, but ultimately they simply strive to survive the experience. Hemingway understands that survival requires a vision of the future and the confidence and desire that there will be a tomorrow.

Hemingway casts survival in two basic frames: "life and death" and "day-to-day." The story begins in a relatively pleasant village (Gorizia) close to the front lines, where active fighting is common. Henry, being an ambulance driver, needs to be near the front but far enough away that the field hospital to which he ferries the wounded will not be shelled. The town is usually quiet and days largely consist of idle conversation and some relatively innocent trash talk. Lieutenant Henry reports on conversations where the priest is often teased, his purity is set against a ribald desire for the good humor of the other men. Such idle back-and-forth allows the soldiers and civilian support to build a rapport, and it passes the time and becomes ritual in a world turned upside down. Ritual helps the men order the world, recast the day-to-day experiences and expectations from the mundane life of tailoring or farming into the mess hall as they come from the battlefield. Rituals like the mocking of the priest give order to the chaotic experience of the battlefield. When such rituals break down, so do the men.

When Henry returns from his injuries, he quickly discovers that his compatriots are deeply demoralized. Upon his return, he is greeted with friendly conversations, but they tend toward the serious and philosophical. The men talk in quieter tones, one-on-one. Henry meets with the priest, then passes Rinaldi, then Gino jokes with him, but the puns fall flat. The officers have given up on their rituals and fallen despondent during Lieutenant Henry's absence. Their desire to survive has almost completely eroded in the absence of sustaining routines. "There isn't anything more," the priest says. "Except victory. It may be worse." Henry responds, "I don't believe in victory anymore." And the priest rejoins, "I don't. But I don't believe in defeat either. Though it may be better." Defeat brings an end to the suffering, the doldrums of the day-to-day horror of war. Defeat brings death; victory means survival and more fighting. When survival is the object of dread, even the shepherd of the soul is lost to the nihilism of war.

While Hemingway writes about the fragility of the social and religious coping mechanisms for survival, he does offer one consistent possibility for his protagonist (and thus his reader). Lieutenant Henry is seriously injured in a mortar attack at the front. He is shuttled to the local hospital, then to a better hospital in Milan. It is not until Catherine joins him there that his survival is ensured. "God knows I had not wanted to fall in love with her. I had not wanted to fall in love with anyone. But God knows I had and I lay on the bed in the room of the hospital in Milan and all sorts of things went through my head but I felt wonderful and finally Miss Gage came in." The doctor who would perform the successful surgery on his leg had arrived. Love, intentional or not, proffers the hope for survival. But Hemingway's alternative to society, religion, and ritual is a bright, hot, and all-too-brief flame.

All one can do is survive a war. There is no safety. No one leaves unscathed. The action of the novel breaks away from the fighting during a temporary retreat. Lieutenant Henry and Catherine diverge from the road their comrades follow only to discover that there is no safety in escape. They survive the war only to be confronted with the simple reality that everyone who is born dies. Ultimately the survival rate for all men is zero. Lieutenant Henry leaves the field alive. He is a survivor, but at the cost of everything, most especially hope in the promise of tomorrow. Hemingway leaves his protagonist and his reader without a future, merely alive. Survival: It may be worse.

Aaron Drucker

HEMINGWAY, ERNEST *The Old Man and the Sea* (1952)

The Old Man and the Sea was first published in the September 1 issue of *Life* magazine in 1952. Two years later it was the only novel to receive explicit mention by the Swedish Academy when they awarded Hemingway the Nobel Prize for literature. Set in a Cuban fishing town, the short novel tells the story of an old man, Santiago, and his four-day-long, perilous, solo pursuit of a great fish.

Santiago's past is full of hardships, yet his bad luck has not made him weary of life. His body shows the traces of years of strenuous work, but his friendship with the boy, Manolin, and their talk of baseball, the lottery, and fishing reveal a persevering vibrancy in the old man. It is their close friendship that seems to keep Santiago alive throughout the novel, even when he is alone in his skiff. The old man's life also depends on the sea. This deep connection becomes literal when he hooks his great fish. If the old man shares a tempered optimism with the boy, he shares a wild desperation with the fish, as they pull each other through the Gulf Stream and toward death. When he returns to the island, both man and marlin have been torn to pieces. Still, Santiago, with the support of Manolin, has triumphed over the sea, loneliness, and even death.

The Old Man and the Sea presents themes such as NATURE, ISOLATION, and STAGES OF LIFE, in multifaceted and complex ways, making the simplicity of the novel's plot and language as deceptive as the tranquil surface of the sea.

Japhet Johnstone

ISOLATION in *The Old Man and the Sea*

Ernest Hemingway's *The Old Man and the Sea* paints an ominous picture of isolation. The old man, Santiago, lives a solitary life in a shack, with a dilapidated skiff for his livelihood and one friend, the boy Manolin, to keep him company. His journey at sea isolates him even more, as he goes "beyond all people" in search of a great fish. Far out in his boat isolation also creeps into the old man's dreams. However, *The Old Man and the Sea* does not create an image of total isolation. The old man is never completely alone, and the bleak images of isolation make his bonds of kinship with the world stand out all the brighter.

The old man's life on the island is isolated both socially and economically from the other fishermen and villagers. Foremost, he has no family. A photograph of his deceased wife serves as a reminder of this loss, but he keeps it under a clean shirt because the sight of the photograph makes him too lonely. Without a family the old man seems all the more lonesome in contrast to Manolin. The boy's family dictates his behavior and influences his opinions. His family is a living part of his world, not something he can hide away. There is no such influence over the old man's decision-making, except maybe a desire for economic ease. As a fisherman, he must catch fish to make a living. Since at the beginning of the story he has not caught a fish in 84 days, his financial resources are lower than ever. He lights no fire at night. He would have little to eat if the boy did not bring him stew and rice. Moreover, his "bad luck" makes him an object of ridicule and pity in the village. In these abject conditions the old man has nobody except for the boy, and he even leaves him behind when he sets out to test his luck on his 85th day at sea.

The old man isolates himself both physically and geographically on his three-day fishing expedition. He refuses to take the boy with him in his skiff. All alone, even with his strong but old body, he suffers from thirst, hunger, and fatigue. He regrets not having the boy with him multiple times during his voyage. Without the boy, drinking, eating, or recuperating lost fishing-line all become Herculean tasks for an old fisherman. With nobody by his side, the old man finds himself in a dangerous position, made more dangerous by his geographic isolation. On his first day he sails out to where only the tops of the island hills are visible; then when he hooks his big catch he is dragged out to where no land is visible at all. The old man reaches his most remote point when he kills the marlin and stops the fish from towing his boat farther out to sea. Without his only friend and far from help, the old man's isolation nearly kills him.

Isolation also haunts the old man's dreams. When the old man finally allows himself to sleep during his second night at sea, he has three dreams. Between two dreams of companionship and pleasure is a dream of discomfort and cold. This harsh dream resembles the old man's life on the island: a chilly, unpleasant night in a shack. The severity of this image contrasts with the two other dreams. The first dream is of a school of porpoises playing in the ocean during mating season. The other dream is of a lion that arrives on a beach alone and is then joined by others. In this dream sequence, the old man's life of solitude appears all the more arduous juxtaposed with these pleasant visions of animal communities.

Though for the old man community and belonging seem but a dream, he is never completely isolated. His poor outsider status on the island does not mean that no one cares for him. Certainly, this is most obvious in his relationship to the boy. But upon his return to the island, it is clear that the villagers do worry about the old man. They sent the coast guard to search for him, and Manolin must tell the proprietor of the Terrace to prohibit any curious parties from disturbing the convalescent old man. Even far out at sea, the old man knows that he is not utterly alone. The kinship he feels toward the turtles, porpoises, wind, and stars is accompanied by his thought, "no man was ever alone on the sea." From the old man's point of view he is surrounded by his "brothers" of the air and of the water. Isolation thus becomes merely a question of perspective.

Japhet Johnstone

NATURE in *The Old Man and the Sea*

The central conflict in *The Old Man and the Sea* is between man and nature. The old man, Santiago, challenges nature when he sets out alone in his skiff to catch a great fish. At sea, he overcomes many trials thanks to his determination and sharp mind. These assets are quintessentially human and are the old man's best weapons against the unpredictable and wild sea. The sea, and all of nature, can grant both good luck and bad. It is a source of fortune and beauty, and also a formidable enemy. But nature is not just the sea, the stars, the marlin, and the sharks; the old man is also a part of nature. His connection to nature is most evident in his own body and his relationship to the marlin. In the end, however, it is the old man, and not the marlin, who makes it back to shore alive. Even with no luck at all, Santiago's resolution is strong enough to bring him back home alive, exhausted, and a hero.

Nature has not been kind to the old man. His work as a fisherman has exposed him to nature's cruelty. The sun has marked his skin with cancer. He knows firsthand the burning poison of jellyfish. When the novel begins Santiago has gone 84 days without catching a fish. On the 85th day he catches a 1,500-pound marlin. Nature rewards the old man with its bounty, but the size of its bounty is almost too much for a single fisherman. When the old man has finally lashed the marlin to his skiff, nature sends its minions: sharks, who devour most of the fish.

Santiago meets all of nature's trials with determination. His years at sea have taught him many "tricks" to counter nature's whims. After almost three months of bad luck, he still goes out to fish daily. While the taut, heavy lines cut across his back as Santiago waits for the marlin to surface, he reminds himself that his advantage over the fish is his intelligence and his unrelenting resolution. Indeed, Santiago does not cut the line. Even when black spots appear before his eyes and sharks attack through the night, he commands himself to keep a clear mind and does not relinquish his catch.

Though nature is often cruel to the old man, he still loves it, especially the sea. Unlike some of the young, brash fishermen, who think of the sea as *"el mar,"* a hostile, masculine opponent, Santiago thinks of the sea as *"la mar."* The sea is a woman, and Santiago feels that, like a woman, the sea is naturally wild. These things do not make him love the sea any less. He also has an affinity for nature's creatures. He feels compassion for the fragile terns whose voices are so delicate. He reveres turtles and hawksbills for their elegance and porpoises for their playfulness. Even the sharks are beautiful to Santiago, though he hates them. Nothing in nature is without some quality that the old man can admire.

The old man himself is one of nature's creatures. If the mind is human, then the body is natural. The opening description of the old man compares his scars to erosion in a desert, and it is as if nature had written itself into the old man's skin. The ebb and flow of luck, which is nature's domain, influences his whole body. Bad luck strikes when his left hand cramps. Suddenly, he has no power over it. In the same way that the old man waits for the marlin to surface, so too must he wait for his hand to uncramp. But the old man's link to nature is more than just his own physical body.

Santiago's most notable connection to nature is the marlin caught on his hook. At each end of the fishing line there is a figure who will not let go of its life. As the old man shortens the line, the spiritual distance between the two also shortens. The old man wonders about the marlin and feels sorry for him. He even wishes to be the fish at one point. Both fish and man parallel each other in endurance and strength. The marlin's determination drags the old man far out to sea. The old man's brings them back. And though the old man lives on, the parallel between the two is not broken by the marlin's death and mutilation. As the townspeople examine and measure the fish's skeleton on the beach, they are also measuring the old man's greatness. This greatness resides in his will power, which can face the sea and all of nature's tricks, with or without luck.

Japhet Johnstone

STAGES OF LIFE in *The Old Man and the Sea*

The Old Man and the Sea does not detail the stages of life in a progressive development from youth to adulthood to old age. Instead, the old man stands at the final stage of life, where death is a real threat, but also where experience has given him a wealth of knowledge. His friend, the boy, is just at the end of the first stage of life, yet he is already wise beyond his years. He lacks only experience and instruction, both of which he hopes to gain from the old man. The years between the old man and the boy do not distance them from one another. The long span of time is full of dreams and fantasies that the two share.

The old man feels the effects of aging. Except for his eyes, which retain a cheerfulness and triumphant shine, everything about Santiago is old. When his eyes are closed he looks lifeless. His conversation with the boy turns frequently to the retelling of stories, but the old man is not senile. His awareness of aging is sharp. He recognizes that age is his alarm clock and wonders why old men wake up so early. Age has also provided him with experience, which in turn has taught the old man many tricks. In spite of his age and his fatigue, the old man battles the sharks that assault his skiff. The old man has a small armament to kill the sharks, but more than these material weapons, he is armed with his mind. And it is not old age that threatens his mind at sea, but starvation, dehydration, and exhaustion.

Manolin represents youth and its benefits. He is capable and lucky. He can procure food for his old friend and help him with his fishing gear. The boy also works on a good fishing boat and regularly catches fish. These qualities contrast with Santiago's stage of life. He often regrets not having the boy with him on his lonely skiff. If the boy were with Santiago, the fisherman would not only have an extra set of hands, but also, symbolically, have his youth to give him added vitality and endurance.

Still, youth alone would not be enough to subdue the giant fish. Even if the old man fondly thinks of the boy and nostalgically remembers his youth, it is the experience that has come with old age that helps him most.

Between youth and old age lies the stage of life during which we gather experience. The old man has this period behind him, and yet keeps it fresh in his memories and dreams. It was a time of love, conquest, and travels for the old man. Some of these memories he returns to fondly, like his sailing to Africa and his arm wrestling triumphs. Other memories he does not welcome, like the memory of his wife. The clearest figure of adulthood however, is not in the old man's past but in the newspapers. Joe DiMaggio is young and strong, and Santiago thinks about him as frequently as he thinks about the boy. The old man wonders how long DiMaggio would stay with a giant fish, and if his bone-spur would cause him much pain. But the old man does not wish DiMaggio, an adult, were accompanying him. He longs for Manolin and youth. Similarly, the boy does not wish to learn from anyone else but the old man. None of the other characters in the novel, real or imagined, can provide the boy with the instruction and companionship of the old man. Nor can they provide the old man with the devotion and admiration of the boy.

By the end of the novel both Santiago and Manolin are on the verge of passing into their next stage of life. For Santiago the next stage of life is death. Though he does not die, his body is wrecked by his expedition. Death seems very near. For Manolin the next stage of life is adulthood. Indeed, the pains that the boy takes to care for the old man show responsibility and maturity. The boy casts off the last remnant of childhood, his obedience to his parents, when he decides to fish with the old man in spite of their orders not to. But more than his renunciation of his parents, the boy's passage into adulthood is marked by his first hard lesson—the lesson of loss. More than the old man himself sees, the boy sees how close to death the old man came. The boy's tears prematurely mourn the loss of Santiago, from whom the boy still wishes to learn "everything."

Japhet Johnstone

HEMINGWAY, ERNEST *The Sun Also Rises* (1926)

Ernest Hemingway's first great novel, *The Sun Also Rises,* was published in 1926. It is the story of a group of American and British expatriates living in Paris after World War I, who struggle to find some meaning in their lives. It begins with a brief description of Robert Cohn, a Jewish writer who worries that he is "not really living." It is narrated by Jake Barnes, an American whose war wounds have left him impotent. Jake is in love with the Lady Brett Ashley, a beautiful, charming, and promiscuous woman. Brett loves Jake as well, but his wound has left them unable to pursue their relationship. She is engaged to Mike Campbell, a bankrupt Scottish veteran. Brett has a brief affair with Robert, who is unable to let her go. The veteran Bill Gorton is, like the others, a heavy drinker. Book 1 of the novel introduces the characters, and highlights Jake and Brett's unhappiness in their frustrated relationship. Book 2 details the group's trip to Spain, beginning with Jake and Bill's fishing trip. They meet Brett, Mike, and Robert in Pamplona for the bullfights. Brett falls in love with the bullfighter Pedro Romero. They enjoy the fiesta for a time, until Robert's jealousy for Brett leads him to punch Jake and Mike, and to severely beat Pedro. Brett and Pedro go away together, but their relationship soon breaks down, and Brett sends for Jake to rescue her. The novel ends with the two lamenting their condition. It is a beautiful expression of ALIENATION, FUTILITY, GENDER, LOVE, and SPIRITUALITY.

James Ford

ALIENATION in *The Sun Also Rises*

A sense of alienation and estrangement is pervasive throughout *The Sun Also Rises.* Jake Barnes is alienated from himself and the world around him. He is alienated from his own body, particularly by the war wound that has left him impotent, unable to consummate his love for Lady Brett Ashley. He tries to explain to his friend Robert Cohn that "you can't get away from yourself." He says that people want only what they cannot have, a sign of the futility of human life and desire. Jake wants Brett to be with him, to run away with him, to live with him despite his wound. Neither can have what they really want. There is a distance between Jake and everyone else, particularly his friends. He is aware of the emptiness around him, but he struggles to live with it. He says that he does not care what life is all about; "All I wanted to know was how to live in it." His passion for fishing and for the bullfights gives a sense of meaning to his life, but they do not make it any easier for him to live with his separation from Brett.

Cohn is also alienated from everyone around him. He talks about his sense that he's "not really living," but his attempts at really living ultimately cost him his only friend. He falls in love with Lady Brett Ashley, who after a brief affair wants nothing to do with him. Cohn is certain of his love for Brett and follows her constantly. First he surprises Brett and her fiancé, Mike, at San Sebastian, where Brett and Cohn had their affair. After being cast off by Brett, Cohn continues to follow her around "like a poor bloody steer." Cohn refuses to believe that his love for Brett does not matter, even as Mike and Brett insist that they do not want him around. Cohn is alienated from those around him by the fact that he is Jewish, by his failure to have fought in the war, and by his naïve insistence that Brett must love him. When Brett turns her affections to the bullfighter Pedro Romero, Cohn finally faces the truth that she does not love him. He punches out Jake, Mike, and finally Romero, before deciding that everything is useless and leaving it all behind.

Brett is perhaps the most alienated character in the novel. She loves Jake, but has a series of affairs with other men and is engaged to Mike. She says it is "hell on earth" to be in love. As Mike says, she "enjoys things" but is not happy. She sees a momentary happiness with Romero, but it quickly fades. She says she wanted Romero but decided that she "was bad for him." Having sent Romero away, she calls on Jake to rescue her so that she can return to Mike.

Brett and Jake are also both alienated from religion and from God. At one point Jake goes into the cathedral to pray, regretting that he's such "a rotten Catholic." His religion does not seem to make much difference to his life. Later he and Brett go to the chapel to pray, but it only makes her "damned nervous," since it never does her any good. Jake says that he is "pretty religious," but that hardly seems sincere given his own difficulties with church and prayer. After Brett's rejection of Romero, it is her sense that she has done the right thing for Romero that is her consolation. It is, she says to Jake, "sort of what we have instead of God." In the most explicit statement about their lack of religious and spiritual beliefs, Jake says that "some people have God," to which Brett responds "He never worked very well with me."

The novel concludes with them drinking more wine, eating more food, and talking around their problems, until Brett finally voices her frustration that "we could have had such a damned good time together." Jake's answer—"Isn't it pretty to think so?"—is the last word in the novel. It suggests that he knows that many of their problems would remain, even if they were together. It shows that he feels estranged even from the idea of their union, that perhaps he doubts whether anything could resolve their feelings of alienation. It seems unlikely that any of the major characters will ever feel at home in the world.

James Ford

FUTILITY in *The Sun Also Rises*

The theme of futility is present from the first words of *The Sun Also Rises*. The two epigraphs that open the novel speak to this sense of the uselessness of human life. Gertrude Stein's comment that "You are a lost generation" is directed at those who suffered through World War I and its aftermath, but the feeling of being "lost" is one that recurs in every generation. The epigraph from Ecclesiastes (which is the source of the book's title) makes this plain: "One generation passeth away, and another generation cometh." In Ecclesiastes, human concerns are a "vanity," a chasing after wind, and this is true throughout the novel as well. The first line introduces Robert Cohn as a Princeton boxing champion, but the narrator (Jake) explains that such things do not impress him. This is an early indication of the larger insignificance of human accomplishments. This focus on Cohn is a curious beginning, for other characters (particularly Jake and Brett Ashley) will be as important in the novel, but early on the focus is on Cohn and Jake's

relationship to him. Cohn is determined to travel, in part because of a novel that he takes too seriously. Jake is world-weary and tries to convince Cohn how futile traveling the world actually is: "All countries look just like the moving pictures." In truth, what Cohn wants is a new life. "Don't you ever get the feeling that all your life is going by and you're not taking advantage of it?" Cohn asks, and Jake replies that he is "through worrying" about life, death, or anything else. Jake has decided that such worrying is futile. Cohn is searching for some larger significance in his life, but for Jake life is the same all over; "Why don't you start living your life in Paris?" is his sensible response. The major characters in the novel are discontent whether in Paris or anywhere else. Bill says later that Vienna "seemed better than it was." Brett says that "one's an ass to leave Paris." Yet they all leave Paris for the fiesta in Spain.

Many of the things that might make life more enjoyable seem tired for Jake and his friends. Drinks, dancing, parties, and in general the night-life all get boring. Even love seems futile, in part because of Jake's condition. Brett says "There isn't any use my telling you I love you" because "talking's all bilge." Jake and Brett long to be together, but his war-wound and her wanderings make a future together impossible. When asked why they don't get married, Jake jokes that "We want to lead our own lives" and Brett explains that "We have our careers," echoing and mocking common explanations for not settling down. Mike's comment later is typical: "This is all awfully amusing, but it's not too pleasant." Jake and his friends enjoy many things, but they rarely are happy. Even their arguments (between Jake and Cohn first, then Cohn and Jake's friend Harvey) amount to nothing. Most of all, human wisdom is futile in the novel. Jake realizes how pointless his own philosophy of life is, thinking that "in five years . . . it will seem just as silly as all the other philosophies I've had." All things pass away, even as the world endures.

This sense that human pursuits are ultimately futile receives fullest expression during the fiesta, where "it seemed as though nothing could have any consequences." There are real consequences, though; for instance, the consequences of love affairs—Jake's emptiness, Mike's loneliness, Brett's unhappiness, and Cohn's violence. Brett knows that Cohn's problem is that "he can't believe it didn't mean anything" when they were lovers, but to her it is meaningless. After Cohn knocks out his friends and beats Romero to a bloody pulp, he finally agrees that "everything" is pointless, saying "I guess it isn't any use." When a bystander is killed during the running of the bulls, a man who had a wife and two children, a waiter is left to express how senseless the death is. "All for sport, all for pleasure," he says. Ironically, the only truly worthwhile activities are casual pursuits, like fishing with friends. Jake is happiest trout-fishing with his friend Bill, and enjoying a bottle of wine (or two) afterward. They find a kind of peace in friendship that is otherwise elusive. For Jake, traditional pursuits like prayer and RELIGION seem empty in comparison. The novel ends with his rescue of Brett, but their relationship is another exercise in human futility. They are right back where they started, lost.

James Ford

GENDER in *The Sun Also Rises*

The Sun Also Rises raises many questions about what it means to be a man. The novel is narrated by Jake Barnes, a man left impotent by his war wounds. Most of the major characters are men, but they spend their time fighting and arguing over one woman, Brett Ashley (the novel's only major female character). When Brett is first introduced in the novel, what is most prominent is how she differs from other women. She has a crowd of men around her and she is quite beautiful, with her "hair brushed back like a boy's." In fact, Jake explains, "she started all that." Another fact that makes her different is her tendency to drink like a man. Count Mippipopolous, one of the many men smitten with Brett, says that she is "the only lady I have ever known who was as charming when she was drunk as when she was sober." Her refusal to follow the rules of polite society often excludes her, such as when she cannot enter the church because she has no hat. Much has been made of Lady Ashley, and the significance of her character. Is she a liberating force, since she is in many ways the center of the novel and refuses to follow societal conventions? Or does she reinforce common prejudices, in that she

seems to be the cause of many of the problems in the novel and often is dependent on men? As Jake says of her, "she can't go anywhere alone." What is clear is that Brett Ashley is a compelling character, and the men of the novel orbit around her. For instance, at the fiesta she wants to dance with a crowd of men, but they keep her in the center of the circle: "they wanted her as an image to dance around." This is symbolic of Brett's relationships throughout the novel. She has a series of affairs, all the while loving Jake. Her final affair is with Pedro Romero, the young bullfighter who in many ways is a symbol of young, powerful manliness. That relationship fails (just as all her others do), in part because Pedro wants her to grow her hair out, to be "more womanly." He insists on marriage, but Brett Ashley refuses to be bound by society's expectations of a woman.

Jake is far removed from the smooth confidence of Pedro Romero. His war wound shadows him throughout the novel, "the old grievance." He is generally good-natured about his condition, but it prevents him from pursuing his relationship with Brett. They genuinely love each other. Whether or not Brett's affairs are the result of his impotence is unclear, but it is certainly an important factor. As she says, "I couldn't live quietly in the country. Not with my own true love." Jake is patient with her, but his situation leaves him decidedly bitter about women in general, and Brett Ashley in particular. He muses that a man has "to be in love with a woman to have a basis of friendship," before concluding "to hell with women, anyway." That conclusion is half-hearted; the one thing Jake can never do is forget about Brett, or the wound that keeps them apart.

One quality that seems indicative of manliness in the novel is *aficion*, the passion that some men (and only men) have for bullfighting. Jake has it, and it is his link to a secret world of men. The hotelkeeper Montoya is an aficionado, as is Pedro Romero. In fact, all the great bullfighters and lovers of the bullfights are aficionados, with a sort of spiritual bond linking them. When Brett's affair with Pedro threatens to weaken his *aficion*, it is the one thing Montoya cannot forgive of Jake and his friends.

Robert Cohn is a man who lacks that passion. In fact, the other men compare him to a steer, which is a young, castrated bull—the symbol of a lack of manliness. They laugh at him for the way in which he follows Brett, just as the steers hang around the bulls waiting for their attention. Ironically, Cohn is the most violent man in the novel, decking his friends and nearly killing Pedro Romero in his frustration at Brett's rejection. Cohn's traditional sense of pride and honor alienate him from the world around him, just as Jake's impotence and Brett's independence alienate them. Gender roles are another way that Hemingway's characters are not at home in the world.

James Ford

HERSEY, JOHN *Hiroshima* (1946)

In the spring of 1946, Pulitzer Prize-winning author John Hersey flew to Japan to interview six survivors of the atom bomb that devastated Hiroshima on August 6, 1945. *The New Yorker* magazine published Hersey's long article in August 1946; the article was later issued as a book, entitled *Hiroshima*. In 1985, Hersey returned to Japan to write a follow-up article on the six survivors. *The New Yorker* also published this piece, entitled "The Aftermath," which was soon added to a revised edition of the book.

Following World War II, many Americans felt intense hatred toward Japan. *Hiroshima* can be read, in part, as a response to that hatred. For example, some of Hersey's readers were Christian, and his inclusion of a Japanese United Methodist minister and a German Jesuit priest among the profiled survivors allowed his readers to see that some differences between American and Japanese cultures, such as religion, were not as vast as believed at the time. The book also sympathetically details the plight of families. One example is a mother suffering from radiation sickness and poverty, who must provide for her three young children. Hersey's journalism made it difficult for the American public to justify prejudice against its former enemies of war because the two cultures, although different, share basic human values and emotions.

The atomic bomb dropped by the U.S. Army Air Force on Hiroshima killed approximately 100,000 Japanese plus foreign civilians and military personnel. Out of this tragedy, the book makes clear, arose tremendous SUFFERING. But selfless acts of HEROISM kept the community together. People also survived by giving friends and strangers HOPE that Hiroshimans would heal and rebuild their lives.

Elizabeth Cornell

HEROISM in *Hiroshima*

Heroism is a bold act of courage. A hero often acts at the risk of his or her own life or well-being. Generally, a person is not conscious of acting heroically, nor does someone perform a heroic deed only to be recognized as a hero. John Hersey's *Hiroshima* is filled with heroes and acts of heroism, large and small. For example, minutes after the bomb explodes over Hiroshima, Mrs. Hatsuyo Nakamura digs her children out of the rubble that was once their house. Her act of heroism is motivated by desperation, love, and maternal instinct. Mrs. Nakamura is a heroine because her effort to save the lives of her children is a selfless one.

Hersey details other remarkable instances of selfless heroism like Mrs. Nakamura's. Father Kleinsorge, who is "apathetic and dazed in the presence of the cumulative distress" caused by the destruction of Hiroshima, learns that the secretary of the diocese is trapped in the second floor window of the burning mission. Kleinsorge shakes himself out of his dazed state and runs into the flaming building. Mr. Fukai wants to remain in the house to die, but Kleinsorge refuses to honor his wish. With the help of a student, he drags Fukai downstairs and outdoors. Since Fukai refuses to walk, Kleinsorge hoists him on his back and they escape from the fire that soon devours everything in the neighborhood. But when Kleinsorge sits down to rest, Fukai runs away, back into the fire. He is never seen again. Sometimes heroic acts are unappreciated or even unwanted by the recipient.

Rescuing people from life or death situations, as Kleinsorge did at the risk of his own life, are clear acts of heroism. But, as Hersey's book shows, heroism is not always associated with high-risk situations. Moreover, heroic deeds do not necessarily have clear-cut beginnings and ends, and often continue for long periods of time. Mrs. Nakamura is a case in point. Widowed by the war, she is sole care-taker for her three children. She has few marketable skills. On top of that, Mrs. Nakamura suffers from serious radiation sickness. She manages to take in some sewing, as well as cleaning and laundering for neighbors, but "she got so tired that she had to take two days' rest for every three days she worked. . . . She earned barely enough for food." She struggles for many years. Her heroism lies in never giving up on herself and her family, despite lingering illness and the bleak conditions that plague her daily existence. Her tireless, selfless efforts pay off: Her children eventually become successful adults. When Mrs. Nakamura retires, she finally takes pleasure in living.

Father Kleinsorge also selflessly gives to others, and does so for the rest of his life. We might say his life is one long, heroic act. Despite the radiation sickness that afflicts him, Kleinsorge serves his church faithfully and tirelessly. He conducts Mass, hears confession, teaches Bible classes, runs eight-day retreats, visits survivors, and even babysits on occasion. Hersey explains that Kleinsorge takes "on himself the Japanese spirit of *enryo*—setting the self apart, putting the wishes of others first." Kleinsorge's colleagues think "he might literally kill himself with kindness to others."

Sometimes heroes receive medals for their courageous acts. Kleinsorge receives nothing but deep gratitude from everyone he touches until his final days, when some of his selfless service to others is paid back. When Kleinsorge is unable to take care of even his most basic needs, he receives loving and round-the-clock care from his helper, Yoshiki-san. Their relationship demonstrates a view of heroism described by Thomas Carlyle, a 19th-century Scottish philosopher. Carlyle wrote that heroes are "leaders of men"; they are "the modellers, patterns, and in a wide sense, creators, of whatsoever the general mass of men contrived to do or attain." One implication of this passage is that common people admire heroism and may wish to emulate heroes. Kleinsorge, "a leader" of people, can be seen as a "modeller" who creates "patterns" of behavior for others to copy. Yoshiki-san's selfless service to the dying Kleinsorge is an emulation of the selfless heroism the priest modeled throughout his life.

The bombing of Hiroshima was a terrible act against humans; but the outcome was not entirely negative. As the feats of heroism described above show, it takes more than a bomb—even a nuclear bomb—to break the human spirit, heroic or otherwise.

Elizabeth Cornell

HOPE in *Hiroshima*

A curtain of flames reflects in the night sky over bombed-out Hiroshima, and a girl rescued from a toxic river shivers. Father Kleinsorge, one of the six survivors profiled by John Hersey in *Hiroshima*, brings her a blanket. But she continues to shiver uncontrollably. The priest brings her another blanket. "I am so cold," she says, "and then she suddenly stopped shivering and was dead." The blanket offers the girl a hope of warmth and life, but her death makes the post-bomb scene feel hopeless indeed. The thousands of slimy, swollen, and discolored human bodies only add to the sense of hopelessness. Reverend Tanimoto, one of the uninjured few, keeps reminding himself that these people "'are human beings.'" In the initial days after the American bombing of Hiroshima, hope feels like a luxury to the sick and dying crowds of people. One doctor is only willing to take care of the slightly wounded. He explains, "There is no hope for the heavily wounded. They will die. We can't bother with them." But glimmers of hope cut through the nightmare. A Japanese naval launch traverses the seven rivers of Hiroshima to announce the imminent arrival of a naval hospital ship. This gives the people cheer and hope. However, no ship arrives.

False hope is common in the desperate days after the bombing, but sometimes even that kind of hope is useful. For example, at the Catholic International Hospital in Tokyo, a doctor presents an optimistic face to Father Kleinsorge, who is very sick. The doctor promises to send Kleinsorge home in two weeks; but privately, to the Mother Superior, he predicts that the priest—and all the "'bomb people'"—will die. He holds little hope, but understands that giving this kind of false hope is the best medicine he can offer. Kleinsorge does survive, however, as do many "bomb people." Perhaps Kleinsorge's deep faith in God gives him hope for survival. Later, he shares this faith with Miss Sasaki, whose long stay at the Red Cross Hospital depresses her. Kleinsorge's words give her hope that all is not lost. After his visit, Dr. Sasaki notices that "she seemed quickly to draw to physical strength" from Kleinsorge's words; soon after she is discharged from the hospital.

Since Miss Sasaki is not a Christian, Father Kleinsorge's religion may seem, to her, like an unlikely resource for hope. But hope often comes from unexpected channels. An unlikely source for all the Hiroshimans comes from Japan's now powerless leader, Emperor Showa. When he announces on the radio that Japan has surrendered to the Allies, thus ending the war, Mrs. Nakamura, like most Japanese citizens, is stunned. The common people have never heard his voice before. They consider their emperor to be more than human: He is a sacred symbol and the embodiment of Japan. The emperor's message uplifts the disheartened Japanese and gives them hope for their country's future. Tanimoto later explains in a letter to an American friend that people believe that to surrender is to make a "whole-hearted sacrifice for the everlasting peace of the world": hope, in other words, for a better future.

With this hope for a better world, the Hiroshimans almost immediately begin to rebuild their city. Dr. Fujii, whose entire medical clinic fell into a river during the bombing, builds a new clinic. It becomes more successful than his original one. Kleinsorge rebuilds his mission and Tanimoto rebuilds his church. Rebuilding is an important way for the survivors to maintain the hope that all was not lost on August 6, 1945. Medical clinics and churches are among the institutions that provide some of the necessary infrastructure and hope the community needs to move on from the tragedy.

By rebuilding their city, the Hiroshimans show faith in their future. They also hope for a future in which peace reigns. Many survivors want to use their experiences to promote peace. But peace is more easily visualized than achieved. Tanimoto works toward establishing a center for world peace. He receives support from organizations in the United States, but encounters resistance in Hiroshima. Moreover, although the destruction caused by the bombings of Hiroshima and Nagasaki should be enough impetus for countries to stop manufactur-

ing bombs, such is not the case, as Hersey makes clear. Scattered throughout "The Aftermath" are italicized sentences indicating when another country acquires the knowledge to develop a bomb. The resistance Tanimoto encounters for his peace center and against the continued development of bombs is not an indication that the peace movement is failing, however. They are indications that the struggle for world peace is complex and difficult. Hope and activity for peace must not be abandoned but constantly renewed with increased vigor and awareness.

Elizabeth Cornell

SUFFERING in *Hiroshima*

John Hersey's book, *Hiroshima*, describes the human suffering caused by the atomic bomb, through details that may otherwise have been lost to history. The six survivors profiled in the book all have suffering in common but, as Hersey movingly shows, each experience of suffering is unique.

For example, most who survive the bombing suffer immediate and severe injuries. But the Reverend Mr. Kiyoshi Tanimoto is not injured; his suffering stems from the guilt of not being injured and seeing the deep suffering that surrounds him. "Excuse me for having no burden like yours" he pleads to the burned and lacerated people he passes as he makes his way into the recently shocked and bomb-blasted city. The human suffering is on a scale unlike anything he has ever encountered. Tanimoto sees people whose burnt skin bears the shapes of the flowers printed on their kimonos. When he assists a woman onto a rescue boat, the skin falls off her hand in "glovelike pieces." The wounded and dying grieve him so much that when, by pure chance, he finally encounters his missing wife and son, "Tanimoto was now so emotionally worn out that nothing could surprise him" and he does not even embrace them.

Miss Toshinki Sasaki, an office clerk, does suffer physical injury. In the attack, a ceiling beam and a heavy shelf of books land on her. Her left leg is twisted and broken. After being rescued many hours later, she is taken outside and given shelter from the rain underneath a large sheet of corrugated iron. She suffers in this bare space for over two days with a "woman with a whole breast sheared off and a man whose face was all raw from a burn." After a while, these people start to smell, but Sasaki—whose leg becomes "swollen and putrid"—is too injured to move away from them. She is at last rescued by friends, who bring news that Sasaki's parents and baby brother are dead, adding more emotional suffering to her ordeal. Doctors at the Red Cross Hospital manage to save her leg, but she is permanently disabled.

Outside medical assistance is slow to arrive in Hiroshima. Only six doctors at the Red Cross Hospital can work, including Dr. Terfumi Sasaki (unrelated to Miss Sasaki). Nurses and medical supplies are scarce. In the dreadful days that follow the bombing, 10,000 injured people make their way to the 600-bed hospital. Confronted with so much suffering, Dr. Sasaki becomes robot-like, "mechanically wiping, daubing, winding, wiping, daubing, winding" the bomb victims. He secretly rests after 19 hours of treating raw flesh and dangling limbs. But an hour later, the wounded find him and chide him for not doing his job. In total, Sasaki works three straight days with one hour of rest. The suffering—his own and everyone else's—is a nightmare he will long remember.

In the years following the attack, the immediate suffering subsides. But the survivors continue to encounter new forms of suffering they never imagined possible. Miss Sasaki's fiancé, who was not in Hiroshima during the bombing, abandons her because she is crippled. Like most survivors, Sasaki also suffers from radiation sickness as well as social and economic ostracism. These people are called *hibakusha*, meaning "explosion-affected person." Non-*hibakusha* often scorn *hibakusha* and believe *hibakusha* can cause disease and bear deformed offspring. On a bright note, the *hibakusha* receive special health services and monthly allowances if they are unable to work. Moreover, thanks to Reverend Tanimoto, some female *hibakusha* with facial deformities (keloids) are selected to travel to the United States for plastic surgery. One *hibakusha* dies from the procedure, but the rest—now dubbed Maidens—are remarkably improved. Unfortunately, when they return to Japan, they become "not only objects of public curiosity but also of envy and spite."

Despite this negative response to the Maidens, what is remarkable are the relatively few instances in the book when people complain about their suffering or condemn the Americans for causing it. The Reverend Tanimoto comments in a letter to an American friend that he "never heard anyone cried [sic] in the disorder, even though they suffered in great agony. They died in silence, with no grudge, setting their teeth to bear it. All for the country." His observation does not mean that no one in Hiroshima complained or condemned the Americans for destroying a beautiful city. It may, however, cause readers to question their preconceived notions of what suffering is and their public and private responses to it.

Elizabeth Cornell

HESSE, HERMANN *Siddhartha* (1922)

Hermann Hesse (1877–1962) began writing *Siddhartha* in 1919 and it was first published in 1922. His life and numerous works, including this novel, were influenced by his parents, who both lived in India before meeting in Germany, as well as by a trip he took to Southeast Asia in 1911. Based on the dates that the Buddha is thought to have lived, this story takes place from approximately 540 to 480 B.C.

Siddhartha leaves his family as a young man with his childhood friend, Govinda, because they are in search of enlightenment. Both decide to become *samanas* (wandering ascetic monks), and during this time they hear about Gotama, who is said to be the Buddha. Govinda decides to follow Gotama's teachings, while Siddhartha continues his journey and reenters the world. He subsequently meets Kamala, a courtesan, and through her Kamaswami, a wealthy merchant, both of whom teach Siddhartha their trades. Feeling unhappy and unfulfilled after becoming a gambler, Siddhartha employs the ferryman Vasudeva, with whom he remains. After many years he sees Kamala, who dies from a snake bite shortly thereafter, and he discovers that she has given him a son. Siddhartha tries to raise his son, but quickly realizes that the son too must leave his father and go out on his own. In the final chapter Siddhartha once again sees Govinda; through a kiss on Siddhartha's forehead, Govinda is able to find the oneness and peace that Siddhartha has already achieved, within himself and with his surroundings.

Christine Rinne

INDIVIDUAL AND SOCIETY in *Siddhartha*

Siddhartha grows up with his family, in a Brahman community, and he must venture out of its confines in order to obtain the wisdom he seeks. He initially believes that withdrawal and social seclusion will offer the solution, then tries living in a large, diverse society, but he comes to learn that moderation leads to his happiness. Siddhartha encounters many types of people throughout his lengthy journey for peace, and he uses these experiences and interactions to decide how and where to spend the remainder of his life. It is only later in life, while living with Vasudeva, that he is able to achieve a balance between these two communal extremes, to understand himself and his environs better, and successfully to conclude his quest.

As a young man Siddhartha decides that he must leave his parents and friends to be happy, and he thinks that he can best achieve this in isolation. He and Govinda renounce material possessions and live secludedly as monks for three years. However, Siddhartha concludes that he must actively experience what he is being taught in order to truly learn and attain wisdom. After seeing Kamala, he decides to reenter society so that she can teach him about the art of love. Though he does well as a merchant, which allows him to meet Kamala's material demands, he does not always follow his mentor Kamaswami's advice; Siddhartha is concerned about more than simply making a profit. Instead, he uses these opportunities to get to know the people whom he encounters, to learn about their motivations, values, and beliefs. Through this process he identifies qualities that he finds both helpful and harmful, in others and himself. After becoming a gambler Siddhartha has what he labels an empty life, until he has a dream about a dead caged bird. It inspires him to abandon this lifestyle as well and once more seek meaning. He briefly considers committing suicide because he cannot find solace or enticement anywhere or in anything or anyone, but he is halted by the sacred *om,* which again evokes tranquillity and serenity in him.

Once Siddhartha experiences both extremes, full withdrawal from as well as complete submersion in society, he is able to find a medium, a place where he interacts with those around him, yet also has the solitude he enjoys. After sleeping by the river Siddhartha sees Govinda, by whom he is reminded that his inability to love has made him ill. Thus when Siddhartha encounters Vasudeva, he accepts his friend's offer and stays with him. He lives and works with the wise man, and it is here that Siddhartha is able to achieve some balance. He learns a new trade and has contact with those who employ his services, but he is not diverted by the negative aspects that had temporarily amused, yet also distracted him previously. It is also during this period that Siddhartha discovers he is a father and tries to establish his own family. His son, however, is unwilling to adapt to a simpler lifestyle, and Siddhartha, like his own father, must learn to let the boy go. Because of Vasudeva's beneficial influence, Siddhartha learns to listen to the river as Vasudeva does and heed its guidance. Once while looking into the water he sees the faces of all who are dear to him: his father, himself, his son, Govinda, and Kamala. Their images and voices unite and he finally achieves oneness. He is also able to pass on this treasure, which he is able to achieve largely because of the lessons he learns from Vasudeva, to Govinda. Although Siddhartha loses many people who are important in his life and development, including Vasudeva, Kamala, and his son, their influence permits him to achieve contentment after decades of longing and searching.

The story concludes with Siddhartha aiding Govinda to also obtain oneness, and the reader is not explicitly told what comes of these two friends, whose paths have yet again crossed. However, they have both finally achieved what they spent their lives in search of: peace with themselves and their surroundings. Siddhartha's path was long and diverse, and included numerous types of societies. It is because of what he learns from each experience that he is finally able to achieve wisdom and happiness. Siddhartha has to find a balance between himself and his surroundings, and learn moderation and acceptance.

Christine Rinne

LOVE in *Siddhartha*

Siddhartha experiences and learns to recognize the value and necessity of love from three groups of people in this novel: his family, his friends, and his lover. To achieve his goal of oneness, Siddhartha lives according to different sets of values and beliefs, and he comes to realize that many people play an important role in his life and are essential to his ultimate happiness. Without loving and being loved he feels alone and dissatisfied, but when he loves, admires, and respects the things and people around him, he is able to achieve peace.

When the story begins Siddhartha is a child and everyone loves him. Though he gives joy and pleasure to others, he is not content. Thus when he is a young man, he fears that his parents' love and that of his friend Govinda will not be enough to satisfy him. Because Siddhartha's father loves him and recognizes that he truly desires to become a monk, he permits Siddhartha to leave the family and join the samanas. Years later, when Siddhartha has a son of his own, he better understands his own father's reluctance. Kamala spoiled their son and the son does not adjust well to his father's simple lifestyle. Siddhartha consequently struggles with his son's choices and must learn to grant him independence. Vasudeva helps Siddhartha realize that he is smothering his son with love, through his kindness and patience, and that he too must permit him to experience the world firsthand.

After Siddhartha and Govinda part, they remain friends and their paths cross twice again. Both times Govinda does not recognize him, but Siddhartha immediately knows that the man is his childhood companion. The first occasion is after he has stopped gambling and is contemplating how to proceed. Govinda sees him and is worried about a man sleeping in the dangerous forest by himself. While they talk Siddhartha realizes how much he loves Govinda and that it was his own inability to love that had made him so ill. Their second encounter takes place at the end of the story, while he is working with Vasudeva. Govinda hears about the ferryman, who is rumored to be a sage, and he goes to see him with the hope that Vasudeva will be able to still his restlessness. When Siddhartha reveals who he is, Govinda asks him to share any realizations he has had. Siddhartha tells him that it is most important to love the world, and though Govinda is skeptical, he obeys Siddhartha's final command to kiss his forehead. Through this act, which was driven by love, Govinda is also able to achieve the oneness for which he had been searching.

Vasudeva becomes an important friend to Siddhartha while on his quest. Their first encounter is brief and takes place after he has left the samanas. He crosses the river but is unable to pay, because these monks do not have material possessions, so Vasudeva asks for his friendship as compensation. After leaving Kamala, more than 20 years later he again crosses the river there. Siddhartha stays with Vasudeva and also takes up his occupation. Here he is finally able to achieve oneness, by learning to listen from Vasudeva and the river. Vasudeva has a successful method to teach Siddhartha what he has been searching for, including how to love others.

When Siddhartha sees Kamala for the first time, he decides that he wants to learn the art of love from her. Though numerous women are attracted to Siddhartha and he is attracted to many, Siddhartha had not yet been in love or had a sexual experience. This changes when he observes Kamala and consequently asks her to be his lover. Through his time with her, he learns that though love can be won, bought, received, or found, it cannot be stolen as he initially threatens; love must be reciprocated if it is to be enjoyed. Although Siddhartha is not aware of it when he departs, Kamala is pregnant and their child will later permit him to experience the joys and pains of a different kind of love.

Siddhartha spends much of his life on a pursuit for wisdom and peace. Though he is loved as a child, he must learn to recognize, value, and reciprocate these feelings. Through his family, his friends, and his lover, many of whom he repeatedly encounters as he grows, Siddhartha comes to acknowledge the importance of each in his life, and their contribution to his wholeness.

Christine Rinne

SPIRITUALITY in *Siddhartha*

The novel follows the main character, Siddhartha, on his quest to achieve peace and oneness. During this process he discovers that he must experience life for himself, instead of following someone else's experiences and teachings, in order to develop and define his own values and ultimately obtain happiness. Over the course of this journey he learns the ways of priests, monks, merchants, and gamblers, but only with Vasudeva does he finally realize his goal. Though Siddhartha does not formally dedicate his life to religion, he is able to find a place and method for practicing his spiritual beliefs that are appropriate and gratifying for him.

During each phase of Siddhartha's journey he learns something about himself and his surroundings that allows him to eventually define his own spirituality. Siddhartha is the son of a Brahman, a Hindu priest and scholar, and while growing up he takes part in the priests' conversations and religious observations. For example uttering the *om,* which begins and ends every Brahman prayer, is a practice that remains central throughout his life. However, he becomes frustrated when the priests do not teach him how to reach his innermost self and soul *(atman).* This dissatisfaction leads him to join the samanas, from whom he hopes to learn how to be empty of all desires, because the passion of these solitary outsiders left an impression on him as a child. Siddhartha and Govinda fast, renounce material belongings, and practice self-denial as monks, but Siddhartha again grows disenchanted after mastering these practices. He feels that many types of people, even alcoholics, could have taught him how to leave his body. He is certain that samanas will never achieve the ultimate goal of nirvana (death without rebirth) through this method. After listening to Gotama, who is said to be the Buddha, Govinda decides to follow his teachings. Siddhartha, however, finds a flaw in his doctrine, namely that he does not tell others how he has achieved salvation. Siddhartha concludes that true knowledge and salvation can never be taught by a teacher, but can be achieved only through personal experience.

Siddhartha consequently decides to reenter society with the goal of experiencing what he has heard about firsthand. While wandering he sees the courtesan Kamala, and he is immediately drawn to her. Though he has been attracted to other women, he decides that he would like to learn the art of love from her. In order to meet her material demands

Siddhartha learns about commerce from Kamaswami. Siddhartha masters these skills and also learns from his customers, who help him define what attributes he finds positive and negative. After attaining monetary wealth he becomes a gambler, but he still does not feel satisfied. Siddhartha again withdraws from society and briefly considers suicide, but he realizes that it would not aid him in achieving his goal either. When he sees Govinda, he is reminded that he needs to love and be loved again, thus Siddhartha accepts Vasudeva's offer and stays with him. Vasudeva is a wonderful listener, and through this practice he has been able to attain enlightenment, an achievement he is able eventually to pass on to Siddhartha. It is during this time that Siddhartha sees Kamala again and meets his son. After her death he tries to rear his son, but the boy does not adjust well to his father's simple lifestyle and runs away. Vasudeva counsels Siddhartha and eventually he is able to let him go. Consequently Siddhartha realizes that what he has been searching for is the wisdom of how to feel and absorb oneness. One day while Siddhartha is in the woods he hears the river laughing, his final step toward peace. When he comes closer he begins to see many faces and hear many voices, but they blend together and he is enlightened. In the final scene Siddhartha imparts his realization to Govinda, something he had hoped many would do for him.

Siddhartha must undertake a lengthy journey to find the spiritual oneness he desires. By living according to different sets of rules he is able ultimately to reach his goal and find a method that is suitable for him to practice his beliefs. Combining the lessons he learns at each stage in his quest, he discovers how much he can learn from his surroundings, and accept and appreciate those around him. Though he is not formally a religious leader, he is able to take what he learns as a student and convey it to Govinda.

Christine Rinne

HESSE, HERMANN *Steppenwolf* (1927)

Hermann Hesse's *Steppenwolf,* which has been called his most popular, most innovative, most influential, and most controversial work, grew out of a personal and artistic crisis. Just before Hesse started composing the novel, his short-lived second marriage to mentally unbalanced Ruth Wenger collapsed, his health deteriorated, and, approaching his 50th birthday, he suffered a severe midlife crisis. In addition, a writer's block that had been precipitated by the revelation of his nom de plume, "Emil Sinclair," kept Hesse from completing his Indian novel, *Siddhartha* (1922). In order to overcome this crisis Hesse underwent psychoanalysis, meeting with Dr. Josef B. Lang, one of Carl Gustav Jung's disciples, numerous times. Hesse also wrote a cycle of poems, entitled *Krisis* (1928), which served as a palliative and which is closely linked with *Steppenwolf.* One of the poems, entitled "Steppenwolf," eventually became part of the novel, with Harry Haller as its fictional author. Considering the novel's genesis, it is not surprising that it is Hesse's most autobiographical work. The book's protagonist shares his initials with the author and many of the locations and characters are based on those known by Hesse. Harry Haller's existential crisis and his attempts at anesthetizing his pain by drowning it in alcohol, drugs, and sex mirror Hesse's life between 1924 and 1926. It was the use of drugs depicted in the novel that caused Timothy Leary in the 1960s to recommend *Steppenwolf* to his followers as preparation for an LSD trip. Moreover, the riveting depiction of the protagonist as an outsider who despises war and technology and who rejects middle-class values, struck a chord with large parts of the American youth in the 1960s and the book became a best seller in the United States.

Karl Stegner

ALIENATION in *Steppenwolf*

The title of Hesse's novel alludes to the protagonist's role as outsider, his alienation from middle-class society. Before we learn his real name, Harry Haller, he is introduced by the (fictional) editor of his writings as "a real wolf of the Steppes, as strange, wild, shy-very shy-being from another world" who is extremely unsociable and who gives off a foreign and hostile air. To the editor, whose aunt takes the stranger in as a lodger and who is a representative of bourgeois values, proud of leading "a narrow, middle-class life, but a solid one, filled with duties"

(20), the Steppenwolf's slovenly, irregular, and irresponsible way of life, which does not seem to serve a practical purpose, is an affront. The editor, an avowed abstainer from alcohol and a nonsmoker, is especially displeased by the Steppenwolf's numerous wine bottles and the ever-present stumps and ash of cigars, which he discovers while spying on the lodger. A stickler for rules and regulations, the editor balks at the Steppenwolf's request not to inform the police of his residence, as stipulated by law. Even though Haller gives poor health as a pretext for his request, his alienation from society, in particular from the bureaucratic constraints of the state, is the true reason for his breach of existing law. Although the Steppenwolf leads a bohemian life which stands in stark contrast to the editor's sense of duty and purpose, the outsider is attracted to middle-class orderliness to a certain degree. When the editor returns home one evening, he finds the Steppenwolf admiring two plants at the entrance of a flat. For Haller the spotlessly clean plants are "the very essence of bourgeois cleanliness, of neatness and meticulousness, of duty and devotion shown in little things." While he declares that he does not laugh at bourgeois life, because it reminds him of his childhood, the Steppenwolf is painfully aware that he is estranged from that world and that it is lost to him forever: "I live a bit to one side, on the edge of things." After an initially negative view of the lone wolf, the editor eventually feels sympathy "for one who had suffered so long and deeply." When the Steppenwolf suddenly disappears, he leaves only a manuscript behind along with the statement that the editor may do with it as he pleases. Because the editor regards the manuscript as a document of "the sickness of the times themselves," he decides to publish it with a caveat to the reader that he considers it for the most part fictitious: He believes that the Steppenwolf has attempted to give deeply lived spiritual events the form of tangible experiences.

Having experienced the Steppenwolf from a primarily exterior perspective, the reader is next confronted with a firsthand, interior view of the outsider's sufferings in "Harry Haller's Records," which bear the caution "For Madmen Only." It is significant that *Verrückte,* the German word for madman, implies displacement and derangement, stressing yet again the Steppenwolf's outsider position. Haller's alienation from middle-class values becomes only too evident when he is invited to the home of a conservative professor. The evening turns into a disaster when the professor unwittingly calls Haller a "bad fellow and a rotten patriot" and when the Steppenwolf insults his hostess by criticizing her favorite portrait of the classical writer Goethe for its sentimentality. For Haller the disagreeable soirée represents his ultimate break with the bourgeois world: "It was my leave-taking from the respectable, moral and learned world, and a complete triumph for the Steppenwolf." The image of the Steppenwolf gains another dimension in Haller's writings. It signifies not only his outsider role but also his untamed, animalistic nature, which is in constant conflict with his intellectual, civilized side. This strife between nature and spirit, which frequently brings Haller to the brink of suicide, is expanded upon in the "Treatise on the Steppenwolf," a detached analysis of his dilemma, which he receives from a mysterious stranger. It not only stresses that Harry consists of a hundred or a thousand selves, not merely two, it also offers humor as the solution. As recommended by the treatise, Haller now commences the "wild zig-zag trail" of exploring those elements of his psyche that he has suppressed. This quest, during which he is assisted by several characters from the margins of society, culminates in the Magic Theater, in which he explores such suppressed facets as sexuality and violence. Thus, even though Haller's alienation from the middle class is exacerbated, the alienation within him is slightly ameliorated.

Karl Stegner

Sex/Sensuality/Eroticism in *Steppenwolf*

One sign of Harry Haller's alienation is his lack of an intimate relationship and his suppression of sexual feelings. The collapse of his marriage to a mentally unbalanced woman, along with Harry's loss of profession and livelihood, constitutes the reason for his withdrawal from society: "Love and confidence had changed of a sudden to hate and deadly enmity. . . . It was then that my solitude had its beginning." The subsequent relationship with his lover Erika is fraught with conflict and is based on desperation rather than love. They see each other only intermittently and each meeting leads to quarrels. Harry concedes that "since both of us were lonely, difficult people related somehow to one another in soul, and sickness of soul, there was a link between us that held in spite of all."

One evening, when Harry is close to committing suicide, he meets Hermine, "a pale and pretty girl" who wears a withered camellia in her hair and who reminds him of his former sweetheart, Rosa Kreisler, and of Hermann, a boyhood friend. The flower is symbolic for Hermine's being a courtesan who is financially supported by several men in exchange for sexual favors. Hermine, however, does not see Harry as a prospective customer but rather as a lost soul who needs to be taught the pleasures of life. She takes on the role of a mother by calling Harry a silly baby who needs someone to look after him. In order to loosen Harry up and to free him from his inhibitions, Hermine teaches him to dance the fox-trot. Soon Harry's feelings of depression lift and he glimpses a ray of hope: "She was the one window, the one tiny crack of light in my black hole of dread. She was my release and my way to freedom. She had to teach me to live or teach me to die." Hermine introduces Harry to Maria, another courtesan, and to Pablo, an exotic, bisexual musician who talks him into experimenting with drugs. Since Hermine represents the female component of Harry's personality, or, in Jungian terms, his anima, he cannot be intimate with her. Hermine states: "I am a kind of looking glass for you, because there's something in me that answers you and understands you" and Harry concedes: "You're my opposite. You have all that I lack." When he finds Maria in his bed as a gift from Hermine, Harry is at first hampered by bourgeois hang-ups: he worries about what his landlady might think. Eventually, however, he learns to enjoy the sensual pleasures the experienced courtesan has to offer: "She taught me the charming play and delight of the senses, but she gave me, also, new understanding, new insight, new love." Harry enters into a sexual liaison with Maria, renting a room specifically for their frequent assignations. Surprisingly, he is not bothered by the fact that he has to share Maria with other men who are paying for her favors. A further indication that Harry is shedding his middle-class inhibitions and prejudices is the fact that his uptight view of bisexuality and homosexuality gradually loosens. Even though he initially rejects Pablo's offer of a threesome with Maria, Harry is not repulsed when Pablo kisses him on the eyelids: "I took the kiss as though I believed it came from Maria, but I knew very well it came from him." Eventually Harry accepts his bisexual tendencies when in the Magic Theater a young, elegant fellow, who represents one facet of Harry's personality, leaps laughing into Pablo's arms, embraces him, and goes off with him. When Harry enters a room, which promises "ALL GIRLS ARE YOURS," he not only relives all the love affairs of his youth, rectifying all the mistakes and omissions he made as a young man, he also accepts Pablo's invitation to "fantastic games for three and four." This experimentation does not leave him conflicted, but rather calm, wise, and expert. In the Magic Theater Harry also encounters Hermine dressed up as his boyhood friend Hermann and falls under her hermaphroditic spell. Even though Harry has come far, he still has far to go. This is revealed when he finds Hermine and Pablo in deep sleep after a bout of lovemaking and stabs her with an imaginary knife in a fit of jealousy. When Mozart, one of the Immortals, stresses that Harry must learn not to take life too seriously, Harry agrees that he still has much to learn: "One day I would be a better hand at the game. One day I would learn how to laugh."

Karl Stegner

VIOLENCE in *Steppenwolf*

Harry Haller's exploration of his violent impulses follows a similar trajectory as that of his sexual and erotic urges. At the beginning of the novel he is strongly opposed to any form of violence and aggression. He is a pacifist who is vilified in newspaper editorials as "a noxious insect and a man who disowned his native land" because he opposes preparations for an impending war, which he predicts will be a good deal more horrible than the last. Harry's violent impulses are turned against himself, and he frequently considers suicide to escape a world that he despises. At the beginning of his manuscript, for example, Harry considers cutting his throat with a straight razor. When Harry is called "a bad fellow,

rotten patriot, and traitor to his country" by a young professor who has invited him to dinner, he suppresses his rage against the ignorant colleague and instead turns it inward, coming close to ending his own life. It is revealed in the "Treatise on the Steppenwolf" that Harry has set his 50th birthday as the day upon which he is permitted "to employ the emergency exit" and that this knowledge makes it bearable for him to keep on living.

After he meets Hermine, however, Harry realizes that it is unhealthy to suppress his violent impulses and he starts exploring them. In the Magic Theater he first enters a door inscribed "Jolly Hunting. Great Hunt in Automobiles." In a darkly comic scene Harry joins the war between men and machines and, together with his school friend Gustav, proceeds to shoot the drivers and passengers of cars. At first, the friends kill and destroy out of a sense of displeasure and despair of the world, but gradually they enjoy the feeling of power and revenge. Ultimately, though, Harry comes to regret that he has unleashed the violence within him: When he is confronted with a harmless, peaceable, and childlike man, "who was still in a state of innocence," Harry is ashamed of his actions.

The theme of violence is explored further in the scene entitled "Marvelous Taming of the Steppenwolf." Harry encounters an animal tamer, who appears to be his "diabolically distorted double" and who forces a wolf to perform circus tricks that run counter to his wild nature: When presented with a rabbit and a sheep, the wolf lies between them and touches them with his paws, forming "a touching family group." A sudden role reversal, however, puts the wolf in charge and lets him recover his wild nature. The animal tamer then turns into a wild animal, tearing the rabbit and sheep limb from limb and chewing the living flesh rapturously. The fact that Harry flees the scene in horror is an indication that he is still unable to accept the aggressive, wild animal within.

Further proof of Harry's continuing inability to come to terms with the various facets of his personality is his act of smashing a gigantic mirror that shows the reflection of a beautiful wolf, who is transformed into Harry himself. In the final scene of the Magic Theater, entitled "How One Kills for Love,"

Harry finds the naked figures of Hermine and Pablo asleep after a bout of lovemaking. He notices a bruise beneath Hermine's left breast that shows the imprint of Pablo's "beautiful, gleaming teeth" and he plunges a knife to the hilt into the bruise in a fit of jealousy: "Before she had ever been mine, I had killed my love." Harry clearly has not yet learned how to channel his aggressive and violent impulses properly. Whereas some critics have interpreted the novel's ending as pessimistic and considered Harry Haller's attempts to explore the sexual as well as violent urges of his personality ultimately a failure, Hermann Hesse himself stressed that he conceived *Steppenwolf* not as the portrait of a man who is in despair but rather as that of a believer. He stated that the story does not lead to death and destruction but rather to healing. Perhaps one can take a clue from the fictional editor of the book who asserts that, even though Harry Haller's experiences greatly upset the outsider and caused him to leave town precipitously, he is convinced that the Steppenwolf did not commit suicide.

Karl Stegner

HINTON, S. E. *The Outsiders* (1967)

The Outsiders introduces a group of friends in the 1950s who live on the poor side of town and have to deal with all of the prejudices and realities of poverty. Ponyboy Curtis is the 14-year-old narrator of this story. While he is the youngest of his brothers, as well as the youngest of all of the friends with whom they associate, he is also the storyteller, both literally and figuratively, and he sees what happens around him more clearly than most of the other characters are able to do.

At the beginning of the story, Ponyboy can see the world only from his own perspective. He believes his oldest brother doesn't like him, and is mean to him as a result. He believes that the Socs, the rich kids, have no problems because they have money. Over the course of the novel, he realizes that his oldest brother is strict with him because he cares so much about Ponyboy and couldn't bear to lose him. Also, he befriends Cherry, a Soc girl, and begins to understand that "things are tough all over." Money doesn't buy happiness, love, or a sense of personal

security. Unfortunately his journey to these realizations (one could say his journey toward maturity or adulthood) includes violence and heartbreak. Two of his good friends are killed during the story, and he watches several other characters deal with less tragic, but still painful, changes. This is a narrative of growth, with the focus on the growing pains.

Kathleen McDonald

The AMERICAN DREAM in *The Outsiders*

The debate over whether anyone can achieve his or her American dream has raged since long before the term was coined in 1913, and continues in full force today. Hinton's *The Outsiders* shows how a group of people whose birth was not fortuitous, who had to fight for every scrap that they had. Their biggest fight comes when they have to face people who can not believe that these greasers have the ability to achieve anything worthwhile, much less the respect to appreciate it if they did.

The two groups in this novel seem to divide on lines of socioeconomic status. The Socs have every material advantage that money and status can provide; the greasers are constantly struggling simply to make ends meet. However, our narrator realizes that this line is porous and allows for movement back and forth. Ponyboy notes that "the only thing that keeps Darry from bein' a Soc is us." When Cherry and Ponyboy discuss their mutual appreciation of watching sunsets, it leads Ponyboy to a realization: "Maybe the two different worlds we lived in weren't so different."

Yet for these characters, this division is very real. Darry, the oldest brother, can not afford to go to college, even with an athletic scholarship. Sodapop, the middle brother, has dropped out of high school to work and help keep the family together after their parents died. It is easy to see how the lack of money and goods has contributed to the problems of the greasers; however, Hinton shows how the exact opposite situation contributed to the destruction of the Socs. Cherry spells out this situation in her first conversation with Ponyboy:

> You greasers have a different set of values. . . .
> We're sophisticated—cool to the point of not feeling anything. Nothing is real to

us. . . . Did you ever hear of having more than you wanted? So that you couldn't want anything else and then started looking for something else to want? It seems like we're always searching for something to satisfy us, and never finding it.

Later that evening, Ponyboy realizes: "the Socs had so much spare time and money that they jumped us and each other for kicks." Ponyboy eventually realizes that this freedom from want or the need to work was what led to the death of Bob, a Soc. In a final encounter between Ponyboy and Bob's best friend, Randy, Randy notes: "most parents would be proud of a kid like that—good lookin' and smart and everything, but they gave in to him all the time. He kept trying to make someone say 'No' and they never did. . . . If the old man had just belted him—just once, he might still be alive."

The ability to achieve individual dreams is implied, especially as characters age. Just before the big rumble at the end of the story, Ponyboy evaluates the greasers assembled for the fight. He recognizes that some actually seem to enjoy being hoods and would likely be hoods for the entirety of their lives. However, when he looks at his brothers and himself, he sees something different:

> I looked at Darry. He wasn't going to be any hood when he got old. He was going to get somewhere. Living the way we do would only make him more determined to get some-where. That's why he's better than the rest of us, I thought. He's going somewhere. And I was going to be like him. I wasn't going to live in a lousy neighborhood all my life.

Although Ponyboy uses a concrete, material example of what achieving his American dream would mean (living in a better neighborhood), the emphasis is not on things but on not being a hood, not simply accept-ing the life that one started with, but being deter-mined and making changes to acquire a better life.

At the end of the novel, Ponyboy has reached the point where he is making sense of what happened. A letter that his friend Johnny had written before he died sums up the belief that the American dream does exist, even for greasers: "And don't be so bugged over being a greaser. You still have a lot of time to make yourself be what you want." Hinton's novel points out how strong the obstacles to achieving the American dream can be, but ultimately supports the premise that innate talents combined with hard work make it achievable for all.

Kathleen McDonald

CRUELTY in *The Outsiders*

Violence pervades *The Outsiders*. If it is not actively taking place in a particular scene, the threat of it constantly exists just under the surface. Physical fights occur, both between individuals and between groups. Characters are beaten, some badly, and several even lose their lives from violent encoun-ters. Most of the characters carry knives or guns in anticipation of meeting violence. Yet cruelty and VIOLENCE are not synonyms. Violence is often a manifestation of cruelty, but each can occur in the absence of the other. Some of the cruelest moments in *The Outsiders* occur without physical violence, yet these moments still disturb deeply.

In the first encounter with Cherry and her friend at the Drive-In, Ponyboy notes the cruel taunting that Dally subjects the girls to, and his discomfort with this treatment. He says:

> I had a sick feeling that Dally was up to his usual tricks, and I was right. He started talk-ing, loud enough for the two girls to hear. He started out bad and got worse. Dallas could talk awful dirty if he wanted to and I guess he wanted to then. I felt my ears get hot. Two-Bit or Steve or even Soda would have gone right along with him, just to see if they could embarrass the girls, but that kind of kicks just doesn't appeal to me.

Ponyboy rightly interprets Dally's motive to be to make the girls in front of them suffer. He notes that Dally "was up to his usual tricks" and is not pleased. His discomfort shows through his ears getting hot and his unwillingness to participate with the much stronger, both physically and in personality, Dally, in teasing these girls, depicting his awareness of how cruel Dally is being.

The girls themselves show their consciousness of Dally's cruelty: "The girls got mad. 'You'd better leave us alone,' the redhead said in a biting voice, 'or I'll call the cops.'" Dally is not impressed with this threat and continues his cruelty by mocking this very legitimate claim for social authority to protect them from unwanted and inappropriate behavior: "'Oh, my, my'—Dally looked bored—'you've got me scared to death. You ought to see my record sometime, baby.' He grinned slyly. 'Guess what I've been in for?'" When Cherry realizes that threatening legal ramifications is unlikely to work, she switches from a threat to a plea: "'*Please* leave us alone,' she said. 'Why don't you just be nice and leave us alone?'" This tactic actually works as Dally saunters away to get drinks for everyone, but this is only because his cruelty was the mask he was using to begin a conversation with the girls. His actual objective was about getting attention from girls who are in a higher socioeconomic class, so the unwritten rules of their teenage society told him they were out of his league. If Dally had approached them directly in a friendly manner and was shot down, he risked being laughed at, both by the girls and by his own friends. For many boys, but especially those concerned about having a tough-guy reputation, being laughed at is the cruelest response of all. Therefore, his outward cruelty to these girls hides his own fear of being the object of cruelty and derision. This is confirmed by the fact that he brings back Cokes for everyone, including both girls, and sits down beside Cherry when he returns. This psychological understanding in no way makes Dally's behavior acceptable, as Cherry shows in the story by throwing the Coke in his face. But knowing a character's motives permits a deeper insight into both the character and the story.

In a later scene, Johnny notes how the absence of violence can be the cruelest treatment of all: "'I think I like it better when the old man's hittin' me!' Johnny sighed. 'At least then I know he knows who I am. I walk in that house, and nobody says anything. I walk out, and nobody says anything. I stay away all night, and nobody notices.'" For Johnny, the only notice his parents ever pay to him is to be abusive. As bad as that physical abuse is, he realizes that the pain of their pretending he doesn't exist is just as bad, if not worse.

In *The Outsiders*, cruelty is a main theme that runs throughout the entire novel. Sometimes it is linked directly to violence; other times it is not. But with or without physical violence attached, the cruelty these characters all have to contend with throughout the novel is frightening in its scope. Great literature makes us think and feel. When we consider how pervasive is the cruelty in this novel, we should do both.

Kathleen McDonald

HEROISM in *The Outsiders*

There is one clear-cut example of heroism in this story: The abandoned church where Ponyboy and Johnny are hiding out from the police catches fire and they rush into the burning building to save several little kids caught inside. While Ponyboy and Johnny are still inside, the building falls apart and a burning beam falls on Johnny, breaking his back. This dangerous choice to save children that they don't even know is an act that results in everyone labeling them heroes. There are newspaper articles written about them, and even when strangers find out that they were only in the church because they were running from murder charges, that is not enough to make people think them less heroic. However, while this is publicly labeled heroism, there are several other acts in the story that are, perhaps, even more heroic, due to their premeditated and less public nature.

When Dally comes to find Ponyboy and Johnny in the church, he tells them that Cherry has agreed to come forward and testify that Ponyboy acted in self defense. Cherry risks her physical safety in order to try to make things right. Although they don't jump her, with tensions running so high after a greaser killed a Soc, she couldn't have been sure that this would be the case, regardless of her motives. Beyond the courage that this physical encounter required, Cherry shows her heroism in a much stronger way. She knows that the rules of this society require her to ignore greasers, as she tells Ponyboy the night they meet: "if I see you in the hall at school or someplace and don't say hi, well, it's not personal or anything." However, that rule is trumped by her feelings of responsibility. She believes that the entire situation is, at least partially, her fault. As the girlfriend of the dead boy, no one would ever expect her to do anything to help the people who killed him. Yet she does. She is willing to testify against her dead boyfriend and her entire social group, to help two boys she barely knows, one of whom killed her boyfriend, just because it is the right thing to do: unheralded heroism.

There is another powerful example of unheralded heroism in this story. Ponyboy's oldest brother, Darry, had the grades for college, but when the boys' parents died, Darry had to make a choice between college for himself and keeping a home together for his younger brothers. Even with Ponyboy's inability to understand Darry in the beginning of the story, he can see that Darry has sacrificed a lot, so that he and Sodapop didn't have to go to foster care. Darry worked hard, sacrificing his own dreams and ambitions, so that Ponyboy and his younger brothers could fulfill theirs.

The story has a major act of publicly declared heroism, yet it is not any more important than any of the other less-heralded heroic acts. It creates a pivotal plot twist that is essential to the conclusion of the story but is equal thematically to the heroism displayed by Cherry or Darry or many of the other characters. In this novel, heroism symbolizes the changes associated with growing up. As you mature, you must take responsibility. You must do this regardless of personal desires or peer pressure. Through this story, Ponyboy (and hopefully the reader) realizes that heroism, recognized or not, requires the maturity to sacrifice.

Kathleen McDonald

HOMER   *The Iliad*   (800–650 B.C.E.)

The Iliad is one of two great epic poems attributed to Homer. Little is known about Homer or the composition of the two works, but *The Iliad* was probably written between 800 and 650 B.C.E. It is the tale of a brief period in the 10th (and final) year of the Trojan War, as the Greeks are besieging the city of Troy. The war began when Helen, the world's most beautiful woman, ran away with a Trojan prince named Paris. Helen's husband Menelaus, together with his brother, King Agamemnon, gathers the Greek armies and sails after Helen. The

Greeks' greatest warrior is Achilles, who is joined by his close friend Patroclus. Other major Achaeans (another name for the Greeks) include Odysseus, the cleverest man alive, and Diomedes, a fearless warrior. The Trojans are led by their greatest warrior, Hector, one of Paris's brothers. Aeneas (who it is said will later found Rome), Glaucus, and Sarpedon are all key Trojan allies. Hector's wife Andromache and his father, King Priam, dread the war's outcome.

The Iliad is the story of "the rage of Achilles" (77). Agamemnon has taken Chryses, the daughter of Apollo's priest, as a prize. When Agamemnon refuses the priest's request for her return, the god Apollo ravages the Greeks with a plague. Agamemnon returns Chryses, but seizes Briseis instead (who was Achilles' prize). Achilles is enraged at this insult and refuses to fight for the Greeks. Without him, the Greeks are unable to win and both sides suffer terrible losses. Eventually, Patroclus fights in Achilles' place and is slain, leading Achilles to seek vengeance on Hector. Achilles slays Hector, even though he knows that he is fated to die soon after. Throughout the story, gods like Zeus, Athena, and Apollo take sides in the fighting and scheme to help their favorite mortals. *The Iliad* is a classic epic of war, exploring a range of themes that include DEATH, FATE, HEROISM, PRIDE, and VIOLENCE.

James Ford

DEATH in *The Iliad*

The main subject of *The Iliad* is Achilles' rage, and the first few lines show that the cost of that rage is death—"hurling down to the House of Death so many sturdy souls, great fighters' souls, but made their bodies carrion, feasts for the dogs and birds" (77). It begins with the plague sent by the god Apollo, "and the corpse-fires burned on, night and day, no end in sight" (79). Achilles' mother Thetis wails that he is "doomed to a short life," but the poem also demonstrates that all human beings ultimately "have so little time" (91).

The gods play with human life in *The Iliad*. Zeus sends a "murderous dream" to tell Agamemnon that Troy is now his for the taking, when in reality his army will be devastated (99). The armies gather for a titanic battle, but instead Paris challenges Menelaus to single combat. Both sides pray for victory, but even more for an end to the war. Instead, the goddess Aphrodite rescues Paris before Menelaus can kill him. The great clash of armies resumes, with "screams of men and cries of triumph breaking in one breath, fighters killing, fighters killed, and the ground streamed blood" (160). Slain heroes are named, while countless others suffer nameless deaths. Antilochus kills the Trojan captain Echepolus, and the slaughter is on. Elephenor tries to strip the dead man's gear and is himself stabbed in the ribs. "His life spirit left him and over his dead body now the savage work went on" (160–161). Meanwhile, Apollo cheers the Trojans on with a cry of "Stab them, slash their flesh!" (162). When not encouraging the slaughter, the gods often save their favorite heroes. Aphrodite saves the wounded Aeneas from Diomedes, who stabs her in the wrist as punishment. Athena saves Diomedes from Ares, and together they spear the god in the belt. Ultimately, death is beyond even the gods' control. The goddess Hera says it best: "Men—let one of them die, another live, however their luck may run. Let Zeus decide . . ." (245). While Zeus is tempted to intervene for his favorites, first Sarpedon and then Hector, both times Hera rebukes him. Zeus concludes, with pity, that "there is nothing alive more agonized than man of all that breathe and crawl across the earth" (457).

Homer's account of death is often brutal and graphic, as when Ajax slashes a man at the nipple "clean through the shoulder" (161). Leucus is gouged in the groin, while Diomedes spears Pandarus right between the eyes. At other times deaths are merely listed. Hector and Ares slaughter seven men in succession, with little detail. But the horrible cost of death—both for the fallen and for their loved ones—is always clear. Diomedes kills the two sons of Eurydamas, and "left their father tears and wrenching grief . . . distant kin would carve apart their birthright" (169). Andromache pleads with her husband Hector "before you orphan your son and make your wife a widow" (210). Both realize that slavery awaits her when Troy falls. The battle is often halted so that the dead can be gathered, the bodies burned. Both sides build their funeral pyres, "their hearts breaking" (228). While souls are said to travel to the House of Death, no details are given, and that

hint of afterlife is no consolation. Patroclus's soul goes down, "wailing his fate" (440), as does Hector's a short while later. Men are ashamed to fail in the defense of fallen heroes, and some of the most vicious fighting is for the bodies of the dead.

Most heroes struggle for an honorable death. Agamemnon calls for retreat as one battle goes poorly, saying it is "better to flee from death than feel its grip," but Odysseus rebukes him for this "nonsense" (372). Similarly, Hector says of a fallen comrade that "he dies fighting for fatherland—no dishonor there!" (403). Great warriors on both sides question the value of war. Sarpedon once calls to Glaucus, if only the two could escape and live forever, he would never fight again; but alas, "the fates of death await us" (335). Achilles refuses a king's ransom to reenter the war, since "a man's life breath cannot come back again" (265). Of course, all his reservations fade with the death of his friend Patroclus. Achilles goes to meet his death, as long as he can kill Hector. The final word on death is Priam's. Hector's father tells Achilles that "all looks fine and noble" for a young man killed in war, but an old man dead is "the cruelest sight in all our wretched lives!" (543–544). Achilles grants Priam 11 days for mourning and Hector's funeral. The poem ends as it began, with the cost of death abundantly clear.

James Ford

FATE in *The Iliad*

Fate is a pervasive theme in *The Iliad,* as all of the mortal characters are conscious of the grim fate—DEATH—that ultimately awaits them. Fate is most often described as driving the characters on to their deaths. This is particularly true for minor characters on both sides of the battle: "destiny guided Amphius on," straight into Ajax's spear (184); similarly for Tlepolemus: "his strong fate was driving him now against Sarpedon," who promptly kills Tlepolemus. Death and fate are closely linked for great heroes as well. Seeing his brother Menelaus seriously wounded, Agamemnon wonders what will happen to the Greeks "if you die now, if you fill out your destiny now." At times the fate of death narrowly misses one hero only to strike another. Ajax hurls his spear at Polydamas, "but the Trojan dodged black fate himself with a quick spring to the side"; the spear strikes Archelochus instead, "for the gods had doomed that fighting man to death" (384).

While *The Iliad* sometimes equates fate with the will of Zeus, at other times fate stands above even the gods themselves. Helen wishes to Hector that she had died as a child, to prevent the destruction of the Trojan War, but the gods dictated otherwise. "Zeus planted a killing doom within us both" (207). As wise Nestor notes, "not a man alive can fight the will of Zeus." The gods also see fate as the will of Zeus. Hera is anguished to see so many Greeks die, "filling out their fates to the last gasp," but it is for Zeus to "decide the fates" (245). Ares, too, is tempted to intervene (for the Trojans), "[e]ven if fate will crush me, striking me down with the thunderbolt of Zeus" (391). Poseidon complains that he should not have to listen to his brother, Zeus, but that the other gods' "fate" is to obey Zeus (394). Even mighty Zeus complains of his "cruel fate" when faced with the death of his son Sarpedon (427). In Greek mythology, the Fates were three goddesses who spun the destinies of mortals in thread. As Hera notes of Achilles, "he must suffer what the Fates spun out." But the nature of fate is rarely clear in *The Iliad*; the gods frequently intervene lest something happen "against the will of fate" (514).

At several points in the battle, Zeus weighs "two fates of death" in his "sacred golden scales" (233). In Book 8, the Achaeans' fate goes down, and Zeus intervenes against them; in Book 22, the fate of the two great champions is weighed, and it is Hector whose fate it is to fall to Achilles. It is Zeus who makes the ultimate prophecy that overshadows *The Iliad*, that Patroclus's death will bring Achilles back into battle, to slay Hector. The fullest statement on fate is Hector's, who is resigned to fate and death. He states that no one can slay him, against his fate; "And fate? No one alive has ever escaped it, neither brave man nor coward . . . it's born with us the day that we are born" (212). Later, though, Hector flees a battle when he senses "that Zeus had tipped the scales against him" (434). At that point, Patroclus might have escaped his fate, had he obeyed Achilles' command to stay near the ships, but "the will of Zeus will always overpower the will of men" (435). Zeus drives Patroclus on, and only Apollo prevents him from taking Troy. Hector slays Patroclus, who

rightly sees that "deadly fate in league with Apollo killed me" (440). He prophesies that soon "death and the strong force of fate" will bring Hector down, in the form of Achilles (440).

Achilles' situation is more complex. Achilles clearly has a choice. His mother (the goddess Thetis) has revealed to him the possibilities, that "two fates bear me on to the day of death" (265). Either he can stay to besiege Troy, in which case he will die soon, and his glory will live forever; or he can head home, to a long life without pride or glory. With the death of Patroclus, Achilles embraces the fate that brings him glory and death. Interestingly, Achilles is not the only mortal aware of his choice. The minor character Euchenor was told by his father (a prophet) that sailing to Troy meant certain death in battle, while staying behind meant a slow death from plague. Like Achilles, Euchenor chose death in battle as his fate. It may be that all mortals have a choice of fates, but only a few realize it.

James Ford

HEROISM in *The Iliad*

As the Greeks' greatest fighter, Achilles is the primary model of heroism in *The Iliad*. His tremendous courage and power distinguish him, leading Agamemnon to describe him as "the most violent man alive" (82). Heroism in *The Iliad* is a matter of honor, won especially through glory in battle. The "godlike Achilles" lives entirely for honor, withdrawing from the fighting when he is slighted by Agamemnon (81). His longing for glory is so complete that he prays for the slaughter of the Greek armies, until he receives the honor he deserves. Heroism requires courage, and no one is more courageous than Achilles. Diomedes (another great hero) argues that "courage, the greatest power of all," stands above honor, ruling, or anything else (252). Both the Greeks and the Trojans are taught courage from birth. Hippolochus tells his son Glaucus, "Always be the best, my boy, the bravest, and hold your head up high above the others" (202), words echoed in Peleus's own advice to his son Achilles (322). In *The Iliad*, to be the bravest often is to be the best.

Heroism is not only about courage, however. While he is not a fighter like Achilles, Agamemnon also expects to be recognized as the best of men (this longing for recognition is the source of their dispute). Achilles calls him "the most grasping man alive" (81), but Nestor explains simply that Agamemnon "has more power because he rules more men" (86). This question of whether greatness consists primarily of prowess in battle or of ruling other men hangs over *The Iliad*. Wisdom in council is another important aspect of heroism in the poem. Nestor is too old to be of much use in fighting, but is still regarded for his wisdom. Odysseus, in particular, "that mastermind like Zeus" (120), manages to combine greatness on the battlefield with the power of persuasion and skill in tactics. Helen calls him "the man of twists and turns" (135), and in some ways he represents the best of both models of heroism.

Hector, the greatest of the Trojans, also represents a balance between the courage of a great warrior and the wisdom of a great ruler. Unlike Achilles, Hector's longing for personal glory is usually tempered by his love for Troy and his fellow countrymen. Hector is heroic in his resignation, knowing the long odds that face his people and their dim prospects for survival. "But I would die of shame to face the men of Troy and the Trojan women trailing their long robes if I shrank from battle now, a coward" (210). His prayer for his son—that he be "first in glory among the Trojans, strong and brave like me, and rule all Troy in power . . ."—is a powerful summation of that heroic code (211). He knows that he is weaker than Achilles but fights nonetheless. His parents beg him not to go forth, but he replies that it is better "to stand up to Achilles, kill him, come home alive or die at his hands in glory . . ." (545). Still, great as he is, even Hector will run from Achilles, until Athena tricks him into fighting.

Heroism is partly men's own and partly a gift from the gods. For instance, Athena grants Diomedes "strength and daring" to "win himself great glory" (164). But this only accentuates Diomedes' usual courage and power. Warriors are often heroic alone, but at times two together are heroic, as when Diomedes and Odysseus embark on their night mission. The fear of shame is an important impetus for heroism on both sides, as Agamemnon rallies the Greeks to "dread what comrades say of you here in bloody combat!" (181). Heroism often involves defending the fallen, although at times that means forgoing the heroic lust for glory. Ajax urges his countrymen to stand fast in defense of Patroclus's body, saying "no heroes either, bolting out of the Argive pack for single combat" (454). Achilles himself raises doubts about the heroic life, complaining that "the same honor waits for the coward and the brave" (262). But those doubts are washed away with the death of Patroclus, when all that matters to Achilles is vengeance, and "great glory" (471).

Priam, the Trojan king, displays his own heroism at the close of *The Iliad*. Achilles refuses Hector's offer to return the loser's body home, with the crushing dismissal, "there are no binding oaths between men and lions" (550). Priam goes to Achilles alone, to ask for Hector's body. Reminded of his own father, Achilles complies, and marvels at Priam's "daring," his "heart of iron" (605). Although too old for battle, Priam's courage is still heroic.

James Ford

HOMER   *The Odyssey*

The Odyssey is the second of the two great epic poems attributed to Homer. Little is known about Homer or the composition of the two works, but *The Odyssey* was almost certainly written after *The ILIAD*. Unlike *The Iliad*, which focuses on a particular event (the conflict between Achilles and Agamemnon) and its immediate aftermath, *The Odyssey* is simply the story of Odysseus—the man, his travels, and his family. The first four books provide the background for his tale by focusing on his son, Telemachus, who travels in search of news of his father, who has not returned from the war in Troy. Odysseus, "the man of twists and turns," has been gone from his home in Ithaca for 20 years (77). Telemachus struggles against a crowd of suitors who constantly feast at his home, pestering Odysseus's wife Penelope to choose one as her new husband. The goddess Athena aids Telemachus in his search, just as she often advises Odysseus. Eventually the poet turns to Odysseus himself, who is held captive by the goddess Calypso (who loves him). The rest of the poem tells the story of his journey home, and of his many adventures—including his visits to the Cyclops, the goddess Circe, and the land of the dead.

Ultimately, Odysseus reaches home, unites with his family, and slays the suitors who have plagued his household. Through it all Odysseus is noted for his cunning as well as his courage, his wisdom as well as his might. *The Odyssey* is a grand adventure story, full of themes like DEATH, FAMILY, FATE, HEROISM, IDENTITY, and PRIDE.

James Ford

FAMILY in *The Odyssey*

While *The ILIAD* is a tale of VIOLENCE and war, *The Odyssey* is a tale of family and home. Odysseus, "his heart set on his wife and his return," does everything he can to make it home from the war (78). The poem begins by focusing on Odysseus's son, Telemachus, his "heart obsessed with grief" at his father's absence (84). A crowd of suitors for his mother, Penelope, are draining his household dry with their constant feasting. The goddess Athena counsels him "like a father to a son," advising Telemachus to leave home in search of news of his father's fate. "Few sons are the equals of their fathers," Athena tells him, but she assures him that he has Odysseus's courage and cunning (102). Telemachus travels to see Nestor, wisest of the Greeks, who recognizes that Telemachus has Odysseus's tremendous eloquence. Nestor sends his son Psistratus with Telemachus to see Menelaus, and one observer says the two young men "look like kin of mighty Zeus himself" (125). The importance of family is highlighted by the joy that Menelaus and his wife, Helen, share. Helen abandoned her child, her husband, and her home when she went with Paris to Troy. Now she realizes her "madness," all the suffering and DEATH that resulted (132). Their reunited family is a model of domestic bliss.

Odysseus himself is certain of the value of family. Although he did sleep with Calypso while on her island, he was an "unwilling lover alongside lover all too willing" (157). Odysseus perseveres through a series of trials and adventures to reach his home. He tells the Phaeacian princess that there is no greater gift than a home and marriage in harmony, with "two minds, two hearts that work as one" (174). His homeland of Ithaca is almost as important as his wife and son. As he says, "I know no sweeter sight on earth than a man's own native country" (212). The family is mirrored in the country, particularly

for King Odysseus, who ruled Ithaca "kindly as a father to his children" (94). But his greatest goal is to be reunited with his wife and son.

Penelope is just as devoted as Odysseus to their family, if not more so. She longs for her husband's return, delaying her suitors for years. In a scheme worthy of Odysseus (and suggested to her by a god), Penelope says she will choose a new husband once she finishes weaving a shroud for Laertes (Odysseus's father). Each night she unravels whatever she wove during the day. The trick works for a full three years before the suitors discover the ruse. Despite Odysseus's charge to choose a new husband when Telemachus's beard begins to grow, Penelope holds out for her husband's return. She is "the soul of loyalty" (409). Her final test for the suitors—stringing Odysseus's mighty bow—is another sign of that loyalty. She longs for the days when her family was whole, when her household was "so filled with the best that life can offer" (409). In *The Odyssey*, family and a happy home are clearly the best that life has to offer.

The importance of a loving family is underscored by the tragedy of Agamemnon, who is killed at his return home from Troy. Aegisthus has conspired with Agamemnon's wife Clytemnestra to murder Agamemnon, and the Greeks regard this as the ultimate betrayal. Agamemnon's only solace is that his son Orestes avenges his death, a sign of how crucial the father-son relationship is to the Greeks. When Odysseus travels to the kingdom of the dead, Agamemnon's ghost begs for knowledge of his son's life. Similarly, Achilles' ghost no longer cares about the glory he won during life. Instead he asks about his father Peleus and his son Neoptolemus. Achilles is thrilled to learn that Neoptolemus is gifted in battle and in counsel. Similarly, Odysseus's parents suffer greatly at his absence. His mother, Anticleia, died of grief and longing while Odysseus was away. His father is also bereft, but he rejoices at his son's return. When he sees his son and grandson "vying over courage," it is the ultimate triumph for the man and a fitting end to the poem (484).

Finally, the emphasis on hospitality reinforces the importance of home and family. Nestor welcomes Telemachus, as does Menelaus—"Just think of all the hospitality *we* enjoyed" (125). The Phaeacians welcome Odysseus and provide him with the means to return home, while the Cyclops violates all the customs of hospitality. Nestor provides essential wisdom: "Don't rove from home too long" (117).

James Ford

HEROISM in *The Odyssey*

The distinctive feature of Odysseus's heroism is the way he combines cunning and wisdom with boldness and power. While many facets of heroism are on display in *The Odyssey*, more than anyone Odysseus balances courage with sense. It is this combination of wisdom and power that enables Odysseus to return home after 20 years at sea.

The poem begins with four books telling of a future hero, Odysseus's son Telemachus. Telemachus has his father's gift of speech and some of his courage, but needs Athena's encouragement before he ventures forth. Athena makes explicit Odysseus's excellence. Posing as Mentor, she marvels "now there was a man, I'd say, in words and actions both!" (102). Many Greek heroes are men of action, a few others skilled in counsel, but few combine the two like Odysseus. As Telemachus relates it, people say that Odysseus pledged his word and "made it good in action" on the battlefield (110). Telemachus wishes that his father could have had a good death in battle, or in old age at home, either of which would mean great fame for the Greek hero. Instead, he worries that Odysseus will be forever lost at sea, a death without glory. Despite his eagerness to defend his house, Telemachus himself lacks glory until his father returns to lead him in battle against the suitors.

Meanwhile, Odysseus is "fighting to save his life and bring his comrades home" (77). Zeus himself says that Odysseus "excels all men in wisdom, excels in offerings too" (79). Despite his wisdom, Odysseus runs afoul of the god Poseidon when he blinds the Cyclops Polyphemus. Odysseus's return home is cursed, and he spends 10 years wandering the seas in his ongoing voyage home. Odysseus's heroism is marked by "a hundred feat of arms," as Menelaus says (129), feats marked by his cunning as well as his courage. Helen tells Telemachus of the time Odysseus snuck into Troy disguised as a beggar, while Menelaus cites the idea of the Trojan horse as evidence of Odysseus's heroism. This combination of cleverness and courage is on full display in Odysseus's retelling of his encounter with the Cyclops. Trapped inside a cave with the giant, Odysseus defeats the Cyclops with clever planning followed by bold action. He gets the Cyclops drunk on powerful wine, works with his men to poke the giant's eye out, and then escapes from the cave by strapping himself and his men to the underside of the Cyclops's massive sheep. In one of his great tricks, Odysseus tells the Cyclops his name is "Nobody," so that when Polyphemus turns to his fellow giants for help his cries make little sense: "Nobody's killing me now by fraud and not by force!" (224). As Odysseus reminds his men later, "my courage, my presence of mind and tactics saved us all" (277). The same qualities eventually enable him to return in triumph, avenging himself against the suitors and reclaiming his wife and home.

While death is not quite as constant or as graphic in *The Odyssey* as it was in *The ILIAD*, the dark side of Greek heroism is still apparent. When Odysseus travels to the House of Death to learn his fate, he sees his mother Anticleia, dead from grief over Odysseus's long absence. He longs to embrace her, but is unable. He sees a variety of heroes long dead, before meeting Agamemnon, murdered by his wife Clytemnestra and her lover Aegisthus on his return home. Finally he sees great Achilles, hero of *The ILIAD*. Odysseus praises Achilles for his greatness in life, and now his power over the dead. Achilles rebukes him, saying "By god, I'd rather slave on earth for another man . . . than rule down here over all the breathless dead" (265). If Achilles himself has rejected the glory of death in battle for the possibility of a long life enslaved, this would call into question the entire ideal of Greek heroism in war. But the reality is that Achilles has little patience for Odysseus's flattery. His adherence to the heroic ideal is shown by the rest of his speech, in which he questions Odysseus about the fate of Achilles's son, Neoptolemus. When Odysseus tells him that his son displayed excellent tactics and great courage in battle, Achilles rejoices, "triumphant" in the knowledge that his "gallant, glorious son" has followed in his footsteps (267). The magnificence of Homer's epic is to recognize and highlight the consequences of heroism while still displaying the glory of those who embrace it. *The Odyssey* proves that heroism is not only a matter of courage, but also the result of wisdom and cunning, particularly in the case of Odysseus.

James Ford

IDENTITY in *The Odyssey*

The Odyssey is the story of Odysseus, "the man of twists and turns" (77). His identity—who Odysseus is—is a central theme in the poem. He is at once a "raider of cities" (192), "the man of many struggles" (184), and "the great teller of tales" (211). While Aeolus calls him "most cursed" and his dead mother says he is the "unluckiest man alive," he is also a great hero who uses his cunning to escape from a series of dangers (232, 256).

Although *The Odyssey* is the tale of Odysseus and his wanderings after the Trojan War, it is not until the fifth book that Odysseus himself appears. The first four books focus instead on his son, Telemachus, who was only a month old when Odysseus sailed for Troy. Now 20 years old, it is his identity that is at issue at the beginning of the poem. Is he ready to become a man, worthy of great Odysseus? After a meeting of the gods, Athena comes down from Mount Olympus to inspire Telemachus to action. The poem is filled with numerous disguises and attempts to hide one's true identity. Athena disguises herself as a stranger, a man named Mentes. Telemachus welcomes the man warmly, questioning who he is, where he is from, and who his parents are. Asked about his own identity, Telemachus is doubtful. He names Odysseus as his father, but then wonders, "Who, on his own, has ever really known who gave him life?" (84). But later when he tells the suitors about Mentes, he has an insight worthy of his father—"deep in his mind he knew the immortal goddess" (91). Athena disguises herself as Telemachus, gathering a crew and securing a ship so that the young prince can seek news of his father's fate. Telemachus travels to Menelaus and Helen, key figures from Homer's *Iliad*, both of whom recognize Telemachus as Odysseus's son before he reveals himself. Helen tells the story of how Odysseus, disguised as a beggar, infiltrated Troy, and she alone recognized him.

Odysseus himself is often slow to reveal his identity. When questioned by Queen Arete, he spins his tale slowly, not revealing his identity until a muse sings the story of the Trojan horse (another of Odysseus's cunning exploits). Finally he makes himself plain, saying "I am Odysseus, son of Laertes, known to the world for every kind of craft—my fame has reached the skies" (212). He recounts to Arete the tale of his encounter with the Cyclops Polyphemus. When the Cyclops first asks who they are, Odysseus wisely answers "Men of Achaea" (219). Polyphemus asks again as he drinks Odysseus's wine and devours his men, and this time Odysseus replies "Nobody" (223). After Odysseus blinds the Cyclops, Polyphemus calls for help and says "Nobody's killing me now" (224). The other giants refuse to help him, and Odysseus's ruse leads to his triumphant escape. But in his hubris Odysseus taunts the Cyclops as they sail away, revealing his true identity. Polyphemus's curse on Odysseus causes years more of wandering and suffering.

Odysseus's return to Ithaca is a series of disguises, ploys, and careful tests of identity. He pretends to be a foreigner, but he meets Athena, who knows the truth. She counsels him not to reveal himself to anyone (advice that hardly seems necessary, given how cautious Odysseus is). Odysseus meets his swineherd, and says he is from Crete. He talks with Telemachus, at which point Athena tells him to reveal himself. Telemachus refuses to believe at first, but finally recognizes his father. Odysseus urges Telemachus to say nothing, "if you are my own true son, born of my blood" (348). Faithful servants recognize him, though. His old hound Argos leaps with joy—and drops dead on the spot. His old maid recognizes his scar when bathing him. Odysseus tests his father when he meets him, then embraces him. Even Laertes asks for "some proof" that Odysseus is who he claims, so Odysseus reveals his scar (478). Odysseus is revealed to the suitors through the test of the great bow. None can string it, let alone fire an arrow through the axes. Odysseus strings it, fires it true, and he and Telemachus slay the suitors. The most significant drama of recognition is between Odysseus and Penelope. He tests her, she tests him, both sounding out the other's true feelings. She says that they have "secret signs" known only to each other, particularly the secret of their marital bed (459). His knowledge of it proves his true identity, and at last husband and wife are reunited.

James Ford

HOUSTON, JEANNE WAKATSUKI
Farewell to Manzanar   (1972)

Jeanne Wakatsuki Houston begins her autobiographical text, *Farewell to Manzanar,* after the Japanese bombing of Pearl Harbor. The stable, FAMILY-oriented life she has known as a child is altered irreparably as her family is interned at the Manzanar War Relocation Center in California. The text recounts the family's life at Manzanar through the perspective of a seven-year-old Wakatsuki who spends three years of her CHILDHOOD at the prison. Because of the text's young narrator, life at the camp is occasionally portrayed as a new adventure where Wakatsuki meets new people and easily adapts to her imprisonment. However, as she ages, the narrator reveals the more sobering side of internment by focusing on her father's emotional and physical decline in the camp and her family's disintegration. Wakatsuki also discusses the key concerns that preoccupied internees, including loyalty oaths, the abrogation of citizenship rights, the dispossession of private property, and the predicament of having emotional ties to two warring nations: Japan and the United States. The book then shifts from the devastating consequences of wartime hysteria to post–World War II society as Manzanar is closed and the Wakatsukis reluctantly leave the camp to return to a hostile society. We follow the narrator's struggles to reacclimate herself into a postwar culture marked by continuing racial discrimination against Japanese Americans as she enters high school and tries to lead a normal teenage life. The book is ultimately a bildungsroman that narrates the trauma of internment and the dissolution of family.

Belinda Linn Rincon

FAMILY in *Farewell to Manzanar*

Farewell to Manzanar is a co-authored firsthand account of how the internment of Japanese Americans during World War II affected Jeanne Wakatsuki Houston's family. Houston's girlhood memory of watching her father and brothers sail off to work as independent commercial fishermen comes to an end as news of the Pearl Harbor bombing spreads. Her father is suspected of delivering oil to Japanese submarines and is interned at Fort Lincoln, North Dakota. It will be one year before she sees him again. This initial separation foreshadows the many struggles that the Wakatsuki family will face to stay physically and emotionally connected.

Weeks after her father is interned, the rest of Houston's family is sent to a camp called Manzanar. Although they manage to remain in the same camp, the stress and indignity of imprisonment begin to change family dynamics as certain traditions erode. For example, the camp system is designed to serve meals to thousands of internees, making it nearly impossible for families to eat together. Camp authorities realize the negative impact this change has on family unity and community morale when sociologists who study camp life propose an edict that orders families to start eating together again.

Houston describes how internment also affected her parents' relationship. Before her father was reunited with the rest of the family at Manzanar, her mother struggled to adjust to the deprivations of camp life as the family was crammed into poorly built wood shacks that failed to protect them against the cold and the dust storms of the desert. The open latrines, inedible food, and lack of schools fill her mother with worry and distraction, which causes Houston to seek attention elsewhere. Her mother eventually adapts and works as a dietitian, but the family's fragile sense of stability ends when Houston's father returns.

Papa becomes a brooding presence who stays in the barracks all day, makes his own liquor, and gets drunk. His depression relates to his time at Fort Lincoln. While he was there, he worked as a translator, which raised suspicions among other internees when he was released from Fort Lincoln before the other men were. Many saw his early release as a reward for collaborating somehow with camp authorities. Papa deals with the shame he feels over these false accusations by drinking. His misery is compounded by his lack of control over his surroundings, his family, and his future. Papa had always been the patriarch who maintained his wife and their nine children. The loss of all their possessions and the stress of internment lead to the further deterioration of the family as Papa takes out his anger and powerlessness by beating his wife. In one pivotal scene, he comes close to killing her when Houston's brother Kiyo intervenes and punches Papa in the face. The confrontation ends abruptly, but not before Houston senses that she has just witnessed her father's downfall from the controlling yet stable authority figure he had once been.

The family faces even more turmoil when brother Woody decides to volunteer for the armed forces, against Papa's wishes. Woody believes that his service will prove to Americans that Japanese Americans can be trusted. However, the issue of loyalty is complicated for families like the Wakatsukis who still have relatives in Japan. Fighting for the United States places some Japanese-American soldiers in the position of possibly fighting against their Japanese relatives. Woody eventually goes off to war, and his trip to Papa's village near Hiroshima ironically reestablishes lost family ties. Papa had left Japan when he was 17 years old and had never returned, leaving his family to believe that he was dead. Woody meets Papa's family and reaches a greater understanding of his father's life.

Houston ends with a description of her return to Manzanar 30 years after its closing. Her family, like many other interned families, tried to forget about Manzanar by never talking about it. However, Houston refuses to bury those crucial yet difficult years in her family's life, taking her own children to visit the site. As she watches her three children look among the scattered traces of Manzanar, she hears the voices of the thousands of internees who endured the injustice of internment. By refusing to silence those voices that include her own family's, Houston ensures that her children will remain connected to their family heritage and will recognize the courage their family displayed in the face of one of the most painful moments in U.S. history.

Belinda Linn Rincon

NATIONALISM in *Farewell to Manzanar*

Ko Wakatsuki's experience as an issei, or Japanese immigrant, is the most poignant examination of nationalism in Jeanne Wakatsuki Houston's *Farewell*

to Manzanar. Before the Japanese attack on Hawaii, Ko had lived in the United States for 38 years, raised a family of nine children, and given up all intentions of returning to Japan. Despite these indelible ties to his new country, he is legally barred from officially joining the nation and is not allowed to apply for citizenship, which makes him vulnerable to other forms of discrimination. For example, while living in Oregon, he is prevented from owning property because of the Alien Land Law. The racial discrimination that he and others experience is exacerbated by wartime hysteria after the Japanese attack. The Wakatsuki family is forced to sell their belongings and move to a prison camp because of President Franklin Roosevelt's Executive Order 9066, which allowed the government to label certain groups as threats to national security and to exclude them from military areas. This order eventually leads to the imprisonment of Japanese Americans in internment camps like Manzanar.

As Japan and the United States went to war, issei like Ko are caught in the middle as they are separated from their nation of birth and denied access to full citizenship rights in their nation of residence. Although Ko is, in some sense, stateless, he feels a deep bond to both nations. Japan holds important family connections and ties to his cultural heritage while the United States, despite its racial discrimination, holds certain financial and social opportunities. Also, with every birth in his family, Ko is bound closer to the United States. During an interrogation at Fort Lincoln, an official asks Ko which country should win the war. Ko responds with a telling analogy: When a child is caught between bickering parents, he doesn't want either parent to die; rather, he wants them to stop fighting. Ko's response shows his emotional attachment to both nations and makes it clear why choosing between them is no simple matter.

However, in the wake of the Pearl Harbor bombing, the United States does demand a choice from Japanese Americans because nationalism depends on loyalty. The United States attempts to confirm Japanese-American loyalty through interrogations and oaths, which have moral and physical consequences. Manzanar internees over the age of 17 are forced to fill out the Application for Leave

Clearance, which contains two questions that are meant to determine the internee's national loyalty. Question 27 asks respondents if they are willing to serve in the U.S. military, and question 28 asks if they would not only swear allegiance to America, but also forswear allegiance to Japan. To answer "No No" suggests that the respondent is disloyal to the United States and would face possible repatriation to Japan as a result—a difficult fate for those Japanese Americans who have lived all their lives in the United States. Many internees fiercely debate the loyalty oath and consider answering "No," not necessarily out of disloyalty to the United States but out of principle. They react to the oath's hypocrisy and protest the idea of pledging allegiance to a nation that demands loyalty but is disloyal to its own people because it condones racial discrimination, inequality, and internment. To answer "Yes Yes" would most likely make male respondents eligible for combat duty. Houston's brother, Woody, answers "Yes" and is sent to the battlefront. Woody, along with other nisei, or Japanese Americans born in the United States, believes that military service is the best way to prove that Japanese Americans can be trusted. Unfortunately, nisei soldiers would prove their national loyalty through blood and sacrifice. Houston notes that nisei soldiers received the highest number of military decorations for their valor and suffered the highest number of casualties and deaths.

Government officials thought the oath would help identify Japanese spies, but Manzanar internees thought it was ridiculous. A real spy, they argued, would not truthfully answer the oath in the first place. Nevertheless, the oath demonstrates how nationalism can sometimes make impossible demands on individuals such as Japanese Americans who are asked to be loyal to a nation that rejects them and that would accept them only if they voluntarily faced death on its behalf. Sadly, the deaths of nisei soldiers did not eliminate the discrimination that Houston and other Japanese Americans experienced after the war ended. Despite being born and raised in the United States, Houston and others in her community continued to encounter the ways in which racism often prevents full national unity.

Belinda Linn Rincon

STAGES OF LIFE in *Farewell to Manzanar*

Farewell to Manzanar describes what it was like to grow up and grow old during the Japanese internment and post–World War II eras. Jeanne Wakatsuki Houston presents her childhood and young adult years in three different phases: pre-internment (age 7), internment (ages 7–10), and post-internment (teen years and adulthood). After the bombing of Pearl Harbor and before her family was interned at Manzanar, Houston moved from town to town in the midst of prewar hysteria. She recalls attending different schools. In one school, Japanese students pick on her because she can not speak Japanese. In another school, she remembers feeling racial hostility from her white teacher. When the government relocates her family, Houston is too young to be insulted by the racism and violation of her and her community's civil rights. In the camp, she enjoys sleeping with her mother in the crowded shack and does not fully appreciate the worry and fear that burden Mama. Mama finds work to earn money and grows distant from Houston, whom she cannot supervise within the chaotic camp. Houston seeks attention from others and soon befriends two nuns. She nearly converts to Catholicism before her father returns from North Dakota. With no school and no parental supervision, Houston's childhood is spent in exploring the camp and meeting new people.

As she grows older in the camp, she has certain experiences that will become important to her personal development. For example, when Papa is reunited with the family, she is affected by his physical and emotional changes. His loss of control and dignity during internment take a heavy toll; he begins to drink and abuse Mama. In one scene, he nearly kills her. Houston witnesses the violent confrontation and feels the pain of her family's disintegration. Her carefree childhood has come to an end.

In the later years of internment, a school is built and life becomes somewhat normalized within the camp as people wait for the war to end. Houston attends school, where children join the band, put on plays, or sing in the glee club. During this time, Houston searches for her own hidden talents and interests as she grows in independence. However, she experiences her most profound moment of independence when she witnesses her parents grow closer after the news of their grandson's birth. Houston describes how she felt oddly separated from her parents and recognized them as not just her parents but as human beings.

By 1945, when the camp closes its gates, Houston is 10 years old and is afraid of the hatred she anticipates from the outside world. She fears that people will humiliate her because of her ethnicity. Her family moves to a housing project in Los Angeles and she attends public school. She goes through the normal stages of adolescence—making friends, fitting in, dating—but with the added pressure of racial discrimination. She is barred from joining the Girl Scouts, her friends never invite her to their homes, and teachers almost prevent her from being carnival queen even though the students vote for her. Her father disapproves of the American styles and values that she adopts in order to be accepted by her peers. However, when she turns 17, she becomes mature enough to know that social acceptance is not as fulfilling as it seems. She enters college and eventually has a family of her own.

Houston's childhood experience of camp life with its emphasis on exploration is tempered by her description of Papa's bitterness and depression. At least two times in the book, Houston states that the camp was her "birthplace" and was his deathbed. We learn about his years as a young man in Japan and his immigration to the United States. He and Mama struggled to raise nine children through the Great Depression and despite laws that prevented them from owning land. Houston recalls how internment accelerated Papa's demise as he went through the stages of his life, moving from a self-sufficient family patriarch to a dependent and emotionally and physically damaged man. He had aged 10 years in the nine months he spent in North Dakota. When internment ended, his attempts to start a business and resume his role as breadwinner fail. He now depends on Woody whose citizenship status allows him to get a fishing license. The roles are reversed: The father must now rely on the son for financial support.

Belinda Linn Rincon

HUGHES, LANGSTON   poems (1902–1967)

Following the Civil War (1861–65), African Americans began migrating to large, industrialized cities in the North (such as Chicago, Detroit, and New York), with the hope that life would improve not only for them, but also for their children. Unfortunately, what they found was the same sort of racism, discrimination, and marginalization that they had experienced in the South. While they were no longer slaves in the physical sense, African Americans continued to be oppressed, as Jim Crow laws (which reinforced black/white segregation) cast a shadow on their initial constitutional victories of freedom, suffrage, and citizenship.

Starting in the 1920s, African-American writers, musicians, and scholars began an active backlash against white domination, especially in the realm of culture. Dispensing with the influences of white America, a group of visionaries from Harlem in New York City—including Zora Neale Hurston, Countee Cullen, Billie Holliday, and Louis Armstrong—began to create artistic and literary expressions that chronicled the black experience. Langston Hughes (1902–67) was, arguably, the most influential of all the Harlem Renaissance literati. The author of countless novels, including *Not Without Laughter* (1930), plays (e.g., *Mule Bone*, coauthored with Zora Neale Hurston in 1931), and short stories (many of them featured in the 1934 anthology *The Ways of White Folks*), he is best known for his poems, which explore themes such as the meaning of the American dream for African Americans, the role of race in America and the definition of freedom, especially for the disenfranchised.

Tanfer Emin Tunc

The AMERICAN DREAM in the poetry of Langston Hughes

Hughes lived in an America that was torn apart by racism and segregation. Despite the so-called "opportunities" for blacks in the North of the 1920s and 1930s, African Americans lived in a differential relationship to the nation. Their experiences with the myth of the American dream did not escape Hughes's perspicacious gaze, and is thus a constant thread in his literary work.

Arguably, Hughes's most biting criticism of the limitations of the American dream is conveyed through "Let America Be America Again" (1938). In this poem, Hughes describes the American values that have come to comprise the "dream"—freedom, liberty, democracy, and equality—all the while interjecting that the dream never actually existed for poor Americans, peoples of color, and "undesirable" immigrants. During enslavement, African Americans were excluded from participating in the American dream (also a theme in the 1931 poem "The Negro Mother"). Forced into a cycle of poverty after emancipation, which included the sharecropping system and a rigid caste system that prevented anyone who was not a white Anglo-Saxon Protestant from advancing, African Americans became the forgotten pioneers whose American dream amounted to nothing more than a nightmare.

Despite the pessimism that runs throughout most of the poem (after all, it was published at the height of the Great Depression when the United States was experiencing record homelessness, unemployment, and general civil unrest, all of it described), Hughes is optimistic for a brighter future: "O, let America be America again—The land that never has been yet—And yet must be—the land where every man is free." Hughes echoes the same sentiments in "I, Too, Sing America" (1925), in which he describes two Americas, one for affluent whites, the other for their "darker brothers" who, as maids and butlers, are sent to "eat in the kitchen when company comes." However, Hughes predicts that one day the tables will turn, and those who are at the bottom of society today, will grow strong and rise to the top (in "Cultural Exchange" [1967] Hughes even dreams of a day when Martin Luther King, Jr., is governor of Georgia).

Hughes also addresses the limitations of the American dream in "Harlem" (1951). This poem, which is framed around "dreams deferred," discusses what happens when dreams are delayed or postponed. According to Hughes, there are two options: They either die from within—or they explode. Many African Americans of his generation were forced to surrender their dreams, and were left with nothing but "crusted" and "sugared-over" syrupy sweet memories of what might have been. In "Har-

lem," Hughes maintains that African Americans can no longer afford to allow their dreams to "sag like a heavy load," or else their dreams will eventually "explode." Although this poem was written before the Civil Rights movement became an organized social force, it is clear that Hughes believes that African Americans are on the cusp of a revolution. Hughes uses the same metaphor—this time of a dream exploding through prison walls—in his poem "Oppression" (1947). In "Sea Calm" (1932), Hughes metaphorically states that the dreams of African Americans will one day be realized, and that all they were experiencing was the "calm before the storm": "it is not good for water to be so still that way."

"Theme for English B" (1951), which was written the same year as "Harlem," also grapples with the nature of the American dream. "Theme for English B" is structured around a writing assignment given to a 22-year-old African-American college student by his white composition instructor. During the writing process, the student realizes that he is the only black student in his all-white class (which is probably at Columbia University, given its proximity to Harlem): at school, he is a token representative of his minority race, but at home in Harlem, he is in the majority. He realizes that because of his race, his page will not remain "white" but will be "colored" by his experiences and identity as an African American. His composition allows him to come to terms with the reality that, in the United States, there are multiple definitions of "American" and the "American dream." Despite the tension between blacks and whites—"Sometimes perhaps you don't want to be a part of me . . . Nor do I often want to be a part of you"—according to Hughes, they should learn to live together in harmony: "You are white—yet a part of me, as I am a part of you." Hughes's message is that as "Americans," people of all races can learn from each other and draw unity from shared experiences. This, in his opinion, is the true meaning of the American dream.

Tanfer Emin Tunc

FREEDOM in the poetry of Langston Hughes

Langston Hughes's poetry provides a theoretical space in which minorities, the marginalized, and the disenfranchised can negotiate freedom despite racial prejudice and their systematic exclusion from the American dream. In "Negro Speaks of Rivers" (1920), Hughes transcends the burdens of slavery and racism, harkening back to a time when his ancestors lived in Africa and were free to bathe "in the Euphrates when dawns were young . . . build[ing their] huts near the Congo . . . [and] look[ing] upon the Nile and the raised pyramids above it" (5–7). While in the United States, the so-called "land of opportunities," they are oppressed and enslaved, back home in Africa they, and not whites, are the masters, possessing ultimate knowledge about their land and its history: "I've known rivers ancient as the world and older than the flow of human blood in human rivers . . . My soul has grown deep like the rivers" (11–13). However, despite the physical and spiritual enslavement of blacks in America, Hughes optimistically believes that the freedom his people experienced in the "old world" of Africa can be recreated in the "new world" of the United States: "I heard the singing of the Mississippi when Abe Lincoln went down to New Orleans, and I've seen its muddy bosom turn all golden in the sunset" (8–10).

Hughes also uses land as a metaphor for freedom in "Freedom's Plow" (1943). In this poem, Hughes asserts that freedom can be derived from working the land, even though the United States—or the "land of the free"—was established on the enforced labor of slaves. Regardless of the fact that African Americans have been systematically deceived by the freedom calls of leaders such as Jefferson, Lincoln, and John Brown, Hughes still maintains that freedom can be achieved through an unwavering belief in the American dream of "life, liberty and the pursuit of happiness": "Keep your hand on the plow! Hold on! If the house is not yet finished . . . Don't be discouraged, builder!" (160–162). As Hughes conveys, "the plan and pattern" of unity, freedom, and democracy are "here"; the seeds of these institutions merely need some nurturing (165). In his poem "Democracy" (1949), Hughes also compares freedom to a seed that needs to be planted and carefully cultivated. However, in this poem, Hughes is more pro-active in his message to African Americans: "Democracy will not come . . . Through compromise and fear" (1, 4). No longer willing to "let things take their course" (11),

Hughes urges his fellow citizens (especially people of color) to end their passivity and "stand on [their own] two feet and own the land" (7–9).

In "Children's Rhymes" (1921), Hughes reveals his thoughts on race and the limits of freedom. While white children can aspire to be president, Hughes claims that this is not an attainable goal for black children. Moreover, "liberty and justice for all" are merely "lies written down for white folks" (11, 12, 14). In reality, "we know everybody ain't free" (9–10). Hughes reiterates this pessimism in "Justice" (1923) when he admits that although African Americans have, for decades, been promised freedom, equality under the law, and democracy, they know that Lady Justice is not "a blind goddess" (1). Once upon a time, she did have eyes to see the injustices inflicted upon the disenfranchised; however, after centuries of abuse, all that remains under "her bandages [are] . . . two festering sores . . . that once perhaps were eyes" (3–4).

Like "Cross" (1959), "Advertisement for the Waldorf-Astoria" (1931) links freedom to race and class. In this case, the freedom to dine at the expensive Waldorf-Astoria Hotel is a "right" bestowed only upon wealthy whites who "got rich" from the labor of the working class (33). While the poor "clip coupons," the rich are "draw[ing] dividends and liv[ing] easy" (34, 36–37). The closest the unemployed will ever get to living this lifestyle is walking by the hotel and stealing a glance inside. After all, looking is free and "democratic," and impoverished people of color—i.e., those most severely impacted by the Great Depression (the time period in which this poem was written)—can not afford much more than that anyway: "Walk through Peacock Alley tonight before dinner, and get warm . . . You've got nothing else to do" (40–41). "Dinner Guest: Me" (1951) also uses the metaphor of food to express the connection between race, class, and freedom. This poem narrates the tale of a "token negro" who somehow finds his way into an all-white, elite dinner party. A spectacle on display, he is "wined and dined" by his hosts who attempt to assuage their white guilt by being "kind" to an African American (3). However, as Hughes conveys, while being a "problem on Park Avenue at eight . . . is not so bad" (19–21), when the party is over and the hosts return to their affluent neighborhoods, "solutions to the problem, of course, [have to] wait" (22–23). To those who are already free, securing the freedom of others is merely "charity work"—a trivial hobby that can always wait for another day.

Tanfer Emin Tunc

RACE in the poetry of Langston Hughes

One of Langston Hughes's most profound statements on race can be found in "Will V-Day Be Me-Day Too?" (1944). This poem, which is essentially a letter written by a black World War II soldier, "GI Joe," chronicles the racial injustices faced by African-American veterans who helped liberate white Europeans, but face death and destruction in their own country. As Hughes illustrates, African-American soldiers freed the Jewish prisoners from concentration camps, and eradicated fascism from Germany and France, but for them, V-Day (Victory Day) will never come, for "Here in my own, my native land, . . . the Jim Crow laws still stand" (42–43). The soldier wonders: "Will Dixie lynch me still, When I return?" Although he believes that "Tan-skinned Yanks, Driving a tank" still have a long way to go to achieve racial equality, in his perpetual tone of optimism, Hughes encourages his fellow brothers, both black and white, to "stand up like a man, At home and take your stand, For Democracy."

In "Minstrel Man" (1954) and "Merry-Go-Round" (1959), Hughes employs the metaphor of the carnival to express the absurdity, and danger, of racial discrimination. "Minstrel Man" conveys the pain and anguish felt by a black minstrel performer who, because of his race, is assumed to be sub-human—a mere spectacle for the entertainment of white people. In this case, the minstrel's black identity is dangerously trivialized by his clownish makeup, wide grin, gay songs, and dancing feet. While on the outside he may seem like a stereotypically content "coon," in reality, he is struggling with an "inner cry" of desperation brought on by his socially constructed inferiority. Those who only see his "feet . . . gay with dancing," would never be able to guess that every day "he dies."

Like "Will V-Day Be Me-Day Too?," "Merry-Go-Round" also presents a biting critique of the Jim Crow system which, for most of the 19th and 20th

centuries, kept blacks and whites entrapped in a vicious cycle of race-based segregation. "Merry-Go-Round" conveys the inner turmoil of an African-American child who wishes to ride the carousel. However, because of years of racist conditioning—"Down South where I come from . . . White and colored . . Can't sit side by side"(4–6)—he automatically seeks the "Jim Crow" section of the merry-go-round. As Hughes illustrates, not only has the child internalized the racist attitudes and practices imposed on him by whites, but also, as a result, he has lost his childhood innocence. Because the merry-go-round is a circular ride, and "there ain't no back," the displaced child asks "Where's the horse . . . For a kid that's black?" In a perfect world, such a question would never be asked, for a black child would be able to sit on any horse he or she desires.

"Cross" (1959) and "Ku Klux" (1935) also deal with the burdens of American racism, especially with respect to miscegenation and white supremacy. "Cross," like Hughes's 1935 play *Mulatto* (he also wrote a poem with the same title), interrogates the "no-man's-land" of race that is often occupied by individuals who, as Hughes expresses, are "neither white nor black." Ultimately, as Hughes conveys, race and class are mutually defining; in "Cross," the narrator's black mother "died in a shack," while his white "old man died in a fine big house." As someone who is "in-between," and unclaimed by both communities, the narrator is left wondering where he will die. Thus we are left to conclude that racial hybridity is incompatible with both social acceptance and personal fulfillment.

Hughes wrote "Ku Klux" as a reaction to the second KKK peak, which occurred between World War I and World War II. The poem chronicles an encounter between a black man and a white KKK member who uses violence to force his victim to "Look me in the face—And tell me you believe in . . . The great white race" (18–20). When the black man tries to resist—"Mister . . . I'd believe in anything . . . If you'd just turn me loose" (5–8)—he is accused of "sassin'" the Klansman, who viciously beats him. By portraying the white supremacist as an irrational and sadistic bigot, and the unrelenting black man as a brave and non-violent individual who arbitrarily becomes the target of racist aggression,

Hughes succeeds in redeeming African Americans as heroes who, even in the face of death, refuse to subordinate their race to the will of the oppressors. It is this lesson of survival against all odds that Hughes ultimately believes will allow the black race to achieve equality.

Tanfer Emin Tunc

HURSTON, ZORA NEALE *Their Eyes Were Watching God* (1937)

Although contemporary critics consider Zora Neale Hurston's *Their Eyes Were Watching God* to be one of the literary masterpieces of the Harlem Renaissance, critics did not like Hurston's novel when it was first published. Known for its use of African-American vernacular, Hurston's novel captures the sound and rhythms of African-American life at the beginning of the 20th century.

Readers of the novel generally remark on the main character's journey from young, innocent womanhood to maturity. The novel begins with Janie's return to Eatonville, the only all-black town in the United States. While her neighbors are curious about what has happened to her, they refuse to ask her and she refuses to tell. Instead, Janie tells her story to her friend Phoebe saying, "mah tongue is in mah friend's mouf," giving Phoebe permission to retell the story if she so chooses. Janie's story is one of growth through the relationships she experiences with men. She "marries" three times, each of which teaches her something about her own identity and what she wants in life.

Henry Louis Gates argues that *Their Eyes* is a "speakerly text" because it requires the reader to "hear" the voices of the characters in the characters' speech. Some readers find the book challenging because of this, but many find it easier if they read aloud. In this way, the reader has a sense of the characters' voices beyond the page.

Nancy Cardona

GENDER in *Their Eyes Were Watching God*

In counseling her granddaughter about the realities of the world, Nanny tells Janie "[D]e white man throw down de load and tell de nigger man tuh pick it up. He pick it up because he have to, but he don't tote it. He hand it to his women folks. De nigger woman is de mule of de world so fur as Ah can see." Although the language that Nanny uses is no longer considered "politically correct," the observation that she makes guides Janie in her journey in the novel. Janie goes from a girl who lives her life according to how others around her tell her to do so, to becoming a woman who makes her own decisions on her own terms.

Janie begins her journey with a decision that has been made for her; after Nanny sees Janie kissing a young man, Nanny decides that Janie needs to be a married woman who will be provided for. She chooses Logan Killicks, a local farmer who owns his farm, house, and organ. Janie chooses to go along with her grandmother's choice, deciding that she will learn to love Killicks. And for the first year, Killicks treats her well. But soon he begins to treat her as just another person who works on his farm. Janie is disappointed that she hasn't learned to love him and tells Nanny this. Nanny responds that Janie should be happy with the stability that Killicks provides, making the best of the life that she has.

Janie refuses to settle for less than her ideal notion of romantic love, so when Joe "Jody" Starks arrives, speaking of an all-black town, Janie's hopes for romantic love are reignited and she leaves Killicks to go with Starks. Janie believes that she will be an equal partner in this second marriage, as Joe seems to be a man of ambition. What she does not know is that he is a man who is interested in his own ambition and is willing to sacrifice Janie's dreams for his own. He becomes mayor and a store owner. He treats Janie as one of his possessions, making her wear her hair in a head scarf and forbidding her to talk with the people who congregate on the store porch. Janie soon learns that Jody's idea of a better life is centered on making his own life better, not theirs as a couple. Janie lives out the marriage, doing as Jody dictates.

When Jody dies, she takes control of her life again. She removes her head scarves and burns them after Jody's funeral, symbolizing her refusal to live according to Jody's dictates. She soon begins to interact with the people on the porch, playing checkers and telling jokes. When she is asked when she will marry again (because certainly she needs someone to take care of her), Janie just laughs because "This freedom feeling was fine. These men didn't represent a thing she wanted to know about. She had already experienced them through Logan and Joe."

The next time Janie goes with a man, it is on her own terms. Even though Tea Cake is 15 years her junior and she fears what the townsfolk will say, she chooses to make herself feel happy. Tea Cake treats her as an equal, taking her fishing and to a baseball game. What's most important is that Tea Cake seems to know exactly what Janie needs: to live her life on her own terms and he offers her just that. They go to the Everglades where they work together, side by side, in the fields.

Janie's final choice of herself comes near the end of the novel, when she must shoot Tea Cake in order to save herself. Even though the townsfolk are talking about her, Janie recognizes that the choices that she has made have been in her best interest. In the end, Janie "pulled in her horizon. . . . Pulled it from around the waist of the world and draped it over her shoulders. . . . She called in her soul to come and see" (184). Janie is able to live her life in the way that she chooses.

Nancy Cardona

ISOLATION in *Their Eyes Were Watching God*

Hurston begins her novel with the tension between the individual and the collective. Janie returns from her "adventures" with Tea Cake a different woman, now able to exercise and enjoy her individuality even as the rest of her community seeks to hold her at arm's length. Despite their rejection of her, the community wishes to know what happened to Janie in her absence. Uninterested in satiating their curiosity, Janie chooses to tell her story to her friend Phoebe, to whom she gives permission to retell her story by saying ". . . mah tongue is in mah friend's mouf."

Janie's story can be seen as a series of moments of isolation from her community, beginning with her marriage to Logan Killicks. Concerned with providing for Janie's needs, her grandmother arranges this marriage to a husband who can provide for Janie's needs. Soon frustrated with her loveless marriage, Janie seeks to make connections through Jody Starks, a man who woos Janie with the promise of living in an all-black community.

Janie's hopes for a better life that is connected to other people does not come to fruition, as Jody insists that Janie hold herself apart from the community. He forbids her from joining in the storytelling and checker-playing that takes place on the porch of the store that he owns. Instead, Janie must remain isolated from the group, symbolizing the superiority of Jody's possessions. This isolation proves frustrating for Janie, but she waits out the marriage and "celebrates" Jody's death by wearing her hair down and participating in the community that congregates on the store's porch. Janie vows to live life on her own terms, never again sacrificing her own happiness for another's. Soon, she meets Tea Cake, a young man who shares Janie's philosophy of living life for the moment.

Janie is finally able to join a community in her marriage to Tea Cake. He teaches her to play checkers and allows her to work alongside him when they go to work in the "muck." In this place, Janie finally is able to bridge her isolation and be accepted by others on her own terms. She makes friends among the women in the community and entertains friends in their modest home. This ideal moment, however, comes to a close when Tea Cake dies in a hurricane. Janie again must assume her position of isolation as she goes on trial for Tea Cake's death. In her return to the town where she lived with Jody, Janie remains isolated from the community. But at this stage, Janie no longer has as great a need to join a community, as her life with Tea Cake has shown her how to live life on her own terms, regardless of what others think. As Janie tells Phoebe, the townspeople have only to do two things, "They got tuh go tuh God, and they got tuh find out about livin' fuh theyselves."

Nancy Cardona

STAGES OF LIFE in *Their Eyes Were Watching God*

Hurston's novel follows the development of Janie Crawford, who begins as an idealistic 16-year-old girl. Over the course of the novel, Janie attempts to define herself as a woman, first marrying for stability, then adventure, and finally for happiness within herself.

At the beginning of the novel, Janie's grandmother catches her sharing her first kiss with a boy.

This kiss is the culmination of Janie's discovery of her sexuality, symbolized by the pear tree in which she sees a bee darting in and out of the tree's buds. "This is love," thinks Janie and so her romantic notions of love and fulfillment are rooted in this first witnessing of nature's cycle. From this experience, Janie believes that she is ready to go out into the world to make her own life. But Nanny changes Janie's future by choosing stability for Janie, instead of romantic love.

Logan Killicks, Janie's first husband, is highly desirable as a husband to the local women. He owns property and can therefore offer Janie a kind of stability that to Nanny is the ultimate sign of freedom. So Janie marries him, hoping that later she will grow to love him. Although he begins the marriage as an attentive husband, Killicks changes and becomes interested only in Janie's ability to help him in the fields. The narrator observes that Janie "knew now that marriage did not make love. Janie's first dream was dead, so she became a woman." In this instance, Janie's understanding of love indicates that fanciful notions about love have to do with young adulthood; women, on the other hand, cannot expect such frivolities and thus must make do with the marriage that they have. Even though Janie comes to terms with her marriage, it does not mean that she has abandoned her idea of romantic love. When Killicks leaves her to go and see a second mule, Janie meets Jody Starks, the man she believes will help her find the love she dreams of. Although she recognizes that Jody does not share her ideas of love in that "he did not represent sun-up and pollen and blooming trees," she also knows that he offers her more because Jody "spoke of far horizon." Janie is intrigued and goes with him to Florida, in hopes of finding a place for herself.

After they arrive, Jody becomes mayor and he buys a store in order to build his wealth. Janie helps him much as she did Killicks, but she soon learns that Jody only wants to show her off as his possession. On the day that he opens his store, he tells her to dress up because "he didn't mean for nobody else's wife to rank with her. She must look on herself as the bell-cow, the other women were the gang." He even requires her to wear a headscarf because "[s]he was there in the store for *him* to look at, not those

others." He sees Janie as his possession that he can lord over the rest of the community. After a fight with Jody, which culminates in Jody hitting Janie, Janie's ideal of love and marriage shatters, leaving her in a loveless relationship until his death some 15 years later when she is almost 40.

When Jody dies, Janie changes back to the women who left Logan Killicks. She looks at herself in the mirror and finds a woman: "She tore off the kerchief from her head and let down her plentiful hair. The weight, the length, the glory was there. She took careful stock of herself, then combed her hair and tied it back up again." Janie's letting down of her hair symbolically allows her to claim herself again. She will no longer live by the rules that Jody, much less anyone else, places before her. Rather, she will live as she chooses, sitting on the porch with her neighbors and playing checkers. Soon thereafter, Tea Cake, a man of about 25, arrives in Eatonville and begins courting Janie. He plays checkers with her, takes her to a baseball game, and shows her that he appreciates her for who she is. Rather than trying to make her work, or use her to show off his wealth, Tea Cake treats Janie as an equal, something she has never experienced before.

Although this "marriage" ends tragically, Janie has not had to sacrifice herself for Tea Cake's image of her. If anything, Janie's choice of herself over Tea Cake when he attacks her signifies a true understanding of her value. As she tells Phoebe at the end of the novel, "Two things everybody's got tuh do fuh theyselves. They got to go tuh God, and they got tuh find out about livin' fuh theyselves." This is Janie's true accomplishment: Her experience of three marriages has taught her how to live for herself rather than for others.

Nancy Cardona

HUXLEY, ALDOUS *Brave New World* (1932)

In his novel *Brave New World*, Aldous Huxley depicts the dystopian vision of a technocratic society. The World State, as it is called, subscribes to the motto of Community, Identity, and Stability. To maintain stability, the World State controls its citizens with the help of the drug *Soma*, which ensures everybody's happiness. The idea of "families" has been abandoned; instead, human beings are produced like cars on an assembly line. From the moment of fertilization on, each citizen has a predetermined fate and abilities according to the caste to which it will belong. Through its rigorous caste system, the World State prevents dissatisfaction in its citizens and guarantees stability.

Nonetheless, such a state also needs leaders. These are members of the Alpha-Plus caste, the only caste whose members are supposed to be able to think freely and experience themselves as individuals, although they cannot give in to their abilities for stability's sake. This circumstance creates a dilemma that traps Bernard Marx and Helmholtz Watson alike. During a visit to a Savage reservation with Lenina Crowne, Marx meets John Savage, illegitimate son of a World State Beta and the Director of Hatcheries. Having been an outcast on the reservation all his life, John is eager to see the World State. Having fallen in love with Lenina, John goes with them when they return to London. However, the principles of the World State and the way in which they are enforced disgust him. After his mother Linda's death, he tries to stir hospital workers into rebellion by throwing their Soma-rations out of the window. This action leads to the banishment of Watson and Marx.

John, on the other hand, is told to stay and finds refuge in a remote lighthouse. When journalists observe John whipping himself—he tries to cleanse himself of the World State—the ensuing stream of tourists drives John into a frenzy. When Lenina appears at the lighthouse, he is so outside of himself that he attacks and beats her. Ashamed and guilt-ridden, he hangs himself that night.

Elke Brown

COMMERCIALISM in *Brave New World*

Instant gratification is a buzzword that characterizes our modern society. However, it also best describes the attitude of the citizens of the Brave New World and their government toward commercialism.

In the World State, citizens are being conditioned to enjoy only things and activities that need to be purchased. When the Director of Hatcheries shows a group of students how conditioning works,

he shows them a group of toddlers who—through electroshocks and sirens—are taught to hate flowers and books. The purpose of this lesson, he explains, is that children will not grow up to spend time reading (an unsocial behavior) or to love nature for nature's sake. Instead, they shall love nature for the opportunities of leisure activities it offers that make them actually consume something. Outdoor sports, for example, such as Obstacle Golf and Tennis, are highly approved of. In fact, each caste has its own facilities that allow its members to participate in these activities. Naturally, according to the philosophy of the World State, those facilities are severely segregated from each other, but, the focus on consumption, in a way, blurs class boundaries in that respect.

In compliance with the World State's motto "Community, Identity, Stability," commercialism provides yet another means to ensure stability in the Brave New World. In their free time, citizens of the Brave New World engage in some social activity, be it sports, dancing, the feelies, or their Solidarity meetings. In case they do not feel up to any of these activities, they take *Soma*, to again be able to act in accordance with the World State's prescribed universal happiness. However, no matter what activity they choose, it will force them to consume something and spend money. This behavior ensures not only a stable and thriving economy, but also provides the World State's citizens with numerous distractions that keep them from actually thinking—a dangerous activity, as the examples of Bernard Marx and Helmholtz Watson illustrate.

Both men are aware of their individuality and experience difficulties with the demanded obedience to the World State's dogmas until they both are exiled from the Brave New World. While Watson rejects commercialism, Marx succumbs to it after gaining a certain amount of popularity when he brings John Savage from the reservation into the Brave New World. When Marx takes Lenina Crowne out on their first date, he gets lost in contemplating the night sky above the English Channel. Lenina, on the other hand, is unable to appreciate the view. It does not mean anything to her because it is free—it cannot be purchased, worn, or consumed in any other way. To appreciate nature that way goes against her conditioning and is, thus, impossible for her.

On their second date, Marx takes Lenina out on the reservation. He indulges in the luxuries of the hotel room and later worries about the bill because he has left the tap of perfumed water running. This instance is, interestingly enough, the only time in the novel that Huxley makes a direct reference to money. It seems that every citizen in the World State, independent of caste, earns sufficient funds to afford a kind of lifestyle that keeps the people in the Brave New World happily consuming. Naturally, this makes sense, for dissatisfied citizens might become rebellious, and that is the last thing any government could wish for.

With its emphasis on consumerism, the World State creates a nation of shopaholics. People who shop are happy—a message that sounds disturbingly familiar if we take a comparing look at our present consumer ideology. The fact that in the Brave New World this consumerism serves the stability of the state and is achieved through questionable methods and at a high price is highly unsettling and intended as a warning sign by Huxley for future generations. However, it cannot be overlooked that Huxley—influenced by communist and socialist ideas—also implies that in order to have a flourishing economy, citizens need to have sufficient money to spend on consumer goods—all citizens, that is, not only the middle and upper classes.

Elke Brown

EDUCATION in *Brave New World*

While we like to think of education as giving people the means and information they need to be able to think for themselves, in *Brave New World* education has become a strict and cruel way of conditioning people from early childhood on. The educational system in Huxley's novel is determined by the World State's focus on productivity and efficiency. Since human beings are predestined from the moment of fertilization to belong to a specific caste, their skills and abilities depend on the caste to which they have been designated. After decanting, the process that replaces natural birth, each citizen enters a caste-specific educational program that hinges on two main methods: actual instruction and hypnopedia.

The World State's focus on productivity and its regard for human beings as a technological resource results in the conviction that each citizen ought to be instructed only as much as he or she needs to know to be able to perform his or her duties as a productive member of society. Thus, for example, children are discouraged from reading books and from loving nature. To the end of producing useful members of society, the World State uses drastic and cruel methods: During a tour the Director of Hatcheries gives to Alpha students, he shows them toddlers who are taught to shy away from books and flowers through the use of shrill sirens and electroshocks that leave them twitching on the floor. This education through traumatization is extremely effective in furthering the goals of the World State: Without knowing why, those children, as adults, will not waste any valuable time with reading (a very solitary, and thus forbidden, pleasure) or on loving nature for nature's sake, that is, without consuming anything.

In matters of life and death, the World State's educational approach is as honest and blunt as it is unorthodox. Because adults do not procreate, sexual activity has become another pastime and, basically, the unavoidable end of a pleasurable evening between a man and a woman in the *Brave New World*. Promiscuity, indeed, is a virtue, not a vice. Therefore, the children in the World State are encouraged to play erotic games and explore their sexuality, only to leave such childish behavior behind as adults.

Similarly, children in the World State are being death-conditioned. In the *Brave New World*, death has been planned for just like everything else. At the age of 60, the system of a person simply shuts down: Worn out from youth-enhancing medications and the use of *Soma*, the person dies in the Hospital for the Dying. This passing away is considered merely the natural end of the process of living. Even after death, a citizen of the World State can still be useful to society because his or her cremated body produces phosphorus, which can be used as fertilizer. To understand death as another contribution to society and as a natural process, the hospital hosts field trips for children to view those who are dying.

In addition to this way of instructing children, the World State relies heavily on hypnopedia: a way of indoctrinating people in their sleep. Having recognized that this method works most efficiently when relaying moral messages, the hypnopedic system, indeed, takes care of "instructing" the citizens from the beginning of their lives. Due to the fact that the messages are absorbed by the person's subconscious, the citizen accepts them as absolute truth. Naturally, all hypnopedic lessons intend to promote and further the World State's aims and principles. Thus, Beta-members, for instance, learn to love being Beta. They feel superior to Deltas and Gammas, but do not aspire to attain Alpha-level. Hence, people are content with their lives and perfectly willing to focus on fulfilling their assigned tasks. Other lessons instill the desire to consume certain goods, have fun, and, if all fails, take *Soma*. The most important lesson, however, is that "everybody belongs to everybody else." This not only supports a high level of promiscuity, it also implies that people are not individuals; they do not have selves.

Education in the *Brave New World*, hence, serves only one purpose: the propagation of the World State's goals. This authoritative, totalitarian approach stands as a warning against a government-controlled educational system in which citizens are indoctrinated, manipulated, and conditioned without the ability or chance to pursue any other paths. Whereas education ideally serves to open doors in people's minds to give them a myriad of choices, the World State closes those doors one by one.

Elke Brown

INDIVIDUAL AND SOCIETY in *Brave New World*
The World State's motto "Community, Identity, Stability" already reveals that IDENTITY and COMMUNITY are linked. In the course of the novel this fact becomes evident. We meet five characters who struggle or have struggled at one point with the tension that arises from the awareness of one's individuality and the demands of the World State to integrate into society to an extent that might require complete denial of an individual self.

Admittedly the one whose individuality is the least tangible, Lenina Crowne often is not included among the characters who have problems with completely rendering their personalities to the World State's demands. However, her case is one of the more interesting ones for, as a Beta, she should not have the same urge to individuality as Alphas do. However, Lenina refuses to obey the rules of sexual promiscuity and develops feelings for John. Despite his violent rejection of her "love" for him (which, in reality, is not romantic love but sex), Lenina appears at the lighthouse to speak to him. The fact that she makes that effort proves a kind of loyalty and devotion that is deemed inappropriate individualism in the Brave New World. Examples such as this one illustrate her struggle with the dogmas of the World State. Because Lenina otherwise behaves impeccably and her struggles are private, not political ones, she does not present a threat and does not have to be removed.

John Savage is usually deemed the most individualistic character in the novel. However, his actions are not so much prompted by the desire to confirm his individuality but, rather, to integrate into society. Not a citizen of the World State, John's denial of the Brave New World at the end of the novel appears to be a rebellious act when, instead, it illustrates his allegiance to the culture of the reservation, which is supposed to cleanse him from contact with the World State.

Similar to John, Bernard Marx wishes for nothing more than social acceptance. At the beginning of the novel, Marx appears as a fundamental rebel against the rules of the Brave New World: He refuses to take *Soma*, prefers to be alone, does not enjoy the customary pastimes, such as Obstacle Golf, and wonders what it would like to be free without the conditioning that ensures the state's stability. Marx increasingly reveals his rebelliousness as hypocrisy— a pretense to make himself interesting. Although he genuinely feels his individuality, Marx, like John, wishes only to blend in with everybody else.

In contrast to Marx, his friend Helmholtz Watson honestly tries to become a separate entity: He wants to create a new kind of poetry that would shake the World State and gladly accepts exile. Watson too does not realize that his conditioning will prevent him from realizing his goal. As Alphas, both Watson and Marx run into the problem that they have the mental capacity to discover their individuality while being forced by their state to fight the need to feel as an individual, which results in their eventual removal from the World State by Mustafa Mond.

Mond is the only character in the novel who not only is acutely aware of his individuality but who also has the opportunity to act as an individual. A highly intelligent and ambitious scientist, Mond is given the choice of banishment or becoming one of the Top World Controllers. Mond also is the one single character who has freedom of choice in the Brave New World: As the person who is in charge, he can decide which rules to obey and which ones to bend. However, his case shows the dark side of this freedom. Following his scientific curiosity, Mond misjudges John's mental fragility. He denies John the chance to join Watson and Marx on an island and thus becomes ultimately responsible for the young man's death.

All of these characters serve as constant reminders that the perfect stability the World State thinks to have achieved is only an illusion. Huxley's satiric novel illustrates that even in the most rigidly controlled environment it is impossible to suppress the need to be, act, and express oneself as an individual. It is this outlook on a world dominated by technology and dehumanized by it, that makes Huxley's work relevant to this day.

Elke Brown

IBSEN, HENRIK *A Doll's House* (1879)

Nora Helmer is the central character in Henrik Ibsen's play, *A Doll's House.* She is considered childish and dim-witted and is treated as if she were a doll—an object of beauty lacking substance—by both her husband and her father. As the play opens, Nora's husband, Torvald, has been promoted to bank manager. Nora is elated, for this means a higher income and less frugality. As the play unfolds, we learn that Nora previously entered into a loan agreement in secret with Nils Krogstad, a morally reprehensible man (according to Torvald) who now works under him at the bank. Nora believes that in taking out this loan and paying it back without her husband's knowledge or assistance, she can prove that she is able to provide financially for her family and should no longer be considered little more than a human doll. Krogstad, however, fears he will lose

his position once Torvald begins his official duties as manager, so he blackmails Nora with the loan documents, threatening to reveal all to her husband, including the fact that she forged her father's signature as co-signer of the loan, unless Nora uses her womanly influence on her husband to ensure that he keeps his job at the bank. Nora fails in her attempts, and after her husband discovers her criminal act and subsequently debases her position as wife and mother, she sees that she has been wronged by his treatment of her throughout their marriage and that she has led an insignificant existence. Nora leaves Torvald to seek a true identity in a life of her own.

Elizabeth K. Haller

ETHICS in *A Doll's House*

The ethics of Henrik Ibsen's central male character perpetuate the chain of events pivotal to the plot of *A Doll's House.* Torvald Helmer passes judgment freely, and he expects his strict moral principles to be upheld by his wife, his friends, and his employees. Torvald's primary concern is with appearances and remaining above suspicion; therefore, it becomes clear to all who know him that deviating from Torvald's rules of conduct would certainly lead him to discontinue any semblance of an acquaintance. This is illustrated most clearly in his relationship with Nora but also in his relationship with Krogstad.

Torvald worries that others will declare him unethical if he continues to retain Krogstad as an employee at the bank once he has taken his post as manager. That they knew each other as children causes Krogstad to take a familiar tone with Torvald, who fears that this familiarity in his new and high-ranking position at the bank will be a cause for ridicule by others in his employ. Anything or anyone that deviates from Torvald's maintaining of the most respectable of appearances is quickly expelled. Additionally, rather than consider the circumstances behind Krogstad's illegal actions, Torvald looks upon Krogstad's forgery as an act of treachery signifying a lack of moral character. He passes judgment on Krogstad's home, stating that he is poisoning his children by his mere presence, instilling in his home an atmosphere of lies and evildoing. A firm believer that a parent's indiscretions are passed down to the children, Torvald criticizes Krogstad for failing to confess openly to his crime and take his punishment, a more morally defensible act than that of perpetuating a lie.

Nora fares no better than Krogstad in her husband's eyes. Torvald's demeaning view of and reference to Nora as a witless and feeble animal throughout enforces his view that it is right for a woman to be beautiful and dependent. That Nora could devise such a scheme involving the forging of her father's signature, the undertaking of a loan, and the procuring of funds to pay the loan indicates that she used her brain rather than her beauty, which undermines Torvald's belief system. As such, he is both threatened by her independence and appalled at Nora's breach of his set code of moral conduct. One has only to look at his reaction toward Nora's financial impropriety to see his willingness to uphold his rules of conduct and all appearances of propriety at all costs, including abandoning his wife.

Torvald is ever one to set forth the propriety of a situation, especially when it comes to matters of money. He is vehemently against borrowing money, believing it to be a form of dependency on outside forces that detracts from the beauty of home life. Nora is unfamiliar with legal matters, including the intricacies involved in her borrowing of money from Krogstad and the resulting bond. She looks only toward how the ends justify the means; therefore, she cannot understand why the law would not and does not consider the circumstances surrounding a crime (such as forgery) that may justify the crime being committed. When she forged her father's signature on the bond, Nora's only concern was in providing Torvald with the retreat to Italy that he needed to restore his health. That she was simply looking to save Torvald's life is of no consequence to him, however, as Torvald sees only the impropriety of his wife's legal and financial indiscretions. Torvald's primary concern, though, remains with appearances and remaining above suspicion, for he knows that the perfect appearance of his home and his moral propriety would be forever tarnished if others became aware of the situation. Additionally, he is convinced that keeping Nora in the home would be a danger to their children, raising them in a poisoned atmosphere of deception. As such, Torvald sees fit to sever all ties with Nora in an attempt to save his children and uphold appearances.

Once he discovers that word will not leak of Nora's impropriety, however, Torvald is quick to revoke his earlier claims of dissolving their marriage, but it is too late for Nora. She points out that though a man will not compromise his honor for a woman, a woman will sacrifice hers for a man. She questions the ethics behind this behavior. It is clear to Nora that, rather than recognizing her forthrightness in seeking financial assistance as an act of desperation to keep him alive, Torvald views it as an act of moral reprehension that could spell the downfall of his position in society.

Elizabeth K. Haller

IDENTITY in *A Doll's House*

In Henrik Ibsen's play *A Doll's House,* Nora is characterized by others as childish, irresponsible, and dim witted. Her identity is formed by and around these characterizations. Her husband, Torvald Helmer, refers to her often as a squirrel, a chirping skylark, and a little spendthrift. Rarely is she considered to possess a solid thought, and at one point she states that everything she thinks seems silly and insignificant; her husband is pleased that she has acknowledged this fact. She states that her father treated her as a doll-child, and her husband treats her as a doll-wife. Nora, however, possesses a secret that she is certain will transform her identity from that of a brainless object to that of a caring and clever business-minded woman. She is confident that once it is revealed that it was not money left by her father that saved Torvald's health by allowing them to move to Italy for a year but rather it was money gained through her own devices, that her husband will then look upon her in a new light, and she will be seen by him and others as a competent woman. Nils Krogstad, the man she entered into the loan agreement with, ends her hopes as he reveals to her his knowledge that she forged a signature on the loan document. He threatens to reveal Nora's identity as a criminal if she does not ensure that Torvald, as bank manager, allows him to maintain his current lower-level position at the bank.

Krogstad is described as a morally corrupt individual who cares little for others and is primarily concerned with his own well-being. He too forged a document in his past, causing him to lose not only his job but his standing in society as well. He has spent the years since that time attempting to regain his reputation, and he is dependent upon his blackmail of Nora to guarantee his standing through retaining his position at the bank. He intends to further rely on this blackmail by revealing the truth of Nora's position to her husband and ultimately usurping Torvald as bank manager. Krogstad claims that his moral corruption arose due to his being a victim of circumstance. Had he not been jilted by Christine Linde, a school friend of Nora's, years before he would have been a different man. His plans to further blackmail Nora and her husband are altered as he encounters Linde at the Torvald residence.

Up to the time she arrives at Nora's home, Linde's identity was made up of being a caretaker to her mother and a provider for her two younger brothers as well as a wife to a man whom she did not love but married for the sake of financial assistance in caring for her family. She was soon widowed and left penniless, leaving her to take any position she could find to continue to care for her family. Once her mother died and her brothers were set in situations in which they could care for themselves, Linde was left alone and empty. She decides to forge a new identity as an office worker to keep her mind busy. It is to this purpose that she comes to Nora asking for assistance in obtaining a position at Torvald's bank, to which Nora complies. It is here that she runs unexpectedly into Krogstad, the man she jilted in order to ensure what she thought would be financial security in marrying another. She states that dire circumstances led her to end their relationship. Linde reveals to him that her life since they parted has not been dissimilar to his—described as a shipwreck. Linde professes a need to reclaim her identity through once again having someone to care for and suggests that she and Krogstad renew their relationship and join forces to once again stand on solid ground.

Although Linde has it within her power to prevent Torvald from learning of Nora's loan agreement, she believes it best to have Torvald read the letter in which Krogstad sets forth the circumstances surrounding Nora's criminal activity. Upon reading the letter, Torvald is immediately struck with how the situation will affect his reputation. It is at this point that Nora realizes Torvald's true identity and his complete disregard for her thoughts and emotions, for he does not express any concern for how the situation may affect her. She once thought of him as a loving and concerned husband, but now she sees that he loves only the thought of being with her, and he is concerned only with his own affairs. Nora decides to leave Torvald, hoping that by doing so she will learn more of the world in which she has been sheltered and transform her identity from that of a dim-witted, overly trusting doll to that of a prudent and sensible human being.

Elizabeth K. Haller

ILLNESS in *A Doll's House*

Henrik Ibsen's main characters in his play *A Doll's House* are all affected by illness, either physical or moral, as it plays a fundamental role in altering each of their lives.

Doctor Rank, once Torvald Helmer's personal physician but now considered the dearest friend of both Torvald and Nora, suffers from a physical illness alluded to as a form of syphilis. Rank's illness is a blatant case of his being physically affected by, or as he believes punished for, his father's moral discrepancies in his philandering and otherwise irresponsible sexual behavior prior to Rank's being conceived. His father's moral illness is passed down to his son in the form of a physical illness. As a result, Rank has not had the opportunity to live a full life and dies at a relatively young age. Rank's life, then, is forever altered through the actions of another. Such is also the case with Christine Linde, Nils Krogstad, Nora, and Torvald.

As a result of her widowed mother's physical illness, Christine Linde, once a school friend of Nora's, finds herself responsible, as the eldest of three children, for the care and well-being of her two younger brothers and her ill mother. To assist her in providing for her family, Linde must choose between marrying Nils Krogstad, the man whom she loves but who is not financially stable, or the man whom she does not love but who could provide financially for her family. She chooses to marry for money, rather than love, and this decision proves a bad one when she discovers her new husband's business ventures are not as sound as she believed. She is soon left widowed and penniless and must take on various menial jobs to support her brothers. If not for her mother's illness, Linde would have been free of the burden of marrying for financial stability instead of love, a choice that ultimately alters her life as she becomes a haggard woman in search of a better position. However, this search ultimately leads her to Nora's door, in hopes of finding employment through Torvald at his bank. It is in coming to Nora's home that Linde reencounters Krogstad, an encounter that leads to their joyous reconciliation by the end of the play.

It was not only Linde's life that was altered by her mother's illness and the resulting ultimatum of marriage, but Krogstad's life as well. Krogstad blames Linde's jilting of him for his resulting moral corruption. After Linde left him for another man, Krogstad entered into an unhappy marriage and was left a widower with several children. He does whatever he can to support them, including blackmail. It is as a result of Krogstad's moral corruption that he enters into a loan agreement with Nora, who then forges her dying father's signature on the loan documents so as not to trouble him with her situation. Krogstad makes it clear that it is not only money he is after but winning a position of respect in the town as well, for his sons are growing and it is imperative that they be given a fair chance to succeed. Krogstad sees maintaining his position at the bank as a necessary step in obtaining and upholding society's good opinion.

Krogstad's loan agreement with Nora is seen by Torvald as her moral demise. He is shamed by her actions and fears what society will think of a man in his position once word is leaked that his wife entered into secret negotiations with a morally reprehensible man behind her husband's back. Torvald chastises her as an unfit mother and a disappointment as a wife. If Krogstad had been a man of high moral character, he would not have entered into such an agreement with Nora without her husband's knowledge. His diseased moral character, then, led to the moral corruption of Nora. Torvald is initially unwilling to forgive his wife for her actions, but he changes

his mind once he discovers that the loan agreement has been made null and void. His response to her situation, however, causes Nora to realize that Torvald will always maintain a tainted moral view of her character, and she decides to leave him.

A chain reaction of events stemming from a physical illness alters the lives of each character—some for the worse, as in the case of Dr. Rank, whose father's philandering led to Rank's early demise, as well as in the case of Torvald, who loses his wife as a result of his reaction to her questionable behavior. But some lives are altered for the better. Although the illness of Linde's mother caused her to choose between love and money, with Krogstad's life also adversely affected in the bargain, it was her coming to Nora for assistance that led to a reunion with the man she originally loved. Consequently, Nora's entering into a loan agreement with Krogstad eventually opened her eyes to her husband's selfish and unforgiving manner, causing her to choose a new and anticipated better life without him.

Elizabeth K. Haller

IBSEN, HENRIK *Hedda Gabler* (1890)

Hedda Gabler is a work of major significance in world drama. It has been continuously performed, adapted, interpreted, and repeatedly translated ever since it was first published in 1890. The play's woman-centered narrative offers uniquely challenging opportunities for a female actor to portray a psychologically charged character.

Its female protagonist's attempt to free herself from the constraints of paternalistic society, a pointless marriage, and her complete disregard for conventional values has always fascinated audiences. Despite her constant manipulation of the lives of others and her narcissistic clash with the demons of her mind and soul, Hedda comes across both as a victimizer as well as a victim of life's ruthless logic.

Ibsen focuses on Hedda Tesman, who has married a promising young scholar for economic security. Her husband's hopes of advancement are in danger from another maverick scholar, Eilert Løvborg. Løvborg loses an invaluable manuscript, which George, Hedda's husband, finds on the wayside and brings home. Hedda quietly destroys Løvborg's manuscript and encourages a frantic Løvborg to commit suicide. Her husband and Mrs. Elvsted dedicate themselves to recovering the lost manuscript through reconstruction and rewriting from notes that Mrs. Elvsted still possesses. Hedda foresees a scandalous involvement in Løvborg's death as he is accidentally killed with the gun that Hedda had given him. Distraught, she commits suicide.

The play's apparent simplicity of design and form and its relatively plain dialogue hides many layers of meaning. It has been valued as an important feminist document for its perceptive social criticism and psychological insights. It continues to grow in public estimation and remains one of the most frequently performed plays with the possible exception of one or two of Shakespeare's plays.

Gulshan Taneja

ETHICS in *Hedda Gabler*

Addressing the audience at the Festival of the Women's Rights League, Ibsen remarked that

> My task has been the description of humanity. To be sure whenever such a description is felt to be reasonably true, the reader will read his own thoughts and sentiments into the work of the poet. They are then attributed to the poet; but incorrectly so. . . . (1880)

Despite an artist's urge to create characters objectively conceived as organic wholes who would, much like real humanity, represent a myriad of hues, works of art often restrict themselves to a limited aspect of human existence to illustrate major principles and eternal truths. Even though there are multiple levels of complexity in the character of Hedda, Ibsen, expectedly, tips the balance to highlight a specific, limited trajectory of his thought on an issue of major importance.

Depending on how one wants to look at it, the character of Hedda can come across as a victim at the hands of patriarchal society, a totally amoral and self-centered human being, a manipulative individual, or a victim of circumstance. Yet there is no doubt that Ibsen's one major thrust in *Hedda Gabler* is the narrow question of the sense of right and wrong in the context of human affairs. In the character of

Hedda, he projects an individual marked by a total absence of any notion of ethical interest. No ethical consideration governs her life, nor does she suspect any in the lives of people she interacts with. In his notes on the play Ibsen described her character as one who makes "Great demands upon life and upon the joy of life" (1889–90).

Hedda's choice of George as a husband is motivated by her growing years—she is already 29—a diminishing flock of admirers, and George's possession of a villa once owned by the widow of a cabinet minister. Even though beyond his means, George secures the villa and goes on a six-month-long honeymoon to please his bride. Hedda is bored with George's academic preoccupations. She loathes him when it appears that he might not get the much coveted professorship at the university, as then she may not have the means to live in style and affluence. She is convulsed with disgust and hatred when she discovers that Løvborg, her former lover whom she had rejected, might secure the much sought after university position. That a mousy Thea, her husband's former sweetheart, Hedda's one-time classmate and friend, had inspired Løvborg with her LOVE and devotion to complete his new book, which would ensure his superseding George, fires her anger even more. She herself had rejected Løvborg's suit, believing he lacked potential for social and financial upward mobility. This for her is now a matter of great gnawing regret. For this she loathes herself even more. Hedda's Machiavellian manipulations result in the destruction of the manuscript and she convinces a traumatized Løvborg to commit suicide.

Løvborg dies in a brawl. Hedda finds herself trapped in a likely social scandal, as it in her pistol that Løvborg uses in the scuffle in which he dies. Her only option appears to be to accept Judge Brack's offer and become his mistress to escape the scandal that could erupt at any moment. Both the possibility of a scandal as well as personal humiliation at the hands of Judge Brack, whom she finds repulsive, shatter her completely and she kills herself.

Ibsen has no illusion that ethical considerations must forever remain supreme. He believes that, to a degree, these are matters of mutually agreed upon beliefs in a community of people. He makes a perceptive remark in a letter to George Brandes, Ibsen's lifelong friend and an academic:

> Greater things than [state] will fall; all religion will fall. Neither the conceptions of morality nor those of art are eternal. To how much are we really obliged to pin pour faith? Who will vouch for it that two and two do not make five up in Jupiter? (1871)

Yet a human being as social animal is a site for an examination of major values that are considered humanity's social and spiritual bulwark. As an artist Ibsen creates a specific situation that shows humanity at work in a sociocultural context. Hedda refers to the manuscript as the intellectual equivalent of a baby and is in fact pregnant when she kills herself. Hedda's actions destroy both babies. Her Lady Macbeth-like ruthlessness lends the play an unusual intensity and determines the contours of her character. It would appear from the architectural design of *Hedda Gabler* that Ibsen's intention is as much to show how self-seeking, egotistical, and heartless human beings can be, as to point to the inescapable fact that self-centeredness can exist only in a context in which altruistic impulse exists, too. Thus, by implication, Ibsen assures us that the finer human urges do exist even though they are forever threatened by their baser counterparts. Thea is moved by love and devotion. George is keen to reconstruct the manuscript that has been destroyed because it will bring honor to a worthy scholar. Yet the strong voices that Ibsen lends to his protagonists, including Hedda, discourage readers from indulging in moral judgments.

Gulshan Taneja

GENDER in *Hedda Gabler*

Contemporary thinkers in Ibsen's time believed that the issue of equality of the sexes was closely bound up with major social reforms and structural changes in society, a view that Ibsen appears to have shared, believing that feminist causes were part of the larger canvas. In a speech delivered before the Norwegian Women's Rights League, Ibsen had said that he must "disclaim the honour of having consciously worked for the women's rights movement. . . . To me it has seemed a problem of humanity in general" (1898). Much earlier, in his notes for *A Doll's House,* Ibsen expressed a similar feeling: "A woman cannot be herself in contemporary society, it is an exclusively male society with laws drafted by men, and with counsel and judges who judge feminine conduct from the male point of view" (1878).

There is, of course, no doubt that the question of feminist reform was never far from Ibsen's thoughts. His wife, Suzannah, was an independent-minded woman. Her mother, Magdalene Thoresen, a playwright and novelist, was her role model. Ibsen himself considered Mrs. Thoresen much ahead of her times. Ibsen's interaction with Camilla Collett, who voiced Norway's most important feminist concerns, and his great admiration for her achievements, led to a deep impact on his own thinking as well as his writings. He, for instance, lent support to the 1884 petition in favor of property rights for married women in Norway.

Despite his humanist liberal attitude to social issues and his concern for larger questions, Ibsen's focus on the female characters in his plays was a major achievement. Ibsen projects the figure of the emancipated woman in almost all his plays. Many of his characters value independence and sexual fulfillment rather than marriage. Often, his female characters are better educated, taking up jobs rather than acting as self-sacrificing cogs in the everlasting domestic wheel of life. They ignore traditional female attire, wear boots and men's clothing, and deglamorize themselves. Some of them are shown using words and expressions traditionally associated with men. They can be blunt and aggressive in their behavior and disregard what people might think of their actions. Ibsen projects powerful and dramatic female characters who do not consider motherhood as their inescapable destiny.

By her upbringing, Hedda is more of man than a woman. She is brought up by her father, a general: "She has to be regarded," Ibsen wrote, "rather as her father's daughter than her husband's wife" (1890). She plays with a pistol, loves horses, and in moments of anxiety, paces up and down as a stereotypical man would do. Her desire for FREEDOM from domination and personal independence are viewed as masculine ambitions. In the play, Hedda reacts angrily to Judge

Brack's reference to her pregnancy. Her extreme sense of vulnerability and aggression that arises out of her sense of being trapped beyond hope, is what projects her beyond the mere victim in a feminist text.

There is little doubt that in *Hedda Gabler*, as much as in all of Ibsen's plays, a woman must not be offered the choice of independence at the cost of ALIENATION from and REJECTION by society. Ibsen's firm commitment is to the view that women must be allowed to make up their own minds and must have the last word on their bodies. Ibsen's contemporaries and early feminists considered his creations nothing short of miracles. His plays shaped the feminist movement in Scandinavia and had deep and lasting impact. The universe that Ibsen created for his characters to inhabit furthers many ends. One of them certainly is his historic contribution to the feminist movement in the 20th century.

Gulshan Taneja

SPIRITUALITY in *Hedda Gabler*

Even though Ibsen's plays are commonly associated with naturalistic theater and material issues of his times, Ibsen had a profound understanding of the human enigma. In his plays he reveals insights into the heart and soul of his characters even when he portrays his characters embroiled against the backdrop of sociopolitical issues of his day.

Hedda Gabler's neurotic personality is accorded an inner logic of its own even as her actions do not accord with conventional expectations. Hedda lives in a secret world of her own, buried deep in her unconscious and observing a code of values that is independent and her own. One can argue that Ibsen's one major interest in creating the character of Hedda Gabler was to delve deep into the depths of the spiritual dimension of humanity.

Despite the day-to-day material web in which Hedda is shown entangled, Ibsen sought to look deeper into her soul. Several readers and scholars have described Hedda as spiritually empty. She makes demands upon life and demands too much. But her focus in life is on the petty and the insignificant. Her demands reveal a mind and heart narrowly confined to the most constricted yearning of which a human being is capable. No finer sentiments inspire

her heart, no deeper philosophical notions fire her mind. Neither RELIGION nor FAITH nor LOVE motivate her in her yearnings. Her desires are the shallowest for a human being and her sensations are the sensations of the lowliest of animals. Ibsen shows remarkable artistic judgment in giving her actions and judgments the hues of apparently common and widely noticeable actions and judgments.

It is easy to miss that the essential purpose of the dramatist in creating such a character was not to show us an unredeemed villain but rather to illuminate the fact that each and every human being is in danger of degenerating into such a soulless being when devoid of spiritual health. It is in this sense that *Hedda Gabler*, as also other plays of Ibsen, must be understood. Elizabeth Robbins, the actress who played Hedda Gabler to great acclaim and had great influence on the way Hedda was perceived in the 20th century, had rightly said: "How should men understand Hedda on the stage when they did not understand her in the persons of their wives, their daughters, their women friends?" And when she goes on to say, "Hedda is all of us," she is pointing to general decay and a widespread spiritual malady that had overtaken the Europe of Ibsen's day and to which *Hedda Gabler* provides a major testimony.

Gulshan Taneja

IRVING, JOHN   *The World According to Garp* (1976)

Constructed as a biography, John Irving's fourth novel, *The World According to Garp*, traces its titular character literally from conception to memory, following him through the ordinary and extraordinary events of his life. Son of fictional feminist icon Jenny Fields, T. S. Garp (named after his biological father, Technical Sergeant Garp) grows up in the privileged environs of the Steering School, surrounded by the excesses of wealth but enclosed by his mother's protective and constant gaze. As he grows into adulthood, the novel allows us to enter Garp's world more intimately, reading the work of the nascent author during the process of composition in a war-ruined Vienna. Understanding Garp's purview by glimpsing the writer's writing recurs as a motif several times throughout the novel, allowing the reader the unusual insight of exploring the somewhat causal, always tenuous relationships between a writer's life and his writing. Irving leads his readers steadily through Garp's eccentric life: chasing down side-street speeders, cooking in the afternoon, fretting fruitlessly about his children, running anxiously and continuously through streets littered with the detritus of suburban angst and frustration. In the most explored relationship in the novel, Garp and Helen's marriage suffers from complications of their own making, from the difficult yearnings of unrealized expectations to infidelity and, ultimately, mortality. When in doubt, Irving's characters *do* something, and inevitably—occasionally tragically—it is the wrong thing. *The World According to Garp* is a comedy in the bleakest sense. Its humor and warmth are punctuated by the human suffering of its title character and his immediate family, but the book never loses its strange brand of optimism.

Aaron Drucker

GENDER in *The World According to Garp*

In Garp's world, women are victims and men lust. In *The World According to Garp* sexual identity is a prescribed role even as gender is constantly transgressed. Much of the novel serves to differentiate between gender and sexual identity. Sexuality, in all its forms, is generated from Jenny Fields's peculiar perspective. Garp's mother is an unlikely feminist, but in the novel, she is the preeminent figure of feminism, the woman who is emblematic of the contemporary, second-wave feminism. She begins her book, *A Sexual Suspect*, with the pronouncement: "In this dirty minded world . . . you are either somebody's wife or somebody's whore—or fast on your way to becoming one or the other." Gender is a state of being, a power position, either owner or owned. Women are told they are owned; men do the telling. It is not an equal relationship, and it has nothing to do with sexual identification, per se. Her appearance is embodied by the nurse's uniform she unceasingly wears. In that symbol of antiseptic femininity, the social and professional embodiment of the caretaker for the sick and injured, she fulfills the gender role of female without, in fact, identifying herself with the feminine. She is essentially asexual

(the act of procreation, for her, was an affair engaged in with a phallus and little else—certainly not a father, in more than the biological sense), and thus she denies and transcends the owner/owned (male/female) binary she actively protests. She engages almost exclusively in homosocial relationships, and though she is not lesbian, she has no interest in men, whom she largely views as victimizers, abusers, or fools. Jenny Fields sets the stage for the curious and often contradictory portraits of gender in *The World According to Garp*.

Garp is the product of Jenny Fields's stern and clinical indifference to social sexuality. In her pronouncement, "Men lust," Garp is no exception. In some ways, his maleness is less complex than Jenny Fields' femininity. Throughout the novel, he carries out several sexual escapades, both licit and illicit. From his first détente with Cushie Percy to his unsympathetic lust for Mrs. Ralph, Garp engages the sexuality of his gender with Jenny Fields's practical simplicity. He identifies himself with the male who cannot (or will not) curtail his sexual desire. His maleness is defined by his sexual needs and conquests. Such an identity is not without limits, however. Encountering the radical, bastardized version of lust—a rapist of prepubescent girls—Garp actively pursues the criminal, catching him (forcibly), and turns him in to the authorities. There is a point, for any man, at which more lust becomes too much lust and desire becomes violation, even in Garp's more open interpretation of sexual propriety. While his inability to keep his zipper shut causes any number of complexities in his life, it is only in regard to sex itself that Garp holds on to gender circumscriptions. In his home life with Helen and the kids, he explicitly disregards traditional gender roles, staying at home to write and care for his children and household while Helen carries on a professional position. He is a loving father and caretaker, even to the point of being ostentatious. While he expresses an awareness of the social reversal—he is embarrassed, for example, when he explains that he is a "writer" and no, you haven't read anything he's written—he is also happy in this role: the active and encouraging parent who protects and pushes his children into their promising future. Though Garp represents a "stay-at-home-Dad" as well as "more lust," he presents only the most straightforward of Irving's male complexities and inversions.

At first, Roberta Muldoon seems the iconic type of Irving's subversive gender politics, with his asexualizing of the feminist and his hypersexualizing of Garp; Roberta Muldoon used to be Robert Muldoon, quarterback of the Philadelphia Eagles and now a transsexual. "He" has become a "she" through the miracles of modern surgery. A six-and-a-half-foot, broad shouldered woman who knows who she is, she is both the theoretical feminist ideal and the ultimate sexual suspect. She also transcends any identifiable—and thus limiting—category. It would not be too grand a pronouncement to say that Roberta Muldoon is the most sympathetic character in *The World According to Garp*. He is the one unfailing, loyal, engaging, protective, giving, generous, and honest person in the novel. Ultimately, being able to dispense with strictures of gender and discovering a self-defined sexual identity is the most successful way to become a good—which is to say, self-aware and fully realized—person, at least according to *Garp*.

Aaron Drucker

GUILT in *The World According to Garp*

In *The World According to Bensenhaver*, the novel character T. S. Garp is working on in John Irving's *The World According to Garp*, guilt abounds. "In Garp's work, guilt always abounds," as it does in Garp's world. This world is shaped and defined by guilt. Characters act to avoid it, to relieve it, and to heal from it. Reeling from Helen's critical reaction to a short story he wrote, Garp's anger and frustration and desire for approval force him to sleep. The narrator explains, "But, actually, he'd had so much on his mind, he'd been confused; he had fallen asleep because he was bewildered. If he'd been able to focus his feelings on any *one* thing, he'd still have been awake when she came upstairs. They might have saved a lot of things, then." Helen wakes him gently, but in his dreams, he is thinking of Mrs. Ralph, his son's friend's mother. He feels the guilt of his virtual infidelity only as a reflection on how it would affect his wife to know that while she was engaging him, he was thinking of another woman. It is impossible to consider guilt sufficiently in *Garp*

without first acknowledging the novel's distinctly adult subject matter. Sex and adultery permeate the matter of the novel, and each major conflict circles around some aspect of sexual transgression. Guilt is a pervasive sensibility in Irving's novel, from the haunting of each character by his or her personal indiscretions or violations to the radical group-guilt of the Ellen Jamesians. There is no one untouched by the undertow of sex and guilt. Surviving the "undertoad" of life's errants and errors, learning to cope, to resolve, and to grow, that is what presses the novel forward. Guilt gives purpose to *The World According to Garp*.

T. S. Garp carries on several extramarital affairs throughout the novel, and Helen engages in only one. She commits to stray with Michael Milton, one of her graduate students, and when they are exposed, she tells Garp that she can break it off cleanly and decently. She explains that, "She felt she had never lost sight of Garp and the children during this indulgence; she felt justified in handling it *her* way, now." Garp takes the kids out to a movie in order to allow Helen the space to handle it her way. But circumstances conspire in the tragic ironies of the characters' lives. Michael Milton insists upon seeing her one last time, and he drives to the Garps' home. She meets him in the front seat of his 1951 Buick Dynaflow, where they engage in a last sexual act—the last gasp of a foolish recreation. Garp calls home, and Helen does not answer. Furious and impulsive, Garp gathers Duncan and Walt and drives them home early. To entertain the kids, Garp is in the habit of shutting off the motor and the lights of his car, coasting into the driveway in the black and the silence, a suburban roller-coaster thrill. In the darkness, he never sees the massive, parked station wagon in the driveway, and his children—thrilling to the rush, unbuckled in the back seat of the family car—are caught completely unaware by the collision.

There is a clear moral for the cuckolding lover, Michael Milton, as the clench of Helen's jaw during the accident proceeds to limit all future indiscretions. In Garp's words, "Three quarters is not enough." One would think Milton would disagree. And yet such a literal emblem for the loss of masculinity that cuckolding represents is typical of Irving's novel.

Milton feels no guilt for his dalliance with a married woman: It is a conquest and a desire that he refuses to relinquish. His lack of guilt is punished in the most disabling, permanent way. His transgression is not participation in adultery but the insistence that, when made public, he refuses to let it go. He feels no guilt; he is not grown up (and now, lacking full sexual identity, he never will be). For Irving, guilt is a maker of maturity, a sign of adulthood. Helen and Garp cannot fully accept their adulthoods, cannot be a mature couple, until they feel and resolve the guilt caused by their indiscretions.

The price of their straying is terrible. Walt is killed instantly. Helen and Garp survive the crash physically intact, injured but alive. Duncan loses an eye. It takes the tragic death of one son and the blinding of another for them to tackle the depth of their guilt, the denials and evasions that sprout from it, when they can finally resolve the failures of their relationship and learn to grow up together. In the relentless pessimism of Irving's novel, of course, this would not be the last terror or tragedy, but it is the central event of the book, and the impetus for denouement of the novel. The resolution of guilt—physical, emotional, sexual, and personal—is the movement of the last third of *The World According to Garp.*

Aaron Drucker

PARENTHOOD in *The World According to Garp*

Garp spends most of his adult life tending to his children's needs and keeping the house in order (not too neat, though) while awaiting his next surge of inspiration. While Helen teaches at a local women's college, Garp writes his first novel "between diaper changes and feedings" and his second in much the same way, though with less success. Garp considers himself a good father (privately, perhaps, better than "good"), and he frequently judges other parents by his own unusually devoted standards. But, in *The World According to Garp,* you can't be too careful.

In the beginning of the novel, there is Jenny Fields, Garp's mother. Meticulous, methodical, and distant, she does not want the burdens of a "normal" relationship, so she impregnates herself by way of an extraordinary affair with the mortally wounded technical sergeant Garp. Fatherless, Garp grows up at the Steering School comparing his caring and cautious but practical and efficient mother to the families of other students, most notably the campus-ensconced Percys. Jenny Fields teaches Garp to disdain relationships like those exemplified by the Percy clan: wealthy, privileged, unfocused, and (thus) valueless. Though the Percy household displays all the trappings of child-rearing, "carpeted and spacious and full of generations of tasteful toys," the parents of the Percy children do not have "the brains to worry about their children as much as they should." Carelessness, the mortal sin of Garp's conception of parenthood, is a prevalent part of the Percys' parenting strategy, and while under the inattentive eyes of the Percy parents, it quite literally ends up biting Garp when Bonkers, the Percys' dog, chews off the better part of his left ear. The Percy children are raised with a casual carelessness that allows, in better minds, the flowering of success, the type expected of wealthy legacy children. On the other hand, this same casual regard for caution allows a freedom in the children that leads to pain, tragedy, and finally to madness. Parenthood, for Jenny Fields, is about being careful. Only when the watchful eye of the parent is missing do children get into trouble. The lesson is not lost on Garp.

Garp and Helen have three children: Duncan, Walt, and later, Jenny. For the narrator, the subjective perspective of Garp's fatherhood is continually explored in the first half of the novel through the protagonist's unceasing cacophony of opinion on other parents' apparent failures. "Mrs. Ralph," the mother of Duncan's friend Ralph, is the epitome of Garp's failed parent. As painted by Garp, Mrs. Ralph is a nasty portrait of single motherhood. Garp's encounters leave him with the impression she is slovenly, drunk, promiscuous, and unmotivated. In an extended episode, Garp concludes that Mrs. Ralph is unfit as a parent, and he will watch his son's sleep-over at Ralph's. While the results are comic, her inaction is innocuous. For all of Mrs. Ralph's faults, even in her unmindful way, Ralph and Duncan remain safe, if not indulging in the quality of cuisine Garp would serve.

However much Garp's theory of parenthood rests on his being careful, *The World According to Garp* inexorably drifts into irony. Protecting his children from a terrible emotional scene when Garp discovers Helen's infidelity, Garp takes his children to see a movie. Intoxicated by the weeknight splurge, the children fumble for "the best view" of their father's daredevil return home—what should be a harmless thrill as the car floats silently down the driveway and into the garage. Except there is a car blocking the safe entrance of Garp's returning vehicle. The results are horrific. For all of Garp's caution, for all his will to safety, for all his plans and initiative, Garp cannot be careful enough to avoid the unknowable, the inevitable position of all parents. Even while his children remain in arm's reach, they can suffer terribly.

In the world according to Garp, parenthood is an impossible contradiction: the setting forth of a new life and the responsibility for its safety. Inextricably bound with terror and fragility, Jenny Fields, the Percys, Garp, Mrs. Ralph, and the panoply of characters try to compensate for their incomplete control of their children's lives. But like all adults with children, parenthood is formed by the character of the parent, and in turn, the children are cast in the image of father and mother. Duncan, the monocular result of the ever-watchful eye, does not have children. He survives his family (Jenny Fields, Garp, Helen, and Roberta) in order to start a family of his own, but with a transsexual woman. Parenthood is not an option for Duncan Garp. Garp was too aggressively careful with his children, as he was too aggressive with all things, and in the end, his desire for a perfect world left it sterile.

Aaron Drucker

IRVING, WASHINGTON *The Sketchbook of Geoffrey Crayon* (1819–1820)

Washington Irving's *The Sketchbook of Geoffrey Crayon*, first published serially between 1819 and 1820, made the author the first American to earn a successful living through his writing. Indeed, Irving is considered the inventor of the short story in America, largely because of this text; however, *The Sketchbook* also demonstrates Irving's mastery of the travelogue, satire, essay, and folktale.

The best-known stories from Irving—"The Legend of Sleepy Hollow" and "Rip Van Winkle"—are included in this collection, but its other selections are equally important. In "The Spectre Bridegroom," Irving proves his ability to work with and meld the genres of the fairy tale and the gothic, while in essays such as "English Writers on America," Irving takes aim at contemporary concerns over English critiques of American culture. In addition, Irving includes sketches of events and people that could easily pass as the field notes of an anthropologist.

Adopting the pseudonym Geoffrey Crayon, as well as Diedrich Knickerbocker, Irving explores such themes as NATIONALISM (and a national identity), GENDER, RESPONSIBILITY, and the INDIVIDUAL AND SOCIETY. Employing various genres allows the text to appeal to a variety of readers and engage them in the debate surrounding issues of the period and today.

Robin Gray Nicks

GENDER in *The Sketchbook of Geoffrey Crayon*

In Irving's *The Sketchbook of Geoffrey Crayon*, he explores the issue of gender and often ties it to responsibility. In Irving's text, men and women have not only different traits, but also different responsibilities. Stories that illustrate these ideas include "The Wife" and "Rip Van Winkle."

One of the earliest stories in the text, "The Wife," follows stereotyped roles for men and women, creating in the heroine a domestic goddess who perseveres in encouraging her husband even in the worst economic circumstances. The beginning paragraph of the text exalts women who maintain the behaviors of the stereotype: "Nothing can be more touching than to behold a soft and tender female, who had been all weakness and dependence . . . suddenly rising in mental force, to be the comforter and supporter of her husband under misfortune, and abiding . . . the bitterest blasts of adversity." In other words, the story sets up the perfect wife as dependent upon her husband, while also able to comfort and support him in the face of "the bitterest blasts of adversity."

From their physical characteristics to their internal dispositions, the wife and husband possess opposing characteristics that, at the same time, complement each other. The title character has "sprightly powers" and a "slender form" in contrast to her husband's "tall, manly person." At first, the husband of the piece refuses to share his financial troubles with his wife. Finally, the narrator explains to him that he is "depriving [him] self of the comforts of her sympathy" rather than addressing it as knowledge to which the wife has a right. Neither man discusses the wife as anything more than someone who wants only to comfort her husband, and as someone who will relish the opportunity to do so. The narrator's understanding of woman's true nature includes that "she will rejoice to prove that she loves you for yourself." He continues his argument by pointing to the "spark of heavenly fire" in woman's heart and to her nature as a "ministering angel" that can appear only when her husband "has gone with her through the fiery trials of this world." Throughout his discussion with the husband about the reasons why the latter should share the truth about his financial situation with his wife, the narrator addresses the wife's role as nurturer and supporter and her responsibility only to "prove" her love for her husband through the "fiery trials" they encounter. Not once does the narrator address the RESPONSIBILITY of the husband to share important life information with his wife and life partner. Clearly, responsibility for the success of the marriage lies with the wife.

This pattern of wifely responsibility is also addressed in "Rip Van Winkle," though the story uses the opposite situation to show what happens when one's wife does not play the role of nurturer and supporter to her husband. Instead, "all the good wives of the village . . . took his part in all family squabbles, and never failed, whenever they talked those matters over in their evening gossipings, to lay all the blame on Dame Van Winkle." Of course, the opposite was actually true because "Rip's composition was an insuperable aversion to all kinds of profitable labour." In fact, it is only because "his wife kept continually dinning in his ears about his idleness, his carelessness, and the ruin he was bringing on his family" that Rip does anything of use. The responsibility of supporting his family financially is his. Dame Van Winkle's responsibility is to buoy his spirits and joyfully support him. Because she instead chooses to "din," the other women cast her as the one at fault in family squabbles.

Rip's first thoughts when he awakens from his long slumber include "dread" at the thought of his wife's reaction. When he learns that his wife has died, "there was a drop of comfort at least in this intelligence." Neither he nor the narrator casts this as a blight on Rip's character, though the narrator does appear to denigrate Rip's laziness. In truth, the only compliment paid to Dame Van Winkle doing her duty as a wife is the recognition that she "had always kept [the house] in neat order." According to the text, the only responsibility she fulfilled as a wife was keeping the house neat and tidy. Otherwise, she failed in her responsibilities. Rip too fails, but his failures are recounted with comic overtones, whereas his wife's are recounted with disdain.

These two tales exemplify the collection's attitude toward gender and responsibility. Men and women have different responsibilities based solely on their genders. When women fail to fulfill these responsibilities, the text disdains them, whereas it looks at men's failures in their responsibilities with humor or sympathy.

Robin Gray Nicks

INDIVIDUAL AND SOCIETY in *The Sketchbook of Geoffrey Crayon*

The Sketchbook of Geoffrey Crayon by Washington Irving demonstrates the importance of the struggle between the individual and society in early America. Several stories in the collection, including "Rural Life in England" and "Traits of Indian Character," deal with this theme.

In "Rural Life in England," the narrator, Geoffrey Crayon, looks at the differences between one's character and behavior in the city and in the country. According to the story, people "who see the Englishman only in town are apt to form an unfavourable opinion of his social character." His relation to others and his need to be formal and civil require him to behave in this negative way. Because he is engaged with others constantly, the Englishman in the city is "absorbed" and "distracted by the thousand engagements . . . in this huge metropolis." He has so many people to see and engage with that he is always "on the point of going somewhere else . . . [and] while paying a friendly visit, he is calculating how he shall economize time so as to pay the other visits allotted in the morning," which makes him appear "selfish and uninteresting," something the narrator blames solely on the city.

On the other hand, in the country, the Englishman reverts to his "natural" state, unencumbered by the strictures and mores of city life. In the country, he "breaks loose gladly from the cold formalities and negative civilities of town" and "he puts no constraint either upon his guests or himself, but in the true spirit of hospitality, provides the means of enjoyment, and leaves everyone to partake to his inclination." In the country, the Englishman can be an individual, whereas in the city, he must be a member of a society with a multitude of "restraints." In the country, different classes move together "more freely [and are] more disposed to blend and operate favourably upon each other." In the city, the social codes forbid the blending of classes, or even the association of one with another. In the country, no such codes limit people's movements and relationships.

In "Traits of Indian Character," Crayon addresses common complaints that whites level against Native Americans as reasons to destroy or "civilize" them. The piece is laden with sarcasm, such as when he praises the American government for "wisely and humanely exert[ing] itself to inculcate a friendly and forbearing spirit towards them, and to protect them from fraud and injustice," and follows it with a footnote explaining that what this really means is that the government removed their power to purchase or sell land "without the express sanction of government." This introduction to society has diminished the character of the Native Americans so that they are "mere wrecks and remnants of once powerful tribes." According to Crayon, white society bears responsibility for the "repining and hopeless poverty, a canker of the mind unknown in savage life," which now pervades Native Americans. They are "drunken, indolent, feeble, thievish, and pusillanimous" because of the influences of society. In other words, these individuals lived a purer and more majestic life prior to their introduction to polite society.

Indeed, Native Americans' lives prior to their introduction to white society were vastly different. The sketch explains, "Their wants were few, and

the means of gratification within their reach. They saw every one around them sharing the same lot . . . No roof then rose, but was open to the homeless stranger." Each individual or "every one" was treated as an equal, regardless of his or her status. Once they began to associate with society, they experienced "vulgar prejudice and passionate exaggeration." The sketch even attributes their "cruelty . . . towards their prisoners" to the white society's "burning their villages and laying waste their slender means of subsistence." Crayon instead lauds the individual character of the Native American as possessing "stern resolution, the unbending pride, the loftiness of spirit, that seemed to nerve the hearts of these self taught heroes." In using the term "heroes," the text sets the societal outsider, the Native American, above those who adhere to the tenets of white society and those who persecute him.

Irving's exploration of the individual and society looks at the individual not necessarily as a single individual but as that which stands outside of the limitations placed upon people within the dominant society. In the country, the Englishman can revert to his true nature. In the past, prior to contact with "society," the Native American was powerful and honorable. According to these two pieces, as well as other texts within *The Sketchbook,* the responsibility for selfishness, greed, hurried relationships, poverty, and a host of other social ills rests squarely at the feet of society.

Robin Gray Nicks

NATIONALISM in *The Sketchbook of Geoffrey Crayon*

Washington Irving's *The Sketchbook of Geoffrey Crayon* contains several sketches and stories that promote a national mythology and literature, building upon the traditions of the folktale and the history of the American Revolution. Two in particular—"The Legend of Sleepy Hollow" and "Rip Van Winkle"—promote this nationalistic impulse.

A prefatory note to the story explains that "The Legend of Sleepy Hollow" was "found among the papers of the late Diedrich Knickerbocker," the pseudonym Irving used when writing his 1809 *A History of New York.* A ghostly tale, "Sleepy Hollow" references the Revolution and the Puritans and uses these allusions to create a sense of place and history. We learn that villagers think the headless horseman "to be the ghost of a Hessian trooper whose head had been carried away by a cannon ball, in some nameless battle during the revolutionary war." Haunted by the specter of history, the villagers and visitors see the ghost no matter their state of consciousness. It is a constant reminder of the nation's fight for independence, and it helps Irving establish some of the first truly American literature dealing with American settings, history, and issues.

Another constant reminder of the nation's history is the collection of books and stories with which Ichabod Crane regales his community. One of Crane's favorite texts, and one in which he fervently believes, is Cotton Mather's *History of New England Witchcraft,* a clear allusion to the witch trials in New England's past. Crane also enjoys entertaining the "old Dutch wives" with tales from Mather's text and other "anecdotes of witchcraft, and of the direful omens and portentous sights and sounds in the air, which prevailed in the earlier times of Connecticut." Though Knickerbocker's description of the scene works to set the tone for the later mysterious events surrounding Crane's disappearance, it also works to establish the text as firmly American. American literature must wrangle with not only the geographic peculiarities of a region, but also the contradictions and blemishes within the history of the nation. By alluding to the problematic history of America, Irving situates his text as one of the first to promote and embody the sort of national literature called for by the editors and writers of his day.

Another of Irving's stories supposedly found among Knickerbocker's papers is "Rip Van Winkle." In this tale, the reader encounters a myth or folktale of the Hudson River Valley, a folktale that the narrator urges the reader to take as "true history" over the "scanty" research found in books on the region. Again, Irving works the Revolutionary War into the fabric of the tale. Having slept through the revolution, Van Winkle encounters a world vastly different from the one he left. Seeing a portrait of General George Washington where a portrait of King George once hung startles Van Winkle, while flyers about rights, elections, congress, and "heroes of seventy-six" simply "bewilder" him.

Most frightening and shocking to Van Winkle are people's inquiries about his voting record, "whether he was a Federal or Democrat?" When he responds that he is a "loyal subject of the King," Van Winkle is unprepared for the violent reactions of the tavern politicians and customers. That a region, much less an entire country, could change so dramatically in 20 years not only shocks Van Winkle, for whom it's been only a day, but also shocks the reader, who may not have fully understood the extraordinary transformation that occurred during and immediately following the Revolution. Through Van Winkle's nap and jarred awakening, Irving's story symbolizes the awakening of America into its freedom, as well as American authors' reliance upon folklore in conjunction with historical fact to develop an "American" literature.

The nationalism promoted in Irving's *Sketchbook* is not a nationalism that declares America the best country, but a nationalism that begs for and works to develop a mythos, literature, and attitude all its own. Other stories work to juxtapose America with England or to disparage English criticisms of America. "English Writers on America" questions the English propensity to condemn Americans for what the English view as lowliness. Instead, Irving praises the American spirit and hospitality toward the English who "under rate a society, where there are no artificial distinctions, and where, by any chance, such individuals as themselves can rise to consequence." Praising America as the proverbial land of opportunity, Irving seizes the opportunity to himself "rise to consequence" as the father of the American short story.

Robin Gray Nicks

ISHIGURO, KAZUO   *The Remains of the Day*   (1989)

The Remains of the Day tells of Mr. Stevens, head butler of Darlington Hall, who takes a six-day motor trip to the West Country (Devon and Cornwall) of

England in 1956. Stevens recounts various strands of stories during the six days: unreliable memories of his working and personal life entwined with his present trip to visit Miss Kenton, a former head housekeeper who left Darlington Hall 20 years ago to get married. Lord Darlington, his previous employer—Darlington Hall was sold to Mr. Farraday, an American, when Lord Darlington passed away—held secret conferences to reconcile the differences between the British and German heads of state after the Great War. However, unknown to Lord Darlington, the Nazis made use of his kind and gentlemanly intentions to propagate their war ambitions. In the first of the secret conferences, Stevens remained at his butler duties even though his father was dying; Stevens thought that this act could be considered as dignified. As the narrative unfolds, it is gradually revealed that Stevens loved Miss Kenton. However, he did nothing to stop her marriage because he was, again, working to prove his dignity. The novel ends with Stevens resolving to make best use of the remains of his days. Ironically, he has not learn from his mistakes and returns to Darlington Hall, determined to please Mr. Farraday. *The Remains of the Day,* winner of 1989's Booker Prize, uses an unreliable narrator to talk of themes like dignity, loss, and NATIONALISM. It was adapted into a film in 1993 that received eight Oscar nominations.

Aaron Ho

AMBITION in *The Remains of the Day*

Ambitions are often unfulfilled and thwarted in *The Remains of the Day:* The characters are unsatisfied and disappointed and their lives empty. Lord Darlington, a rich aristocrat, desires neither occupational fame nor financial success. Although he dabbles in politics, it is perhaps inaccurate to say that he is ambitious politically since he has no interest in holding a governmental office. Whatever political meetings he arranges, he does so in his capacity as an aristocrat. If he has an ambition, it is that he aspires to be a gentleman. After the Great War and despite fighting the Germans, he remains a great friend to Herr Bremann because Lord Darlington believes that they are both serving their respective countries—something a gentleman would never fail to do. Being forgiving and sympathetic, virtues

a gentleman should possess, Lord Darlington agonizes over the way Germans were mistreated in the Treaty of Versailles. When Herr Bremann can no longer endure the hardships and commits suicide, Lord Darlington bring about a series of meetings in attempts to end the suffering of the Germans—against his godson Mr. Cardinal's advice. Unknown to Lord Darlington, he has been manipulated by the Nazis; he is Hitler's most valuable pawn in England. In the end, Lord Darlington's friends shun him and he dies a lonely death.

Like Lord Darlington, William Stevens, the father of Mr. Stevens who was the head butler of Darlington Hall, came to a tragic end because of his ambition. Although it is not immediately clear (because the narration is mediated through Stevens), William, by neglecting his family and investing his energy in his career, proved that he was ambitious. William's ambition was so ingrained into his way of thinking that even when he was 72, he still put his work before his family. For example, when Stevens inquired about William's health, William avoided Stevens's inquiries and diverted the subject to work. Because of his ambition, William was estranged from his son. On his deathbed, William said to Stevens twice: "I hope I've been a good father to you." Stevens's silence on the topic implies that he has not been a good father. Inculcated with William's work ethics, Stevens was on duty and did not stay by his father's deathbed. William's ending is as tragic as Lord Darlington: Both die alone.

Stevens, like his father, aspires to be at the top of his profession. For Stevens to achieve his dream of becoming an excellent butler, he has to have "dignity," a term Stevens discusses throughout the novel. Stevens's idea of "dignity" is that a butler should always put his work before his personal life and never lose control over his emotions. He believes he has achieved the acme of the butler profession, especially in two instances, his father's death and Miss Kenton's acceptance of Mr. Benn's marriage proposal. On both occasions, because he had to see to the smooth running of important conferences, he ignored his inner life and sacrificed his happiness for his ambition to be a dignified butler. He did not accompany his father as William was dying. He did not stop Miss Kenton from accepting Mr. Benn's proposal although he was deeply in love with her. (His love for her was so deep that even after 20 years of her marriage, he hoped to reconcile with her.) Ironically, at the end of the novel, after he has regretted his actions, his ambitious ways are so ingrained in him that all he can think of is how to please his new employer, Mr. Farraday.

Like Stevens, Miss Kenton believed that marriage was the death of one's career. When Lisa, a favorite maid of Miss Kenton's, eloped with the footman, Miss Kenton confided in Stevens: "[Lisa's] so foolish. She might have had a real career in front of her . . . So many young women like her throw away their chances, all for what?" Later, however, Miss Kenton, realizes that it is worth sacrificing one's ambitions for love and marriage, a realization Stevens, blinded by his pursuit of ambition, can not reach. Hence, even when Miss Kenton taunts Stevens with Mr. Benn's marriage proposal, Stevens does not stop her from accepting it.

All four of the characters—Lord Darlington, William, Stevens, and Miss Kenton—believe that familial ties are antagonistic to the fulfillment of ambitions. (Even Lord Darlington had fallen out with his godson because the former persisted in helping the Nazis.) They choose to put their ambitions as their first priority but come to regret their decisions: They realize love and kinship are more important than their ambitions but can no longer salvage the situation.

Aaron Ho

ETHICS in *The Remains of the Day*

Kind deeds never go unpunished in *The Remains of the Day*. After the Great War, Lord Darlington becomes acquainted with a German friend, Herr Bremann. Despite being enemies during the war, neither Lord Darlington nor Herr Bremann bear each other any grudge because they know they were doing their duty. Due to the Treaty of Versailles, signed in 1949 after the armistice that stopped the war, Germany suffered economically. With each passing visit, Herr Bremann gets thinner. His eyes have a haunted look. Eventually, he shoots himself and his family is dispersed. Lord Darlington, a gentleman who takes badly to Herr Bremann's suicide, desires to put an end to the injustice Germany has suffered. He pulls several heads of state together to sympathize with the Germans. Unknown to him, he is being manipulated by the Nazis in bringing about another war. Although Lord Darlington is morally upright, he dies lonely and broken.

Like Lord Darlington, William Stevens, Mr. Stevens's father, was punished for trying to do the right thing. When three gentlemen he was driving were gossiping about his employer, he stopped the car and opened the door. Instead of threatening the trio, he kept silent. Only when they, on their own accord, promised not to badmouth William's employer did he resume his chauffeuring duty. This incident demonstrates William's loyalty but also his reticence and ineloquence. Yet, like Stevens, William was so responsible and loyal that he always put his duties before his personal life. Since William was Stevens's subordinate, whenever Stevens tried to show concern for William, William would often be businesslike and cut Stevens off. However, on William's deathbed, he regrets the moral propriety with which he has conducted his life. He says to Stevens, "I hope I've been a good father to you. I suppose I haven't." Like Lord Darlington, William led a life guided by strong moral values but died with regret.

Like his father, Stevens's ethical code of conduct does not allow him to indulge his personal feelings while he is on duty; Stevens aspires to be known for his dignity. Even though he attempts to define the word "dignity" throughout the novel, for him the meaning is ultimately tied to work alone. For him, "dignity" is the ability of a butler to be composed in trying situations. For example, Stevens did not stay by his father while he was dying because Stevens was on butler duty. Or when Miss Kenton, the housekeeper whom Stevens loved, announced that she was going to accept a marriage proposal, he did not stop her partly because he was, again, on duty. Perhaps it could have been predicted that—since he had neither family nor friends—he was likely to follow in the footsteps of Lord Darlington and his father: They had abided by a set of moral principles but ended in despair and regret.

It is, however, difficult to call Stevens entirely ethical. He schemes, prevaricates, lies, and eavesdrops on private conversations. He is petty, proud, spineless, vain, and megalomaniacal. For instance, the readers are informed that the purpose of his motor trip is partly business: He wants to recruit Miss Kenton as he had made several mistakes and claimed he was short-staffed. As the novel progresses, the readers discover his aim is to see, or even to woo, Miss Kenton. His mistakes were made because he was getting old. On the trip, he meets with several naïve country people who mistake him for an aristocrat. He does not correct them. He even denies that he worked for Lord Darlington. During the trip, he reminisces about his 35 years of working for Lord Darlington. He firmly believes that the management of the household would have immense repercussions on the secret conferences Lord Darlington held. He compared his preparations the way "a general might prepare for a battle." In one of these preparations before an important conference, he continuously checked on and tried to find fault with Miss Kenton's work because he had a row with her previously. At this particular conference, he eavesdropped on a conversation: "I paused for a second to listen at the door . . it is common practice amongst many professionals. That is to say, there is no subterfuge in such an action, and I for one had no intention of overhearing."

Whether the readers should trust Stevens's explanation or not is an impossible matter to decide since he prevaricates. What Ishiguro does in the novel is refuse to moralize: Even though Stevens lied, the readers sympathize with him; and even though Stevens, William, and Lord Darlington abided by a set of moral rules, they ended up badly.

Aaron Ho

REGRET in *The Remains of the Day*

Although only one character explicitly expresses regret, most of them wish they could have done things differently. The novel starts with Mr. Stevens, the head butler of Darlington Hall, who goes on a six-day motor trip along the West Country in 1956. His aim is to recruit Miss Kenton, a former head housekeeper for Darlington Hall. Throughout the six days, he reminisces about his life from before to after World War II, culminating in a tearful confession: "[Lord Darlington] chose a certain path in life, it proved to be a misguided one, but there, he chose it, he can say that at least. As for

myself, I cannot even claim that . . . I can't even say I made my own mistakes." Since Stevens is a guarded narrator, this confession is especially poignant in expressing his regret: He rues his personal and working life. For instance, when Miss Kenton told Stevens of her marriage proposal, he did not stop her, even though he loved her, because of his work ethic. He refused to leave his butler duties to resolve his emotional entanglement because Lord Darlington was holding a conference of paramount consequences. In this conference, Lord Darlington was committing a grave mistake. He was being used by the Nazis to bring the British prime minister and German ambassador together for talks to advance German war plans. Stevens put such great unquestioning trust in Lord Darlington that he did nothing (within his limited powers) to warn his employer. In the end, he regrets his decisions over his love life and career. He goes on the trip to recruit Miss Kenton because he thinks her marriage is over. He lies, denying that he ever worked for Lord Darlington. However, Miss Kenton is only having a tiff with her husband and his lies about his work are exposed. What is most unfortunate about Stevens's life is that he does not learn from his mistakes. At the end of the novel, Stevens decides that he ought to have a positive attitude and make best use of the remains of the day. Ironically, he returns to his new employer, Mr. Farraday, determined to please him.

Stevens learned his work ethic from his father, William Stevens, who was also a butler. Like Stevens, his father sacrificed his personal life for his work. William was cool and unaffectionate to Stevens. They seldom talked to each other. On William's deathbed, he said to Stevens, "I hope I've been a good father to you. I suppose I haven't." Stevens did not comfort or even reply to his father directly. By circumventing the issue entirely, Stevens tacitly agreed with his father.

The sense of regret isn't restricted to the Stevenses. Miss Kenton, too, regretted. The relationship between Stevens and Miss Kenton was like a tug-of-war: Although both parties clearly had feelings for each other, neither wanted to be the first to admit to them. In an attempt to evoke a reaction from Stevens, Miss Kenton started to go on regular dates with Mr. Benn. When Stevens asked her about these dates, instead of getting angry for invading her privacy, she was relieved "as though she had been long awaiting an opportunity to raise the very topic." Stevens then discontinued the informal "meetings" they had after work. Miss Kenton, in another bid to win this tug-of-war, announced that her suitor had proposed to her and she intended to agree. Stevens did not stop her. Twenty years later, when Stevens meets her on his motor trip, she explains to him the reason she left (but eventually returned to) her husband thrice: "I get to thinking about a life I might have had with you, Mr. Stevens. And I supposed that's when I get angry over some trivial little thing [with her husband] and leave." But she goes on to explicate that "one can't be forever dwelling on what might have been" and returns to her husband in the end. However resolved she is to bear her past mistakes, she sometimes regrets the past so much her restraints breakdown. For example, she writes to Stevens: "The rest of my life stretches out like an emptiness before me."

The wistful and nostalgic tone of the novel reflects the regret that is felt by the characters. While Stevens, Stevens senior, and Miss Kenton are regretful, they deal with the emotion differently. Stevens senior died with regrets. Miss Kenton bravely admitted that she had regretted her decision in marriage but lived on with her decision, while Stevens continued to delude himself, to live a lie.

Aaron Ho

JACKSON, SHIRLEY   "The Lottery" (1948)

"The Lottery" tells of a small, nameless town's annual summer ritual. On every June 27, the father of every family draws a slip of paper from a black box. One slip has a mark on it. When one family is selected, every member of that family then draws another slip of paper, one of which, again, is marked. When it is determined who has selected the marked paper, that individual is immediately, inexplicably, and unemotionally stoned—presumably to death—by the entire village, including their own family members. The individual stoned this particular year is Tessie Hutchinson, wife to Bill Hutchinson,

mother to Bill Jr., Nancy, and little Davy, to "whom someone gave . . . a few pebbles." The story concludes with the haunting line: "'It isn't fair, it isn't right,' Mrs. Hutchinson screamed, and then they were upon her."

We identify with Tessie Hutchinson prior to her death because she arrives late to the ritual and then jokes with the crowd that she didn't want to leave dishes in the sink. The oldest man in the village, aptly named Old Man Warner, admonishes those who would do away with "The Lottery." This shows us that some of the villagers dislike the practice but continue anyhow. Mr. Summers and Mr. Graves ceremoniously lead the tradition, and there are a dozen or so other minor characters that comprise those present during the ritual.

As one of the most famous American short stories of the 20th century, "The Lottery" is brief, sparsely detailed, and relies less on character development than on its shocking finale for its emotional power and unsettling insights into human behavior.

David Michelson

INDIVIDUAL AND SOCIETY in "The Lottery"

A central conflict represented in "The Lottery" is between an individual, Tessie Hutchinson, and her society—the small, nameless village. Although the village is made up of individuals, once the rationale for the lottery is shared by a large number of people, an individual like Tessie becomes helpless to protest against a practice that the collective has deemed "right" and "necessary." However, Tessie is not simply a victim of collective cruelty; the story shows quite clearly that Tessie—even as a victim—has the same potential to do to another what is done to her.

On the one hand, Tessie is clearly an individual who becomes the victim of an outdated social practice. The purpose of the lottery is to select an individual to be sacrificed, but readers are never told why this is necessary. One presumes that this ritual performed a function in the past—that is, that the society benefited from an individual's sacrifice. Yet in the story's modern setting of factories and post offices, it seems the functionality has vanished while only the selected individual's burden remains. The ritual's apparent non-functionality supports our feeling that Tessie is a victim of a practice that should have been changed long ago. Our sympathy for Tessie as the victim is furthered by the fact that she is the only character who is individualized by the author. Tessie shows up late to the ritual, setting herself apart physically from her society and drawing our attention to her, and then jokes with the crowd about leaving dishes in the sink, which as a moment of light comedy, allows greater identification with her than with any other character. The fact that Tessie's final words are, "It isn't fair, it isn't right!" serves to underscore her role as an individual victim of her society.

On the other hand, Tessie's behavior—this year and in the past—is not that of an innocent victim. "The Lottery" is an engaging story, in part because it shockingly demonstrates the power society can exert over an individual's morality. Although we see her as a victim, it is tragically true that Tessie Hutchinson would have unthinkingly stoned any other member of her village were they to have drawn the marked slip of paper. In fact, one has to assume that she has participated willingly in the stoning of another individual each and every year. Although we feel sorry for her having been selected this year, her victimhood is complicated by the reality that, until today, she was part of the society that was enacting a cruel fate on another individual.

Part of the terrible power a society can wield over an individual resides in how quickly it can make a single person do something in the name of self-preservation that they would never do otherwise. Tessie shows this after her husband, Bill, is found holding the marked paper. Tessie exclaims "There's Don and Eva . . make *them* take their chance!" Eva is Tessie's eldest, married daughter, and in a frantic effort to save her own life, Tessie suggests that Don and Eva should be included in her family's drawing of lots. Even though she knows this would be against the rules of the lottery, she offers it up in a last-ditch effort to increase her own chance of survival. Thus, we see that, despite garnering our sympathy as a victim of a cruel social practice, Tessie is not without fault. Whereas, generally, being part of a society bestows benefits on individuals, "The Lottery" reverses this expected dynamic and shows how viciously selfish even a mother can become toward her own children when her life depends on it.

Whether we are to blame Tessie's society for forcing her to protect herself in this seemingly self-ish manner, or whether we are to look to Tessie as the locus of her own moral control, is the core of the moral quandary that the story asks us to engage. That Tessie embodies aspects of both victim and victimizer—in varying degrees depending on the context—demonstrates the complex potentialities of humans' moral nature, and shows that such issues are not easily resolved even though they are recurrent problems we all face as individual agents living in a social world.

David Michelson

TRADITION in "The Lottery"

In many respects, the central theme of "The Lottery" is tradition. While tradition is commonly thought of positively as social glue that holds families and communities together, Shirley Jackson's story offers a dark reminder of the dangers of following traditional practices uncritically.

The opening paragraph informs us that the lottery occurs in many towns. Although "in some towns there were so many people that the lottery took two days and had to be started on June 26th" the shared time of year suggests that a popular, recurring tradition is about to unfold. To normalize the lottery as a stable convention of village life, Jackson tells us that the early summer ritual is conducted by the same man every year—Mr. Summers—who also oversees other aspects of traditional life such as "the square dances, the teen-age club, the Halloween program."

The conventional nature of the lottery is under-scored further by the author's detailed description of the items involved in the ritual, and the villagers' specific reactions to changing them. Even though the "original paraphernalia for the lottery has been lost long ago," the townspeople still use an old, rick-ety box for drawing slips of paper. The box is older than the oldest man in the village, and any discussion of making a new box is met with disapproval, as "no one liked to upset even as much tradition as was represented by the black box." Affinity for what the box represents is motivated, in part, by a traditional "story" that recounts how the current box contains pieces of the original box used by the founders who "settled down to make a village here." One might say that the box symbolizes tradition: It is based on a story, is passed down from generation to generation, changes very slowly over time, but nevertheless is believed to serve an important function within the community.

Jackson conveys her cautionary message on tradition by establishing a tension between the brutality of the ritual practice and the fact that it has lost much of its specificity and functionality over the years. Indeed, "the people had done it so many times they only half-listened to directions," and over the years certain parts of the tradition "had been allowed to lapse" and "had changed with time." At one point, a villager named Mr. Adams mentions that "over in the north village they're talking of giving up the lottery." Mr. Adams's mere mention of another town abolishing the tradition is met with howls of disapproval by the aptly named "Old Man Warner": "Pack of crazy fools . . . listening to the young folks, nothing' good enough for *them*. Next thing you know, they'll be wanting to go back to living in caves." Old Man Warner's dictum—"Lottery in June, corn be heavy soon"—suggests that the ritual might once have held a functional, agricultural purpose that now seems outdated, given the modern setting of the story, complete with coal plant, bank, and post office. Like the tattered box, Old Man Warner may also represent tradition, which is continually threatened by and hostile to new ideas and attitudes, here represented by "the young folks." At the end of the day, it seems that tradition itself is reason enough to continue the lottery; Old Man Warner reminds us: "There's *always* been a lottery," and to think of changing it, well, "Nothing but trouble in *that*."

Rereading the story, one cannot help but read Old Man Warner's words ironically. We know that the lottery is "nothing but trouble," and as there is no convincing explanation for why one villager has to die a horrific death each year, the fact that "people ain't the way they used to be," might actually be a positive step away from blindly following a tragic tradition. Nevertheless, the arbitrary violence that punctuates the end of the story serves to reinforce the author's highly negative opinion of some traditions and human beings' willingness to uphold them—even to murderous ends.

The author further expresses her condemnation of unthinking tradition with sarcasm "although the villagers had forgotten the ritual and lost the original black box, they still remembered to use stones." The troubling, ironic cruelty attributed to the followers of the tradition is Jackson's way of condemning the violence potential latent in those who too gullibly accept custom. In so thematizing convention, the author encourages us to discuss and debate traditions in our own towns and cultures, and to imagine ways in which they might benefit from some collective rethinking.

David Michelson

VIOLENCE in "The Lottery"

If we examine the literal language used to describe the events that transpire in "The Lottery," the only act of violence—if we can even call it that—occurs at the very end of the story, when, after Tessie is selected in the annual lottery ritual, "a stone hit her on the side of the head." Despite this simple description of violence, the story's implied violence—a continued, brutal stoning-to-death suggested by the final line, "and then they were upon her"—has a tremendous power to unsettle even the most hardened of readers. After all, "The Lottery" concludes with the assumption that the community stones Tessie Hutchinson to death. However, it is not evident that this is in fact the case. Might they simply want to scare Tessie? Is she to be stoned until she is hurt, perhaps to teach her a lesson? Or will the stones fly until she dies? Most readers of "The Lottery" assume the worst case scenario because of a series of textual clues that slowly add up to, but in no way solidify, the conclusion that Tessie is executed. Such inferences drawn from the text, fueled by our imaginations, have made "The Lottery" one of the most enduring nonviolent representations of violence in American short fiction. The implied violence at the end of the story is made all the more terrible by two factors: first, our growing realization of having been duped by the story's tone; and second, the means of killing Tessie is purposefully brutal.

In its effect on readers, "The Lottery" sneaks up on us like a wolf in sheep's clothing. The opening pages paint a commonplace setting and the tone of the story is initially one of happy anticipation.

Indeed, the weather is pleasant, everyone is chit-chatting, and even the subtle foreshadowing of events to come—the fact that the boys are picking smooth, flat rocks and putting them in their pockets—is easily dismissed as an innocent activity that one can expect in such a town. By the middle of the story, however, it becomes clear that beneath the veneer of happy small-town life resides a discontent in the village. It is curious that Old Man Warner admonishes those who would give up "The Lottery" and Tessie becomes increasingly adamant that the lottery is not fair. Significantly, we are not told why some villages want to give up the lottery ritual, and we struggle to determine just why someone would not want to win a lottery, which usually results in something good. The possibility of violence at this point in the story is remote if not incredible; but, drawn this far into the tale, we have been at least initially primed for a modestly incongruous ending. When we learn that Tessie is to be stoned to death, and that all of the village—including her husband and children—will participate, everything we have assumed thus far is thrown into confusion. The initially happy tone, which has slowly been weakening to worry, finally erupts into horror. Our presuppositions about family life, small-town living, and good-neighborliness must struggle to reconcile how we went from sunny day to vicious stoning. This sneaky, gradual shift is accomplished, fundamentally, through a clever manipulation of tone by the author.

The form of violence suggested by the end of the story serves to punctuate this tonal inconsistency with a giant exclamation point. Stoning is a cultural practice that most Americans read about only in books. It is exotic, terrible, and a brutal way to die. Jackson could have just as easily ended the story with Tessie drinking a painless, fast-acting poison. Alternatively, she could have exiled Tessie from the village or had her work for somebody else as a servant for a year. The potential conclusions were many, but the author decided upon a form of extreme violence. Critically, this is not violence for violence's sake; Jackson is not simply trying to shock us. While the strong suggestion of stoning is literally violent, the figurative meaning of this violence gestures beyond itself in ways that literary symbolism

typically does. The violence serves to draw attention to the author's deeper concerns about the possibly deadly costs that follow from blindly following tradition, and the impact of unfair social practices on the individual. For a story that represents no actual violence, "The Lottery" has the power to make us imagine extreme harm enacted upon an individual, thus serving to unsettle our common assumptions about the contexts in which people harm others. If we can get past the jolt of the violence that punctuates the end of the story, we can begin to examine the origins of our revulsion, and the power of fiction to elicit such feelings.

David Michelson

JACOBS, HARRIET   *Incidents in the Life of a Slave Girl, Written by Herself* (1861)

Incidents in the Life of a Slave Girl was written in 1861 by Harriet Jacobs and is the only novel-length slave narrative by an African-American woman. Unlike other slave narrators, Harriet Jacobs did not publish the book under her own name, instead used the pseudonym Linda Brent. It details the particular brutalities faced by female slaves, particularly sexual abuse, and is unique in that it addresses a specific audience, white women in the North. As a young girl, Linda is unaware of her status as a slave; her father, Uncle William, and grandmother, Martha, protect her. As she reaches adolescence, she is constantly harassed by Dr. Flint, her owner, and Mrs. Flint, his wife. The narrative describes Dr. Flint whispering sexually explicit remarks to Linda and accosting her sexually; Mrs. Flint recognizes her husband's sexual pursuit of Linda and becomes increasingly more abusive toward her. The only person Linda can turn to is her grandmother. When Linda wants to marry another slave, Dr. Flint denies her request; in a final attempt to be free of his torments, she decides to have two children, Ellen and Benny, with Mr. Sands, a white politician. Dr. Flint attempts to use her children to get her to submit to him; rather than run away and leave her children, Brent spends seven years hiding in the garret over her grandmother's house. During that time, her grandmother takes care of her, and she and her family write false letters to Dr. Flint in order to make him think that she is free in the North. At the end of the narrative, Linda escapes to the North with her children, and Mrs. Bruce, her employer, ultimately buys her freedom for $300. The narrative was published with a foreword by Lydia Maria Child, and it implores its imagined audience, white northern women, to use their moral influence to assist the abolitionist cause.

Courtney D. Marshall

GENDER in *Incidents in the Life of a Slave Girl*

In *Incidents in the Life of a Slave Girl,* Harriet Jacobs, an escaped slave, documents the sexual abuse she underwent while enslaved and her dramatic escape in which she spent seven years imprisoned in a garret above her grandmother's house. Though the book is autobiographical and by definition self-affirming, Jacobs chooses to hide her identity behind the name Linda Brent, because she believes that making her story public, while imperative, is not a usual activity for a woman. Jacobs's narrative is different from other slave narratives because it takes as its focus the issues of female enslavement and the particular trials that women face. Her story focuses on the rights of women to protect their bodies and families and to keep their children. Throughout her narrative, she describe struggles for freedom in which women play major roles. *Incidents* is also unique in that it addresses a specific audience—white female readers in the North—and speaks for black women still held in bondage.

In the opening of *Incidents,* Harriet Jacobs makes it clear that she is writing her book to an audience of white northern women. At this time, women could not vote, but, according to the gender ideology of the time, they could effect moral change in their male relatives who could. Jacobs attempts to bridge the gap between free white northern women and herself by making a series of critical comparisons. She compares her experiences with first love with that of her readers, asserting the futility of the slave woman ever finding love with someone who respects her. Later, she asks her northern reader to compare her New Year's Day with that of the slave woman who sits in her cold cabin with her children waiting to see if any or all of them will be sold away from

her the next day. According to 19th-century gender standards, motherhood was very important. Slave women were not allowed to have control over their bodies or their children, and in this example, Jacobs hopes that by appealing to her readers as mothers they will find further commonalities with her and want to effect change.

Jacobs realizes that because she is a slave, she cannot experience girlish innocence, motherhood, or romantic love without being worried about the slave system taking them away; her circumstances lead her to make choices that put her at odds with gender conventions. Enslaved women and their children could be separated at any time; even if they belonged to the same owner, strict labor policies and plantation regulations severely limited the development of the mother-child relationship. In an era when women were not supposed to talk about sex, she says she was prematurely aware because of the foul words Dr. Flint begins to whisper in her ear. She prays to die in order to escape Dr. Flint's advances, particularly after he builds a house for her in the woods and orders her to live there. The most controversial decision she makes in order to escape Dr. Flint is to become involved with Mr. Sands, a visiting white politician, and to have two children with him. She believes that Dr. Flint will be jealous of her love and finally stop harassing her; however, this is not the case. Dr. Flint threatens Linda by promising harm to her children; because she wants to protect her children from Flint, she decides to escape.

Throughout the narrative, Jacobs holds herself out for judgment by her readers, but repeatedly argues that enslaved women should be held to a different moral standard. At the same time, she argues that the slave system is inherently criminal because it keeps her from fulfilling her ideas of true womanhood. Because she is a slave, she cannot have a stable marriage with a man who supports her, a home protected by law, or literacy that would allow her to read the Bible and share its teachings with her children.

The institution of slavery also distorts standards of masculinity. Dr. Flint, Linda's master, is depicted as a lascivious, godless man who pursues her for decades, and Mr. Sands reneges on his promise to free them. At the same time, her uncle and brother are punished and imprisoned for asserting their masculinity. After Linda gives birth to her daughter, she feels great pain because she believes that, though slavery is terrible for men and women, it is worse for women because they have their particular hardships to undergo.

Today, Jacobs's story is the most female-authored slave narrative. Its attention to the ways in which slavery corrupted gender roles and standards in the antebellum South makes it key for understanding slavery's effects on southern society.

Courtney D. Marshall

JUSTICE in *Incidents in the Life of a Slave Girl*

Where can a slave find justice? According to Harriet Jacobs, not in the American legal system because this system relies upon injustice and deception. In "The Trials of Girlhood," she asserts that women of the North can advocate for slaves even though they themselves do not live on southern soil. Laws protect the free woman from insult, violence, and even death. She writes that fiends "bear the shape of men," differentiating her imagined audience for the callous male audience who would seek to keep her enslaved. She imagines a loving female audience that would see itself as diametrically opposite of this group. In this passage, she positions herself as a witness to slavery's wrongs—and the female audience as a jury who must condemn slave practices.

As Jacobs well knew, various laws worked to deny slaves legal justice. Though slave laws varied, basic restrictions included the inability to vote, run for office, or petition the government. Her grandmother lent $300 to her mistress, but when the mistress died and she came for repayment, the mistress's son-in-law, Dr. Flint, tells her that the law forbids the recognition of a contract involving a black person. Jacobs notes that the Flint family did keep a candelabrum bought with the loaned money and that she is sure that a fiction has already been concocted as to its whereabouts. The beauty of the candelabrum is juxtaposed with the ugliness of the lie on which it was gained. The incident in the book strengthens Jacobs's argument about the way that slaves are cheated. Dr. Flint also cheats Jacobs's grandmother when he decides to sell her instead of granting her the freedom her mistress had promised her.

There is also no justice when it comes to Dr. Flint's harassment and her eventual freedom. Jacobs appeals to divine justice as a stand-in for that of humans, while making repeated references to American ideals of law. When Dr. Flint abuses her, she says that slavery is like jail, but worse because, unlike a jail sentence, it does not end. Though his wife knows that he is abusing the narrator, the wife does not help her. Jacobs repeatedly holds her own experience out for judgment by her readers so that abolition and justice will become a reality for all enslaved people.

She juxtaposes herself with her white female northern readers whose purity is protected by the home and the law. For her, womanhood is linked to questions of justice, and the differences between white and black women derive less from nature than from circumstances and legal status. Jacobs's focus on the law and justice helps her to motivate northern women to see slavery as a national problem. By staging a literary reaction to legal realities, Jacobs's text expands our understanding of the cultural and historical moment.

SEX in *Incidents in the Life of a Slave Girl*

In *Incidents in the Life of a Slave Girl*, Harriet Jacobs deploys a slave girl's testimony along with the stories of several other women and men in order to generate multiple pictures of slavery's treatment of sexuality. As an enslaved African-American woman, Linda and other slaves were confronted with stereotypes about their hypersexuality. At the time she lived, white slaveholders invented the mythology of Jezebel to rationalize the rampant rape and sexual abuse of slave women. In addition, southern law did not consider the rape of slave women a crime. Because of her awareness of this stereotype, she is reluctant to discuss her sexuality in the narrative.

When Linda is 15, her master Dr. Flint begins to make sexual advances toward her. She uses biblical imagery and compares her awakening to sexual matters to the serpent's tempting of Eve. Jacobs describes him as "[peopling her] mind with unclean images, such as only a vile monster can think of." Because he is her master, he has power over all areas of her life, including her sexual identity. Later in the narrative, he refuses to let her marry a fellow slave and hatches a plan to build a small, secluded house for her. While he tells her that moving into the house will help make her a lady, she knows that he wants to have here there so that he can have unchecked sexual access to her. It is at this point that she decides to have sex with another man in order to show him that she is not interested in him. It is interesting that their relationship in this section of the narrative is more like a romance novel, with Linda painted as the object of desire between two romantic rivals.

Even though the slaveholding culture does not respect her right to sexual autonomy, the women in the narrative hold convictions about sexual propriety. As a result, Linda's narrative oscillates between dealing with the realities of sexual abuse and the pull to be a proper 19th-century woman, chaste and pious. Linda is afraid to tell her grandmother about becoming pregnant by a white man because she feels that she will be ostracized for rejecting the values her grandmother instilled in her. These are the same values that she claims Dr. Flint tried to destroy when she was younger. At this point in the narrative, Jacobs also begs her readers not to judge her too harshly. She does not go into details about the sexual relationship she has, but she says that slave women should not be held to the same sexual standards as white women because their sexual propriety is not respected by the culture. They are taught to be duplicitous and secretive.

Jacobs's text reminds us that enslaved men are also subject to sexual abuse. In the chapter on the Fugitive Slave Law, Luke is chained to his master's bed and partially clad (only a shirt). When his master becomes sick and too weak to beat him, he sends for the constable. The abuse Luke suffers is tinged with sexual impropriety. He thinks "Some of these freaks were of a nature too filthy to be repeated." By including his story, Jacobs demonstrates the ways in which slave laws regulated sex and used it as a weapon.

Courtney D. Marshall

JAMES, HENRY *Daisy Miller* (1878)

When *Daisy Miller* appeared in 1878, it became Henry James's most popular story, and it still ranks among the most-often read of his works today. In this novella, James explores the international theme, studying ways that Americans act toward each other in communities abroad. At the end of his career, between 1907 and 1909, James revised *Daisy Miller* and included the new version in his collected works, known as the *New York Edition*.

This story follows Annie P. "Daisy" Miller, a young woman from New York, as she travels with her mother and her brother, Randolph, on her first European tour. Although the Millers are wealthy, other Americans in Europe consider them inferior because they do not understand the social rules of the upper class. In Vevey, a resort town in Switzerland, Daisy meets Winterbourne, a fellow American, who is surprised that she acts so independently. Studying her actions, he first labels her an innocent, uneducated girl but later considers her a calculating flirt. Winterbourne's aunt, Mrs. Costello, refuses to meet the Millers, and his friend in Rome, Mrs. Walker, also rejects Daisy, because she will not follow social conventions. For instance, Daisy ignores Mrs. Walker's warning by choosing to walk in public with Mr. Giovanelli, a lower-class Italian man. After the two visit the Colosseum, a site rich in symbolism, one evening, Daisy will die of malaria; Winterbourne learns of her innocence—too late.

Through Daisy's tragic story, James explores themes of COMMUNITY, FREEDOM, IDENTITY, INDEPENDENCE, INDIVIDUAL AND SOCIETY, INNOCENCE AND EXPERIENCE, REJECTION, RESPONSIBILITY, SACRIFICE, and SOCIAL CLASS.

Melanie Brown

FREEDOM in *Daisy Miller*

Freedom emerges as a significant theme in James's novella when Daisy, flirtatious but naïve, chafes against the social expectations of American expatriates she meets in Vevey and Rome. There, Daisy finds that middle-aged socialites and seemingly eligible bachelors conduct themselves according to social rules that she does not understand. The rules governing young women's behavior prove more restrictive than those she grew up with in New York, where Daisy was free to move about in public and to choose with whom she spent her time. Although valued in America, her nouveau-riche liberties offend the wealthy expatriates' European sensibilities and result in Daisy's downfall.

In Vevey, the Millers act as freely as they did at home. Randolph, Daisy's younger brother, traverses the first-class hotel's grounds with a pointed walking stick that he thrusts indiscriminately into landscaping and ladies' dresses. Mrs. Miller, having met all of Daisy's many gentlemen callers in New York, does not realize that she should curtail her daughter's plans to visit the castle of Chillon alone with Frederick Winterbourne, an expatriate visiting from Geneva. Daisy ignores the implication of Eugenio, her European courtier, that to do so would be improper and enjoys the attention she attracts as she leaves the hotel with Winterbourne and without a chaperone.

The Millers' actions sit better with some guests of the hotel than with others. Winterbourne struggles to be cautious when he realizes that Daisy will accompany him alone on their tryst. Having lived so long in Switzerland, he is taken by Daisy's insistence on her freedom to do as she wishes. Mrs. Costello, Winterbourne's aunt, however, pronounces the Millers uneducated and "horribly common." Upon learning that the young woman intends to visit Chillon unchaperoned, Mrs. Costello declares herself "honestly shocked" at Daisy's behavior. When she realizes that Mrs. Costello will not receive her, Daisy masks her disappointment not by conforming to the older woman's restrictive social rules but by acting even more freely in ways that she considers "natural."

This tension between the expatriates' expectations of social modesty and Daisy's American sense of social freedom emerges again in Rome. There, Daisy finds a vibrant atmosphere, with gentlemen callers, dinners, and dances. Although she enjoys this scene, the socialites around her, including Mrs. Costello and Mrs. Walker, are appalled by her interactions with "third-rate Italians" and "regular Roman fortune-hunters."

One afternoon at Mrs. Walker's apartment, Daisy announces her intention to walk to the Pincio, a public park with views of the city, to meet her most energetic suitor, Giovanelli. Winterbourne, stunned by Daisy's willingness "to exhibit herself unattended to [the crowd's] appreciation," hastily agrees to accompany her. When, upon spying Giovanelli,

Winterbourne warns her to beware of him, Daisy replies coolly, "'I've never allowed a gentleman to dictate to me or to interfere with anything I do.'" This credo reveals the value Daisy places on her freedom, but Mrs. Walker seeks to curtail that independence. She pursues Daisy in her carriage, but the latter refuses her invitation to drive about the Pincio: when warned that her behavior is not customary in Rome, the young American replies, "'If I didn't walk, I'd expire.'" Thus, James's naming of Mrs. Walker proves ironic, as she attempts to control Daisy's freedom of movement—"'You should walk with your mother, dear'"—from the vantage point of her carriage.

As Daisy increasingly alienates herself from Rome's expatriate social set by persisting with Giovanelli, Winterbourne attempts to negotiate her shifting status among his peers. When he encounters the couple late in the evening inside the Colosseum, he feels Daisy has gone too far, both scandalizing and endangering herself by appearing unchaperoned and by courting the "Roman fever," or malaria, of the city's swampy lowlands. When he turns away, Daisy cries, "Why it was Mr. Winterbourne! He saw me and he cuts me dead!" Her observation proves prophetic. The Colosseum becomes a symbol of her death at the hands of a Roman society that seeks to inhibit her freedom, even as Daisy cannot see the dangers of a land with customs different from her own. She explains, "'I was bound to see the Colosseum by moonlight—I wouldn't have wanted to go home without *that*.'"

In the end, she does not go home at all. Felled by malaria, Daisy is buried near the city wall; at her funeral, Winterbourne and Giovanelli remember her as a young woman "'who did what she liked.'" Throughout the story, the names Daisy and Winterbourne evoke a struggle between vibrant innocence and frozen custom. Although Daisy dies at the end of the story, as an ironic symbol of the freedom she treasured, her grave rests among "the April daisies" that grow wild by the city wall—after the winter born.

Melanie Brown

RESPONSIBILITY in *Daisy Miller*

In Europe, Daisy Miller seeks the adventure and company of society, but she does not understand (or, in some cases, chooses not to follow) social conventions, finding them too constricting. Given her ignorance of how and why to follow social expectations, who is responsible for educating her about them? Is her mother, also unaware of these rules, responsible for her daughter? Does that responsibility fall to the men and women—Mrs. Costello and Mrs. Walker, Winterbourne and Mr. Giovanelli—around her in Vevey and Rome? Or, is Daisy finally responsible for herself, for her education, and, in the end, for her own death?

The women in Daisy's community, older, married, and long-time residents of Europe, cultivate society's exacting regulations, and they shun Daisy for not conforming to them. Mrs. Costello feels responsibility and allegiance not to Daisy but to her social set. When Winterbourne realizes that his aunt will ignore the Millers, Mrs. Costello explains, "I wouldn't if I hadn't to, but I have to.'" She also feels responsible for her family, refuting Winterbourne's generalization that all American girls—including Mrs. Costello's granddaughters—act as innocently and as ignorantly as Daisy Miller. Conversely, Mrs. Walker feels personal responsibility, at least temporarily, for Daisy. She warns the girl that walking in public with Mr. Giovanelli is socially dangerous, but Daisy takes her walk anyhow. Mrs. Walker even follows the couple in her carriage in an "attempt to save" the girl but to no avail (46). When Daisy not only rejects her advice but also arrives with Mr. Giovanelli hours late at Mrs. Walker's next party, the woman relinquishes any responsibility to Daisy and vows never to invite the girl to her home again. Mrs. Miller, the only other woman who might help Daisy, is as ignorant of social conventions as her daughter and thus proves helpless to guide her into society or, in the end, even to save her life.

Although men offer Daisy more companionship in the novella, they do not accept responsibility for her social education. To the contrary, both Winterbourne and Mr. Giovanelli seem to enjoy Daisy's breaking of restrictive social rules. The latter enjoys strolling about the Pincio in Rome with the girl, while Winterbourne acknowledges that he is able to take liberties with Daisy Miller that are unavailable to him when he socializes with young, single women in Geneva. A student of sorts during his months in Geneva, he makes a study of Daisy, drawing on his and others' observations of the girl in vain to classify her as either innocent and uncivilized or as flirtatious and even immoral. Accordingly, he is, in turn, thrilled and repelled by Daisy's insistence on acting independently, and he wavers between defending and deriding her. But when he spies her with Mr. Giovanelli at the Colosseum late at night, he feels relieved to settle on one definition—immoral—and offers her a final piece of advice: to take medication to avoid contracting malaria. His advice comes too late; after Daisy's funeral, Winterbourne momentarily feels some responsibility for her loss. He tells his aunt that, having lived so long in Europe, he "was booked to make a mistake" in his dealings with a young American girl. His return to Geneva suggests that knowing Daisy has left no impact on him and that his sense of responsibility is fleeting.

Despite the responsibility those around her might bear, Daisy Miller is responsible, at least in part, for her actions. Even when told of social conventions, Daisy often ignores them. She seeks to shock Winterbourne by proposing to visit the castle of Chillon with him at night. "'That's all I want,'" she tells him, "'a little fuss!'" She ignites more than a little fuss, however, when she rejects all advice given her. She chooses to meet Winterbourne in a crowded hotel lobby for their daytime trip to the castle, and she persists in spending time with Mr. Giovanelli, declaring herself improper for declining Mrs. Walker's offer of a ride home from the Pincio (48). When Winterbourne offers her the last of his advice, Daisy rejects this suggestion as well, telling him she does not care if she falls ill. In the end, Daisy's death results from her initial ignorance and eventual forthright rejection of social rules as defined by ex-patriate Americans in Europe. Given her nouveau riche status, however, Daisy could not know the rules of this rarefied society, and so responsibility falls, as well, on those characters who refused to take upon themselves her cultural education.

Melanie Brown

SOCIAL CLASS in *Daisy Miller*
Daisy visits Geneva expecting to find people and social events similar to those she has experienced

back home in New York, but she discovers that her understanding of appropriate social behavior clashes with the expectations of expatriate American high society. Upon meeting Winterbourne in her first-class hotel in Vevey, she tells of dinners hosted in her honor, some of them by men, in Manhattan. Vevey offers little, in contrast to the lively landscape of New York, and Daisy expresses her disappointment in the town's wholly absent social scene. Indeed, her compatriots in the hotel have avoided making the Millers' acquaintance, a rejection best represented in the character of Mrs. Costello, Winterbourne's aunt.

During their first meeting, Daisy confides in Winterbourne that she hopes to know his aunt, a wealthy woman who, as Daisy learns from conversations with one of the hotel's maids, is "very exclusive." Mrs. Costello, however, has no intention of crossing Daisy's path; as she tells Winterbourne, the Millers are "the sort of Americans that one does one's duty by just ignoring." Indeed, the Millers hail from a rising class of newly rich Americans, their wealth so newfound that Daisy's father must forego travelling to Europe in order to continue making money to finance his family's tour. The Millers' nouveau riche status contrasts sharply with the wealth of the socialites they meet abroad, all of whom experience the freedom of leisure bought by fortunes inherited rather than earned. Later in the novella, Mrs. Costello makes a condescending reference to the source of the Millers' income when, in speaking to Winterbourne, she pretends to forget Daisy's name, calling her instead Miss Baker and Miss Chandler before finally settling on Miss Miller. Emphasizing the labor-intensive jobs of baker, candlestick maker, and mill operator, Mrs. Costello here delivers a veiled critique of the Millers' reliance on business. Winterbourne acknowledges his aunt's dismissal of Daisy in Vevey, where he "at once recognised [sic] from her tone that Miss Daisy Miller's place in the social scale was low."

Daisy seems to confirm her status on her trip to the castle of Chillon. Visiting the castle with Winterbourne and without a chaperone, Daisy does not practice discretion, choosing to meet her companion in the crowded hotel lobby where sundry guests and servants watch her come down the stairs and leave unattended with a man. During their trip, Winterbourne feels both anxious and exhilarated about breaking the social code, but Daisy's straightforward demeanor and lack of self-consciousness surprises him. For Daisy, this excursion provides a delightful diversion from the otherwise dull social atmosphere of the hotel, where her desire for society goes unmet due to inexplicable—from her perspective—class boundaries.

In Rome, Daisy spends much time with Giovanelli, an Italian with a reputation among elitists, such as Mrs. Costello and Winterbourne's friend, Mrs. Walker, for courting American heiresses in search of fortune. Daisy, however, enjoys the lively company of Giovanelli and his social circle, especially after her relatively quiet weeks at Vevey. When Daisy asks Winterbourne to accompany her to the Pincio to meet Giovanelli, the American sees him for the first time and characterizes him in class terms as "a music-master or a penny-a-liner or a third-rate artist," all denigrating descriptions of the artist of no account who works for pay. More astounding to Winterbourne and to his social set is Daisy's persistent interest in Giovanelli; Winterbourne is appalled that Daisy does not realize the man's low status. Mrs. Walker expresses similar indignation when Daisy rejects an effort to salvage the girl's reputation. In an effort to clarify for Daisy the upper-class view of her behavior, Mrs. Walker travels to the Pincio in her carriage to warn the girl against being reckless and unreasonable, but Daisy waves off the carriage to continue her walk with Giovanelli.

She pays dearly, twice, for rejecting the tenets of high society. First, a few days later, at Mrs. Walker's party, the hostess turns her back on Daisy, a public and humiliating sign that the girl is no longer welcome in Mrs. Walker's company. Second, a few weeks later, Daisy again spurns the advice of those around her in favor of visiting the Colosseum by moonlight, only to contract a fatal bout of malaria. At her graveside, Giovanelli tells Winterbourne that, despite appearances and upper-class assumptions, Daisy would never have married him, leaving Winterbourne to feel that he had misjudged her.

Melanie Brown

JAMES, HENRY   *The Portrait of a Lady* (1882)

The Portrait of a Lady is the story of Isabel Archer, a girl from Albany who visits her uncle's family in Europe and eventually marries a wealthy compatriot. After her arrival in 1871, Isabel soon receives two marriage proposals: one from Lord Warburton, a neighboring estate-owner, the other from Caspar Goodwood, a businessman she has met in America. Isabel turns down both suitors because she does not want to commit herself yet. Some time later, in Italy, her friend Madame Merle introduces her to Gilbert Osmond, who is generally regarded as a cold-blooded loafer, and to everyone's surprise she accepts his marriage proposal. The last part of the novel opens in 1876, three years after their marriage. In the meantime, Isabel has found out that Osmond was interested only in her money; he is treating her coldly and tyrannically. The turning point of the novel occurs when Isabel learns that Osmond's daughter, Pansy, is actually Madame Merle's child, and that the former lovers plotted her marriage to provide financially for Pansy's future. Against her husband's will, Isabel goes to England, where the novel ends on an equivocal note: Isabel turns down Goodwood once more and seems to have decided on returning to her husband, but her exact plans remain unclear. Written in an elegant, realistic style, *The Portrait* is an initiation story with the "international theme" typical for James: a likable but naïve American is confronted with the complicated world of upper-class Europe.

Timo Müller

AMBITION in *The Portrait of a Lady*

Ambition is mostly considered a bad quality in the James universe. It is often associated with narrow-mindedness, egotism, and intrigue. In many of James's works, but especially in *The Portrait of a Lady* and in his later novels *The Wings of the Dove* (1903) and *The Golden Bowl* (1904), the plot is driven forward by the ambitious scheming of one of the main characters. This character always has villainous traits, and none more so than Gilbert Osmond, who is one of the greatest villains in 19th-century fiction. His ambition is powerful and all-encompassing. Of rather obscure origins himself, he wants to rise in the social hierarchy of expatriate Italy by connecting himself with wealthy and/or respected people. He has forced his sister into an unhappy marriage with a useless and disloyal Italian count just to associate his family with the aristocracy. He marries Isabel for her money alone, and in the last part of the novel is bent on pandering his daughter to Warburton (who is both wealthy and an aristocrat) even though Warburton is still interested in Isabel, not in Pansy. The scheme is revealing in several respects: Osmond not only encourages a former suitor's interest in his wife, but also is willing to have this suitor around on a permanent basis and to pander his own daughter to a man who clearly doesn't love her.

Osmond treats people like he treats his artifacts and pictures, as objects to be acquired and show-cased in pursuit of his societal ambition. He expects his entire family to behave perfectly at all times in order to maintain an aristocratic appearance. His ruthless demands transform both Pansy and Isabel into subdued, anxious, and altogether unhappy servants to Osmond's ambition. Osmond does not shy away from using the people closest to him in his intrigues. He knows that Madame Merle is anxious for her daughter's future, so he has her befriend wealthy girls like Isabel and introduce them to him. Later on, he tries the same trick with Isabel herself when he orders her to encourage Warburton's interest in Pansy. Unlike Madame Merle, Isabel refuses to make other people pay for her mistakes. Instead of propagating the determinism typical of naturalist fiction, James here indicates that the individual can overcome his or her limitations and weaknesses. The same principle is at work at the very end of the novel, when Isabel refuses Goodwood's offer of an easy way out and returns to Italy to help Pansy struggle against Osmond's crushing ambition.

This is not to say that Isabel's own ambitions, which she voices early in the novel, are regarded altogether uncritically. When Isabel comes to Europe to be "as happy as possible," she comes across as rather selfish and superficial herself. She refuses to listen to her friends' advice when she sees her pursuit of happiness endangered, and it is this obtuse ambitiousness that helps Osmond entrap her in his marriage scheme. The other two contestants for Isabel's hand are also ambitious in a questionable way.

If Goodwood was less focused on his business, for instance, he might have a better chance of winning Isabel's hand. But as it is, his overpowering ambition prevents him from truly understanding Isabel and her motives. Warburton, on the other hand, is really not ambitious at all but pretends to be in order to make himself more interesting and to relieve the boredom of his aristocratic lifestyle. He advocates radical socialist views but never follows them up in practice, which makes him appear insincere and discourages Isabel—and us, the readers—from taking him seriously. However critically they are regarded, the ambitions of Isabel, Goodwood, and Warburton are still depicted in a much more sympathetic way than the ambitions of Osmond. All the other characters are ambitious up to a certain point; when they realize that they are hurting others they always put their ambitions in second place. In contrast, Osmond is never willing to put his ambitions in second place; for him, his ambition is always more important than the happiness of those around him.

Timo Müller

FREEDOM in *The Portrait of a Lady*

Isabel's loss of her freedom is one of the central themes of *The Portrait of a Lady*. Having been raised by an independent-minded father, she comes to Europe to move freely and have new experiences. Her attitude is expressed in a key passage early in the novel, when Isabel tells her aunt that she wants "to know the things one shouldn't do" because she wants to have the choice to do them or not. She turns down two suitors so that she can enjoy her freedom and travel. Ultimately, she makes the wrong choice. She marries Osmond and loses not only the ability to go where she wishes but her freedom of mind as well. Osmond is a master psychologist and manipulator. In his world there is no freedom for anyone. Everything—his wife and daughter, just as his house, garden, furniture, clothes, and so on— must conform to social expectations and be supervised at all times to keep up a perfect appearance. Osmond has perfect control even over his speech and can mimic anyone and he expects the same of everyone around him. Madame Merle has already become very good at it, and when we encounter Isabel some years into her marriage, she has lost her

refreshing, cheerful manner because she is afraid to displease her husband. Pansy, too, is unusually quiet and self-controlled: Osmond sent her to a convent for years in order to train her. This environment is the exact opposite of Isabel's untroubled childhood. Instead of preserving her freedom, she has become imprisoned in body and mind.

Obviously, Isabel's notion of freedom has been a mistaken one. James suggests that there can be no such thing as complete freedom: We cannot just do what we want but have to be considerate of those around us. This sensitivity is the only way to find out who wishes us well and who doesn't. Freedom must always be a reflected freedom. It presupposes a knowledge of the limits society sets us, otherwise it is just naiveté. Isabel is a naïve person when she comes to Europe. She has been brought up on stories and abstract ideas. While she has read a lot of books, she has not learned how to read people, as she herself puts it in retrospect. Her judgment is severely limited, so that she is much less free in her choices than she thinks she is.

Even at the beginning of the novel, Isabel is less self-reliant than she appears. She is influenced by a number of people, many of whom have one-sided or naïve ideas of freedom. Her father left her to herself for most of her childhood, which certainly gave her a lot of freedom but equipped her with little knowledge of the adult world. In England, she encounters Lord Warburton, whose freedom is an irresponsible one: He claims to support reforms for the benefit of the working class, but really he is content to enjoy his wealth and keep out of politics. The most momentous mistake is Ralph Touchett's. For Ralph, freedom requires financial independence. He persuades his dying father to leave Isabel a fortune so that she can try out everything that interests her. It turns out, however, that her wealth makes Isabel above all a target for fortune-hunters like Osmond; since she has never learned to judge people she is easy prey. Basically, Ralph's notion of freedom rests on the same error as Isabel's: He thinks that once you have enough money, you can do what you want, regardless of other people. But one of the things we learn from the novel is that there is no such thing as absolute independence. Human beings are "social animals," and in modern society there are too many social ties and unspoken expectations for anyone to enjoy complete freedom.

However, James is no bleak pessimist. At the end of the novel, Isabel has acquired the kind of knowledge and experience that she needs to assert herself. She rises above her husband's control when she decides to visit Ralph in England, and she takes another step forward when she decides to go back to Italy instead of escaping to America with Goodwood. Under her guidance, Pansy will be able to learn all the things that Isabel learned too late. If Isabel has lost her freedom, she will at least secure a better fate for her stepdaughter.

Timo Müller

INNOCENCE AND EXPERIENCE in *The Portrait of a Lady*

For Isabel Archer, the journey from America to Europe is a journey from innocence to experience. Back in Albany, she spent most of her time in her cozy, protected home reading novels and philosophy books. In Europe, on the other hand, she has to manage her own life, and it turns out that her innocent youth has hardly prepared her for that task. She goes to Europe because she finds it "picturesque"—one of her favorite words—and expects to see some castles with real ghosts in them. When she has to deal with European high society, its unspoken codes and its complicated structure, she is completely off her guard. Over and over again, she forms wrong opinions of people she meets and cannot distinguish false friends from real friends. She turns down the advice of her experienced, well-meaning aunt but accepts the advice of Serena Merle, who is dishonest and interested only in her own gain. Instead of judging people by what they say and do, she tends to project her own naïve ideas on them: She is fascinated by Madame Merle, who plays the piano and talks about interesting things, whereas the sound advice of her aunt and cousin sounds slightly boring to her. Calculating and experienced, Osmond knows how to make use of Isabel's lack of judgment. He has no personality of his own but plays along with Isabel's romantic ideas, so that he appears to her as an ideal guide and companion: She "waited, with a certain unuttered contentedness, to have her movements directed; she liked Mr. Osmond's talk, his

company; she felt that she was being entertained." Isabel's naïve innocence leads her to make the great mistake of her life. It is only after her marriage to Osmond that she realizes how dull, dishonest, and incapable he really is.

When she finds out about the love affair between Osmond and Madame Merle, Isabel turns away from her husband and begins to judge her situation more objectively. She sheds all the innocent, romantic ideas of her childhood and begins to behave as an adult rather than as Osmond's immature child-wife. This can best be seen in her relation to Pansy: Up to this point, Isabel has been Pansy's playmate rather than her stepmother, but now she assumes responsibility for the child. When Osmond wants to marry Pansy to Lord Warburton, Isabel's former suitor who still cares more for her than for Pansy, Isabel prevents the scheme through her passive resistance; when Osmond reacts by sending Pansy to a convent, Isabel visits her and promises to protect her as best she can. This might be one reason why Isabel decides to go back to Italy in the end: She wants to protect her innocent stepdaughter from the selfish scheming of Osmond and Madame Merle, just as she would have needed protection herself some years earlier, when she fell for their plot and married Osmond.

The opposition of innocence and experience is related throughout the novel to the opposition of America and Europe. The Americans who come to Europe (Isabel and her friend Henrietta) are portrayed as somewhat naïve but innocent in a positive sense: They are honest, outspoken, friendly, and sociable. The Europeans appear more experienced in comparison. They are more careful and self-controlled, which in some cases means that they can deceive, manipulate, and take advantage of others, but also that they are more agreeable and better at judging people. Basically, there are three types of Europeans in the novel: native Europeans who embody the rich culture and history of the continent (Lord Warburton), Americans who have moved to Europe and have preserved their innocence to some extent (the Touchett family), and Americans who have assimilated to Europe and become corrupted and false as a result (Osmond, Madame Merle). Instead of presenting a one-sided, stereotypical picture of Americans and Europeans, James shows that there are different ways of dealing with innocence and experience, and that one needs to develop one's own way in order to lead a successful life. Isabel's mysterious decision to go back to her husband at the end of the novel also illustrates this assumption: Instead of dodging responsibility once again, she decides to face the consequences of her mistake and thus finally grows into mature dignity.

Timo Müller

JAMES, HENRY *The Turn of the Screw* (1898)

On January 5, 1895, Henry James entered the St. James Theatre in London as the final curtain came down on the opening night of his play *Guy Domville*. Already depressed because he was having trouble successfully publishing his fiction, he moved to the stage in answer to the audience's call for the author; he was jeered. Despite James's humiliation, the play ran for several weeks. In the psychological crucible of the following months, James wrote the first notes for *The Turn of the Screw*. In contrast to the complete vulnerability James experienced on the stage of *Guy Domville*, James creates a web of ambiguity in this terrifying tale that is anchored in three realities: the actual, the psychological, and the supernatural.

In *The Turn of the Screw*, the narrator's acquaintance, Douglas, shares the manuscript of a friend of his sister. The text recounts the young woman's travails after she is interviewed and hired as governess to an orphaned brother and sister who live in an isolated country house with Mrs. Grose, the housekeeper. The governess comes to learn that her predecessor, Miss Jessel, and groundskeeper, Peter Quint, died under mysterious circumstances. Mrs. Grose appears to insinuate that the couple had had a tryst, and that they were corrupting influences on the children. The crux of the plot is the governess's attempt to save the children from these "ghosts." In the end, she fails.

The simplest way to read the tale is as a ghost story, a fiction type to which James was no stranger. The early "The Romance of Certain Old Clothes" (1867) and the late "The Jolly Corner" (1908) are examples of his mastery of this genre. *The Turn of the Screw*, however, is different in that it may be read as a psychological thriller filled with Freudian subtext and sexual innuendo, heightened by the characters' circumstances of isolation. A classic struggle between good and evil or innocence and experience, critics agree that James's story is among the first "modern" tales in English.

Ellen Rosenberg

INNOCENCE AND EXPERIENCE in *The Turn of the Screw*

Henry James regularly wrote fiction driven by the themes of innocence and experience. A New Yorker, born in 1843, he frequently traveled to Europe with his wealthy family, attending a variety of European schools, being tutored at home, and visiting the monuments of the Old World. In between trips, James was schooled in America. The differences that he observed between the two worlds developed into a view that Americans were essentially naïve, unsophisticated, and inexperienced, while Europeans were cultured, knowledgeable, and experienced, though sometimes to the point of dissipation. As a young man, James returned to Europe and eventually chose to live in England for the rest of his life.

His life as an American abroad influenced his writing, and the question of innocence and experience often takes place on the societal level. In *The Turn of the Screw*, we have characters whose passage into knowledge may be viewed as a maturational necessity: Sooner or later, we all grow up. The book takes place in America, but it is allied to James's transatlantic novels in which individuals of narrow experience come to know a wider world that operates under exacting social laws. This thematic tie comes to us through the governess, who is herself naïve at the beginning of the story and parallels American innocents in James's other works. She comes from a poor, religious, but educated background and is too young to have been initiated into love. She finds herself in the resplendent setting of Bly, in the employ of the wealthy, decadent, and impatient bachelor who sparks her passions. This emotional ember marks the beginning of her passage out of innocence. Similarly, Mrs. Grose comes from a plainer background, but she is the salt of the earth and knows her place in society. She also passes from innocence to experience. Though the guardian and children of Bly are Americans of privilege, they parallel James's 'civilized' Europeans. Thus, they have a taint of corruption due to their class, and it is not surprising that the children may be acquainted with wickedness.

Flora and Miles are different from James's typical innocents. They are not strangers to a culture who might commit a social error; instead, they are so "beautiful," "lovely," "angelic," "with charming little 'table manners'" that even Miles's unnamed actions at school are minimized by the governess and Mrs. Grose as the healthy "naughtiness" of a little boy. What, then, is the wickedness or corruption of which they are accused?

If the story is read as supernatural, then Quint and Miss Jessel are ghosts who were evildoers in their lives. The governess believes the children see the apparitions, although they never say they do. She thinks they have been initiated into dangerous, probably sexual, knowledge. In chapter 6, Flora and the governess are sitting at the lakeside. Suddenly, the governess sees on the opposite bank, "a figure of . . . horror and evil: a woman in black, pale and dreadful." Flora's back is to the figure, and she is sticking a twig into a piece of wood with a hole in it, perhaps to make a toy boat. The governess watches her "attempting to tighten" the twig into place. The governess says she "apprehended" what Flora was doing, but does not specify. Is Flora simply a child at play, or is she making a boat as a sign that she wants to join Miss Jessel in death? Perhaps her actions illustrate sexual intercourse. In the latter two choices, the child is damaged if not damned, which is why the governess believes she must save Flora from crossing over to the other side. Later, after a second appearance of Miss Jessel, Flora denies ever having seen her, turns in terror of the present governess, holds onto Mrs. Grose for protection, and soon falls ill. When the housekeeper reports to the governess the next day, she says, "From that child—horrors! . . . she says things—!" The governess feels justified in her suspicions. Flora must be taken away from Bly. Perhaps Flora will recover, but she will not be innocent of the events that have

transpired. The governess is now alone in the house with Miles.

In the final scene, the governess confronts Miles about stealing her letter to the guardian about Miles's dismissal and Flora's derangement. Quint appears at the window, as if he has come to draw Miles to his death. The governess blocks Miles's view of the window, forces him to admit stealing the letter, and then presses him to reveal what he did at school. He tells her he has said things to other children that he liked. He realizes that she is preventing him from seeing the window. He asks if Miss Jessel is there. The governess tells him it is Quint. Miles struggles to see the valet, seems to fall, and the governess grabs him, as if to protect his soul from being taken by Quint. When she rises, Miles is dead, "his little heart dispossessed." The last word is ambiguous: Either the governess has won Miles's soul and he is no longer possessed by a demon or, literally, his heart has simply stopped and she has scared an innocent to death.

If the story is read as a psychological tale, then the children are innocent from beginning to end. Obsessed with the tryst between Miss Jessel and Quint, stimulated by her infatuation for the guardian, the mad governess is the source of evil who sees sexual meaning in all the acts of the children. In the end, she destroys the two to keep them from becoming normal, sexualized adults.

Ellen Rosenberg

ISOLATION in *The Turn of the Screw*

The theme of isolation manifests itself throughout *The Turn of the Screw*. The setting of the story is a lonely countryside house, far from neighboring homes. While the governess's first impression of Bly is of an open, fresh-looking estate with lawns, bright flowers, and twittering birds, within a day she feels fearful of its remoteness and size. By the end of the first chapter, she thinks that the little household is "as lost as a handful of passengers in a great drifting ship." She senses something ominous stirring in the breath of the house, and is soon keeping a written account of "what was hideous at Bly," which she now experiences as a great emptiness. If the house is physically isolated, it is also cut off from civilization in time as well; the books in the library are a century old.

The characters, too, are marked by varying degrees of isolation. The governess comes into a position of authority at this family home, but it is not her home and there is almost no family intimacy. The children are orphaned and consigned as wards to a man who has no patience to take care of them. Her employment as the children's governess puts her into a position like that of a mother, but without the ties and tender bond of maternity. She is a hired worker, a fact that forever isolates her from the children. While the governess has suppressed feelings of attraction for the children's young, handsome bachelor guardian who hired her, she is, in fact, nothing to him. A condition of her employment is that she never have contact with him, that she relieve him entirely of the unwanted burden of caring for his orphaned niece and nephew. So while James tempts us by dangling an eligible bachelor, a loner, who could ostensibly be the children's new father and the governess's helpmeet, he sets narrative restrictions that prohibit those attachments and relationships from being formed.

The other characters are isolated in different ways. At the moment the governess arrives, Flora has been alone with Mrs. Grose, the housekeeper. Miles has been separated from Flora and placed at a private school, although he has just been expelled. When he returns to Bly, the children pair off, and we learn by mid-tale that the governess suspects that they are not engaging merely in childish activities, such as reading to one another, but are talking of the apparitions and conniving somehow to position themselves to be corrupted by the two evil spirits. The governess, struggling with a rising sense of alarm at dangers unnamed, compensates for her conditions of near-total estrangement from real connections by throwing herself into a too-adoring care for Flora and Miles. From the children's perspective, this clutching and sobbing young stranger must have been a frightening and smothering presence.

The theme of isolation works on the level of language and image as well. James is careful to word Mrs. Grose's—and the children's—responses to the governess in such a way that the reader can perceive that the governess is imagining their thoughts. Speaking of the children, the governess says to Mrs. Grose,

"They're not mine—they're not ours. They're his and they're hers."

"Quint's and that woman's?"

"Quint's and that woman's. They want to get them . . . ."

"But for what?"

"For the love of all the evil. . . . to keep up the work of demons. . . ."

"Laws!" said my friend under her breath. The exclamation was homely, but it revealed a real acceptance of my further proof of what, in the bad time—for there had been worse even than this!—must have occurred."

The governess reads agreement into Mrs. Grose's response; but "Laws!" (meaning "Lordy") could just as easily be Mrs. Grose's shock at the governess's madness. This disconnection of language reinforces the isolation underlying the characters' experiences. The governess's state of isolation plays upon her mind, feeding her anxieties and desire for connection. The governess's visions are solely hers. Of course, James's point is to pose the question of whether the ghosts are real or specters that arise from the governess's agitated psyche.

Trapped in her own nightmare, seeking reassurance where none exists, the governess manages to alienate—and frighten—both Flora and Mrs. Grose. As they prepare to abandon Bly under the governess's belief that they are under siege by demons seeking to control the children, the ultimate state of isolation is achieved. To cut Quint off from possessing Miles, the governess cuts Miles off from life and cuts off the vestiges of connection to the household and her position. We have learned from Douglas in the frame story that, although the governess continued to find other similar work arrangements, she will finally die without ever really belonging anywhere or to anyone.

Ellen Rosenberg

SEXUALITY in *The Turn of the Screw*

Henry James's works embody the Victorian perspective, even while *The Turn of the Screw* is clearly modern in its psychological approach. This tale especially reflects contradictory sets of ideas about sexuality, sensuality, and eroticism that shaped social attitudes while Victoria was queen of England (1837–1901). The Victorians insisted upon public morality, modest dress, and restrained social behavior guided by strict etiquette, while also valuing physical appearance and beauty. This prim code drove normal impulses underground and intensified curiosity, sometimes infusing the commonplace with unconscious desires. The sexuality that is never explicitly addressed in the tale actually works to increase its presence in the unconscious minds of the characters. It creates a wild emotional underground that pulses with love, sexual awakening, sexual desire, sensuality, eroticism and the dangers that these impulses represent.

The first hint of these themes comes in the little story that frames the governess's tale. The author guesses that the governess was in love, and Douglas affirms it, but tells the author that neither he nor the governess ever spoke of it. The theme of unspoken love gets top billing with the theme of horror: Douglas was in love with the governess; the governess was in love with the handsome guardian of the children. She experienced a sexual awakening in her two limited interviews with the guardian, much as Miles probably experienced a sexual awakening at school. The guardian employs the governess to go to Bly, his country estate, but insists that she must never contact him. She promises to follow that instruction, and when he takes her hand at the end of the interview, she feels "rewarded." Off she goes to Bly, vibrating with an awakening sensuality that is doomed never to be spoken of, no less fulfilled.

The unnamed governess redirects the sexual interest aroused by her employer by focusing on loving and, in her word, "possessing the children." A byproduct of her erotic arousal, however, is that, shortly after arriving at Bly, she begins to see "apparitions." Often these sightings occur just when the governess is dreaming of the gentleman who had hired her. The "ghosts" of the story, then, can be understood as representations of the governess's own guilty conscience. In a prim Victorian world, sex must be repressed, but the energy has to go somewhere.

At Bly, the governess's only adult companion is the housekeeper, Mrs. Grose, who is taking care of the guardian's little niece, Flora. The child, whose name means "flower," is described as being pure, and

she represents a pre-sexual openness to the world around her. Ominously, we learn that there had been a previous young and beautiful governess, Miss Jessel, whom the governess believes had tried to corrupt Flora. Jessel had gone away, ostensibly for a holiday, and then she died.

So, too, the valet, Peter Quint (whose two names suggest masculine and feminine sexual parts) has died mysteriously. Mrs. Grose insinuates that the two had been lovers. Flora's brother Miles is about to return home permanently because he has been expelled from school for reasons unknown. The housekeeper and the governess speculate that he did or said something that posed a threat to the other students. What could a "lovely" 10-year-old boy, on the brink of adolescence, have done? The implication is that something unclean transpired between Quint and Miles, and Miles has carried this corruption into his behavior at school. Mrs. Grose, moreover, later confirms that Miles had gone off with Quint alone for many hours at a time, and when questioned about it, he denied having been with Quint. The governess concludes that Miles was engaged in an "intercourse" that he was concealing. While intercourse can mean something as simple as communication, the double entendre (a word that can be understood in at least two ways, one of which is sexual) feeds the governess's imagination. She never says, but seems to believe, that Miles has said or done something of a sexual nature.

In her sexualized maternal role, the governess feels it is her charge to save the children from these "ghosts," which are actually the governess's own sexually "wound up" thinking.

She surmises that Jessel became pregnant by Quint and probably died in childbirth. Later, Quint died from a fall (with the suggestion that he might have been murdered), but not before Miss Jessel tried to initiate Flora or Quint had corrupted Miles. The children never admit to "seeing" the ghosts. In one instance, Flora stares off into the distance. The governess decides that she must be seeing Miss Jessel, come back to get or sexualize Flora. The governess's hysteria can be tracked by a literal reading of her sentences. She projects her own sensual and sexual fears onto the household, finishing their sentences with her own erotic conclusions.

Close examination of the language shows that none of the governess's suppositions about what is happening are ever confirmed by another character; nothing sexual has happened, except in the governess's mind. We can imagine Miles's terror at the end of the tale as the governess (believing herself to be saving Miles from Quint), hurls herself onto him. No wonder his heart stopped.

Ellen Rosenberg

JEFFERSON, THOMAS *Notes on the State of Virginia* (1784)

Thomas Jefferson composed his *Notes* as a way of explaining to Europe that America is a vibrant new country and introducing the facts about the state of Virginia. He uses copious figures, illustrations, and listings to show that he does not present information based on pure observation; rather, he is a man of science and supports his statements with evidence. Eventually, his *Notes* will help demystify some false accounts about this side of the Atlantic.

This trait of relying on facts becomes the benchmark of the *Notes*. In fact, to make his descriptions convincing, Jefferson begins with particularly detailed records about Virginia. He is interested in defining boundaries, revealing minute details of natural objects, and eventually classifying things. For example, he relies on facts to refute notions rumored in Europe that animals on this side of the Atlantic are usually smaller and lighter. The *Notes* also serves as an ethnographical account. Jefferson is conscious of the race issue of the time, and he tries to give a vivid, though somewhat prejudiced, depiction of the Native Americans and the African slaves. At the same time, he also tries to present a slightly balanced view about them, since the American people are also regarded as "primitive" by European standards.

The *Notes*, therefore, exceeds its original purpose of mere question and answer. In fact, it becomes a fascinating record of natural history in the 18th century.

Huang-hua Chen

NATURE in *Notes on the State of Virginia*

For Jefferson, nature has many aspects. He begins the *Notes* with descriptions of Virginia, ranging from her natural resources to various geographical features and records. In part to answer Mr. Marbois's 22 queries about the present state of America, Jefferson emphasizes America's spectacular scenes and enormous amount of natural treasures throughout the *Notes* in order to denounce the common notion that the colonies are just an extension of European culture and that nothing here is particularly different from, or may be inferior to, Europe.

One can quickly catch a glimpse of how Jefferson sets out to demystify false impressions of America. Virginia, according to him, is "one third larger than the islands of Great Britain and Ireland." Even her natural resources are far greater than that of Europe. In query six, he denies count de Buffon's idea that animals in the new world are "smaller," of "few species," and have often "degenerated" due to the hotter and more humid weather. Jefferson counters Buffon's argument by including various tables that compare the differences between the old world and the new world. As it turns out, almost all the animals in the new world are heavier and of more varieties. He suggests that nature has a way of balance with every living being, and that "below these limits they cannot fall, nor rise above them." He goes on to say that "what intermediate station they shall take" may depend on some external factors, but "the manna of heaven would never raise the Mouse to the bulk of the Mammoth." Such is the view on nature that Jefferson generally adopts. For him, nature is almost comparable to a kind of deity, and it will follow the rules of reason and balance. That is why, when asked of the extinction of the mammoth, he vehemently denies such a possibility. He states, "such is the economy of nature, that no instance can be produced of her having permitted any one race of her animals to become extinct." In other words, nature is like a perfect equation behind every living being, always operating in harmony, and it is impossible to suppose an unreasonable nature that is subject to any weakness.

Yet, nature is not always as predictable as he would like. Jefferson admits that "nature has hidden from us" her works. All one can do is resort to "experience" if necessary. This therefore results in two different kinds of attitude toward nature. The shell fossils found in the mountains of Virginia, for example, can be explained by his careful scientific explanations, his "experiences," so to speak. In other words, nature is still well within the boundary of reason and harmony. At the same time, in the possibility of a "great convulsion of nature" that heaves the bed of the ocean to the heights of the Andes, Jefferson hesitates to make such an inference. For him, nature is harmonious and well-balanced, and for such radical change to take place is utterly unthinkable.

Perhaps a good example of the contradictory attitudes toward nature can be seen from his experience on a natural bridge, an incident he mentions in query five. He describes the bridge as "the most sublime of Nature's works." The sublime is an interesting concept that is brought up in the 18th century. "Sublime" usually indicates fear and horror, a feeling or a phenomenon too great to be named. Jefferson tells us that "you involuntarily fall on your hands and feet, creep to the parapet and peep over it. Looking down from this height, gave me a violent head ache." Yet, when he is below it, he changes his tone: "so beautiful an arch, so elevated, so light, and spring as it were up to heaven." As much as he wants to acknowledge the mystery of nature's many faces, he balances them with a reserved picture of elegance and beauty. Jefferson seems to urge us to step away from the violent side of nature and focus more on its "reasonable" and "pleasant" side. He seems to warn us that what rushes into our senses—nature's sublime—is not necessarily the essence of nature; and if we are able to look further and pay more attention, we might just find the true nature of nature.

Huang-hua Chen

RACE in *Notes on the State of Virginia*

In a response to Buffon's claim that the aboriginal people of North America are generally inferior to the people living in Europe, both in mind and body, Thomas Jefferson defends the Indians with scientific proofs. To Buffon, because of the warmer climate on this side of the Atlantic, Native Americans are feeble, of small stature, and lack character. After commenting on their physical attributes, he goes on to suggest that they have no community, no morality, no love, and only harsh rule. Buffon's opinion is not uncommon to an 18th-century European, but

it is also fabrication at best. Jefferson refutes these opinions, and he backs himself by using his own experiences with Native Americans. In query six, he continues to present evidence where Native Americans are not that different from the white settlers of the time. He mentions that their affections are genuine, and they are honorable and brave in battle. He even wonders at his neighboring Indian monuments and produces a detailed account of them in query 11.

What may be of curiosity to us, though, is the way in which Jefferson ends that particular section of the query. Having established his argument, he then diverges to talk about how it is incorrect to assume that the Indians lack intelligence. Given enough time and the use of letters, the Indians might be able to produce great works of literature as well. He refutes Buffon's idea that the western side of the Atlantic can produce only inferior products, because, with only a little time, America has produced Washington and Franklin and the like. It is here that one starts to detect the hidden agenda of Jefferson's seeming racial equality, because both Native Americans and white settlers are susceptible to the constant scrutiny and doubt of the Europeans. In other words, by identifying with Native Americans, Jefferson is also making a case for the capability of the emergent American culture. Jefferson is not alone in the 18th century. Rousseau, for example, has a similar idea of "noble savages," which suggests that because of the lack of a contaminating civilization, they are without pretense and corruption. Using this notion, Jefferson tries to counter the prejudices of the old monarchial Europe.

However, Jefferson also has prejudices of his own, and again they partially derive from the 18th-century world view. While he talks of the emancipation of African-American slaves, he would also suggest that the best way to achieve it is through re-allotting them elsewhere instead of incorporating them in the colonies. Jefferson worries that an American society with both races will result only in more conflict because of racial tensions. Other than political reasons, however, Jefferson brings up other aspects, which he calls physical and moral. In query 14, he mentions that the difference between blacks and whites is "fixed" and goes to explain what he sees as the disparity in physical beauty between the two races. Unlike his treatment of Native Americans, he now spends several pages listing the physical differences of black slaves and how these physical attributes somehow affect their abilities and morality. He suggests, for example, they require less sleep and are more ardent in desire. Because of their more primitive nature, he says, they are more feeling than they are thinking. He talks of famous black literati of the time, but they are always inferior according to his standards. In other words, the racial difference becomes the ground on which Jefferson judges their mental and moral capacity.

This view of racial difference as set in nature hinders Jefferson from realizing true equality. It also echoes Alexander Pope's idea of a "Great Chain of Beings," meaning the world is a hierarchical structure created by God. It would then be unwise for the two races to mingle together. For Jefferson, there is a definite racial hierarchy among the white settlers, Native Americans, and African Americans. But despite his historical limitations, Jefferson does recognize the injustice of racial oppressions, and as an Enlightenment thinker, he at least takes the first step toward eliminating the racial barriers and turning them into mutual understandings.

Huang-hua Chen

RELIGION in *Notes on the State of Virginia*

Thomas Jefferson's *Notes* is not a religious piece per se, but it is definitely filled with religious sentiments and views. While the *Notes* is mostly concerned with the miscellaneous affairs of Virginia, there is usually a religious subtext that the reader can detect. Whether or not it is specific to a Christian world view is another matter.

One can start to sense this religious undertone when Jefferson describes his experience of the sublime in the Blue Ridge Mountains. This idea is important in the 18th century because, while this is the age of reason, the sublime represents that which is beyond the reasonable boundary, religious experience being something that does cross this boundary. The 18th century produced several philosophical works on the sublime, and Jefferson seems to be preoccupied as well. While remarking on the dynamic pictures of the Shenandoah Valley, Jefferson states

that "the piles of rock on each hand, but particularly on the Shenandoah, the evident marks of their disrupture and avulsion from their beds by the most powerful agents of nature, corroborate the impression." That the world we live in changes over time is not something Jefferson is willing to give up, according to his religious belief. But how do you reconcile the obvious contradiction between the sublime and the harmonious world? He proposes to look at the "small catch of smooth blue horizon, at an infinite distance in the plain country" because here "the eye ultimately composes itself." Through this experience of the sublime, Jefferson seems to say that while religion or religious experience is sometimes said to be incomprehensible to finite beings such as us, it is only because of our limited capacity. When we look at the big picture, not the mere "impression," we will be able to find the reasonableness of the world we live in.

This world view is reminiscent of Alexander Pope's famous dictum, "Whatever is, is Right." Both are influenced by Christianity and try to grapple with a world filled with obvious contradictions. This subtext can be seen when Jefferson observes the fossil bones of mammoths. He asks his readers whether he should omit references to the extinction of mammoths, saying. "Such is the economy of nature, that no instance can be produced of her having permitted any one race of her animals to become extinct; of her having formed any link in her great work so weak as to be broken." For Jefferson, nature is very much the work of God, and to some extent, an equivalent of God, and for nature to be broken down is utterly unthinkable. This idea that religious truth can be found in nature is not uncommon, but in the context of Christianity, nature often represents the work of God and thus indicates a sense of harmonious order or hierarchy.

This parallel between a natural order and religion can be found in Jefferson's attitude toward slaves. It is important to know that Jefferson adopts an abolitionist attitude. But again, the religious subtext plays into the decision as well. While he supports the emancipation of the slaves, he does it because he learns from religion and history that the world is constantly in cyclical movement. Here we find the perfect example where nature and religion come together. Just like the natural world where things like the four seasons and day and night often remind us how harmony reigns, so Jefferson invokes the will of God as the constant in history. He states that we need to free slaves in order not to incur the wrath of God for taking away the liberties of these people; otherwise "a revolution of the wheel of fortune, an exchange of situation" is possible as willed by God. In other words, Jefferson's religious truth is deeply rooted in the observation of nature.

Too often religion plays an important role in dictating how Jefferson perceives the world. As the *Notes* reveals, Jefferson, as an 18th-century man of science, still struggles between religion and empirical truths. At the same time, the religious subtext within the *Notes* remains a positive one that depicts a balanced and harmonious world.

Huang-hua Chen

JONES, LEROI (Amiri Baraka [from 1968]) *Dutchman* (1964)

Dutchman is a fierce, angry, sometimes shocking punch to the gut of American values, still as raw and provocative as it was the year it was published. It is a one-act play about difference and deception. Can racial tensions in this country ever be healed when both the conflict and the attempts at resolution are based on lies?

The play focuses on two individuals—a black man and a white woman—who spar, dance, and ultimately crush the possibility of racial harmony or understanding in a claustrophobic society, symbolized by the subway car in which they ride for the duration of the play. Lula chats up Clay as they ride to an unknown destination. While they talk, the upper hand rests with Lula, as she invites herself along with Clay, tells him how to address her, and (literally) tells him what to say. Clay plays along, excited by her language games, until she turns especially vulgar and violent. She begins to insult him and speak racial epithets—she accuses him of being a buck and an Uncle Tom, and, briefly, the power shifts to Clay. He erupts, accusing her of a foolish self-deception and an anger that has no intellectual foundation. He threatens Lula, stating his desire to kill her and other smug whites who think they

understand race. Lula then stabs Clay and gets other passengers to help throw him off the subway at the next stop. Soon, another young black man walks by her, and so the trauma and the violence promise to be repeated.

Sharyn Emery

IDENTITY in *Dutchman*

Is identity inextricably linked to race? Can we separate racial identity from a person's personality, or would that create an inaccurate picture of who a person is? In *Dutchman*, LeRoi Jones plays with the notion of identity as we watch Clay and Lula dance around each other—lying, seducing, insulting, but not revealing their true selves until the end of their doomed subway ride. Authentic identities ultimately clash then, and so society continues wearing a mask, afraid of the violence the truth might cause.

Clay presents himself as a mild-mannered, young African-American man. He is educated, curious, and polite, but intrigued by Lula's games. He pretends both innocence and concern as their interaction warms up, caught between genuine desire for Lula and disbelief in the things coming out of her mouth. As the play progresses, he cannot keep up his white-bread façade, as Lula's insults (which grow more racist each moment) elicit an angry, murderous response. It is only in the final moments of *Dutchman* that Clay presents his true identity—he lays into Lula for her phony understanding of black life and culture, claiming he wishes he could kill her for her vile ignorance. In this last monologue, Clay reasserts his own black authenticity and finally, forcefully, tells the truth. As he speaks, he claims African-American artists played music as a way of shielding their own angry identities from white audiences and crowds. Clay, as the voice of Jones, argues that these white patrons do not understand identity—that of the singer or themselves. The musicians cannot possibly spend their time murdering white people, so they play jazz instead. The play sets up those patrons as believing themselves to be hip and understanding, but instead they are self-deluded fools, or like Lula, murderous liars.

Lula participates in this game of shifting identities, as well. Ironically, Lula loosely takes on the form of the trickster, a figure from African-

American (and African) folklore. She transforms herself over the course of the play, covering up and revealing very little about her true self until she murders Clay at the end. She fools him for a while, causing him to think they might have a chance at a romantic relationship, but he eventually catches on to her underhanded motives. Lula wants to bait Clay into admitting desire, or anger, or some other emotion that can justify her bloodlust, and so she tries on different identities, trying to draw out of him the response she wants. Clay appears to be so good natured and straightforward that this proves hard; it is only after she calls him an Uncle Tom that he explodes and that both characters reveal their true selves.

Clay reacts violently to the racist insult, restraining an increasingly excited Lula and shoving another passenger who tries to become involved. The show of violence is precisely what Lula had been waiting for. When Clay stands up for himself, and finally tries on the full mantle of black manhood, Lula stabs him. The two authentic identities cannot survive together; the subway car was fine when both individuals were lying about themselves, but when the truth was exposed, the tinderbox of racism was ignited, leaving Clay dead and another young black man vulnerable to Lula's next game.

Jones asks us to think about our authentic identities, and what role deception plays in racial contexts. Can there be racial harmony and truthful utterances about the state of race relations at the same time? *Dutchman* seems to indicate that it is not possible, that if we face each other honestly, the truth about the African-American experience will prove angering and difficult for white America, which will lead to the destruction of black men. It is a bleak outlook, one that seems about to be repeated at the end of the play. Lula strolls over to another young African-American man on the subway, greeting him in her deceptive first guise, waiting for him to give himself away so she can enact another crime. Perhaps it need not be seen as automatically bleak, however. The black conductor greets this new young man as a friend, as a comrade, as an African-American brother. This exchange could be interpreted as a moment of truth, a moment when two African-American men honestly exchange a greeting and show their true selves to the world, regardless of who may see. If we can focus on their interaction, the outlook is less painful and violent—for everyone.

Sharyn Emery

INDIVIDUAL AND SOCIETY in *Dutchman*

LeRoi Jones's *Dutchman* takes place on a subway car that is a symbolic representation of society. The specific urban location of the subway is not revealed, for it is meant to take on a somewhat mythical quality, a place both real and unreal at the same time. Thus, the theme of the individual's relationship to society comes to the fore, made evident by the use of just two major characters, Clay and Lula. An individual's actions reverberate within society, just as society affects individuals every day.

Because the two individuals cannot reconcile the tension and anger between them, the play rather darkly suggests that the race problem in America will not be solved on an individual level. Larger societal changes are necessary, as evidenced by the continuation of Lula's seductive destruction after Clay's death. She gets ready for another victim and another crime, and the subway conductor's minstrel shuffle indicates a continuation of societal expectations. Thus, it is clear that the individual characters are also actors playing up those expectations (at least for the first half of the play), since Lula correctly reads Clay's personality and background from the start, and they begin a sort of stereotypical dance until Clay's righteous anger overwhelms the situation. Lula paints Clay as an upright, dull, educated African American, who she surmises "acts white" most of the time. For various reasons, Clay plays along, partly because it's somewhat true and partly because he's interested in Lula and wants to continue the conversation. It is this sublimation of his fuller, more complex individual IDENTITY that Clay practices on a daily basis to get by in a racially charged society. At least, that is, until Lula's racial invectives become stronger and louder. The buildup of anger allows Clay to step out of what society expects and speak the truth, no matter how painful it sounds.

Clay's outburst of personal expression illustrates how difficult it is for the individual, particularly the individual of color, to be heard in society. The conversation up to that point had virtually been scripted by Lula—she was determining what Clay said and when he said it. Clay, as a young African-American man, doesn't have a strong individual voice—not one that society is willing to listen to, at least. Clay ultimately has to make a choice as to whether to remain a faceless member of society or to step up and claim his individuality in the face of majority OPPRESSION. He attempts to choose the latter, which leads to his death. Clay's cruel FATE seems to be a bleak harbinger for the ability of individuals to be heard and to be able to express themselves. Society is against him, as shown by the willingness of the other subway passengers to help Lula throw Clay's body off the train. No one stands up for themselves, or for Clay. They move en masse, with no regard for the individual victim.

Of course, the irony in the play is that Clay has to speak for the entire community of African Americans in his dealings with Lula. He cannot ever achieve a truly individual personality—whether he is acting the part for Lula, or speaking up for Bessie Smith and black artists, Clay is a collective representation. Whether for good or ill, Clay must stand up with a collective, rather than an individual, message. This is a double-edged sword; there is unity in the collective identity, but no individual strength within the racist society, a situation borne out when Lula sets her sights on the next young African-American man in the subway car. The men are helpless against Lula, who exercises the power of life and death over them; society ends up winning, but at least one individual puts up a fight.

Sharyn Emery

RACE in *Dutchman*

Like the arrival of the rumbling subway car in which it is set, racial violence is inevitable in LeRoi Jones's (now known as Amiri Baraka) play *Dutchman*. As Clay and Lula spar, flirt, talk, and dance, their interplay slides from a sexualized male-female dynamic to one grounded in white-black racial conflict. The work is, most simply, a play about race. Clay struggles to maintain several racialized guises against the barbs hurled by the temptress Lula. At the start, Clay is somewhat naïve about the role race plays (and will play) in his interactions with the apple-eating white woman, but as the play advances

and he dons various guises, Clay becomes more hip to the game, more aware of his "true" race, and of the true black man at his core. Unfortunately, that awareness comes at a price, and Clay pays for his earlier naiveté with his life.

When he first steps onto the subway car he is a Booker T. Washington-type intellectual, buttoned up and focused on the future. Lula reads these qualities in him right away, stereotyping his neat clothes and polite demeanor, and proclaiming him dull and familiar—a young college man on his way to a party. Clay falls for this reading, confirming Lula's attempts to "read" his racial identity. She chides him for looking foolish and "inauthentic," skinny and pasty-faced. By challenging his racial "authenticity," Lula is able draw Clay into her game. She eventually bores of this racial persona, and expertly maneuvers Clay into his next guise, by playing to his desires for sex as well as his desire to be seen as an authentic black man.

At Lula's prompting, Clay becomes a sexualized black "buck" figure, tempting the white woman while being tempted by her. This is reflected in the rapid back-and-forth Lula traps Clay into, as she virtually scripts him into desiring her—thus creating the image of the sex-crazed Negro hunting the white woman. She demands that he invite her to the party he's attending, and imaginatively playacts their entrance into that event. She entices Clay with the phony script of their date, then turns the tables when Clay expresses genuine interest—she claims to be too wild for him and forces him to prove that he can handle her. This forces Clay into playing the "wild buck," a highly destructive, yet long-standing racial stereotype. The very thought of a black man with a white woman is at the core of America's lynching history, and the image of the sexually aggressive black man will come back at the end of the play, when Lula uses it to her murderous advantage.

Lula eventually works herself into a frenzy, baiting Clay with harsher language until he has to physically restrain her and silence her insults. Thus, Clay ends the play as a proud African American, rejecting Lula outright and taking a political stance for black culture and against white supremacy. He (re)claims the blues, sex, and poetry for black culture, spewing invectives against Lula's (white) ignorance. It is at this juncture in the play that the worst racial epithets are spoken. Lula calls Clay "Uncle Tom Big Lip" and "Uncle Tom Woolly Head," while charging him to ignore the first racial guise (buttoned up middle-class intellectual) and act the black part—to act like the "nigger" she screams he is. Clay refuses further advances on Lula and declares her foolish and undesirable; he thus rejects the racial role she tried to force him to play, and this results in his murder. Lula, humiliated and defeated in her twisted racial game, stabs Clay and enlists the help of others to dispose of his body. She asks the other passengers to get Clay off of her, thereby linking racism to a supposed sexual attack.

Sadly, his death is neither martyrdom nor wake-up call—his body is dumped off the subway car and Lula immediately sets her sights on the next black man she sees. Thus, *Dutchman* can be read as a cautionary tale for young black men to resist the temptation to wallow in racial stereotypes to attract women, or to refuse to allow white America to determine their racial identity; young African-American men must know who they are before taking on the world. It also showcases the need for black men to remain on guard against white seduction, regardless of what form it takes.

Sharyn Emery

JOYCE, JAMES *Dubliners* (1914)

Dubliners is a collection of short stories about the people who live in the city of Dublin. When questioned about the stark nature of his stories, James Joyce replied, giving us an insight to authorial intention:

> It is not my fault that the odour of ashpits and old weeds and offal hangs round my stories. I seriously believe that you will retard the course of civilization in Ireland by preventing the Irish people from having one good look at themselves in my nicely polished looking-glass. (xv)

Most of the stories have no plot, in the traditional sense of the term, and have as their central focus the people in them. The stories touch on a myriad of issues, such as identity, both personal and national, religion as it affects the average Irishman, personal relationships in their various forms, and the struggle to come to terms with one's place in the world. Through magnificent storytelling and characterization, Joyce takes the reader on a journey, not only through the city, but also through the psyches and emotional labyrinths of his various characters. Despite being a collection of individual short stories, persons and places move seamlessly across stories. Not only are people interconnected and bound to society, they also cannot seem to escape their circumstances. Such is the fate of the Dubliners that Joyce portrays in this collection, adding to the poignancy that pervades the text.

Throughout Joyce's literary career, national identity remained a prime concern, and all stories deal with this issue in one form or another. More important, the concept of "nation" is explored from the perspective of the common person affected by its political and cultural anxieties. In some stories, this is dealt with directly, such as "Ivy Day in the Committee Room," which gives the reader an insight into the politics of Ireland. In "The Dead," national identity is explored through the cultures, literatures, and languages one adopts. In other stories, such as "Araby," nation is explored in a more subtle manner. Related to nation is the issue of religion, explored in the stories "The Sisters" and "Grace." As with issues of nation, Joyce is concerned with religion as it affects the common person. More important, Joyce explores the emptiness of religion in the modern world, and how humans seem to have drifted further and further away from meaningful fellowship with God. Family is another concern that runs through all of Joyce's work. In this collection, family is seen, more often than not, as a source of oppression. In "A Mother," the mother figure is portrayed as an overbearing, authoritarian, and unreasonable person, and the daughter a meek young girl who allows her mother to make decisions on her behalf. In "Eveline," a young lady makes a promise to her dying mother to look after the family, a promise which later makes it impossible for the young lady to leave Ireland. In "Counterparts," one is given an insight into domestic violence, and in "A Little Cloud," individual hopes and dreams are unfulfilled due to the pressures of marriage and family. As a result of the tensions mentioned above, Joyce's characters often find themselves alienated and isolated from others around them. Joyce neither resolves these conflicts, nor provides a solution to the solitude felt by his characters, but leaves readers to contemplate the universality of these conditions.

Wern Mei Yong

FAMILY in *Dubliners*

Family in *Dubliners* is more often than not portrayed as a source of oppression. In "Araby," a young boy, in love with a young lady, wants to go to the night bazaar to buy her a gift. He is unable to do so because he has to wait for his uncle to return home, and give him some money. By the time the boy goes to the bazaar, it is almost closing and most of the stalls have closed. The night bazaar, with its exotic connotations, presents an escape for the boy, just as his infatuation for the lady is a means of escaping the drudgeries of everyday life. His uncle does not seem to take the boy's desire to go to the bazaar seriously, and Joyce reveals at one point, very curtly and simply, that "He had forgotten." The brief sentence adds a sense of finality and poignancy to the lack of control the boy seems to have over his own desires, as their fulfillment is tied to the whims of others. Family, in this sense, stands in the way of the fulfillment of the boy's desires, and at the end of the story, the boy finds himself alone in darkness, a "creature driven and derided by vanity," and his "eyes burned with anguish and anger."

In "Eveline," Joyce continues to explore the idea of family. The story begins with a description of Eveline:

> She sat at the window watching the evening invade the avenue. Her head was leaned against the window curtains and in her nostrils was the odour of dusty cretonne. She was tired.

Here, Joyce portrays an image of a young girl trapped; just as the evening is seen to invade the avenue, we get a sense of the young girl being overwhelmed by her surroundings. The pervasive odor of the curtains that fills her nostrils suggests the immense pressure domestic life seems to have on her. This pressure is reinforced by the brevity and finality of the closing sentence of the paragraph. We learn that Eveline, on the last night of her mother's illness, had made a "promise to her mother, her promise to keep the home together as long as she could." Having had enough, she decides "to go away, to leave her home" and to "explore another life with Frank" in Buenos Aires. Life in Dublin consists of constant "squabble for money," "hard work to keep the house together," and domestic violence. Buenos Aires, at the time a thriving and wealthy city, offers a means of escape for Eveline; but, apart from being Frank's wife, we are not told what she will do in Buenos Aires. At the very moment the ship is about to leave the pier, she finds herself unable to leave with Frank: "She set her white face to him, passive, like a helpless animal. Her eyes gave him no sign of love or farewell or recognition." Comparing her to a "helpless animal" suggests her powerlessness and paralysis. Eveline is indeed trapped, since whether in Ireland or Buenos Aires, she will continue to live a life of subjection to the will of others, with little autonomy or freedom of her own. Eveline does not leave Ireland because of the guilt she would bear were she to break her promise to her mother to look after the family.

A similar force of oppression symbolized by the family is seen in the story "A Little Cloud." The story begins with Chandler's meeting with his friend in a public space, and ends with tension and conflict within himself in the private, domestic space of the home. At the beginning of the story, we see Chandler getting ready to meet his friend, Gallaher, after an eight-year absence. As the story progresses, Chandler finds himself and his life to be inadequate, small and impoverished in comparison to the life of Gallaher, who has left Dublin. That he is referred to as "Little Chandler" further enhances how limited and small his life and personality are in comparison to Gallaher, who is described as a man of presence who has achieved a certain degree of success in life. As with other stories in the collection, the main protagonist understands that "if you wanted to succeed you had to go away. You could do nothing in Dublin." He expresses envy at his friend's newfound life in London, and is resentful of the factors that hold him back from what might have been a lucrative literary career. This is symbolized by the "books of poetry upon his shelves" that he had bought in his bachelor days, before he was committed to family life.

After his meeting, he returns home and begins to examine with a different eye his surroundings. He looks at a photograph of his wife Annie: "He looked coldly into the eyes of the photograph and they answered coldly. Certainly they were pretty and the face itself was pretty. But he found something mean in it." Glancing around the room, he sees the same meanness in the furniture around the room, all "too prim and pretty." The meanness again recalls the limitedness and smallness that characterize Little Chandler's life. At this moment he experiences a detachment from the woman he married, unable to form a human connection with her or the home they now share. As he falls deeper into contemplation, his eyes fall on a volume of Byron's poems and he begins to read. He realizes in despair that any dream of a literary career is merely an illusion, at which point his child awakens and begins to cry. Chandler tries to silence the child without success. The realization of the illusion, together with his inability to silence the child, a symbol of that which has held him back, is too much for Chandler to bear. The child begins to scream, and Chandler tries as hard as he can to soothe the child, with no success. He gets a fright imagining the child dead, and the possibility of him being the cause of its death fills him with terror. Annie returns to the room. She takes the baby back and, with an accusatory tone, asks him what he did to provoke the child. Chandler is reduced to a stuttering mess of guilt, for having made the child cry in a fit of anger and frustration. Annie departs the room with the child, leaving Chandler alone.

Like "Araby" and "Eveline," this story ends with Little Chandler left alone to contemplate the frustrations of being tied down by family. By opening the final paragraph with "Little Chandler," the reader is reminded of the smallness and insignificance of Chandler and his individual hopes and desires. As in the other two stories, there is an apparent conflict, of having to look to the demands of family duty, which seem to trump the fulfillment of one's own hopes and dreams.

Wern Mei Yong

ISOLATION in *Dubliners*

Many of the characters in Joyce's *Dubliners* experience one form of isolation or another. In the story "A Painful Case," James Duffy is introduced as someone who "lived in Chapelizod because he wished to live as far as possible from the city of which he was a citizen." There is a clear juxtaposition between being a citizen of Dublin and his deliberate self-exile from Dublin. Furthermore, he lives in a room that is "uncarpeted," suggesting a lack of warmth, and whose walls "were free from pictures," pointing once again to a deliberate attempt to keep his world separate from any intrusion by the outside world. His room is described as being sparse and lacking personality, and he had "neither companions nor friends, church nor creed."

> He lived a little distance from his body, regarding his own acts with doubtful side-glances. He had an odd autobiographical habit which led him to compose in his mind from time to time a short sentence about himself containing a subject in the third person and a predicate in the past tense.

Duffy eventually meets Mrs. Sinico, with whom he forms a relationship. Mrs Sinico is married, and their relationship is kept in confidence from society, which again reinforces the notion of isolation. Their meetings often take place in "a little cottage outside Dublin," where they "spent their evenings alone." They would speak late into the evening, till darkness enveloped them in the "dark discreet room," and they were united in "their isolation."

In their last meeting before Duffy puts an end to the relationship, Mrs. Sinico had "caught up his hand passionately and pressed it to her cheek," which took Duffy by surprise. Mrs. Sinico's yearning for companionship counters Duffy's belief in the "incurable loneliness" of humankind, a way of life he has come to accept. One suspects that it is the only way of life familiar to him and therefore desirous to him. Because of their incompatible attitudes, Duffy puts an end to the relationship.

Four years go by and Duffy one day reads in the paper that Mrs. Sinico has been killed by a train. Instead of expressing sympathy, he expresses revulsion:

What an end! The whole narrative of her death revolted him and it revolted him to think that he had ever spoken to her of what he held sacred. . . . Not merely had she degraded herself; she had degraded him. . . . Just God, what an end!

The lack of sympathy Duffy expresses is shocking, and his criticisms of Mrs. Sinico are ironic. While it seems evident to him that Mrs. Sinico was "unfit to live," it is not evident to him that his own life resembles more a kind of death sentence in its isolation and monotony. Furthermore, it is not Mrs. Sinico who lacks "strength of purpose," since her apparent suicide is an act of free will. Duffy, on the other hand, for fear of having his familiar world interrupted by the passion displayed by Mrs. Sinico, puts a stop to their meetings.

In "The Dead," Gabriel Conroy ends the story feeling utterly alone and isolated from everyone around him. The story begins with a sense of fellowship and community, with a party thrown by Gabriel's two aunts, Miss Kate and Miss Julia. It is attended by friends and family, and throughout we are presented with life, warmth, laughter, and fellowship. Gabriel, however, seems not to fit in with the company he is among. This is due to his sense of himself as being better educated than those around him. His fondness for Miss Kate and Miss Julia may be described as slightly condescending and patronizing: "What did he care that his aunts were only two ignorant old women?" When thinking about what to include in his speech, he is

undecided about the lines from Robert Browning for he feared they would be above the heads of his hearers. Some quotation that they could recognize from Shakespeare or from the Melodies would be better. . . . He would only make himself ridiculous by quoting poetry to them which they could not understand.

In this arrogant manner, Gabriel sets himself apart from everyone else. His isolation, in a sense like Duffy's, is a kind of self-exile.

After the party, Gabriel and his wife Gretta are walking through the snow back to their hotel, and watching her in front of him, he feels a sudden desire rising within him for her. When they arrive home, Gabriel tries to express his affection for her, in hopes that she will respond in a manner matching his own desire. She does not, and after much prompting she finally reveals to him that she is upset because the snow outside has reminded her of a lover in the past who had died of ill health. Gretta reveals that the boy had come to see her the night before she was due to leave Galway, exposing himself to the rain, which eventually caused his death. Gabriel is humiliated by the revelation, and the events of the evening leading up to this moment compound themselves into driving him into further isolation. He "saw himself as a ludicrous figure, acting as a pennyboy for his aunts, a nervous well-meaning sentimentalist, orating to vulgarians and idealizing his own clownish lusts, the pitiable fatuous fellow he had caught a glimpse of in the mirror." Like Duffy in "A Painful Case," the extent of his isolation is so great that he experiences a kind of alienation even from himself, as he indulges in a moment of self-loathing. Like Duffy, his isolation is also guided by selfishness, and is to a certain extent self-imposed as a result of pride and arrogance. Like Duffy, it prevents him from being sympathetic toward his wife.

At the end of the story, Gretta finally falls asleep, and Gabriel quietly contemplates the inevitable loneliness of humanity. He imagines the death of Aunt Julia, and compares death to a "shade," a kind of darkness that creeps over us all, and how "one by one they were all becoming shades." Gabriel's own isolation becomes a meditation on universal isolation: "His soul swooned slowly as he heard the snow falling faintly through the universe and faintly falling, like the descent of their last end, upon all the living and the dead." The snow descends upon the universe, forming a blanket of isolation under which humanity is buried.

Wern Mei Yong

RELIGION in *Dubliners*

The collection *Dubliners* opens with the story "The Sisters," and with the introduction of three terms that characterize the collection as whole. These terms, italicized to draw attention, are *paralysis*, *gnomon*, and *simony*. The final term, "simony," refers to putting religion to non-religious, profitable ends. Religion therefore becomes empty of anything meaningful. In "The Sisters," the narrator recalls his relationship with the late Father Flynn. We are told that Father Flynn had taught the narrator a great deal about history and various aspects of religion. More important, Father Flynn used to pose challenging questions to the boy:

> Sometimes he had amused himself by putting difficult questions to me, asking me what one should do in certain circumstances or whether such and such sins were mortal or venial or only imperfections. His questions showed me how complex and mysterious were certain institutions of the Church which I had always regarded as the simplest acts.

Although the narrator goes on to list various ritual acts performed by priests as "the simplest acts" he used to take for granted, Joyce is also trying to tell us that one should never take anything we see or hear for granted, especially where it concerns religion. Faith and belief must be accompanied by rigorous examination and assessment of the dogmas presented to us, so that we are not merely following them blindly.

Toward the end of the story, one of the sisters, Eliza, informs us that Father Flynn died because "the duties of the priesthood was too much for him." Father Flynn was a "disappointed man"; but what initiated Father Flynn's spiritual and physical deterioration was "that chalice he broke . . ." which fortunately "contained nothing." The chalice, in the Catholic faith, contains the consecrated wine, believed to be the blood of Christ, and breaking it is a sign of disrespect. Whereas the sisters believe this to have been the cause of Father Flynn's guilt, leading to mental instability and eventually death, the narrator and reader understand otherwise. The chalice may be read as a symbol of the Church and religion. Its emptiness symbolizes that Church and religion are empty of meaning, that there is nothing beyond the words and symbols of the Church. When a man drinks the consecrated wine from the chalice, his fellowship with God is sealed. The lack of wine seems, therefore, to symbolize the severance

of the bond between man and God. This is the cause of Father Flynn's disappointment, and perhaps a cause for his gradual spiritual and mental deterioration. When the narrator looks into the coffin, he sees Father Flynn clutching the chalice loosely, possibly suggesting Father Flynn's own loss of faith in the relationship between man and God.

That no one seems to have any clue as to why Father Flynn died is all the more significant and ironic. They think that "there was something gone wrong with him. . . ." This illustrates how little the sisters, and those around him, were aware of his concerns, and by implication how little they were aware of their own spiritual poverty. Ironically, it is not Father Flynn but themselves who had "gone wrong" spiritually.

Another story that deals with the emptiness of religion is "Grace." Briefly, the story is an account of the efforts of a group of businessmen to convince one of their acquaintances to give up his damaging habit of excessive drinking. Their intention is to convince Tom Kernan to attend a religious retreat for businessmen, during which he might regain God's grace. The word *grace* itself takes on several meanings in the story. First, it refers to the freely given, unconditional favor and love of God. Second, it refers to an allowance of time after a debt is due to be paid, before any charges or further penalty are brought against the debtor. Third, it refers to the moral strength one has to perform one's duty. Last, but not least, grace refers to the elegance of one's manners. The several meanings come together in Joyce's tale. At the beginning, Kernan is shown to be very drunk, behaving in a manner lacking in physical grace, as well is in social grace. In his excessive debauchery, he has certainly fallen out of God's grace. His businessmen friends, in their visit to try to convince him to attend the retreat, display a degree of moral strength in their concern for their friend. As the story progresses, we begin to see how the material aspects of the term *grace* begin to enter into the picture, with the steady introduction of gossip of members of the business community. It becomes quite clear that asking the stubborn Kernan to attend the retreat directly is bound to be met with failure, and the only way is to broach the subject indirectly, via his interest in the business community. This builds up to the end of the story, when the men are gathered together for the retreat.

Among those who attend the retreat are Mr. Harford, the moneylender, Mr. Fanning, the registration agent and mayor of the city, and Michael Grimes, the owner of three pawnbroker shops. These businessmen are here at the retreat to address their spiritual poverty, a price paid for the increase in their worldly riches. The priest, Father Purdon, cites Luke 16: 8–9, in which Jesus tells men to befriend "the mammon of iniquity." After reading the text, Father Purdon begins by validating his appropriation of the text: "It was one of the most difficult texts in all the Scriptures, he said, to interpret properly." He then goes on to explain that this command was made to men like those sitting before him, called to serve God through their material, business means. What he leaves out, however, is the latter part of the verse, where Jesus says that one cannot serve two masters at the same time: money and God. Father Purdon chooses to interpret only the section of the verse that he thinks the men of the business community would appreciate, instead of reproaching them outright, as he should do as a responsible religious leader. His selectiveness is an example of the "simony" Joyce mentions in "The Sisters," where a religious text is interpreted and used to suit one's ends.

Father Purdon also uses the metaphor of accounting to describe the relationship between these men and God: "He came to speak to business men and he would speak to them in a business-like way. If he might use the metaphor, he said, he was their spiritual accountant." This has the effect of reducing the relationship to a mere transaction, a balancing of records. Ironically, God's grace, being freely given, is a unilateral gift and not a matter of "set[ting] right my accounts." These men cannot earn God's grace, and certainly not through befriending "the mammon of iniquity." By the end of the story, we come to understand the superficial nature of the retreat, and see it for what it really is: It is less about receiving God's grace than it is about justifying their material and business concerns in the eyes of God.

Wern Mei Yong

JOYCE, JAMES *A Portrait of the Artist as a Young Man* (1916)

A Portrait of the Artist as a Young Man, one of the most celebrated novels of the 20th century, is the COMING-OF-AGE story of Stephen Dedalus. It deals with issues of ALIENATION, RELIGION, and MEMORY. As a very young boy in Ireland, Dedalus witnesses the adults in his life clash over politics and religion, two subjects forever intertwined in the life of that country. Shortly after the novel begins, he is sent away to Clongowes College, a boarding school run by the Christian Brothers religious order. Here Stephen experiences both camaraderie and brutality, creating internal contradictions that will color his entire life. Stephen feels both drawn to and separate from his family, his church, his school, and his country, and he will spend the majority of the novel trying to resolve these contradictions and discern his purpose in life.

As a teenager, Stephen seriously considers the priesthood. He is deeply affected by the teachings of the priests who surround him during his schooling. He alternates between extreme self-loathing for his weakness and a desire to live what he sees as the spartan life of a priest. As he grows older, he begins to understand that what he is drawn to is not religion, but the intellectual life. He ends the novel having broken free of the constraints of his country and his religion, and determined to understand his place in the world.

Jennifer McClinton-Temple

ALIENATION in *A Portrait of the Artist as a Young Man*

Stephen Dedalus may well be one of the most alienated characters in modern literature. From the early part of his life, he thinks of himself as being different from all the others who surround him—his family and the other boys at school. He is constantly looking in from the outside, but rarely is the reader given the impression that he wants to join in the action. More often, he just wants to be left alone; however, being left alone is not a happy state for Stephen, either. Isolation does not offer him solace. He feels that he is inexplicably and torturously different, and thus feels alienated from all around him.

For the reader, Stephen's account of his alienation starts at school. The other boys often seem to be in on a joke he has missed. His school friend Athy points out that his family name, which is Latin, is "queer" and sets him apart, as does his first name, derived from St. Stephen, the first martyr of the Church. Stephen martyrs himself throughout the novel, but always for the sake of being different, being unlike the rest of the crowd, as though he is willing to suffer as long as it will bring him distinction. When he falls ill at Clongowes, he thinks of himself as Charles Stewart Parnell, the "uncrowned King of Ireland," who was ultimately alienated from his beloved Irish people when the Catholic Church condemned his relationship with Kitty O'Shea. Parnell's fate is memorably argued about by Stephen's family in the Christmas dinner scene near the beginning of the novel.

As Stephen grows older, he slowly comes to recognize, if not understand, his alienation. He thinks, even while he is still a child himself, "the noise of children at play annoyed him and their silly voices made him feel . . . that he was different from the others." So different in fact, that he sees himself, on more than one occasion, as less than human. He feels as if he is turning into a beast, with his soul "fattening and congealing into a gross grease." Later, struck by nightmares and paralyzing guilt, he feels as if he might be an "inhuman thing" moved by "bestial" desires. It is the indoctrination by Catholicism that leads Stephen to such depths of despair, but even after he has moved beyond his fears of eternal damnation, he remains alienated from others. He realizes, at the moment one of the priests at his college suggests to him that he consider the priesthood, that, although this is an invitation he has long awaited, he could never be part of such a community. He thinks, "His destiny was to be elusive of social or religious orders . . . He was destined to learn his own wisdom apart from others or to learn the wisdom of others himself wandering among the snares of the world."

Stephen's status as an alien only strengthens as he grows to adulthood. Even as he makes friends as a young man, he continues to feel he is set apart from them. Just as the country of Ireland is set apart from the rest of the English-speaking world, Stephen senses that, although he may look like the others, he is clearly and undeniably not one of them. He connects this alienation to his Irishness on several occasions. He realizes, all at once, how foreign to the Irish is the English tongue, when Stephen refers to a funnel as a *tundish* and the dean of the college exclaims that he has never heard such a word. Stephen thinks, "The language in which we are speaking is his before it is mine . . . I cannot speak or write these words without unrest of spirit." However, unlike many of his fellow Irishmen, Stephen does not allow this alienation from the English to unite him in solidarity with his countrypeople. On the contrary, it only makes him feel further alienated. When his friend Davin is trying to convince him to join with the nationalist cause, he fights even that connection, saying "When the soul of a man is born in this country there are nets flung at it to hold it back from flight. You talk to me of nationality, language, religion. I shall try to fly by those nets." Stephen, like Joyce himself, sees the connection between himself and his country, but refuses it in favor of the all-consuming need to think things through for himself.

Jennifer McClinton-Temple

MEMORY in *A Portrait of the Artist as a Young Man*

Much of *A Portrait of the Artist as a Young Man* uses a narrative style known as stream-of-consciousness. In this style, the narrative reads as though the reader were hearing the main character's thoughts as they occur. Not all of the text is written in this unique style, but even when the narrator is writing in third person (that is, using a narrator who is not a character in the text, but who is privy to the action) the reader still feels as though main character Stephen Dedalus's name is an open book laid before us. With such a narrative, memory, with its inaccuracies, eccentricities, and emotional power, emerges as an important theme.

The text begins with Stephen's first memory. He says, "Once upon a time and a very good time it was there was a moocow coming down along the road and this moocow that was coming down along the road met a nicens little boy named baby tuckoo . . . ." Stephen's father had told him that story, and clearly the comfort and safety Stephen associates with his infancy resonates as he begins the first part of this story, in which he will leave that safety and encounter the world of boarding school.

Much of the first part of the text takes place at Clongowes Wood College, a boarding school run by Jesuit priests. Stephen's recollections are brought forth in a way that is often difficult to understand. Seemingly unrelated thoughts run into one another, dialogue (always without quotation marks) abruptly abuts passages of description, and references to people and places in Stephen's past are made with no explanation or identification. However, while this technique can be difficult to follow and provides for a challenging text, it is far more evocative of childhood and the past than would be a more traditional narrative. For instance, when Stephen gets ill from having been pushed into a ditch at school, he continues to remember one particular detail: that another student once saw a rat jump into that same ditch. Stephen repeats the detail of the rat twice, even though he did not see it himself. He also reminds himself later, as he is starting to feel ill and the prefect checks his head for a fever, "that was the way a rat felt, slimy and damp and cold." Stephen returns again and again to the rat that he never even saw because, when he fell into the ditch, that thought, the thought of the big, slimy rat swimming in the same water as him, was the first thought that entered his head, and it would stick with him for days after. Although instances like this in the text might be difficult to understand because they run counter to how narrative usually works, they actually enhance the reader's understanding of Stephen's memories, because that *is* how memory usually works.

It is this complex system, the way in which memory works, that Joyce explores so deeply in *Portrait*. Images from Stephen's past come to him throughout his life, in times of crisis, in times of reflection, and the narrative gives one the sense that these images are ever changing. Frequently, Stephen "reminds" himself who he is, saying, for instance: "I am Stephen Dedalus. I am walking beside my father whose name is Simon Dedalus. We are in Cork, in Ireland" (92). That he must tell himself who he is reflects the unreliability of his memory. As he ages,

the memories of his childhood grow less vivid and less recognizable. He thinks of himself as a child, "a little boy in a grey belted suit," and is unsure what relationship he bears to that little figure.

This confusion forces Stephen into the present, and as the narrative progresses, he lives less and less in his memories and more in his actions and thoughts as they are happening. He continues to attend school, and his studies become increasingly sophisticated. He spends most of his time with his friends or alone, as he gradually pulls away from his family and the attendant memories they might evoke. He thinks of himself as a different person, saying of his childhood, "I was someone else then." As the novel ends, Stephen has moved beyond living in the present and is now concentrating on the future. However, the narrative gives us the sense that this is artificial—that one cannot leave the past behind entirely. In the last few pages, Stephen's diary entries as he prepares to leave home are littered with images from the past, some arguably trivial. Such as, "I go now to encounter for the millionth time the reality of experience." It is clear that he will be unable to do that without recognizing his past.

Jennifer McClinton-Temple

RELIGION in *A Portrait of the Artist as a Young Man*

Much of *A Portrait of the Artist as a Young Man* deals with Stephen Dedalus's struggle to understand Catholicism, its hold on him, and its proper place in his life. For Stephen, every facet of his life is permeated by religion. The indoctrination he receives at Clongowes Wood College and later, with the Christian Brothers and the Jesuits in Dublin, leaves him successively in fear for his mortal soul, determined to become a priest himself, and, finally, indifferent to the Church.

As a young boy, Stephen is taught, as are his classmates, that he is a "lazy, idle little loafer" like all boys. He is beaten by Father Dolan, the prefect of studies at Clongowes, for breaking his glasses. Father Dolan claims that Stephen must have broken them on purpose to avoid work. Stephen knows that this punishment is "unfair and cruel," but because Father Dolan is a priest, he feels conflicted. This scene, early in the text, sets up the conflicting role priests will have in Stephen's life. He fears them, and instinctively knows that many of the teachings to which he is subjected in his life run counter to what he knows about himself; however, at the same time, he admires the commitment and the sacrifice of the priesthood, and even considers that this role in life might be his some day.

Joyce makes clear that Stephen's admiration of sacrifice is misplaced, and perhaps driven by his own self-loathing. This self-loathing is not necessarily caused by the Catholicism that surrounds him, but it certainly is exacerbated by it. Joyce implies in the text that it is the dual condition of being Irish and being Catholic that keeps Stephen from breaking free. When he is very young, he is present as the adults in his family argue about Ireland, politics, and religion. Charles Stewart Parnell, the most important political leader in Ireland, has married a divorced woman, Kitty O'Shea—and indeed been the cause of her divorce—and the priests and bishops of Ireland have declared that the Catholic faithful must disavow allegiance to him. Stephen's father and family friend Mr. Casey believe that the priests should stay out of politics, but Mrs. Riordan, whom Stephen calls Dante, believes the opposite. She says, "A priest would not be a priest if he did not tell his flock what is right and what is wrong." She follows this with "The bishops and priests of Ireland have spoken, and they must be obeyed." It matters not, to her, what the best course is politically; it matters only what the priests say. The men at the table do not agree with her, but they too are conflicted, as they continue to call themselves Catholics despite being unable to follow the priests' edict. The Irish, it seems, are governed by two masters—the English and the Roman Catholic Church—and in this case, at least, the two are in collusion to keep the people oppressed.

This position of inferiority confuses Stephen, for he rightly believes himself to be of extraordinary disposition (thus, the "artist" in the title). At a religious retreat, he begins to sink to what is perhaps his most confused state. The speaker tells the boys they should be in fear for their immortal souls and gives an extended and quite graphic description of hell. He speaks to them of the "boundless, shoreless, bottomless" torments: the darkness, the foul,

unbreathable stench, the fire, and ultimately, the demon tormentors themselves. Stephen leaves the retreat devastated, incredulous, yet convinced that he could be one of the sinning, damned creatures bound for this hell. He begins a life of self-denial, constantly atoning for his worldly nature. He forces himself to never consciously shift position in bed, so as to cause himself pain; he purposefully seeks out bad smells; he walks with his eyes downcast, so as never to see beauty or meet the eyes of women. Stephen believes he may one day be a candidate for the priesthood, but as soon as a priest inquires about this interest, he realizes that such a life repulses him. He says, "He was destined to learn his own wisdom apart from others or to learn the wisdom of others himself wandering among the snares of the world."

Jennifer McClinton-Temple

KAFKA, FRANZ   *The Metamorphosis* (1915)

The Metamorphosis begins with the transformation of Gregor Samsa into a giant insect. Samsa is an ordinary man with family and work responsibilities who dreams of a different life. His transformation into an insect provides Samsa with the life-changing opportunity that he desires. This transformation also changes Gregor's family by forcing them to accept financial responsibility for themselves. This change in the family dynamic makes Gregor an outsider in his own family, and the subsequent abuse he suffers leads to his death. It is only after his death that Gregor and his family achieve peace. Kafka's story is a critique on the sacrifices that an individual must make to keep the family unit going. *The Metamorphosis* addresses the dehumanization of work and family life through Gregor's transformation. As a normal man, he is confined to his job and his family responsibilities. As an insect, he is allowed to forego these responsibilities and live a life free from work. Gregor's metamorphosis provides him with the opportunity to become a master of his own fate. Subsequently, Gregor's family are also transformed, from their financial dependence on Gregor to financial independence from him. *The Metamorphosis* allows Gregor a measure of liberation from the confines of his previous life and allows Gregor to achieve salvation in death.

Sumeeta Patnaik

FAMILY in *The Metamorphosis*

The transformation of Gregor Samsa into a monstrous vermin is the catalyst that opens and closes Franz Kafka's *The Metamorphosis.* Gregor awakens from unsettling dreams to find himself transformed into a monstrous insect. This nightmare transformation condemns him to be forsaken by his family. Gregor is his family's main breadwinner and his transformation makes him unable to work, forcing his family to pick up the financial slack. Gregor's family, his father, mother, and sister, come to resent him and see Gregor as a burden. It is through their neglect that Gregor eventually dies, unable to free himself from the burden of his familial responsibility. Upon his death, the Samsa family is ironically freed from the same burden that condemned Gregor to his nightmare existence. Family is a central theme in *The Metamorphosis,* with each family member contributing to the eventual demise of their central caregiver, Gregor; it is his sister, Grete, who gets a chance to have the life that Gregor was not allowed to lead.

Awakening to his newly transformed state, Gregor's devotion to his family is shown immediately as he attempts to get ready for work despite his changed appearance. Gregor works as a traveling salesman, a job he despises but maintains, to save his family the embarrassment of having to deal with the financial burden brought on by his father's failed business. During his attempts to go to work, Gregor muses upon his dislike for his job and working for a boss whose paranoia over his employees' performance causes him to send his head clerk to Gregor's home with veiled threats of being fired. This occurs, despite the fact that Gregor has never missed a day of work and was not late even on the day of his transformation. Gregor does not want his family, particularly his younger sister, Grete, to be subjected to this kind of work environment. Despite his best efforts, his transformation forces them to enter the workplace. In doing so, his family members are transformed from their dependence on Gregor to the financial

independence they had previously been resistant to obtaining.

As his family works toward financial independence, their feelings toward Gregor change from sadness to outright hostility to relief at his death. Family members deal with Gregor's transformation differently, thus highlighting their true feelings toward Gregor prior to his metamorphosis. Gregor's father, Herr Samsa, claimed to be an invalid after his business failed, and relied on his son to step in and become the family provider. After his transmutation, Gregor recalls his father's previous attitude toward his son as loving, with his father embracing him each time he returned from a business trip. Yet, Gregor realized that his altered appearance immediately changed his father's attitude toward him and that Herr Samsa regarded Gregor as a burden that was only to be tolerated. Gregor's delicate mother, Frau Samsa, is initially horrified by her son's changed appearance, yet she attempts several times to care for him, even fighting with her daughter to keep Gregor's room the same in case he should return to his former self. However, Frau Samsa yields to her husband and daughter's wishes that Gregor disappear and the family be rid of the burden of caring for him.

Finally, Gregor's sister, Grete, is his greatest champion, until she wants to be rid of the burden of caring for him. After Gregor's initial metamorphosis, Grete is the family member who takes care of him. She brings him food, cleans his room, and shelters him from their angry parents. Yet her devotion extends only to a certain point; like Gregor, she desires a life free from burden. In the end, she betrays him by demanding his removal from the apartment and their lives. Upon hearing his sister's words, Gregor's resentment toward his family fades and he dies peacefully, thus freeing his family of their great burden.

Gregor's desire for a new life is quelled by his family's financial debt. In an effort to pay off these debts, Gregor works for his father's creditor as a traveling salesman, but he is, in effect, an indentured servant to his family's debts and their needs. After Gregor's metamorphosis, his family assumes the financial burden and surprisingly discovers that they are not only capable of contributing to the family's financial situation, but they also actually had a small savings from Herr Samsa's failed business. Nevertheless, when Gregor is unable to contribute financially to his family's care, he is no longer considered a viable member of the family; therefore, his previous contributions do not count when his family is in such financial crisis. In *The Metamorphosis,* financial debt transforms the Samsa family from a close, loving family to a family that betrays their son when he is no longer able to care for them. Gregor's transformation actually brings him freedom from his familial obligations, but his loyalty to his family leads to his death. Kafka's story is a critique on family dynamics and the sacrifices that must be made to keep the family unit going.

Sumeeta Patnaik

FREEDOM in *The Metamorphosis*

Gregor Samsa's transformation from human being into monstrous insect is the event that opens and closes Franz Kafka's *The Metamorphosis.* Gregor awakens from terrible nightmares to find himself transformed into a grotesque insect. This shocking transformation allows Gregor the freedom that he was never allowed to have as a human being. Gregor provides his family's primary financial support and his transformation does not allow him to work, thereby forcing his family to become financially responsible. Once Gregor's transformation condemns his family to the same burden of providing, it is then that the family realizes the depth of the responsibility Gregor has shouldered. Ironically, Gregor's family comes to resent him for not sustaining his financial responsibility, thereby ensuring them freedom from work. Freedom is a central theme in *The Metamorphosis,* with Gregor's transformation into an insect providing him with the freedom that he was unable to find as a human being. Furthermore, Gregor's transformation also provides his family with the freedom to pursue new lives after Gregor's death.

Upon awakening to his newly transformed state, Gregor's first thought is his anger at having to work at a job that he so despises. As a traveling salesman, he works long hours and rarely finds time away from work. Indeed, Gregor fantasizes about quitting his job and telling his boss exactly how he feels about his position. Nevertheless, he does not admit how much he dislikes his job, as he fears being unable to financially provide for his parents and sister. Gregor's dislike of his job deepens when the head clerk from his firm arrives and proceeds to make veiled threats of having Gregor fired from his job despite the fact that Gregor has never missed a day of work in five years and was not late even on the day that he was transformed. Even with his best efforts to retain his position, Gregor ultimately loses his job due to his transformation, and the financial burden falls back on his family. Yet, Gregor finds the freedom that his familial and financial responsibility did not previously allow.

Gregor's transformation from a human being into an insect allows him to gain a personal appreciation of himself. Prior to his change, Gregor rarely did anything for himself. Even his father admitted to the head clerk that he encouraged Gregor to take some time out for himself, but that Gregor often spent evenings at home either with his family or planning his work schedule for the next day. Gregor's transmutation allowed him time to gain an appreciation for himself. Physically, Gregor discovers that he is much stronger than before and does not tire as he did in his human form. As Gregor discovers that he has become physically stronger, he also learns that his parents are physically stronger than he previously knew. Gregor's transformation forces his parents into the workplace. Before Gregor's transmutation, his father claimed to have been an invalid and his mother that her asthma prevented her from engaging in work. His sister, although physically strong, is spoiled by the family. Now that Gregor's parents and sister are forced into the workplace, they discover, along with Gregor, that they are physically capable of work and are able to contribute to the family income. This allows Gregor the freedom to spend his days resting, sleeping, and watching the world from his window. Furthermore, Gregor's transformation allowed him to learn more about his family, particularly his father. Before Gregor's transmutation, Gregor was the primary breadwinner in the house as his father had lost the family business. After Gregor's change, he learns that his father had a small savings left from the business that could help provide for the family for about a year. While Gregor is relieved to learn that his family will not starve, he is also hurt to learn that his father had the means to make Gregor's life easier and chose not to do so. Gregor's transformation allows him to learn more about his family, thus freeing him from the burden of caring for them. Gregor dies peacefully. His transmuted state allows him to finally escape from familial and financial responsibilities.

Gregor finds freedom through a physical change that allows him to become a stronger individual. In finding his personal strength, Gregor also discovers a great deal about his family, including that they are capable of providing financially for themselves. Gregor's transformation allows him freedom from working as an indentured servant to his family's debt and needs. Although his transmutation keeps him a prisoner in his room, he has obtained a new kind of freedom where he is finally allowed time for himself. In *The Metamorphosis*, freedom transforms Gregor from workaholic in debt to his family's financial needs into a being that has time for contemplation and relaxation. Kafka's story is a critique on family responsibility and the individual cost that must be paid in order to keep the family unit going.

Sumeeta Patnaik

SUFFERING in *The Metamorphosis*

Gregor Samsa's hideous transformation from a human being to an insect is the action that opens and closes *The Metamorphosis* by Franz Kafka. Gregor awakens from terrible nightmares to find himself transformed, and this shocking transformation allows Samsa to alleviate his suffering and escape from his humdrum existence. Prior to his transformation, Gregor worked at a job that he disliked in order to support his family financially. Once he is transformed, Gregor's family must take on Gregor's responsibility and provide an income for the entire household. Freed from his financial responsibility, Gregor's suffering is relieved and he learns a great deal about himself and his family. Still, Gregor experiences a different kind of suffering through his transformation, and his death is the catalyst for change in his family.

Awaking from his terrible dreams, Gregor's first thought is to carry on as normal. He tries to get ready for work and does not allow his mother to come into the room. Even after the head clerk comes to find out why Gregor is late for work, Gregor attempts to convince the head clerk that he is ready to work, so he will not lose his job. Unfortunately, once his situation becomes known, it becomes clear that things will have to change. Having worked for several years at a job that he dislikes, Gregor finds his newly changed physique allows him the freedom to sleep, daydream, and watch his family experience the suffering that Gregor experienced in the workplace. Despite his freedom, Gregor worries about his family's ability to provide financially for themselves. He discovers, as his family does, that each member of the Samsa family is capable of working. This discovery changes the family's view of each other and of Gregor. Now that he is no longer financially viable, Gregor is viewed as the cause of his family's suffering.

Previously, Gregor bore the burden of the entire family's existence. As the family breadwinner, Gregor was under enormous pressure to provide for each of his family's needs. Five years prior to his transformation, Gregor's father lost his business and became an invalid. At that time, Gregor's mother was ill with asthma and his sister, Grete, was too young to work. Therefore, Gregor took on the role of providing financially for his family. In spite of his love for his family, Gregor was miserable in his position and often fantasized about finding ways out of work. Gregor's transformation provides him with that freedom at the expense of his family's needs. Ironically, Gregor's family experiences the same type of suffering at work that Gregor experienced prior to his change. However, instead of feeling sympathy for Gregor's suffering, his family comes to resent the burden of having to care for Gregor. As a result, Gregor is subjected to abuse from his family. He is isolated and his father often threatens Gregor when he tries to interact with the rest of the family. Even Gregor's sister, Grete, who initially cares for him, also comes to resent this care and asks their father to help her rid them of the monstrosity Gregor has become. Sadly, Gregor comes to agree with his family's sentiments and decides to end his own life. Gregor's death allows him to find peace and allows his family to become financially independent and move on. Gregor's sister, Grete, achieves what her brother was unable to achieve in life: independence from family needs.

Gregor's suffering both as a human and as an insect allows him to become stronger. Although Gregor physically suffers before his untimely death, his transformation into an insect allows him to gain personal satisfaction. For a time, Gregor emerges from his transmutation physically and emotionally strong and self-confident while his family suffers through financial hardships. This change in the family dynamics creates resentment toward Gregor that leads to his death. Gregor's death, like his transformation, serves to provide change for the entire Samsa family. Kafka's story is a critique on family responsibility and the cost an individual must pay in order to keep the family unit going.

Sumeeta Patnaik

KEATS, JOHN   poems   (1795–1821)

Easily one of the most talented of the romantic poets, John Keats's career is all the more remarkable for having ended so soon. His first notable poem, "On Looking into Chapman's Homer" (1816), was published when he was only 21 years old. In the space of four years he went on to compose some of the most memorable poems in the English language, including "La Belle Dame sans Merci" (1820) and "Ode on a Grecian Urn" (1820). Keats's remarkable career was cut short by tuberculosis; he died in 1821 at age 25. At his request, his gravestone bore only the inscription "Here lies one whose name was writ in water," a last poetic nod to the transience of art and life.

Keats's poetry is distinguished by its melodic lines and sensual, concrete imagery. Highly conscious of both the importance of art and the fragility of life, Keats's poems focus on the contradictions of lived experience—the connection between pain and pleasure, for example, in "Ode to a Nightingale" (1820), or the relationship between love and death in "The Eve of St. Agnes" (1820). Like other romantic poets, Keats was interested in the themes of nature, art, love and death, but his treatment of these themes is characterized by a celebration of the physical world and thoughtful acceptance of the limitations of human existence.

Siobhan Carroll

DEATH in the poetry of John Keats

John Keats was no stranger to death. By the time he was 15, he had lost a brother, his grandmother, and both his parents. Having witnessed so much death, Keats looked to art as a means of achieving immortality on Earth.

In "Endymion" (1818), Keats retells the Greek legend about a man put into an eternal sleep of youth. "Endymion" begins with a famous rejection of death and transience: "A thing of beauty is a joy for ever: / Its Loveliness increases; it will never / Pass into nothingness; but still will keep . . . a sleep / Full of sweet dreams" (l.1–4). These lines summon up the image of a sleeping Endymion, but also extend that idea to beauty itself. Keats insists that death can be transcended through the creation of beautiful objects. For example, he describes a group of dancing Greeks as being "not yet dead, / But in old marbles ever beautiful" (l.71–72). On the one hand, Keats's description brings death into the poem, reminding us that the people we are reading about are going to die. On the other hand, the next line reminds us that the ancient Greeks continue to "live" in the form of marble sculptures that preserve their beauty.

Keats returns to the idea of art transcending death in his famous "Ode on a Grecian Urn" (1820). The speaker is captivated by the way the artwork on an ancient urn captures an ideal moment of life. The trees depicted on the urn will never shed their leaves (l.21) and the musician will never grow old or die. At the same time, the speaker is also aware that the people who knew the stories behind the pictures are dead (l.39–40). The ode concludes with the poet reflecting that the art he is looking at will also probably outlive him and his generation (l.46–7).

"Ode to a Nightingale" (1820) begins with the speaker sinking into sleep while listening to the song of the nightingale. Caught up in the pleasure of the experience, he feels himself losing touch with his body, as though he has been poisoned or drugged (l.1–3). He wishes he could follow the nightingale's song out of the world, leaving behind his misery and pain. He doesn't want to live in a world of transience, where joy and beauty fade and "youth grows pale, and spectre-thin, and dies" (l.36). The poet wonders what it would be like to die at this moment, when he is peaceful and happy: "Now more than ever seems it rich to die, / To cease upon the midnight with no pain" (l.54–55). He reflects on the irony that the birdsong will continue after his death, becoming a requiem he can no longer hear. This in turn leads the poet to think about the immortality of the nightingale. Although the bird is not literally immortal, its song has remained the same across centuries. Like the Grecian urn, it is an example of beauty that will survive the poet, just as it has survived listeners before him.

Keats's poems published after his death reveal a bleaker perspective. In "When I Have Fears that I May Cease to Be" (1848), the speaker discusses his fear that he will die without achieving his life's ambitions and without seeing his lover again. Whereas in other poems, art offered the speaker comfort in the face of death, here the poem concludes with the isolated speaker unable to do anything but "stand alone, and think / Till love and fame to nothingness do sink" (l.13–14). The final line implies that either the poet's fears will fade or that he will die and his dreams will cease to matter.

"This living hand, now warm and capable" (1848) is one of Keats's most chilling poems about death. The poet asks the reader to reflect on the hand that is composing the poem. If it could, that hand, once dead, would "haunt thy days and chill thy dreaming nights" (l.4) until the reader would wish himself or herself dead and the poet alive again. The final lines of the poem—"see here it is—/ I hold it towards you" (l.7–8)—are a powerful acknowledgment of the failure of art, because we cannot, of course, see the hand of the desperate poet pleading for life, nor can we save him.

In "Sleep and Poetry" (1817), Keats asks to be spared death for 10 years so that he can study poetry and fulfill his dreams (l.96–97). Sadly, Keats was dead in four years, consumed by tuberculosis by the age of 25.

Siobhan Carroll

LOVE in the poetry of John Keats

Keats's poems demonstrate that the poet held varying attitudes toward love during his short life. Some of his poems idealize love, portraying it as a power that can elevate the lover into a state approaching divinity. Other poems bypass idealism in favor of bawdiness and celebrate SEX and sexuality rather than transcendent love. Finally, in the poems Keats wrote toward the end of his life, we can see the poet questioning his early idealization of love and sometimes expressing frustration with the way his new relationship competes with his long-held poetic ambitions.

Keats's idealization of love can be seen in poems like "The Eve of St. Agnes" (1820). In this poem, the sexual encounter and then escape of the two young lovers is described in very romantic terms: "Into her dream he melted, as the rose / Blendeth its odour with the violet" (l.320–321). At the end of the poem, the lovers flee into the night, leaving the dreary world of religious and parental control behind them.

Keats also wrote several poems that celebrate sex and sexuality more overtly. "Over the hill and over the dale" begins innocently enough, describing a journey "over the bourn to Dawlish" (l.1–2). In the second verse, however, we meet "Rantipole Betty" who "Kicked up her petticoats fairly" (l.5–6). The poem's sexual innuendo becomes clearer when the speaker suggests to Betty that "I'll be Jack if you will be Jill" (l.7). Betty, agreeing, sits "on the grass debonairly" (l.8). Comedy ensues when Betty panics several times about being interrupted by passersby, but the frustrated speaker is finally able to persuade her to "lay on the grass" (l.12) like a "Venus" (prostitute). The poem concludes by asking who would not want to go to Dawlish and "rumple the daisies there" (l.19). The poem is characteristic of Keats's writing about sex: It is bawdy in its innuendos and the sexual encounter itself is implied rather than described.

In 1818, Keats fell in love with Fanny Brawne. His poems from this point onward show both excitement over his romance with Fanny and an increased consciousness of the less-than-ideal aspects of relationships. Keats's poems written to Fanny celebrate her beauty and his love for her, but also express concern over the toll their relationship may take on his poetic career. In "To Fanny" (1848), Keats praises "One-thoughted, never wand'ring, guileless love, / Unmask'd, and being seen—without a blot!" (l. 2–3). Keats adopts the excessive tone of courtly romance, claiming that if his lover remains cold and distant he will die, or worse, continue to live on as his lover's "wretched thrall" (l. 11) and "Forget, in the mist of idle misery, / Life's purposes" (l. 12–13). The last lines of the poem dwell on the way the speaker's lovesick SUFFERING has impacted his life, leading "the palate of my mind" to lose its sense of taste and leaving "my ambition blind" (l. 12–14). The last line is significantly Keatsian: The worst thing that love threatens to do to the speaker is to rob him of his poetic ambition.

Cynical poems like "Modern Love" (1848) are quick to criticize what Keats perceives as the shallowness and commerciality of romantic relationships: "And what is love? It is a doll dressed up / For idleness to cosset, nurse and dandle" (l. 1–2). The poem seems to mock Keats's earlier idealism—"silly youth doth think to make itself / Divine by loving" (l. 3–4)—and expresses anger over lovers' tendency to read high drama into their shallow relationships.

> Fools! If passions high have warmed the
> 　　world,
> If queens and soldiers have played deep for
> 　　hearts,
> It is no reason why such agonies
> Should be more common than the growth
> 　　of weeds. (l.11–14)

However, having sneered at those who want to believe that "Cleopatra lives at Number Seven" (l.9), the speaker concludes by seeming to wish his idealism back intact, as symbolized by his demand that lovers "make me whole again that weighty pearl" (l.12) which their excesses have presumably destroyed. In that respect, Keats's poems seem never to stray far from Keats's early, idealistic celebration of love as a state approaching divinity.

Siobhan Carroll

NATURE in the poetry of John Keats

Romantic poets are generally characterized as being interested in the relationship between human beings and nature. John Keats is no exception to this rule.

One of his earliest poems, "On the Grasshopper and the Cricket" (1817), begins with the line "The poetry of earth is never dead" (1). Keats likens insects to the singing poets of the earth and claims that their song never truly ceases, for when the grasshopper's voice is silenced by winter's frosts the cricket's voice takes over: "from the stove there shrills / The Cricket's song, in warmth increasing ever, / And seems to one in drowsiness half lost, / The Grasshopper's among some grassy hills" (12–14). Although natural life involves the passing of seasons and, eventually, death, nature has built-in mechanisms that ensure the continuity of beauty from season to season and year to year.

Keats returns to the relationship between nature and mortality in his famous poem "To Autumn" (1820). Although autumn, as the forerunner of winter, might seem like a gloomy season, Keats hails it as the "Season of mists and mellow fruitfulness" (1). In wording that echoes that of "On the Grasshopper and the Cricket," the poet first asks "Where are the songs of spring?" (23) before concluding that, although the sounds of new life are beautiful, those of autumn also have their charms: "Think not of them, thou hast thy music too" (23–24). However, a potentially negative note appears elsewhere in the poem, when Keats reflects on autumn's production of "later flowers for the bees / Until they think warm days will never cease" (9–10). Unlike humans, bees and other forms of natural life are both blessed and cursed by ignorance of their mortality.

In "Ode to a Nightingale," Keats expounds further on the natural world's ignorance of present and future woes. As a human, the speaker in the poem cannot help but be aware of the misery of others, and as a result feels that "to think is to be full of sorrow" (27). By listening to a nightingale, which is ignorant of the cares and troubles of the world, the speaker is temporarily able to forget his human perspective: "fade far away, dissolve, and quite forget / What thou among the leaves hast never known / The weariness, the fever, and the fret / Here, where men sit and hear each other groan" (21–24). Nature, however, cannot provide a lasting refuge for the poet. The speaker is eventually awakened from his trance and enters back into consciousness of human pain and mortality.

In "Ode on a Grecian Urn," Keats contrasts the world of nature with the world of art. Examining the illustrations on an ancient piece of pottery, the speaker is struck by the way in which art has frozen a beautiful moment in time, arresting both the progress of seasons and the advance of death. Unlike the trees in "To Autumn," the painted trees on the urn will never feel the touch of winter: "Ah, happy, happy boughs! That cannot shed / your leaves, nor ever bid the spring adieu" (21–22). Likewise, the humans depicted on the urn will never grow old and die, but will remain "for ever panting and for ever young" (27). Ultimately, however, the poem expresses ambivalence toward art's interruption of the natural cycle. The human figures on the urn seem trapped rather than liberated by immortality—"Bold lover, never, never canst thou kiss" (17)—and the poet dubs the urn a "Cold Pastoral" (45), acknowledging that the frozen trees and figures lack the vivacity and warmth of real life.

Keats's poems, like the work of other romantic poets, express admiration for the natural world and portray nature as a means of escaping the troubles of modern life. Unlike other romantics, however, Keats emphasizes the mortality rather than the regenerative aspects of nature. Rather than reminding the poet of his individuality, nature in Keats's poetry reminds the poet that he is part of the natural world and thus is bound to die.

Siobhan Carroll

KEROUAC, JACK *On the Road* (1957)

On the Road is the quintessential American travel novel. It has inspired countless readers to drop everything and hit the road in search of themselves, enlightenment, or just a cheap buzz. Its (now somewhat dated) romanticized version of life on the road is irresistibly tempting for anyone with even the faintest hint of a travel bug. It is also a love letter of sorts to America, highlighting the adventure and fascination inherent in her vast landscapes.

The late 1940s and 1950s saw the beginning of the interstate road system in America, which eventually connected all major cities through a series of linked roads. Although not an interstate, Route 66, which provided a direct route between Chicago and California, was part of the U.S. Highway System. Published in 1957, *On the Road* was a major factor in the romanticization and mythologizing of these new roads, as it showed how the roads connected people from all social and economic classes. Sal Paradise and his friends have the country opened up for them in a way unavailable to previous generations.

The novel has never been out of print, and is a staple of the American high school reading list. It is particularly popular with young people at a crossroads in their life: They identify with the choices Dean Moriarty and his friends must make as they mature. Dean keenly observes that his travels are directly related to his maturity: "I was halfway across America, at the dividing line between the East of my youth and the West of my future. . . ."

On the Road presents several different themes throughout the various strands of the story line. Most evident is the idea of freedom—freedom from responsibility and perhaps from "adulthood." The novel also questions and redefines the notion of the "American dream," which took on a completely new meaning in postwar society. The relationship between the individual and society is also examined: To what extent should we follow what is expected of us by society? The examination of these considerable notions helps make the novel an intensely personal read.

Georgina Willms

The AMERICAN DREAM in *On the Road*
The year 1945 saw the end of the fighting of World War II. Soldiers returning to America had witnessed some of the harshest combat the world had ever known. The sheer amount of casualties is a testament to the extreme horror and brutality witnessed by these men. Returning home, they sought the quiet and normalcy that they had left behind—regardless of whether that had been their reality before they had left for war. This quest for normalcy, combined with the advent of the suburbs and a zeal for material possessions, led to a new lifestyle ideal—a new "American dream."

The idea of an "American dream" was by no means new; versions of it had been around since Europeans first settled the New World. In general, it involves some degree of "success," usually material success. In the 19th century it became associated with immigrants coming to America, looking for "the land of opportunity" and its "streets paved with gold." (This is still a common image of the United States.) But in the aftermath of World War II, the "American dream" took on a new look: the returning soldier, leading a nice, uneventful life with a submissive wife and the newest and best material possessions (kitchen appliances, televisions, and automobiles being some examples of the technological advances that became "must-haves" for the suburban life.

However, not all returning soldiers felt this need for material wealth and success. Some aimed for a more aesthetic, pleasure-driven lifestyle. Very little mention is made of Sal Paradise's military career in *On the Road*, but we are told that he was in the war, in the navy. (Paradise was Jack Kerouac's alter ego; Kerouac himself received an honorable discharge for medical reasons from the U.S. Navy in 1943, after serving a minimal amount of time.) The attitudes and experiences described in *On the Road* are a reaction to the sense of normalcy craved by the middle classes. Sal and his friends are also searching for contentment, but in a very different way.

This anti-middle-class stance is manifested most clearly in the character of Dean Moriarty (based on Kerouac's friend Neal Cassady). By having Dean be the son of a bum, and having him live the life of a tramp, Kerouac is making a clear statement about the unimportance of material things. Dean rarely has his own place to live, his car is the only thing of value he has ever owned, and he does not seem to make any concentrated effort to make a living. Yet he is viewed by Sal as a symbol of freedom and happiness; Sal aspires to be like Dean, to be thrilled by life without material concerns. If the American dream is a quest to find happiness through the acquisition of material goods, then Neal is the anti-American dream—happiness through the denial of materialism.

If this is the case, then it must be noted that as the novel wears on Sal becomes increasingly disillusioned with Dean's lifestyle. He begins to see it as immature, self-centered, and indifferent to the needs, wants, and comforts of others. It can be read as Sal maturing, wanting more out of life than what the road can offer him. It is on the final big trip, to Mexico, that Sal comes to terms with this dissatisfaction. On this trip the friends come face to face with real poverty, meeting people who live without even the possibility of the material comforts that Sal, and even Dean, take for granted. Sal realizes that Dean has made the choice to live the way he does.

So what does this say about the American dream? Sal and Dean have to leave America to realize what they have (at least Sal does—left alone in Mexico by Dean while ill, he gradually turns his back on the road lifestyle). Their last meeting in New York City is sad and disjointed; they can no longer understand each other, no longer communicate. Sal has become more settled, more "acceptable" by society's standards, although he has learned a lot from his time on the road. Dean is still the same, manically looking for the next thrill, unconcerned with material matters. Instead of offering a judgment on this, Kerouac presents both sides equally, suggesting that one can learn from both. The "American dream" is, was, and always will be to some extent unattainable, as evidenced by the inclusion of the word "dream." What Kerouac suggests is that this dream is fluid, not static, and that everyone can make it work for themselves, because we all define our own dreams.

Georgina Willms

FREEDOM in *On the Road*
In the late 1940s and 1950s Americans were busy redivising their definition of "freedom." Years of depression, war rationing, and austerity had taken their toll on the populace, and the economic upturn the country experienced in the early 1950s led to previously incomprehensible levels of economic comfort. As often happens, people soon began to feel "trapped" by their belongings. People spent their new money on appliances, cars, and fancy homes, and then found they must work hard to maintain them. Soon a backlash began against this economic complacency.

The promise of freedom is an essential part of the appeal of *On the Road*. Since its publication, people have been inspired by the book to take off on their own trips, leaving their lives and the consequent responsibilities behind. It is, of course, to some extent a fantasy—your problems will follow you wherever you go (as our heroes find out numerous times). But the vast landmass that is America holds the promise of autonomy, independence, and a (possibly hedonistic) escape from daily life. Contemporary readers who embark on extended road trips are looking for an escape from their mundane daily lives.

Economic freedom is one of the essential freedoms enjoyed by the protagonists of *On the Road*. At a time when the economy was booming, thanks to postwar industry, an increasing emphasis was being placed on personal economic success. Capitalism and materialism were at an all-time high. By turning their backs on this phenomenon, and not joining the so-called "rat-race," Dean and his friends freed themselves from this tyranny of wealth. This economic freedom is personified in the character of "Old" Dean Moriarty, Dean's father, a character who never actually appears but is discussed, searched for, and virtually deified by Sal and Dean. A tramp, he is thought to wander the roads, with no money, no prospects, and, most important, no ties. While he may seem a somewhat sad character for this, the reverent tones used while speaking of him imply that his life represents the pinnacle of economic freedom for which the characters are striving.

Sal and his cohort also exemplify a kind of political freedom. In postwar America things were changing rapidly, and one of the prominent changes was the relationship between the races. While the Civil Rights movement in America would not become a national concern until the 1960s, by the late 1940s there were already developments in these relations. The culture of segregation that had been prevalent since the late 19th century was beginning to collapse. Sal, Dean, and the others seem, to some extent, oblivious to any tensions between the races, as they befriend African-American characters in several cities, and display an appreciation for black culture that was rare at the time. Sal's escapade in California with the Mexican workers also gives him insight into the many problems faced by other races and cultures. *On the Road* succeeds not only in highlighting positive aspects of other cultures, but also in presenting a more relaxed relationship between the races.

Of course, the pursuit of personal freedom is at the core of *On the Road*. All of the characters are try-ing to free themselves from the constraints placed on them by society, family, and by themselves. While it may seem that the characters are repeatedly running away from their problems, they are also running to an imaginary, nirvana-like existence where they are free to live as they please. To some, this may sound immature. To others, it is at the heart of any spiritual journey.

In the end, the novel both propagates and destroys the hope of tremendous freedom from daily life. Mexico is the most ambitious trip the friends embark upon, and Sal's illness combined with Dean's eventual abandonment of him does not make for a happy conclusion. However, the night that Sal, Dean, and Stan spend outside becomes a sticky, hot, insect-ridden dreamscape in which Sal comes as close as he can to pure freedom. After this moment of awareness in the desert, Sal returns to New York and begins to lead a considerably more "proper" life—but a life forever changed by his experiences on the road.

Georgina Willms

INDIVIDUAL AND SOCIETY in *On the Road*

On the Road is an intensely personal story told as a first-person narrative through the point of view of Sal Paradise (a pseudonym for author Jack Kerouac). All of the action is seen through Sal's eyes, and we are privy only to his version of events. Because of this, it is possible to align oneself with Sal, as many readers do. A main theme threaded throughout the book is that of society: What constitutes a "society," and how does one determine one's place in it? All of the characters in the novel struggle with these questions to some extent, but none more than Sal. The novel is, in a sense, the story of Sal's struggle with where he feels he belongs. Sal's struggle becomes synonymous with that of the country itself: "This is the story of America. Everybody's doing what they think they're supposed to do."

Sal's domestic situation in the beginning of the novel seems to indicate that he has already spent a fair part of his life contemplating his role in a larger society. We are told that he has been married and is only just recovered from an illness relating to the break-up of the marriage (no doubt a nod to Kerouac's own experience with mental illness). He is at a crossroads in his personal growth, and happens to meet Dean Moriarty at a time when he is looking for something "more" out of life. Sal recognizes the lifestyle that Dean leads is outside the norm and free from the normal responsibilities and trappings of adulthood. He is tempted by the promise of an almost child-like existence. By joining Dean on the road Sal succeeds in temporarily postponing the moment when he has to decide how he fits into society.

When contemplating one's place in society it is always tempting to revolt against the laws and norms dictated by that society. Deciding to place oneself in opposition to the prevailing society is an easy way out. A cursory glance at Dean's life may give the impression that he has chosen this path; however, we eventually realize that he is outside of society as a whole, so he has no need to consciously fight against it. Sal is also tempted by this battle against society, most conspicuously when he is living in San Francisco with Remi Boncoeur. Remi habitually steals from the barracks they are meant to be guarding, and Sal eventually joins him. As Sal states: "I suddenly began to realize that everybody in America is a natural-born thief. I was getting the bug myself." We also see the effects of taking this path when Sal visits Old Bull Lee (a fictionalized William S. Burroughs) in New Orleans. Bull Lee is a drug addict, and this section of the book contains the most references to drug-taking. Taking illegal drugs is a most obvious and time-honored way to place oneself in direct opposition to society. Sal is tempted by this path but, again, does not take it.

Sometimes instead of trying to find one's place in society, or consciously railing against it, a character is firmly entrenched outside of society. This is the case with Dean, who has never conformed and never will conform to the norms of society. He marries, but has no intention of honoring his vows. He pays no mind to the kind of ties that would usually hold a person down, instead preferring to follow his own lead traveling across the country and back whenever the fancy strikes him. For the most part, Sal and the others seem to understand that this is how Dean is, and bear him no ill will for it. In fact, it is exactly this remove from society and its rules that attracted Sal to Dean. In Dean, Sal sees an escape from society.

What Sal eventually realizes, is that this is in Dean's nature; he was raised by a transient father and had no roots growing up. He has had no role models and never learned about personal responsibility. While this life outside of society may seem appealing for a while, Dean is eventually shown to be an intensely unhappy character, whom Sal comes to pity, rather than adore.

Georgina Willms

KESEY, KEN   *One Flew Over the Cuckoo's Nest* (1962)

Written during the 1960s and tapping into many of the concerns of the contemporary counterculture Ken Kesey's *One Flew Over the Cuckoo's Nest* explores themes such as identity, heroism, and the corrupt nature of authority.

The novel is set in a mental institution ruled over by the authoritarian Big Nurse, a tyrannical figure who controls every aspect of her male patients' lives through fear and intimidation. Big Nurse allows her orderlies to abuse the patients and uses electro-shock therapy as a means to punish them when they disobey her. Among those in the hospital is the paranoid half-white, half–Native American, Chief Bromden. Bromden narrates the novel, which centers on the appearance of a new patient, Randle P. McMurphy, who will come to challenge Big Nurse's iron grip.

McMurphy's subversive nature leads him to rebel against the rule of Big Nurse, the Chief's name for Nurse Rached. He does this by restoring a sense of self-worth and dignity in the other patients. While McMurphy is ultimately lobotomized for his disruptive actions, his rebellion is still a triumph as it causes Big Nurse to lose control over the men. McMurphy's success is most obvious in Chief Bromden's escape from the hospital. At the end of the novel Bromden is able to lift a cast-iron work unit off the ground and throw it through a window, something he would not have been able to do before McMurphy had rebuilt his confidence.

David Simmons

HEROISM in *One Flew Over the Cuckoo's Nest*
The idea of heroism is an important element in *One Flew Over the Cuckoo's Nest*. The novel contains a

subtle but in-depth exploration of how we construct our heroes, what it means to be "heroic," and the results of this process on those who are singled out for such adulation.

Right from McMurphy's initial appearance we are told how the other characters conceive of him in a heroic mold. Chief Bromden thinks that McMurphy is a giant sent to rescue them from Big Nurse and notes that the rest of the patients "get a big kick out of going along with him." As the story progresses McMurphy takes on the appearance of a religious or spiritual hero, analogous to the figure of Jesus Christ. Harding, a patient leader, suggests that McMurphy could "work subconscious miracles." McMurphy organizes a fishing trip for 12 of the other men, "his dozen people," and upon being given electroshock therapy on a cross-shaped table he jokingly asks the attendant whether he gets "a crown of thorns." In addition to these religious allusions, the plot of the novel, in which McMurphy sacrifices his own life for the good of the other men, has obvious echoes of the biblical story of Jesus.

While the traditional hero is often a superhuman individual marked out by his superior strength or physical prowess, the novel frequently highlights how normal McMurphy is. Perhaps most significantly, at one point in the early part of the novel McMurphy is unable to lift a heavy control panel off the ground. While we are never convinced that he will be able to achieve such a Herculean feat, his declaration to the other patients that he "tried though" has its own heroic significance, given the manner in which McMurphy encourages the men to stand up for themselves to Big Nurse.

McMurphy's subversive actions and anti-establishment attitudes mark him out as an antihero, a common figure in American novels of the 1960s. Indeed, *One Flew Over the Cuckoo's Nest* explores America's relationship with the antiheroic. Once Big Nurse learns of the patients' adoration of McMurphy she attempts to discredit him. She tries to downplay McMurphy's heroism by ridiculing the idea that he is savior-like: "And yet," she went on, "he seems to do things without thinking of himself at all, as if he were a martyr or a saint. Would anyone venture that McMurphy is a saint?" However, such is the patients' love of McMurphy that when Big Nurse

tries to suggest McMurphy is manipulating them for the worse the patients refuse her suggestions: "I feel *compelled* to defend my friend's honor as a good old red, white, and blue hundred-per-cent American con man." Harding's comments imply that the patients both realize and embrace McMurphy's supposed moral failings. Though the hero conventionally embodies the values of the establishment that he belongs to, the novel's depiction of the hospital ward as a corrupt, abusive, and dehumanizing place means that we, like the patients, have little problem in siding with McMurphy over Big Nurse and her staff.

Interestingly, the novel also suggests that the patient's worshiping of McMurphy has negative effects for him. As the story reaches its conclusion Chief Bromden realizes that the role of hero might have more drawbacks for McMurphy than he and the other patients initially thought: "I wondered how McMurphy slept, plagued by a hundred faces like that, or two hundred, or a thousand." The sense that McMurphy is trapped by the needs the patients have of him is also made apparent. When McMurphy has a chance to escape from the ward but refuses, the Chief suggests: "It was like he'd signed on for the whole game and there wasn't any way of him breaking his contract."

Ultimately McMurphy is successful as a hero, saving the other patients from Big Nurse. Though in one sense he "loses" his battle against Big Nurse and is lobotomized at her command, by the end of the novel he has managed to pass on his life-affirming sense of self-belief and self-worth to the other men. This positive message enables the patients to overcome their fear of Big Nurse and face the prospect of leaving the hospital for good.

David Simmons

IDENTITY in *One Flew Over the Cuckoo's Nest*

As the novel begins we are introduced to the narrator, Chief Bromden, as the orderlies on the mental ward are mocking him. The staff thinks of him as a child and treats him like an object, calling him "Chief Broom," this introduction is indicative of the novel's preoccupation with identity and the various ways in which society attempts to control us by denigrating certain peoples and lifestyles. For the Chief suggests that those who work on the ward are only a small part of a much larger organization called "The Combine" that is trying to make everyone and everything in American society the same: "like, for example—a train . . . laying a string of full-grown men in mirrored suits and machined hats, laying them like a hatch of identical insects."

As the story progresses we learn that the Chief's conflicted sense of identity is due not only to being undermined by those in authority but also to an internal crisis concerning his mixed race ethnicity. As a half-white, half-Native American, the Chief seems torn between two ways of being. Unable to find an identity that he feels comfortable with, the Chief instead acts as he thinks others expect him to: "I was just being the way I looked, the way people wanted. It don't seem like I ever have been me." The Chief's identity crisis also represents a larger issue concerning the destruction of American Indian identity. We are told that the removal of the Chief's father from his land was partially instigated by his white mother who became the dominant force in the relationship. This led the Chief to take his mother's surname instead of his father's, an act that is symptomatic of white assimilation of indigenous cultures.

The other patients, oppressed by Big Nurse, share the Chief's confused sense of identity. Nurse Ratched controls the patients, instilling in them a belief that they are abnormal and need to adjust in order to fit into "normal" society, as one of the patients sarcastically states "Not talk me into it, no. I was born a rabbit. Just look at me. I simply need the nurse to make me *happy* with my role." Harding, in particular, is important here, the novel implying that he is a closet homosexual unable to declare his homosexuality for fear of ridicule by the wider society.

While Big Nurse manipulates any sense of identity the other patients have, she is largely unable to control McMurphy in a similar manner. The appearance of McMurphy is markedly different from our introduction to the Chief. While Chief Bromden is presented as a repressed and downtrodden character, McMurphy's individuality lends him a strength of personality and belief in himself that the other patients initially lack. The Chief says that McMurphy "sounds like he's way above them, talk-ing down, like he's sailing fifty yards overhead, hollering at those below on the ground. He sounds big" and suggests that he is this way because "He hadn't let what he looked like run his life one way or the other, any more than he'd let the Combine mill him into fitting where they wanted him to fit."

In opposition to the harmful practices of Big Nurse, McMurphy tries to restore the other patients' confidence, turning them from "rabbits" back into men. He does this by encouraging the men to believe in their own self-worth and by teaching them that it is Nurse Ratched who is in the wrong. McMurphy's independent actions and the positive effects they have on the other patients suggest that a strong sense of "who we are" is important to our personal well–being. Indeed, the novel ends with two events that demonstrate this belief. First, the Chief smothers the lobotomized McMurphy in order to prevent Big Nurse from using McMurphy as a tool to control future patients, and, second, the newly restored Chief is able to escape from the mental institution by hurling a cast-iron control panel through a window. Both actions represent a desire to state the importance of the individual maintaining control over his or her own identity in the face of society's attempts to change it. As the Chief notes at the end of the novel "I been away a long time."

David Simmons

OPPRESSION in *One Flew Over the Cuckoo's Nest*

Reflecting the anti-authoritarian ethos of the 1960s, the novel suggests that society tries to control our actions through oppressive practices. In the book we are presented with numerous examples of those with power attempting to tell characters with less power how to behave. Most obviously this occurs through the characters of Big Nurse and her orderlies, who are effectively employed with the sole purpose of controlling the patients. While the structure of the hospital system means that the staff must tell those under their care what to do, the novel suggests that Nurse Ratched goes beyond mere supervision and instead seeks to rule over all elements of the patients' lives.

At the start of the novel we are introduced to the narrator, Chief Bromden, as the hospital orderlies are mocking him. We soon learn that this abuse is not particular to the Chief and that the staff at one time or another have mistreated all of the patients on the ward. There is institutionally sanctioned rape, with the orderlies habitually inducting new patients onto the ward by abusing them. The Chief tells us about Ellis and Ruckly, two patients that have been irreparably damaged by electroshock therapy, and about Mr. Taber, a former patient whose refusal to endure the abuse dealt out by the staff led to his being given a frontal lobotomy.

While the majority of the oppression in the novel takes place on the ward as a direct result of Big Nurse's practices we are also presented with examples outside of the hospital where oppression has taken place; Billy Bibbit's emotional development as a young man has been repressed by an overprotective mother while Harding has repressed his homosexuality for fear of the negative repercussions of "coming out" in a society that still frowns upon being gay. The novel repeatedly provides us with examples of minorities being criticized or treated poorly by the majority within society, as Harding notes: "the great voice of millions chanting 'Shame. Shame. Shame.' It's society's way of dealing with someone different." Chief Bromden is a pertinent example of this. The Chief recollects his childhood and the manner in which white society (including his own mother) tried to oppress his father and the tribe to which they belonged. Such is the effect of white oppression that the Chief chooses to withdraw from the world by pretending that he is deaf and dumb.

Indeed, whether or not we choose to read the hospital ward as a representative microcosm of wider society, the novel seems to be heavily criticizing what it believes is the repressive nature of postwar America. This sentiment is made overt by Chief Bromden's belief in "The Combine," a secret state-sanctioned organization that is trying to engineer society so that everyone looks the same, lives the same lifestyle, and behaves in the same way.

McMurphy, the (anti-) hero of the story, comes onto the ward to free the other patients from Big Nurse's oppressive regime. McMurphy, it seems, has escaped the oppression of society if only due to his refusal to be a part of it. The Chief notes: "logging, gambling, running carnival wheels, travelling light-footed and fast, keeping on the move so much that the Combine never had a chance to get anything installed." However, as the novel progresses we learn that McMurphy has also suffered from oppression. Growing up, McMurphy was in and out of prison and work farms for not conforming to society's rules. Furthermore, the novel implies that the total reliance the other patients have in McMurphy's saving them becomes an oppressive force, leaving the character trapped into a course of action that will eventually lead to his death.

McMurphy has been able to retain his "sanity" only through the realization that it is those in authority who are in the wrong rather than him, and he subsequently leads the other patients to freedom by getting them to realize this too. Indeed, it is an irony that by the end of the story we view many, if not all, of the patients on the ward as being less "sick" than those who have oppressed them for so long.

David Simmons

KINCAID, JAMAICA   *Annie John* (1985)

Kincaid's text tells the coming-of-age story of Annie John, whom we meet as a 10-year-old Antiguan girl at the beginning of the novel. She will grow up to become a strong-minded 17-year-old whom we leave, at the end of the novel, as she is about to move from her island to the "motherland" (England) to get an education. Annie John is, from early on, a successful student. She does very well in the colonial school system and, as a young girl, strives to meet the expectations of her surroundings, especially her mother with whom she has a strong, loving relationship. However, this relationship will erode as Annie grows older and slowly separates from her mother, who grows strange, even foreign, to Annie. The new experiences Annie lives through outside the home and her school, the freedom she finds away from her mother and often without her knowing, the unsettling emotions Annie begins to feel for young girls around her—all these events combine to further wear away the mother-daughter relationship and to unveil and confirm Annie's strong desire for change and difference, her longing for an "elsewhere."

The following themes—COMING OF AGE, IDENTITY, INNOCENCE AND EXPERIENCE—all offer perspectives from which to reflect upon Annie's journey toward adulthood, a journey paved with many obstacles that acquaint or reacquaint the reader with the difficulties a smart and unconventional young girl encounters when confronted with the high expectations of a traditional family and community.

Sophie Croisy

COMING OF AGE in *Annie John*

The term *coming of age* implies a series of changes in the life of a child or adolescent. Generally, these changes are synonymous with upheaval. Annie John goes through a series of transitional moments (she grows from child to young adult) that greatly modify her self-image and destabilize her relationship with her surroundings. The text takes her through a series of realizations that come to deconstruct the truths she had relied on as a child and leave much room for uncertainty in her life.

Her first real intrusion from the world of adulthood happens through death. The death of a schoolmate—Nalda, 10 years old—forces Annie to depart from her childhood world of carelessness and ignorance when she realizes that "until then, I had not known that children died." Even if it is a consciousness-raising event, her attitude toward that death is rather detached as she turns drama into a subject of gossip: "At school, I told my friends about this death. I would take them aside individually, so I could repeat the details over and over again." Though she is confronted with death, she does not express any real sensitivity to it and intellectualizes the experience without feeling for the dead and the mourners. It is only when death gets close, and when her father tells her the story of his grandmother's death that she merges knowing and feeling in her reaction to death. Her slowly developing ability to know and feel at the same time shows maturity in Annie John, though this union of logos and pathos in dealing with life events will remain, throughout her growing up, a difficult process for Annie.

On an anatomical level, Annie's growing up implies bodily changes that lead to a mis-recognition of her own self in the mirror: at 12, "small tufts of hair had appeared under my arms, and when I perspired the smell was strange, as if I had turned into a strange animal." Anatomical disturbances highly perturb Annie, who often comes to feel "too big and too small at once" as if the constant changes that come with growing up leave her in a middle place between childhood and adulthood where nothing is familiar, recognizable. This liminal position gets so disturbing and damaging that Annie falls sick. While bedridden and feverish, Annie looks at the pictures around her room: "none of the people in the wedding picture, except for me, had any face left. In the picture of my mother and father, I had erased them from the waist down. In the picture of me wearing my confirmation dress, I had erased all of myself except for the shoes." Her sickness is without a name, but it is a symptom of a transition that involves a mis-recognition of her body and surroundings. The erasure of parts of the people from the pictures she looks at symbolizes this mis-recognition: Annie is not as she used to be, nor is her life, nor are her parents' attitudes toward her. This new state of things materializes in her mother's change of attitude toward Annie from the moment she turns 12 onward: no more dressing in a fabric similar to her mother's, and no more "childish" ritual of looking through an old trunk full of things from the past. Thus, Annie experiences the end of a harmonious relationship with her mother and reads her mother's change of attitude as a complete rejection, which plays a role in Annie's developing her "transition sickness."

Annie's unclear position between childhood and adulthood is exemplified through her constant change of attitude toward life: She goes back and forth between feelings. She is a child when she hates her mother for breaking their strong bond and thus betraying Annie's love, but she is an adult when she begins to see her mother as a woman with a life of her own—not just as the object of Annie's affection. She can reject the present and the unavoidable march into adulthood by sometimes wishing that "everything would fall away . . . no future full of ridiculous demands," but she can also welcome the future as she dreams of leaving her family and friends behind and traveling to Belgium. She will eventually accomplish her goal of going abroad though she remains, when she departs at 17, torn between a childish attachment to the past and the prospect of an independent life on the old continent, the life of a young adult.

Sophie Croisy

IDENTITY in *Annie John*

Annie John, from the very start of the story, does not show a personality that would compare with the image her mother (and main caretaker) has of her as a child. Neither, as she grows up, does she become the young lady her mother wants her to become. Through a series of trials, Annie John constructs her own identity outside the frames of reference her mother would like to impose on her (so that she can become a proper young Antiguan lady with a good education and a good husband to boot). As a girl of 10, her attraction to beautiful things and beautiful people and her desire to control them leads her to show both kindness (mainly the type of kindness that brings forth her intellectual superiority) and violence (she hurts the thing she loves in an attempt to control it). This behavior is made visible by her relationship with Sonia, a school friend: "I loved very much—and so used to torment until she cried—a girl named Sonia . . . I would try to get to school early and give her my homework so that she could copy it . . . I thought her beautiful and I would say so . . . At recess, I would buy her a sweet . . . Then I would pull at hair on her arms and legs—gently at first, and then awfully hard, holding it up tight with the tips of my fingers until she cried." This love-hate relationship with beautiful girls her age is a running motif throughout the novel (her schoolmate Gwen and a wild girl she names "the Red Girl" will be Annie's adolescent crushes), as are the cruelty, lies, and disobedient behavior resulting from an unquenchable curiosity, an attraction to the forbidden, and a desire for independence and freedom fed by an intelligence way above average. For instance, still at the age of 10, she lies to her mother about her whereabouts in order to go to a funeral and see a dead body after having been forbidden to go. Later on, she will "go to the lighthouse behind my mother's back" and experience the height, the danger, the dizziness when at the top accompanied by her love, the Red Girl, of whom her mother knows nothing. In order to keep her mother and father happy, how-ever, she lies and cheats so they will not know what she thinks, who she is, what she really wants. She constructs her true identity away from and outside of her parents' ring of control.

She puts her intelligence to good use as she always performs wonderfully in the English school system of Antigua, which makes her family really proud. However, even though she takes in the education received through that system and uses the system for advancement, she has a mind of her own and is critical of this system and its colonial context: She knows quite well what England, the motherland, did to her African ancestors, though she keeps her critiques to herself. Among other things, she secretly loves looking at the "Columbus in Chains" picture in her history book "to see the usually triumphant Columbus, brought so low, seated at the bottom of a boat just watching things go by." Her intelligence also helps her become a respected and feared leader among her girl friends outside the classroom. She is the strong and bold mind upon which the group relies, a group infused with Annie's love for independence, misbehavior, and her dismissal of the rules, regulations, and expectations of the adult world: "We were sure that the much-talked-about future that everybody was preparing for us would never come, for we had such a powerful feeling against it, and why shouldn't our will prevail?" As she grows up, Annie continues to refuse the intrusion of the inconvenient rules of the adult world, but as always, in front of her mother and family, she tries to "pass" as a proper young lady. Nonetheless, she feels a secret love for other girls and is happy with her secret wanderings and her manipulative ways, so much so that even as she grows into a young adult, she manages to preserve and further develop this self-constructed identity based on self-trust and the rejection of traditional notions about life and expectations for women. When Annie is 17 and about to leave for England, she can hardly hide her feeling of repulsion when her mother tells her, "you are a young lady now, and we won't be surprised if in due time you write to say that one day soon you are to be married.'" "'How absurd!'" are the words of Annie in response to her mother's commentary, a response that fur-ther emphasizes Annie's clear departure from her family's envisioning of her future, of her identity—her sexual identity, among other things.

Sophie Croisy

INNOCENCE AND EXPERIENCE in *Annie John*

The young Annie John's innocence loses ground little by little as important life experiences become crucial sites of knowledge for Annie, who is becoming a young adult. The first noteworthy moment of knowledge is Annie's first encounter with DEATH, the death of one of her schoolmates: "until then, [she] had not known that children died." Not only does she find access to knowledge about this universal and omnipresent concern for humankind, and thus slowly departs from the self-centered and careless world of CHILDHOOD, but she also comes to know death on a more physical level: She goes to funerals to witness death and try to understand its implications for the dead and the living

School is also the place where her own knowledge of life gets expanded and exacerbated through sharing knowledge with others. It is with her classmates that Annie regularly goes to the churchyard after a week of school: "we would sit and sing songs, use forbidden words, and, of course, show each other various parts of our bodies. While some of us watched, the others would walk up and down on the large tombstones showing off their legs." Socializing with schoolmates is the occasion for breaking the rules of language and behavior, which implies a loss of innocence: no more blind acceptance of the rules of life at home and life in school when these rules limit the acquisition of new knowledge. School is the place where knowledge is produced, where experience happens. There, Annie learns about pleasing others, specifically teachers, in order to have what she wants. She learns about playing "the good student" and she performs her misdeeds knowing that this protective veil of quasi-perfection will take her out of many uncomfortable situations. She thus learns hypocrisy, but whatever she does, her actions get redeemed by the fame she manages to acquire through excellence in school: "I was soon given responsibility for overseeing the class in the teacher's absence . . I would never dillydally with a decision, always making up my mind right away about the thing in front of me. Sometimes, seeing my old frail self in a girl, I would defend her; sometimes, seeing my old frail self in a girl, I would be heartless and cruel. It all went over quite well, and I became very popular."

Starting to listen to and observe her close surroundings is also an important aspect of knowledge production for Annie. The people closest to her are her parents, and her growing up leads to her questioning the validity of her parents' teachings: "Often I had been told by my mother not to feel proud of anything I had done and in the next breath that I couldn't feel enough pride about something I had done." The REJECTION of her parents' many double standards and their hypocrisy leads to Annie dismissing their authority, disobeying them on every occasion she gets, manipulating them, and even stealing from them. Her realization that her father had other women and other children before her mother and herself came into the picture, her witnessing her parents having sexual intercourse, her listening to her father's stories about his harsh childhood, all these elements render mother and father less perfect and more human, and Annie's observations give birth to an emotional distance between parents and daughter.

This witnessing of their imperfections marks the end of Annie's innocence and the beginning of her involvement in the complications proper to the world of adults, a world she learns to know and live in, and at the same time rejects because of its falsehood. It is a world that focuses on appearances, on the way you look and behave in public (Annie both uses this knowledge for her own good and rejects it when she sees it in others); hence her mother's rough reaction when Annie, then 15, only briefly talks to a boy she used to know when she meets him in the street on her way back from school. Their innocent conversation is interpreted by her mother, who saw the scene, as improper behavior: "it had pained her to see me behave in the manner of a slut (only she used the French patois word for it) in the street and that just to see me had caused her to feel shame." Annie, when old enough to do so, will decide to leave her island and its strict rules in order to live a less static, less restricted life and not have to play the hypocritical game of perfection anymore.

Sophie Croisy

KINCAID, JAMAICA *A Small Place* (1988)

Kincaid was born and raised in Antigua while it was still a British colony. She received a British education and learned the British view of history. Leaving Antigua at 16 to become an au-pair (live-in babysitter) in New York, she did not return to Antigua for 20 years. By that time, Antigua was no longer a British colony but had become an independent nation, with a freely elected black government. However, the average Antiguan was worse off than before, buildings were in disrepair, the government was corrupt, and the people seemed unable to believe that anything could change for the better. A tiny minority of well-to-do white people still exerted a tremendous negative influence on the island's native inhabitants, the descendants of slaves who had begun to arrive shortly after Columbus discovered the island in 1493.

Kincaid begins her essay from the point of view of a white male tourist from North America or Europe. She shows how the tourist commodifies Antigua and Antiguans in the same way the British colonizers did—the island and its inhabitants become things to be consumed, to be experienced for a price. Because the tourist feels so superior to the poor ignorant native, tourism to third-world nations is a form of imperialism, very similar to the attitude of innate superiority adopted by white British colonial officials. The corrupt black government, which is now impoverishing Antiguans even more, learned its methods from the colonizers. The very poor Antiguans who continue to freely elect the same corrupt government are, after six centuries of degradation by slavery and colonialism, passive, ignorant of any world history or political theory that could change their lot, and unable to imagine that they have the power to change anything.

Barbara Z. Thaden

COMMODIFICATION/COMMERCIALIZATION in *A Small Place*

Jamaica Kincaid begins her acerbic commentary on the life of the inhabitants of a tiny island by looking at it through the eyes of a tourist. Antigua is an island of breathtaking beauty, a popular tourist destination because the constant drought, a bane to the poor islanders who must conserve every drop of water, almost guarantees sunny weather for the tourists fleeing their cloudy and cold climates. The tourist sees the beauty of the island commodified for his consumption, but does not see the government corruption responsible for this commodification, and does not notice the poverty and ignorance in which the inhabitants live because their government (the post-colonial, post-British government) has robbed them of their wealth and land.

The government is all too ready to allow the commodification of the island's only natural resource—its beauty—to enrich itself. It sells large pieces of land to foreign investors, who build ugly condominium communities designed for foreigners on Antigua's "commodity," the land itself. The tourist thinks he is eating fresh, locally grown vegetables and locally caught seafood, while in reality this food, a commodity like any other, has first been shipped to Miami for "processing," then sent back to Antigua, at a hugely inflated price, to sell for a profit, a profit that finds its way into American and not Antiguan hands.

To the tourist, Antigua itself is a commodity, something to be purchased and enjoyed for a week or two. The native Antiguans also are, for the tourist, commodities to be enjoyed, as he watches them creating small souvenirs from scraps of cloth, observes their quaint and, to him, primitive customs, and their colorful (but incorrect) use of the English language. But the Antiguans know they are being commodified, being sold along with the tourist package as local scenery and culture. They know that the tourist can never imagine them as people like himself. He cannot imagine that the native Antiguan hates and despises him, because she is too poor to leave Antigua and tour other places where she could feel superior. Antigua is not only a home but also a prison. "Every native of every place is a potential tourist," writes Kincaid: Every native would like to escape the monotony and boredom of his or her own life. But almost every native everywhere is not able to do this; capitalism, the creator of commodities, has not left the native with the resources necessary to live comfortably in his homeland, much less to travel as a tourist to another country and be diverted by the natives there. The tourist, who makes of the natives a "commodity," is an ugly human being to those being commodified.

Poor people, people like the native Antiguans (the descendants of slaves), distrust capitalism, commodification, and the wealth that both can bring, because the rise of capitalism in the Western world is a direct result of the slave trade, a fact that is omitted from history books. As slaves, the natives of Antigua were not the capitalists, but quite literally the capital, the commodity that was traded and made the white capitalists wealthy. Nothing the author can imagine can ever make up for this centuries-long commerce in human flesh that is her only heritage. Commerce has robbed her of her country, her language, and her culture. She can never know from what part of Africa her ancestors came, what language they spoke, what customs they had. She can write only in the capitalist's language, study the capitalist's version of history, and try to express her great grief and rage that wealthy whites still do not recognize the magnitude of their crimes and still see and treat black inhabitants of third-world nations as intellectual and cultural inferiors.

Barbara Z. Thaden

JUSTICE in *A Small Place*

There is no justice in a small place for those who live there permanently, at least for the vast majority of those who are the descendants of slaves. The essay begins with the injustice of the natives having to endure, still, the wealth and arrogance and ignorance of their former enslavers and colonizers, whose descendants are now visiting as "tourists." For the white, wealthy tourist Antigua is an island paradise, while for its natives it is an island prison.

There is injustice in the fact that the former oppressors still own all the profits of their cruelty and ruthlessness. The white nations still possess the wealth created by enslaving Africans and using their free labor to enrich themselves. There is certainly no justice in seeing that, even in post-colonial Antigua, the wealthiest inhabitants are still white or foreign or both, while the "natives" to whom the country now supposedly belongs still live in the most humble poverty. There is no justice in the main source of legal income being tourism, white tourism, where the role of the black Antiguan is to

be the perfect servant and where the perfect education is being a graduate of the celebrated Hotel Training School.

Living under a freely elected, inefficient, corrupt black government and knowing that the former white rulers are saying, "We told you so," is a bitter injustice, as is the fact that the only way to become rich in Antigua is to be a corrupt government official, one whose wealth comes from being bribed by those who have money. Drug dealers and white foreigners buy up the land and build things only tourists and foreigners can enjoy, like condominiums, gambling casinos, and private clubs.

There is no justice in the descendants of slaves being robbed of their native language and their native culture and religion so that they have only the oppressor's language in which to complain, the oppressor's God to pray to, and the oppressor's history (in which they play no discernible part) by which to understand their place in the world. There is no justice in being forced to memorize a history in which all the heroes are really your greatest enemies—those who discovered lands to conquer, their Indian populations to eliminate and replace with African slaves, to create empires and enrich themselves at the expense of everything you and your ancestors ever had. And nothing imaginable can ever make up for this greatest of all injustices, the enslaving of an entire race and the erasing of their entire history and culture, creating a commodity out of people who once had a language and a culture of their own but for centuries were not allowed even to own their children, much less speak their own language or practice their own religion. "Even if I really came from people who were living like monkeys in trees," writes Kincaid, "it was better to be that than what happened to me, what I became after I met you."

Injustice is apparent everywhere in Antigua—in the identities of those who own the grand mansions (corrupt government officials, drug lords, whites) and in the way the average black Antiguan is forced to live. Roads are in disrepair, schools are so ill-kept that they look like a row of latrines covered in dust, sewage is dumped directly into the Caribbean because the island has no sewage system, and the only hospital on the island is in such a state of filth and collapse that wealthy Antiguans fly to New York for medical care and poor Antiguans consider it a death sentence to be taken to such a place.

This state of injustice has existed for centuries. First, the black Antiguans were slaves, then they were the colonized, forced to maintain a very low position in society, and now they are the victims of a corrupt black government. Kincaid is dismayed that what at first seems like progress—the slaves are emancipated, the colony becomes a free, self-governing nation—is not progress at all. Instead of being miseducated, the population now seems uneducated, and their will to effect positive changes seems paralyzed.

Barbara Z. Thaden

OPPRESSION in *A Small Place*

The history of Antigua is a history of oppression. Discovered by Christopher Columbus in 1493, the tiny, surreally beautiful island in the Leeward Islands was colonized by "human rubbish from Europe," those unhappy, unsuccessful-at-home white people who, to satisfy their avarice, immediately brought African slaves to Antigua to toil on sugar plantations. The author writes as a descendant of those African slaves, whose history and culture and language and religion is nothing but the history and culture and language and religion of slavery and oppression. When England outlawed the slave trade and then slavery itself in its colonies, those who had become wealthy through the slave trade continued to become even wealthier through oppressing and exploiting the formerly enslaved Africans.

The Barclay brothers, for example, who had become wealthy through slave-trading, became even wealthier as bankers by investing the savings of the former slaves and lending it back to them with interest. The white, colonial government, which ruled until 1947, educated all former slaves using the British curriculum, which emphasized the grand history of Britain and the benighted condition of the Africans who were rescued from savagery and transported to this British colony to become Christians and to become civilized (eventually) but to always be so much less than, so far below, any white British subject precisely because they had needed to be rescued from savagery in the first place.

Allowed only the most menial positions (laundress, waiter, servant), these black Antiguans lived in grinding poverty while white Antiguans lived in luxury. Even emigrants from the Middle East and Jewish refugees from Hitler's racist extermination policy of World War II in Europe came to Antigua and oppressed those black Antiguans whose ancestors had been there since the time of Columbus.

What really infuriates Kincaid is that after Antiguans gained their independence from Britain and became a self-governing country, the average Antiguan was even worse off under the newly elected black government than he had been under the British. She asks, "Have you ever wondered that all we ever learned from you is how to corrupt our societies and how to be tyrants?" The reason, to her, is obvious. To the natives, the British government had always seemed to be only a tyrant and kidnapper and thief, who took what was not its own and made laws to enrich itself and oppress its former slaves. The average black Antiguan was educated to know his inferiority, his inability to really fight off this white capitalism, which impoverished most of the islanders, so that when a black government did come to power, it knew only how to sell itself to the highest (white or foreign) bidder and enrich itself through corruption. The people of such a small place have no history with which to compare this, no cultural or national identity with which to counter such a government, not even a self-imposed morality by which to judge themselves. Because they live in a small place, they are not aware of much that is going on in the world, and because they are the descendants of slaves, they have either been denied an education entirely or educated and indoctrinated into the belief that they are inferior while the white race is naturally superior and magnanimous enough to allow the black inhabitants to live in the shadow of their superiority and benefit from the greatness of their culture. Thus, while Kincaid mourns the wreck of the once magnificent library where she used to read as a girl, and blames the corrupt black government and the uncooperative wealthy white citizens for allowing it to remain in disrepair, she at the same time acknowledges that everything she read there reinforced the greatness of British culture, British history, British government, the English language, and Britain itself, while completely leaving out any history of her own ancestors, how they arrived in Antigua, how they were treated, and how the British Empire grew wealthy through slavery in its colonies. This great mental as well as social and physical oppression has left her people with a profound feeling of powerlessness, an incomplete understanding of cause and effect, and a belief that they can only be victims of circumstances that they cannot control. Antiguans must learn to understand that they are capable of taking control of their destiny, and whites must acknowledge the atrociousness of their crimes and their responsibility for the misrule that is affecting so many freed British colonies, so that both peoples can become fully human, neither victim nor victimizer.

Barbara Z. Thaden

KINGSOLVER, BARBARA *The Bean Trees* (1988)

Barbara Kingsolver's debut novel, *The Bean Trees*, first published in 1988, has since become a landmark text in environmental and ecofeminist literature. The narrative follows the life of Marietta Greer, a teenager living in Pittman County, Kentucky, who works at the local hospital until she saves up enough money to buy herself a Volkswagen bug so she can leave town and avoid getting pregnant. On her trip west she passes through Taylorville and renames herself Taylor. She continues westward, driving through Oklahoma, where a Cherokee woman abandons a baby girl in Taylor's car. Taylor names the baby Turtle and discovers that the baby has been physically and sexually abused. Taylor's car malfunctions when she arrives in Arizona where she meets Mattie, the owner of a tire repair shop. Mattie gives shelter to illegal immigrants above her shop, among them Estevan and Esperanza, a couple fleeing from Guatemala where they had to abandon their daughter Ismene when guerrillas kidnapped the child to force them to betray their colleagues. In Arizona, Taylor finds work with Mattie and room and board with Lou Ann Ruiz, another single mother whose husband has abandoned her and her child, Dwayne Ray.

As the story progresses Turtle develops a fondness for anything related to nature and is able to identify fauna and flora easily. Edna Poppy, a blind neighbor babysits Turtle often, and one night a prowler attacks the little girl. Though Edna saves Turtle from harm, a social worker threatens to take Turtle away when she discovers Taylor has no legal papers of guardianship. Taylor travels to Oklahoma to find Turtle's parents, together with Estevan and Esperanza, who are in danger of being discovered in Arizona and are hoping to find asylum elsewhere. When Turtle's parents cannot be found, Estevan and Esperanza pose as her parents before a judge, once again being forced to metaphorically give up their daughter. The couple remains in Oklahoma finding sanctuary in a church and among the Native Americans. Taylor obtains legal guardianship of Turtle, returning with her to Arizona to start a new life.

This quest narrative explores themes of ABANDONMENT, GENDER conflicts, NATURE, immigration, ecofeminism, ecocriticism, and ALIENATION.

Lourdes Arciniega

ABANDONMENT in *The Bean Trees*

The theme of abandonment permeates Barbara Kingsolver's *The Bean Trees*, propelling the narrative forward and becoming a strong motivator for several characters' emotional growth. Abandonment surfaces from the start of the novel when the reader meets the protagonist, Marietta Greer, and learns that Marietta's father abandoned her mother when she became pregnant. Marietta refuses to conform to the fate of other teenage girls of the town who become pregnant, drop out of school, and lead fruitless lives. Marietta gets a job, buys a used car, and abandons her mother to travel and carve an alternate life for herself. Abandonment plays an important role in her social development because when she travels she not only breaks all social ties with her past, but also her first action upon leaving Pittman County, Kentucky, the town where she grew up, is to discard her given name and rename herself Taylor.

As Taylor continues to travel through Oklahoma and Cherokee territory, she meets an Indian woman at a bar who abandons her niece in Taylor's car. Taylor, who is running away from the risk of becoming pregnant, now finds herself a surrogate mother to a girl whom she names Turtle.

Taylor drives farther west until she reaches Arizona, where she is forced to stop when her car breaks down. There she finds work with Mattie who runs a tire shop and befriends Estevan and Esperanza, illegal emigrants from Guatemala who seek shelter in Mattie's home after guerrillas kidnapped their daughter in their home country. These guerrillas blackmailed Estevan and Esperanza, asking them to give up their friends if they wanted to see their daughter alive. Unwilling to lead their friends to certain death, and willing to sacrifice the life of one to save 17 others, the couple was forced to make an unbearable choice, to abandon their daughter and flee to the United States.

In Arizona, Taylor also befriends Lou Ann Ruiz, another single parent who was abandoned by her husband Angel when their son Dwayne Ray was born. Lou Ann and Taylor become an unusual family unit as two single mothers who struggle to raise their children on their own. A few months later, Angel asks Lou Ann to move with him to Montana and live with him in a yurt or to allow him to return. Lou Ann, who has by now found a job, refuses to leave Arizona or to take Angel back.

Turtle, who was sexually and physically abused before being abandoned with Taylor, personifies the strongest and most poignant example of abandonment in the novel. This early abandonment proves to be lifesaving for the little girl as she clings like her namesake mud turtle to Taylor, who struggles to bring some normalcy into her life. However, just as Turtle is emerging from her emotional shell, she is once again attacked while in the care of a blind woman. Although Turtle comes to no physical harm, she is emotionally scarred and withdraws once more. As a result of this incident, Social Services questions Taylor's guardianship of Turtle and the agency threatens to remove the little girl from the only stable home environment she has known. To legally adopt Turtle, Taylor has to show proof of abandonment.

In the meantime, Estevan and Esperanza face legal problems of their own as they cannot stay in Arizona unless they can produce documented proof that their life was in danger in Guatemala, but as Mattie says "when people run for their lives they frequently neglect to bring along their file cabinets of evidence" (159). For these refugees, abandoning their homeland and their daughter was not a choice but a cruel twist of fate.

Taylor is able to use the immigrant's lack of documentation to save Turtle by convincing Estevan and Esperanza to pretend they are Turtle's parents before a judge, so that they can fool him into believing that they are giving up Turtle's guardianship to Taylor. This second "abandonment" of Turtle, a child whom the couple had grown to love as their daughter proves to be both cathartic and heartbreaking for them, as this time they find power in the right to make a decision without being blackmailed.

The characters in *The Bean Trees* face familiar, social, governmental, and even spiritual abandonment. They are able to overcome their hopeless situations by cultivating emotional and social relationships that ensure they will not face an uncertain future on their own.

Lourdes Arciniega

GENDER in *The Bean Trees*

Women have traditionally remained within the domestic sphere, taking care of family and home, feeling marginalized and unable to access jobs in the public arena. Barbara Kingsolver challenges this conventional depiction of women by creating a fictional world that foregrounds strong, independent female characters who epitomize women's conflicting and conflicted roles within a patriarchal society.

Marietta Greer, the protagonist of *The Bean Trees,* comes from a strong-willed female lineage, descendants of Cherokee. Alice Greer is raising her daughter Marietta Greer as a single parent after her partner abandoned her. Alice supports Marietta's desire to leave the hopeless Pittman County in which they live, and encourages her to get a job and buy a car. Marietta refuses to become an unwed teenage mother like many of her schoolfriends and instead leaves town, asserting her independence and authority by renaming herself Taylor. The fact that Taylor is a gender-free name represents Taylor's unwillingness to be defined and confined by a name. The Greer women's strong will, stubbornness, and non-conformity foreshadow Taylor's unusual naming of her own daughter Turtle.

When Taylor arrives in Arizona she befriends Mattie, another unconventional female who runs a tire shop and a shelter for illegal immigrants. Mattie becomes a mother figure for Taylor and Turtle, combining an earth-mother image with a strong sense of social activism. In spite of her fear of exploding tires, Taylor works for Mattie as an apprentice mechanic to support Turtle and herself, once again working in a job that would traditionally be reserved for men. Taylor also shares a house with Lou Ann Ruiz, another single mother who has been abandoned by her husband. These two women create a family where the only male is Lou Ann's infant son. Taylor adopts the male role in this functional unit by working outside the home while Lou Ann takes care of domestic matters. As the novel progresses, though, Lou Ann becomes increasingly aware of her female strength by recalling her pregnancy and by being outraged at the doorknob in a strip joint representing a female body part which has to be pushed in to make it work: "like a woman is something you shove on and walk right through." Lou Ann eventually finds a job in a salsa factory as a line worker and is later promoted to manager. When her husband asks her to move and live with him in a yurt, she refuses to give up her newly found independence. Although Lou Ann dates other men, she is not interested in living with them and by the end of the novel she and Taylor have solidified their matriarchal family unit with Taylor's legal adoption of Turtle.

There are very few men given prominent mention in the novel. Most, like Turtle's unnamed attackers, are portrayed as violent predators. Angel Ruiz, Lou Ann's husband, is a selfish, lazy drunkard, so much so that even his own mother doesn't like him. The men Taylor meets during her trip west patronize her by criticizing her outspoken manner and try to scare her in an attempt to redress the gender balance. "I never could figure out why men thought they could impress a woman by making the world out to be such a big dangerous deal" says Taylor, logically pointing out that "we've got to live in the exact same world every damn day of the week, don't we?"

Estevan, Esperanza's husband, is the only man portrayed sympathetically. He is ironically lauded for his non-masculine qualities, such as sensibility and a willingness to express his love for his wife. Taylor becomes attracted to him precisely because he doesn't exhibit any of the stereotypical male attributes she has come across. Unlike Angel Ruiz, Estevan prioritizes family, friendship, and loyalty. His career itself is teaching English as a second language, which places him as a service provider, one who can be both empathetic and patient. Estevan also shatters myths about illegal immigrants by demonstrating through his flawless English that he is industrious, willing to embrace a foreign language, and to integrate himself within the community.

Illegal immigrants, American Indians, and the women in the novel are marginalized members of the society they inhabit. Taylor takes pride in her Cherokee blood and derives strength from this tribe's history of physical endurance and cultural survival. The novel highlights the strong association between the Native Americans' tradition of nurturing and protecting nature and women's roles as homemakers and caregivers. Taylor and Lou Ann Ruiz survive and succeed by creating strong bonds with their children and other women, and by nurturing themselves and those around them, instilling in them a love and respect of nature and all its creatures.

Lourdes Arciniega

NATURE in *The Bean Trees*

In *The Bean Trees*, Barbara Kingsolver depicts nature as an omnipresent character symbolizing the emotional turmoil faced by the main female protagonists. On the one hand, Mother Nature cradles and nurtures Turtle, Taylor, Estevan, Esperanza, and Lou Ann, giving each of them hope through her neverending cycle of rebirth, and yet this cycle also entails facing death. The women in the novel have a fierce, protective love for their children, greater even than their love of men. These women as single parents or single females have symbiotic relationships representative of nature's interdependence. The blind Edna depends on Virgie Mae to be her eyes and she in turn counteracts Virgie Mae's abrasive manner. Lou Ann helps Taylor embrace her natural abilities while Taylor instills self-confidence in Lou Ann.

When Mattie Greer renames herself Taylor, at the beginning of the novel, she experiences a rebirth as she takes command of her identity and the way she wants society to view her. As she travels west, Taylor also reacquaints herself with her Indian heritage by mailing a postcard of two Indian women to her mother, foreshadowing her own adoption of Turtle. Taylor also names the baby "April Turtle," giving her a first name signifying springtime and natural birth. When her aunt abandons her with Taylor, Turtle finds a second chance at life. Turtle herself repeats this cycle of reproduction and rebirth with her first word "bean," signifying her faith in the eventual appearance of a tree from the dried up bean in her hand. The tree will itself reproduce the natural cycle of life and represents the interdependence that its parts have with the whole. The wisteria tree, for example, which grows on almost barren soil, represents endurance and stubbornness, whereas the cereus flower, which blooms only once a year and can be smelled by Edna, represents the fragility of existence. This flower blooms only in the dark and needs to be left alone because, if it is plucked, it loses its fragrance, highlighting the precariousness of its roots.

This ecologically themed novel also foregrounds the idea of place and establishing roots. Most of the women who come to Arizona were born elsewhere. When Lou Ann's grandmother visits, she brings water from Tug Fork to baptize Dwayne Ray. Water symbolizes continuity and life, and yet Angel pours the water down the drain before it can be used, depicting him in opposition to natural life. Esperanza and Estevan had to uproot themselves from Guatemala and can find only temporary shelter in Arizona before fleeing to another land with a body of water, the Lake of the Cherokees. Taylor leaves Kentucky to find Turtle outside a bar and needs to return to Cherokee land to legally claim her before she can live in Arizona with her.

Turtle delights in learning the names of all the plants, and cares faithfully for the vegetables in her garden. Yet she also brings death into her cycle of life when she buries her dolls. At first Taylor thinks Turtle is burying the dolls and hoping more dolls will spring up, but later on she realizes that the baby is repeating her mother's burial at a cemetery. Turtle depends on all the women she meets whom she calls by their name with "ma" added to it, thereby acknowledging their mothering role in her life.

When Esperanza bonds with Turtle during their trip to Cherokee land, Esperanza finds in Turtle a surrogate for her daughter. For Esperanza however, this rebirth is accompanied by death, as she must come to terms with her permanent separation from her daughter Ismene by symbolically giving Turtle to Taylor at the end of the novel.

Kingsolver associates Turtle with nature (particularly birds) throughout the novel, as when Estevan tells an Indian story of how people survived in heaven with awkwardly shaped spoons by feeding each other. Estevan feeds Turtle and she takes the food "like a newborn bird." When Taylor takes Turtle to see a doctor and he tells her of the terrible abuse the girl suffered, Taylor sees a bird outside the doctor's window where it has made a nest inside a cactus, surviving amidst painful surroundings. Turtle utters her first word after seeing how Taylor and Lou Ann stop on the road to let a mother quail and her chicks pass by. Finally, after Turtle is attacked, a sparrow finds itself trapped inside the house but the women manage to set it free so that it becomes a harbinger of Turtle's own resilience and survival.

Nature is featured in the novel as an entity to be feared and respected. The protagonists are in awe of the flowers that bloom once a year, the vegetables that spring from dried up seeds, the wonders of a summer rainstorm in the desert. Because of their affinity with the Indian heritage and their interest in ecological conservation, Taylor, Turtle, and Lou Ann learn to nurture and respect their environment and its inhabitants.

Lourdes Arciniega

KINGSOLVER, BARBARA *The Poisonwood Bible* (1998)

The Price family moves from Georgia to the Congo on the eve of Congo's independence from Belgium. Baptist preacher Nathan Price has a Christianizing mission to fulfill in Kilanga. This mission, eventually jeopardized by the Kilanga community's unwillingness to accept Price's Christian authority and by the political turmoil raging in the country, turns into a life-changing experience for Orleanna, Nathan, and their four daughters. They will have to survive a brutal cultural shock as well as diseases, natural catastrophes, hunger, political instability, and other upheavals. This experience will turn into a test of faith. The members of the Price family will face this test not as a family kept together by a deeply suffocating patriarchal figure, but as separate individuals growing and gradually freeing themselves from the grasp of that absolute ruler. As the Congo sees its hope for democracy vanish after independence, the Price family disintegrates into nothingness: The fallen father is left behind somewhere in the Congolese jungle, and the girls-turning-into-women construct their lives away from each other and beyond the limits once imposed upon them by a conservative Christian father. This text can be further analyzed through three main themes: ETHICS, FAMILY, and GUILT. The notion of ethics plays out in the roles played by the text's Christian figures in the Christianizing/colonizing process. Family is evoked by the disintegration of the traditional Christian family outside the Christian world. Finally, the theme of guilt is the focus of the life choices of the members of the disbanded Price family who, years after the fall of their family and the democratic Congo, reflect (or not) upon their responsibility in the demise of both.

Sophie Croisy

ETHICS in *The Poisonwood Bible*

In *The Poisonwood Bible,* Kingsolver conducts a thorough critique of Christian ethics through the intervention of multiple characters with a different vision of Christianity, of its potential salvaging role, and of Christians' ethical responsibility in the world.

Baptist preacher and missionary Nathan Price's strict ethics, constructed upon traditional Christian beliefs and teachings, are quite ascetic. Price is a tyrannical, self-proclaimed messianic figure who carries the word of God and thus must be respected and obeyed. He won't hesitate to force upon the Kilanga community the idea of a baptism day in the Kilanga River even though he knows that the river is infested with crocodiles and thus deadly to the children. His attachment to Christian ritual is obsessive, and when Kilanga children start dying fast from an epidemic of Kakakaka (dysentery), his daughter Adah cannot help noticing that "he doesn't seem to mind the corpses so much as the

soul unsaved" since none of the dead children had yet been baptized. His behavior here exemplifies his daughter Rachel's description of him as being a man carrying "numerous deadly weapons" inside him, these weapons being a patriarchal and colonialist frame of mind.

There are, however, Christian characters in the text whose idea of Christianity's role in the colonial and postcolonial Congo evolves through the relationship they build with this country. These Christian characters offer a positive and modern image of Christianity, participate in a critical analysis of Christian beliefs and ethics, and question the intrinsic goodness and worthiness of traditional Christian values and some of the people practicing them. As Brother Fowles once tells Orleanna Price, "For certain Mrs. Price, there are Christians, and then there are Christians."

Orleanna Price was raised a Christian and believed in the goodness of the evangelizing task before coming to the Congo, but she comes to distrust her husband's ambition because of his incapacity to reconcile faith and life, to communicate and build a relationship with the leaders of the Kilanga community toward which he shows no respect. Unlike Reverend Price, Brother Fowles, a missionary who had come to the Kilanga community to preach the gospel before Nathan Price, was able to build a relationship with the chief of the Kilanga village, Tata Ndu. His role as a missionary was not to impose an ethics of life based on Christian teachings, but to engage in conversations with Tata Ndu about ethics and share Christian values with him, hoping that some would be adopted by the community. Although Brother Fowles never managed to convince Tata Ndu that there were great benefits in monogamy, "each of those wives [in the community] has profited from the teachings of Jesus. In my six years here I saw the practice of wife beating fall into great disfavor. Secret little altars to Tata Jesus appeared in most every kitchen, as a result." Brother Fowles has a very pedagogical approach to missionary work, a communicative approach always respectful of his interlocutor's opinion.

Leah Price marries a Congolese man and discards, little by little, all of her father's Christian values. She comes to see these values as entirely unethical because they are attached to her home country, the United States. She learns to her horror that the leader of her country, President Eisenhower, has been actively engaged in arranging the murder of Congolese politician Patrice Lumumba. She says, "What sort of man would wish to murder the president of another land? None but a Barbarian. A man with a bone in his hair." Leah also points to the inhumanity of white Christians who, despite their supposed attachment to Christian principles, lose their credibility as Christians by supporting racial hatred: "It's dawning on me that I live among men and women who've simply always understood their whole existence is worth less than a banana to most white people."

Kingsolver shows in her text the sometimes dubious ethical goal of Christian representatives who turn Christian teachings into deadly dogma, who hold onto a vision of Christianity that does not take into account the need to adapt in an environment where traditional Christian rituals and values just cannot fit. The novel's leitmotiv, "Tata Jesus is *bangala*" (Mister Jesus is poisonous), summarizes well the impact of Christian "ethics" upon the Congo: Christian nations organized the murder of Patrice Lumumba who was elected prime minister after the Congo's independence from Belgium, and was killed because he wanted political and economic independence for the Congo against their will.

Sophie Croisy

FAMILY in *The Poisonwood Bible*

The Price family is a traditional 1960s Baptist family from the South of the United States. The father and preacher Nathan Price is a patriarchal figure, only breadwinner and master of the household, who makes all the important decisions and expects obedience from wife and daughters. He is obsessed with "the education of his family's souls" and "views himself as the captain of a sinking mess of female minds" who, though unfit for education in his opinion, must at least learn the ways of the Bible in order to stay away from sin. He is a strong, masculine, patronizing, self-proclaimed messianic figure whose purpose in life is to spread the word of God and enlighten his congregation as well as his family.

When the family moves to Kilanga, Congo, in order for the Reverend Price to conduct a Christianizing mission and teach the ways of the Western world to the Congolese, the reluctance Nathan Price encounters exacerbates his desire to convert and submit the inhabitants of that region of Congo, as well as his daughters, to the law of the Almighty. His mission turns into an obsession and he becomes "a potter with clay to be molded" who now ignores the feelings and difficulties of his children and wife in adapting to a foreign environment. As Orleanna Price notices, "He was hardly a father . . . Their individual laughter he couldn't recognize, nor their anguish." Nathan Price's lack of interest in his family on the one hand and his growing cruelty toward them on the other (a cruelty born out of his failure to Christianize the Kilanga people, to own them through conversion as he owns or wants to own his own family) lead to a progressive dissolution of the Price family. The father's gradual abandonment of his family (when he was once its cement) leaves the daughters very much free to discover the new world in which they now live. They are free to redefine the concept of family outside the framework offered to them by their upbringing in the American South. Leah, for example, notices that the children of a Kilanga family, especially the girls, work and are concerned with issues that in an American family are adult issues, such as finding food and building houses. Thus, the Price daughters become the household food gatherers. They take up the traditional role of the father who, absent most of the time, cannot be the breadwinner anymore. More important, they prove themselves quick to learn and apply themselves as they manage to find ways to survive in a deadly environment. Moreover, as the situation becomes more and more dire for the Price family after the devastating aftermath of independence, as Europeans are chased down and killed and internal wars are raging after the death of real-life leader Patrice Lumumba. Orleanna Price, usually an obedient and passive wife, takes on a new, active position as decision-maker in the family, daring to speak her mind in front of her husband and getting ready to take her daughters outside the Congo. Once the sole commander of his family, Nathan's estrangement from its members and their gradual rejection of his teachings in an environment that requires other frames of thinking and looking at the world than those imposed by this Baptist preacher, make him and his patriarchal and colonizing attitude obsolete.

Not only does the concept of the traditional Christian family collapse in this novel, as it finds no room in an environment that cannot sustain it, but we also witness the crumbling of the "nation as family" ideal. The Price daughters are betrayed by their American Christian education, which does not apply in the Congo, and by their own nation and its government, a government that becomes the root of all evils in the Congo (which becomes known as Zaire) since it actively participates in the demise of the Congolese democratic process with the assassination of Patrice Lumumba and the rise to power of a dictator. As Leah notices after independence, "The United States has now become the husband of Zaire's economy, and not a very nice one: exploitative and condescending, in the name of steering her clear of the moral decline inevitable to her nature" (543). In the same way as the Price daughters were subdued and devalued by a father who embodied American Christian values, Zaire after independence is subdued and devalued through a violent (though silenced), economic and political colonizing intervention of the United States.

Sophie Croisy

GUILT in *The Poisonwood Bible*

For Orleanna and Leah Price, guilt is the result of introspection—a kind of critical inquiry into one's past and present behavior that brings to consciousness the errors committed in dealing with one's surroundings. Guilt is thus the consequence of a moral and political awakening, an awakening that takes place for them in 1960 in the Congo. Adah, who does not need to feel guilt, embodies moral consciousness: She is never complicit with her father's sadistic Christian enterprise and always lays a critical eye on the world and its cruelties. For Rachel and Nathan Price, however, their lack of guilt toward others is evidence of mental stasis and of the absence of moral and political consciousness. Neither Nathan Price nor his daughter Rachel ever seem to wake up to the horrifying events happening

in the lives of the people who are closest to them: their family and the Kilanga people.

When she first arrived in the Congo, Orleanna Price did her best to fit in a foreign environment, focusing on the day-to-day needs of her family without learning from the Congolese people living around her. Her lack of participation in the outside world is one of the main aspects of her guilt when, years later and back in the United States, she recollects her time in the Congo: She was only "a captive witness" (10) then. She recollects this forced detachment from the Congolese world and its rules, intricacies, dangers—a detachment that she sees as the reason for her younger daughter's death: Ruth May was bitten by a snake placed in their garden by Tata Ndu, an important figure in the Kilanga community, and the nemesis of Nathan Price. If she had had the strength to rise against her husband's Christian fanaticism, the Kilanga community might not have turned against him, and the snake might never have been put in their garden.

Her daughter Leah's guilt draws from a childish, blind belief in her father's words and teachings. Her childhood actions were essentially centered around one goal: to be the best Christian daughter she could ever be. However, the months spent in the Congo give birth to a desire to know and learn what lies beyond the patriarch's ethnocentric envisioning of the world, hence her being torn for a long time between her daughterly duty and her need to understand the Congo, its inhabitants, their customs, and their pains. She eventually chooses the path of knowledge and consciousness, marries a Congolese man, and dismisses her father's monolithic Christian education as well as her cultural inheritance as an American. Her guilt also lies in her belonging to a culture that promotes values and a way of life that it does not always uphold when economic interests are at stake. The United States government indeed participates in the demise of the democratic Congo (and other African nations) under the eyes of Leah who remains in Africa all her life to see, among other things, the United States "trying to bring down Angola's sovereignty" in the 1980s to gain control over its oil and diamond industries.

There is no room for guilt in Adah Price's frame of thinking, only room for thinking and trying to point out "the sacred ignorance" (212) of Christian Americans who want to impose their ways of believing in a foreign land. The workings of her mind are never limited by the cultural prison in which Nathan (and to a certain extent Rachel) is content to dwell throughout his life, a prison filled with prejudices and ready-made answers to the problems of the world. His self-proclaimed messianic mission cannot suffer to stray from the Christian path he has envisioned and imposed upon his surroundings since his return from World War II: There, he was the only soldier in his regiment to survive the Bataan Death March. To redeem himself, he dedicates his life to saving the souls of his family and congregations in order to please God, which takes him to the brink of madness, drives him to endanger his congregation, and makes him lose his humanity. He feels guilty toward God, but never toward the human beings he hurts in his quest to please God. His older daughter Rachel follows the path of inhumanity as she spends her life, after leaving the Congo, trying to make a profit in Africa by using and abusing Africa's economic opportunities and people. She will, among other things, acknowledge and participate in the South African apartheid system.

Sophie Croisy

KINGSTON, MAXINE HONG
Tripmaster Monkey: His Fake Book   (1987)

The central character in *Tripmaster Monkey* is Wittman Ah Sing, a recent college graduate and fifth-generation Chinese American living in 1960s San Francisco. Like his namesake, poet Walt Whitman, he is a creative and free thinker. He also embodies the title character, the Monkey King, from traditional Chinese myth, as both are rebellious and mischievous and both bring truths to the people. The Monkey King aids in bringing the Buddhist sutras to China from India, and Wittman brings the truth about Caucasian perceptions of Chinese Americans and the necessary actions Chinese Americans need to take. Wittman finds himself disillusioned with the modern world: capitalism, the Vietnam War, and especially contemporary views of Chinese Americans. The bulk of the novel follows Wittman as he tries to come to terms with the opposition

between what he wants out of life and what is expected and/or available to him.

Wanting more than anything to be a poet and playwright, he feels trapped in his dead end job. Wittman comes to realize that he must push forward with his play if he ever wants to escape the rote business world. Securing a location to stage the play, he calls upon his friends and family, who swarm together to help flesh it out over the next several months and to enact the characters. The end production is a seven-night event, each night a continuation of the previous, wherein his cast enacts traditional Chinese and Chinese-American myths, stories, and history. Wittman's play also creates and enlarges these stories and histories, commenting on Caucasian perceptions of Chinese Americans. Following the play's conclusion, Wittman speaks to the crowd about perceptions and stereotypes of Asian Americans, challenging his audience to make changes. Through his play and speech, he encourages Asian Americans to claim their place in American society and whites to reevaluate their views.

Lisa Wenger

COMMODIFICATION/COMMERCIALIZATION in *Tripmaster Monkey*

There is nothing Wittman Ah Sing likes about commercialism. In fact, Wittman sees the entire corporate world as a complete waste of his time. He is miserable in his job as a sales clerk in the toy department, despite the fact that it earns him a living and that he has to work only three days a week. The work is rote and mundane, which is captured in his wife Taña's diatribe about her own job, where at 8 A.M. "'this chime goes off. . . . We have to be at our desks. It goes off again at ten-fifteen, coffee break, and ten-twenty-five, end of coffee break, and at twelve noon and twelve-forty, and at two-fifteen, second coffee break, and two-twenty, end of coffee break, and five o'clock—commute hour.'" The corporate/commercial world turns them into unthinking machines, performing repetitive actions that leave no room for creative or intelligent thought. Taña's only salvation during the day is the short unpaid coffee and lunch breaks she receives. For Wittman, the customers, mothers who continually dump their children on him while they run other errands, also are unbearable. Unlike most of his fellow Asian-American classmates, Wittman graduated from college with a degree in liberal arts. If anything, this education has taught him to question everything about capitalism, and the only thing he can think is "[w]hich way out? Which way out?" Blaming his "malcontentedness" on his education, Wittman knows this world offers him no creative outlet, but rather more of the same for the rest of his life. Having failed managerial training, there isn't even any hope for a promotion, which would at least change his job duties. Wittman tries to make the best of his situation. Believing he can at least educate customers, he lectures a grandmother about the evil of toy guns. In the end, the woman is extremely irritated and still buys the gun.

Accompanying his manager, Louise, to a toy convention, Wittman views commercialism's pointlessness firsthand. The first half of the convention is wasted with idle chitchat and eating; as far as Wittman can tell, nothing productive occurs. The conference also is solely about upcoming releases in the Mattel toy line. The second half of the convention is full of self-important business people spouting statistics and reading from pie charts. All these charts offer nothing, for they are purely guesses as to who will buy what and how much. Furthermore, the conference is not even promoting a necessary product, but rather something that is purely for children's entertainment. While he tries to pay attention to the speakers at first, Wittman soon finds that "his mind died . . . [and] the next thing he knew, he was aware of not having listened for some time." Trying to inject some meaning into the trivial proceedings, he asks the speakers if Mattel donated anything to the needy. His question is ignored, and instead another business person leads the crowd in chanting the Mattel slogan.

Wittman is depressed when he is fired after returning to the store. Placing Barbie Bride in a sexual position, he winds up a toy monkey and places it on top, horrifying the mothers. He is not so miserable over the loss of the job itself but of the income, especially since most of his friends have successfully navigated the corporate world. Wittman cannot even escape this world through his social life. Attending his friend Lance's party later that night,

Wittman realizes the theme itself is business, with most partygoers wearing suits. While Lance expects Wittman to network and easily come away from the party with a new job, Wittman has absolutely no desire to do so. In fact, he realizes that "he didn't want to do business whatsoever. There has got to be a way to live and never do business." He is delighted when he learns that he can apply for and subsist on unemployment. Suddenly, his dream of writing and producing his own play seems attainable, and he actually finds that he respects himself more for not crawling back to the capitalistic "monster" that has consumed all his friends.

Throughout *Tripmaster Monkey*, the artistic and creative is celebrated, particularly for the way it can challenge thoughts and ideas. The commercial, on the other hand, is critiqued for offering little of value to the world, other than a steady paycheck. Knowing he must find a job to support Taña and himself, his derision for the corporate world still shows at the end. As he tells his audience, when asked during job interviews why he wants to join a corporation, he thinks, "'[t]hey don't understand, I don't want to. I have to.'" Understanding that he must join the corporate ranks to survive, he also uses this as motivation for creative works, works through which he knows he can ultimately escape.

Lisa Wenger

IDENTITY in *Tripmaster Monkey*

Wittman Ah Sing is secure in and proud of his identity, a fifth-generation Chinese American. The problem lies in the way whites view him and other Asian Americans. Whites automatically assume all Asian Americans are "F.O.B.s" The acronym, for Fresh off the Boat, is a slang term often applied to newly arrived Asian immigrants, indicating that they have not assimilated into American culture. In this way, the whites differentiate between what it means to be American and Asian, while completely overlooking the Asian-American identity. Wittman knows there is nothing "Eastern" about him or other Asian Americans, yet they must continually reinforce and defend their identities.

Continually lumped in with new Asian immigrants, Wittman's frustration grows, for he is so far removed from that culture. As he relates, "[i]mmigrants. Fresh Off the Boats out in public. Didn't know how to walk together. Spitting seeds. So uncool. You wouldn't mislike them on sight if their pants weren't so highwater, gym socks white and noticeable . . Uncool. Uncool." Wittman hates the way their ignorance of American ways and customs makes them stand out. Furthermore, they do nothing individually, which Wittman also mocks, taking pride in his "American independence." Given the F.O.B.s' conspicuousness, Wittman and other Asian Americans are frustrated when whites group them in this category, stripping away their identities.

That the Asian Americans of Whittman's generation, born and raised in the country, are fully Americanized is evidenced through the older generations. When he visits his mother, all his aunts are gathered at the home for mah-jongg (a traditional Chinese game where participants build suits from a set of tiles). While they talk in Chinese among themselves, "[t]hey spoke English to him and to the dog. American animals." They recognize that he is not Chinese but Chinese American, and as such, that some Chinese customs and language are lost to him. Consequently, they firmly identify Wittman as Chinese American, thereby validating his identity in a way the whites do not. This Americanization is illustrated further when Wittman approaches an uncle about using the Benevolent Association's building to stage his play. Communicating in Chinese, the trouble arises when Wittman wants to tell the man he is writing a Chinese-American play. He suddenly thinks, "[i]s there a Chinese word for Chinese American? They say 'jook tsing.' They say 'ho chi gwai.' Like 'mestizo.' Like 'pachuco.'" Chinese indicates China, a place where there would be no Chinese Americans, hence no need for such a word. The generic terms signifying the mixing of cultures, though, do not rob Wittman of his identity. Instead, they allow him to talk about and define it. He first does so when he switches to English, a language more his own. Next, he begins giving the uncle examples of the stories his play will tell, stories that combine the two cultures. Accordingly, the missing Chinese word gives him a way to provide deeper insight into his identity.

Through his play and its staging, Wittman demands recognition of his Chinese-American identity, of all Asian-American identities. Drawing on and embellishing myths and stories from both Chinese and Chinese-American culture, he draws attention to the way culture, and in conjunction identity, is reinvented and reshaped. In fact, when friends and family come to rehearse the play, they bring costumes and props, things collected from both Asian and American homelands. The story he tells of his family's name also is a striking example of this. Wittman relates to his audience that he is an American Ah Sing, and "'[p]robably there are no Ah Sings in China. You may laugh behind my family's back, that we keep the Ah and think it means something. I know it's just a sound. A vocative that goes in front of everyone's names. . . . Everyone has an ah, only our family writes ours down." This change in the family name, the switch from the *ah* as verbal only to both written and verbal, shows the modification in culture and identity upon arriving in America. While the *ah* is an important reminder of Chinese identity, it also is a shift away from it toward a new Chinese-American identity.

As Wittman emphasizes throughout the novel, he is not Chinese but American. His features alone do not make him Chinese, something many whites assume. This is something he reinforces to his audience at the end of his play, saying, "'[t]ake a good look at these eyes. Check them out in profile too. And the other profile. Dig the three-quarter view. So it's not Mount Rushmore, but it's an American face.'" Wittman rallies his audience to celebrate and vocalize their identities, challenging the preconceptions that surround them.

Lisa Wenger

RACE in *Tripmaster Monkey*

Race preoccupies many of the Asian-American characters in *Tripmaster Monkey,* including Wittman Ah Sing. Despite being born and raised in America, Wittman is constantly asked questions about how long he has been in America and whether or not he speaks English. As many Asian Americans find, whites view Asian Americans as "foreign," "exotic," and "oriental." They play on and perpetuate stereotypes of Asian Americans, seen most strikingly in the racial joke Wittman overhears from a table of whites at a restaurant. Because of their appearance and skin color, Asian Americans also do not fit the "standard" image of an American. As Wittman comments to his audience after his play, "'[t]hey think that Americans are either white or Black. I can't wear that civil-rights button with the Black hand and the white hand shaking each other. . . . I'm the little yellow man beneath the bridge of their hands and overlooked'" (307–308). Consequently, Asian Americans remain the perpetual outsiders, never quite American no matter how many generations their families have been in the country.

What disgusts them even more is the stereotypical portrayal of their race in literature and film. Wittman admires the poet Jack Kerouac, but derides a reference Kerouac makes to "twinkling little Chinese." Even worse are the depictions of Asian Americans in film, especially the bucktoothed, face-painted Chinese landlord in *Breakfast at Tiffany's* played by the white Mickey Rooney. Other than "comic" roles, as Wittman points out, "'[o]ur actors have careers of getting killed and playing dead bodies.'" The roles for Asian-American actresses are not any better, playing off the idea of the submissive Asian woman. After a recent audition, Wittman's actress friend Nanci Lee remarks, "'I know what my part will be—an oriental peasant. You only need high heels for the part of the oriental prostitute. . . . And the director says, 'Can't you act more oriental? Act oriental.'" Roles for Asian Americans are limited, minor roles, never leading characters. Furthermore, these Western actors are criticized for not acting Eastern enough, something the white directors believe should come naturally based on their looks. What further annoys Wittman is that so many leading fictional characters have no race associated with them, meaning Asian Americans could easily play their film adaptations, yet such roles are never offered to them. Taking what small steps he can to counteract this, Wittman decides that, in his imagination, all such characters will be Chinese.

These white perceptions and stereotypes carry over to the way Asian Americans view themselves. This is particularly evident through the women. Most, as Wittman drily comments, are unavailable,

searching for the perfect, successful white husband. What he abhors even more is that they hold themselves up to a white standard of beauty, particularly when it comes to their eyes. When a former classmate, Yoshi Ogasawara, is told her eyes are beautiful, she replies "'[n]o. Oh, no, they're not. . . . I'm going to have them operated on for double lids. I have single lids. These are single lids.'" What she is talking of is the fold in Caucasian eyelids that is missing in her own. The whites listening to Yoshi have no idea what she is talking about, but Wittman is disgusted and walks away. Later he chastises Asian-American women for these alterations, alterations that often only leave a scar, rather than the desired fold. Wittman knows that the "slanty" eyes are one of the big factors leading to the white view of Asian Americans as exotic and foreign; however, he also knows they need to celebrate their features as well as loudly proclaim their own American identity.

Even though Wittman embraces his features, he still worries over white views. He purposefully wears green after being told it reflects harshly on "yellow" skin. Rather than deflect his color, he instead wants to call attention to it. Yet he tenses when Taña begins talking about his body and features, positive she is going to say something derogatory. Surprised when she does not, he thinks, "[g]ood. She did not tell him that she liked 'yellow' skin or 'slanty' eyes. She did not say he was 'mysterious.'" Wittman still keeps his guard up, expecting the worst. Later, he further betrays the influence Caucasian perceptions have on him. After having his picture taken with Taña in a photo booth, he thinks that she "looked like a blonde movie star; Wittman looked like a wanted bandito. El Immigrante, his wetback passport picture i.d." Despite his bravado, Wittman, at times, cannot help but make comparisons to himself, finding himself lacking.

In the end, Wittman rants against white racial assumptions. Understanding how race and identity are connected, he commands his audience, both white and Asian American, to set aside and call out racial stereotypes, to challenge modern ideas of what is and isn't American, for Asian Americans to abandon white standards of beauty, and for the theater to challenge Hollywood typecasting.

Lisa Wenger

KINGSTON, MAXINE HONG *The Woman Warrior* (1975)

The Woman Warrior: Memoirs of a Girlhood among Ghosts is Maxine Hong Kingston's first published book. Usually considered a memoir or an auto-biographical novel, it received the National Book Critics Circle Award for nonfiction and has been extremely popular as a textbook for high school and college classrooms. The first three chapters are based on the stories the unnamed narrator heard from her mother, Brave Orchid, about what happened in China before her mother left for the United States in 1939. The first chapter, "No Name Woman," is about the narrator's forgotten aunt who transgressed through an extramarital affair and pregnancy and killed herself and her child to eschew a life as the rural community's outcast. The second chapter, "White Tigers," chronicles the career of a legendary Chinese woman warrior, Fa Mu Lan, whom the narrator is expected to emulate even as a young woman living in the United States. The third chapter, "Shaman," recollects the narrator's mother's life in China as medical student and then successful doctor. The last two chapters of the book, "At the Northern Palace" and "A Song for a Barbarian Reed Pipe," show processes of successful or failed adaptations by Chinese immigrants to American ways of life, with the last chapter suggesting ways in which Chinese traditions can be modified to inform and enrich the lives of young Chinese Americans as well as better their relationships to their immigrant parents. The major themes highlighted in the novel include race/ethnicity, gender, tradition, survival, identity, alienation, coming of age, and family.

Tomoko Kuribayashi

GENDER in *The Woman Warrior*

The gender issues in *The Woman Warrior* almost exclusively concern women and reflect the novel's focus on intercultural conflicts experienced by Chinese immigrants to the United States and their American-born children. Kingston's five chapters present two possible exemplary social roles for women as defined by mainstream pre-communist Chinese culture: Women should be slaves and/or good wives (note that the two can be synonymous) or they can be women warriors, trained in traditional martial arts for the specific purpose of avenging their families. The patriarchal belief that women are to be subservient because they are innately inferior is often articulated in Kingston's narrative in the form of traditional sayings such as "Girls are maggots in the rice" and "It is more profitable to raise geese than daughters." The first chapter of the book, "No Name Woman," informs the reader of the punishment meted out to a woman in a Chinese village, actually the narrator's paternal aunt, who got pregnant through an extramarital affair: Her family's house was raided by villagers and she killed herself and her child to avoid a lifetime of ostracism while her lover or possible rapist got away scot-free. The narrator's mother, Brave Orchid, narrates this story as a warning about what can happen to the young daughter if she fails to follow the strict rules set up for women's social and sexual conduct.

At the same time, Kingston's narrative proffers multiple stories featuring women warriors who far surpassed men in their bravery, intellect, and strength. One important example is Fa Mu Lan, the legendary warrior, who went through rigorous training in martial arts in order to avenge her family and village against oppressive rulers. Another major example of a heroic woman is the narrator's own mother who, after the deaths of her first two children, acquired medical knowledge by attending a school of midwifery in China. Brave Orchid also proved to be a woman warrior as an immigrant to the United States where she had six children well into her forties and worked extremely hard to support her family. One possible way these two opposite models for women's lives—slave and warrior—can be reconciled is how Fa Mu Lan is said to have done it: After avenging her family and village against the evil emperor and baron, the woman warrior willingly became an obedient wife and daughter-in-law, pledging to work hard in the field and the house and to give birth to many sons. It must also be noted that Fa Mu Lan had to hide her gender while in battle since women soldiers were totally forbidden in Chinese culture.

Traditional Chinese culture also dictates that sexuality or individual sexual desires, both male and female, be suppressed to protect the harmony and well-being of the entire community; men and women are to be like brothers and sisters to each other. That goes against the message Kingston's narrator and other daughters of Chinese immigrants in northern California receive at school. If they are to be considered socially appropriate and get dates in the United States, they need to cultivate a more overt, yet still respectable kind of sexuality, or what they call "American-feminine," which includes speaking less loud than Chinese, both women and men, traditionally do.

Further confusion as to what Chinese culture regards as truly desirable in a woman is generated by the explicit contrast of Brave Orchid and her sister, Moon Orchid. While Brave Orchid is hardworking and intelligent and is thus valuable as a man's helpmate, she is not gentle or soft, the way her useless and timid younger sister is. One can also assume their other sister, Lovely Orchid, who owns a shoe business in Hong Kong, is the pretty one, representing yet another ideal type of woman. The American-born narrator, presumably Kingston's double, suffers both from Chinese culture's contradictory expectations for women—to be slaves as well as warriors—and the different standards of ideal femininity endorsed by Chinese and American cultures. Her confusion and resultant self-hatred erupt in the most startling way in the scene where the young narrator torments another Chinese girl at school who is "Chinese-feminine" like Moon Orchid: totally silent and always neat but entirely helpless. After many years of frustration, the narrator is able at least in part to resolve the intercultural gender confusion by seeing herself as a woman warrior who wages battles against oppressors of her family through the words she writes.

Tomoko Kuribayashi

SURVIVAL in *The Woman Warrior*
The theme of survival has several major applications in Maxine Hong Kingston's memoir/autobiographical novel. The first three chapters of the novel, "No Name Woman," "White Tigers," and "Shaman," depict what is required for survival in Chinese society. The first chapter concerns the narrator's paternal aunt, whose existence has been forgotten. Her own family wipes her from memory as punishment for the trespasses of adultery and ensuing pregnancy for

which she killed herself after her family's house was raided by angry villagers. The lesson to be learned from this story, at least as the narrator's mother, Brave Orchid, intended it to be, is that the well-being of the entire community comes before the happiness or desires of an individual, especially in times of hardship like a poor harvest or political unrest. The value placed on roundness by Chinese culture is expressed in round moon cakes and round doorways, symbolizing the importance of communal harmony and family wholeness for which individuals' rights and freedoms must be sacrificed.

In "White Tigers," the main character, whom the American-born narrator imagines herself to be, is a young Chinese girl who is trained by an old couple in the mountains to become a woman warrior, skilled in martial arts, so that she can avenge her family and fellow villagers against the neglectful emperor and the wicked baron. She starts her training by learning to be utterly quiet so that every creature in the world of nature will let her learn its hiding and fighting skills. At the mid-point of her 15-year stint with the elderly teachers she endures a solitary survival test in which she must subsist on meager provisions and withstand extreme cold for many days. Later, even as an accomplished woman warrior, successful in her campaign against the evil governors and fulfilled in marriage and motherhood, she must survive on the battlefield by hiding her gender, as she would be executed if found to be female.

In the third chapter "Shaman," the narrator's mother in her younger days shows extreme resourcefulness and bravery, which helps her confront the resident ghost at a Chinese school for midwives and earn fellow students' respect. One major way that somebody can show courage and strength is the ability and willingness to eat anything, including wild animals and perhaps even monkey brain. Even in her later days as an immigrant to the United States, the narrator's mother cooks such unusual creatures as skunks and turtles for her American-born children. It is equally important to be able to "not eat," when fasting is the appropriate choice. In addition to her mother's detailed example, Kingston's narrator lists a number of fantastic eaters from China whose abilities were thought to bring rain during a draught or conquer evil ghosts.

The theme of survival in the United States as immigrants and as immigrants' children is foregrounded in the last two chapters of *The Woman Warrior*. The narrator's mother, once a successful midwife/doctor in China, must now make a living running a family laundry business; in her old age she works as a tomato picker even though she does not need the pay. Those who are not able to adjust and to work hard like Brave Orchid literally lose their minds. For example, Brave Orchid's younger and less practical sister, Moon Orchid, who is brought to California from Hong Kong by her determined sister, becomes delusional and has to be committed to a state mental asylum. Kingston's narrator also describes other "crazy" women of which the immigrant community seems to have had plenty. One of them, Pee-A-Nah, was an angry witchwoman who chased children as they picked berries in a slough. There was also Crazy Mary who, left as a toddler in China when her parents emigrated, was later brought over as a disturbed 20-year-old; she was not able to learn English and help her parents out as had been hoped for. On the other hand, one could risk overadjusting and losing one's Chinese roots completely as is seen in the case of Moon Orchid's husband, who has become extremely Americanized, married to a young Chinese-American woman, and practicing dentistry in a sleek office in downtown Los Angeles. He sounds, looks, and even smells like an American-born and proclaims his Chinese wife is like a character in a story he read long ago. Immigrants' children, including the narrator, must find ways to survive without losing their connections to their families' past, to straddle two widely different cultures and languages and their often conflicting values.

Tomoko Kuribayashi

TRADITION in *The Woman Warrior*

Tradition is one of the main concerns of Kingston's memoir or autobiographical novel, which is narrated from the viewpoint of a Chinese immigrant daughter growing up in northern California in the 1950s and '60s. The many first-generation immigrants that surround the narrator, especially her mother, hope to instill traditional Chinese values in the younger generation, but are often disappointed at the rude-

ness and lack of formality found in the youth. When the mother, Brave Orchid, laments that her teenaged children are not "traditional" toward their long-lost aunt, Moon Orchid, she means that they are not polite, especially to their elders, since being respectful to one's social superiors is an essential part of traditional Chinese culture. The American-born children are also audacious in that they look at people's eyes directly whereas the correct way in China is to have an unfocused gaze. Since the older generation plans and hopes to return to China one day, they think it important for the children not to lose the traditional ways.

One major tool that the older generation uses to communicate their beliefs and customs to their offspring is "talk-story," that is, telling stories like the one about a legendary female warrior, Fa Mu Lan, or the more private one about an ill-starred aunt, both of which the narrator hears from her mother. Ghosts and food—both important Chinese traditions—are also featured frequently in the stories. Even Chinese opera and songs may be considered a kind of "talk-story," a communal and musical way of handing down traditional values and history. Yet the American-born children are often confused as to what is socially and culturally expected of them. For one, the parents, who by Chinese custom tend to be oblique in their statements or to state the exact opposite of what they mean, do not clearly delineate the guidelines for maintaining Chinese tradition. To make matters worse, the younger generation is often less than fluent in Chinese and does not know the meaning of words their parents use in their "talk-story," and the parents do not bother to explain each and every word, even when asked. The first-generation immigrants also withhold some information because they fear deportation and other retaliation if their "secrets" are to be leaked through their "American" children who do not know when to remain silent.

Gender issues highlight the theme of tradition. The young narrator suffers from much confusion and fear because she is told that in China a woman should be a slave and also be a woman warrior—two seemingly contradictory roles. The narrator does not want to be a slave or to accept the often vocalized Chinese belief that women are innately inferior, and is afraid that she will be sold off as a slave or a wife as soon as her family returns to China. Nor can she figure out how to become a woman warrior in a land where there are no obvious evil rulers as in Chinese stories of female heroism.

In the end Kingston's novel suggests that traditions need to be handed down as well as modified as the times change and as people settle in new places. The reader is informed that even in China old traditions are being destroyed by the Communist government, depriving the first-generation immigrants of any hope that they might return to their homeland. The narrative also suggests that second-generation Chinese Americans need to explore new options, including more formal education, in the absence of arranged marriages and close-knit rural communities. The last chapter of the novel, "A Song for a Barbarian Reed Pipe," artfully expresses the cultural and generational reconciliation the narrator and her mother reach, through its final episode about a Chinese female poet and warrior, Ts'ai Yung, who was kidnapped by a barbarian and bore him two children. Her children, who spoke no Chinese, initially laughed at her when she spoke her native tongue. One day, however, she sang a song about her family in China, the emotional significance of which the barbarians understood without comprehending the words. Later, freed from her 12-year captivity and returned to her family, Ts'ai Yung translated the barbarians' songs, one of which becomes part of Chinese culture. Kingston's narrator concludes the narrative with the comment, "It translated well." This ending suggests that Kingston's narrator and her mother, or the older and younger generations of the Chinese-American community, are finally able to understand what each other values despite the linguistic and cultural barriers.

Tomoko Kuribayashi

KIPLING, RUDYARD *Kim* (1900–1901)

In one sense, Rudyard Kipling's *Kim* is a simple adventure story told against the backdrop of the British Raj. From quite a different perspective, it is the most ancient story of all—the quest for enlightenment and escape from the Wheel of Life. Kim is torn between these two extremes in the story, as he strives to become a faithful *chela* (servant in Hindi) to a Tibetan lama, as well as a cunning spy of the British empire. This crisis of identity reflects the uncertain destiny of India herself, perched between the ancient and modern worlds: For however indifferent Kipling himself was to India's independence, Kim ends his story with the possibility (if not realization) of becoming a free agent. Having helped the lama find his river, he is still a number in the imperial system, charting the unknown peripheries of the British empire. Yet he remains an "Indian" in the truest sense, as no language or caste is unknown to him; the staggering diversity of this ancient world is a story he can recite at will. How he tells this story—and for whose benefit—is the true subject of *Kim*, with its emphasis on timeless waters and wheels that spin beyond the reach of history and the maps of empire.

Joshua Grasso

INDIVIDUAL AND SOCIETY in *Kim*

Halfway through the novel, when Kim is being initiated into the rules of the Great Game by the "horse-dealer," Mahbub Ali, he is told:

> Among Sahibs, never [forget] thou art a
>   Sahib, among the folk of Hind,
>   always [remember] thou art—
> "What am I? Mussulman, Hindu, Jain, or
>   Buddhist? That is a hard knot."

Like the novel itself, Mahbub Ali refuses to answer this question, simply confiding to Kim that he is "my Little Friend of all the World." Perhaps what makes this work so compelling, and Kim such a rich figure in English literature, is his ability to become everyone, both Sahib, Hindu, and Muslim, in one of the most racially divided corners of the British empire. As the opening of the novel explains, Kim is the illegitimate child of an Irish soldier and an English nursemaid; however, like the young Kipling himself, Kim is thrust into the culturally diverse world of India, where he quickly learns to speak dozens of "languages," which he can use to adopt any caste or religion. Yet where does this leave Kim? Initially, he seems clearly marked for the "Indian" world, as he cavorts with servants and street urchins and has little interest in tracing his roots—though he speaks vaguely of a "Red Bull and a Colonel," along with "nine hundred devils" who will whisk him off to his destiny. This confusion of his racial identity (the Red Bull was the emblem of his father's regiment, and the 900 devils his brothers in arms) is the first time we realize that our native guide is playing an even greater game than he realizes.

If we read *Kim* as the story of a boy's adolescence, then Kim comes of age under the tutelage of two mentors: the Teshoo lama, a Buddhist pilgrim seeking a fabled river, and Mahbub Ali, a horse-dealer who is secretly an agent of the British empire. While the lama believes that Kim is his *chela*, or spiritual aide, Mahbub marks him out as the prize "colt" to be broken into the subterfuge of the Great Game. Throughout the novel, Kim teeters between these wildly disparate worlds, in awe of the lama's devotion but longing for the "dignity of a letter and a number—and a price upon his head!" which Mahbub's profession could bring him. His confusion is compounded when he is discovered by his father's regiment, which sends him to a mission school to become a proper Sahib. As a boy of English pedigree—however dubious—he has a racial imperative to become English in language, manners, and thought. Yet the great irony is that he is cultivated by Mahbub, Lurgan Sahib, and other functionaries because of his ability to be *other* than English; in essence, his ability to be "the Friend of all the World," blending in everywhere, and going where no Englishman can travel. When the lama learns the truth of his heritage, he exclaims: "A Sahib and the son of a Sahib . . . But no white man knows the land and the customs of the land as thou knowest. How comes it this is true?" In other words, can a "Sahib" truly see India as an Indian? Can a man live in both worlds, being a proper Englishman even while he salaams among Muslims on a secret mission?

Kim's crisis of identity is expressed in one of the most remarked upon passages in the novel. When he becomes a free agent of the Game, able to live or die by its fortunes, Kim reflects: "Now am I alone—all alone . . . In all India is no one so alone as I! . . . Who is Kim—Kim—Kim?" The repetition of his name is telling: The name is not familiar to him, nor is his identity as a secret agent, using India as a disguise (something artificial) when the "disguise" simply comes naturally to him. Kim constantly has to remind himself: "One must never forget that one is a Sahib, and that some day . . . one will command natives." Yet these Peter Pan-like dreams of adventure and entitlement are shattered when he views India not as a thing to be mapped and collected (the Game), but as a timeless, sentient world. Though the novel closes with Kim's career still uncertain, we cannot forget the passages when Kim "sees" himself in its diversity and abundance: "This was seeing the world in real truth; this was life as he would have it—bustling and shouting, the buckling of belts, and beating of bullocks and creaking of wheels, lighting of fires and cooking of food, and new sights at every turn of the approving eye . . . India was awake, and Kim was in the middle of it, more awake and more excited than anyone."

Joshua Grasso

NATIONALISM in *Kim*

Kipling once said that "India will never stand alone," suggesting that an India without Britain could never exist. In many ways, *Kim* is the literary expression of this statement, as Kipling's India is a *British* India, whose hero, for all his native insight, is racially English. Throughout *Kim*, the idea of nationalism works in several ways, defining the British against the so-called "Oriental" character, as well as Britain's rival, Russia, which seeks to invade India in the "Great Game" of empire. We see this early in the novel, when Mahbub Ali reflects that "Kim could lie like an Oriental." The narrator also delivers winking asides about the customs of Indians, to whom "All hours of the twenty four are alike," suggesting how the punctual English traveler is frustrated at every turn. The effect of these passages is curious; while they can easily be read as racist, it is important to separate the rhetoric from the narrator and his technique. Kipling's strategy is an uneasy way of maintaining his national ethos while writing of worlds and people that only a native could know; he keeps them at arm's length, drawing from a fund of Oriental lore that allows him to remain safely "English" in his exotic narrative.

For whatever fears England had about "going native" in India, it was undeniably part of the British landscape, a landscape that was darkened by the threatening shadow of Russia. Behind the scenes of Kim's coming-of-age story is the Great Game, the struggle for a central Asian empire that involved Britain and Russia for much of the 19th century. In the novel, Kim intercepts Russian spies surveying the northern boundaries of British India. When one of them encounters Kim's fellow spy, Hurree Babu, the Russian reflects: "He represents little India in transition—the monstrous hybridism of East and West . . It is *we* who can deal with Orientals." This "hybridism" reveals the Russians' contempt for India and Indians, who should be racially and culturally segregated from the ruling class. Hurree Babu—as well as Kim—is a man of two worlds, able to speak and act English as readily as any number of languages and dialects. Our Russian speaker finds this "monstrous," as he sees the Oriental character as a fixed, exotic specimen—thus echoing a famous Kipling poem: "Oh, East is East, and West is West, and never the twain shall meet." However, his ignorance of the Eastern character is revealed when he tries to barter for—and then seize—the lama's sacred drawing of the Wheel of Life. A comic melee ensues, with Kim soundly drubbing the buffoonish Russian, a scene that is rendered as vividly as a modern political cartoon.

However, in Kipling's novel only the British rulers can truly understand and value Indian culture. From the very first chapter, Kipling introduces us to the curator of the Lahore museum (supposedly based on Kipling's father), who has painstakingly collected the artifacts of Indian history. His knowledge is shown to be equal to that of a true native, the Teshoo Lama, who gratefully accepts his gift of spectacles. This gift is telling, as the association of glasses with sight suggests that the curator—an Englishman—must help the native "see" his path to enlightenment. Likewise, Kim's English mentors, such as the mysterious Lurghan Sahib, are virtual encyclopedias of Indian culture, with impressive collections of art and weaponry. This idea of knowing India is reflected in the Great Game itself, where British agents must methodically map every square inch of Indian soil. To truly rule a country, the Game

suggests, it must be collected, classified, and labeled on future maps. Thus, Kim's work in the Great Game is the truest expression of his nationality as a British subject.

Of course, India's "hybrid" subjects are exactly that—hybrids, setting foot in both worlds, though of questionable cultural/racial origin. Kipling is not oblivious to this dark undercurrent of colonialism, as seen in Hurree Babu's attempts to publish scholarly papers in England and join the Royal Society. Not surprisingly, he is rejected for the same reason Kim is sent to school to become a proper Sahib: Kim belongs by birth to a world that Hurree Babu can never aspire to, despite his learning and experience. He must serve the Empire tirelessly and, ultimately anonymously, offering colonial information that will be published under an Englishman's name. As something of a hybrid himself, Kipling was keenly aware of the impossibility of being both Indian and British, particularly in a world that wanted a stable, English subject. Kim's destiny seems to follow a similar path of anonymity, fading into the background of the Great Game as the one person who can truly experience the diversity of Indian life.

Joshua Grasso

SPIRITUALITY in *Kim*

In a book that has long been interpreted as a colonial adventure tale, spirituality plays a major role, particularly as it shapes the dichotomy between Kim's Indian and English identities. Though Kim seems aloof from RELIGION, he is drawn to the most spiritual figure in the book—the Teshoo Lama, who recruits Kim for his sacred quest. However, many critics have found it upsetting that the voice of Indian spirituality in the novel is Buddhist. After all, the dominant religious philosophy of India is Hinduism, Buddhism being a relatively late import from China. Yet what would seem an embarrassing lapse on Kipling's part has surprising relevance in the novel. In the opening pages, the lama seems to emerge from the mists of time, prompting even Kim (otherwise a shrewd judge of nationality) to remark: "but he is no man of India that *I* have ever seen" (6). As a figure who cannot be named with a specific race or class, he assumes an almost mythic dimension, a "type" whose memory lingers in the collective unconscious. This type is less a stock colonial figure than a living embodiment of the wisdom of the *Ramayana,* the *Dhamapada,* and other Indian epics that symbolize the Eastern quest for enlightenment. His very presence in the novel evokes a tradition outside of history (and certainly the British Raj), speaking in a language ridiculous to some, incomprehensible to others, but utterly transformative to a select few—including Kim.

His outsider status as a Buddhist also complements Kim, whose quest is complicated by his own racial and national uncertainty. Not surprisingly, the lama recognizes this "otherness" and immediately dubs him his *chela,* a spiritual aide on his quest to enlightenment. This becomes clear in chapter 9, when the lama tells Kim a *jataka,* or fable, concerning one of the Buddha's previous incarnations. The fable concerns an elephant captured by a king and fitted with a tremendous leg iron. None of his brother elephants can remove the leg iron, so the elephant abandons himself to rage and despair. Yet one day he discovers an abandoned calf in danger of being trampled by the herd; the elephant protects and nurses the foundling for 35 years, all the while enduring the pain of the leg iron. When the calf is grown, it notices the leg iron and asks what it is. When the elephant explains, the foundling dashes the iron in a single blow of his trunk. The lama moralizes this tale by explaining: "the elephant was Ananda, and the Calf that broke the ring was none other than The Lord himself." On its most immediate level, the fable explains the relationship between the lama and Kim. The lama, who lives in the world of epics, sees Kim as yet another incarnation of The Lord, and himself, Ananda. By rescuing this poor calf, in danger of being crushed by the Wheel of Existence, he will reveal Kim's true nature as *chela* and guardian. Of course, the fable functions on a more symbolic level as well: India can be seen as the elephant, held fast by the empire's chains. To free herself (the fable suggests), India must not look to the kings, or the children of kings, but to her orphans—children like Kim, born of two worlds, without clear distinctions of race or caste.

Though Kim does not "convert" to the lama's creed, their travels together test Kim's faith as a Sahib and an agent of the Game. Increasingly, he sees India not as a world of maps and boundaries, but as a timeless, mythic landscape. Embarking on his second journey with the lama, Kim observes

> [t]he clamour of Benares, oldest of all the earth's cities awake before the Gods, day and night, [beating] round the walls as the sea's roar round a breakwater . . . Kim watched the stars as they rose one after another in the still, sticky dark, till he fell asleep at the foot of the altar. That night he dreamed in Hindustanee, with never an English word . . .

Coming soon after his education at St. Xavier's, this passage reaffirms Kim's spiritual ties with India, which does not speak his adopted language. Perhaps realizing this, the lama ends the novel with the following prediction for Kim: "Let him be a teacher; let him be a scribe—what matter? He will have attained Freedom and the end. The rest is illusion." The implication is that Kim has found his inevitable path on the Way, which will lead to a spiritual awakening for himself—and quite possibly, an entire nation of pupils. Kipling may have been unable to write this ending, but he does give the last word to the lama, echoing the eternal procession of sages, seekers, and stories that color the Indian landscape.

Joshua Grasso

KNOWLES, JOHN *A Separate Peace* (1959)

John Knowles first published his award-winning novel *A Separate Peace* in 1959. The novel takes place in New Hampshire during World War II at the fictional Devon School. The work is set up as a frame story; an adult Gene Forrester returns to Devon, which he attended in his youth. He reminisces while wandering around the campus and recounts the events of one particular summer session and the following semesters, which make up the bulk of the book.

The main characters in the story are the teenaged Gene and Phineas. The teenage Gene is uptight and academic, while "Finny" is charismatic and athletic. Though polar opposites in temperament, they become best friends and even form a "secret society" whose initiation ritual involves jumping from a tree branch into a river. Early in the story, Gene begins to resent Finny's charm, thinks the latter intends to sabotage his studies, and, subsequently, causes Finny to fall from the aforementioned tree limb and break his leg. The remainder of the story involves the students' dealing with the emotional fallout from this incident. From these events, Knowles explores the themes of INNOCENCE AND EXPERIENCE, COMING OF AGE, GUILT, VIOLENCE, and IDENTITY.

The struggles faced by Gene and his friends resonate still today with those who are going through or have gone through the transition from child to adult. The novel's timeless themes will likely continue to do so with future readers.

Ryan Neighbors

COMING OF AGE in *A Separate Peace*

The journey to adulthood is often filled with struggles, suffering, and lessons learned. John Knowles's *A Separate Peace* is largely about this coming of age, the journey from adolescence to adulthood. The novel follows several boys at a New England private school in the 1940s as they study and prepare to go to war. This journey is most clearly seen in the protagonist Gene. The novel begins with an adult Gene revisiting the school where he spent his adolescent years. He recounts for the reader his time spent at the school, centering around one particular summer and a friendship that changed his life. That friendship with a boy known as Finny helped him discern certain undesirable characteristics about himself and grow as a person.

In the beginning of the novel, the adolescent Gene is a smart, disciplined boy, focused on his studies. Since he is not the most brilliant student in the school, he has to work hard to succeed and hopes to be head of the class. He dislikes breaking the rules and feels nervous when he does, such as when he rides to the beach with Finny and jumps with him from the tree into the river. In short, Gene wants to conform. His conformity is not the sole aspect of his personality, however; he also is consumed with envy of Finny.

Finny, on the other hand, stands out among the other boys because of his charismatic and mischievous nature. He is a superb athlete, though he does not seek athletic glory for himself. He is also a natural leader, forming a secret club with the other boys. Finny leads what seems like an effortless life and is the epitome of a non-conforming individual.

Gene, at the same time, admires and loathes him for this. At times early in the novel, we see Gene apparently wanting to be Finny. He even tries on Finny's clothes at one point while the latter is away. At other times, Gene believes that he and Finny are in a contest to see who is the best boy at Devon—Finny with his athletics or Gene with his grades. After Gene flunks a math test following a trip to the beach, he begins to think Finny is not really his friend at all and is intentionally trying to hurt his studies. Gene fluctuates from wanting to be like Finny to despising him for the very thing he admires, his individuality.

When Finny comments sincerely on how he wants Gene to succeed, Gene realizes that the hatred he has held for Finny is unfounded. Apparently, Finny is above hateful competition. The revelation angers Gene even more. This anger leads Gene to jostle the limb when Finny is preparing to jump in the river, causing him to fall and shatter his leg.

This incident is the first turning point in the story for Gene. The secret hatred he has felt for Finny melts away and is replaced with guilt, even though he will not admit it to himself. Through the rest of the novel, Gene seemingly becomes more like his friend. With Finny's help, he trains to become a star athlete at Devon, in effect taking the athlete's place at the school. However, Gene's denial of the part he played in Finny's accident, as well as his inability to acknowledge and cope with his guilt, prevents him from growing into maturity. It is not until Gene is confronted about the accident that he truly begins the process of change.

After Gene is recognized as the cause of Finny's fall, the two friends are able to talk openly and honestly in the infirmary before the latter's surgery, perhaps for the first time in over a year. Gene apologizes to his friend, finally freeing himself from his denial and guilt. Finny forgives him, and Gene is able to accept his friendship. When Finny dies during the surgery on his leg, Gene reacts stoically, realizing that his own old self has died with his friend.

Gene has suffered and caused suffering. The hatred, jealousy, guilt, and self-denial have left him. For the first time in his life, he can grow into adulthood, symbolized by the war that all of the boys face after graduation. He can now live his life without fear or resentment.

Ryan Neighbors

GUILT in *A Separate Peace*

John Knowles's *A Separate Peace* focuses on schoolboys at fictional Devon School in New Hampshire. It plays out as a flashback when the adult Gene reminisces about his time spent at the school, particularly his relationship with a boy named Phineas, or Finny. The pair become fast friends. Despite their contrasting personalities, they spend most of their free time together, break the school rules together, and even form a secret society, centered on jumping from a tree branch into the river. However, most of their relationship, particularly in the last half of the book, revolves around the guilt Gene feels toward Finny.

Their relationship changes at the end of the summer session where the adult Gene begins his flashback. This change is what leads to Gene's guilt. After becoming friends with Finny, Gene begins to feel jealousy and resentment toward him because of his charismatic and non-conforming nature. He also begins to think that he is in a competition with Finny to be the best boy in the school and that the latter is intentionally trying to sabotage Gene's studies to win the competition. Eventually, Gene realizes that Finny is above his petty jealousy, which makes him angry. The next time the pair perform the ceremony of their secret society by jumping from the tree into the river, Gene jostles the limb, causing Finny to fall and break his leg.

Gene immediately feels guilty about his action, particularly after hearing that Finny will never play sports again. He tries to confess his guilt to Finny at the infirmary and later at Finny's house, but Finny won't believe it. He has absolute faith in his friend. Gene has to rescind the confession.

Gene, however, continues to feel guilty when he returns to Devon for the winter session. When Finny returns weeks later, he pressures Gene into taking his place as the star athlete since Finny can no longer play. It is implied that Gene's guilt plays into his consent to train. They even plan for Gene to compete in the 1944 Olympics.

Gene's guilt returns to the forefront of his mind, however, after a friend, Leper, enlists in the military. He leaves the military shortly after enlisting, having gone slightly mad. When Gene goes to visit him in Vermont, Leper says that he knows what really happened to Finny. This accusation causes the schoolboys to have a mock trial to decide if Gene is really guilty. Finny says that his MEMORY of the event is blurry; Gene says that he does not remember. Leper, however, accuses Gene of causing the accident. Finny says that he does not care, leaves angrily, and falls down the stairs, re-breaking his leg.

It is only after Finny and Gene talk in the hospital that they are able to reconcile. Gene assures Finny that there was no hatred in his action; he acted blindly on impulse. Finny forgives him, and they are able to resolve the situation. Even though Finny dies during his surgery, Gene finds peace and forgiveness, freeing himself of the guilt that he felt for so long.

As has been shown, guilt is central to the conflict of the novel. Gene's guilt stems from the first major incident that occurs in the story, Finny's breaking his leg. From then on, that guilt determines how the pair relates to one another. This focus on guilt culminates in the mock trial, Finny's reinjuring his leg, and Gene eventually gaining forgiveness from Finny.

Not only is Gene's guilt central to the conflict, but it also serves as the central catalyst for Gene's change in the novel. It promotes his COMING-OF-AGE. Gene begins the novel as an immature and self-centered person. However, he grows from his early vindictiveness, experiences guilt about hurting Finny, and finally gains redemption and feels better about himself. By the end of the novel, he is a more mature, well-rounded person because of the guilt that has plagued him and his ordeal with Finny.

Ryan Neighbors

VIOLENCE in *A Separate Peace*

John Knowles's *A Separate Peace* deals with the relationships between two boys at a fictional school in New England during World War II. These two boys begin the novel as very different people. Gene is immature and competitive. Finny is carefree and charismatic. Knowles illuminates many themes through the relationship between the two boys, including the theme of violence. Violence mainly appears in the text in two aspects, through the incident at the tree and through the war that the boys are preparing to face after graduation.

The incident at the tree is perhaps the most important scene in the book, and it is the sole location of actual physical violence taking place. In the beginning of the book, Gene and Finny become friends, despite their differences. Through the next several chapters, Gene begins to be jealous of Finny. Finny is a natural athlete, and everyone likes and admires him. Gene also starts to believe that Finny is acting like his friend only to keep Gene from his studies. Because of this, he becomes more competitive toward Finny. This jealous competition comes to a head one evening while the pair are performing their ritualistic jump from a tree branch into the river. Finny makes a sincere and kind remark to Gene, and the latter realizes that their competition has been only in his imagination. This realization makes Gene angry. When Finny reaches the end of the branch, Gene bends his knees, causing Finny to fall and break his leg.

Admittedly, this is a minor act of violence. Physical contact is not even made between the two boys involved. However, the ramifications of this act propel the novel forward. It leads to Finny's inability to play sports and Gene's subsequent GUILT. It also leads to Finny's death and Gene's maturation.

In addition, the act itself is very telling of Gene's character at the time it occurs. In the beginning of the book, Gene often is competitive, jealous, and petty. When he realizes that Finny does not share those qualities, he lashes out. Instead of discussing the issue with Finny, he causes him to break his leg. Gene responds as a child, showing his immaturity. Interestingly, though, it is the repercussions of this act that enable him to grow as a person. Through Finny's forgiveness, Gene becomes more mature and comfortable with himself. Though Gene's violence shows his immaturity, it becomes a vehicle for his growing up.

The second example of violence in the novel is the war that the boys face after graduation. During the time frame in which the story takes place, both the Pacific and European theaters of World War II are in full swing. However, the novel only alludes to the war. In the story, no soldiers die and no guns are fired. The war is present solely in how it affects the boys at the school. Many of the boys respond to the war with fear and hatred, but others have more specialized reactions. For example, Brinker boasts about the prospect of going to war, while Leper, who chooses to enlist before graduation, eventually goes AWOL and becomes insane, pointing to the possible consequences of violence.

The implications of these two examples of violence in the novel seem to contradict each other. Gene's act of violence in breaking Finny's leg shows his immaturity, and he grows up only after his remorse and Finny's ensuing forgiveness. In a sense, he matures only after moving past violence. On the other hand, what awaits the boys in the adult world is violence. What is supposed to represent maturity to them, i.e., being an adult, carries with it some of the greatest death and destruction the world has ever seen. Perhaps the idea is that life is a war, and the key to maturity is picking your battles and dealing with them responsibly. Or perhaps Knowles is suggesting that humanity has some growing up to do. Either way, the violence in the story has a lasting effect on all the characters involved and on us as readers.

Ryan Neighbors

KOSINSKI, JERZY   *The Painted Bird* (1965, 1976)

Jerzy Kosinski's *The Painted Bird* brutally portrays a child's struggle for survival during wartime. Set in German-occupied eastern Europe during World War II, the novel tells the story of a young boy sent by his parents from his home in the city to the countryside, where they hope he will be kept safe. The boy, whose name we never learn, is instead forced to wander from village to village seeking shelter. Because of his dark complexion, he is in danger not only from the occupying Nazi army but also from villagers who often torment him. The boy is six at the start of war, 12 at its end. Although he survives the war, he leaves the novel a much-changed character, one warped and damaged by his experiences.

Kosinski's novel is episodic in its structure, organized around the boy's encounters with new people, new places, and new trials that he must face. Important characters in these episodes include Olga, a village healer, Lekh, a bird catcher, Garbos, a farmer, Gavrila and Mitka, soldiers in the Soviet army, and the Silent One, a war orphan who befriends the boy. Much like a folktale, the novel pits a young and helpless protagonist against a cruel world.

Although Jerzy Kosinski was Polish by birth, *The Painted Bird* was written in English after his immigration to the United States. Because Kosinski was born to Jewish parents and survived the war in hiding, many people have assumed the novel to be semi-autobiographical. However, Kosinski insisted in his preface to the second edition that the book was entirely a work of fiction, arguing that "Facts about my life and my origins . . should not be used to test the book's authenticity."

James Wyatt

IDENTITY in *The Painted Bird*

As the nameless narrator of Jerzy Kosinski's *The Painted Bird* seeks shelter in different villages, the peasants that the boy meets speculate about his ethnic identity. They consider the dark-haired and olive-skinned boy "a Gypsy or Jewish stray." The novel is set in eastern Europe during World War II, when the occupying Nazi army made sheltering a Jew or a Gypsy a crime punishable by death, and the villagers worry about the consequences of taking the boy into their communities. In addition, the villagers often identify the boy according to superstitious traditions: They fear and despise him because they believe that he possesses dark powers. Marta, his first protector, believes him to have "Gypsy or witches' eyes," which "could bring crippling illness, plague or death." Olga the Wise calls him "the Black One" and says that his eyes have the power to cast and remove spells.

In this way, the boy's identity is determined not by his inner self but by his outward appearance, which differs both from that of the villagers and from the Aryan ideal of the Nazis. The book's cen-tral metaphor makes clear this relationship between one's appearance and one's identity within society: when Lekh, the bird catcher, enraged by Ludmila's absence, paints a bird in bright colors and releases it, the bird tries to return to a flock of its own species; however, the flock regards the rainbow-colored bird as an intruder and viciously attacks it. Likewise, the boy is tortured and tormented by the villagers because they believe him to be different from themselves. The importance of this metaphor is stressed as we learn of the trains that pass through the forests near the villages carrying prisoners destined for concentration camps—prisoners who have been deemed subhuman due to their race or religious background.

The boy himself, separated from his family and removed from his previous society, becomes unsure of his identity. As he wanders throughout the war from village to village, he comes to believe in the view that the villagers have of him. Taken to an encampment of German soldiers, the boy stares directly into the eyes of one of them, believing that this might cast an evil spell. Later, when the boy witnesses the Kalmuks' horrific attack on a village, he believes that the villagers must be right about his evil nature: "I realized why God would not listen to my prayers, why I was hung from hooks, why Garbos beat me, why I lost my speech. I was black. My hair and eyes were as black as these Kalmuks'. Evidently I belonged with them in another world."

As an outsider at the mercy of others, the boy tries on various identities, attempting to find the key to power and control in society. He adopts variously a belief in evil, in the power of prayers of indulgence, and even in the power that the Germans possess. He identifies himself most strongly, however, with members of the Soviet army, the troops that move in from the east and push the Germans westward. From them he adopts Gavrila's Stalinist view of humanity and Mitka's philosophy of revenge. Forced to leave the regiment and to join an orphanage, the boy clings to this identity, refusing to part with his Soviet army uniform. He tells the teachers at the orphanage that his language is Russian and refuses to learn to read and write in his mother tongue.

Kosinski's novel suggests that our identities are malleable, formed by our experiences and by the images that others have of us. So strongly has the boy been shaped by the war that, when he is reunited with his parents, he is ambivalent toward them and unable to adapt again to the family life he once knew.

In this regard, it's interesting that Kosinski never specifies the boy's name, his home country, or his ethnic background. Although many readers have identified the setting as Poland, Kosinski's home country, and the boy as Jewish, as was Kosinski, the book is ambiguous on these points. Much like a fairy tale or a fable, the boy is cast into a hostile landscape, but not one that is readily identifiable. Perhaps Kosinski's novel challenges us to see something of ourselves through this device. Perhaps by trying specifically to identify the boy and his country, we repeat the mistakes of the villagers, that is, we risk seeing the boy as a member of a group rather than seeing his inner humanity.

James Wyatt

INDIVIDUAL AND SOCIETY in *The Painted Bird*

The Painted Bird is the story of an individual's struggle against a society that perceives him as different. The boy, dark-haired and dark-complexioned, is constantly threatened and abused by the villagers he meets, who are blond and light-skinned. Because of the boy's appearance, the villagers fear and despise him. Garbos worries that the boy is casting Gypsy spells. The carpenter is afraid that the boy's black hair will attract lightning. Others make the sign of the cross when they see him in order to ward off evil. As a result of the villagers' fears, the boy is pelted with stones, thrown into a manure pit, whipped, and nearly drowned.

It is this relationship between the individual and society that is illustrated in the novel's central metaphor: Lekh, the bird-catcher, enraged by Ludmila's absence, paints bird after bird "in still gaudier colors, and release[s] them into the air to be killed by their kin." The relationship between the painted bird and its flock is a metaphor for the way that society treats those that it perceives as different. Just as the birds tear apart the individual that they fail to recognize as one of their own, so too do humans. Ludmila, whom Lekh imagines as a "strange-colored bird," lives apart from society

and does not obey its conventions, taking countless lovers. As a consequence, the women of the village set upon her and brutally kick and beat her to death. In much the same way, because the Nazis perceive them as different, Jews and Gypsies are sent to concentration camps.

In Kosinski's novel, society demands conformity. The boy realizes this fact and dreams of inventing tools to change people so that they conform to the norms. Reflecting upon the trains leading to the death camps, the boy asks, "Wouldn't it be easier to change people's eyes and hair than to build big furnaces and then catch Jews and Gypsies to burn in them?" Even when he is rescued by the Russian army, the boy worries that the Soviet system will demand a similar kind of conformity. He notes that "Only the group, which they called 'the collective,' was qualified to determine a man's worth and importance" (192), and he therefore worries that "just as my black hair and eyes were held against me by the peasants, my social origin could handicap my new life with the Soviets."

And yet the metaphor of the painted bird also describes the desire of the bird to return to its flock. Even as the boy faces danger in the villages, he needs and desires companionship. He relies upon others for protection and for food, and he longs to be accepted and loved. At the novel's end, although the boy's experiences throughout the war have led him to desire isolation, he still feels compelled to return to his parents when they at last find him in an orphanage. Upon seeing his mother and father for the first time in many years, he realizes that he "suddenly felt like Lekh's painted bird, which some unknown force was pulling to its kind." However, the boy soon decides he "would much prefer to be on [his] own again, wandering from one village to the next."

The boy's experiences throughout the novel lead him to believe that life within society is impossible. After he is thrown into the manure pit, the boy becomes mute, a condition that seems emblematic of his inability to communicate with others. Near the end of the novel, the boy makes clear his feelings about society: "Every one of us stood alone . . . It mattered little if one was mute; people did not understand one another anyway." And yet despite this pessimistic view of society's relationship to the individual, the book does end on a small note of optimism. The boy, living in the mountains apart from his parents, answers a ringing telephone and feels that "somewhere at the other end of the wire there was someone who wanted to talk with me . . . I felt an overpowering desire to speak." Although the boy has clearly been altered by his experiences during the war, perhaps we can find hope in the fact that he regains his voice, hope that the boy may yet be able to communicate with and participate in society.

James Wyatt

VIOLENCE in *The Painted Bird*

Even the most jaded reader of *The Painted Bird* must be shocked by some of the novel's depictions of violence. The images are gruesome: Garbos tortures the boy by suspending him just above the jaws of a vicious dog; the miller blinds a rival by plucking out his eyes with a spoon; the Kalmuks (Soviet deserters who fought with the Germans) rape the women and children of a village. That a young boy, alone and unprotected, is witness to—or often subjected to—such violence makes these depictions even more shocking. Some readers may feel that the novel's violence is overstated, perhaps even obscene, so perhaps we should consider the problem Kosinski faced in writing about World War II: How does one begin to convey the magnitude of the Holocaust?

Surprisingly, the violence that the novel depicts is generally *not* that of concentration camps and of the occupying German army. In fact, the boy is met with relative kindness by one of the German soldiers, who, when ordered to kill the boy, instead sets him free. Although we are made aware of the trains carrying Jews and Gypsies to the camps, the violence we witness is largely associated with the villagers that the boy encounters. Those whom we might expect to shelter the boy instead despise and violently abuse him. The pattern is set early in the novel when the boy, seeking help, enters a new village: He is kicked by one peasant and whipped by another. In response, the crowd "howl[s] with laughter." In each new episode of the novel, the boy encounters new forms of abuse and violence.

The novel therefore describes not simply the violence of war, but also the violence of human nature. Kosinski presents us with a world in which people are intrinsically harsh, cruel, and animalistic. In fact, we are often shown that there is little or no difference between human and animal behavior. Garbos, who wants to kill the boy, is closely linked to his dog Judas, who attacks the boy. The murder of Ludmila by the village women reminds us of how Lekh's painted bird is torn to pieces by the flock.

In such a world, where individuals are despised for being different and where only the strong can survive, the boy necessarily learns to be violent. To save his own life, he is forced to kill, escaping from the carpenter by pulling him into a bunker filled with rats. From Mitka, the Russian sniper, the boy learns a philosophy of revenge when several soldiers from Mitka's regiment are killed at a party by drunken peasants. Mitka in response takes up his sniper rifle and kills a number of the villagers: "Only the conviction that one was as strong as the enemy and that one could pay him back double, enabled him to survive, Mitka said. . . . If someone slapped you and it felt like a thousand blows, take revenge for a thousand blows." The boy and the Silent One seem to follow this philosophy when they plot the murder of a farmer who beat the boy. In their attempt to kill the farmer, they derail a passenger train, killing perhaps hundreds of others. At the novel's end, when the boy is at last reunited with his family, his parents are shocked by his violent behavior. They look at him with wordless incomprehension after he breaks the arm of his adopted brother.

The novel is in this way a strange coming of age story: The boy matures and loses his innocence; however, his experiences during the six years of the war leave him violent and vengeful. Likewise, the other children in the orphanage, who have also lived through the horrors of war, have been badly damaged by their experiences. Violence, it seems, begets violence. A boy nicknamed Cannon kills a girl by throwing a heavy boot at her. Other boys gang-rape a nurse.

The Painted Bird suggests to us that violence is a tool we use to gain power over others. Before the boy and the Silent One derail the passenger train, the boy considers the power at his disposal. He says, "I recalled the trains carrying people to the gas chambers and crematories. The men who had ordered and organized all that probably enjoyed a similar feeling of complete power over their uncomprehending victims." Moreover, by juxtaposing the violence of the villagers with the violence of the German army, Kosinski cautions us that the Holocaust was not simply a product of Nazism. Violence and cruelty were not simply the result of the war. Rather, they are a part of nature, and our distrust of those who are different can too easily lead to atrocities.

James Wyatt

KUNDERA, MILAN   *The Unbearable Lightness of Being*   (1984)

The Unbearable Lightness of Being is a masterpiece of European literature, written by Milan Kundera, a Franco-Czech novelist born in Brno but living in France since 1975. The novel was written in 1982 (Czech title: *Nesnesitelná lehkost bytí*) but first published in 1984 in France; Czech censorship had prevented the author from publishing it in his homeland. The novel is set in 1968 Prague, and aims to be a fresco of the situation of artists, intellectuals, and leading figures in communist Czechoslovakia after the tragic events of the Prague Spring and the subsequent invasion by the USSR. The novel's main character is Tomas, a renowned surgeon who loses his position for writing an insignificant article, published in an unknown journal, that is accused of criticizing Czech communists. The other most prominent characters are Tomas's wife Tereza (a photographer and, later, a barmaid), his lover Sabina (a painter), and Sabina's lover Franz (a college professor).

The novel portrays a passionate love affair, entangled with crucial historical issues and some philosophical adagios—such as the reflection on Parmenides's concepts of "lightness" and "heaviness"; or the considerations on *"Einmal ist keinmal"* ("what happened once might as well have never happened at all"). Analyzing the relationships between Tomas and Tereza, Tomas and Sabina, Sabina and Franz, set against the misery and tragedy of an oppressive political regime, the narrator

offers a masterful exploration of such themes as love, identity, and oppression, in which all nuances are given voice.

Tania Collani

IDENTITY in *The Unbearable Lightness of Being*

In Kundera's *The Unbearable Lightness of Being,* readers are faced with a sophisticated reflection on identity. On the one hand, characters do everything not to identify themselves with their parents and their own homeland; on the other hand, when they are away from their own country, their feeling of self-dispossession becomes "unbearable," and they feel a natural need to go back to their origins, to their original identity. This feeling is particularly evident in the stories of the two female characters of the novel, the unconfident Tereza and the crackling Sabina.

From the beginning of the novel, Tereza looks at herself in the mirror, trying to find out as many differences as possible between her mother and her. She hates her mother, and all her choices are influenced by the comparison. Tereza's revulsion toward her heritage has a parallel with her hate toward the weakness of her own country, which resigned itself to the invasion of the Soviet Union. After the Prague Spring of 1968, the equilibrium of the whole country changed radically in August 1968. Since Tereza identifies herself neither with her personal roots (her mother), nor with her social roots, she decides to fly to Switzerland: "one thing was clear: the country would have to bow to the conqueror . . . The carnival was over. Workaday humiliation had begun."

During her short Swiss exile, Tereza feels the sensation of losing her roots: It is one thing to "hate" her country and her mother, it is another thing to be "indifferent" to both. She cannot bring herself to become a fashion photographer, after having reported the horrible events of Prague, even though everyone seems indifferent to what happened in Czechoslovakia: "Being in a foreign country means walking a tightrope high above the ground without the net afforded a person by the country where he has his family, colleagues, and friends, and where he can easily say what he has to say in a language he has known from childhood."

Little by little, her radical feelings change, becoming more mature and more complex. The sense of hate toward the humiliation of President Dubcek's speech to the nation, diminishes as time goes by: "Thinking in Zurich of those days, she no longer felt any aversion to the man The word 'weak' no longer sounded like a verdict." Through deep introspection, she manages to understand that she has nothing to share with Switzerland, with its valuation of success at all costs, and that she cannot resign herself to being a fashion photographer: "She realized that she belonged among the weak, in the camp of the weak, in the country of the weak, and that she had to be faithful to them precisely because they were weak." That's why she decides to go back to her country, even if she is aware that her decision will affect her and her husband's future. Once back, she is confronted by another huge loss of identity: All the leading figures before 1968 have been replaced by people who consented to the invasion. Tomas, once a famous surgeon, becomes a window washer; Tereza becomes a barmaid and she works with a former diplomat, who keeps on his desk a photograph of his meeting with a smiling Kennedy. Everything is different from what it was before; but her suffering is more bearable than her lack of identity.

On the contrary, the painter Sabina worships her feeling of unfaithfulness toward both her father and communism. Her identity is not formed by moralist lessons, but by beautiful ideas: "Betrayal means breaking ranks and going off into the unknown." She doesn't feel any particular sense of loss connected to the political situation. Once she "allowed herself to be taken along to a gathering of fellow émigrés," and she loathed their meaningless speeches: "she asked herself why she should bother to maintain contact with Czechs. What bound her to them? The landscape? If each of them were asked to say what the name of his native country evoked in him, the images that came to mind would be so different as to rule out all possibility of unity." Sabina's aesthetic perspective prevents her from feeling a sense of belonging to a nation due to shared political views. Since only personal values count for her, her only link to her country is the image of the "cemetery" and her friends, Tomas and Tereza.

When she finally learns that Tereza and Tomas died in an accident, she feels that "the last link to her past had been broken."

Tania Collani

LOVE in *The Unbearable Lightness of Being*

In Kundera's *The Unbearable Lightness of Being* the reader is faced with two main types of love: on the one hand, the main love affair between Tomas and Tereza, ending with their marriage and a life together; on the other hand, the love affair between Tomas and the painter Sabina, which is primarily based on sex and on the thrill of eccentricity and instability.

In both cases, it is interesting to see how all characters are (metaphorically) sterile, and content to be involved in sterile love stories: Only Tomas has a son "by mistake" from his first wife, but at no moment does he feel compassion for him or regret at having left him with his mother. Halfway through the novel, when Tereza and Tomas are already fallen into misery because of the communist regime, she tells him, relieved: "I'm beginning to be grateful to you for not wanting to have children." However, seen through Sabina's eyes, the fact of not having children is also a way to escape the holy decree "Be fruitful and multiply."

The main love affair between Tomas and Tereza is characterized by a huge tension between Tomas's infidelity and Tereza's will to change his nature. Nonetheless, however unfaithful, Tomas is truthfully in love with Tereza, and he feels all the frightening "symptoms" of love: "But was it love? The feeling of wanting to die beside her." Tomas's spur to infidelity responds to a philosophical issue he is confronted with from the beginning of the novel: "What happens but once . . . might as well not have happened at all." A consequence of this assumption is the fact that people live only one life, which means that they can make mistakes, but have no chance to do better in another life. That's why Tomas cannot avoid going to bed with a large number of women: He wants to test all possibilities of material love, even though he doesn't debate his love and relationship with Tereza.

As a matter of fact, Tereza is the first woman, after Tomas's divorce, to spend a whole night with him: "He fell asleep by her side. When he woke up the next morning, he found Tereza who was still asleep, holding his hand." And Tomas is perfectly aware that "spending the night together was the corpus delicti of love." This awareness marks a real transformation in Tomas's life of inveterate bachelor and Casanova; he has never felt the same "compassion" he now feels for Tereza. As the text itself suggests, "metaphors are dangerous," and "a single metaphor can give birth to love": The association between Tereza knocking on Tomas's door carrying two heavy suitcases, and the biblical "child put in a pitch-daubed bulrush and sent downstream," is the main cause of his love for her. In Tomas's philosophy, making love with a woman is not linked with the passion of sleeping with her: "love does not make itself felt in the desire for copulation (a desire that extends to an infinite number of women) but in the desire for shared sleep (a desire limited to one woman)."

The love affair with Sabina is very deep as well, even if they both decide to leave their relationship to the status of infrequent meetings. Tomas loves Sabina because she accepts him as he is, without being jealous for his other dealings. She is a thorough individualist but, at the same time, she is capable of great abnegation. Her love and esteem for Tomas stretch to the point of helping Tereza to find a good job as a photographer, even if she is inexperienced: "When Sabina herself introduced Tereza to everyone on the weekly, Tomas knew he had never had a better friend as a mistress than Sabina." When Tomas meets Sabina in Zurich, while on voluntary exile from Czechoslovakia, he thinks that his life with Sabina and Tereza is marvelous: "he thought happily that he carried his way of living with him as a snail carries his house. Tereza and Sabina represented the two poles of his life, separate and irreconcilable, yet equally appealing." He is eventually forced to choose, for Tereza goes back to Prague and he can either be completely free in Zurich, or join Tereza and be oppressed by the communist regime. He chooses the second option, bidding farewell to Sabina and Zurich's "unbearable lightness" to go back to his "heavy" roots, Prague and Tereza, even though his choice is irreversible.

Tania Collani

OPPRESSION in *The Unbearable Lightness of Being*

Kundera's novel covers the whole spectrum of human oppression: from oppression caused by intricate LOVE relationships, down to the sense of subjugation induced by a peculiar political situation (both of them seen through Tomas and Tereza's eyes), and the aesthetic oppression caused by the standardization of ugliness (shown from the painter Sabina's perspective).

The theory that opposites attract is undoubtedly true for Tomas and Tereza. Tomas is in fact a modern Casanova who is really in love with his wife, Tereza, but cannot avoid having sexual relationships with other women. Loving women's bodies is seen by him as a natural impulse, and he manages not to confuse physical attraction with real love. On the contrary, Tereza is faithful to him and thinks that real love shows itself through monogamous relationships. She is perfectly aware of Tomas's unfaithfulness, and she spends all her life trying to stop her husband from seeing other women. That is to say, she is oppressed by this situation, because she knows that Tomas loves her, even though he makes love to other women. As a result, she oppresses Tomas by intervening in both their lives, trying to change this state of things.

Tereza is haunted by her own jealousy, especially at night: Her recurrent dreams bring out all her anxieties about her relationship with Tomas. In one case, Tereza dreams of being ordered by Tomas to stand in a corner while he makes love to Sabina: "the sight caused Tereza intolerable suffering" and, in order to alleviate "the pain in her heart by pains of the flesh, she jabbed needles under her fingernails." In another case, she dreams of being sent to death by Tomas himself, who ordered her and another group of naked women to march around a pool; as Tereza tells Tomas, "you never took your eyes off us, and the minute we did something wrong, you would shoot." Tereza's lack of quiet sleep is of course due to his husband's inconsistency: "first he disavowed his infidelities, then he tried to justify them."

Tereza's accounts of her restless nights induce a strong sense of subjugation in Tomas. First of all, he understands that since Tereza lives with him, he has no more private life, as proved by the fact that she reads his secret lovers' letters. When Tomas accuses her—"So you've been rummaging in my letters!"—not only does she not deny it, but also she lays it on thicker: "Throw me out, then!" The sense of oppression felt by Tomas emerges quite clearly in the following sentences: "He was in a bind: in his mistresses' eyes, he bore the stigma of his love for Tereza; in Tereza's eyes, the stigma of his exploits with the mistresses." Burdened with that same sense of oppression, Tomas comes back from Zurich to Prague in order to join Tereza, after his fleeing from the communist regime. He is perfectly aware that he cannot live without her, but as soon as he enters his apartment in Prague and meets Tereza, with the consciousness that he can never go back, he "felt no compassion. All he felt was the pressure in his stomach and the despair of having returned."

The oppression provoked by the communist regime interferes not only with Tomas's private life, but also, and above all, with his social life. While before 1968 he was a renowned surgeon, when he decides to go back to his homeland to join Tereza, his professional career deteriorates until he has descended all the way down the social scale to window washer. This descent to the lowest social classes is due to a critical article that Tomas wrote shortly before the arrival of Soviet tanks in Prague. Asked to retract his statement, he refuses because he feels a deep sense of oppression: "he was annoyed with himself and at his clumsiness, and desired to avoid further contact with the police and the concomitant feeling of helplessness."

This widespread sense of oppression is sublimated in the point of view of the painter Sabina, who translates the idea of dominant ugliness in aesthetic terms—the *kitsch*. This ugliness starts in music and touches all fields of visual life: "she discovered that the transformation of music into noise was a planetary process by which mankind was entering the historical phase of total ugliness . . . The omnipresence of visual ugliness would soon follow." The concept of *kitsch* contains also the political and social feeling of mass oppression: It implies that bad taste and arrogance inexorably penetrate all levels of life, subjugating the individual's inclinations to a general sense of conformed beauty.

Tania Collani

KUREISHI, HANIF   *The Buddha of Suburbia*   (1990)

The Buddha of Suburbia (1990) is Hanif Kureishi's first novel and established his reputation as a fiction writer. It won the Whitbread Award for Best First Novel and in 1993 was adapted into an acclaimed BBC television series, following the success of Kureishi's screenplay for *My Beautiful Laundrette* (1985).

The novel describes and investigates the experiences of first- and second-generation immigrants in the society of 1970s suburban England. Through the characters of its chief protagonists, it also becomes an examination of the psychology of mixed race. The narrator of the novel, Karim, struggles to find acceptance in British society as a racial hybrid, born of an Indian Muslim father, Haroon, and a British Christian mother, Margaret. He intertwines his tale with that of Jamila, the daughter of Haroon's neo-conservative friend, Anwar, and his Pakistani wife, Jeeta. Karim's journey toward self-identification involves a new understanding of being "English" and of the transitions from adolescence to adulthood to maturity.

The novel's opening depicts how Karim's natural teenage anxieties are reinforced by the gradual dissolution of his parents' marriage and interracial tensions in the suburbs. In his new existence as Oriental philosopher and spiritual guide to upper-middle-class suburbanites, Karim's petty bureaucrat father, Haroon, becomes involved with the dilettantish Eva. As this adulterous liaison develops, Margaret's sister, Jean, and brother-in-law, Ted, support her decision to divorce Haroon, because it endorses their essential race-based snobbery. Their inflexible attitudes, like Anwar's patriarchal behavior, are the target of Kureishi's satire. Karim's relationships with Jamila, her child-like husband Changez, and Eva's rock-star son Charlie stabilize his own ideas about life, but the true realization of his individuality comes from within him.

Through these characters and their interactions, Kureishi explores themes like PARENTHOOD, REJECTION, and SPIRITUALITY. *The Buddha of Suburbia* at times comes close to being stream-of-consciousness, but its inherent confusions are always negotiated by the quasi-authoritative voice of its narrator.

Divya Saksena

PARENTHOOD in *The Buddha of Suburbia*

Hanif Kureishi's novel, set in suburban England of the 1970s, becomes an exploration of the role of parenthood in forming the characters of its chief protagonists, as well as an examination of the parents themselves. The narrator of the novel, Karim or "Creamy," tells of struggling to find acceptance in British society as a hybrid, born of an Indian Muslim father, Haroon ("Harry"), and a British Christian mother, Margaret. He intertwines his tale with that of Jamila or "Jammie," the daughter of his father's old childhood friend, Anwar, and his Pakistani wife, "Princess" Jeeta. As a teenager, Karim becomes aware that Haroon, by day a petty bureaucrat, is in the evenings and weekends establishing a parallel identity as an Oriental philosopher and spiritual guide to suburbanites. In this secretive, subterranean existence, Haroon becomes involved with Eva who, seeking spiritual comfort as she recovers from breast cancer, ends up providing sexual solace to Haroon. When Karim accompanies his father to one of his group meetings, he witnesses Haroon and Eva's passionate sexual activity, and for the first time begins to realize the extended nature of parenthood in his life. He has himself a sexually loaded relationship with Eva's son Charlie, slightly older than him and an aspiring punk rocker. When Haroon moves in with Eva, Margaret decides to live temporarily with her sister Jean and brother-in-law Ted. Although his younger brother Allie sides with their mother, Karim prefers to divide his time between Haroon and Eva, Margaret and her relatives, and Jamila's parents, Anwar and Jeeta. Hence, his adolescence is defined by at least three sets of parents, biological, surrogate, and adopted. As he puts it, "It comforted me that there was always somewhere less intense, and warmer, where I could go when my own family had me thinking of running away."

More than comfort, Karim derives practical advantages from revolving among these different avatars of parenthood as he enters his adult years. Influenced by Charlie, he decides to drop out of college, frustrating his father's vicarious dreams of studying medicine. His participation in Eva's scramble up the suburban social ladder and her indirect entry into the London social scene is rewarded when Eva introduces him to Shadwell, who needs a new actor to play Mowgli in an avant-garde production of *The Jungle Book*. While Karim enjoys the sensation of being the center of attention, he also struggles with ambiguous feelings toward Shadwell, who becomes his surrogate father for a while, supplying him the adult perspectives and practical guidance that Haroon has always been incapable of providing.

Visiting his mother, Karim shares her helplessness in her divorce, trying to understand her desire to resume the humdrum but secure middle-class existence that Ted and Jean still maintain. As a parent, Margaret initially exhibits all the traits of traditional, self-sacrificing mother. While Karim resents her surrendering Haroon to Eva without fighting for her rights as wife, he sometimes despises her for being too accommodating of her husband's demands. Deriving his essential selfishness from her as much as from Haroon, Karim fears that Margaret's "weakness and unhappiness" will infect him; he does not realize that his own youth, his "life and spirit could stimulate her." Hence when she moves back into the home she shared with Haroon, she immediately begins to claim it as her own space. She leaves her job at a shoe store and becomes a doctor's receptionist. Celebrating the preview of his debut as an actor, Karim is surprised to see his mother dance barefoot to the Jackson Five in a nightclub in London's West End: "I'd forgotten how happy she could be . . . I'd never seen Mum dance before." He has to accept that parenthood for Margaret is now only one aspect of her life.

With Anwar and Jeeta, his substitute parents, Karim can enjoy the benefits of a traditional Indian cultural background. Jeeta evolves from being a subservient wife to becoming the dominant business partner. However, she cannot prevent Anwar from emotionally blackmailing Jamila into an arranged marriage with Changez, a stranger from India. Anwar regards parenthood as a means to achieve his own desires. His hunger-strike, "self-inflicted frailty" is a deliberate manipulation of his daughter into providing him with a son-in-law and grandchildren to help expand his Indian grocery store. Trapped in his concepts of traditional male parenthood, he terribly underestimates Jamila, taking her obedience for granted: "It was as if, in some strange way, it was beneath his dignity to take an interest in her."

Changez turns out to be a gross, balding, congenitally lazy man with only one good arm. Symbolically, his atrophied arm represents the withering of Anwar's paternal dreams, since Jamila will be a wife in name only.

Returning from America to Eva and Haroon, Karim realizes that "you never stop feeling like an eight-year-old in front of your parents." He takes a perverse pleasure in revealing his mother's new love-life to his father in front of Eva, in revenge for their betrayal of parenthood. He wants Haroon to experience the despair he has felt at the inevitability of change. At his party to celebrate his new part in a soap opera, when Eva and Haroon announce their forthcoming marriage, Karim feels happy and miserable at the same time. Eva will be his official new mother at last, and a semblance of parenthood, upgraded from suburban anonymity to urban celebrity, will be restored to him. But sadly, his obsession with parents has now changed to a realization of his own power as an individual.

Divya Saksena

REJECTION in *The Buddha of Suburbia*

In Hanif Kureishi's novel *The Buddha of Suburbia* the racially hybrid narrator Karim, or "Creamy," born of an Indian Muslim father, Haroon ("Harry"), and a British Christian mother, Margaret, struggles with issues of acceptance and rejection in British society. Similarly, Jamila, the daughter of Haroon's old childhood friend Anwar and his Pakistani wife "Princess" Jeeta; Jamila's husband Changez; and Charlie, the punk-rock star son of Haroon's girlfriend Eva, all go through rejection of traditional attitudes and ideals while trying to establish their own identities in an adult world. When the novel opens, Karim discovers that Haroon, by day a petty bureaucrat, has in the evenings and on weekends established a parallel existence as an Oriental philosopher and spiritual guide to upper-middle-class dilettantes; this becomes the initiation point for a series of rejections that establish an important theme in the novel.

Haroon has begun to image himself as a reincarnation of the original Buddha, becoming the Buddha of the suburbia, a spiritual god-man who promises upper-middle-class Britishers relief from all the ills and pressures of modern life. As such, he feels he must renounce his wife and family. Unlike the original Buddha, he creates a parallel family with Eva and Charlie. His wife rejects his idea of connected parallel homes and turns back to her own culture, where she can trade on sympathy from her peers and relatives as the rejected wife of a foreign immigrant. Although her sister Jean and brother-in-law Ted lament her original rejection of her own white society to marry Haroon, they are supportive of her rejection of Haroon's foray into spiritualism. Jean's negative attitude to Haroon transmits itself to Karim's younger brother Allie, so that when the family breaks up, Allie goes with his mother "crying and yelling, 'Bugger off, you Buddhist bastard!' as he left with Mum and Jean." Allie's desire to be a ballet dancer and attend an expensive school also signifies his rejecting both the working-class norms of his mother and the "aristocratic" quasi-intellectual aspirations of his father. Allie ends up working for a clothes designer, and tries to convince Karim that "no one put people like you and me in camps and no one will. . . . Let's just make the best of ourselves." His rejection of both his cultural polarities has led him to a new acceptance of his hybridity, an acceptance that Karim seeks but finds elusive. As Karim says, after their childhood rivalry, he is strangely attracted to the adult Allie: "I liked him now; I wanted to know him; but the things he was saying were strange."

Instead, Karim prefers the relatively straightforward rejection of all ideals that Jamila undertakes in her journey through adolescence into adulthood. Jamila imbibes a quantity of radical ideas from her old teacher Miss Cutmore, then "started to hate Miss Cutmore for forgetting that she was Indian." She shares with Karim the essential alienation of second-generation immigrants from the mainstream society. Both surreptitiously explore alternative identities while experimenting with ways of rejecting their ethnicity: "Yeah, sometimes we were French, Jammie and I, and other times we went black American. The thing was we were supposed to be English, but to the English we were always wogs and nigs and Pakis and the rest of it." Jammie is certain of at least one fact: While she cannot physically prevent her parents from running her life, she can devote her energy to finding as many ways as possible to reject and subvert parental authority and eventually get her own way.

While Karim admires her militant attitudes, he is often fearful of her extreme radicalism. Hence, when she rejects the arranged marriage with Changez, an unseen groom from India, Karim is torn between understanding her turbulent emotions and sympathizing with Anwar. Jamila rejects outright her conjugal relationship with Changez. Her rejection stems not from his external repulsiveness or the physical deformity of his polio-withered arm, but rather she rejects him largely due to her commitment to her radical ideology. At the end of the novel, when she is living in a commune and allowing Changez to serve as a domestic help and unpaid nanny to her baby daughter, she also forces him to reject the traditional patriarchal norms he has cherished all his life. When Karim puts it to him, "I am asking how you, Changez, you with your background of prejudice against practically the whole world, are coping with being married to a lesbian." Changez is stupefied by the realization that he has indeed unwittingly rejected all the ideals of his Indian upbringing.

Eva's son, Charlie, is one of the few characters in the novel who succeeds in his ambition. At the height of his success as a rock star, he turns his back on his London fans and moves to a faster, drug-oriented life in New York. He rescues Karim from a failing dramatic career and offers him a permanent place in his home as his assistant. However, after a while, Karim finds himself rejecting all that Charlie and his wild lifestyle have to offer. When they argue, Charlie claims that by embracing New York he is rejecting the narrow-minded prejudices of life in England: "So shocked, so self-righteous, and moral, so loveless and incapable of dancing. They are narrow, the English. It is a Kingdom of Prejudice over there. Don't be like it!" Ironically, when Charlie and Karim go out together in New York, they become "two British boys in America," identifying themselves by the culture they claim to have rejected.

Karim also rejects the excesses of sexual experimentation he observes Charlie undertaking. He gradually realizes that his time in New York has helped heal his emotional wounds of being rejected by the mainstream theater in England because of his

mixed race. He also realizes he shares with his father the experience of being a social outsider, a minority, which paradoxically gives them both the strength to survive against social odds. Thus, he comes to understand that

> Dad had always felt superior to the British: this was the legacy of his Indian childhood—political anger turning into scorn and contempt . . . and he'd made me feel that we couldn't allow ourselves the shame of failure in front of these people. You couldn't let the ex-colonialists see you on your knees, for that was where they expected you to be.

The realization that his father has not rejected his essential Indian identity even after more than 20 years in England makes Karim understand that he has "inherited from Dad a strong survival instinct" (250). It gives him a deeper insight into his father's and his own characters and provides him the resolution to reject all the material advantages of being Charlie's sidekick. It also completes his emotional healing. Therefore, he can take the risk of returning to England with only the faint possibility of a television career ahead of him. Finally rejecting the idea of a career in theater, he can pursue and achieve success in the new medium of television, playing a racially relevant part in a sitcom. He can also reenter the world he had once turned away from, and accept not only that his mother has a white English boyfriend, but also that Eva and his father are about to be married. In rejecting the shallowness of materialistic living, Karim feels he has discovered greater depths for true emotional life within himself.

Divya Saksena

SPIRITUALITY in *The Buddha of Suburbia*

By its very title, Hanif Kureishi's novel *The Buddha of Suburbia* becomes an investigation of the working of spirituality in suburban England of the 1970s. The narrator of the novel, Karim or "Creamy," describes his struggle to find acceptance in British society as a hybrid, born of an Indian Muslim father, Haroon ("Harry"), and a British Christian mother, Margaret. Their lives are inextricably linked with Jamila or "Jammie," the daughter of his father's old childhood friend Anwar and Anwar's Pakistani wife "Princess" Jeeta, Jamila's husband Changez, and Charlie, the punk-rock star son of Haroon's girlfriend Eva. Early in the novel, Karim discovers that Haroon, by day a petty bureaucrat, has in the evenings and on weekends established a parallel existence as an Eastern philosopher and spiritual guide to upper-middle-class suburbanites. He has begun to image himself as a reincarnation of the original Buddha, becoming the Buddha of suburbia, a spiritual god-man who promises relief from all the ills and pressures of modern life.

Hence, almost from the beginning, Kureishi takes up the theme of spirituality in his novel, juxtaposing different social and religious positions and showing how the essential pacifism of Buddhism transcends differences in its appeal to modernity's pursuit of the higher life. Spirituality, in a narrow sense, concerns itself with matters of the spirit, and involves not only non-physical or abstract concepts (or even abilities) but also contrasts these with humankind's fundamentally earthly (or material and worldly) nature. Herein lies the attraction of Haroon, otherwise a nondescript, insignificant man, to the troubled upper-middle-class socialites like Eva. Tiring of what they perceive to be their worldly ambitions and excitements, they seek a new form of stimulation and they find it in Haroon's partly obscure utterances. Coming from his more pragmatic view of his father as an incompetent homemaker and ineffectual disciplinarian, Karim is astonished to see these socially influential people surrender themselves before Haroon and acclaim him as their spiritual master.

An important defining characteristic of spirituality is a perceived sense of connection of oneself to a greater metaphysical reality, of the individual soul to a greater entity through the medium of a master or guide. This connection creates an emotional experience of awe and reverence, leading to a sense of release into a perfect state such as Nirvana. Hence, spirituality relates to matters of mental sanity and psychological health, sometimes focusing on mystic personal experiences through collective activities like prayer and listening to a spiritual discourse. This is how Haroon conducts the com-

munal meetings organized for him by Eva. To be fair to Haroon, however, Karim acknowledges that his father has always wished to be valued: "Beneath all the Chinese bluster was Dad's loneliness and desire for internal advancement." Marginalized in his daytime world of British bureaucracy, and in his cross-racial home life, spirituality is an escape as much for Haroon as it is for his worshipful audience.

However, among many definitions spirituality can mean perceiving or wishing to perceive life as "higher," as more complex than a merely sensual worldview. Many spiritual traditions, accordingly, share a common concept: the "path," "work," or method of subjugating one's physical, animal nature to the rest of existence or the cosmos to become free from the lower ego and more fully one's "true" self. However much Haroon exhorts his followers to this "Path or Way," he does not adhere to it himself, for Karim sees him making passionate and illicit love with Eva in the garden away from his invited audience. This sensual relationship leads to his divorce from Margaret and moving in with Eva. As he leaves home, his younger son Allie shouts tearfully at Haroon, "Bugger off, you Buddhist bastard!" The phrase reveals not only the deeply rooted suspicion of Haroon's philosophy in his English wife and her relatives, but also their feeling of betrayal by him under the guise of his spiritual activities.

Earlier, Margaret's brother-in-law Ted has experienced Haroon's alleged powers when he tries to dissuade him from continuing his "Buddhist" spiritualism: "Buddhism isn't the kind of thing she's used to. It's got to stop." Haroon responds by putting Ted through a spiritual experience of his own, forcing him to confront his own workaholic nature and his fear that his wife, Jean, will leave him. Ted collapses, almost weeping from the force of the emotions he encounters in himself, and Haroon is able to tell his wife happily: "I've released him." The incident reinforces Haroon's belief in his own spiritual abilities and is another step in his reinvention of himself as a suburban guru, embarking on an exploration into the meaning of becoming fully human.

Once Eva and Haroon move to London, they proceed to establish him more firmly as spiritual adviser. Now their targets are not the middle-aged suburbanites of Beckenham, but the much more influential and financially rewarding urban socialites. Haroon has learned by now to distinguish between the transformational spirituality he attempted in Beckenham, where he tried truly to transform his disciples' approach to life, and the "feel good" spiritualism he can practice in London on jaded sophisticates who merely want someone to listen to them, support them, and receive a reward for doing so.

Divya Saksena

KUSHNER, TONY *Angels in America: A Gay Fantasia on National Themes* (1992)

Angels in America: A Gay Fantasia on National Themes comprises two full-length dramas: *Part One: Millennium Approaches* and *Part Two: Perestroika.* Though separate works, *Perestroika* joined productions of *Millennium Approaches* already running in London and New York in November 1993. It is a historical drama and a work of magical realism that follows individuals through personal struggles and despair caused by an America teetering on the edge of a new millennium.

As a historical drama, *Angels in America* illustrates the past and present of an American landscape in the late 1980s for viewing by an audience through a critical lens. The past is shown as a literal passing, through the funeral of a Jewish woman from the "old country." The present is captured through a hypocritical, fictionalized politician. And finally, it is a small group of lonely people who navigate the difficulties of their lives, coming together to remember the past in order to make the choices that can lead to progress and life over stasis and death at the work's conclusion. Magical realism (a literary technique that fuses the supernatural with the real), on the other hand, is employed to show forces beyond the material and real through characters speaking with the dead and the interaction of Prior Walter and the Angels.

The drama follows the characters of Prior Walter; Louis Ironson; Belize; Roy Cohn; and Joe, Hannah, and Harper Pitt and illustrates complex and difficult relationships that develop from the individual struggles each faces. Through these characters, Kushner explores themes such as HOPE, ILLNESS, and ALIENATION.

Brian Stiles

ALIENATION in *Angels in America*
Tony Kushner illustrates the theme of alienation throughout *Angels in America* to make a social and political statement about the state of America in the 1980s. In this manner, alienation is used on two levels, through the alienation of the audience and the alienation of the characters within and among themselves.

The form of the play is envisioned as Epic Theater, or Theater of Alienation, in which the audience engages with the play, aware that the work is making a social and political statement and that theatergoers should examine it critically. It accomplishes this by staging the play in such a way as to make the audience aware of the issues the work addresses. It pointedly avoids presenting the story as escapist entertainment.

Angels in America strives to demonstrate the social, political, and economic isolation of marginalized communities, particularly the gay COMMUNITY. The characters of Prior, Louis, and Belize are denied a substantive voice in society because of their sexual orientation. The community they represent is further ostracized because of the HIV/AIDS epidemic. Economic and political alienation is best illustrated through the availability of azidothymidine (AZT) and the fictionalized Roy Cohn. In the play, he is a powerful voice for a socially conservative movement who hides his homosexual desires and activities. Ultimately contracting AIDS, he is in a position to acquire the medication for treatment because of his position of power and influence. As Cohn is in the hospital dying, Belize, a nurse, takes some of Cohn's large supply of the rare AZT. This is the only realistic way to get the drug to those who need it but are unable to get it, like Prior Walter, an openly gay man with AIDS.

For many of the characters, such as Prior, Louis Ironson, and Belize, being gay places them outside of mainstream society. Other characters, Joe, Harper, and Hannah Pitt, are Mormons who are not fully prepared for "modern" American life as they travel to and try to live in New York City. And as stated before, Roy Cohn is a closeted and hypocritical homosexual who embraces and works toward policy that furthers the alienation of communities that do not conform to generally accepted behavior. Eventually, each character has to reconcile his or her role in American society, and this ends with Prior, Louis, Hannah, and Belize coming together to work toward a "new" community of memory and acceptance. The play is further complicated with the appearance of the Angel who announces to Prior that God is gone from Heaven. This adds a sense of the spiritual alienation of a modern America.

In addition to the social and political issues, the characters of the drama are individuals who serve to represent people in various stages of alienation, or estrangement, from themselves and others, emotionally and physically. The two characters that have the most difficult time navigating through life for the extent of the play are Prior and Joe Pitt, who is a Mormon married to Harper and struggling with his sexual identity. For all the characters, though, relationships are tenuous and are broken while new relationships are formed. The relationships are severed due to the different characters' emotional and physical barriers that are the cause of estrangement with each other and in some cases with themselves. Louis plays a major role when looking closely at the characters of Prior and Joe. Louis leaves Prior because of his inability to handle the emotional and physical issues of having a partner sick with AIDS. Joe struggles with his sexuality as it goes against his religious beliefs, and the struggle to repress his homosexual desires harms his marriage. Eventually, Louis forms a purely physical relationship with Joe after abruptly leaving Prior, and for Harper, her already fragile mental and emotional state are further harmed as she learns of Joe's actions. The cycle continues as each character's personal struggles affect the next.

Prior, as a man who is separated from his former life, his former partner, and society because of his sexuality and illness, finally realizes that he cannot simply exist, he must do something. As he rejects his role as prophet and in turn chooses life over death, he reveals, "I'm thirty years old . . . I haven't *done* anything yet . . ." (131). As a prophet, he has

no opportunity to do anything—he would exist as a memory. But he is part of a marginalized community that is politically impotent and in desperate need of a voice that merges memory and progress. And in the end, it is Hannah, Joe's mother, joining Louis, Belize, and Prior at Bethesda Fountain, who articulates the social and political statement of the drama that the characters embody. She says, "You can't live in the world without an idea of the world, but it's living that makes the ideas" (144). This is the essential issue—action without thought or thought without action—that Prior reconciles with the words, "The Great Work Begins" (146). Alienation, or estrangement, whether personal or political, takes many forms and in all cases is destructive for the individual as well as the community.

Brian Stiles

HOPE in *Angels in America*

Tony Kushner presents his audience with an American landscape that is, at best, socially and politically ambivalent, and at worst hostile to its citizens who lack a recognized social identity. Set primarily in the second half of the 1980s, the prevailing conservative climate offers little hope to the play's characters who are either gay and dealing with the HIV plague or dealing with moral conundrums of identity. Despite the personal problems and bleak reality of these characters' lives, the work concludes with the words, "The Great Work Begins" (146). For the characters gathered with Prior Walter at Bethesda Fountain, the sense of working, or progressing, toward a better future offers hope of a benign future, one that is more accepting socially and politically for people that have long been pushed to the outer fringes of social consciousness.

The play loosely centers on the character Prior Walter, a 30-year-old homosexual man whose health is rapidly deteriorating due to the effects of HIV. Of any of the characters, he has reason to despair; he knows he is going to die as he has seen many of his friends suffer that fate. Furthermore, when he tells Louis, his partner of four years, Louis quickly abandons him. As *Millennium Approaches* ends, the first of the two plays that make up *Angels in America,* an Angel arrives in Prior's bedroom and announces her presence. And as *Perestroika,* the second play, begins he is anointed a prophet, one who is to "lead" America to stasis.

This angel is not a messenger from God—God has, in fact, abandoned both the heavens and earth—but from the Permanent Emergency Council of the Continental Principalities, Heaven. Prior's problem arises because that current society is an uncaring, oppressive, and alienating force, so stasis is not an option. In fact, it is impossible. With the Angel imploring Prior to lead people to stand still, which for him would be death, it seeks the halt of progress. But in this explanation she reveals the very nature of why there is cause for hope. She says to Prior, "YOU *Think.* And You *IMAGINE!*" (*Perestroika* 42). This is revealed to be uniquely human.

Prior initially rejects the role of prophet and in doing so makes his claim for life despite the terrible condition of his deteriorating health and of the ambivalence of society. He says to the council, "We live past hope. If I can find hope anywhere, that's it, that's the best I can do" (133). In other words, life is hope; life is change, and Prior wants to live.

Beyond Prior, the many characters in *Angels in America* are in situations where hope seems lost to them. Louis and Belize are openly gay and are outcasts in American society. They are at risk and sensitive to the HIV plague that provides a constant atmosphere of fear, illness, and death for their community; Joe Pitt is a conservative lawyer, a Mormon, and a man struggling with his sexual identity; Harper and Hannah, Joe's wife and mother respectively, are Mormons in various stages of disillusionment with their personal lives and roles in society; and finally, Roy Cohn represents American hypocrisy. At different points in the plays, the characters are left alone in their confusion and suffering.

Each individual moves through crises of physical, emotional, and spiritual nature. The status quo offers only a lonely and hopeless situation. But as the title of the second play, *Perestroika,* or "restructuring," suggests, it doesn't have to be that way. As different characters meet and interact, they find ways to comfort and help each other. This is often awkward and difficult, but the results are seen at the conclusion of *Perestroika,* and not without the casualties that mark any struggle.

The concluding scene begins with Prior, Louis, Belize, and Hannah. The initial discussion shows the progress of political movements across Europe, such as the fall of the Berlin Wall, but in Russia in particular. The changing of a whole political structure is ". . . a leap into the unknown." This in many ways embodies the notion of progress in that you hope to change for the better, but ultimately it is the unknown we work toward, hopefully bearing in mind the past while moving forward.

Angels in America is not a work that illustrates hope in any simple, uplifting way. Instead, it engenders the hope of merging history (memory), theory (ideas), and action. It is the hope for "more life" that Prior embodies.

Brian Stiles

ILLNESS in *Angels in America*

Angels in America begins in 1985 at a time when the HIV/AIDS virus is reaching epidemic proportions within the gay community in America. The work traces the lives of four of the five primary male characters, Prior, Louis, Belize, and Roy Cohn, who are directly affected by the disease. The play is unapologetically straightforward and graphic about how HIV/AIDS manifests itself physically, emotionally, and politically.

The play is anchored around the life of Prior Walter, who has contracted AIDS. The first sign of infection for him appears as "K.S." or Kaposi's sarcoma. His illness is further brought to life through the graphic portrayal of additional lesions, loss of weight, and bloody bowel movements. While dealing with the physical manifestations of the disease, he must also cope with being abandoned by his longtime boyfriend, Louis.

Through the character of Louis, Kushner illustrates the difficulty relationships encounter when faced with a frightening and mostly fatal situation. At this time, the outcome of Prior contracting AIDS would be a painful and humiliating death. Louis leaves because he cannot deal with what the future holds for Prior.

Belize is another openly gay character. He is a nurse and has a firsthand knowledge of what the gay community faces when dealing with HIV/AIDS in the 1980s. He is Prior's friend and announces his intention to stick with him no matter what. Belize is better equipped than Louis to deal with Prior's deteriorating physical condition, as he has witnessed it "lots" of times before (*Millennium* 25). Because of his experience as a nurse dealing with AIDS patients, he knows the common treatments such as radiation for the lesions and the experimental drug azidothymidine (AZT), and how they are harmful in and of themselves. In addition to his insight and knowledge, he provides emotional support and care and ultimately a link between Prior, Roy Cohn, and the only viable form of treatment, AZT.

The stigma attached to HIV/AIDS in the mid- and late eighties is manifested through the fictionalized account of Roy Cohn. This character is a powerful and politically connected man who is a closeted homosexual who has AIDS. He is adamant to his doctor that his symptoms are related to liver cancer, as he says, "AIDS is what homosexuals have. I have liver cancer" (*Perestroika* 46). He dies during the course of the play from the effects of AIDS but not before he secures a large quantity of the extremely rare AZT. Because of his secrecy about his prognosis, nobody knows he has the AZT except his nurse, Belize.

Roy Cohn's portrayal helps to establish the outsider status of gay men during the time period of the play through his words and inferred actions as well as the difficulty in obtaining fair treatment. Belize is amazed at his ability to obtain AZT as he witnesses the hospital giving a placebo to patients. As Roy dies, Belize liberates the secret stash to help Prior, his friend, but more significantly one who is not connected, powerful, and privy to this type of treatment.

In focusing on the illness of HIV/AIDS, *Angels in America* provides an all-encompassing view of the plague that ravaged a largely ignored and marginal community. The graphic description of the physical effects endured by those infected and the references to the many gay men who had died already are reminders of the pain and suffering this illness brings. The additional portrayal of the emotional struggles of the men, both those infected and those knowing the infected, adds another level of depth and understanding to the struggle through this illness.

Though the personal stories are important to recognize and explore in *Angels in America*, the disease during this time was also a political issue, illustrated through Roy Cohn. Roy embodies the hypocrisy of the medical and political communities. Those individuals who are most in need are denied the type of care that can be secured by the powerful. Those most in need at this time, the homosexual community, are considered second-class citizens, as demonstrated through court cases referenced in the play as well as Roy's emphasis on labels and how they affect status.

As Prior struggles for his life, it is a struggle that encompasses his physical existence as well as the political future of himself and others like him. HIV/AIDS is not a personal illness; it is an illness of society as well.

Brian Stiles

LAWRENCE, D. H.   *The Rainbow* (1915)

The Rainbow is a major modern novel distinguished by an innovative departure from the realism of its author's earlier fiction. Although it is concerned with the traditional subjects of courtship and marriage, Lawrence eschews traditional modes of characterization, delving into the psychology of his characters, stressing instinct, sexuality, and, above all, the unconscious. His psychological approach is informed by a religious sensibility, often relying on biblical imagery and an incantatory style of writing. The results are striking, hypnotic scenes whose dream-like effects reveal the unconscious drives of Lawrence's characters.

The Rainbow tells the story of three generations of the Brangwen family in the English Midlands, concluding at the turn of the 20th century. The novel begins with the famous prologue, a poetic overview of the Brangwens, portraying their farm life and, in the case of the women, their aspirations. In each generation the principal characters struggle with relationships: first, Tom Brangwen and his Polish wife Lydia Lensky; next, Will Brangwen and Lydia's daughter from a previous marriage, Anna Lensky; and finally the daughter of Will and Anna, Ursula Brangwen, and her two lovers, Winifred

Inger and Anton Skrebensky. The novel is devoted mostly to Ursula, whose story continues in Lawrence's *Women in Love* (1920).

The Rainbow was banned as obscene soon after publication, but it is now generally recognized as a significant novel because of its innovative form and its bold thematic treatment not only of marriage, sexuality, and the unconscious, but also of education, gender and industrialism.

Mitchell R. Lewis

COMMODIFICATION/COMMERCIALIZATION in *The Rainbow*

In the late 19th and early 20th centuries, commerce in England was dominated by industrialism. Lawrence introduces the theme of industrialism after the prologue, beginning with the description of a canal constructed across the Brangwen farm that connects "the newly-opened collieries of the Erewash Valley." The Brangwens receive financial compensation for this trespass on their property, but Lawrence indicates that this canal serving the collieries is the beginning of an "invasion" into what is described as a pastoral paradise for the Brangwen men. Soon, a colliery is built on the other side of the canal, followed by a railway line. With this development come "red, crude houses plastered on the valley in masses, and beyond all, the dim smoking hill of the town." The Brangwens are "astonished" by the commotion, becoming "strangers in their own place," always aware of the sound of "the rhythmic run of the winding engines." Driving home, they see "the blackened colliers trooping from the pit-mouth," and during the harvest they endure the "faint, sulphurous smell of pit-refuse burning." The industrial invasion contaminates the countryside, disrupting the vital interchange between the Brangwens and their farm. Lawrence suggests a fall from paradise, contrasting industrialism with nature as he reveals its deadening influence.

The subject of industrialism comes up again when Ursula introduces Winifred Inger to her Uncle Tom. A manager of a new colliery, Tom lives in Wiggiston, a former hamlet in agricultural country that has been transformed into an industrial town, much like the towns in the vicinity of the Brangwen farm. Colliers hang out in gangs, looking like "spectres," while the town itself is characterized by a "homogeneous amorphous sterility." The buildings and roads are uniform and regimented, yet for all this order there is "no organic formation." The order is mechanical, not vital. It is imposed, not growing out of the life of its inhabitants. The same is true of the "great, mathematical colliery on the other side of town." It also imposes itself on the workers, who have come to believe that "they must alter themselves to fit the pits and the place, rather than alter the pits and the place to fit themselves." Tom and Winifred derive a perverse pleasure from "serving the machine," worshiping it, feeling "free from the clog and degradation of human feeling." Ursula, on the other hand, rejects "the great machine which has taken us all captives." She would see the colliery destroyed and the men out of work, "rather than serve such a Moloch as this." She is equally appalled with Tom and Winifred and "their strange, soft, half-corrupt element."

As Ursula's reactions suggest, Lawrence's portrayal of industrialism emphasizes the sacrifice of the individual to the machine. In this regard, it is linked to the novel's general concern with the modern world's attempt to subordinate the individual to society. The novel repeatedly uses terms associated with the colliery to describe society's negative influence. Anton Skrebensky, for instance, views London as an "ashen-dry, cold world of rigidity, dead walls and mechanical traffic, and creeping, spectre-like people," and he himself becomes a person in whom "only the mechanism of his life continued." Ursula's school is also described in similar terms, the teachers "compelling many children into one disciplined, mechanical set, reducing the whole set to an automatic state of obedience and attention."

The industrialism theme takes on its full value in Ursula's concluding vision of the rainbow. First, she sees "the stiffened bodies of the colliers, which seemed already enclosed in a coffin," and the houses of a colliery town, "which seemed to spread over the hillside in their insentient triumph, a triumph of horrible, amorphous angles and straight lines." Then she imagines that the colliers have a "rainbow arched in their blood," and it is this rainbow that is prompting a new germination that will cast aside the old world. The industrialism imagery thus serves as a contrast to the rainbow imagery. The old world to be swept away and replaced by a "new creation" takes the form of industrialism. In fact, it can be said that the system against which all of Lawrence's characters are fighting, whether they know it or not, is industrialism. It is linked to the education system, as well as to the personal frustrations of Lawrence's characters. It is a system opposed to individual fulfillment, and Lawrence attempts to counter it with a religious sense of the instincts of humanity.

Mitchell R. Lewis

EDUCATION in *The Rainbow*

The prologue to *The Rainbow* introduces the subject of education, stressing differences of gender and class. The Brangwen men are satisfied with farm life and the rhythms of nature, but Mrs. Brangwen desires more for herself and particularly for her offspring. She notices that the local vicar's children take precedence over her own because of "education and experience." It is "this higher form of being" that she wants for her children, who face a life of anonymous toil among the working classes of the English Midlands. In spite of this noble aspiration, later linked to the suffragette movement, the Brangwen family's educational experiences tend to be negative ones. In fact, Lawrence suggests that instinct, intuition, and experience are more important than formal education.

In grammar school, for instance, Tom Brangwen is "more refined in instinct" than his peers, but "he could not learn deliberately." Tom does emotionally respond to literature when read to by his teacher, but he is ashamed and angered by his inability to read books, regarding them as hateful "enemies." Rage and humiliation are also the results of his experiences with composition and mathematics, in spite of his "instinct" for the latter. Tom is even "bullied" by his Latin master, resulting in a "horrid scene" in which Tom "laid open the master's head with a slate." The grammar school labels Tom a "hopeless duffer at learning," but clearly it fails to take into consideration Tom's sensitive nature and class background.

Like Tom, Anna Brangwen also resists her formal education. She is "intelligent enough" and proud, but when she is at a young ladies' school, she feels that "she ought to be slinking in disgrace." Anna questions her schoolmistresses, who act like "representatives of some mystic Right," and she does not see "why a woman should bully and insult her because she [does] not know thirty lines of 'As You Like It.'" As a result, her teachers almost make her believe in "her own intrinsic inferiority." As in Tom's case, Anna is singled out and humiliated for being different.

Lawrence touches briefly on how Will Brangwen enjoys teaching woodwork in night school, but his most extensive treatment of education comes in the case of Ursula Brangwen, the principal character of the last half of the novel. As a child, she imagines herself "on the hill of learning, looking down on the smoke and confusion and the manufacturing, engrossed activity of the town." In this regard Ursula clearly embodies the aspiration of Mrs. Brangwen, but her "instinctive" intelligence and her "bitter contempt of all teachers and schoolmistresses" combine the family traits of Tom and Anna, respectively. Seeking her independence like many suffragettes of the time, Ursula becomes a teacher at a working-class elementary school. She strives to be personal with her students, but she finds that they are rebellious and that she herself is simply a tool of a disciplinary institution, its focus on authority and regimentation resembling a "prison." Ursula reluctantly subordinates herself to her institutionalized role, becoming "nothing but Standard Five teacher."

The unruliness of her students and the goading of her authoritarian headmaster, Mr. Harby, prompt Ursula to seize control of her class by making an example of Vernon Williams, a student whom she viciously canes. The scene recalls the episode between Tom and his Latin master, the novel once again portraying the combative relationship between teacher and student. Lawrence suggests that the educational system coerces students and teachers alike into obedience, creating resentment, frustration, and anger all around. A professional woman educated out of the working class, Ursula finds herself in "the ignominious position of an upper servant hated by the master above and the class beneath."

While her sister Gudrun enjoys a measure of success at art school, Ursula finally attends university for the sake of "pure education, not for mere professional training." She thinks of her studies in religious terms, viewing the professors as "black-gowned priests of knowledge," but she soon becomes disillusioned. In the end, Ursula sees college as a "sham workshop" in which "the religious virtue of knowledge [has] become a flunkey to the god of material success." Ursula fails to get her degree, but she embraces the changing times around her, finding hope for tomorrow symbolized in a rainbow. Her education, Lawrence suggests, will come through the experience of living her life, not through school.

Mitchell R. Lewis

GENDER in *The Rainbow*

Lawrence's novel addresses the subject of gender in its portrayal of Ursula Brangwen's attempt to win her independence in the "man's world." She fights the social constraints against her, resisting the "limited life of herded domesticity" and insisting on "the right of women to take equal place with men in the field of action and work." In effect, Ursula criticizes the way in which society defines women. With her education she hopes to break through society's barriers to become a financially independent, modern girl. Her friends help her to learn about the women's movement and its effort to reform society, but she eventually grows discontented with the movement, believing that allowing women to participate in society is not sufficient social reform for women or even for men. Lawrence's essentially religious view of gender allows little room for social accommodation in any form. Unable to practically discuss gender and society, Lawrence depicts an apocalyptic vision of the future in which women and men are liberated from the present into an unspecified utopian world. It is an image of fulfillment to come for men and women *as* men and women.

Lawrence's reservations about the women's movement can be seen in his portrayals of Winifred Inger and Maggie Schofield. A teacher, Winifred is proud and free and she is "interested in the Women's Movement," but she is also a "modern girl whose very independence betrays her to sorrow." Similarly,

as a teacher, Maggie is "free," but there is "something like subjection in Maggie's very freedom." She is a "great suffragette, trusting in the vote," but she suffers from "a heavy, brooding sadness that was almost meat to her." Maggie and Winifred have achieved a measure of success, breaking into the professional class, but they remain fundamentally unhappy because of the inevitable compromises they must make with society. Winifred even goes so far as to marry a manager of a colliery, taking a "perverse satisfaction" in serving "the machine" of industrialism.

In contrast, Ursula does not compromise with society, having a "strange, passionate knowledge of religion and living far transcending the limits of the automatic system that contained the vote." For her "the liberty of woman meant something real and deep," but the present form of society does not allow for it, even if women were fully emancipated. The implication is that Lawrence wants radical social reform, not social accommodation for women. The scope of that reform is suggested by the novel's persistent use of apocalyptic imagery derived from the biblical story of Noah. Images of flooding, arks, and rainbows abound in *The Rainbow*. In fact, the novel concludes with Ursula's apocalyptic vision of a "new creation" in which the rainbow becomes a symbol of a desire for fulfillment and freedom that is hard to define in material terms. It involves the complete destruction of the old world and a transformation of personal relationships and the body.

As this imagery suggests, Lawrence's view of men and women is essentially religious in nature. Going beyond personality and society, Lawrence delves into the unconscious desires of his characters, portraying them as caught up in a religious ritual beyond time and space. This use of ritual is especially noticeable when Anna and Will Brangwen stack sheaves of corn at night, the scene and formal language suggesting a fertility ritual. The two arched sheaves leaning together also recall the religious rainbow imagery, which Lawrence uses to describe the proper relationship between men and women. Lawrence's religious view of gender can also be seen in Tom Brangwen's assertion that "an angel is the soul of man and woman in one: they rise united at the Judgement Day, as one angel." It is also apparent in the novel's peroration on the "risen body" in which the narrator becomes a resurrected Christ embracing and kissing Mary Magdalene. This need for the resurrection of the flesh echoes the apocalyptic imagery of the novel, reinforcing the kind of radical social transformation that Lawrence envisions. Lawrence suggests that if the women's movement amounts only to jobs, money, and the vote, unhappiness will remain until the distinctive religious natures of women and men are fulfilled. Lawrence also suggests that men and women are fulfilled *as* men and women through their personal relationships with each other, not through social accommodation.

Mitchell R. Lewis

LAWRENCE, D. H.   *Women in Love* (1920)

D. H. Lawrence's *Women in Love* continues the story line of *The Rainbow* (1915), but it abandons the latter's historical form to focus on Ursula and Gudrun Brangwen and their lovers, Rupert Birken and Gerald Crich, respectively. The novel contrasts the two relationships, the first leading to marriage, the second to assault and suicide. *Women in Love* also explores the friendship between Rupert and Gerald, with homoerotic overtones. Conceiving of personal relationships as combative, *Women in Love* is a disturbing meditation on the psychology of love. Its characters are largely unconscious, driven by the need for power, control, and authority.

Eschewing the linear narrative associated with realism, *Women in Love* is episodic. Its chapters usually focus on symbolic incidents that develop its thematic concern with love. Among the famous incidents are Rupert throwing stones into a pond in "Moony," Gerald's cruelty to a horse in "Coal-Dust," and Rupert and Gerald wrestling in the nude in "Gladiatorial." In each case, the incident is vividly described, but it resonates with a meaning beyond the literal, like a dream.

Because *The Rainbow* was banned, Lawrence had problems getting *Women in Love* published, but many now regard it as Lawrence's greatest novel. It

is also considered an important work of modernism because of its episodic form, its use of symbolism, and its concern with the unconscious. *Women in Love*'s thematic exploration of love leads inevitably to the discussion of gender and sexuality, but it also touches on industrialism.

Mitchell R. Lewis

COMMODIFICATION/COMMERCIALIZATION in *Women in Love*

Lawrence takes on the subject of commerce, in the form of industrialism, in his treatment of the Crich family. The dying patriarch of the family, Thomas Crich, is a great coal-mine owner in Beldover, a small Midlands town surrounded by mining villages and pits. Feeling responsible for his colliers, Thomas tries to enact the Christian principles of love and charity. He treats the miners as if they are closer to God than he is, making them "his idol, his God made manifest." While he makes an enormous profit from the mines, Thomas views the welfare of the minors as more important than profit, the mines being "primarily great fields to produce bread and plenty for all the hundreds of human beings gathered about them." His sense of duty, moreover, leads him to institute an open-door policy for the poor, whose requests for charity he never denies.

Although all their basic needs are satisfied, the miners eventually become discontented with their meager share of the profit. Similar situations arise in other mining communities. Meanwhile, the mines are not producing as well as they had, and thus not paying as well. As a result, the Masters' Federation to which Thomas belongs forces him to close his mines in order to compel the workers to accept a reduction in wages. Resisting the lock-out, the workers organize, animated by egalitarianism, the idea that "All men are equal on earth." Riots break out, and a "war" ensues between the masters and workers. After the workers set fire to a pit, soldiers suppress the riots, restoring order and breaking the will of the miners.

During the course of the riots, Thomas sympathizes with the workers, reluctantly closing the mines. He can see that the "disequality" between master and worker is wrong, but "he could not give up his goods, which [are] the stuff of disequality." The conflict breaks his heart, destroying his illusions about his relationship with the colliers. The riots and their aftermath reveal Thomas Crich to be good natured, idealistic, and charitable, but also sentimental, deluded, and, finally, more materialistic than he had thought. As much as he values Christianity, Thomas also values property, profit, and his class status.

When Thomas becomes ill, retreating into a solipsistic religiosity, his son Gerald takes over as director of the firm, at a time when the mine is more run down than ever. Like his mother Christianna, Gerald despises his father's charitable disposition, having no sympathy for the workers. In fact, during the riots he longs to go out with the soldiers to shoot the miners. Educated in the science of mining at a German university, Gerald successfully modernizes the coal mines, increasing their efficiency and output. Where his father was sentimental, Gerald is coldly rational but also darkly sadistic. He accomplishes his "great reform" not for the money but for the satisfaction of dominating nature. He envisions himself in a "fight with Matter," in a struggle to "reduce it to his will." Gerald extends this domination to his employees. Conceiving of the miners as mere "instruments,"Gerald takes pride in "the stream of miners flowing along the causeways from the mines at the end of the afternoon, thousands of blackened, slightly distorted human beings with red mouths, all moving subjugate to his will." Subordinating nature and humanity to his designs, Gerald sees himself as the "controlling, central part" of a smoothly running machine. He becomes the "God of the Machine," completing the contrast with his father, who saw the miners as a manifestation of God.

In this brief family history Lawrence captures his sense of the problems of industrialism. He portrays the class conflict and exploitation endemic to industrialism, along with the masters' failures of understanding and empathy. He reveals the dehumanizing of the working classes, as well as the sentimentalism and megalomania of the ruling classes, who are also dehumanized by their lust for power. He shows how the scientific method can be a tool for ruthlessly dominating humanity as well as the environment. He also links the desire for control and power to sexual politics. As *Women in Love* shows, Gerald takes the same approach to Gudrun as he does to his mines. He tries to dominate and control her. He also tries to dominate and control himself, exhibiting a strange combination of nihilism and repression. Ironically, after Gerald commits suicide, freezing to death in the Alps, he becomes simply "cold, mute Matter."

Mitchell R. Lewis

GENDER in *Women in Love*

In *Women in Love* Lawrence portrays men and women as "perfectly polarized," each sex having "a single, separate being, with its own laws." According to this essentialist view of gender, men and women recognize in the other a fundamentally "different nature." It is a nature, moreover, that is unknowable, beyond conscious understanding. The result, in the case of heterosexual relationships, is a mutual recognition of "the immemorial magnificence of mystic, palpable, real otherness." A vitalist who scorned scientific knowledge, Lawrence suggests that even in their sexual relationships, men and women never really know each other. Drawing on religious and metaphysical language, Lawrence typically portrays relationships as ineffable experiences in which human beings encounter each other's absolute but impersonal natures. Lawrence insists on the possibility of mutual fulfillment, but his emphasis on gender-difference complicates the issue. In fact, Lawrence finally depicts heterosexual relationships as violent power struggles over who has authority and control. Thus Lawrence's emphasis on gender difference is linked inseparably to a focus on gender hierarchy. His characters battle for dominance over the other, driven by a largely unconscious will to power.

The battle between the sexes is repeatedly thematized in the novel. For instance, Ursula thinks that Rupert is "a bully like all males," while he considers her an arrogant "queen bee," a mother who desires "to have, to own, to control, and to be dominant". Rupert also reflects on the "female tyranny" of Hermione. Similarly, while watching Gerald dance, Gudrun resolves "to combat him" until one triumphs over the other. Considering himself dominated by Gudrun, Gerald thinks, "If only I could kill her—I should be free." The artist's model, the Pussum, finally, intends "to capture Halliday, to have complete power over him."

Complementing the thematic discussion of the will to power in relationships are numerous instances of hostility between men and women. Gudrun strikes Gerald, feeling "in her soul an unconquerable desire for deep violence against him," while Gerald himself assaults her at the end of the book, taking "the throat of Gudrun between his hands" and "watching the unconsciousness coming in her swollen face, watching her eyes roll back." Gudrun lives, but she drops to her knees, "like one executed." Earlier, two lovers are found drowned in a lake, the woman's "arms tight around the neck of the young man, choking him." Filled with hatred, the rejected Hermione hits Rupert over the head with a "ball of lapis lazuli," an act from which she derives "unutterable satisfaction." The cruel Loerke has to slap his female model to make her docile enough to pose in the correct way for his sculpture. Even the men fight with each other, as attested by the homoerotic wrestling match between a nude Gerald and Rupert in the "Gladiatorial" chapter. In each case there is a disturbing mingling of aggressive and sexual instincts.

Symbolic instances of violence are also in *Women in Love*. The fight between the domestic cat Mino and a wild female cat symbolizes the relationship between Rupert and Ursula, as the latter realizes. Bismarck, a rabbit, becomes a symbol for the mindless cruelty in men, as he scores the wrists of Gudrun with Gerald watching. Rupert's throwing rocks at the reflection of the moon in a pond is a symbol of his aggression toward Ursula, who secretly witnesses the event, "dazed" as if she were Rupert's target. Before throwing the stones, Rupert curses goddesses like "Cybele" and "Syria Dea," strong maternal images he associates with Ursula. Perhaps the most striking symbolic act of violence is Gerald's mastering a female horse in the chapter entitled "Coal Dust." His amusement at controlling, terrifying, and torturing the horse is indicative of the sadism seen in his relationship with Gudrun. It also expresses

his repressions and self-destructive masochism. As Lawrence makes clear, Gerald is driven by a kind of nihilism that the author associates with reason, SCIENCE, and industrialism.

Underwriting Lawrence's portrayal of gender is a persistent concern with the primitive, as seen, for instance, in the African "negro statues," particularly the one of the woman giving birth, "conveying the suggestion of the extreme of physical sensation, beyond the limits of mental consciousness." If gender is absolute and impersonal, Lawrence suggests, it is also primitive, consisting of largely erotic but violent instincts that lead to combative relationships.

Mitchell R. Lewis

SEXUALITY in *Women in Love*

Lawrence's *Women in Love* presents a complex picture of human sexuality. Typically Lawrence portrays sexuality as a mystical experience, a timeless ritual linked to mythology and the unconscious. He also links sexuality to primitivism, a theme developed in relationship to African art. Lawrence's main assertion is that sexuality is impersonal and even "inhuman." It transcends personality and knowledge, allowing for a fulfilling mystical communion in which each participant is still decidedly other. The ideal experience appears to be represented in the relationship between Rupert and Ursula. Lawrence describes their sexual relationship in religious terms, characterizing it as "ineffable" and as "mystically-physically satisfying." He portrays Rupert as one of the "Sons of God" and as a potent "Egyptian Pharaoh," and he also describes Rupert's embrace of Ursula as "the fingers of silence upon silence, the body of mysterious night upon the body of mysterious night, the night masculine and feminine." It is a sensual communion, described in the archetypal language of religion and mythology.

This mystical, heterosexual experience, however, is complicated by Rupert's unfulfilled need "to love a man purely and fully." The "problem of love and eternal conjunction between two men" undermines Rupert's relationship with Ursula. He believes that his relationship with her will not be complete until he has an "eternal union with a man too," and he desires such a union with Gerald. Ursula considers this need a "perversity" and cannot understand why she is not enough for him. While Rupert often indicates that his desire for men is simply a need for male friendship, Lawrence clearly suggests that it is homoerotic.

An early if indirect indication of this homoeroticism occurs after Hermione assaults Rupert with a ball of lapis lazuli. Disgusted with Hermione and women in general, Rupert wanders through a valley, removes his clothes, and proceeds to walk "to a clump of young fir-trees, that were no higher than a man." What follows is a symbolic homoerotic experience with the fir-trees: the "soft sharp boughs beat upon him, as he moved in keen pangs against them, threw little cold showers of drops on his belly, and beat his loins with their clusters of soft-sharp needles." In addition, "a thistle . . . pricked him vividly." Rupert also clasps "the silvery birch-trunk" to feel "its smoothness, its hardness, its vital knots and ridges." The experience leaves him feeling that he "did not want a woman—not in the least."

A more direct representation of homoeroticism is evident later when Rupert and Gerald wrestle in the nude. As the two fuse into a "tense white knot of flesh," Rupert's "great subtle energy" attempts to "penetrate" Gerald's body, to fuse them into "oneness." The insistent repetition of the word "penetrate" carries obvious homoerotic overtones, and the reiteration of the word "knot" echoes the earlier scene with the fir-trees. In the end, Rupert and Gerald clasp hands, each thinking that the "wrestling had some deep meaning to them—an unfinished meaning."

The novel concludes with Rupert mourning the death of Gerald, as he argues again with Ursula about his need to love a man. Ending the novel in this way, Lawrence suggests that the relationship between Rupert and Gerald may be the real focus of the novel, not their relationships to Ursula and Gudrun. Reinforcing this position is Lawrence's suggestion that the heterosexual relationships are Oedipal in some way. Rupert thinks of Ursula as an oppressive "queen bee" or "Great Mother," while Gerald seeks solace from Gudrun like "an infant . . . at its mother's breast." Perhaps the aggressive behavior toward women seen in both Gerald and Rupert is simply a function of their repressed homosexuality.

What is clear, in any case, is that Lawrence perceives himself to be exploring the topic of sexuality at a time when traditional Western sexual mores are no longer acceptable. Rupert, in particular, is trying to negotiate relationships with Ursula and Gerald for which he has no precedents. He is trying to take the "love-and-marriage ideal from its pedestal," to do away with "the exclusiveness of married love," and "to admit the unadmitted love of man for man," to create "a greater freedom for everybody, a greater power of individuality both in men and women." The novel's conclusion leaves these complex issues unresolved.

Mitchell R. Lewis

LAWRENCE, JEROME, AND ROBERT E. LEE *Inherit the Wind* (1955)

Jerome Lawrence and Robert E. Lee's play *Inherit the Wind* has become a standard of American drama. Inspired by the trial of Tennessee schoolteacher John Scopes, who was charged under a Tennessee law that forbade the teaching of evolutionary theory in schools, the play chronicles a titanic struggle for free speech and free thought as lawyers Henry Drummond and Matthew Harrison Brady argue over Scopes's fate.

Though Scopes is in the middle of the plot, Drummond occupies its moral and thematic center. Drummond is the play's model for tolerance, healthy skepticism, and reasoned faith. He is at once a crusader against bigotry while at the same time finding the compassion to understand, and even admire, what is noble in the bigots he fights against. In his most powerful speech Drummond declares that an "idea is a greater monument than a cathedral," a notion that summarizes the play as a whole. The greatness of humanity, Lawrence and Lee suggest, is in its ability to fashion transcendent concepts, enduring ways of understanding the world. The physical things of the world are transitory and fleeting by comparison.

But though ideas may be monuments, they should not, the authors imply, be monolithic and unchanging. Instead, the play calls on us to cherish our ideas even as we critique them. When Drummond's questions about the Bible lead Brady to feckless mumbling ("I do not think about things that . . . I do not think about"), Drummond has a devastatingly witty rejoinder: "Do you ever think about things that you *do* think about?" (emphasis in original). Here again, the line emblematizes the play: It is not enough to think. We must, collectively, challenge ourselves to be critical of our own views and those of others, no matter how treasured they may be—to think about, in short, the things we think about.

Todd Pettigrew

HOPE in *Inherit the Wind*

In a crucial exchange near the end of Lawrence and Lee's *Inherit the Wind,* attorney Henry Drummond muses that it might be nice to have cases that were sure things, prompting Cates (the character who represents Scopes) to joke that Drummond "sure picked a long shot this time." Cates's status as a long shot, in turn, leads Drummond to a dreamy recollection of his "first long shot," a childhood rocking horse called "Golden Dancer." As Drummond relates, Golden Dancer was a beautiful toy that the young Drummond coveted and when his working-class parents managed to scrape together the money to buy it for the child's birthday, the horse turned out to be worthless: "It split in two! The wood was rotten, the whole thing was put together with spit and sealing wax!"

In a drama played out in the shadow of the Bible, the Golden Dancer story functions as a parable of false hope. Like the inheritance of the prodigal son, the rocking horse is too beautiful to resist but ultimately worthless. At the same time, the gold in Golden Dancer and the fact that it is an animal, recall the Golden Calf made by the Israelites in the wilderness, a false idol that tempts the true believers away from the path of righteousness. Drummond draws out the moral for Cates explicitly: "whenever you see something bright, shining, perfect-seeming . . . look behind the paint!"

At the same time, Golden Dancer is Drummond's "first long shot," and though Drummond admits that it is tempting to get rich by taking only easy cases, the fact that he comes to Hillsborough to help Cates, his most recent long shot, implies that, while Drummond has learned the lesson of Golden Dancer—do not be misled by false hopes—he has not been embittered by his childhood disappointment either. One can still retain hope in truth and in progress, according to the attorney; against the childish infatuation with a shiny toy, the play juxtaposes Drummond's fervent belief "In a child's power to master the multiplication table," which he claims contains "more sanctity" than the empty prayers of the Hillsboro faithful.

Inherit the Wind ultimately suggests that there is a reason for hope in the world, even in a world replete with false idols and false prophets. At the same time, hope is always a risk, always a long shot where one may, as Drummond says, "ride like fury, just to end up back where I started."

Todd Pettigrew

JUSTICE in *Inherit the Wind*

In a play that seems to be centered on justice—it begins with an accusation, dramatizes a trial, and ends with a verdict—what is most striking is the drama's suggestion that justice in any real sense is largely impossible or, at the very least, always deferred.

From the outset, it is clear that much of the support for the case against the play's central, if not main, character, Bertram Cates, arises not from a desire to see a legally fair outcome, but from the fact that the case brings notoriety and that, as a shopkeeper says in the first scene, "means business!" Similarly, Matthew Harrison Brady's decision to prosecute the case seems to be as much about reviving his reputation as a defender of traditional values as it is about justice. His status as a three-time presidential candidate in days gone by is pointed out early on by Meeker, and reporter E. K. Hornbeck assesses Brady as a "Yesterday-Messiah" who has come to Hillsboro merely "To find himself a stump to shout from." When others fear the arrival of Henry Drummond, Brady welcomes him, because he knows where a Goliath like Drummond fights, "headlines follow."

Even those on Cates's side are not always interested in justice, per se. Hornbeck uses the trial to showcase his acerbic wit and to indulge his own narcissism, calling himself the "most brilliant reporter in America today" and describing his article on Cates as a "Brilliant little symphony of words." While other characters in this play speak prose, Hornbeck speaks in verse.

If there is a hope for real justice dramatized in *Inherit the Wind*, it is embodied in Drummond himself. The play's most moving speeches about truth and civil liberties come from Drummond—"an idea is a greater monument than a cathedral"—and Drummond's devastating examination of Brady and his religious views unravels Brady's case, his standing, and ultimately his life. Though Brady has described Drummond as a Goliath, it is Brady himself who is exposed as an overvalued Philistine mindlessly reciting the names of the books of the Old Testament and whining about being laughed at.

Still, for all Drummond's arguments and legal agility, the verdict comes down against his client. And while the sentence is so small as to be practically nominal, even that decision is not reached through a thorough consideration of the legal issues. Drummond himself knows that "A lot of people's shoes are getting hot" as the trial goes on, and the judge's sentence is clearly influenced by the mayor's reminder that "November ain't too far off" and that it "wouldn't do no harm to let things simmer down." The fine of $100, then, is not so much a meting out of justice as a politically motivated compromise. Cates is guilty but goes unpunished, and his murky status is made all the murkier by Drummond's determination to appeal the decision, an appeal we never see. Even Cates himself is left questioning, "Did I win or did I lose?" And while Drummond insists they have won in the court of public opinion, the great lawyer still admits that there really is no final justice: "You don't suppose this kind of thing is ever finished, do you?"

Todd Pettigrew

RELIGION in *Inherit the Wind*

Religion wafts through nearly every line of *Inherit the Wind*, from little Melinda's denunciation of Howard's account of evolution—"You was a worm, once" he taunts; "that's sinful talk," she scolds in return—to Henry Drummond's lyrical eulogy of his former adversary: "Matt Brady got lost. Because he

was looking for God too high up and too far away." In between, the entire plot turns on a law that privileges religion to the exclusion of science, and every major character is described in religious terms one way or another. E. K. Hornbeck wryly confesses to be the worst kind of infidel, since he writes for a newspaper, and where Bert Cates is vilified throughout the play as a sinner, Drummond is denounced as being "perhaps even the Devil himself!"

The locus of traditional religion in Hillsborough is the Reverend Jeremiah Brown. Brown's religion is fundamental and punitive, and his Old Testament zeal is as intoxicating to his congregation as it is appalling to the audience. At the prayer meeting he calls on the "Lord of Righteousness and Wrath" to "Strike down this sinner, as Thou didst Thine enemies of old, in the days of the Pharaohs!" Brown's faith of violence and vengeance is too extreme even for Brady who reminds the Hillsborough congregation that "God forgives His children. And we, as Children of God, should forgive each other." Brady's gospel of forgiveness has limits, though, for the next day finds him decrying "the teachings of Godless science" and demanding that the "full penalty of the law is meted out to Bertram Cates" with nearly as much exuberance as the local minister.

Brown's opposite for much of the play seems to be Drummond himself, who, though he is introduced by Hornbeck as "the most agile legal mind" of the century, can be understood by the stunned townspeople only in religious terms: "agnostic," "Godless," "an agent of darkness" are the preacher's words, and that account goes uncontradicted early on. When he arrives, the real Drummond turns out to be just as horrifying to the Hillsborough faithful as the bogey-man that Brown sketches. Drummond calls the Tennessee lawmakers "clockstoppers" who want to dump "a load of medieval nonsense" into American law. He calls Brown's religion a mere commercial "product," and stuns the court by claiming that "Right" has no meaning for him at all. But during the climactic cross-examination of Brady, Drummond makes it increasingly clear that his supposed agnosticism is really a misunderstood ecumenicalism. His problem with Brady is not that

Brady thinks he hears the voice of God, but that Brady seems to think it impossible that anyone else—including Cates and Darwin himself—can hear God speak too.

"The Bible is a book. A good book. But it's not the *only* book," Drummond insists (emphasis in original). And though Hornbeck calls him a fraud for sustaining faith alongside his skepticism, Drummond shows his satisfaction with his many-booked view of the world by placing the Bible next to his volume of Darwin in his briefcase as the curtain falls.

Todd Pettigrew

LEE, HARPER   *To Kill a Mockingbird* (1960)

A classic since its publication in 1960, *To Kill a Mockingbird* is now considered an essential part of the American literature curriculum. Harper Lee was awarded the Pulitzer Prize for her portrayal of the American South and the effects of intolerance. Drawing upon autobiographical elements of her life for her only novel, Lee tells the story of a young Alabama girl who learns her world is far more complex than she ever imagined.

Jean Louise "Scout" Finch is the main character of *To Kill a Mockingbird,* a preteen tomboy whose EDUCATION in the world comes from Atticus, her father, Jem, her older brother, and Charles Baker Harris, her friend known affectionately as Dill. Atticus, with the help of Calpurnia, his cook, does his best to raise his children. A lawyer by trade, Atticus often helps Scout with her understanding of the world, though his lessons do not always agree with Scout's reality. Observing the lives of Tom Robinson, a black man accused of raping a white woman, and Boo Radley, the town of Maycomb's mysterious recluse, leads Scout to the bitter understanding that terrible injustices exist despite the efforts of truly good people such as Atticus. In her novel Lee examines such themes as RACE, CHILDHOOD, JUSTICE, PARENTHOOD, SOCIAL CLASS, and PREJUDICE.

To Kill a Mockingbird challenges readers to see the world from the perspective of the less fortunate. Scout exchanges her naïveté for wisdom, using both

tragedy and triumph to help her transition. Accordingly, Lee's novel is a poignant yet uplifting depiction of the journey from innocence to experience.

Chris Gonzalez

CHILDHOOD in *To Kill a Mockingbird*

It is fitting that a novel that depicts so many facets of childhood should be narrated from a child's perspective. *To Kill a Mockingbird* is the recounting of several formative childhood events by an adult woman named Jean Louise Finch, who was known as "Scout" during those years. Child figures dominate the list of characters, each of them with their own set of circumstances through which they must navigate. Scout and her brother, Jem, differ from the other children in Macomb in that they are fortunate to have a parent who truly has their best interests at heart. The rest of the children in the novel all have parents (or parental figures) who overlord or, at worst, endanger their charges. Scout slowly begins to recognize that not all children have a parent like her father Atticus, and that this key ingredient dictates not only a childhood but also an entire lifetime, as the tragic lives of Boo Radley and Mayella Ewell exemplify.

Scout's first perception that her childhood is not the norm comes when Walter Cunningham is a guest in her home. A boy whom Scout has fought with on the school playground, Walter cannot help but pour syrup on every bit of his food while at the Finch house. Displaying her innocence, Scout cannot fathom why Walter does this to his food, ridiculing him to the point of shame. And although Calpurnia scolds Scout for this, telling her if Walter "wants to eat up the tablecloth you let him," there is more to this moment than mere gentility and etiquette. Scout cannot perceive that Walter is a child who does not have the luxury of syrup as a regular part of his dinner table, that he is less fortunate than she. This episode initiates a series of lessons for Scout on the subject of childhood. Scout discovers, for example, that Dill's childhood is not what it seems. Though he insists he comes from a loving home, his reality is exposed when Scout and Jem find him hiding under a bed in their room, starved and wild-eyed, having run away from home. Dill's situation is all the more tenuous in light of Boo Radley, or worse, Mayella Ewell, for they are adults whose lives went horribly awry due to thwarted childhoods.

Boo Radley and Mayella Ewell serve as the two main plot points of *To Kill a Mockingbird;* Boo's story is the overarching narrative that frames Scout's story, with Mayella's tragic encounter with Tom Robinson—and Atticus's heroic defense of Tom—nestled within this larger story. Mayella Ewell is a teenager on the verge of womanhood, the daughter of Bob Ewell, an angry man who lives near the city garbage dump and does not value EDUCATION. His children have a history of attending only the first day of class, lice-ridden and surly. Scout does not know much else about the Ewell children, but during the trial recognizes that Mayella is starved for attention. Her desperate need for human contact pushes her to clumsily seduce Tom Robinson, a handicapped black man who is later accused of raping Mayella. She is but one example in *To Kill a Mockingbird* of the consequences of a childhood gone wrong.

Likewise, Boo Radley suffers from overzealous parents. Derogatorily called "foot-washers" (those of the Baptist faith who interpret the Bible literally) by some members of the Maycomb community, the Radley parents have overprotected Boo his entire life, effectively isolating him from the rest of the community. As a result of not knowing (or seeing) him, the Finch children and Dill believe Boo is more monster than human, letting their imagination get the better of them. The truth of the matter, as Scout later discovers, is that Boo lives vicariously through the Finch children. He begins by leaving small tokens of affection, such as chewing gum and a broken pocket watch, within the hollow of an oak tree for the children to find. Later, Boo places a blanket on Scout's shoulders on one of the coldest nights in Maycomb's history. Boo's affection and protection of the children culminates when he stabs Bob Ewell, who attempts to enact revenge against Atticus, who he believes has humiliated him beyond repair during Tom Robinson's trial. Boo, who did not have a childhood in which he had loving parents to care for him, cannot help but lovingly watch over Scout and Jem.

Ultimately, it takes the death of Bob Ewell at the hands of Boo Radley for Scout to understand that terrible things may befall children even when they have loving parents. Even Atticus, the stalwart representation of reason and JUSTICE in *To Kill a Mockingbird*, is astonished at Bob Ewell's brazen attempt to kill two innocent children. Lee's novel takes the nostalgic idea of a carefree childhood and razes it with carefully crafted representations of characters whose childhoods withered on the vine, affording Scout the opportunity to cherish and appreciate her own.

Chris Gonzalez

JUSTICE in *To Kill a Mockingbird*

There are few characters in literature that embody moral uprightness and human kindness as much as Atticus Finch, attorney and father of the narrator of *To Kill a Mockingbird*. Scout Finch often turns to her father for an explanation of the confusing ways of the world, and Atticus unhesitatingly does so with patience. He is a character who represents fairness and an unwillingness to compromise his ETHICS no matter how difficult the situation may be. As a child, Scout's sense of justice seems to favor a physical imposition upon those who offend her. Indeed, Scout's outspokenness is fueled by her ability to back it up with her fists, something she later resists because it disappoints Atticus.

The concept of justice is difficult for anyone to grapple with, let alone a child. Yet Atticus has a penchant for explaining complex ideas in a manner his children can comprehend, as in his dictum for shooting birds. "Shoot all the bluejays you want, if you can hit 'em," he tells his children, "but remember it's a sin to kill a mockingbird." Thus, Atticus gives Scout her most important lesson on justice, as the title of the novel indicates. The mockingbird represents a creature whose sole existence is to bring some goodness to the world through the songs it sings. To kill a mockingbird is an injustice of the worst kind. Additionally, the two characters analogous to the mockingbird are Boo Radley and Tom Robinson.

Handicapped due to an accident with a cotton gin, Tom also has the misfortune of having to pass by the Ewell house twice daily on his way to and from the cotton fields where he works. Mayella often calls Tom to perform various odds and ends as a pretense so she can talk to him, until one night she convinces him to come into the house. Mayella is desperate for the attention of a man, any man, so long as it is not her father, who has an incestuous relationship with his daughter. Though incredibly selfish, Mayella's action is laden with pathos. She has been robbed of the opportunity for a normal life with normal relationships, and in her desperation she reaches out for a black man, knowing the consequence for Tom should he be caught alone with her. There is no justice for Tom, who is caught in an untenable circumstance. If he angers Mayella by denying her what she wants, she can claim anything to get him in trouble. If he obeys her, as he does, he is still accused of violating a white woman.

Atticus tells Scout that he will be unable to win Tom's case. When Scout begins to ask how this can be, Atticus answers, "Simply because we were licked a hundred years before we started is no reason for us not to try to win." Despite already knowing the outcome is predetermined—an injustice that strikes against the very purpose of the legal system—Atticus would be doing Tom an injustice himself if he does not attempt to win his case with every effort he can possibly muster. As he later tells Jem, "The one place where a man ought to get a square deal is in a courtroom, be he any color of the rainbow, but people have a way of carrying their resentments right into a jury box." Tom is later found guilty and is shot attempting an escape, paralleling the image of killing a mockingbird. Even the manner of Tom's death seems an injustice, for he is shot 17 times.

There is no justice for Mayella's crime of falsely accusing Tom, unless, of course, the manner of her existence is justice itself. The Ewell place has only one beautiful feature amongst its filth, the six red geraniums that most of Maycomb believes to be Mayella's work. The geranium is often cited as a flower that symbolizes stupidity or folly and is therefore apropos for such a character as Mayella. Her father, Bob Ewell, who is ostensibly responsible for Tom's death, is stabbed by Boo Radley, the unseen protector of the Finch children. Ewell receives justice at the hands of Boo, and Atticus breaks from legal protocol this once in deciding not to turn Boo in to the authorities. In fact, it is Sheriff Heck Tate who delineates the justice of the situation: "There's a black boy dead for no reason, and the man responsible for it's dead. Let the dead bury the dead this time, Mr. Finch. Let the dead bury the dead."

Scout learns for herself the complex nature of justice when Atticus labors with how he chooses to interpret Bob Ewell's death. Atticus cares less for how his decision will affect him than how it will impact Scout and Jem. Morally, he knows leaving Boo Radley out of the events is the right course of action. It is only when Scout expresses her understanding of what it means to kill a mockingbird that Atticus is at peace with his decision.

Chris Gonzalez

RACE in *To Kill a Mockingbird*

Scout Finch, the narrator of *To Kill a Mockingbird*, recounts the experiences of several summers of her youth in Maycomb, Alabama, at the height of the racially segregated South. As a young, pre-teen girl, Scout's upbringing does not reflect the racist attitudes of her community, thanks to her father, Atticus. His training as a lawyer and his uncompromising integrity help Atticus instill this same approach to race in his children, but it is his employment of Calpurnia as the family cook that truly allows Scout to appreciate all human beings regardless of skin color. Calpurnia, whose name alludes to Julius Caesar's loyal wife, serves as the mother figure for the Finch family. While Atticus deals his lessons to Scout in the erudite manner of an attorney, Calpurnia often explains things to Scout in a folksier way. Thus, Scout receives her true EDUCATION not from school but from the best representatives of each COMMUNITY—Atticus, one of the most highly respected attorneys in Alabama, and Calpurnia, whom Atticus describes as having "more education that most colored folks." When she speaks of the family, Calpurnia does not segregate herself from the Finches, using pronouns such as "we" and "us." And although there is tension between Scout and Calpurnia, it is never race-based, but merely the typical resistance a child might have to a parent or authority figure. Atticus empowers Calpurnia with the respect and dignity afforded any person, and consequently his children do not treat her with the same disdain Mayella Ewell shows Tom Robinson, for example. Rather, Scout has an appreciation for Calpurnia's authority, confessing, "On my part, I went to much trouble, sometimes, not to provoke her."

Racist attitudes are not found solely within the white community of Maycomb. One Sunday morning while Atticus is away, Calpurnia brings the Finch children with her to church, the First Purchase African M.E. Church, so called "because it was paid for from the first earnings of freed slaves." It is at First Purchase that Scout feels the sting of racism herself when a woman named Lula chastises Calpurnia for toting white children into a black church. Scout agrees with Jem's suggestion that they leave a place where they are not wanted, but Calpurnia's invocation of hospitality prevails, proclaiming, "They's my comp'ny." Calpurnia's adherence to the law of hospitality is a great equalizer of sorts, for it is the exact rationale she uses to excoriate Scout after she ridicules Walter Cunningham at the dinner table earlier in the novel. Scout is stunned to realize that Calpurnia resides in two worlds and must be essentially two different people depending on where she is. During her visit to First Purchase, Scout learns not only about Calpurnia's duality but of the unfortunate Tom Robinson, who stands accused of raping Mayella Ewell, a young white girl.

Atticus is given the task of defending Tom, knowing full well the chances of winning are almost nonexistent. The Finch children see firsthand the malignity of the community when a lynch mob (which Atticus calmly diffuses) attempts to murder Tom. During the trial, Scout, Jem, and Dill sit in the balcony with members of the black community, a physical manifestation of their ability to transcend race. Despite clearly demonstrating that Tom was incapable of raping Mayella with only one arm—the left one having been obliterated in a cotton gin years before—Tom is found guilty and sentenced to death. Scout discovers that in her world it is not fact that matters within a situation but the color of one's skin; truth is on Tom's side, but the inexorable power of racism is on Mayella's. The Ewells, a disgrace irrespective of their skin color, who live near the city garbage dump and literally exist off of its trash, still wield more power than the likes of a hardworking black man such as Tom Robinson. During the cross-examination of Tom, Dill can no longer stand how Tom is degraded and must be escorted out of the courthouse by Scout. It is Dill who intuits the perverseness of the situation, the debasement of a man because of the color of his skin. Additionally, Dolphus Raymond, a white man whom all of Maycomb believes to be a drunk, explains to Dill and Scout that he puts on an act in order to give people a rationale that explains why he prefers to spend his time in the black community. Racism is so pervasive in Maycomb that people cannot believe a white man would carry on as Dolphus does through his own volition. He, like Calpurnia, must lead a dual existence.

So much of *To Kill a Mockingbird* is about Scout's education in a world riddled with flaws. Scout, as her name indicates, is someone who gathers information and examines it diligently. She represents the potential of the South, if it only has the courage to face its shameful legacy of slavery and racism, the type of courage people such as Atticus and Tom display in Lee's novel.

Chris Gonzalez

LESSING, DORIS   *The Golden Notebook* (1962)

The underlying plot of Doris Lessing's *The Golden Notebook* is the story of Anna Wulf's life, which is told in the five different parts of the novel called *Free Women.* Anna is a writer who lives with her young daughter, Janet, and her best friend Molly who, like Anna, is divorced and has a child, but Tommy lives with his father.

Anna suffers from a writer's block, but undertakes to document different areas of her life in five different diaries: "a black notebook which is to do with Anna Wulf the writer; a red notebook, concerned with politics; a yellow notebook, in which [she makes] stories out of [her] experience; and a blue notebook which tries to be a diary." The novel alternates among these different narratives, and we do not get to know about events in a chronological order but need to put together different pieces of information to get a fuller view of Anna's life.

Lessing has noted that, although she thought the name of her novel clearly indicated what she intended to be the main theme, it has been overlooked in most of the critical writings on the novel. When Anna is unable to keep the different parts of her life clearly separated—which is her intention with the different diaries—she, on the verge of becoming insane, brings them all together in the writings of the golden notebook.

Eva Lupin

GENDER in *The Golden Notebook*

The Golden Notebook contains five parts called "Free Women," and the novel opens with the sentence, "The two women were alone in the London flat." These references to gender, which are echoed throughout the plot, have produced innumerable readings of the novel as a feminist text despite Lessing's assurance that her intentions were completely different. In any case, gender is clearly a theme in the novel.

The two women referred to in the opening sentence are Anna Wulf and her best friend Molly who are both "bringing up children without men." Together with Anna's daughter Janet they live in an apartment where they occasionally let one of the rooms to male tenants. Although Molly also has a child, Tommy, the two women's roles as mothers are strongly marginalized, and the narrative seems to emphasize their lives as "free women." Their world is a female realm where men come to visit, but where the more traditional fate of women, that of marriage, is avoided. And while marriage in the early sixties—when the novel was first published—was even more of a norm than it is today, Anna and Molly meet different men throughout the novel.

That Anna is torn between her role as a free woman and her role as a mother is especially clear in one of the scenes where she wakes up next to her present boyfriend Michael. As she wakes up she becomes aware of the need to get Janet off to school before Michael will wake up and ask for breakfast. For a moment she is jealous of the fact that while she is worrying about details, such as getting Janet going and buying the tea that is missing from the cupboard, Michael "will spend his day, served by secretaries, nurses, women in all

kinds of capacities, who will take this weight off him." Her double roles become even more obvious when they start to make love, aware that Janet is moving around in the other side of the apartment. After they've finished Michael remarks: "And now, Anna, I guess you are going to desert me for Janet?" Anna fights the resentment she feels by reminding herself that his remark is impersonal, and a sign of "the disease of women in our time." Clenching her teeth she tells herself: "If I were a man I'd be the same."

The two women's living arrangement and their close friendship appears to offer a way of living without men; yet they both seem to fear complete autonomy and the men they have relationships with are often the dominating type. Saul, one of the men to whom Anna is drawn and who she calls a "real man," is in truth misogynistic and oppressive; and Anna is not the only female character in the book who is drawn to such men. Anna's husband, for example, has met a new woman whom he treats badly by cheating on her; and one of the main plots in the novel that Anna is writing is about another man having a mistress. Overall, women are depicted as rather weak and dependent on men, while the novel's men are powerful and dominant; it seems that women's attraction for these men helps to select the kind of men who will continue to oppress them.

The novel also deals with homosexuality, but Anna expresses her preference for heterosexuality when she lets the room to a gay couple and worries about Janet's well-being. A "real man" would "spark tensions, set a balance," she muses, thinking that Janet would be better off with a heterosexual tenant than she is with the "charming, friendly perceptive young man Ivor." Her thoughts, however, are ambiguous and she wonders at herself feeling uneasy "when [she sees] Ivor with Janet because he's like a big friendly dog, or a sort of harmless elder brother." All men, however, assume superiority over women, and the two gay men's exaggerated use of female attributes mocks women and becomes a way to show their domination over them. After having overheard their mocking ways one night, Anna finds herself devastated and asks herself: "And when had this new frightened vulnerable Anna been born?" The question is soon answered by herself. "She knew: it was when Michael had abandoned her"; she then "[smiles] at the knowledge that she, the independent woman, was independent . . just so long as she was loved by a man." In the end Anna is so hurt by the ways of the homosexual couple that she feels forced to make them leave her house.

What this passage illustrates is not so much the novel's stance toward gender, but the centrality of this issue in the plot. The novel offers many different ways to think about and approach gender issues; and it focuses the reader's attention on areas in women's lives that before this novel was written had not been so openly described in literature.

Eva Lupin

IDENTITY in *The Golden Notebook*

Identity is a central issue in *The Golden Notebook*, and Anna Wulf, the protagonist, often refers to the question of who she is in her writings. Quite early in the book she discusses the characters in the novel she is writing and reflects on how once again she is touching upon a subject that often occupies her mind to the verge of obsession: "I mean, of course, this question of 'personality.'" One thing that astonishes her about the characters she is creating for her story is their complexity. No matter what adjective I use for a character, she thinks to herself, I could just as well use the opposite. But how can a person be both kind and ruthless, both cold and warm? Anna's conclusion is that she knows nothing about the characters she is describing and that words become irrelevant. This leads her to the acknowledgment that she accepts amorality as a stance because she does not care. All she does care about, she says, is to describe her characters so that the readers feel that they are real.

Just as Anna struggles with the complexity of her characters, so is she struggling with the difficulty of combining the different sides of her own personality. And structurally this thick novel mirrors her struggle by consisting of the four different notebooks she keeps. Being a writer, a political activist, a single woman, and a mother, she struggles to map out her own personality in writing, by keeping "a black notebook which is to do with Anna Wulf the writer; a red notebook, concerned with politics; a yellow notebook, in which [she makes] stories out of [her] experience; and a blue notebook which tries to be a diary." Through her writings she tries to structure and categorize different sides of herself, and these notebooks combine into the novel we keep in our hands. In this way the novel suggests that identity is a matter of story telling.

In the beginning Anna manages pretty well to keep order by keeping the content of her different notebooks apart; the further into the novel we get, however, the more the stories in the notebooks blend and blur together. Writing about Ella, one of the characters in the novel she is writing, for example, Anna notes: "I, Anna, see Ella. Who is, of course, Anna. But that is the point, for she is not." The confusion of characters interests Anna, and she continues her musings: "The moment I, Anna, write: Ella rings up Julia to announce, etc., then Ella floats away from me and becomes someone else. I don't understand what happens at the moment Ella separates herself from me and becomes Ella. No one does. It's enough to call her Ella, instead of Anna." When the novel starts Anna is suffering from a writer's block, which makes it hard for her to continue writing the novel she is working on, but as Anna realizes the connection between herself and her characters, her writer's block starts to give way.

The entries in Anna's notebooks are fragmentary, presented to the readers who sometimes need to provide missing pieces of information themselves. Readers sometimes realize the context of scenes, or the impact of them on other incidents, only in retrospect, and consequently we do not get a clear picture of who Anna is, but we, like Anna herself, end up searching for clues about her identity. Similarly, Anna, by reviewing her different life situations and her responses to different situations, slowly gets a more comprehensive picture of who she is. Toward the end, the only way for Anna to keep her sanity is to acknowledge and allow for a blurring of the different narratives, and she does so by making it all the same story in what she names *The Golden Notebook*. Together then, Anna and the reader are presented in this last notebook with a writer who has come one step further in the effort to make all the sides of her personality into a more integrated version of herself.

Eva Lupin

ILLNESS in *The Golden Notebook*

In *The Golden Notebook* writing and mental illness seem to be connected. The narrator, Anna Wulf, is keeping four different notebooks where she compartmentalizes different areas of her life. The novel has nine sections, these different notebooks and five different parts called *Free Women,* which can be read as a novel on their own. This fragmented way of telling the story seems to offer a way into the consciousness of the narrator, who struggles at times to keep the different parts of her life separated from each other. Each notebook contains things related to a certain area of her life; and the way she is dividing her life into compartments illustrates the feeling she has of herself cracking up, while her effort to try and keep the different stories separated in effect also keeps her from falling apart.

In the beginning of the novel, Anna seems to have little trouble deciding what kind of experiences belong in which notebook; but further into the novel we discover that Anna is beginning to confuse her stories, and is having big difficulties keeping them apart. The blurring of lines is a phenomenon Anna notices in so many different areas that it becomes symptomatic to the novel. At one point she identifies with the situation of fellow women to the point that she is having difficulties separating herself from the history of other women; at another time she gets her different stories mixed up; and sometimes she has a problem separating her own person from the characters in the novel she is writing. In addition, she remarks that the "normal" person in the family is the sickest one; only his/her strong personality causes the other members to act out the illness for him/her. Immediately after noticing this, she comments that she is recording her observation in the wrong notebook.

As the story becomes more and more fragmented, Anna's consciousness appears to be affected in the same direction. As long as her writings are clearly divided into separate stories she experiences a sense of well-being; but as the stories begin to spill over into each other Anna is becoming more confused. One of

her notebooks, her blue diary, is supposed to simply record reality, but Anna realizes that her intention is harder to achieve than she anticipated. Words, she discovers, are not neutral and do not allow for a simple straightforward reporting of events; she says that she most have been mad to think that she would succeed.

Once she starts fighting her impulse to keep her writings separated, and instead allows for them to blend by dissolving all boundaries between them, she starts to feel as a whole person again. Toward the end of the book, the man she is living with is watching as she spreads out her notebooks on her bed, and he asks her why she keeps four of them. Anna answers that, apparently, it has been necessary for her to split herself up but that from now on she will be using only one. And talking to her lover at the end of the novel, she comments on how they both have personalities that include everything: art, politics, literature, and so on. Madness, she says, is when she is unable to keep all of these in view at the same time but goes on to concentrate on only one thing. The last parts of the novel become more and more dreamlike, and Anna remembers and experiences events from all the stories that were previously separated from each other but are now all coming to life at the same time. Stories and characters become difficult to distinguish from each other until Anna's consciousness collects itself in something that resembles peace. But although we might sense that the story goes from chaos to order, from disintegration to wholeness, from illness to well-being or ultimately from madness to sanity, the novel more than anything else refuses to make these distinctions and toward the very end Anna concludes: "I was, in other words, sane again. But the word sane meant nothing, as the word mad meant nothing." When words lose their meaning, opposites dissolve into each other and, ultimately, become the same thing. Thereby no one can decide anymore who is ill and who is not.

Eva Lupin

LEWIS, C. S.   *The Lion, the Witch and the Wardrobe* (1950)

The Lion, the Witch and the Wardrobe is the first and best known book of *The Chronicles of Narnia.*

Though second in the chronological order of the series after *The Magician's Nephew*, it was published first, in 1950.

Set in the early '40s, it is the story of four siblings: Peter, Susan, Edmund, and Lucy Pevensie, who are sent to the English countryside to escape the London bombing during World War II. While playing hide and seek, Lucy discovers, inside an old wardrobe, the enchanted realm of Narnia, ruled by the evil White Witch who has cast a spell on the whole country to keep it in an eternal winter with no Christmas. The other children do not believe Lucy's story until they all hide in the wardrobe and find themselves in Narnia. The kids, who (according to an ancient prophecy) can save Narnia, begin a troubled journey, helped by Mr. and Mrs. Beaver and Father Christmas, to meet the lion Aslan, the true king. Edmund, tragically, leaves them to join the White Witch. Aslan offers himself to the Witch in Edmund's place but, because Aslan is an innocent victim, he may return to life. In the final battle, the children defeat the White Witch, with the help of Aslan and other magical creatures, and become kings and queens of Narnia. They rule for a long time, but when they go back to England through the wardrobe only five minutes have passed since they hid in the wardrobe.

The Lion, the Witch and the Wardrobe is a delightful fairy tale for both children and adults in which C. S. Lewis explores such themes as JUSTICE, HEROISM, GUILT, TIME, and NATURE in a light, yet significant way.

Chiara Sgro

HEROISM in *The Lion, the Witch and the Wardrobe*

Heroism is one of the most important themes in *The Chronicles of Narnia* and, in particular, in *The Lion, the Witch and the Wardrobe*. Though the words "hero" and "heroism" are never mentioned in the book, the story of Peter, Susan, Edmund, and Lucy follows the main steps of the classic hero's quest typical of the tradition of epics and medieval romance. Moreover, although they are not directly referred to as heroes the children, as well as Aslan, have all the characteristics of the hero: loyalty, courage, and complete self-sacrifice in service of the mission. For

this reason, in *The Lion, the Witch and the Wardrobe*, heroism is strictly linked to self-sacrifice and the story is full of great and small acts of heroism until the mission—to defeat the White Witch and restore peace in Narnia—is completed. The characters, just as the heroes of ancient poems, are called to acts of self-sacrifice for a greater good and regardless of the consequences to their own lives.

Lucy's adventures in Narnia and the rebellion against the White Witch begin with a small act of heroism done by Mr. Tumnus. Indeed, he decides not to hand Lucy over to the Witch though he perfectly well knows that this disobedience will lead him to imprisonment and maybe death. It is when Lucy goes back to Narnia with her brothers and sister and discovers that Mr. Tumnus has been captured by the Witch that they begin their adventure through Narnia to meet Aslan and help him defeat the false queen. Their travel—like the voyage in a hero's quest—will be characterized by challenges and trials necessary to reach the final goal. As in the tradition of epic and romance, they will be helped in their tasks by magical or special helpers. Indeed, they begin their actual travel to the Stone Table—which recalls the Round Table of the stories of King Arthur and his Knights—with the help of Mr. and Mrs. Beaver. The help and support the two little creatures offer the children, leaving their home and challenging the Witch's power, is yet another act of heroism. This act highlights the novel's revolutionary idea that everyone can be a hero by doing something, small though it may be, for the greater good.

The story also calls attention to the novel detail of children as heroes and saviors of a nation. For this reason, Peter, Susan, Edmund, and Lucy are treated and presented as the heroes of epic poems. In particular, the encounter with Father Christmas is crucial to the identification of the children as heroes and to the understanding of the particular kind of heroism being expressed by C. S. Lewis. Father Christmas gives Peter, Susan, and Lucy precious gifts that will help them complete their mission. These gifts are not only weapons but also special objects that will have a particular significance and use later in the story. The gifts belong to the tradition of heroic poems and make the children become real heroes. Peter receives a sword and a shield, as did ancient knights; Aslan uses this sword, which recalls other famous swords such as Excalibur and Durendal, to knight him after Peter kills the wolf. Susan is given a bow with arrows, another typical weapon of epic and romance stories, and a horn. The horn in such a story is usually given to valiant warriors to call the army to battle or to ask for help, and indeed, Susan uses her horn to call Peter to his first battle. Lucy receives a dagger for self-defense and a bottle full of a magic cordial that can heal all kinds of wound; in receiving this magic object Lucy becomes the healer, another typical figure in the heroic poems. She will heal all the creatures wounded in the final battle and end the series of deaths caused by the White Witch and her evil deeds.

Father Christmas's advice on how and when to use the precious gifts introduces another important idea: The children will have to do their best to complete their mission no matter how difficult it will be and how much it will cost them. This is a recurrent idea in the story. Aslan himself, during his first meeting with Peter, Susan, and Lucy, when they ask him to save Edmund, underlines that "all shall be done" but it will probably be harder than the children think. Aslan's words are the perfect expression of Lewis's idea of heroism as sacrifice and responsibility. This idea culminates with Aslan's extreme self-sacrifice to save Edmund and satisfy the Deep Magic demanded by the White Witch. The heroism of the lion recalls Jesus's heroism and makes Aslan a Christ figure. The lion must suffer humiliation and death in order to save Edmund as Jesus faced agony and gave his life to save the human race. In the epic poems written in the Middle Ages, pure and brave knights such as Gawain, Perceval, or Galahad are often compared to Christ. Lewis, however, goes one step further and rewards his literary hero with an actual resurrection. Apart from the theological significance of this innovative conception of heroism, the main idea is that personal suffering and sickness cannot be a deterrent for the heroism/sacrifice required by the situation. When Peter has to kill the wolf who has attacked Susan, he declares that though he is about to be sick it makes no difference to what he has to do. Thus, in *The Lion, the Witch and the Wardrobe*, heroism cannot be detached from sacrifice and responsibility.

Edmund himself, after being rescued by Aslan, understands that acting only to satisfy one's own pleasure is not right. For this reason, in the final battle he is the one who fights with the greatest enthusiasm and until the battle is over, regardless of the serious wound that threatens his life. At the end of the voyage and when the battle between the good and the evil forces is won, as in the typical hero's quest, the children are rewarded and crowned kings and queens of Narnia.

Chiara Sgro

JUSTICE in *The Lion, the Witch, and the Wardrobe*

Justice is often pictured symbolically, as a blindfolded liberty-figure holding a scale to depict the balance of righteousness. C. S. Lewis's *The Lion, the Witch, and the Wardrobe* develops the major theme of justice through the depiction of the consequences and sacrifices required to save Edmund from his own faults and choices. Righteousness requires an honest, moral, and ethical personality, which Lewis shows is lacking in all human characters.

Edmund, the prime example, is a traitor on so many levels: He lies about the time Lucy found him in Narnia, betraying her and leaving her open to Peter and Susan's ridicule; he sides with the White Witch even though he knows she is the evil ruler about whom Lucy's friend Tumnus has warned her; and, because he is not the center of attention when all four children are at Beaver's, he abandons them to go tell the White Witch where they can be found, placing his own siblings' lives at risk. Therefore, when the White Witch demands justice, according to the Deep Magic or the Laws written on the Stone Table, Edmund stands condemned by his own actions.

Peter, Susan, and Lucy are frantic for Edmund's safety and ask Aslan if something can be done to save him. Because Aslan is the King of Narnia, as a parallel Jesus Christ, he can reveal the Deeper Magic from "before the dawn of time," implying he existed, like Christ, "before the beginning." While justice says the consequence or cost of Edmund's treachery is sacrifice upon the Stone Table (and since the White Witch is not willing to give up her supposed victory over the Old Sayings—that two sons of Adam and two daughters of Eve would sit enthroned over Narnia—which are parallels to prophecies of the Old Testament of the Bible), it seems that Edmund must die for justice to be served.

But Lewis shows that there is another way. If someone else would lay down his life for Edmund to pay the price or consequences of the law, then justice would be satisfied, but the person (or beast in this case) has to be suitable—a perfect person, not someone who already owes a price to justice for himself. Since Aslan is the son of the Emperor of the Sea, like Jesus is the son of God, he makes a perfect substitute. He more than satisfies the demands of justice and the law.

The justice theme requires consequences to be paid in other character's lives in the story as well: Tumnus, the faun Lucy met in her first encounter with Narnia, must spend time frozen in stone in the White Witch's castle—not because he betrayed the Witch, but because he intended to betray the Lion and the Old Sayings by helping the White Witch, telling her when he saw human children. Just because he changes his mind and regrets luring Lucy into his tree hovel, Tumnus is not exempt from the consequences of his actions. This is another way in which Lewis shows that wickedness, even when only contemplated, as Tumnus did, has severe consequences.

However, justice is not necessarily negative as it works out for the Beavers. Mr. and Mrs. Beaver are rewarded for their actions—supporting the Lion by helping the children safely meet Aslan on the hill that holds the Stone Table. First they receive a new sluice gate for their dam from Father Christmas, who all children know gives gifts only to "good little girls and boys"—showing that even mythological and legendary characters must follow the logic of justice. Then the Lion commends them in the same way that Jesus says those who do right will be told: "Well done, thou good and faithful servant" (Matthew 25:21).

The scales are balanced when wrong is punished and right is rewarded. Edmund's consequences are paid upon Aslan's death as a perfect substitution sacrifice; Tumnus must bear his consequences in a death-like frozen state until he's forgiven and saved by Aslan overcoming the White Witch's power by rising from the dead; and the Beavers receive their positive consequences for remaining true to what is right. Justice and balance are restored, and righteousness reigns at Cair Parieval at the end of the novel.

Susan K. Jaeger

NATURE in *The Lion, the Witch and the Wardrobe*

The Lion, the Witch and the Wardrobe is set in Narnia, an imaginary world created by C. S. Lewis as the background for his *Chronicles of Narnia*. As opposed to the ordinary world, where Peter, Susan, Edmund, and Lucy come from, Narnia is a mythical world in which nature, in its widest meaning, functions as one of the protagonists of the story rather than as a mere background for the plot. Throughout the book the four main characters have to deal with the natural elements and the magical creatures living in this secondary world, in order to fulfil their mission and save Narnia from the White Witch.

From the very beginning of the Pevensie siblings' adventures in Narnia, nature is one of the prominent features of the story, functioning both as the contact point between the primary and the secondary world and the complication that puts in motion the whole plot. Indeed, before the children realize that they are in a different and magical world, Narnia's natural environment is the first thing they get in touch with, a natural environment that is seemingly the same as that of the primary world, that is, 20th-century England. The wardrobe leads to a wood covered in snow. The apparent ordinariness of the snow-covered trees makes the entrance of the characters into the secondary world soft and the suspension of disbelief in the reader easier, in spite of the awkwardness of finding a wood in a wardrobe. The seasonal difference—in Narnia it is evidently winter while in England it is summer—and the presence of a lamppost in the middle of the wood beyond the back of the wardrobe are elements that give both the characters and the readers a hint of the very special nature of the place. But the Narnian winter is also the complication that sets the whole plot in motion: The White Witch has cast a spell that makes the winter perennial and Christmas forbidden. A deadly and endless winter is the form evil has taken in Narnia. The White Witch controls the country through nature: The natural environment is at her complete mercy until the four Pevensie children arrive to fulfil the prophecy and Aslan comes back to Narnia. Their mission acquires a new significance if one reads the story by paying attention to the role of nature: The final goal of Peter, Susan, Edmund, and Lucy is not merely to destroy the White Witch and her evil magic but also to renew the whole country, to give Narnia a new birth, a new beginning. The children must set nature in motion again, giving Narnia and its magical creatures the safe course of the seasons and take nature back to normal.

Of course, what is normal in Narnia is a mythical scenario in which flora and fauna are alive in the widest meaning of the word: Animals talk, trees are spies in the pay of the White Witch, and the dryads, nymphs, and fauns of the primary world's mythology are real. Therefore, nature in all her forms takes part in the story. Natural elements and magical creatures fight on both sides, either supporting the evil power of the Witch or resisting it. The rebels gather around Aslan, the true king of Narnia but also a lion, king of the animals. Nature changes as Aslan approaches and spring wins over winter. The natural environment rejoices in the return of the true king and life starts to blossom again in Narnia, to the utmost disappointment of the White Witch. It is not by mere chance that, after the nocturnal sacrifice, Aslan comes back to life at dawn. While Lucy and Susan weep over the lion's death, nature stops for a second: a moment of silence and mourning before the new dawn. This image is powerful and can be considered the climax of the nature images in the book and of the story itself. The birds start to sing in the wood and a pale light appears on the horizon. Soon the red light of dawn changes into gold and the sun peeps out. The moment of Aslan's resurrection coincides with sunrise. It is more than just a new day: It is the new beginning for Narnia and the Narnians, the final goal to which the children and the good creatures have struggled throughout the story and the necessary step toward the final victory and the resolution of the conflict between good and evil.

Chiara Sgro

LEWIS, SINCLAIR *Main Street* (1920)

Sinclair Lewis's *Main Street* is important because of its depiction of Carol Kennicott of Gopher Prairie, Minnesota, one of American literature's few truly individualistic female characters. Carol is independent and self-reliant, intelligent and creative, a thinker and a planner. She sincerely wants to do something in her life; she wants to maintain her individuality and also be of service to the community around her, even if this service places her in conflict with the community she wants to improve. Carol is akin in a number of ways to such self-assertive literary heroines as Nathaniel Hawthorne's Hester Prynne in *The SCARLET LETTER* and Henry James's *DAISY MILLER.* But Carol manages to maintain her individualism more than many independent heroines, who find they must submit to societal constraints or who, perhaps, even perish by the time their stories are concluded.

The second reason for *Main Street*'s permanence is its depiction of the "revolt against the village" theme, an early-20th-century theme that perfectly complements the theme of the independent woman. This motif—which is also seen in Sherwood Anderson's *WINESBERG, OHIO* and Edgar Lee Masters's *Spoon River Anthology,* as well as in *Main Street*—underlies depictions of small-town life as narrow-minded, intolerant, and stultifying, and as requiring conformity.

Carol's husband, Dr. Will Kennicott, gives Carol the wherewithal to try to achieve a modicum of independence from the constrictions of small-town life. But at the same time, since he is deeply fond of Gopher Prairie, he is part of the problem. And thus, finally, the novel expands into additional themes, such as marriage and the family. In short, *Main Street* is, thematically, a wide-ranging piece of literature.

Gerard M. Sweeney

FAMILY in *Main Street*

In much of classic, pre-Civil War American literature, especially the literature of the romantic period, family is a subject of relatively slight importance. In the fiction of Edgar Allan Poe, for example, there are very few references to family; and in those tales where family members are mentioned—characters such as Madeline Usher, the sister of Roderick Usher in "THE FALL OF THE HOUSE OF USHER," and the unnamed wife of the narrator of "The Black Cat"—the family member appears only briefly and then dies before the tale concludes. In James Fenimore Cooper's Leatherstocking Tales, the author's most widely known character, Natty Bumppo, substitutes for the family he lacks a type of wilderness brotherhood with Native Americans such as Chingachgook and Uncas. In these relationships, there is both comradeship and loyalty; but what Cooper is depicting is male bonding, not family.

Family becomes much more important in realistic, post-Civil War American literature, in the fiction of writers such as William Dean Howells, Henry James, and Edith Wharton. Parents, children, husbands, and wives are all central in most of the major and minor fictions of the period. It is in this tradition that *Main Street* is to be found; but at the same time the novel reveals strong romantic currents in its depiction of the heroine as an orphan. In short, family in *Main Street* is simultaneously a realistically drawn social phenomenon and, more abstractly, a force that powerfully affects an individual's life.

Like the major—and mostly male—characters of classic American literature, Carol Milford Kennicott begins her career as "an orphan; her only near relative was a vanilla-flavored sister married to an optician in St. Paul." Her mother died when Carol was nine, and her father passed away four years later. These biographical facts, summarized briefly in the first few pages of the novel, come to have an enormous impact on the character, and thus the destiny, of the heroine.

Carol's "independence from relatives" is a major factor underlying her rejection of her first marriage proposal, an offer proffered by Stewart Snyder, a fellow student at Blodgett College. In rejecting him, Carol says, "No! No! You're a dear, but I want to do things. I don't understand myself but I want—everything in the world! . . . Stewart dear, I can't settle down to nothing but dish washing!"

Doing "nothing," or being "vanilla flavored" like her married sister, is what the independent Carol ardently wants to avoid. Ironically, the opposite—doing something—becomes connected for Carol with her acceptance of the marriage proposal of Dr.

Will Kennicott of Gopher Prairie, Minnesota. Will clearly realizes the importance Carol places on doing things, and so he strikes this note as part of his proposal: "Come on. Come to Gopher Prairie. Show us. Make the town—well—make it artistic. . . . Make us change!" Thus for Carol, in becoming engaged to Will, marriage is not so much a matter of family as it is an opportunity to be an urban planner, to do something for, to help to improve, the small town of Gopher Prairie.

But Gopher Prairie resists the improvements Carol envisions; and Carol resists—we are not certain whether by choice or by her nature—the benefits of family life. When she first contemplates the possibility of pregnancy, she reacts with revulsion: "I'd hate it! I'd be scared to death! Some day but—Please, dear nebulous Lord, not now!" Carol's original love of Will, such as it was, transmutes into fondness. This she admits to herself one day while she walks home from a visit to Guy Pollock, a bachelor to whom Carol is attracted: "I am, I *am* fond of Will, and—Can't I ever find another word than 'fond'?" Shortly after this soliloquy, Carol asks Will for a monthly allowance, stating her request in quasi-legalistic language: "Either I'm your partner, in charge of the household department of our business, with a regular budget for it, or else I'm nothing." *Fondness* and a *partnership*: both terms suggest that the family in *Main Street* is decidedly less than ideal.

And it remains less than ideal, as is characteristic of a family in a realistic novel. Will engages in an essentially meaningless affair with one of the Gopher Prairie women. And as for Carol, the birth of a son, Hugh, does strengthen her familial feelings; and therefore, for a time, she feels "no apparent desire for escape." But eventually she does escape, with Hugh, and with Will's acquiescence, to Washington, D.C., where she remains for two years. But this arrangement, a type of compromise, is ultimately not satisfactory, in large measure because it amounts to only half a family. Even as she leaves Gopher Prairie for Washington, Carol realizes that she "had her freedom, and it was empty." And so she returns to Gopher Prairie, pregnant with a daughter who will, Carol hopes, go to Vassar and "become a feminist leader or marry a scientist or both." Thus the novel ends with not the ambiguity of romantic literature, but with a great deal of ambivalence. In short, Lewis presents family life as positive, as productive, and as moderately fulfilling; but at the same time he portrays it as frustrating, as limiting, and perhaps even as a bit unnatural.

Gerard M. Sweeney

INDIVIDUAL AND SOCIETY in *Main Street*

In 1841, Ralph Waldo Emerson, one of America's greatest advocates of individualism and self-reliance, wrote the following: "Society everywhere is in conspiracy against the manhood of every one of its members. . . . The virtue in most request is conformity. . . . Whoso would be a man, must be a nonconformist." These words, written roughly six decades before the publication of *Main Street,* could be said to summarize one of the novel's major themes: the conflict between the individual and the society of which he or she is a part.

This conflict can be seen in the novel's depiction of three important characters, each of whom finds a different way to deal with the individual-versus-society conflict. First, there is Miles Bjornstam, the town handyman and jack-of-all-trades. When the novel's main character, Carol Kennicott, first meets Miles, he is living in a one-room shanty that can easily remind the reader of Henry Thoreau's cabin in *WALDEN.* Miles soon becomes a friend of Carol; and Carol quickly comes to admire—and, indeed, feel exhilarated by—Miles's independence of spirit, an independence that is frequently at odds with the narrowness of Gopher Prairie society. Miles sums up his brand of classless and free-thinking individualism as follows: "Yeh, I'm probably a yahoo, but by gum I do keep my independence by doing odd jobs, and that's more 'n these polite cusses like the clerks in the bank do." Miles eventually marries Bea Sorenson, a country girl who is both Carol's friend and her housemaid. This marriage is a happy one, resulting in the birth of a son, Olaf; and thus it serves to help anchor the independent Miles in the social world. But Bea and Olaf suddenly die of typhoid fever; and Miles, his anchors gone, leaves Gopher Prairie for Canada.

In short, Miles Bjornstam, having become even more isolated by his tragic losses, asserts his indi-

vidualism by escaping from the society he has come to dislike intensely. Another way of dealing with the individual-versus-society conflict represents the exact opposite of Miles's way: succumbing to society, allowing society to defeat—even to obliterate—one's sense of individualism. Guy Pollock, another friend and confidante of Carol, chooses this path. A bachelor, Guy is one of Gopher Prairie's lawyers, and this very fact serves to hinder any conspicuous manifestations of individualism, since Guy's profession involves a commitment to the rules and regulations of the society of which he is a part. A handyman such as Miles Bjornstam can live on the outskirts, both literally and figuratively; but a lawyer is far less able to do so.

But it is not exactly Guy's profession that saps the man's individualism. Rather, it is something more insidious, a phenomenon he refers to as the "Village Virus." This, as he describes it to Carol, "is a germ which—it's extraordinarily like the hookworm—it infects ambitious people who stay too long in the provinces. You'll find it epidemic among lawyers and doctors and ministers and college-bred merchants—all these people who have had a glimpse of the world that thinks and laughs, but have returned to their swamp." Several years before Carol's arrival in town, Guy realized that his life in Gopher Prairie was becoming more and more an empty husk. So he decided to leave. But, unlike Miles Bjornstam, Guy Pollock found that he could not leave; he discovered that "the Village Virus had me, absolute." And so he concludes his brief history by describing himself as "a living dead man."

It is, finally, the novel's main character, Carol Kennicott, who manages to avoid the Village Virus of Guy. Here we should note that Lewis cannot have his heroine escape from society in the manner of Miles—because she is a woman and also, more significantly, because she is a wife and a mother. After all, Lewis wants to present Carol as a realistically flawed character, but at the same time maintain the reader's empathy for her. But Carol does "escape" for a time; to Washington, D.C., where she works for about two years for the federal government. As a result of this temporary "escape," as a result of her realizing from a distance that Gopher Prairie is, after all, not such a reprehensible society, and also as a result of the gentle encouragement of her husband, Carol finally returns to Gopher Prairie. And there she manages to achieve what Miles Bjornstam and Guy Pollock could not achieve: a type of compromise between being an individual and being a member of a larger social unit. In the novel's conclusion, Carol's "active hatred of Gopher Prairie had run out," and "she again saw Gopher Prairie as her home."

Gerard M. Sweeney

SOCIAL CLASS in *Main Street*

Perhaps the most interesting—and certainly the most original—of the many minor characters in *Main Street* is Erik Valborg. Erik comes to Gopher Prairie after leaving—really, escaping from—farm life and the stern management of his father. In Gopher Prairie, Erik becomes a tailor; he expresses bookish and artistic interests he could not express on the farm; and finally he leaves the stultifying Gopher Prairie for Hollywood and the motion picture industry, there changing his name to the softer "Erik Valour." The most striking and original characteristic of Erik lies in his gender identity. Erik has a pronounced feminine nature. He is described by one of Gopher Prairie's matrons as "the most awful mollycoddle—looks just like a girl"; and he is jokingly referred to as "Elizabeth." He describes himself as being "crazy about fabrics—textures and colors and design" (364); and his original goal is to work as a designer of women's dresses. But for the town of Gopher Prairie, Erik's most defining characteristic is that he is "nothing but a Swede tailor." In other words, Erik is defined not by his uniqueness; rather, he is defined—and dismissed—by his social class.

In miniature, the town's labeling of Erik Valborg illustrates much about the novel's depiction of Americans of the early 20th century. In Gopher Prairie, residents' opinions about others and also their relationships with others are rigidly controlled by conceptions of social class.

The social class we see the most is the town's upper class. This is to be expected because the novel's main characters, Carol and Dr. Will Kennicott, are members of this class, as are most of the people with whom they associate. This class is composed of the town's professionals (chiefly the doctors) and the entrepreneurs (chiefly the business owners) and, of course, their wives. Indeed, it is the wives who voice most of the upper-class comments. This is the case because the wives are the characters most in contact with Carol, and most of the novel is presented through her perspective. Carol converses with the upper-class wives at meetings of the Jolly Seventeen, the women's social group, and the Thanatopsis Club, the women's cultural society. These meetings illustrate that Sinclair Lewis can be alternately light-hearted and severe in his social criticism.

The more light-hearted side of Lewis can be seen in his depictions of the intellectual pretentiousness of Gopher Prairie's upper-class women. These women think of themselves as the guardians of culture. So they have meetings to discuss literature, but the discussions never rise above the simplistic. All of the English poets, for example, are discussed in a single meeting, although there are no references to or quotations from actual poetry. Similarly, one single meeting is scheduled for a discussion of "English Fiction and Essays," thus suggesting that, for these women, a topic so enormous in scope and cultural importance can be adequately treated in a matter of minutes. All of this is humorous, but there is also an acerbic side to Lewis's social satire. This we can see in the discussions Carol hears about the immigrant and working-class members of Gopher Prairie society. On this subject, the upper-class women are brutally mean-spirited. One woman reports her husband's assertion that the Scandinavian mill-workers "are perfectly terrible—so silent and cranky, and so selfish, the way they keep demanding raises" (99). And then another woman adds this about the Scandinavian house servants: "They're ungrateful, all that class of people. . . . I don't know what the country's coming to, with these Scandahoofian clodhoppers demanding every cent you can save, and so ignorant and impertinent. . . ."

What we see here is not merely class differences, but real class animosity. And the animosity flows not only from the upper class toward the lower class, but also from the lower class toward the upper class. We see this late in the novel when Adolph Valborg,

Erik's father, unjustly accuses Carol of seductively luring Erik away from life on the farm: "Women like you—you're worse dan street-walkers! Rich women like you, wit' fine husbands and no decent work to do—and me . . look how I work, look at those hands! But you, oh God no, you mustn't work, you're too fine to do decent work."

Main Street depicts class tension, animosity, and even class hatred. We should remind ourselves that *Main Street* is Sinclair Lewis's depiction not merely of a single small town, but of all American towns, and so of America itself. And thus the ultimate questions about the text are these: Is *Main Street* an accurate historical depiction of the way America was in the early 1900s? To this, the answer is Yes. Is *Main Street* also a predictive depiction of America as it is now? The answer to this is one the reader must decide.

Gerard M. Sweeney

LONDON, JACK *The Call of the Wild* (1903)

The Call of the Wild is the story of a dog's transformation from domesticated creature into wild animal. Raised on a California estate, Buck loses his freedom when a gardener's helper captures him and sells him to Klondike gold hunters. The kidnapping throws Buck into basic training as a sled dog, where he has to learn how to deal not only with humans and their cruel, punishing ways, but also with an awakening sense of his innate natural instincts as a wolf descendant.

The novel explores themes of freedom and nature and their impact on identity. Buck's loss of freedom inspires a fast learning curve during his forced tutelage in the Klondike, if only so he can survive. Nature demands efficiency and requires a way of being that is devoid of morality. These external influences set Buck on a breathtaking pace and conflicted path to recover who he is. Indeed, Buck's identity struggles come from the very fact that he was forceably removed from his California estate—he did not seek out the wilderness—where he would never have heeded any "call," no matter how innate his ancient wild identity. Because his freedom was taken from him, Buck never has control over his

life—he can only adapt. Raw nature triumphantly wins out, for Buck chooses to return to the wild. His natural and domesticated identities are reconciled, in that he transforms into a near-mythical superwolf, embodying the best of both his former dog self and his more recent wild self.

Lori Vermaas

FREEDOM in *The Call of the Wild*

For the first four years of his life, Buck enjoys a comfortable existence in a prosperous home, one where his master grants him the freedom to roam around the grounds at his pleasure. Unlike the other dogs, he is "neither house-dog nor kennel-dog. The whole realm is his" and "he stalked [it] imperiously," like a "country gentlem[a]n." However, one day a gardener's helper, Manuel, kidnaps Buck in a gambling scheme that eventually leads to his relocation in Alaska. He puts a rope around Buck's neck, an act signifying his enslavement. Buck has enjoyed so much freedom, however, that he does not understand the meaning of a rope, and initially accepts it "with quiet dignity." Soon after, he realizes its oppressive power, particularly when the rope is given to a stranger, who ignores Buck's growling protest, or "command" of "displeasure," by "tighten[ing]" the rope even more.

So begins Buck's loss of freedom and his subjugation to a system of power relations between man and dog out in the wild where men—especially those who carry tools—are masters and dogs are their slaves. Indeed, various tools regulate the system, including restraints like the rope and a cage. For the next two days Buck endures caged train travel, wherein he snarls and throws himself against the cage while human guards make fun of him and act like animals themselves, "growl[ing] and bark[ing] like detestable dogs." After the two-day trip, when a man in a red sweater frees Buck from the cage, Buck tries to attack him. But the man deftly beats him with a club at each charge, effectively training Buck not to attack men who carry these particular tools. Having "never been struck by a club in his life," Buck "did not understand" the training regimen at first, but after going a couple of rounds, he learns the lesson. When Buck's bloodied body finally acquiesces, the man tells him "you've learned your place, and I know mine. . . . fearlessly pat[ting]" Buck on the head. The club is "a revelation" to Buck, for it teaches him a "lesson . . . [that] in all his after life he never forgot. . . . It was his introduction to the reign of primitive law. . . . [that] a man with a club was a lawgiver, a master to be obeyed, though not necessarily conciliated." This particular tool, above all the others, effectively signifies his loss of freedom and its replacement with obedience to humans.

After being assigned to a sled dog team, Buck notices that another tool, the harness, has a regulatory effect on all the dogs, "utterly transform[ing]" the pack into "new dogs" and focused beings, "the toil of the traces [becoming] . . . all that they lived for." These tools of oppression and degradation, but especially the club, thus collectively teach Buck to accept his new station and lack of freedom. As a sled dog member, he is locked "in the struggle for mastery" against all men with tools.

Throughout the novel, London consistently stresses the importance of who is mastering whom, a hierarchy that involves even the dog pack. Feeling that leadership "was his by right," and desiring it more than escaping a clubbing, Buck ascends to pack leadership. And he excels at it, in that he excels "in giving the law and making his mates live up to it"—in essence, constraining their freedom. Buck thus recovers some of his freedom by circumscribing or controlling others. He has indeed learned the lesson well.

Nature also limits Buck's freedom. It constantly calls to him, a hypnotic lure that constricts his loving friendship with John Thornton. Nature's unrelenting siren call traps him in the uncomfortable position of having to choose between Thornton and a life in the wild. His decision not to choose until Thornton dies—to let fate decide—reinforces his dependent condition. Furthermore, nature's primary lesson, that a being "must master or be mastered" to survive, only reinscribes an unequal system of power relations. Thus when Buck gains his freedom after Thornton's death, his escape into nature requires him both to heed the "call" of the wild and its tenet to "kill or be killed"—leaving him subject to another law, if not the law of the club anymore.

Lori Vermaas

IDENTITY in *The Call of the Wild*

Before his capture, Buck was confident in his identity as "king,—king over all . . . humans included" at Judge Miller's place, "a sated aristocrat" and "country gentleman" who "stalked imperiously." After being kidnapped in California and sold as a working dog in Alaska, however, he is thrown into a whirlwind of experiences, all of which convolute his sense of who he is and even who he thought he was. Caged, he turns into a "raging fiend," "so changed . . . that the Judge himself would not have recognized him." His enslavement precipitates his devolution into a primordial animal, one who eats much more quickly, never shows weakness, and steals. As a result, his body changes: "his muscles . . . hard as iron."

Buck's gradual change into a more primitive being sets him on a path of self-discovery, for it connects him to an entirely new, yet eerily familiar part of his self-identity. It stimulates responses that feel frightening to him "without effort or discovery," particularly the desire to kill. While helping his pack to track and kill a snowshoe hare, he realizes that the urge came to him "with a sense of familiarity. He seemed to remember it all," the "old instincts . . to kill things . . . the blood lust, the joy to kill. . . . was nothing new or strange, this scene of old time. It was as though it had always been, the wonted way of things." Buck's close connection to these dormant, "long dead" ancestral memories of primitive existence soon manifest spiritually, especially when he sits near the campfire, where he is able to meditate and sleep and dream back in time to "memories of his heredity." He time travels in these slumbers, visiting past lives and primitive companions who are all unrecognizable, yet nevertheless possess "a seeming familiarity."

Regardless of Buck's embrace of the primitive in himself, he struggles with these changes, particularly when he meets John Thornton. Although by now Buck is a significantly transformed dog, whose physical prowess and instinctual shrewdness intimidate Thornton's men, under Thornton's guardianship he enters a more emotional existence or identity, in that he discovers love for the first time. Thornton had saved his life, so Buck is very much devoted to him. The time he spends in his camp reawakens memories of his former life as a domesticated dog, which places him in conflict—he's caught in the middle between his two identities. Buck well understands that "there [is] no middle course. He must master or be mastered; . . . to show mercy was a weakness. Mercy did not exist in the primordial life. It was misunderstood for fear, and such misunderstandings made for death. Kill or be killed, eat or be eaten, was the law." His is an either/or existence and love its complicator.

Confronted with these realizations, Buck tries to find some kind of compromise by going out on a series of reconnaissance missions to find himself. He travels back and forth between the domesticated and wild worlds for days at a time, transforming back to a more docile version when he returns to camp, and undergoing an "instant and terrible transformation . . . as soon as he [is] within the secrecy of the forest. . . . a thing of the wild, stealing along softly, cat-footed, a passing shadow," patient and stealthy in his pursuit of prey. He straddles spirit worlds as well, London referring to him as "the Evil Spirit" and "The Fiend incarnate"; a Native American tribe later mythologizes him as "Ghost Dog."

But the precariousness of his dual identity haunts him. When he hears the call of the wild—a wolf howling—for the first time clearly, the sound is irresistible. It "impels him to do things, and ultimately masters him, but only after Thornton is murdered." No longer fettered with a tie to his beloved friend, Buck capitulates to the call. He becomes a super-sized wild version, "a gigantic wolf" with a "long wolf muzzle . . . larger than the muzzle of any wolf," his head "the wolf head on a massive scale." Having inherited the best traits of his St. Bernard father and shepherd mother, his amalgamation improves on them and makes him a superior version of wild animal, more than a perfect compromise between his past and present identities.

Lori Vermaas

NATURE in *The Call of the Wild*

London describes and discusses two versions of nature, domesticated and primordial. The former exists on Judge Miller's estate in Santa Clara Valley, California, a manicured and expansive landscape that induces laziness and sleepiness. Buck's home

for his first four years, the estate is relaxed and leisurely, a spread whimsically "half hidden among the trees" whose "gravelled [sic] driveways . . . wound about through wide-spreading lawns and under the interlacing boughs of tall poplars." It is a picturesque place where man lives comfortably and in harmony with nature, with architecture well integrated into the natural surroundings. The servant's cottages are "vine-clad," part of a larger complex of "an endless and orderly array of outhouses, long grape arbors, green pastures, orchards, and berry patches"— descriptive of a pastoral scene of fecundity and growth. In these brief, opening scenes nature is a playground for Buck—he swims when he wants and goes on "rambles" with the judge's children and grandchildren. He is nature's master.

His upbringing in the warm and inviting South-land, however, strongly contrasts with the cold, harsh Northland on which London focuses for the novel's remainder. The wild is nature's raw and thus truer form, a cruel environment that dominates its subjects. The difference is evident during Buck's first encounter. Stepping onto the *Narwhal*'s deck after sensing the "change," he steps into snow, a mushy, muddy substance he has never experienced before. While sampling it with his tongue, it "bit like fire."

Buck discovers that nature is a brutal, immoral place that privileges the strong and runs on suspicion and ruthless competition. In the wild, morality is irrelevant, even pointless, because "flung into the heart of things primordial . . . , all was confusion and action, and every moment life and limb were in peril. There was imperative need to be constantly alert . . . dogs and men . . . were savages . . . who knew no law but the law of club and fang." The law is thus one of survival, kill or be killed, eat when you can, take care of yourself only, trust no one—and it is all marked by speed. Fights occur suddenly, once weakness is sensed. The docile Curly goes down in a heap of mauling dogs, whose vicious lesson Buck learns early on. After Curly's death, Buck realizes that out here "the way" is "no fair play. Once down, that was the end of you. Well, he would see to it that he never went down."

Given that nature is a harsh taskmaster, only the fittest survive, which creates incredibly efficient creatures. Along with becoming sleeker and stronger—with feet that had grown "hard to the trail"—Buck's digestion improves immensely: "He could eat anything, . . . and [after a meal], . . . the juices of his stomach extracted the last least particle of nutriment; and his blood carried it to the farthest reaches of his body, building it into the toughest and stoutest of tissues." Other physical processes improve: "sight and scent became remarkably keen, while his hearing developed . . . acuteness," such that he could hear "the faintest sound and knew whether it heralded peace or peril"; and he developed "an ability to scent the wind and forecast it a night in advance"—"no matter how breathless the air."

Indeed, living things waste nothing in the wild. Buck realizes this one evening when he notices that other dogs bury themselves in snow at night to keep warm. They carefully plan and carry out work and action, an economical approach inbred by nature that demands the development of a cunning "patience that was nothing less than primitive," the kind that enables an animal to wait out a prey's actions in order to find a moment of weakness. An ancient way of being, patience does not waste effort, because wasted energy is deadly. Patience also pairs with a "blood lust, the joy to kill," a prime ingredient of primordial nature, which drives Buck to kill a bear and then later a moose.

As described by London, nature is a nonhuman place, and Buck enters it fully only after Indians kill his beloved master, John Thornton. It is a stern, eternal urge or way of being, whose "call" is inevitable and "irresistible"—the ultimate master, patient, stealthy, and "cat-footed"—its apotheosis the form of "a long, lean, timber wolf" whose howls ultimately secure Buck's return.

Lori Vermaas

LONDON, JACK *White Fang* (1906)

White Fang is the companion to *The CALL OF THE WILD*, in that its plot reverses the protagonist's journey—this time humans capture a wolf and transform him into a domesticated animal. Such a setup enables Jack London to again examine behavioral adaptation via principles of Darwinian evolution. He shows how chance, nature, and external influences function as forces that shape all animals' evolution in the struggle for existence.

Born in the Alaskan wilderness to a wild she-dog and a pure-bred wolf, White Fang soon loses his freedom when Indians capture his mother and him. Having just begun to recognize his natural instincts as a wolf, he starts a new training—that of obedience to humans, not nature. Using three different owners, Gray Beaver, Beauty Smith, and Weedon Scott, London details White Fang's evolution from wolf to domesticated wolf, making *White Fang* an explication of behavioral development.

The novel explores themes of OPPRESSION, IDENTITY, and NATURE and their effect on behavior. Although nature is a force that controls one's destiny and sense of life purpose and identity, other oppressors, particularly humans, exert equal influence. With each new owner, White Fang learns to distrust many of his instincts, ultimately becoming an example of how nurture trumps nature. With such an approach, the novel also tracks White Fang's search for himself and how he fits in the world. Civilization wins out, not triumphantly, but reassuringly, for White Fang ultimately settles rather comfortably well into his new identity as a California estate watchdog.

Lori Vermaas

IDENTITY in *White Fang*
With White Fang as a case study, London posits that identity is contingent on outside influences. He argues that with heredity as one's "clay," "environment serve[s] to model the clay, to give it a particular form." Thus external forces, particularly situations and relationships, alter identity. White Fang's sense of himself shifts constantly as he encounters all manner of stimuli, particularly obedience training by humans. The first event that initiates White Fang's identity struggle as either a wolf or domesticated dog is his and his mother's capture by Indians. By impressing him with their "mastery and power," the Indians eventually mold White Fang "into a dog that was rather wolfish, but that [also] was a dog and not a wolf."

The collision of wolf and dog in him soon transforms him from an inquisitive and loyal wolf cub into a conflicted and vengeful wolf-dog. "The clay of White Fang had been molded until he became what he was, morose and lonely, unloving and ferocious, the enemy of all his kind," because life in a dogsled camp had influenced him to live this way. For instance, "had Lip-lip," a particularly aggressive sled dog, "not existed, he would have passed his puppyhood with the other puppies and grown up more doglike and with more liking for dogs." His attack style does not betray his wolf heritage, however, for it retains a silent and stealthy strategy: he "never barked . . . [but] dr[o]ve straight at the intruder." Eventually, he even learns to reject his roots, thus more fully accepting his identity as a domesticated animal. After a couple of ill-fated attempts to reconnect with his mother in the wild, he finally ignores her cold snarls—having outgrown even her.

Character develops only through fateful circumstance (nurture over nature), creating an irresponsible world—a place where only results, not accountability, exist. After Beauty Smith (whose very birth name misidentifies his character) deviously arranges White Fang's purchase, London elaborates on how one is not culpable for identity or behavior. He comments that "Beauty Smith had not created himself, and no blame was to be attached to him. He had come into the world with a twisted body and a brute intelligence. This had constituted the clay of him, and it had not been kindly molded by the world." Similarly, because White Fang knows only that he must obey and be with his master, regardless if he is, like Smith, "a veritable, if terrible, god," he transforms into a fight dog. Faithfulness is the strongest quality in White Fang's clay, but with Smith he becomes hateful, molded "into a more ferocious thing than had been intended by Nature." His fights are put on exhibition, and he is christened "The Fighting Wolf." Thus nurture is stronger than nature, with individuals the victims of their environment, devoid as they are of free will.

Then two miners, Weedon Scott and Matt, forcefully purchase and thus save White Fang from Smith. They begin the slow and painful process of remolding his behavior, almost giving up and shooting him until they recognize his intelligence. The new stimuli for his behavior modification are "kindness," freedom, and physical petting. However, White Fang's final transformation, which London claims was "nothing less than a revolution," is possible only because of his childhood experiences with men: "The seal of his dependence on man had been set upon him . . . Early . . . when he turned his back on the Wild and crawled to Gray Beaver's feet." During this period, "White Fang was in the process of finding himself . . . [and] his nature was undergoing an expansion . . . His old code of conduct was changing . . . [and] oft-times [he] elected discomfort and pain for the sake of his god" (pining for Scott when he left home to travel; submitting himself to Scott's hand during petting, although he regarded hands as something to avoid and distrust because they usually wielded a club). "Now, with the love-master, his snuggling was the deliberate act of putting himself into a position of hopeless helplessness . . . an expression of perfect confidence, of absolute self-surrender." In this final incarnation, White Fang comes to be known as the "Blessed Wolf."

Lori Vermaas

NATURE in *White Fang*

The novel opens with a stark description of nature, saying that its "dark spruce forest frown[s]" and leans, "black and ominous." It is a mute landscape out in the wild, "the land itself . . . a desolation, lifeless," suffocating under "a vast silence," "lone and cold." If there is any spirit or levity, there's only a hint of it in a sinister laughter—"a laughter more terrible than any sadness"—evidence of its devilish sense of humor, one unimpressed with its subjects' struggle to survive, for it "laugh[s] at the futility of life and the effort of life." Such is "the Wild, the savage, frozen-hearted Northland Wild."

This kind of nature is a killer, a combatant who always wins, is puffed up with winning, and who "conquer[s]." Indeed, wild nature goes so far as to abhor action, because that shows signs of life: "it is not the way of the wild to like movement. Life is an offense to it, for life is movement; and the Wild aims always to destroy movement. It freezes the water [and] . . . drives the sap out of the trees." Man is a particular nemesis, since man "is the most restless of life."

Nature is unrelentingly cruel, its ruthlessness embodied in the wolf pack, which in the first three chapters patiently and inexorably stalks Henry and

Bill's sled and their dogs, tormenting them with the inevitability of being killed, one by one. It is ominous and judgmental, a "land of desolation and mockery and silence" that "crushe[s]" the men on the sled "with the weight of [its] unending vastness." Such power and immensity reinforces humans' insignificance. Henry and Bill soon recognize their irrelevance when they begin perceiving "themselves [as] finite and small" and deathlike, their frozen faces seeming like "ghostly masques." After the wolves attack and eat Bill, Henry begins to notice his own body, and momentarily is bemused at the wonder of its workings. But then he realizes that out in nature "this living flesh . . was no more than so much meat, a quest of ravenous animals, to be torn and slashed by their hungry fangs, to be sustenance." Man is nature's servant, and nature the ultimate master.

Since nature is in control, it predestines all living things—it has plans. One Eye's "urge of an impulse" to find a lair is an instinct passed down from his forbears. "He did not question it, nor puzzle over it," he simply obeys it. Such is also the case when his gray cub kills and eats the ptarmigan's young and fights off the devastated mother. During the attack, he recognizes his destiny: With "the fighting blood of his breed . . . up in him and surging through him," he realized "his own meaning in the world; he was doing that for which he was made—killing meat and battling to kill it. He was justifying his existence." Nature had "equipped" him for this.

It also equips other instincts and urges, even those that devastate the closest of relationships. After the gray cub matures, as White Fang, he comes upon his mother. Having been separated from her, he bounds toward her "joyously." But she snarls at him and rushes him three times, laying "his cheek open to the bone." Such behavior is not the mother's fault, for "a wolf-mother was not made to remember her cubs of a year or so before. So she did not remember White Fang. He was a strange animal, an intruder; and her present litter of puppies gave her the right to resent such intrusion."

Along with plans, nature also has laws: "the law that forbade [the cub to] . . . approach . . . the [cave's] entrance"; "the law of meat" ("the aim of life,") "EAT OR BE EATEN"; "*oppress the weak and obey the strong*"; and "the law of forage," which deemed that all wasted meat "belonged to the dog that found it." Nature's rule is so complete that each living thing accepts these laws and each of their own motivations without question. London elaborates on this blind acceptance as "a method," an "act of classification." As a cub, White Fang "was not in the least disturbed by desire to find out . . . reason[s] . . . . Logic and physics were no part of his mental makeup." "Single-purposed" and cruel, nature is a lonely and treacherous place for its inhabitants.

Lori Vermaas

OPPRESSION in *White Fang*

Soon after a male gray cub (White Fang) and his mother come upon an Indian camp, one of the Indians, Gray Beaver, recognizes the mother as a wild dog he recently lost. He calls out her given name, Kiche, whereupon she immediately crouches, whimpers, and wags her tail. Her submissive reaction impresses upon the cub man's more powerful, magical, even godlike presence, one whose "mastery and power" instills in him "an overwhelming sense of his own weakness and littleness." The Indians claim the cub and capture his mother, thus initiating the cub's oppression and, significantly, his acceptance of it.

Gray Beaver names the cub White Fang, another example of oppression, in that naming is an act of ownership. The newly christened wolf slowly adjusts to the camp's hierarchy. With his mother tied up, White Fang learns to defer to humans, such that whenever "they walked, he got out of their way. When they called, he came. When they threatened, he cowered down." "Such was the lesson" of his oppression, to learn to "plac[e] . . . his destiny in another's hands, a shifting of the responsibilities of existence."

His training continues after the Indians untie Kiche. Although submissive to humans, White Fang is still in the early stages of accepting his subordination, and so he tries to lure his mother out into the woods and to freedom. But so complete is her conditioning that she stops at its edge, imparting on her son another significant lesson. A different call has transfixed her, an "other and louder call, the call of the fire and of man." She returns to camp, leaving White Fang whimpering softly with confusion and mournful nostalgia, so fragrant is the air filled with the familiar scents "of his old life of freedom before the days of his bondage." After this incident, Gray Beaver presently sells Kiche, and uses the moment of her transfer as a way to imprint more strongly White Fang's subordination. When the cub follows Kiche into the canoe and ignores Gray Beaver's calls to return, the Indian recaptures and beats him mercilessly to instill permanently the "lesson of . . . bondage," that man is the "lord and master over him." No longer free, "obedience, rigid, undeviating obedience" becomes the law. Thus "insidiously, and by remote ways, as well as by the power of the stick and stone and clout of hand, were the shackles of White Fang's bondage being riveted on him."

Even when given the opportunity to escape, White Fang's participation is so complete that, much like his mother, he chooses to return, the Indians now his adopted pack. Indeed, he's changed too much to live free in the wild. Out in the wilderness, he feels overwhelmed with loneliness and scared of danger lurking. Ruined by living in the camp, by accepting bondage, he has "softened" and "weakened"—even as he has evolved in the interim into a savage, vicious wolf. He is a deaf and dumb mute in the wild, for "there was nothing to do, nothing to see nor hear"—except the call of man, which rises within, "an overpowering desire for the protection and companionship of man." London phrases it so innocently, yet it is bondage, plain and simple. His dependence and despondency are so great that he relocates the former site of Gray Beaver's tepee, the Indian camp having moved on elsewhere. Sitting in its center, White Fang lets out a howl—but unlike his mournful cry for the loss of freedom when his mother would not follow, this cry grieves over the loss of man and his bondage. When he finally finds Gray Beaver, much like his mother before him he grovels toward him, "surrender[ing] himself, voluntarily, body and soul. . . . his own choice." "He had given himself" to these gods.

In all of these situations, White Fang is complicit in his oppression, because he learns to accept his role unquestioningly in the hierarchy, even finding meaning, purpose, and, later, love as justification. He exhibits obedience, "faithfulness and willingness." He establishes a "covenant" with humans, whose "terms were simple. For the possession of a flesh-and-blood god, he exchanged his own liberty. . . . a service of duty and awe," an "allegiance . . . greater than . . . love" until his pairing with Weedon Scott.

Lori Vermaas

LOWRY, LOIS   *The Giver* (1993)

Lois Lowry's novel *The Giver* is the story of Jonas, an adolescent boy growing up in a seemingly perfect society. As the story opens, Jonas is nervously awaiting the Ceremony of Twelve, where he will learn the assignment that will determine his adult occupation. At the ceremony, Jonas discovers that he has been selected for an important but mysterious job. He is to be the Receiver of Memory, a human receptacle for the past memories of the world. The old Receiver of Memory has now become the Giver, transmitting memories to Jonas. Through these memories, Jonas's positive vision of his contented, monotonous life begins to disintegrate.

The society Jonas lives in practices "Sameness," a condition that leaves people comfortable and safe, but leaves no room for choice. The people of Jonas's community follow a strict, voluminous set of "Rules," which dictates every aspect of life. As a result of Sameness, people have lost the ability to see color, hear music, and even feel deep emotions, such as love. Through his training as the new Receiver, Jonas begins to see past Sameness. He sees color, and feels the joys of variety and love. Even though Jonas also experiences some of the things his society protects him from, such as pain, starvation, and war, he decides that Sameness makes life meaningless. In an attempt to eradicate Sameness and restore memories to all the people, Jonas flees the community. Lowry does not tell us if Jonas lives and frees his people from Sameness, but instead leaves the ending ambiguous.

Cheryl Blake Price

FAMILY in *The Giver*

In the futuristic world that Lois Lowry creates for her novel, *The Giver*, the family is a very specifically defined unit consisting of a father, mother, one daughter, and one son. The family structure is carefully governed by the community, which allows no exceptions to be made to the standard family unit. While this type of nuclear family may be familiar, and even attractive, to an American audience, it also takes choice and variety out of society. As the novel progresses, it becomes revealed that the family in Jonas's community is a fabricated, and rather meaningless, construction.

Families in Jonas's world are not created by mutual choice; instead, all the decisions regarding the family are made by a group of Elders. When members of the community come of age, they are permitted to apply for a spouse; however, they are not allowed to choose one based on feelings of love or affection. A committee of Elders makes the decision for the couple, weighing their individual strengths and weaknesses for an optimal combination. After three years of observation, the couple is allowed to apply for the first of their two children. Again, the infant is chosen by the Elders and delivered into the family unit in a special annual ceremony. When the family is ready, another child (always the opposite gender of its sibling) is applied for and placed. Older adults who have completed their family raising go and live in the House of Childless Adults.

Even the day to day aspects of family life are highly structured and uniform throughout the entire community. Many of the activities are ritualized, such as the sharing of feelings and dreams. Disturbingly, these activities are also a way in which to monitor behavior and ensure that the community rules are followed. After sharing a dream that hints at his emerging sexuality, Jonas is promptly given a pill that suppresses these feelings. Here, the family unit is acting as the enforcer of the larger community standards, illuminating that the family is, indeed, just a smaller version of the outer community and that there is no safe haven from rules and regulations.

As Jonas begins to receive memories from the Giver that offer a different view of family life, he realizes that one important element is missing from this type of family: love. Love is not a driving force for the joining of spouses and the rearing of children. Rather, joining together to raise children is portrayed as a duty to the community. Even the process of birth is mechanized, with the result that parents and siblings do not have a biological link to each other. Children are genetically engineered and created anonymously through Birthmothers, which creates an absence of blood kinship ties. Yet it is not the artificial creation of the family that bothers Jonas, but the lack of feeling that he finds in the family unit. As Jonas's mother tells him, the word "love" has become "a very generalized word, so meaningless that it's become almost obsolete." As she goes on to explain, parents feel pride and enjoyment, but not love, for their children. The hollowness of this structure, and the insubstantial bonds it creates, can be illustrated by the lack of extended family in the community. Once children are grown, they move away from their parents and rarely, if ever, interact with them again. There are no family celebrations where aunts, uncles, cousins, and grandparents join together and share their lives; in short, there is no depth of emotion tying people together. Beyond childrearing and rule indoctrination, the family seems to offer no other benefit to the people.

Jonas decides to leave the community because, without love, he finds no meaning in life. He undergoes a painful realization that his family and peers can never feel the same way he can because they do not experience deep emotion. The uniform and cautious way the community has chosen to create families leaves them cold and empty. Even though in American culture, the combination of father, mother, son, and daughter is often idealized, it is not compulsory—people can choose the ways in which they create their families. When Jonas flees the community, he takes Gabriel, a toddler his family has temporarily been caring for, with him. With this action, Jonas is symbolically creating his own family; he rebels against the control and uniformity of his past life. What this seems to suggest is that families can combine in many different ways, as long as there is the bond of love.

Cheryl Blake Price

FATE in *The Giver*

In the opening of Lois Lowry's *The Giver,* the protagonist Jonas is worrying about his future. Shortly, a group of Elders from his community will announce their decisions regarding the job placement of Jonas and his 12-year-old peers. As Jonas so precisely states, he is not frightened but apprehensive about the choice they will make for him. Jonas's apprehension arises because he has no input in this process; someone else will be making one of the most important decisions of his life. In fact, someone else will make every major decision in Jonas's life; the Elders have already chosen his parents and sibling, they will select his future job, and when he comes of age they will provide him with a pre-determined wife and children. Choice, even in everyday life, has been mostly eliminated for the majority of people in Jonas's community.

The idea of choice is ultimately bound up in how the theme of fate operates in *The Giver.* Broadly, there are two traditional ways of thinking about fate. The first is that fate is pre-destined; people cannot alter or change their destinies. The Elders of Jonas's community are a personification of this type of fate. Since the Elders make everyone's major life-decisions, this gives the impression that fate is unchangeable and that people have to submit to the choices made for them. The people in the community are conditioned not to desire choice; as a product of his upbringing, Jonas also feels this way at first. He believes that "we don't dare to let people make choices of their own" because "we really have to protect people from the wrong choices." As a future Elder, Jonas can see some good in taking away choice from the people.

However, there is another way of thinking about fate that challenges Jonas's previously held beliefs, which is the view that fate is changeable and can be influenced by personal decisions. Jonas realizes this as a possibility only after he begins his training as the new Receiver of Memory. When the Giver begins transmitting memories from the past, Jonas comprehends that another way of life is possible. This causes some confusion for Jonas, because he both perceives positive reasons to let people have control over their fates, and also recognizes that it could be dangerous. Yet, when Jonas discovers the community's dark secret of mandatory Release (killing) of twins, abnormal children, and the elderly, he

decides that people should have a right to make their own choices. Together with the Giver, he makes a plan to bring memories, and therefore choice, back to the people. In effect, Jonas wants people to have control over their own fates.

Although he and the Giver had carefully constructed a plan to return memories to the whole community, Jonas takes emergency action when he finds out that Gabriel, a baby that had been living with his family, has been scheduled for Release. Hastily, Jonas takes Gabriel in the middle of the night and leaves the community. In an attempt to change his own fate, as well as that of the community, Jonas hopes that once he is gone his memories will go back to the people. However, alone and with no support, limited supplies, and a young child to care for, Jonas ironically begins questioning if he made the right choice: "Once he had yearned for choice. Then, when he had had a choice, he had made the wrong one: the choice to leave. And now he was starving." Yet, even as he longs for the comfort of Sameness, Jonas continues to believe in the redemptive power of choice.

The ending of the novel, in which Jonas suffers from forces outside of his control (such as treacherous weather and starvation) again calls into question how much power a person can have over his or her own fate. The ambiguous ending does not reveal if Jonas reaches Elsewhere and safety; in other words, the reader never knows if Jonas's real fate is the one that he wanted. Lowry never discloses if people can really have control over their fates or if our destinies are all pre-determined. However, what remains clear throughout the novel is that the artificial fate created by the Elders for the people in the community should never be tolerated. While people may have control over their own fate, these decisions should not be left up to other people.

Cheryl Blake Price

SCIENCE AND TECHNOLOGY in *The Giver*

In the futuristic society that Lois Lowry creates in *The Giver,* science and technology play a subtle but important role in shaping the story. Although there have been many scientific advances, Jonas lives in a community that is not dependent on science. Much of the technology in this society—computers, televisions, cars—is rare or absent in the wider community; instead, the emphasis is on simple, communal living without the advantages of technology. However, as the novel progresses, the community emerges as actually quite advanced because references are made to jet planes, genetic engineering, and climate control. In fact, science and technology are important in creating a constant state of conformity, referred to as "Sameness."

Everything in the community is under strict regulation to promote Sameness and create an environment of uniformity. Jonas lives in a house identical to that of his friends; he wears standard-issue clothing and rides a mass-produced bicycle. Family life is regulated, and there are no exceptions to the rule that each family includes a mother, a father, and one sister and brother. Identical meals are delivered daily and cleaned up by Laborers. A book of rules is kept in every home, and small rule infractions are announced over the community speaker, drawing attention to and causing embarrassment for the offender. More grievous transgressions are tolerated only twice before the guilty citizen is Released, or executed by lethal injection. Yet not only criminals are Released; anyone who does not conform to standards or is too sick or elderly to contribute to society is also Released. Everything and everyone in the community has a useful purpose, and technology helps to create a perfectly ordered society.

This monotony encompasses not only material things but also the landscape and the people. Anything natural, which could cause discomfort or inconvenience, has been eradicated. Technology has been used to level hills, regulate climate, and control sunshine. Except for a fish hatchery, the community is also devoid of animal life, suggesting that humans have excluded or driven native wildlife to extinction. The stuffed animals such as bears and elephants that children receive as "comfort objects" are considered to be mythological creatures. The people have manipulated science to completely control nature, and the Giver's memories make Jonas realize that the world was once very different.

The humans of the community are also tightly regulated by technology. The use of genetic engineering has eradicated different racial or ethnic groups; therefore, most people are similar looking.

The standardization of haircuts and clothing supports this similarity because this community does not accept individualization. In addition, social harmony is established by the numbing of emotions, particularly romantic feelings such as love and desire. All adults are required to take a special pill that effectively controls their sexuality. Spouses are chosen by a committee of Elders, and children are born only to specifically designated "Birthmothers." As a reaction to these changes, people have lost creative abilities and can no longer see colors or hear music.

While the technologies make the community an extraordinarily safe place to live, life can be dull and repetitive. Individuality is never celebrated because everyone is expected to conform to community standards; in fact, talking about personal accomplishments is discouraged. When Jonas begins receiving memories and seeing colors, he feels sad that his family and his peers cannot enjoy the beauty that has been revealed to him. Soon, he realizes that the lack of variety in his world is a true loss to the enjoyment of life. The Giver explains to Jonas that long ago the community chose to give up uniqueness in order to take the dangers of unpredictability and chance out of life.

While it appears that this community may have many advantages over our contemporary society, such as low crime, Jonas's world is ultimately presented as a dystopia, a society that has gone too much to one extreme. Since science has a role in creating this society, *The Giver* can be seen as a cautionary tale about the misuse of technology. Humans in the book have learned how to control nature, but they have destroyed the animals and natural landscape that once existed. Art, books, and music do not exist, and Jonas sees that the people's lives are without meaning or true enjoyment. As our society makes huge advancements in technology, Lowry's book warns about the results of scientific exploitation.

Cheryl Blake Price

MACHIAVELLI, NICCOLÒ *The Prince* (1513, 1532)

The Prince is one of the most widely known works in the "primer for princes" tradition, which provides advice to rulers on domestic and foreign policy. It was written in 1513 during a year of forced exile for its author but was not published until 1532, five years after his death.

The Prince is a brief treatise on statecraft in the form of loosely organized essays. It was written at a time when the Italian states were devastated by wars and the machinations of foreign powers. Machiavelli's objective was to exhort Italian rulers to restore Italy's lost glory and establish a unified, stable, and peaceful state. Unlike medieval literature in this genre, Machiavelli does not invoke the concept of an ideal ruler or notions such as the divine right of kings. He was an acute observer of the contemporary political scene. He believed that lessons of the past and the current situation demanded that a ruthless ruler wrest political power, eliminate his rivals, put an end to factions, throw out foreign political powers, avoid mass discontent, and strengthen national religion to bind people together. What counted in politics was success and not virtue. He recommends the use of harsh measures to register the impact of authority as most men, he believes, are simple, greedy and wicked. The state, he insists, must subordinate moral principles to its survival and the welfare of its citizens. For him the ultimate good of the people justifies unethical conduct on the part of a ruler.

Machiavelli's blatant dismissal of the virtuous, the idealistic, and the moral from the world of politics earned him much opprobrium even though his pragmatism paved the way for a "scientific" attitude to politics.

Gulshan Taneja

ETHICS in *The Prince*

Even though *The Prince* was written in 1513, it was initially read in manuscript form and was published only in 1532, five years after the death of its author. Yet, by the time an English translation appeared more than a hundred years later, in 1640, *The Prince* had already earned great notoriety for its advocacy of an amoral attitude to gaining and retaining political power, so much so that the name of the author of *The Prince*, Machiavelli, came to be used as a synonym for diabolical scheming. Elizabethan and Jacobean drama are full of "Machiavellian" politicians, villains, and murderers. Machiavelli himself earns specific mention in Shakespeare's *Henry VI*, Marlowe's *The Jew of Malta*, and Webster's *The White Devil*, among others. Macaulay remarked: "We doubt whether any name in literary history be so generally odious" as that of the author of *The Prince*.

The image of Machiavelli as a wily and evil adviser to cruel, scheming princes refuses to go away. Yet a careful reading of *The Prince* would convince the reader otherwise. Machiavelli did not wish to compose a primer for an ideal prince to create an ideal state for a morally upright and virtuous and law-abiding citizenry. His understanding of historical precedence, as well as his experience as a diplomat and a statesman, convinced him that living realities and practical politics are different from ideal constructs. A utopia was certainly far from his mind. He makes no mention of such notions as the divine rights of a king or the belief that a king must be like a father to his children. His was an impassioned response to a 16th-century Florentine political situation (no different from the other Italian city-states) marked by chaos and anarchy and the maneuverings of foreign powers. The situation had been made worse by the weak and ineffective rulers of Italian city-states. Machiavelli was an acute observer of the political scene. He sought a solution to revive the Italian nation that then lay in fragments, bereft of the glory that he believed was her due.

He believed that for the creation and maintenance of a unified nation-state, a ruthless ruler must rise and wrest political power by hook or by crook, eliminate his rivals through fraud or, if necessary, violence. He firmly repudiated the primacy of morality as the basis of an enduring state and advocated that moral principles must be subordinated to the survival of the state and the welfare of its citizens. As most men are self-centered and greedy, a prince must therefore be ready to lie, cheat, or treat his subjects with force and cruelty in the interest of a stable society and lasting peace. He believed that moral behavior was necessary only if it benefited the prince's people and that rulers must only appear to be virtuous, as men are prone to obey leaders who appear to be so.

The attitude that marks Machiavelli's maxims and the sheer clarity and simplicity with which he puts forth his ideas about the rejuvenation of a sick state through force, fraud, and dissimulation were enough to shock the readers of his work. One can argue that a subversion of values was far from the mind of this much maligned yet celebrated Florentine statesman and diplomat. *The Prince* is not a detached academic exercise in political philosophy, motivated solely by negation. It does not, therefore, set out to undermine the significance of well-entrenched humanistic values. In advocating immorality, Machiavelli merely recognized the world as it was, and men as they were, and merely sought to achieve a specific end. In the giddy world of politics, what counted was success, not virtue. Moreover, virtue did not lead to success.

Thus, even though he exhorts the prince to be ruthless to the masses, he insists that the prince must build his state on the goodwill of the people, be sensitive to their susceptibilities, and bind the citizens together and achieve stability by nourishing a national religion. A prince "will be despised if he has a reputation for being fickle, frivolous, effeminate, cowardly, irresolute. . . ." He should "strive to demonstrate in his actions grandeur, courage, sobriety, strength."

Machiavelli's objective was not idealistic, but practical and earthly. In his appreciation of life, here rather than hereafter, and an essentially secular, realistic, and modern outlook, he was much ahead of his time and showed remarkable courage of conviction. His intention was not to subvert ethical values but to ignore them as they appeared to serve no practical purpose in the context of the anarchic political developments of his time.

There is thus much in *The Prince* to suggest that subversion of humanistic values is not central to it. The gap that had existed between the medieval, scholastic interpretation of ethics and the world of reality drew attention to itself as it impinged upon the minds of thinkers in post-medieval times. Ethics—the moral principles that must guide and govern man's actions—in the context in which Machiavelli places them, receive a new definition as they are subjected to the challenge of the changing times.

Gulshan Taneja

NATIONALISM in *The Prince*

There is some truth in scholarly assertions that, as Machiavelli was as a citizen of Florence, all his concerns for the state as well as the welfare of the citizen in *The Prince* are focused on the city where he was born and where he spent most of his adult life. The nation, thus, for him was Florence. Yet Machiavelli drew a line between the Italians and the *barbari*, the foreigners. He looked upon all Italians and Italian city-states as bound together culturally and racially as one people.

A strong current of nationalistic sentiment suffuses *The Prince* and gives it its fundamental motivation. Machiavelli witnessed destructive factional feuds within Florence as well as other Italian city-states. Commerce forced Naples, Milan, Venice, and Florence to fight for control over Italy. Repeated French and Spanish inroads into the Italian territories over the centuries had destroyed Italian sovereignty. Weak rulers, an indifferent populace, and inadequate military resources had further debilitated a once glorious civilization. The Italian nation was not only marked by conflicts and dissension in the 16th century, it was also fated to remain a nation in bedlam, commotion, and disarray until the end of the 19th century. The decline and fall of this civilization from its great Roman past to a state bereft of all glory, stability, and peace was a sorry spectacle to behold.

Machiavelli was saddened by the murky politics of his day. Fired by his admiration of Rome and Roman institutions, and thus inspired, he goes on to call upon a brave prince to "introduce a new order bringing honour to himself and prosperity to one and every Italian." ". . . leaderless, lawless, crushed, despoiled, torn, over-run, . . . Italy is waiting to see who can be the one to heal her wounds . . . and cleanse those sores that have now been festering for so long." When Machiavelli says in a letter to Guicciardini that he loves his country more than his soul, he speaks from his heart.

Only a unified nation, politically independent and intellectually free, can lead to a stable and peaceful society working for the welfare of its citizenry. Only then does it become possible for citizens to live harmoniously. But before its people can so benefit, a nation has to define itself as an independent political entity, able and powerful to withstand the assault of its natural enemies, both from within and without. Hence Machiavelli's insistent call for a savior whose political objectives he defines with ruthless clarity and much attention to detail.

He also developed a deep-rooted belief in the inability of the common man to rise above his immediate interests—his own safety and comfort. He therefore advises the prince to discipline masses into obedience through ruthless control. The larger interest of the nation-state condoned resorting to suppression and CRUELTY. A prince must project himself as determined to achieve his objectives. A compelling self alone can lead to public triumph. Rule of law, authority, and discipline are indispensable to a ruler who would be feared and obeyed.

Machiavelli viewed history as a constantly moving cycle. If nations decayed and declined, the princes had a patriotic obligation to be defiant, take charge, and rejuvenate a sick society. He observed the current realities of political life and concluded that nothing short of extreme measures would suffice for extreme situations. He firmly understood that people do not live in utopias but in the harsh realities of time and space. He abandoned the inherited medieval thinking that glorified ideals and values for their own sake, and sought a context for people to live in the present and live in peace.

It is interesting to note that Machiavelli, in the context of the politics of his day, did not see an inescapable connection between moral goodness and legitimate authority; but, contrary to popular belief, he did not support political amorality for its own sake. Machiavelli had a larger purpose before him. Much ahead of his time as he was, he brought to bear a sense of political realism and secular thinking upon his mission.

Unlike the earlier medieval writers on statecraft, Machiavelli maintained that common morality and high ideals must be pursued only to attain preconceived objectives. A nation survives and flourishes through leadership, military power, and disciplined masses. A prince must appear to be "compassionate, faithful to his word, kind, guileless, and devout." But he must subject higher ideals to sordid political realities and political strategy: " . . . one who adapts his policy to the times prospers, and likewise . . . the one whose policy clashes with the demands of the times does not," Machiavelli maintained. Thus Machiavelli abandons the medieval predilection for political idealism and its emphasis on RELIGION as an integral part of political thinking. Machiavelli's

views had a great influence on the early modern debate surrounding "reasons of state"—the doctrine that the good of the state itself takes precedence over all other considerations.

Machiavelli has aroused much disagreement over the justness of his remedies. He was a passionate patriot, a democrat, and a believer in liberty. As a visionary, he argued for the emergence of the modern, centralized, political state. What is beyond doubt is his passionate desire to make it possible for a nation to sustain itself politically for the welfare of its citizens.

Gulshan Taneja

RESPONSIBILITY in *The Prince*

Machiavelli, in *The Prince,* is not detached or cynical or irresponsible. In fact, he shows a great sense of responsibility both as an author and as an individual in his role in the larger socio-human context in which he existed. He was a politically concerned citizen with much experience in matters of statecraft. He believed that a citizen lived within the compass of a family, community, and state. He, therefore, had an obligation to help sustain the structures that sustained him. He, it could be argued, fulfilled his obligations as a citizen. He reflected upon the state of affairs in Florence and offered counsel, which, in his view, it was the responsibility of every informed citizen who benefited from organized social and political institutions, to provide. Despite Machiavelli's putative moral predilections, the essential import of his counsel is positive: "Well organized states and wise princes," he maintains, "always take great pains not to make the nobles despair, and to satisfy the people and keep them content; this is one of the most important tasks the prince must undertake."

The question of responsibility presented itself to Machiavelli as a complex issue. He felt that it was the responsibility of a prince, by virtue of being a prince, to secure, defend, and maintain the state. Even though Machiavelli never says that a prince's actions are above ethical considerations, he understands that being a prince requires that the ruler fulfill his responsibility as a prince even at the cost of subverting traditional values. A prince is nothing if not responsible for the welfare of his citizens. Such a clear delimitation of the role of a prince in a society requires that he meet his obligations even if his personal values go against his beliefs.

It has been rightly pointed out that our choices are determined, on the one hand, by a desired course of action, and, on the other, in the light of desired ends. While preferences are spontaneous, choices are deliberate and, far from being free, are determined by facts of history as perceived in the present. *The Prince* clearly registers the authorial preoccupation with certain specific ends in this context. If the ends require dismissal of moral and ethical considerations, the course of action would thus be determined in the light of the ultimate goal a citizen sets for himself and for which advice is proffered, even if the advice is uncommon, controversial, or even unethical. Machiavelli asserts in his *Discourses:* "When the very safety of the country depends upon the resolution to be taken, no considerations of JUS-TICE or injustice, humanity or CRUELTY, not of glory or of infamy, should be allowed to prevail. But putting all other considerations aside, the only question should be 'What course will save the life and liberty of the country?'"

The Prince focuses much on the failure of the citizen to understand, accept, and fulfill his responsibility to the state. A citizen prioritizes his personal or familial needs over those of the state and acts against the larger interest of the community. The citizen's failure to understand the significance of his choices can lead to the collapse of the systemic structure. A prince must work against these tendencies, and thus act cruelly only to be kind.

Confronted with a choice, it would be assumed, and rightly so, that the questions of metaphysical and ethical responsibility weighed less with Machiavelli than those involving sociopolitical and legal obligations.

Machiavelli emerges here as an example of how a responsible citizen must act. What he preaches to the prince, he exemplifies with his own practice. He projects himself in *The Prince* as a model of a concerned citizen, an individual whose concern for the state is not influenced by preconceived notions of RELIGION and church and natural predilection to put himself and his family first.

The Prince was written at a time when Italy was devastated by wars and the machinations of foreign powers. Its author's objective was to exhort the Italian rulers to restore Italy's lost glory and create and maintain a unified state. An expression, clear and effective, of his intention and objectives in no uncertain terms, an unabashed and ruthlessly mechanical attitude with which he endorses means, fair or foul, to attain one's political objective—has lent the seminal work and its author a diabolical image. Yet that image does not explain its author's profound understanding of the needs of the times and the remarkable sense of responsibility with which Machiavelli addresses the problems facing his fragmented nation-state.

Gulshan Taneja

MALAMUD, BERNARD   *The Natural* (1952)

Bernard Malamud's 1952 baseball novel *The Natural* tells the story of Roy Hobbs, whose only desire is to be known as the greatest ballplayer who ever lived. Set in the pre–World War II era, it invokes the Golden Age of American sports and images of iconic players such as Babe Ruth, Ted Williams, and Shoeless Joe Jackson.

What makes Roy Hobbs's story unique is the interruption in his career. As a young man, he is on his way to a tryout with the fictional New York Knights. After an encounter with a fictional version of the then-greatest player, Babe Ruth, Hobbs is shot by a psychotic female fan.

Flash forward and a 34-year-old Roy Hobbs finally arrives in New York, contract in hand. However, the owner has brought him there to sabotage the team for financial reasons, not to save the ailing franchise. Hobbs's skills are undiminished and, using the Wonderboy bat he made from a lightning-struck tree, he leads the struggling Knights into contention.

Tempted by the lure of money and a beautiful woman, Hobbs goes into a slump at the plate and agrees to take part in the sabotage of the team. In the championship playoff game, Hobbs finally realizes he cannot compromise the game he loves and strives to win. Unfortunately, the flawed hero, like poetry's mighty Casey, strikes out.

The film version has Hobbs coming through with a prodigious home run to win, but the novel has a beaten Hobbs walking away, his reputation ruined by the rumors of his throwing the game, even though he tried his best in the end.

Ronald C. Thomas, Jr.

ETHICS in *The Natural*

Ethical behavior can be described as a balancing act performed on a sliding scale between two fixed values, the ethics of aspiration and the ethics of obligation. Aspiration is the higher point, the striving to be the best a person can be, to do the right thing, regardless of cost. Obligation is the lower, the meeting of the minimum requirement for proper behavior. Anything falling short of obligation lies in the area of unethical behavior.

In Bernard Malamud's *The Natural,* baseball player Roy Hobbs inhabits a world where many of the characters fall short of ethical behavior, and Hobbs learns what that can cost him as a player and as a man. Hobbs is one of the most gifted baseball players of all time, coming up as a young man in the pre–World War II Golden Era of American sports, crossing paths with a character who is a clear homage to Babe Ruth. Hobbs is himself a combination of Ted Williams and Bob Feller, a pure hitter who can also throw a blazing fastball. Just as he is about to get a shot at the Major Leagues, Hobbs is shot by a deranged female fan. The bulk of the novel tells the story of his attempt to return to the game he loves as a middle-aged, unknown rookie.

The first ethical problem presented is the very idea of whether an older player should even get a shot at playing pro ball. When 34-year-old Hobbs arrives at the fictional New York Knights practice, the manager, Pop Fisher, says Hobbs belongs in an old folks' home, not a big league ball park. However, Hobbs has a contract signed by the team owner and chief scout so he has to get a chance to play. This addresses the issue of age in pro sports, where older players with proven track records are sent away to make more salary cap room for younger and less expensive players. When economics and demographics outweigh on-the-field ability, the system is no longer based on merit and becomes unethical.

A second ethical problem surrounds the profit motive in pro sports when compared to the will to win. The year before Hobbs joined the Knights, Pop Fisher was forced to sell part of his shares in the team to the new majority shareholder, Judge Banner. In an effort to bring down the value of the team and force Pop to give up the rest of his shares, the Judge has forced a variety of profitable but uncompetitive transactions on the Knights. A 34-year-old left fielder may have been one more way to turn the Knights into a cellar-dweller in the standings, but Banner has not reckoned on Hobbs's undiminished skills as a player. Again, this parallels modern pro baseball, where the Florida Marlins twice dismantled their roster after winning World Series in 1997 and 2003; and a generation before, the Oakland Athletics did the same thing in 1975, after winning three straight World Series. Those were both decisions of making money rather than fielding a contending team. The New York Yankees under George Steinbrenner look like an aberration because they'll pay what it costs to put the best possible team on the field.

The third and largest ethical problem in the novel is players on the take, accepting payoffs to throw games—hearkening to real-life and the infamous Chicago "Black Sox" scandal of 1919, when several White Sox players conspired to lose the World Series to the Cincinnati Reds. To keep the Knights down, Banner has made deals with several key players such as outfielder Bump Bailey and pitcher Al Fowler to make errors or strike out at key moments to assure the team will not win a championship. Prior to a deciding game against the Pirates, the judge offers Hobbs $25,000 to throw the game. Hobbs negotiates a deal for guaranteed future money, too, as he needs wealth to keep one of his love interests in the style to which she has become accustomed. However, in the course of the game, Hobbs realizes he must do the right thing and comes up at a key point late in the game. Unfortunately, like Mighty Casey, he strikes out. The next day, the newspapers print the rumor that Hobbs was throwing the game, never knowing that he did try to redeem himself but failed.

In real life, a child is said to have come up to Shoeless Joe Jackson, the greatest player on the scandalous Sox, banned from baseball and the Hall of Fame, and asked the player "Say it ain't so, Joe." At the end of "The Natural," a child echoes that, asking Hobbs, "Say it ain't true, Roy." In a modern era when sports are rocked by continuing scandals, the ethical questions raised by this novel are still relevant.

Ronald C. Thomas, Jr.

GENDER in *The Natural*

It might seem that a baseball novel should draw its influences from masculinity, replete with images of horsehide balls, bats hewn from tall trees, and muscled men striving on fields of grass and clay. However, the drama in Bernard Malamud's classic *The Natural* is driven by the central character Roy Hobbs's relationships with women, much more so than by his actions on the diamond.

At age 19, Hobbs is a baseball prodigy on his way to a tryout with the Chicago Cubs in the golden era of American sports, the 1920s. On the train, a lovely but mysterious woman named Harriet Bird strikes up a conversation with Hobbs. She probes to find out more about him; flattered by the attention, Hobbs announces his intention to be recognized as the greatest ballplayer who ever lived. Later, Bird contacts Hobbs and lets him know that she is staying in the same hotel. Bird invites Hobbs to come up for a rendezvous and he is eager to collect on the first of many such assignations that he feels his athletic ability and fame should bring him. However, she pulls out a pistol and shoots him. Unbeknownst to him, she is a serial killer who is "collecting" top athletes by luring them sexually and then shooting them. Here, Malamud presents Roy's career as having been destroyed by a woman, a sexual predator.

The novel fast-forwards to 16 years later when a middle-aged Roy Hobbs appears with a contract in hand to play for the fictitious New York Knights. Hobbs is successful with the Knights, until he becomes involved with the treacherous Memo Paris, girlfriend to his teammate, Bump Bailey. When Bailey dies in a collision with the outfield wall, she becomes available. Placing his sexual needs ahead of his game, Hobbs finally achieves his goal of cashing in on his talent and begins a torrid affair with Memo Paris. However, the long nights and high living take a toll on his performance in the batters'

box. Benched for his poor performance, Hobbs finds Memo has turned cold on him, too. An opportunity for salvation appears in the bottom of the ninth against the Chicago Cubs. The Knights are losing and the manager turns to Hobbs as a pinch hitter. Taking two quick strikes, Hobbs notices that, out of all the fans in the stands, one woman in a red dress stands when he is at the plate. He wonders if that one woman could be doing that because she believes in him. Strengthened by that thought, he lashes out for the game winning hit.

The lady in red, Iris Lemon, meets Hobbs outside the ball park, and he opens up to her about his bad luck with bad women, even telling about how Harriet Bird shot him. In this intimacy, she reveals that she has also had rough luck in life, as an unwed mother, now a grandmother. Taken aback momentarily, he still makes love to her by Lake Michigan, thinking that if he captures her "sexual magic" he will also recapture his "baseball magic." However, the idea of dating someone's grandmother forces Iris out of his mind and he seeks to resume his pursuit of Memo, whose devotion to wealth and the "good life" is becoming increasingly apparent.

When Hobbs is offered money to "fix" future games, he takes it, thinking that this will solidify his relationship with Memo. Memo covers him with kisses and gratitude for selling out and Hobbs is racked with guilt.

In the playoff game, Hobbs makes good on his agreement not to help the Knights win. In his first times at bat, he strikes out weakly. However, late in the game, he is heckled by a fan and the stinging remarks get under his skin. Not without his skills, Hobbs figures there's nothing wrong with trying to line a foul ball off the heckler's head. After missing with one attempt, Hobbs drills another powerful shot at the heckler, who ducks, and the sizzling baseball strikes a woman in the head. It is Iris, who has come to support Hobbs at this crucial time.

The game is suspended long enough for Hobbs to rush to Iris's side. As she is taken away to be x-rayed, she exhorts Hobbs to win, not just for her but for the baby she is carrying, their child, conceived the night she broke him out of his slump. In the at bat, he strikes out but still has one more chance left in the ninth inning. He is determined now to get three good swings, to give his best. However, his best is not good enough and he goes down on strikes to lose the game.

As he was leaving the ballpark, the first rumors of his having been in on throwing the game (just like the real Shoeless Joe Jackson of the Chicago White Sox had done) were coming out. Even though he had tried to win in the end, he could never overcome the truth.

Ronald C. Thomas, Jr.

HEROISM in *The Natural*

If we think of heroes as those who sacrifice themselves for some greater good, Bernard Malamud's classic novel *The Natural* is not a very heroic tale. Although there are heroic allusions and undertones, it is the tale of a middle-aged baseball player trying to recapture the lost glory of an interrupted career. The protagonist of the piece, Roy Hobbs, is no heroic righter-of-wrongs; he is a gifted athlete who wants to make his mark as the greatest baseball player of all time.

The term "sports hero" is really a non sequitur and sports star or idol is a more appropriate usage. Still, Hobbs's story is set in the Golden Era of American sports, the pre–World War II period that produced iconic figures such as Jack Dempsey, Red Grange, and Babe Ruth. The Babe even makes a fictionalized cameo appearance in *The Natural* under the nickname of the Whammer. As a young man, Hobbs is on his way from Oregon to New York for a big league baseball tryout and is riding on the same train as the Whammer. At a train stop, there is a spontaneous event where Hobbs pitches to the Whammer before a crowd of onlookers in a field by the train tracks. Just like Casey batting in the classic poem, the Whammer strikes out.

Once back aboard the train, Hobbs is approached by a beautiful woman, Harriet Bird, who observed the impromptu confrontation. She speaks to him of Homer's epics and Lancelot, with an extra irony being that Hobbs is headed for the fictional New York "Knights" baseball club. This imagery will return later in the novel.

Hobbs is unfamiliar with literature but he proclaims his intention to surpass the Whammer and be known as the greatest ballplayer who ever lived. This remark also connotes the real-life sports legend, Hall of Famer Ted Williams, who wanted people to say when he passed "there goes the greatest hitter who ever lived." Williams attained many records in baseball and likely would have earned more if he had not done tours of duty as a Marine Corps fighter pilot in both World War II and Korea. Williams's biographers often stated that he was the real-life version of movie hero John Wayne.

Halfway across the country, Hobbs's train stops in Chicago, and Bird invites him up to her hotel room. Instead of the tryst he is expecting, Hobbs is cut down by a silver bullet fired from Bird's .22 pistol. The silver bullet has ties to heroic legend, as well, through the Lone Ranger and its use against werewolves. In Hobbs's case, the stomach wound ends his hopes of a baseball tryout. Elsewhere in the novel, it is established that Bird has been gunning down other great athletes, such as an Olympian and an All-American football player. As an obsessive fan, her psychosis leads her to attempt to "possess" these great athletes for all time through her shootings.

An additional heroic theme employed in *The Natural* is found in Roy Hobbs's trombone case. Inside this piece of luggage is "Wonderboy," the baseball bat he fashioned himself from a tree struck by lightning. Just like King Arthur's sword Excalibur or Thor's hammer Mjolnir, Wonderboy is an undefeatable weapon in Hobbs's hands. Mythic heroes are often identified with their weapons, such as David's sling, Wyatt Earp's Buntline special, or Luke Skywalker's lightsaber. For Roy Hobbs to have the same iconic status, he must also have such a weapon, and his bat fits the bill.

After years away from the game due to his injuries, Hobbs finally arrives at the New York Knights with bat in hand, as well as a contract. However, his arrival is not like Aragorn's return of the king in the *Lord of the Rings* trilogy. Hobbs is not here to rescue the struggling team; in fact, he is there because the team's owner wants to sabotage the club for financial reasons. Saddling the team with an over-the-hill rookie is one of many underhanded tactics employed. So, Hobbs is no savior and is not readily accepted until he finally gets into the lineup and shows what he can do. As he becomes a recognized star, the team even adopts the lightning bolt logo from Hobbs's bat into a patch they wear on their sleeves. Baseball players can be a superstitious lot and the bolt symbol becomes a good luck charm.

At the peak of his abilities, Hobbs begins an affair with Memo Paris, a noted gambler's girlfriend. Even the name Paris evokes the Trojan War hero and rival of Achilles. As Hobbs enjoys the romance, his playing skills suffer, and he enters a protracted batting slump. Just as Samson was laid low by Delilah (and Hobbs himself was done in earlier by Harriet Bird), a woman proves his undoing. In Hobbs's myth, he also endures temptation. The club's owner, the gambler, and Paris, all pressure him to throw a championship game for money. The lure of easy money and lust for a woman turn him from his heart's desire to be known as the greatest player ever.

At the end of the novel, he has a chance for redemption in the climactic game. In his final at bat, he realizes that he cannot compromise himself any further. Unlike the spectacular home run so well-known from the film version, Hobbs strikes out in the novel. The rumors of his having been involved in a potential fix of the game leak to the papers. Just as the real-life Shoeless Joe Jackson was immortalized in infamy by the child's phrase, "Say it ain't so, Joe," Hobbs is also made into a tragic antihero with the remark "Say it ain't true, Roy."

Ronald C. Thomas, Jr.

MARLOWE, CHRISTOPHER *Doctor Faustus* (1592)

Doctor Faustus, undoubtedly Marlowe's best-known play, is the story of a brilliant man who sells his soul to the devil. In return for an eternity in hell, Mephistopheles, the devil's right-hand man, agrees to serve him for 24 years. Although the story was already familiar from European folklore and a recently translated German work, Marlowe's version is the earliest known dramatization. Written in 1591 and performed the following year, *Doctor Faustus* was not published until 1604, 11 years after Marlowe's untimely death. Full of devils, fools, and magic tricks, the play demonstrates Marlowe's mastery of stage spectacle as well as the powerful verse and imagery that made him a rival to Shakespeare.

The success of Marlowe's version may have been due in part to the fact that England had been undergoing religious turmoil for more than 50 years, and Faustus questions many of the same religious doctrines that had been under attack since the start of the Reformation. In addition, the expanding middle class in England was experiencing a period of great prosperity and opportunity in which a talented man like Faustus—or like Marlowe himself—could realistically hope to move up in the world. Additionally, the playwright's reputation intrigued the public; he was under investigation for atheism when he was stabbed in a tavern quarrel, and speculation continues that his work as a government spy or counterspy led to his murder. *Doctor Faustus* addresses the themes of AMBITION, RELIGION, PRIDE, and EDUCATION, themes as relevant today as they were in late 16th-century London.

Deborah Montouri

AMBITION in *Doctor Faustus*

In the prologue to *Doctor Faustus,* Marlowe clearly announces ambition as a major theme. The chorus tells us that the play will focus on Faustus's fortunes and, using a familiar allusion, likens him to Icarus, a mythological youth who stole the wax wings his father devised but made the mistake of flying too close to the sun; the wings melted and Icarus fell to his death. The figure of Icarus has long been used to represent overreaching ambition, a fault revealed in Faustus's first soliloquy. Considering his occupational choices, he reviews and rejects medicine, the law, and divinity because none can bring him the power and lasting fame that he desires. While a physician may earn wealth and fame for his cures, ultimately, Faustus argues, he cannot make men live forever. He reduces a lawyer's work to mere drudgery and finds divinity useless, as all men must sin, die, and be eternally damned. It is not surprising that Faustus, believing that "A sound magician is a mighty god," settles on black magic, for who but a god has the ultimate power over life and death?

Before Faustus sells his soul to the devil and secures the services of Mephistopheles, his ambitions—aside from pleasing his own craving for wealth, exotic foods, and beautiful women—are relatively noble. He expresses NATIONALISM and a desire to share his good fortune in plans to build a protective brass wall around Germany, drive the invading prince of Parma from the provinces, pay the soldiers fairly, and provide the scholars with silk garments. But his ambitions soon become even more godlike as he imagines reshaping the physical world itself, pulling the continent of Africa to meet with Spain. Additionally, Faustus would restructure the hierarchy of power by making all the earth's rulers subservient to his will.

Once he has signed over his soul to the devil, Faustus's fine ambitions rapidly decline into parlor tricks and vengeful pranks: making Alexander the Great and Helen of Troy appear, fetching out-of-season grapes for the duke of Vanholt's pregnant wife, tossing about platters and goblets at the pope's feast and boxing him on the ear, setting antlers on a disdainful knight's forehead, selling a horse that will turn into a bale of hay when ridden into water, and sending devils to torment an old man whose only offense was begging Faustus to repent and ask for God's mercy. In the end, none of these acts will benefit mankind or bring Faustus the eternal fame he craves.

Through the characters of Wagner, Robin, and Rafe, Marlowe subtly mocks Faustus's lofty ambitions. Wagner, Faustus's servant, observes the results of Faustus's study of magic and determines to gain a measure of power for himself. As Faustus binds Mephistopheles to serve him for 24 years, Wagner proposes that Robin serve him for seven; when money cannot persuade him, Wagner calls up two devils. Although frightened, Robin proposes that he will accept the position if Wagner will teach him, too, how to raise up devils. Instead, he is offered the ability to turn himself into any creature—a parallel to Faustus's request that he may be invisible at will. Immediately, he imagines turning himself into a flea that can crawl into women's most private places. Later, Robin steals one of the conjuring books for the purposes of setting the parish maidens to dance naked before him and getting his master's wife to sleep with him. Like Wagner, Robin desires a servant, and he persuades young Rafe to serve him by promising him sex with the kitchen maid. Robin and Rafe's ambitions seem comical in comparison to Faustus's; however, Faustus's objectives, though

stated in loftier language, are similar. One of the first requests he makes of Mephistopheles is for a wife, but he is content with a devil in the shape of a "hot whore," and his last request is to have Helen of Troy for his mistress. By drawing parallels between these fools' fleshly ambitions and those of Faustus, Marlowe demonstrates that, despite his supposed superiority, he is driven by the appetites and sins common to all men.

Marlowe may have intended *Doctor Faustus* to be a warning to the ambitious self-made man so prominent in early-modern London society—a contradiction, perhaps, considering the playwright's own ambitions and his reputation as a scoundrel, blasphemer, and man of questionable appetites. Ironically, Marlowe is best remembered for this creation of a character whose excessive ambition led him onto the path of self-destruction.

Deborah Montouri

PRIDE in *Doctor Faustus*

As the prologue tells us, Faustus is a man of exceptional talents and intellect. Coming from humble beginnings, he earned a place in the university, where he excelled in argument and was awarded a doctorate in theology. He has learned that any theory, true or false, can be defended using the principles of logic and the power of language. His skill in debate, however, combined with his confidence in his own mind, results in an exaggerated pride, or hubris, that brings about his fall.

We first encounter Faustus as he considers the various professions that he might pursue. But what appears to be an exploration is really a one-sided debate in defense of the path he has already chosen: magic and the occult. While Faustus admits that doctors can earn gold and fame, he rejects the occupation because the dead cannot be brought back to life, ignoring the satisfaction to be gained through lessening others' suffering. Similarly, he scratches the legal profession off his list because he views lawyers as mere servants hired to make money for others through loopholes and technicalities. Finally, he casts off divinity because it cannot prevent men from sin, death, and damnation, but it is his deliberate partial reading of the Scriptures that allows him to ignore the possibility of salvation and eternal life.

To put it simply, because of his pride, Faustus seeks only a profession that will make him "a mighty god," not a useful human being, and that profession, he believes, is sorcery.

When Faustus tells Valdes and Cornelius that he will follow their profession, he claims that, rather than their words, it was his own imagination that persuaded him—yet another example of his pride. He believes that his superior skill in magic has conjured up Mephistopheles, but the devil tells him that he comes whenever anyone abuses the Scriptures, God, or Christ. This point is reinforced when Wagner, Faustus's servant, and Robin, a foolish stable boy, also conjure up devils, proving that the intellect of which Faustus is so proud has nothing to do with his SUCCESS.

There is little doubt that Faustus's pride in his own mind leads to his damnation. In his first conversation with Mephistopheles, Faustus asks how Lucifer, once God's favorite angel, became the prince of devils. The answer should serve as a warning: "O, by aspiring pride and insolence, / For which God threw him from the face of heaven" (1.4). Yet Faustus scoffs at this and other warnings throughout the play, which his reason cannot accept. When contemplating the power he will gain through his bargain with the devil, Faustus devises a plan to improve upon God's creation by moving the continents and oceans. Believing that he can correct God's "mistake" is a demonstration of extreme but wrongheaded pride in his own brilliance.

Ironically, despite this pride in the superiority of his mind, the play depicts Faustus as a man strongly tied to his body and easily seduced by his physical senses. His language is infused with words suggesting sensuality, and in one insightful moment he observes of himself, "The god thou servest is thine own appetite" (2.1). Lucifer and Mephistopheles soon learn that, whenever Faustus considers calling on God to forgive him, he can be easily diverted with threats of physical pain or offers of sensual pleasure. In one such scene, Lucifer first threatens to command a team of devils to tear him limb from limb and then calls up an amusing pageant of the Seven Deadly Sins—significantly led by Pride.

Faustus's greatest displays of pride occur in his moments of doubt, when he contemplates the seriousness of damnation and the possibility of gaining God's pardon. Inevitably, he concludes that his sins are so great that they are unforgivable. He brushes aside the Good Angel's advice and repays an old man who encourages him to repent by sending devils to torment his body. At his last supper, his scholarly friends also beg him to ask forgiveness, but he replies that his sin can never be pardoned. In his last soliloquy, he seems about to repent, but instead of simply asking pardon, Faustus attempts to strike a bargain with God similar to that he made with Lucifer: to serve a term in hell if he will be promised heaven in the end. Ultimately, he is damned because his pride will not allow him to believe that the promise of Christ's sacrifice—forgiveness of sins and eternal life for those who believe—is his for the asking.

Deborah Montouri

RELIGION in *Doctor Faustus*

When Christopher Marlowe wrote *Doctor Faustus,* England was still reeling from decades of religious turmoil, and intolerance for those whose beliefs diverged from the Church of England was still the rule. Henry VIII had broken with the Roman Catholic Church in 1533, declaring himself the head of the new state religion, closing abbeys and monasteries and confiscating church property. His son, Edward VI, continued these reforms, but when Mary I became queen in 1553, she forcibly returned England to the Catholic fold, making Protestant martyrs of nearly 300 subjects who refused to abandon their faith. When Elizabeth I, who ruled when the play was written, reinstated the Anglican Church in 1557, she promised tolerance for dissenters, but all subjects were expected to outwardly conform. Repeated Catholic plots to overthrow or assassinate her led to greater restrictions. Quakers, Methodists, Lutherans, and those of other Protestant sects were also expected to conform, and anyone who spread dissenting doctrines was liable to be charged with heresy. Blasphemy and atheism, for which Marlowe himself was being investigated at the time of his death, were also considered crimes against both church and state.

In this context, *Doctor Faustus* can be read as propaganda for the Anglican Church—a warning against false doctrines and independent thought. In the opening scene, when Faustus ponders his choice of occupations, he casts aside divinity, using Scripture as evidence for its ineffectiveness. The problem, however, is that he takes verses out of context and therefore misinterprets the text. "The reward of sin is death," he reads, ignoring the conclusion, "but the gift of God is eternal life through Jesus Christ our Lord" (1.1). By determining first his own beliefs and then interpreting the Bible to fit them, Faustus represents the official view of the new Protestant sects and the danger in allowing ordinary persons to interpret the Scriptures independently. Although Faustus believes that his conjuring has called up Mephistopheles, he is informed that the devil always comes of his own accord whenever he hears the Scriptures, God, or Christ abused. The play is blatantly anti-Catholic as well. Faustus commands Mephistopheles to exchange his devil's appearance for that of a Franciscan friar, for "that holy shape becomes a devil best" (1.3). In the third act, Faustus and Mephistopheles create havoc at the pope's banquet, tossing about platters of food, boxing the pope on the ear, and beating the friars who curse him. This not only mocks the gluttony of the cardinals but suggests that the rituals of the church—the pope crossing himself for protection, the friars' chanted curse—are ineffectual.

Faustus relies on his intellect to convince himself to sell his soul to the devil, even when the most obvious evidence should warn him against it. Mephistopheles tells him directly not to proceed, warning from his own experience that once one is separated from God, hell is everywhere. But Faustus insists that hell is a fable. In a mockery of Christ's "contract" with God the Father (dying for the sins of mankind), Faustus is required to sign the devil's contract with his own blood. The blood, however, congeals; although Faustus rightly interprets this as a warning, he completes his signature and blasphemously declares, *"Consummatum est"*—"It is finished," the last words of Christ on the cross. Immediately, he sees an inscription on his arm warning him to flee, but Mephistopheles distracts him with gold coins and dancing devils.

At several points throughout the play, Faustus doubts the wisdom of his decision and struggles with his conscience. His Good Angel advises him to cast off the devil and call upon God for mercy, but his Bad Angel easily convinces him that the power he has gained is worth any price and that his sins are too great for God to forgive. As the end of the contract nears, an old man attempts to persuade Faustus to repent but, instead of praying for mercy, he asks for time to think. When Mephistopheles arrives, threatening to tear him to pieces for his disobedience, Faustus asks Lucifer's pardon and bids the devils to torment the old man. Mephistopheles replies that although his faith will protect his soul, they will inflict what pain they can upon his body, "which is worth but little." Again, Faustus misses the point: that physical pain is temporary but the soul is eternal. In a final soliloquy, Faustus seems to understand what lies ahead. He wavers between calling on Christ and begging Lucifer's forgiveness, but the play ends as he is carried away by devils.

Deborah Montouri

MARSHALL, PAULE *Brown Girl, Brownstones* (1959)

Like Betty Smith's *A TREE GROWS IN BROOKLYN* published 16 years earlier, *Brown Girl, Brownstones* is an autobiographical *künstlerroman*, focusing on a girl growing up in Brooklyn, New York. Paule Marshall's heroine, Selina Boyce, is a black daughter of Barbadian immigrants. By adding the dimension of race, Marshall expands the scope of the conventional coming-of-age narrative; by focusing on West Indians, she complicates the exploration of the American dream; and by examining a girl's efforts to negotiate gender and sexuality, she contributes to the growing canon of feminist literary texts.

Brown Girl, Brownstones is written in lush, highly figurative prose. Marshall freely uses dialect to capture the accents and idioms of her Baja (the colloquial name for Barbadians) characters. Set just before, during, and immediately after World War II, the novel uses the war as a backdrop to intensify its exploration of numerous conflicts: black versus white, rich versus poor, immigrant versus native, male versus female, realist versus idealist. Within Selina's family, a war rages between her mother and father—the mother grounded in a pragmatic effort to thrive in Brooklyn, the father lost in a dream of Caribbean grandeur. The mother triumphs, but only at the cost of being called "Hitler" by her daughter.

At the conclusion of *Brown Girl, Brownstones,* Selina embarks for the West Indies. Unlike Francie in *A Tree Grows in Brooklyn,* who goes off to the Midwest to claim an education, Selina, unable to find herself reflected in "America," chooses to embrace her Afro-Caribbean roots in order to establish a firm foundation for her own future and resolve the conflicts that have marked her childhood.

Joyce Zonana

COMING OF AGE in *Brown Girl, Brownstones*

At the beginning of Paule Marshall's debut novel, *Brown Girl, Brownstones,* its heroine Selina Boyce is a lonely, awkward, bookish girl of 10; at its conclusion, she is a poised young woman of 20, a dancer and a writer, choosing to pursue her vague yet pressing dream of "love, a clearer vision, a place." Selina, like so many characters in coming-of-age novels, leaves family and friends and familiar territory to chart an unknown path in her quest for an authentic life.

Selina's coming-of-age is fraught with difficulty: She must find her way as a female, as an immigrant, as a person of African descent, and—most acutely—as someone who has grown up in a household ripped apart by conflict. As she matures, she must find a way to integrate her identities and come to terms with the competing claims on her allegiance. What kind of woman will she be? What kind of Bajan? What kind of black? What kind, ultimately, of an adult?

In the book's opening scene, Selina, on the verge of adolescence, is a "neuter" figure with no clear gender identity and little self-esteem. Possessed by a sudden desire to "declare herself" to the world, she bursts into her sister's room, only to be rebuked by the older girl who is ostentatiously "sick" with her menstrual period. Not much later, Selina becomes aware of her best friend's small breasts and the fact that she bleeds every month "from below." Feeling trapped in her "hard flat body," Selina becomes jealous of the other girls, seemingly "joined against her in their cult of blood and breasts." But soon enough she herself matures physically; by 15 she has breasts of her own and—after a homoerotic interlude with her best friend—has begun to long for intimacy with a boy.

Yet physical maturation is not the same as "coming of age." Many more things must happen before Selina can claim her womanhood. Even choosing to have a passionate illicit affair with a young Bajan artist does not confer that status on her; it is, in the end, her decision to leave her lover and to articulate her own moral vision that marks her initiation into adulthood.

One of the central difficulties Selina faces as she matures is the question of which parent with whom to identify: "the mother," Silla, or her father, Deighton. Silla is a hard-working, bitterly pragmatic woman, "the collective voice of all the Bajan women, the vehicle through which their former suffering found utterance." To Selina, she represents winter in the midst of summer; she imagines that the mother's dark presence causes even the sun to give way. Deighton, Selina's apparently more cheerful father, is ever the optimistic dreamer. Building sunlit castles in the air, he enchants Selina with visions of the white house with "tall white columns . . . like some temple or other" he plans to build on land he has inherited in Barbados. When Silla determines to wrest this land from Deighton, so that the family might "buy house" in Brooklyn, she does so at the cost of alienating her daughter, who clings fiercely to her doomed father.

Selina identifies with her father in part because all the models of black womanhood available to her are flawed: the bitter mother, the carefree but ineffectual Suggie, the wounded Miss Thompson, the self-satisfied 'Gatha Steed. Selina wants a life that will take her outside the realm of unremitting work, careless sensuality, long-suffering victimization, or bourgeois respectability; she does not see how she can have the freedom and authenticity she seeks without entirely rejecting the older women in her community.

It is not until her devastating experience of humiliation by a wealthy white woman that she recognizes that she is "one with . . . the mother and the Bajan women, who had lived each day what she had come to know." In this shattering moment, Selina embraces her blackness, her immigrantness, and her femaleness, realizing that she can integrate, rather than bifurcate, the ways of "the mother" and the father. Although she will not choose the path of her mother, she now has compassion for her. And with this compassion she is freed to shape an authentic adult identity that integrates masculine and feminine, dream and reality, vision and fact. No longer "neuter," Selina is now an androgynous whole, an adult who will work to create a world in which the black, female, immigrant self can embrace—and be embraced by—all of life.

Joyce Zonana

RACE in *Brown Girl, Brownstones*

Race—or, more precisely, skin color—is an inescapable social marker in *Brown Girl, Brownstones,* profoundly affecting the lives of the novel's Bajan protagonists. Having left Barbados to escape the ravages of colonialism, these descendants of African slaves are treated as "dark intruder[s]," or, even worse, "nonexistent" beings in the United States, where they hoped to find equal opportunity. Silla Boyce argues that "power is a thing that don really have nothing to do with color," but her daughter Selina comes to believe that whites abuse blacks because they confuse dark skin "with what they feared most . . . the heart of darkness within them and all its horror and fascination." The novel suggests that until *all* people learn to embrace the "darkness within," even as they fight the "illusion" of surface racial difference, the ideology of white supremacy will "intrude" into "every corner" of black life, "tainting . . . small triumphs" and "exulting at . . . defeats."

Told almost entirely from the point of view of its central black characters, *Brown Girl, Brownstones* offers only occasional glimpses of what lies behind the inaccessible white faces that surround the Bajan immigrants. Early in the novel we hear from Maritze, a poor white woman who lives in the same brownstone as the Boyces: "foreign black scum," she calls them, and we understand what the Bajans are up against. Later, a rich white woman condescends to Selina: "'Oh, please say something in that delightful West Indian accent for us!'" she demands, and Selina recognizes that, to people like this, her "real face"—neither black nor white but human—can never emerge.

Both of Selina's parents, Silla and Deighton Boyce, grew up in Barbados, where "the white man own everything." Silla's memories center around her people's inability to make headway "no matter how hard you work." For Deighton, the most devastating effect of white racism is his psychological humiliation: "utterly unmanned . . . before he was yet a man," he cannot forget the white faces "that had always refused his request for a clerk's job." In New York, Silla, focused on "buying house," can brush aside the insults of white children; but Deighton, still dreaming of "something big," continues to be wounded by the demeaning treatment he receives. In the end a shattered man, he finds consolation only in the cult promises of "Father Peace," a black preacher who claims to be "God Incarnate."

Selina, born in the United States, escapes colonial brutality, but she must still come to terms with racism. As a child, she watches whites flee the "dark sea" of West Indians moving into the neighborhood. She fantasizes about acquiring the "beauty and gentility" of the white family that had occupied her brownstone. But when she glimpses herself in a mirror, she sees that she is "a dark girl alone"; sure that she does not "belong here," she imagines that she is "something vulgar in a holy place." Thus we see that by the age of 10, she has internalized the white supremacist ideology that identifies white as good and black as bad, white as beautiful and black as ugly, white as genteel and black as vulgar. As she grows older, Selina maintains this internalized racism. She goes to college, becomes a bohemian artist, and tries to distance herself from what she sees as the vulgarity of the Bajan immigrants.

Several incidents force her to reevaluate her stance. When she learns how Miss Thompson received the festering "life-sore" on her foot, Selina wants to "avenge the wrong." As a young woman, Miss Thompson had been attacked by a "big red cracker with a shovel" who saw her as an "uppity nigger." Miss Thompson urges Selina to join her "people" in the Association of Barbadian Homeowners and Businessmen, but Selina resists. She joins the association, but only to assert her superiority to it. Not until she is utterly humiliated by a white woman who reminds her that she is "only a nigger after all," does Selina realize her oneness with Miss Thompson, with "the whores" and the "flashy men" on Fulton Street, and with "the mother and the Bajan women." Selina at last embraces her blackness even as she pursues her dream of self-expression and fulfillment, working to undo—rather than internalize or deny—the ideology of white supremacy that has shaped her life and the lives of her people.

Joyce Zonana

SEXUALITY/SENSUALITY/EROTICISM in *Brown Girl, Brownstones*

Sexuality, sensuality, and eroticism play a central role in *Brown Girl, Brownstones*. In the third paragraph, the narrator invites readers to envision, behind the forbidding façades of the Brooklyn brownstones, "bodies crouched in the posture of love." At the conclusion, when the central character, Selina Boyce, chooses to seek "the center of life," we see her nipples growing hard as she walks down Fulton Street. Along the way, we encounter numerous scenes of sexual desire and its fulfillment or frustration, we witness at close hand Selina's sexual initiation, and we are offered vivid descriptions of the lush Caribbean landscape that stirs the senses and opens its inhabitants to a full and free participation in life.

Sexuality in *Brown Girl, Brownstones* is quite explicit. Most of the characters unabashedly embrace and act on their desires, and the narrator describes their action in graphic language: A woman's body is "warm and impatient" as she she pulls her lover down "between her insistent thighs"; a man, after caressing a woman's breasts, "burrow[s] his face into the warm oblivion of her stomach." The action of the novel begins on a Saturday night, a time for "love in dark rooms." Those who, like Selina's mother Silla, are excluded from that "circle of love" feel "old and barren." Yet the narrator shows that such exclusion stems from a choice: Silla, consumed by grief, resentment, and a hard determination to triumph over life, has closed herself to her own "burst[s] of passion."

The intense sexuality of the Bajan immigrants grows out of the sensuality associated with the sun, the landscape, the food, and the music of their island life in Barbados. This life in and of nature is erotic as well; even in New York the natural world embodies a bursting energy identified with life itself. Thus, on a spring morning, the adolescent Selina senses

> the earth swollen with life and heaving in its blind act; she smelled the sad, sweet, fecund musk of birth. All over the ruined yard green tufts nudged toward the sun and their own brief life. New leaves craned in the wind. Aching, she thought of the lovers tonight in the pavilion and the silence that would seem loud with the sound of their mouths and hands.

Earlier, in Prospect Park, she associates the sun, the growing grass, a woman's menstrual blood, and the passion of young lovers.

The strong sexual emphasis of the novel is embodied most fully in Suggie, a woman whose "domain" is "love, its rituals and its passions." "'You're a summer woman,'" 10-year-old Selina tells her neighbor. Suggie spends each Saturday night carousing in her creaky bed; she has no steady man, yet she is defiantly indifferent to the gossip of her neighbors. Suggie's voluptuousness is "so natural that it was innocent." Her passion emerges directly from her continued identification with the Caribbean landscape. Even in Brooklyn, as she prepares a traditional meal of cuckoo—cornmeal, okra, and codfish—"she could see the yam patch . . . and the mango tree with its long leaves weighted down by the dusk, and beyond, all down the soft-sloping hills, a susurrant sea of sugar cane."

Suggie's sexuality also emerges from music and dancing. She recalls her youth in Barbados: "Dancing—the music licking sweet—and sea-bathing" and "loving-up," and she encourages Selina to follow her example. We will not be surprised or judgmental (like her mother) when Selina enters into a passionate affair at the age of 17 and becomes a dancer.

Paule Marshall portrays sexuality as a redeeming, essential force, associated with freedom and full participation in life. Yet for the novel's Bajan characters in Brooklyn it is also compensatory. The characters use sex as a means of escape from their difficult lives as disenfranchised, black-skinned, poor immigrants in a hostile white world. Suggie's passion-filled Saturday nights "nullify" her week of alienating housework; Deighton turns to his "concubine" to prove his manhood and forget his humiliations; even Selina's young lover Clive seeks "to rid himself of his pain in her," and Selina herself finds life "tolerable" because of him. The gloomy brownstones, and the racist society they embody, contain and inhibit a fully joyous, positive, free expression of eroticism. Thus at the conclusion of the novel, Selina turns her back on Brooklyn and is headed toward the sunlit landscape of Barbados, toward "love, a clearer vision," and "the center of life," choosing a sexuality that will not be so much an escape as a full embrace of life.

Joyce Zonana

McCARTHY, CORMAC *All the Pretty Horses* (1992)

The first novel in his Border trilogy, *All the Pretty Horses* is Cormac McCarthy's tale of two Texan boys and their journey into Mexico. A National Book Award winner, the novel introduces readers to John Grady Cole, one of the main characters of the Border trilogy, and his quest to live a life of ardent-heartedness in an age of increasing modernization and urban communities. Accompanying him on this quest is his friend Lacey Rawlins and a young boy they meet in Mexico named Jimmy Blevins. Primarily a coming of age story, *All the Pretty Horses* explores the experience of facing the world as it is rather than what you would have it to be.

When John Grady's mother inherits the family ranch and decides to sell it, John Grady leaves the Texas ranch with Rawlins to head to Mexico in search of a more rustic lifestyle and work as ranch hands. During their time in Mexico they witness the execution of a friend, spend time in prison, nearly die from prison fights, flee from Mexican authorities, fall in love, and abandon love. At its conclusion, the novel leaves John Grady disillusioned about his journey and the actions he took, and Rawlins content to live a new life in Texas. Cole's story is completed in the final book of the trilogy, *Cities of the Plain* (1998). *All the Pretty Horses* explores the roles of NATURE, COMING OF AGE, and the power of FATE through the journey of John Grady Cole and Lacey Rawlins into a wilderness.

Alan Noble

COMING OF AGE in *All the Pretty Horses*

When John Grady Cole and Lacey Rawlins head out to Mexico as young men, they leave to fulfill their desire for adventure and for a lifestyle generally forgotten in the United States. Their ideal life would be spent roaming the countryside and raising horses. As they pursue this romantic longing for a bygone era, they are confronted with forces that challenge their view of the world and people; through adapting to these challenges they mature. John Grady's love for and inability to be with Alejandra, the murder of Blevins, and his own killing of the Mexican prisoner while in the penitentiary contribute to his maturing into manhood.

Throughout the first hundred pages of *All the Pretty Horses* John Grady's preoccupation is with horses, male companionship, and a rustic lifestyle. When Alejandra rides by him on her black horse, we are told that his world is altered forever in the space of a heartbeat. His world is altered in three senses. First, Alejandra becomes the first woman he truly loves. While John Grady had experienced infatuation before, it is not until he sees this beautiful young girl in Mexico that his desire for romance drives his actions. No longer can he be content merely with roaming through empty deserts or raising and training horses; he has experienced sexual attraction and his priorities must be changed. Second, his world is altered because until that point he had desired only things that could be obtained. Before this, his world was filled with things that were fundamentally controllable and uncomplicated: horses, cattle, and young men. But his love for Alejandra forces him to confront a world of pride, tradition, and culture, personified in Alejandra's grand-aunt the Duena Alfonsa. In this world, his wishes are not enough to secure his desires. Although John Grady tries desperately to remain with Alejandra, he is ultimately unable to overcome her grand-aunt and father. When he is forced to acknowledge that he cannot be with her, he understands that "all his life led only to this moment and all after led nowhere at all." Just as his idealistic view of love is challenged, Blevins's execution alters his conception of human morality.

When Blevins is unjustly executed by a corrupt Mexican police captain, John Grady and Rawlins are both deeply affected. The captain justifies his action by explaining that violence is the only way for a man to establish respect. The willingness of the captain to kill another person in order to retain his status as a feared man calls into question the boys' naïve view of honor and justice. As Rawlins leaves Mexico to return home, he recalls Blevins's execution. John Grady attempts to assure Rawlins that he will feel better when he returns home, but Rawlins disagrees, saying "I don't think so." The senselessness of Blevins's death forces the boys to alter their view of human morality; both John Grady and Rawlins come to understand the horrible brutality of which humans are capable.

In the penitentiary, John Grady's courage and manliness are tested when he is forced to kill in self-defense. This event marks his final movement from an uninitiated, naïve boy, to a man willing to shed blood. Once imprisoned, Rawlins is badly hurt in a fight and is taken away by the prison guards. Alone in the penitentiary, John Grady goes to visit an influential convict named Perez in order to get information about his injured friend. Perez tells John Grady that the world wants to know if he is "brave." Soon after this exchange, he is attacked by an assassin. Barely managing to survive, John Grady is forced to kill the assassin in self-defense. This test of skill and strength proves that he is a man, but at the cost of his conscience. Near the end of the novel he visits a judge and relates to him his feelings on having killed a person. Although he knows that he acted in self-defense, he continues to be bothered by the event. He proves to the world that he is brave, but the cost is too great.

Although John Grady is awakened to the beauty of love and sex, he learns that no matter how ardent he is in his desire, there are some forces too great to overcome. The profound senselessness of Blevins's execution alters both John Grady and Rawlins's belief in the relative honor and morality of people. But perhaps the most drastic change in John Grady is his realization that courage is necessary to life, and yet often requires regrettable actions. John Grady's

movement into adulthood is a painful process as he learns the futility of passion, the brutality of humans, and the tremendous cost of bravery.

Alan Noble

FATE in *All the Pretty Horses*

One of the central issues McCarthy engages in *All the Pretty Horses* is whether or not humans have free will to act in the world. These issues are primarily worked out through the character Jimmy Blevins. Early in the novel, Jimmy Blevins is convinced that it is his fate to be killed by lightning if he is exposed to a storm. In the process of fleeing from the lightning, Blevins loses his horse and gun, setting in motion a series of events that culminate in his execution. Blevins fulfills the prophecy of his death in trying to circumvent it. Ultimately, however, McCarthy seems to imply that the person who actually controls the boy's destiny is the Mexican captain who kills him.

Blevins's story focuses on the question of whether or not a person can escape his fate, and while Blevins manages to avoid being struck by lightning, the events that unfold as a result of the storm lead to his execution, suggesting that humans are incapable of freely choosing their fate. Soon after John Grady Cole and Lacey Rawlins meet the young Blevins, a storm brews. Blevins informs his companions that he must find shelter from the storm or else he'll "be struck sure as the world." He explains to Cole and Rawlins that his family has a long history of being struck by lightning, and thus it is his fate to suffer the same consequences if he remains exposed to the storm. Blevins hides from the lightning under the cover of a dead cottonwood. In the ensuing storm Blevins escapes without being struck by lightning, but his horse runs off, taking his gun with him. Because Blevins believed that it was his fate to be struck, he loses his horse and gun; in the process of regaining his possessions from the man who found them, he kills in self-defense. Although Mexico does not have the death penalty, a family member of the man Blevins killed makes arrangements with the police captain to execute him in order to protect his family's honor. This family member cannot bring himself to kill the boy, so the police captain is compelled to execute Blevins to protect his own honor.

Blevins's prophecy that he would be struck "sure as the world" is fulfilled in the novel in the sense that it is the lightning that causes him to make choices that lead to his death. Honor, family history, and a desire for justice confine Blevins's actions to the choices that lead to his execution. He even tells us that he, "aint done nothin that nobody else wouldn't of." In this sense, Blevins's life seems to have been controlled by some sort of fate; although he made decisions, he didn't seem to have any real options. However, in a description of the police captain, we learn that it is he who actually has free will in the novel: "the captain inhabited another space and it was a space of his own election and outside the common world of men." The space of his election is the position he holds as a police captain who can choose who lives and who dies. Cole and Rawlins come to view the police captain as a man whose life is outside of the control of fate because he is willing and able to take the lives of other people according to his own judgments; thus, he is outside the world of men, like Blevins, who are obligated to factors like family honor, justice, and ethics.

From the story of Blevins it seems that the only person who is really free in the world is the person who is willing and able to kill others outside of any governance of justice, ethics, or morality. Blevins acts in accordance with his sense of justice, pursuing the items that belong to him and killing only in self-defense. The result of his actions is that his fate is controlled by others, like the police captain, who are willing to kill mercilessly. In *All the Pretty Horses* humans can have free will, but only if they are willing to take the lives of others into their own hands; otherwise their fates will be controlled by those who are willing to kill.

Alan Noble

NATURE in *All the Pretty Horses*

Since the novel is set primarily in the desert lands of Texas and Mexico, nature is central to both the plot and themes of *All the Pretty Horses*. When John Grady Cole and his friend Lacey Rawlins leave their homes in Texas to recover a more traditional lifestyle in Mexico, the natural landscape of the desert becomes the setting of their maturity. Before leaving, the boys are forced to recognize that a new era is beginning in Texas, symbolized by the death of John Grady's grandfather, owner of the family ranch where ranching and working closely with horses and cattle is no longer profitable. The desert and the people who dwell in it demand a vibrant will to survive from the boys, unlike the safe and settled lives they left in Texas. During their journey, they are forced to carry guns both to shoot game and to protect themselves, they are forced to ration their food and water, survive the elements, and they learn to discern between people who are friendly and those who might cause them harm. Nature, as symbolized by the desert, is a place where a person can test his or her will, a place where the desire to survive is tried against the powerful forces of the environment and man. There is a sense that the boys would be unable to mature into men if they remained in Texas where their courage would not be challenged. The desert landscape provides a place of testing that draws an essential passion to live from John Grady and Rawlins. This passion is also symbolized in the horses that populate the novel.

Early in *All the Pretty Horses,* we are told that what John Grady "loved in horses was what he loved in men, the blood and heat of the blood that ran them." Here, as throughout the novel, horses are used to symbolize unquenchable passion and natural beauty. The heat of a passionate and ardent life is reflected in the blood of both the horses and the men that ride them. John Grady believes that what defines a horse is its ability to live an untamed life in the wild. Several times John Grady dreams of beautiful, wild horses running through fields and mountains, unrestrained by man, given only to their own passion to run. This ardent lifestyle, which is symbolized in the horses, is shown to have negative effects as well. When John Grady and Rawlins go to work at Don Hector's ranch in Mexico, John Grady's greatest pleasure comes not from watching Don Hector's horses roam wild on the mountains, but from breaking them so that they can be ridden. John Grady gains pleasure out of conforming the will of the horses to his own. At one point, John Grady whispers into a horse's ear that he alone is the commander of the mares. While he is attracted to the unbridled spirit of nature he finds in wild horses, he also takes great pleasure in taking command of that wild spirit. Another way this ardent lifestyle is challenged in the text is when an older Mexican ranch hand tells John Grady and Rawlins that horses innately love war, just like men. The boys came to Mexico pursuing a romantic life of passion, something they believed existed in nature and the older traditions, which drew them to horses and ranching; however, they discover that such a lifestyle leads both to an exciting life and to violence and warfare.

While the rest of Texas and America slips into settled lives and more modernized occupations, John Grady and Rawlins seek to return to a time where the wills of men were tested against nature. Their journey through the desert into Mexico tests their resolve and allows them to mature as men. The desert symbolizes the brutal forces of nature, which demand greatness from men. In addition, horses function as the primary symbol of nature in *All the Pretty Horses,* and their defining characteristic is their passionate wills. For John Grady, the beauty of a horse is found in its desire for freedom and its courage, qualities that he also admires in men. While he loves horses and admires their freedom, John Grady seems to be happiest when he is taming them. Thus, the wild passion of nature that both boys seek is something to be controlled and not admired from a distance. The boys also learn that the passionate will they attribute to a horse's beauty is the same will that causes them to love war. In this sense, nature and the ardent will that defines it are not shown to be inherently good or peaceful, but rather are capable of producing violence and bloodshed as well as beauty and passion.

Alan Noble

McCULLERS, CARSON   *The Heart Is a Lonely Hunter*   (1940)

In the years preceding the United States entry into World War II, the lonely residents of a small southern town attempt to understand each other despite social differences. Bereft of a close friend, who falls ill and goes to a hospital, the deaf mute John Singer becomes a customer at the local café, where several townspeople seek him out. The quiet owner of the all-night café, Biff Brannon, finds in Singer an ideal listener to his philosophical observations of life, even as his own life seems to pass him by. Roy Blount, an itinerant labor organizer and alcoholic, finds sanctuary for a time at the café and comes to believe that Singer sympathizes with his obsession for socialist reform when the local workers fail to do so. Similarly estranged from his family and the black community by his beliefs in Marxist revolution, the aging doctor Copeland finds solace in Singer's company. The young and artistic Mick Kelly believes that she has found in Singer a kindred soul with whom to share her passion for music, which she seeks out on solitary walks around town. While characters' separate quests illustrate themes of American business, communism, socialism, and artistic expression, they do not find lasting fulfillment in Singer or in their failed attempts to understand each other. Singer himself silently mourns the absence of his sick friend while his visitors see him as a source of comfort. McCullers's novel thus explores universal themes of community and individualism while grounding them in specific economic, political, and artistic movements of late-1930s America.

Tim Bryant

ALIENATION in *The Heart Is a Lonely Hunter*

The friendship of the two mutes, Spiros Antonapoulos and John Singer, introduced in the opening pages of *The Heart Is a Lonely Hunter,* demonstrates the alienation one can experience even when not alone. Although very different, the two men are always together. The self-indulgent Antonapoulos steals food from his cousin's shop and generally spends his days seeking his own physical comforts. In contrast, the attentive Singer is more aware of others' needs, including those of his friend, whom he accompanies around their nameless southern town after leaving work at the silversmith. While Singer is more aware of others' feelings and feels a great need to communicate his thoughts to his friend, Antonapoulos is uncommunicative in word and deed, never committing a selfless act on behalf of his friend or anyone else. Despite Singer's deep need to communicate, it is doubtful that his friend understands him completely or even cares to do so. Thus, the psychological nature of their alienation from each other displays itself as the paradox of physical closeness but emotional distance. The repeated juxtaposition of physical proximity with emotional detachment highlights the novel's theme of alienation as a consequence of one-sided communication and unequal relationships throughout the novel.

After Antonapoulos's cousin has him taken away to a sanitarium, Singer makes two changes in his life that cause him to become physically, if not emotionally, closer to several other people in town. Moving into the Kelly household as a boarder, he attracts the attention of the young girl Mick Kelly, who believes that he knows about music, her own passion, even though Singer is deaf. Second, Singer starts taking his three daily meals at the New York Café, where he attracts the attention of the owner, Biff Brannon, and one of his customers, Jake Blount. The two men separately visit Singer in his room at the Kellys', where Brannon asks Singer philosophical questions and Blount drunkenly rails about political inequalities that consume his life. Each of these visitors is alienated from any sense of community and so seeks out Singer, who is also an outsider. Yet, alienation persists in these unequal relationships based on one-sided communication. Singer listens, but gives little response to his visitors' communications, ironically filling the role that Antonapoulos had filled for him. That is, while his visitors speak of their innermost thoughts and assume that he understands them perfectly, they do not really know what Singer is thinking. The act of communicating deeply personal thoughts leads to alienation, rather than relationship, in these similarly one-sided examples.

The difficulty of resolving the problem of alienation is demonstrated by the scene in which several of Singer's visitors arrive at his lodging all at the same time. Although they know each other from town, Mick, Biff, and Jake have nothing to say to each other and so leave Singer's room when it is clear they cannot speak to him alone. Another of Singer's visitors, Dr. Copeland, demonstrates this persistent alienation from society, where the individual finds himself unable to communicate personal beliefs and feelings to a wider group. As a father, Junius Copeland attempted early in life to teach his four children to be leaders of the African-American people. Instead, his passion for political and social uplift has alienated him from his children, who fear his passionate outbursts about politics so much that they seldom visit him in his old age. As is the case with Singer's other visitors, Copeland's very passion about life is, paradoxically, what alienates him from others and prevents him from sharing that passion in a meaningful way.

As indicated by the fact that Dr. Copeland names one of his children Karl Marx, there is a political dimension of alienation at play in the novel. As the historical Karl Marx argued, workers are alienated from a meaningful existence because they do not have control over their working lives. Mick's passion for music subsides after she acquires a full-time job to support her family. Biff spends his days at the café, his life dominated by the cycle of his business, which never closes. Blount tries to rally local workers to unionize, but they laugh at him as an outsider. Copeland himself decides to leave town and spend his remaining days on the family farm, having exhausted himself in service to a people from whom his political consciousness has alienated him. In these various ways, characters come to be alienated from their communities, their aspirations, and their beliefs.

Consequently, Singer does not become a figure around which the variously alienated characters overcome their loneliness, but rather the means by which the terms of isolation are defined. Although Biff cares for Mick, she avoids him, believing that he hates her. Blount and Copeland both obsess over political injustices and revolution, but they fail to discuss their ideas productively and part in anger. The ultimate consequence of this incurable alienation is Singer's suicide near the novel's end. McCullers's novel affirms the strength of the human spirit, which can feel most passionately, but reminds the reader that the cost of such passionate insight is often loneliness and alienation.

Tim Bryant

LOVE in *The Heart Is a Lonely Hunter*

As suggested by the title of McCullers's novel, love is a solitary, difficult search for fulfillment. The cause of this difficulty is not that characters do not love, but that they feel love too strongly for objects they cannot obtain. Consequently, lonely characters suffer unrequited love for others who do not love them in return, incomprehensible love whose reasons cannot be grasped, and frustrated love for goals that cannot be accomplished alone. In their own ways, all are lovers and hunters for love.

Examples of unrequited love begin with the two friends John Singer and Spiros Antonapoulos. As deaf mutes, the two men are prevented from communicating with a wider society, but find comfort in a loving friendship. However, the two do not really love the same things or on the same terms. Antonapoulos's primary love is for physical comforts, such as rich food and drink, where Singer take his greatest joy in speaking to his friend after work. Antonapoulos often appears to care and understand little about what his friend tells him; nevertheless, Singer seeks his happiness in his friend. Thus, one friend's love is almost inconsequential to the desires of the other.

The owner of the New York Café, Biff Brannon, shares a less understandable love with his wife, Alice. Running the café 24 hours a day, the couple split 12-hour shifts and thus never see or talk with each other for more than a few minutes per day. Yet, Biff feels a deep love, which he cannot express in words, for the wife he never sees. When Alice dies, Biff feels that he is done with love and lacks a clear idea of what else is left for him to do with his life. He does not know what he seeks, but only that he is still searching for something to give his life meaning. Biff thus demonstrates the extreme example of a lover for whom the search is far stronger than the chance of finding a satisfying object to love.

The young Bubber Kelly suffers from a similarly inexpressible and tragic love. Fascinated at the sight of the beautifully dolled-up Baby, Bubber pleads for the little girl to cross the street so that he can touch her hair. When she refuses, Bubber shoots her with his gun without understanding what he does. His desire to touch something beautiful, which causes him unconsciously to pull the trigger, thus ends in tragedy. He harms the object of his love as well as the innocence of his own life. Captured when he attempts to flee town, Bubber returns home lonely and mean, even less able than before to seek love or give it to others. The flawed attempt to express his

desires thus causes the young boy to be even more greatly set apart from finding love.

The third kind of lonely love is that which sets an individual on a quest to improve the lot of others. The deeply flawed Roy Blount demonstrates this kind of love in his zeal to organize the workers and make socialist reforms for their benefit. When the local tradesmen reject Blount's political activism, he continues to pursue his political theories in discussion with others. Chief among his desired audience is Dr. Copeland, whose own beliefs in Marxist revolution demonstrate his love for his family and the black community, at the same time distancing him from them because they do not agree with his politics. While the men's love for social justice and reform give the two a reason to work together, they go their separate ways after disagreeing about particulars on how to proceed with real reforms. The search for the ideal, just world thus seems more important to these lovers of justice than accepting anything less.

McCullers's novel demonstrates that the lonely business of love can be unrequited, inexpressible, and frustrating. One of the few instances of reciprocated love is Mick's love for her father. Mr. Kelly is himself a lonely man, the head of a poor family struggling to stay ahead financially and together emotionally. Yet, the love shared by father and daughter is one of the novel's few instances of two lonely characters loving each other and recognizing in each other both love and loneliness. It is this mutual recognition of the nature of love that affirms the reasons why the lonely heart continues its hunt.

Tim Bryant

WORK in *The Heart Is a Lonely Hunter*

Work can give purpose to life or stand as an obstacle to pursuing one's true desires. The characters of McCullers's novel face work's dual potential for self-expression and frustration. Workers' lives are defined in part by their jobs, even as individuals try in a variety of ways to find purpose beyond their working lives. Work thus shapes identity both as a means of self-expression and as a limitation to what an individual can accomplish. The work that characters do expresses both their hidden desires as well as the circumstances that prevent them from fully realizing their hearts' desires in life.

The regularity of work shapes several characters' lives for good and ill. Perhaps the most obvious example of lives dominated by work are those of Biff and Alice Brannon, who run the New York Café. Since their business stays open 24 hours a day, seven days a week, the Brannons never see each other except for a few minutes each day when one goes to bed and the other awakens to start a 12-hour shift. Although the two share a life of constant work, the actual organization of that work keeps them apart. Ironically, their permanent state of living close but separate lives gives the rest of the town a place to go at any hour and not be alone. The Brannons' shared work ethic to keep their business open all hours defines their married life as one of separation, in which only a few passing moments are not governed by the demands of work.

Difference in work ethics can also demonstrate a distance between characters who might otherwise seem close. John Singer and his friend Antonapoulos demonstrate a profound difference in work ethics. Singer's job as a silver-engraver requires delicacy and concentration, while Antonapoulos, who helps at his brother's grocery, is an unreliable worker who is known to steal from the store more often than doing any real work. Antonapoulos shows a similar laziness in his friendship with Singer, barely paying attention to his friends' stories, but Singer still derives great satisfaction from the friendship. The friends' behaviors on and off work are thus consistent in themselves, but unequal to each other. Nevertheless, this pair of workers makes a working, if not healthy, friendship for a time.

Dr. Copeland is extremely self-conscious about his work, including his position as a doctor in the black COMMUNITY and, what he considers his true work, leading his people to greater FREEDOM through political self-awareness. However, Copeland's self-appointed mission to preach Marxist revolution, and so expand his work to include curing social and economic ills, is unsuccessful because his beliefs distance him from his community, even his own family. His grown children spend their money, earned at work, on commercial products and dances, which Copeland considers wasteful and detrimental to true freedom of the mind. The doctor's own definition of meaningful work as political and serious thus conflicts with the ideas of the community he wishes to lead. Because Copeland's definition of meaningful work goes beyond what his community will accept from him as a doctor, he considers himself a failure in his true life's work.

More than any other character, Roy Blount desires to change society's definition of meaningful work and reorganize the relationship of work in the lives of the people. As an itinerant worker and socialist, Blount travels from town to town, working odd jobs, as he attempts to organize workers into labor unions. However, Blount's altruistic goal to improve the lives of his fellow workers fails because his political views, like Copeland's, differ greatly from the community of workers, who grow hostile to him and his ideas. Blount loses both his ability to work, when he is fired for being a trouble-maker, and his ability to help workers because their ideas about work are too different from his own. His drunken talk about workers' rights is an attempt to work out his vision of just working conditions, which never come to fruition.

Mick Kelly's father represents a more modest worker who holds few hopes of changing the circumstances of, or future prospects for, better work. As the head of a poor family that survives more from rent paid by boarders than from wages, the figure of Mr. Kelly is a small but effective reminder that work was and is, for many Americans, more often about economic SURVIVAL than self-expression. The fact that Mick eventually goes to work to support the family, trading her dreams of a musical education for a meager paycheck, shows the less fulfilling reality of working life, which places individuals' deepest desires against social and economic realities beyond their control.

Tim Bryant

McCULLERS, CARSON *The Member of the Wedding* (1946)

Carson McCullers's third novel, a small book with an unimposing title, mixes a commonplace event, a brother's wedding, with a young girl's journey into adolescence. It is the summer of 1944, the middle of World War II, in a small southern town, and the novel introduces and develops only three characters:

Frances Addams, a gangly, androgynous, and motherless 12-year-old tomboy; her bespectacled and ethereal six-year-old cousin, John Henry West; and Berenice Sadie Brown, the Addams's black cook, housekeeper, and caretaker. The novel is divided into three parts, each depicting a different day and a different leg in Frankie's journey. Frankie's father, a widower whose wife died giving birth to Frankie, appears only briefly. He is a jeweler, a shadow father preoccupied with his business and his own gray thoughts, who only absentmindedly engages with his child. This coming-of-age novel weaves itself around the wedding of Frankie's older brother, Jarvis, a soldier who returns from duty in Alaska to marry Janice Evans from nearby Winter Hill. During the three days encompassed by the novel, McCullers presents us with the grander themes of ABANDONMENT, LOVE, DEATH, IDENTITY, SEXUALITY, and innocence as seen, experienced, and interpreted through the eyes of Frankie Addams. While the effects of war and racial bigotry are never far from the surface of this novel, what concerns McCullers most is Frankie's internal emotional struggle as she wrestles with her fantasies and fears, and grapples with who she is and what place she holds in the world.

Connor Trebra

ABANDONMENT in *The Member of the Wedding*

"It looks to me like everything has just walked off and left me." These words, spoken by Frankie Addams, punctuate the repetitive conversations she has each evening with Berenice Sadie Brown, the Addams's cook and caretaker, as they discuss the disappearance of Frankie's tomcat Charles. Of all the complex themes found in McCullers's novel, that of abandonment permeates the work, even to its ending. Frankie, her father, Berenice, and John Henry each undergo profound levels of loss that deeply affect their lives and drive their actions.

Berenice Sadie Smith has lost four husbands. The first, Ludie Smith, whom she loved the deepest, died early in their marriage, and since that time she has searched for him in men who appear in her life trailing physical reminders of him—his coat, his hands. These subsequent marriages have ended badly, with men who break their vows, commit violence, and lose themselves to alcohol. In addition, as a black woman, she has been abandoned by the dominant white society within which she lives. And she will leave the Addams family to marry yet again. However, when she does, the Addams family will themselves have left their home, and John Henry, too, will be gone.

Royal Quincy Addams, Frankie's father, is a widower who lost his wife during the birth of his daughter. As she watches him in the morning, Frankie notes that he appears as one who "has lost something, but forgotten what it is that he has lost." He is a man who "deserved a little peace and quiet before he put his nose down to the grindstone." A man who has "ears to hear with" but "[does] not listen." Late in the evenings, Frankie hears him as he stumbles about his room, appearing the next morning with a face "pale as cheese" and eyes "pink and ragged," who hates the sound of his own cup rattling against its saucer. This physical description suggests a man whose sleep is often disturbed and who may drink in order to medicate his feelings. He is a man whose "saggy-kneed grey trousers" and distracted air reflect an inner sadness and numbing confusion. In his struggle to dampen his own emotional pain by focusing intently on his work as a watchmaker, he has closed the door to the deeper needs of his daughter, and leaves her alone to struggle with her emotional challenges.

John Henry is only six, yet there is something that suggests a lonely maturity, and there is a strange pensiveness, even aloofness, that hints at a sense of sorrow beyond his six years. His mother and father are never mentioned, and there is a sense that he has been forsaken. He depends on the love found in the Addams's hot summer kitchen, in the caring of Berenice, and in the sometimes begrudging affection shown by his cousin Frankie. Frankie often comments on a sense of loneliness and fear that emanate from John Henry, and it is this perhaps more than blood relations that connects the cousins. Both are children whose place in the world seems tenuous; despite their age difference, they are drawn together in mutual support and commiseration.

Frankie has been unintentionally abandoned, first by her mother and then by her father, who, while continuing to provide for her, seems to have emotionally left his only daughter. Similarly, the summer has intensified a sense of isolation and separateness for Frankie. Rejected by her female friends for her awkward tomboyish ways, and no longer completely content with the companionship she once found in John Henry and Berenice, her sense of loss is compounded by the abandonment of her brother who, through his engagement and impending marriage, chooses another woman over the sister who idolizes him. It is the sense of connectedness that drives Frankie throughout the book. Frankie becomes acutely aware of the loss associated with death; in addition to the death of Ludie Smith, she enumerates a formidable list of those who have passed on: her mother, her grandmother, the son of a family friend killed in Italy, a neighbor, Lon Baker, who is murdered in an alley, a shopkeeper, and a telephone company repairman.

Conner Trebra

COMING OF AGE in *The Member of the Wedding*

It is early Friday evening, the endless dog-days of August 1944. In a summer suspended by waiting and uneventfulness, the revelations of the next three days will alter Frankie Addams's life significantly. Frankie sits in her kitchen with Berenice Sadie Brown and John Henry West. She is bare-footed, wearing a BVD undervest and blue gym shorts, with brown, crusted elbows and wild hair grown out from an early summer crew-cut. She has become restless and discontent since the spring, noting an unnamable shift in her world. She is distressed by her significant physical growth. No longer able to pass comfortably through the shaded scuppernong grape vines, under which she and John Henry once sat escaping the oppressive heat, she fearfully calculates that by age 18 she will become a nine-foot-tall freak. Indulging in childish pastimes holds no interest for her; she rejects her role as the leader of the swimming pool diggers and no longer writes plays while sitting in the arbor. While too old to continue sleeping with her father, she is "too young and mean" to be included as a member of a club composed of slightly older girls. One moment she is lashing out at Berenice and John Henry, the next she is sitting in the black cook's lap seeking comfort. Frankie is nearly 12

and five-sixths years old, teetering on the brink of maturity, and the maelstrom of feelings she experiences embody the space found between childhood and adolescence.

Earlier, her brother Jarvis and his fiancée Janice stopped by on their way to Winter Hill where they are to be married that Sunday. Their visit invokes a nameless, squeezing feeling in her heart, and Frankie remarks aloud that the "world is a sudden place" and thinks of how it is always "fast, loose, and turning." The wedding becomes an escape from the unpleasant endless monotony of her life, as well as a vehicle for her completion. She has found the "we of me." By the end of the evening her desire and plans to join the couple in their marriage consolidate.

Awakening Saturday morning, Frankie has changed her name to F. Jasmine; this reflects a decidedly more feminine and mature character and mirrors the "JA" of the engaged couple. Dressed in "her most grown and best," F. Jasmine spends much of the day wandering the streets downtown, impulsively telling strangers about the wedding and her plans. On seedy Front Street, while chasing after the elusive organ music of the monkey-man, she meets a red-headed soldier, on leave and drunk. In his stupor, he mistakes Frankie for an older girl, which both titillates and frightens her, and asks her to meet him at the Blue Moon Hotel later that evening. During her last supper with Berenice and John Henry—she will not be returning after the wedding—she shares cigarettes and talk of love and philosophy with the black cook. It is as F. Jasmine that she commits what she fears is murder by hitting the red-headed soldier on the side of the head with a pitcher as he makes unwanted sexual advances toward her.

On the day of the wedding F. Jasmine's plans, to join the newly married couple in their life together, fail miserably. Dressed in an orange satin "grown woman's evening dress" and silver shoes, F. Jasmine wishes only to be "known and recognized for her true self." Yet the adults at the wedding continually refuse to see her as grown and insist upon calling her Frankie. However much passion she feels, in the final moments, F. Jasmine is unable to express her love and yearning to either her brother or his bride. As the couple makes their way to the car that will carry them to their honeymoon, and away from her forever, the child Frankie throws herself to the dusty ground begging them to "Take me, Take me." Once back home, the grief-stricken Frankie steals her father's pistol and wallet and runs away from home only to discover that she knows not where to go or how to get there. She is found by the Law at the Blue Moon where, by chance, she learns that the red-headed soldier is alive and well. As the novel closes, Berenice is moving on, John Henry is dead from meningitis, the Addamses are moving to the suburbs, and Frances emerges—"a child no longer," mad about Michelangelo, her newest friend Mary Littlejohn, and perhaps her own unknown future.

Connor Trebra

COMMUNITY in *The Member of the Wedding*

Although the community in which Frances Addams lives remains unnamed, Carson McCullers's novel teems with the names of places both near and distant. Frankie's immediate world remains small, inhabited by the family's cook and children's companion Berenice Sadie Brown, her young cousin John Henry West, her father Royal, and a handful of Berenice's friends and family. However, time and place foster a growing awareness of the world outside Frankie's hometown. The omnipresent radio broadcasts heard in the Addams kitchen detailing the events of World War II thrust exotic places into the forefront of Frankie's mind: "China, Peachville, New Zealand, Paris, Cincinnati, [and] Rome." In addition, the impending marriage of brother Jarvis, previously stationed with the army in Alaska, to Janice Evans contributes to Frankie's growing restlessness. The desire "to leave the town and go to some place far away" from the smells, sounds, places, and people Frankie knows so very well becomes irresistible. In *The Member of the Wedding*, Frankie Addams is at war with her feelings about the primacy of the familiar and the promise of the unknown. She feels both apart and separate from all around her: Yet, it is this small community and the people in it who support her in her greatest moment of crisis as she crosses the threshold between innocence and experience.

To escape, Frankie constructs a fantasy: She will join her brother Jarvis and his bride Janice; the three will "go into the world and . . . always be together" where she will be freed from familiar bonds and free to forge new ones. On the morning before the wedding, as the new F. Jasmine takes a final stroll through the familiar streets, we witness the bittersweet and complex relationship she has with her community. Yet, despite Berenice's admonitions to the contrary, Frankie feels safe enough to walk these streets alone. Perhaps it is the influx of soldiers from the nearby army base, who fill the sidewalks with "glad, loud gangs" as they walk hand in hand with "grown girls," which adds a flavor of adventure and danger. F. Jasmine knows the town intimately, from the glittering sidewalks and neatly striped awnings of the main street, to Front Street with its glaring cobbled brick surface, its pawnshop and "secondhand clothing store," and warehouses, to the "grass-lawned houses and the sad mill sections and colored Sugarville." These landmarks are crushingly familiar with "the same brick stores, about four blocks of them, the big white bank, and in the distance the many-windowed cotton mill," and Frankie feels as "free as a traveler who had never seen the town before."

Although the people Frankie meets are "mostly strangers to her," they are also recognizable. With each passer-by, "[a]n old colored man, stiff and proud on his rattling wagon seat, . . . a lady going into MacDougal's store, . . . a small man waiting for the bus . . . a friend of her father's called Tut Ryan," Frankie feels "a new unnamable connection, as though they were known to each other." She realizes that she wants these familiar faces "to know her," and because it is easier to "convince strangers of the coming to pass of dearest wants," she begins to compulsively reveal her plans to escape. It is this "thrill of speaking certain words—Jarvis and Janice, wedding and Winter Hill"—that compels her to enter the "neon glow" and darkness of the Blue Moon tavern and hotel catering to the soldiers from the nearby base.

Although the people and sights Frankie encounters throughout the novel introduce an element of familiarity, it is not an entirely comfortable familiarity; there is always an element of distance in McCullers's writing. Frankie recognizes houses, streets, shops, and individuals, nearly all of which afford her an opportunity to reminisce about how the "old Frankie" interacted with them; still the members of the community, outside her family, remain nameless. There is the "street preacher, a known town character" (84), the "little crown of [Mexican] children" (73), the woman sweeping the front porch of a "lace-curtained boarding house" (74), the Portuguese bartender, the Law, and the redheaded soldier. Both the "old Frankie" and the new F. Jasmine desire visibility and connectedness to her community: to be known and embraced for who she is and who she will become. In order to do so she feels she must reject the known and look to the unfamiliar, the exotic, and the dangerous in order to establish a presence. Community is both a blessing and a curse.

Connor Trebra

McMURTRY, LARRY   *Lonesome Dove* (1985)

Originally published in 1985, *Lonesome Dove* won the Pulitzer Prize for author Larry McMurtry. The sprawling western also spawned additional books in the saga, *Comanche Moon, Dead Man's Walk,* and *Streets of Laredo,* as well as a television mini-series and a syndicated spin-off series.

It tells the story of the first great cattle drive from Texas to Montana, led by two former Texas Ranger captains, Woodrow Call and Augustus McCrae. Call is taciturn, slow to speak, and unrevealing of his feelings. McCrae is the more gregarious and rambunctious of the two partners.

Much of the conflict of the story comes from the supporting characters. Former Texas Ranger Jake Spoon, an old comrade of Call and McCrae, suggests the cattle drive as a moneymaking adventure. However, it is also his accidental shooting of a dentist in Arkansas that brings the sheriff from Fort Smith, July Johnson, into the story. Spoon ultimately leaves the cattle drive and joins an outlaw gang. Once Call and McCrae catch up with the gang, they are forced to hang the outlaws, including their old friend.

The climactic sequence in the book tells of McCrae being mortally wounded by Indians near the end of the cattle drive and Call taking his partner's body back home to Texas for burial.

While not based on historic events, it captures the spirit of that time in the West, presenting an authentic picture of the historic cattle drives by figures such as Charles Goodnight.

Ronald C. Thomas, Jr.

ETHICS in *Lonesome Dove*

The ethical themes in *Lonesome Dove* are more authentic in their portrayal of the actual time period of the American westward expansion than in the western movies of the 1940s or the television westerns of the 1950s. There are no Hollywood cowboys like Gene Autry or Roy Rogers in this book; the characters created by Pulitzer Prize-winning author Larry McMurtry inhabit a territory closer to where real people like Wyatt Earp and Wild Bill Hickock walked. While the female characters in the book fulfill some of the literary archetypes of the shrewish wife, cheating spouse, whore with heart of gold, and sturdy frontier widow, it is the cowboys who present the ethical conflicts that were a part of everyday life in the real Wild West. There are no true white hats or black hats but different shades of gray, just as the gunslingers of the past sometimes plied their trade as outlaws or lawmen as they drifted from town to town.

The central characters, retired Texas Ranger captains Woodrow Call and Augustus "Gus" McCrae, clearly stood for the side of right in their former careers and do so throughout the cattle drive adventure in this novel. However, each has an unspoken ethical code they exemplify in their actions and the way they interact with other characters. For the reserved Call, work provides value and meaning to life and a man is known by what he does. For the cantankerous Gus, plain talk is valued, even if his sharp tongue bites a bit into those he cares about. These character traits provide a way of viewing all of the other characters in the book against one of these two standards, Call's work ethic and Gus's rough honesty. The ways in which they express these values, Call's stoicism and Gus's gregariousness, provide verbal examples of the ethical frames through which each man sees the world.

The journey for Gus and Call comes in the form of another Ranger comrade, Jake Spoon, who suggests that there is money to be made in assembling a herd of cattle and driving it up to new territory in Montana. For two former lawmen attempting to scratch a living out of the dusty south Texas land near the town of Lonesome Dove, there is no money to buy a herd. An ethical irony occurs when Call, Gus, Spoon, and some hired cowboys cross the border into Mexico essentially to rustle a herd from the Mexican Pedro Flores. The justification is that the cattle and horses were probably already stolen from Texas and Call and Gus's outfit was just stealing them back. Two wrongs do not really make a right, but it is close enough in this world of ethical equivalency.

Spoon provides another ethical example in contrast to Call and Gus. Even though Spoon had the idea of the cattle drive, he was drawn more toward gambling and living on the edge of the law than the hard work of the drive. As he drifts further away from his former comrades, he falls in with an outlaw gang led by the sadistic Dan Suggs. Spoon had thought he was throwing in with a gang of bank robbers, but Suggs leads them into horse theft. Suggs next commits a brutal killing of two farmers, including hanging and burning the bodies. When Call and Gus eventually cross paths with the Suggs gang, they administer rough frontier justice, hanging the four members of the gang, including their old comrade Spoon. In the West, horse stealing generally was met with summary hanging; stranding a man on the frontier without a horse was a virtual death sentence and horse thievery was considered a capital offense (the cross-border rustling by Call and Gus's outfit notwithstanding).

Even though Spoon had committed no killings himself, he is in for the same sentence as the rest of the Suggs gang and he knows it, even though he pleads his case to Call and Gus. Guilt by association might be considered a logical fallacy, a legal defense, and an ethical failing by 21st-century standards, but in the late 19th century, if you threw in with the gang, you were in for the same fate. The four outlaws are lined up on horseback, nooses around their necks, waiting for the end under a stout hanging tree. Gus takes the task of whipping the horses out from under the outlaws. Spoon, in that final moment of clarity, knows his life has come to no good and spurs his own horse out from under

himself. Gus understands that Jake has balanced his own scales.

Toward the end of the cattle drive, Gus is attacked by Indians while scouting ahead. Ultimately, arrow wounds force a doctor in Montana to amputate his right leg while Gus is unconscious from the infection. Had the doctor not been a drunkard, he would have taken both legs to save Gus from the spreading gangrene. By the time Call locates Gus, the infection has become irreversible. Gus says that he would never have allowed the doctor to take both legs. In this scene, Gus acts out a problem of medical ethics that persists to this day. At what point does someone have the right to forgo treatment and die in what he determines to be dignity?

The final part of the novel deals with Call's epic trip from Montana to bring Gus's body back home to Lonesome Dove, Texas, to be buried. For Call's sense of ethics through silent action, he has to endure any hardship to honor his friend's deathbed request. In the arduous, 2,500-mile journey, Call comes close to dying himself. The act of burying his friend sorely taxes Call and provokes him to say, once the task is done, that he will be more careful about what he promises in the future. Still, with Call's ethic of work and loyalty, the reader is left with no doubt that he would do it again.

Ronald C. Thomas, Jr.

GENDER in *Lonesome Dove*

Given only a cursory look, McMurtry's 1985 novel, which won the Pulitzer Prize the next year, would certainly be characterized a "men's book," obviously in the western genre. McMurtry's saga draws much of its human drama from its cast of interesting female supporting characters. It is the interaction of the women with the male leads that spurs much of the interpersonal conflict, the plot twists and turns, and, by these devices, reveals more about the men than the reader could ever glean from their taciturn cowboy ways. The female characters in *Lonesome Dove* run the spectrum of archetypes from the shrew to the whore-with-a-heart-of-gold, from the long-suffering-but-loyal-wife to the attracted-to-bad-men to the long-lost-love. However, McMurtry does not turn these recognizable character types into clichés or cardboard stand-ups for his male leads to read lines with. His women actually seem to talk and act and react like real women would, a great accomplishment for a male writer, let alone one working in a traditionally male-oriented genre.

While McMurtry has said that he got the idea for the fictitious name of the south Texas town of Lonesome Dove off of a church bus, the term "soiled dove" was Old West slang for the prostitutes of the day. This is a convenient connection, as one of the most important female characters in the story is Lorena "Lorie" Wood, a prostitute in Lonesome Dove. She turned to that profession after being abandoned there by a previous lover. With a firm will and optimistic nature, Gus McCrae takes a liking to her company. Jake Spoon takes a liking to her physical pleasures. Once Spoon convinces the Rangers that there is big money to be made in taking a herd of cattle and horses up to Montana, Lorie sees that going along with Jake is her way out.

However, Jake is rough to her emotionally and physically, and it is Gus who keeps a kindly eye out for Lorie along the way on the cattle drive. Eventually, Jake leaves the cattle drive completely, never having been much for hard work, and falls in with an outlaw gang. On the way to Montana, Lorie is abducted by the renegade Blue Duck, an old nemesis of Gus and Call from their Texas Ranger days. It is Gus who rescues her and Lorie stays with the drive all the way. She never does go on to her eventual goal of San Francisco, which represents respectability and stability, but she finds that in the company of these cowboys and, in the end, a home.

Another of Jake's indiscretions spurs a couple of other female characters to bring Sheriff July Johnson into the main plot. In Fort Smith, Arkansas, Jake gets into a gunfight and accidentally shoots the sheriff's brother, Ben. Ben's widow, the shrewish Peach, demands that July bring Jake Spoon back to Fort Smith to face justice. Even though July Johnson knows it was an accidental shooting and no judge would convict the ex-Ranger on such a charge, July goes on the manhunt just to escape from his sister-in-law's nagging.

However, as soon as he leaves, his pregnant wife, Elmira, uses this opportunity to run away from home and seek out her old lover, an outlaw named Dee Boot. In a weakened state from her harrowing travels, Elmira arrives at a farm run by a woman who is caring for her comatose husband and two daughters. The woman, Clara Allen, takes her in and sees to the delivery of July Johnson's son. Elmira abandons the inconvenient offspring of the man she never loved and finds Dee Boot just in time to see him hanged for his crimes. Shortly afterward, she and one of the hunters she is traveling with are killed by Sioux and the reader never quite understands what made her such a hard woman. Along the trail of Jake Spoon, July Johnson learns that his wife has gone off in search of Dee Boot so he abandons the manhunt to go after his wife and he, too, winds up at the Allen farm.

As the cattle drive works its way north, the plotlines that had been twisting independently finally intersect. Call and Gus bring the cattle drive through at the Allen farm and it is here that the reader learns that the long-lost love that Gus has often mentioned is Clara. He had proposed to her 30 times back in Texas, but she preferred the stable, if unremarkable, life of a farmer's wife in Nebraska. Now, however, her husband is comatose from having been kicked in the head by a horse and she is running a farm with only two teenage daughters to help.

Clara is representative of the strong pioneer women that settled the American frontier, who traveled westward in Conestoga wagons and raised their families in sod houses and log cabins. The various story lines find a strong nexus here, just as the historical western families found their strong center in the character of the women that held them together. After a tender and melancholy reunion with Gus, Clara constructs a new family out of the various elements that have come through her place. July Johnson stays on as the man of the house, as Bob Allen has passed away, and awkwardly tries to court Clara as they raise his baby. Lorie stays on, too, as Clara sees only her character of the present and not her deeds of the past. One of the trail hands, Dish Boggett, takes a job as a farmhand to stay close to Lorie because of his long-standing crush on her.

As Captain Call takes his epic trip back to Lonesome Dove with the body of Gus McCrae to bury him back in Texas, he plays out the finale in what most readers would see as one of the ultimate man-to-man bonding legends. However, a closer reading of *Lonesome Dove* reveals that while the men might have started on a straight path, it was the women whose characters gave the book many of its interesting twists and turns.

Ronald C. Thomas, Jr.

JUSTICE in *Lonesome Dove*

Justice, the blind balancer of right and wrong, is put to the test in Larry McMurtry's sprawling epic of the West, *Lonesome Dove*. This is far more than a classic white-hat, black-hat story about good guys and bad guys. The characters inhabit a world that features lots of gray areas and concepts of justice are malleable things.

The two central characters, Captains Woodrow Call and Augustus McCrae, are retired Texas Rangers. One of the most respected law enforcement agencies in the world, the Rangers have had, from their frontier beginnings to the present day, a nearly free hand to travel the length and breadth of the state to investigate, pursue, and arrest any criminal. Only a very few men, those with a finely honed sense of right and wrong, can be entrusted with that circular badge. Throughout the novel Call and McCrae's sense of justice is needed to resolve various conflicts on a cattle drive from Texas to Montana.

It is another former Ranger, Jake Spoon, who presents the idea of a cattle drive to his former comrades, a money-making adventure. Spoon is already on the wrong side of justice, having just left Arkansas after the accidental shooting of a dentist. Spoon has been drifting since leaving the Rangers, gambling his way from one town to another. In a showdown with a mule skinner, Spoon's shot had accidentally hit a resting rifle and that rifle's shot killed the dentist who was walking on the other side of the street. His current reputation as a gambler and gunfighter would outweigh any benefit-of-doubt Spoon might have enjoyed as an ex-Ranger. Spoon's character and actions provide much of the tension in the novel about the nature of justice.

As Call and McCrae mount the cattle drive, the hard work involved doesn't suit Jake Spoon. He'd rather be drinking, gambling, and womanizing so he abandons the drive that he suggested. In the course of this, he joins a gang headed by the sadistic Dan Suggs. Suggs is clearly an evil character who not only shoots down a farm family whose only offense was being farmers but also sets their bodies on fire and burns down the farm.

When Call and McCrae's cattle drive brings them into the same area, they discover the charred remains. Even though they are no longer active Rangers, their duty is clear and they track down the Suggs gang. Once the gang is subdued, rough justice is summarily dispensed via strong rope and a tall tree. Spoon was not an active participant in the atrocities and initially tries to plead his case. However, Call and McCrae do not waiver, as Spoon has cast his lot in with the Suggs outfit and will have to share in their punishment.

Justice is also represented through the character of July Johnson, the Fort Smith, Arkansas, sheriff. The dentist was his brother but it was the dentist's widow who pressures July into going into Texas after Spoon. Even though it appears to be an accidental shooting, July reluctantly agrees to go after Spoon. In this instance, justice becomes a matter of personal vendetta.

July's mission is diverted from Spoon when he learns that his wife, Ellie, has seized this opportunity to run back to her former man, the outlaw Dee Boots. Again, justice becomes personal as July abandons the pursuit of Spoon to track down his runaway wife. After traveling with buffalo hunters upriver and becoming mortally ill, Ellie finally finds Boots in a jail cell charged with killing a boy. The man she thought would hold the key to her freedom from domestic life is himself a prisoner, truly a case of poetic justice.

Another character who represents the cyclical nature of justice is the half-Comanche, half-Mexican outlaw Blue Duck. A long-time adversary of Captain Call, this renegade kidnapped Jake Spoon's girlfriend (who had been traveling along with the cattle drive). McCrae leads a party to rescue her, but Blue Duck escapes. At the end of the novel, McCrae has died and Call is transporting the body back to Texas when he learns that Blue Duck is in custody in New Mexico, sentenced to hang. As long as it is on his way to Texas, Call decides to stop over and see the hanging. This intended moment of closure does not take place as Call had hoped. Blue Duck escapes from custody on the way to the gallows but breaks his neck in a suicidal leap to cheat the hangman. Despite already being dead, Blue Duck's body is hanged by the local sheriff because that was the sentence. Call witnesses perverted justice served twice as Blue Duck kills himself and then his body is hanged anyway.

In the world of *Lonesome Dove,* while the scales swing wildly back and forth between instances of terrible injustice and righteous rewards for the just, the principle of justice wins out in the end.

Ronald C. Thomas, Jr.

MELVILLE, HERMAN "Bartleby, the Scrivener: A Story of Wall Street" (1853)

In the summer of 1853, his writing career at low ebb following the critical and popular failure of *Moby-Dick* and *Pierre,* Herman Melville began writing short stories. "Bartleby, the Scrivener: A Story of Wall Street" was immensely successful among readers and critics when it was published in 1853 in *Putnam's Magazine;* today it remains a prime object of Melville scholarship.

"Bartleby," like most of Melville's fiction, is told in the first person. The narrator, a character in the story, defines the action of the tale, sets out its parameters, and provides his own interpretation of events. Besides Bartleby and the lawyer, the other characters are Turkey, Nippers, and Ginger Nut, scriveners and workers who are part of the factory-like office and perform tedious work for little pay. Through these characters Melville explores such themes as RELIGION, COMMERCE, IDENTITY, ISOLATION, WORK, and the INDIVIDUAL AND SOCIETY.

The tyranny of the marketplace had a personal relevance for Melville, and many critics have observed that Bartleby's behavior as a scrivener closely parallels Melville's own writing career or, by extension, the position of any artist in a commercial world. Other people mentioned as a model for the character of Bartleby include Henry David Thoreau, Nathaniel Hawthorne, and Melville's brother, Alan. The number and variety of parallels show how open "Bartleby" is to multiple interpretations.

"Bartleby, the Scrivener" is a many faceted tale, and the reader can thrill to the spookiness of the cadaverous Bartleby, match wits with the lawyer in trying to decide how to deal with the problem, or challenge the narrator's version of events, for the lawyer reveals much that he does not acknowledge.

Susan Amper

COMMERCE in "Bartleby, the Scrivener"

The title character of "Bartleby, the Scrivener" is representative of alienated workers in the 19th-century commercial marketplace, damned by dollars and deadened to life, and the lawyer, who serves as the tale's narrator, is revealed as a materialist and capitalist. The story can be read as an attack on the excesses of industrialization and commerce. The tale announces itself in its very subtitle as "A Story of Wall Street," the financial center of American capitalism. The lawyer, too, identifies himself first in terms of his vocation. He is a financial attorney, who does "a snug business among rich men's bond, and mortgages, and title-deeds," and who boasts acquaintance with, and admiration for, that quintessential capitalist, John Jacob Astor. Besides working for capitalists, the lawyer is one himself. The Wall Street business he owns is the image of 19th-century industrialism: a dim and dismal workplace in which underpaid workers labor at dull, repetitive jobs. The office is not literally a factory, yet the building, in the lawyer's words, "hums with industry." The scriveners might be regarded as white-collar workers, yet they are paid piecework—four cents per 100 words—like factory workers. They earn, the lawyer himself admits, "so small an income" that a man could "not afford to eat, drink, and own a decent coat at the same time." The lawyer's focus on money is further revealed in his many references to it. He tells the reader how much his office boy, Ginger Nut, earns, how much the scriveners, Turkey and Nippers, are paid, the price of ginger cakes and how many of them Ginger Nut receives for purchasing them for Bartleby. After Bartleby's continued refusal to work, the lawyer attempts to induce Bartleby to vacate the premises by offering him $20, and at the Tombs prison, the lawyer pays the grub-man to give Bartleby the "best dinner" he can.

The socioeconomic dimension of "Bartleby," established before the title character's arrival, is developed in the subsequent relationship between him and the lawyer. It is a development in which the demands of the marketplace triumph over all other human concerns. Bartleby, however, eventually refuses to do any work at all, repeating the phrase, "I would prefer not to," making him economically useless and causing his employer to give him notice. But Bartleby refuses to leave, and the scrivener becomes a permanent, non-paying lodger in the lawyer's office. However, business considerations, in the form of negative opinions expressed by business associates, intercede. Fearing for his professional reputation, the lawyer moves to new offices, leaving Bartleby behind. This action leads inexorably to Bartleby's removal to the Tombs, followed by his death.

The connection between Bartleby's refusal to copy and a similar reluctance on the part of the other scriveners is particularly significant. In order to make the social point, Melville attempts to extend Bartleby's story from the individual to the more general. The difficulty faced by the other lawyer who moves into the narrator's vacated law offices and then by the building landlord helps widen the social frame. So does the narrator's allusion to the murder case of Colt and Adams, to which he compares his troubles with Bartleby. Melville here makes the socioeconomic nature of his story explicit through the narrator's opinion that the murder could have occurred only in a business setting, never in a private residence or public street: "It was the circumstance of being alone in a solitary office . . . entirely unhallowed by humanizing domestic association" that "greatly helped to enhance the irritable desperation of the hapless Colt."

Commerce, then, leads to death. The lawyer consistently refers to Bartleby using death images. Describing their first encounter, the lawyer characterizes Bartleby as "pallidly neat"; thereafter the lawyer applies the terms "ghost," "cadaverous," "morbid moodiness," and others. Bartleby's desk faces a wall and the view, according to the lawyer, is deficient in what landscape painters call "life." And later he speaks of Bartleby's habitual staring out of the window as his "dead-wall revery." Long after Bartleby is dead and the lawyer has discovered that he worked in the Dead Letter Office he returns to the money and death images, "a bank note sent in swiftest char-ity—he who it would relieve, nor eats nor hungers any more. . . . On errands of life, these letters speed to death." Such sentiments reveal that the lawyer is still reducing life to materialist terms. Bartleby's life and death express the widespread existence of a mechanistic, life-deadening, freedom-denying set of values emphasized in America by increasing industrialization and commerce.

Susan Amper

IDENTITY in "Bartleby, the Scrivener"

An essay on identity in "Bartleby, the Scrivener" would seem to point to a discussion of the title character; however, the unnamed lawyer, who also serves as the tale's narrator, writes that "Bartleby was one of those beings of whom nothing is ascertainable"; Ultimately, the story proves to be not about Bartleby at all, so much as it is about the lawyer. He wants the reader to identify him as a good Christian, employer, and friend, yet he comes off in the end as a self-serving Everyman. Instead of discussing Bartleby, the lawyer promptly turns to discussing "myself, my employees, my business, my chambers, and general surroundings." Before Bartleby appears, the reader is introduced to the lawyer's other employees, Turkey, Nippers, and Ginger Nut. That the relationship between these clerks and their employer establishes a baseline against which to interpret the lawyer's subsequent behavior toward Bartleby is indisputable. A careful reading of the story reveals that the lawyer's acceptance of his clerks' imperfections is less a matter of God-like beneficence than of complacency.

For their part, the clerks do not seem at all content to "bear the yoke." Turkey's lunchtime drinking and his afternoon excesses, which include splitting his pens and throwing them on the floor suggest a powerful impulse to escape from his duties. With Nippers this impulse is made explicit, as the lawyer himself concludes that the clerk's real object in constantly readjusting his writing table is "to be rid of a scrivener's table altogether." The two scriveners' reluctance to write obviously prefigures Bartleby's refusal.

The introductory section of the story, then, quickly establishes a reality that lies beneath and largely contradicts the narrator's pleasant representations. These contradictions touch particularly on the character and behavior of the narrator himself. Specifically, the identity that the lawyer reveals in this introductory section appears in several facets, and each facet establishes a dimension or level of meaning on which the rest of the story plays. Thus the lawyer is revealed as a materialist, and the story develops the clash between his materialism and the SPIRITUALITY represented by Bartleby. The lawyer is shown for a hypocritical Christian, and this theme is developed in the rest of the story. The lawyer is also identified as a capitalist, and the story plays with perfect consistency as an attack on the excess of industrialization. And beneath all these levels is the question of just what these different identities reveal about the lawyer.

The narrator, after much soul-searching, suggests that he and Bartleby share "the bond of a common humanity." Such feelings induce the lawyer to accept Bartleby, when the latter refuses the order to leave, as a permanent, non-paying lodger in the lawyer's office. This is the first time the lawyer has acted from personal rather than business motives. He considers this favor to Bartleby as his special religious "mission in this world."

The lawyer's initial indulgence of Bartleby seems motivated by kindness, and his subsequent actions, such as his offer of money and his offer to take Bartleby home with him, appear to go beyond self-interest, although these are open to question. The money may simply make it easier for the lawyer to fire Bartleby; taking him home may seem the easiest way out of the embarrassing situation in which the lawyer finds himself. He has already told the reader of his "profound conviction that the easiest way of life is the best." We can hardly credit him with Christian charity if he is acting only so as to minimize his own discomfort. The lawyer's position toward Bartleby, however, is not without sympathy. As readers we can see that Bartleby is impossible, and we feel that Bartleby is odd, but we are convinced that he is honest. And we know that when Bartleby says "No," he is telling us the truth.

The narrator, however, cannot face this truth. He is one of those who says "Yes": to the discipline of the marketplace; to the good opinion of the well-to-do; to the pieties and proprieties of a casual Chris-

tianity. For Melville, this means the lawyer lies, and it is this deception about his true identity that is the focus of the story. For it becomes clear that the narrator rather than Bartleby is the real representative of humanity. It is not his failure to live up to Christ's teaching that makes him so human, but his evasion of the truth about himself and the nature of life. In creating this lying narrator, Melville has found a true Everyman.

Susan Amper

RELIGION in "Bartleby, the Scrivener"

A Christian reading of "Bartleby, the Scrivener" is invited by the overwhelming number of religious allusions in the story, which include the lawyer's repeated explicit references to Christian principles as the guide for his behavior toward Bartleby. These begin as more humanistic than strictly religious, with the lawyer's recognition that "both I and Bartleby were sons of Adam." They become more expressly Christian with his recollection of the divine injunction: "A new commandment give I unto you that ye love one another." Subsequently the view becomes downright Calvinistic with the lawyer's suggestion that his situation has been "predestinated from eternity. And [that] Bartleby was billeted upon [him] for some mysterious purpose of an all wise Providence."

Another reference linking the lawyer with organized religion is the lawyer's "indulgence." The reference lies in the sale of indulgences by the Catholic Church, a practice that precipitated the Reformation. The connection between these two concepts becomes more explicit in a passage in which the lawyer in effect attempts to purchase his own indulgence of Bartleby as future investment for his soul: "To befriend Bartleby; to humor him in his strange willfulness, will cost me little or nothing, while I lay up in my soul what will eventually prove a sweet morsel for my conscience."

The Christian themes in the story become more interesting, and more complex, when readers consider the imagery that identities the character of Bartleby with Christ himself. Bartleby's general demeanor, including his "wonderful mildness," is reminiscent of Christ's. His association with a source of natural light coming into the office from above suggests Christ as "the true Light" (John 1:9). The ginger nuts that are his only food are described as "wafers," a reference to the Eucharist. The lawyer also refers to the "advent of Bartleby" and to the fact that he is "always there." Bartleby is further associated with Christ by the number three, which recurs frequently in the New Testament. Christ is tempted three times, rises on the third day, and is part of the Trinity. Bartleby's first refusal to proofread occurs the third day after his arrival, and on that earlier arrival —and again later—he repeats the phrase, "I would prefer not to" three times. When the lawyer tells Bartleby he must leave, the scrivener spends three days before refusing.

Another suggestion of Christianity is the parallel between the lawyer and the apostle Peter. This identification rests chiefly on the passage in which the new tenant and the landlord of the lawyer's vacated offices attempt to make the lawyer assume responsibility for Bartleby. In reply, the lawyer denies Bartleby three times, as Peter did Christ. The phrasing of the denials reinforces the comparison: "I do not know the man," said Peter (Matt. 26:72). "I know nothing about him" the lawyer declares.

If the lawyer represents Peter, then his office and his profession can be viewed as the church that Peter founded. Numerous allusions link law documents with religious documents and law ritual with church ritual. The layout of the lawyer's chamber suggests a church. The end of the office that faces a white wall and is illuminated by "a spacious sky-light shaft, penetrating the building from top to bottom" resembles a church altar. The screen between the lawyer and Bartleby, through which they can converse without seeing each other, resembles a confessional. The lawyer's failure to recognize Bartleby as Christ, even while describing him in explicitly Christian terms, is ironic. The image of Peter enhances this then, for Peter represents recognition as well as denial. He appears in the Gospel not only as the apostle who denies Christ but also as the first one to recognize Him as the Messiah. That Melville deliberately intended this association is suggested by another reference to Peter in "Bartleby." This is the office key that the lawyer attempts to get from Bartleby. A common Petrine symbol in church iconography, the key references Christ's promise to give Peter "the keys of the kingdom of heaven" (Matt. 16:19). Significantly, this promise was made as a direct response to Peter's first recognition of Christ as the Messiah. The fact that Bartleby never does give the lawyer his key points to the fact that the lawyer, unlike Peter, fails to recognize Bartleby for who he really is.

Susan Amper

MELVILLE, HERMAN   "Billy Budd, Sailor" (1886, 1924)

"Billy Budd, Sailor," written in 1886 but not published until 1924, tells the unfortunate tale of a shining young sailor and the tragedy that befalls him. The protagonist, Billy Budd, is well-liked by the overwhelming majority of his crewmen and captains. Early in the tale he is transferred from his position aboard the *Rights of Man* and moved to HMS *Bellipotent*. On this ship he feels scrutinized much more than on the former, and the sight of a disciplining causes him to be even more meticulous in his duties. While he gains the love of the majority of his fellows, the master-at-arms John Claggart seems to bear him ill will. Billy finds out about Claggart's dislike from an older sailor named Dansker, but Billy, always seeing the good in people rather than evil, believes the suspicions to be false. An accident in which Billy spills food on Claggart appears to reinforce this, as Claggart reacts in a friendly manner. But an incident with a mysterious stranger leads Claggart to accuse Billy of treason. Billy, unable to verbally defend himself against the accusations and establish his innocence, lashes out and kills Claggart, which leads to Billy's own hanging. Neither the captain nor the crew wishes to punish Billy in this way, but the captain feels the need to adhere to the law for fear of mutiny. Papers pick up on the story and talk of Billy as treasonous, but the captain and the crew, aware of Billy's innocence, tell a different story and the sailor becomes a legend of sorts.

Ronald Davis

INDIVIDUAL AND SOCIETY in "Billy Budd, Sailor"

Billy Budd epitomizes the individual removed from greater society. Initially, Billy's blackness separates him from the majority of the society around him, but rather than portray Billy as the victim of deliberate racism, Melville describes Billy's skin tone as part of the sailor's beauty. His dark ebony skin distinguishes him in much the same way that his height and his jovial nature do. Another aspect of Billy's character that sets him apart is the overwhelming approval and fondness that other characters have for him. They seem to understand their distance from the perfection that they believe exists in Billy Budd. Everyone looks up to him, from fellow sailors to sea captains, but they also seem to see him as a better version of themselves, as something to strive toward. Billy's position at the center of his crew is short-lived, however, as he is taken from his ship, *Rights of Man,* and is ordered to serve aboard HMS *Bellipotent.*

Immediately, Billy is removed from a society of which he was the center and thrown into a society in which he is the outsider. Throughout the story, his actions reveal his uneasiness in his new position, and seeing another crew member being disciplined strikes fear into Billy's heart. The lashing causes him to put even more effort into fulfilling his duties; while he does well, he still feels as if he is being watched more than other crew members. Despite his uneasiness with his new crew, Billy attains a level of popularity similar to that which he enjoyed upon *Rights of Man.* Yet his displacement causes his behavior to change; when he is thrown into situations that make him nervous, his feelings of ISOLATION cause him to lose the power of speech. At these times Billy seems to view his difference in a negative way. His anxieties about his isolation, and the physical effects of them, eventually lead to tragedy. When Billy confesses his feelings of anxiety to another crew member named Dansker, the older sailor reveals that the ship's master-at-arms, John Claggart, bears ill will toward Billy. Initially Billy's innocence prevents him from believing that Claggart would dislike him, as he has never given Claggart any reason for doing so.

Billy's innocence, and his lack of familiarity with a meaner, rougher society, causes him to continue on with his duties and fall victim to a fiendish plot. When isolated from the crew and asked to "cooperate" by a mysterious stranger one night, Billy's naiveté causes him not only to threaten uncharacteristic VIOLENCE, but also to lie to others about the meeting itself. His feelings of separation, both from the plot developing aboard the ship as well as from the rest of the crew, cause his anxieties to heighten once again. He feels a sense of isolation when the stranger attempts to gain his help and again later when Claggart goes to Captain Vere with accusations of Billy's treason. When confronted with these accusations, Billy begins to stutter, and rather than defend himself logically and calmly, he lashes out, killing Claggart with one blow. His individuality, once a source of happiness for him, has now made him feel and act as an outsider. His rash actions separate him from society once and for all, as he is immediately sequestered and put on trial. During his trial, Billy remains unable to speak for the most part, but maintains his innocence and his sorrow at the death of Claggart. He also speaks to his anxiety, explaining that his inability to communicate at the time of the initial accusation was what caused him to lash out. Despite inner conflict, Captain Vere decides that Billy must be punished for the act and he is hung the next morning at dawn. Unlike many who face execution, Billy approaches it with calmness, and he utters praise, rather than a condemnation, of his captain just before he drops. These actions reinforce his goodness and individuality, even in the face of tragedy. While papers tell of his death as punishment for mutiny, word spreads of Billy's inherent goodness and his story becomes a sort of legend.

Throughout the story, Melville depicts many different versions of individuality. While many are drawn to Billy's individuality for its difference, Claggart is put off by it, thus making the master-at-arms an individual in a different sense. Nevertheless, Melville displays the differences in individual personalities and shows the many dimensions and forms that individuality can take.

Ron Davis

VIOLENCE in "Billy Budd, Sailor"
In "Billy Budd, Sailor," Melville situates his discussion of violence in the context of HMS *Bellipotent,* a late-18th-century British warship. Fear of mutiny runs high on this ship, as well as many others, due

to tales of recent uprisings, and this fear leads to stricter punishments for mutineers. While captains feared their crews because of their potential for violence, the crews also feared captains because of the violence that captains could practice against them. These two aspects of mutiny play into the central plotline of this tale.

Melville describes Billy Budd, the main character, as a beautiful, loyal, powerful sailor. His looks and manner are in stark contrast with the taxing, violent life of a naval warship. Yet Billy proves on more than one occasion that he is quite capable of thriving. Billy's strength and innocence represent the two sometimes conflicting sides of his personality. Captain Graveling of *Rights of Man* is sad to let Billy go when the sailor joins *Bellipotent.* Before parting, Graveling shares a story in which Billy's two sides are aptly shown. Once before, another sailor attempted to push Billy around. At first, Billy tried to reason with the other man, "Red Whiskers," but he hit Billy, and Billy retaliated with similar violence and gave the man a sound beating. Afterward, the man came to "love" Billy Budd, just as all the other crewmembers did. Most often, Billy leans toward violence when he cannot articulate his thoughts and feelings; when he grows flustered, he suffers from awkward and intense bouts of stuttering. This quality is partially responsible for Billy's downfall.

After Billy transfers to *Bellipotent,* he is accepted by the majority of the crew. However, violence surfaces again in the form of a punishment given to another crew member. The man fails to show up for his post and is lashed for it. Billy is "horrified" by the punishment, and he resolves to never do anything that would cause him to earn the same fate. Afterward, though, Billy continually finds himself getting in minor trouble for light offenses, so the fear of a violent lashing constantly hangs over his head. Violence eventually comes to Billy due in part to the workings of John Claggart, the ship's master-at-arms. Claggart has not taken to Billy and, for some reason, bears malice toward him. Melville suggests that Claggart's jealousy of Billy's innate heroism is the cause of bad will, and Claggart shows intelligence through the way in which he deals with Billy. He is not overtly violent toward Billy, but treats Billy kindly, to the point that the newer crew member is surprised to find that Claggart bears him any ill will at all. For example, one day at lunch, Billy accidentally spills his soup on the deck, and the mess runs right at Claggart's feet. Claggart refers to the accident as "handsome," playing on the generally accepted view of Billy; the crew laughs and the incident passes, but Claggart does not forget it.

Claggart concocts a plan to use the fear of mutiny to enact violence toward Billy. One night on the ship, Billy is clandestinely summoned to a remote area, where he is asked by an anonymous figure to "cooperate" and is offered money to do so. Although Billy doesn't understand what is happening, he does know that something is wrong and he threatens the figure with violence. Soon after, Claggart goes to Captain Vere with warnings of a mutiny, citing Billy as ringleader. When Billy is told of the accusations against him, he immediately begins to stutter. Unable to find words to defend himself, he turns and hits Claggart in the forehead, killing him almost instantly. This forces Vere to take action against Billy, and a drumhead court is appointed. Fear of mutiny is used to invoke a quick judgment against him; even though the lieutenants think the trial is a sham, they refuse to speak out against Vere because this too would be seen as mutinous. Billy is found guilty not of the attempt to mutiny but of the act of killing Claggart and is hung the next morning at dawn.

Violence is a central theme in "Billy Budd, Sailor." It provides the basis for the major turning points of the story; the fear of violence and the manipulation of that fear move the story toward its climax. Billy's inability to avoid violence when words fail him leads to tragedy, though Melville also shows that Claggart's manipulation of fear is a form of violence as well.

Ronald Davis

WORK in "Billy Budd, Sailor"

The majority of the narrative of "Billy Budd, Sailor" takes place within the confines of "work." When the story begins, Billy, the main character, works aboard *Rights of Man,* a merchant vessel, and he is somewhat of a legend for his work ethic. Melville compares his working silhouette to that of Greek warriors because Billy is extraordinary in both appearance and output. Soon, he is drafted into the service of the Royal Navy. At both jobs, with the merchants and the Royal Navy, Billy puts forth a decent effort at becoming a "good worker," although he is much more the darling of the former ship. In fact, when he is on the merchant ship, he is responsible for all normal duties, but his presence brings with it a calming effect. With Billy around, the other sailors feud much less, and the threat of mutiny decreases. His mere presence eases tensions between other sailors, and because of this he has an unofficial job as "peacekeeper." During his time on *Rights of Man,* Billy fulfills both of his jobs very well and is well respected by the crew. All are sad to see the good worker go.

Billy does not fare nearly as well on his second ship, HMS *Bellipotent.* From the very moment the two ships part, he finds himself in some trouble. As his former crew sails away, he shouts a farewell, which is against the rules of the navy. Having never been bound by such strict rules before, Billy is immediately seen as less of an ideal worker. As the story progresses, he often finds himself getting rebuked for minor infringements of the rules. After witnessing a lashing given to another crewmember who broke the rules, Billy does his best to take on the role of "good worker" among his new crew, although something, or someone, always prevents him from attaining the same high position he held on the more lenient *Rights of Man.*

Work takes another form for the captain and his lieutenants, as the fear of mutiny runs high throughout this tale. The story is set at a time, Melville tells us, when mutiny was common, and part of each captain's job was not only to quell actual mutinies, but also to dissuade any activity that could potentially lead to a mutiny. This is part of the reason for the strict nature of things on board *Bellipotent* and also for Billy's inability to be the good worker he was before. On his former ship, his presence helped to ease the fear of mutiny, making his old captain's work less demanding. Captain Vere, however, has to be on the lookout constantly, and as Billy hasn't been able to ease the tension aboard this ship, Vere's work is much more stressful.

Billy's work and Vere's work come into direct conflict via Claggart, the ship's master-at-arms. One of Claggart's jobs is to keep order on the lower decks, which suggests that he would appreciate Billy's peacekeeping abilities. However, he develops a dislike for Billy, and because of this, Claggart makes it his mission to try and harm the young sailor. After an incident involving a mysterious figure, Claggart lies to Vere and claims that Billy is planning to take part in a mutiny. Vere's job compels him to investigate this rumor. When accused, the innocent Billy grows angry and, unable to express himself with words, lashes out and kills Claggart with a single blow. Vere now has no choice but to reprimand Billy; not doing so would put him in direct conflict with his designated duties and would show weakness to the rest of the crew. Vere forms a jury aboard the ship, a trial takes place, and Vere is forced to sentence Billy to be hung. Still a good worker, good sailor, and good spirit, Billy respects the decision and sings the praises of his captain just before he dies.

To Billy, work is the key to good behavior and good citizenship. Aboard his first ship he is the ideal worker in more ways than one. However, when the ethics of work become twisted by Claggart's jealousy and deceitfulness aboard Billy's second ship, Billy is doomed to die. Because one man distorts the concept of work, two other hard-working men are put into difficult positions. Billy's severe emotional response, while perhaps warranted, leads to severe retribution, all in the name of duty.

Ronald Davis

MELVILLE, HERMAN *Moby-Dick* (1851)

Published in England and America in 1851, *Moby-Dick* is a masterpiece of American literature. It is the first-person narrative of a figure known to the reader only as Ishmael, who in a highly indirect fashion tells of his tragic adventures on board the whaling vessel, *Pequod.*

After informing the reader what drove him to go to sea and how he came to Nantucket in search of joining a whaling vessel, Ishmael introduces *Pequod*'s captain, Ahab. A lifelong whaleman, Ahab has recently encountered and fought the famous white whale, Moby Dick, losing his leg in the process. When Ahab recovers and sets back out to sea, he becomes obsessed with destroying the white whale, and through the power of his magnetic personality enlists *Pequod*'s crew to join in his vengeful hunt for Moby Dick. Prominent figures in the novel's drama include Starbuck, Ahab's first mate (who futilely tries to oppose his captain's mad plan for revenge); Stubb, the second mate; Flask, the third mate; and the ambiguously sinister Fedallah.

Moby-Dick's structure is complex and can be difficult to follow. The novel's early chapters focus on Ishmael's motives for going whaling, yet Ishmael quickly recedes from the novel's action once he and Queequeg board the *Pequod*. The narrative begins to focus primarily on the drama of Ahab's hunt for Moby Dick, and the development of Starbuck, Stubb, Flask, Fedallah, Queequg, Tashtego, Daggoo, and Pip as characters. Yet Ishmael does not disappear altogether from the text. The many seemingly tangential chapters devoted to educating the reader about matters related to whales and whaling are provided by Ishmael, who punctuates the story of Ahab's tragedy with his occasional reflections and meditations. Though difficult to perceive, the novel's structure has a deep unity: It weaves together the varied "cetological" speculations of Ishmael (which often have a deeply philosophical character) with the compelling story of Ahab and his quest to destroy Moby Dick.

Essentially, *Moby-Dick* is the story of two people on two different quests. It is the story of Ahab in his mad quest to destroy his nemesis, the white whale; and it is also the story of Ishmael the survivor, who continues to seek in the whale a symbolic clue that would help him comprehend the mysteries of life and the universe.

Aaron Urbanczyk

RACE in *Moby-Dick*

The mid-19th-century whaling industry was literally global; consequently it was multicultural as a matter of practical necessity. Thus, Melville does not exaggerate in populating *Moby-Dick* with figures from many and diverse continents, countries, and cultures. The economic dynamic of race relations, as Ishmael unabashedly observes, places white Americans at the pinnacle of economic privilege, while all other racial groups are essentially exploited as cheap labor: "not one in two of the many thousand men before the mast employed in the American whale fishery, are Americans born, though pretty nearly all the officers are. . . . [The] American liberally provides the brains, the rest of the world as generously supplying the muscles" (chapter 27). The fascinating racial pairing in *Moby-Dick* gives evidence of this socioeconomic racial dynamic. Most of the significant powerful white characters are explicitly coupled with at least one racially diverse counterpart: Starbuck with Queequeg; Stubb with Tashtego; Flask with Daggoo; and Ahab with Fedallah and Pip. Indeed, the comic pairing of Ishmael with Queequeg as fellow bedmates who become best friends and shipmates early in the novel offers a scathing critique of Western society's cultural and religiously imperialistic presumptions and hypocrisies vis-à-vis non-Western cultures and religions. While Ishmael maintains the superiority of his "infallible" Presbyterianism (chapter 10), he comes to admire the nobility and humanity of his pagan (and cannibal) friend, even to the point of joining Queequeg in worshiping his idol, Yojo (chapter 10).

Yet Melville's representation of racial difference does not reside merely at the level of highlighting cultural imperialism and economic exploitation. Racial difference becomes a favorite trope for Melville to delve into the complex topics of human psychology, ethics, metaphysics, and religion in *Moby-Dick*. Non-white ethnicity becomes, in certain sequences in the novel, the equivalent of pagan infidelism and moral evil. For instance, in chapter 96, "The Try-Works," the pagan harpooners gathered by night around the flaming try-works appear particularly demonic to Ishmael's imagination, and Ahab deliberately calls upon his non-white, non-Christian harpooners (Queequeg, Tashtego, and Daggoo) when he blasphemously baptizes his harpoon "in the name of the devil," using their blood (chapter 113). Further, Fedallah and his crew, Asian in ethnicity, are described as "tiger-yellow" in complexion, "like the aboriginal natives of the Manillas—a race notorious for a certain diabolism of subtlety" (chapter 48). Once Fedallah surfaces from his hiding place below deck, he is ever described in the novel as a demonic shadow to Ahab, leading *Pequod*'s captain to his doom with perverse council and evil intent.

Yet in crafting *Moby-Dick,* Melville doesn't content himself with easy and predictable racial binaries. As already evidenced in the humorous and humane friendship between Ishmael and Queequeg, racial whiteness is not always clearly good, and non-white ethnicity is not always clearly evil or inferior. In particular, blackness and whiteness become fluid and often paradoxical tropes for psychological, metaphysical, and religious realities of enormous complexity. Blackness appears early in the novel as a theological trope for sin and damnation; Ishmael comically wanders into an African-American church where a preacher discourses on the "blackness of darkness" (a reference to the darkness of damnation in Matthew 8:12). Yet blackness serves also as a metaphorical curative for Ahab's mono-maniacal hatred of Moby Dick. Pip, the disenfranchised young black cabin-boy on *Pequod,* goes crazy when abandoned in the ocean during a whale hunt, and his very insanity and vulnerability, which Ahab calls a "holiness," endear the boy to Ahab. When Pip catches Ahab by the hand shortly before Ahab's final confrontation with Moby Dick, Ahab proclaims "There is that in thee . . . which I feel too curing to my malady" (chapter 129).

Whiteness itself is also an unstable and complex category in the novel. While whiteness often signifies socioeconomic power, privilege, and advantage, it also signifies psychological horror, nihilism, and even atheism. In chapter 42, the "Whiteness of the Whale," Ishmael initially affirms the conventional significances that his era associated with whiteness (e.g., racial superiority, feminine purity, kingly royalty, the power of God); yet he proceeds to undercut such affirmations by turning the significance of whiteness completely on its head in his attempt to explain why Moby Dick's whiteness terrifies and appalls him. Whiteness, to Ishmael in certain moods, represents "by its indefiniteness . . . the heartless voids and immensities of the universe, and thus stabs us from behind with the thought of annihilation" (chapter 42). Ishmael goes on to call it the "all-color of atheism," and, asserting that whiteness is "the visible absence of color" and that all color is merely an optic effect produced by light in the human eye, he shudders to think that reality is actually a blank white by which "the palsied universe lies before us a leper."

In summary, Melville's use of race in *Moby-Dick* is masterfully complex, ranging from commentary upon societal injustices to plumbing the depths of the human soul.

Aaron Urbanczyk

RELIGION in *Moby-Dick*

The religious dimension of *Moby-Dick* should be obvious to even the casual reader. Many characters have biblical names; the novel is populated with references to Christian and non-Christian religions; and even whales themselves, particularly Moby Dick, are frequently described using religious imagery. This religious context gives Ishmael's narrative of Ahab's quest for vengeance an epic and cosmic dimension. Ishmael's search for meaning and truth becomes theological (a search for God and ultimate truths), and Ahab's obsessive hatred for Moby Dick becomes akin to blasphemous impiety (a perverse rejection of the divine order).

In naming his characters, Melville drew from the religious richness of the Bible. Ishmael is named after the spurned son of Abraham and Hagar. This allusion gives Ishmael's character a rich depth; he is the universal seeker and survivor who like his biblical namesake is both excluded from God's covenant (through Abraham) and sustained by God in the wilderness of exile. On the other hand, Melville's use of biblical allusion places Ahab in the tradition of defiant, blasphemous, and idolatrous authority figures (the kings Ahab and Jeroboam) who were prophetically warned by God to amend their wicked ways. Captain Ahab's namesake is King Ahab, a wicked and idolatrous Hebrew king; and Elijah, the crazed prophet who utters cryptic warnings to Ishmael and Queequeg before they board *Pequod,* is named after the famous Hebrew prophet who rebuked King Ahab for his idolatry.

Melville also makes use of sacred worship space and preaching in the novel to lend its tragic action a religious dimension. In chapter 2, Ishmael (still in New Bedford) accidentally stumbles into an African-American church where "a black Angel of Doom was beating a book in a pulpit" and preaching "about the blackness of darkness." Ishmael visits a second worship space, the famous "Whaleman's Chapel" in New Bedford, where he hears Father

Mapple preach on the story of the prophet Jonah and the whale (chapters 7–9). This visit is a strange paradox for Ishmael: The chapel is filled with marble tablets memorializing the dead lost at sea, which Ishmael finds almost an invitation to despair; yet Father Mapple's sermon concludes with a meditation upon redemption for those who, like Jonah (and unlike Ahab), accept God's punishment and repent of their sins. Preaching becomes a darkly ironic farce out at sea as dramatized in Stubb's insistence that the black cook, Fleece, preach to the sharks who are feasting upon the carcass of a recently killed whale (chapter 64). The whale itself is placed at the center of sacred space and religious worship in the novel. In chapter 102, Ishmael records visiting a third sacred temple. The pagan temple is both worship space and object of worship, for it is the skeletal remains of a whale itself.

Ishmael's visit to a pagan temple suggests another important religious dimension of *Moby-Dick*. The novel incorporates numerous Christian denominations and pagan religions into its fabric, sometimes for comic and satirical ends, but ultimately to emphasize the vastness and primordial significance of humanity's striving to know the divine. Ishmael was "born and bred in the bosom of the infallible Presbyterian Church," though he has no qualms in joining Queequeg in worshiping his idol, Yojo (chapter 10). Bildad, Peleg, and Starbuck are all Quakers, and Ishmael lampoons the doctrinal rigidity of their religion by humorously telling Bildad that Queequeg is a born member and deacon of "the First Congregational Church" (by which Ishmael intends all of humanity and not a religious communion). The crazed prophet Gabriel is a Shaker (an English Christian sect that came to America in the late 18th century). *Pequod* is also populated with pagans, including Queequeg and Fedallah (who is referred to as the "Parsee," indicating his alignment with an Indian strain of Zoroastrianism).

In processing the complex religious framework of his experiences, Ishmael distances himself from his doctrinaire Presbyterian roots. While at times feeling the draw of nihilism and atheism (see chapters 42 and 49), Ishmael does not reject the religious quest altogether. He tends to remain a seeking skeptic who does not claim absolute religious knowledge.

He remains one who ever strives to understand the inscrutable workings of God in his creation.

Perhaps the whale himself best represents the complexity of religious representation in *Moby-Dick*. The whale is the phantom in Ishmael's soul (see the end of chapter 1) who represents the divine, the mysterious, and the unknowable; and the whale remains the object of Ishmael's lifelong quest for knowledge and wisdom. Father Mapple describes the whale as the agent of God's wrath and justice (chapter 9). Ishmael asserts that the whale is immortal (chapter 106) and in his imagination compares the whale to both Satan and Yahweh (chapter 86). Moby Dick himself is referred to by Gabriel as the Shaker God incarnate (chapter 71), and Ishmael calls the white whale a "grand god" (chapter 133). The paradox of seeking religious knowledge is best expressed by Ishmael's musings upon the whale: He states emphatically of the whale "I know him not, and never will" (chapter 86), yet he also avers "unless you own the whale, you are but a provincial and sentimentalist in Truth" (chapter 7).

Aaron Urbanczyk

VIOLENCE in *Moby-Dick*

Moby-Dick is a novel permeated with violence and the trauma existing in the wake of great violence. Ahab, captain of the whaling vessel *Pequod*, was wounded body and soul by Moby Dick. Prior to the beginning of the novel, Ahab had fought with Moby Dick, losing his leg in combat with the famous white whale. During the long return home following this incident, Ahab became obsessed with exacting revenge upon Moby Dick. Ahab was so traumatized by this event that he began to see the white whale as a symbol for all that is evil and inexplicable in the world. In chapter 41, Ishmael observes: "all evil, to crazy Ahab, [was] made visibly personified, and made practicably assailable in Moby Dick." Ahab was mentally and physically scarred by his encounter with Moby Dick, and obsessive violence is Ahab's overwhelming response to this traumatic event. Thus, after the *Pequod* again sets sail and is safely out at sea, Ahab dramatically reveals that he has now devoted his life to hunting down and brutally annihilating Moby Dick, and that he will use any means available to usurp the will of his crew members into sharing his quest. Though obsessed with violent revenge, Ahab does have moments, such as in chapter 132 ("The Symphony"), when he meditates upon the futility of his many years hunting whales. Yet Ahab cannot avert his mind and soul from his obsession with destroying Moby Dick. When Ahab finally tracks down his nemesis and does battle with Moby Dick for three consecutive days, the white whale not only destroys Ahab, but also sinks *Pequod*. With the exception of Ishmael, everyone on board the ship dies because of Ahab's insistent desire to continue the cycle of retributive violence by doing battle with Moby Dick.

When the narrative begins (an indeterminate number of years after his adventures with Ahab), Ishmael is a veteran of the whale fishery and has clearly seen his share of fighting and bloodshed. Yet Ishmael, unlike Ahab, is not defined by an obsessive impulse to destroy. Rather, Ishmael is a survivor, who remains curious not only about whales in particular (which explains the many chapters on whales and whaling), but also about the mystic and symbolic significance of the leviathan, the ocean, and nature in general. Ishmael finds that all created nature is a deep paradox: It seems to alternate between violence and peace; chaos and tranquillity; and kindness and vicious cruelty. As Ishmael observes in chapter 119, "Warmest climes but nurse the cruelest fangs"; all within nature alternates between nourishing life and destroying it. Referring to the "horrible vulturism of earth!" (chapter 69) and the "universal cannibalism of the sea" (chapter 58), Ishmael frequently meditates upon how nature exists in a cycle of predatory violence, where the weak become the prey of the strong. Yet Ishmael also observes that in the midst of violence and chaos, nature affords life-affirming nourishment, what Ishmael calls an "eternal mildness of joy" (chapter 87). Indeed, Ishmael finds that he has been returned to a primitive, even savage, state by his many years of violent whale-hunting: "Long exile from Christendom and civilization inevitably restores man to . . . savagery. Your true whale-hunter is as much a savage as an Iroquois. I myself am a savage, owing no allegiance but to the King of Cannibals" (chapter 57). He comes to realize that the human person, like nature, is divided between the desire for peace and the urge

for violence, and Ishmael ultimately longs for peace. In chapter 58, he proclaims "as this appalling ocean surrounds the verdant land, so in the soul of man there lies one insular Tahiti, full of peace and joy, but encompassed by all the horrors of the half known life. . . . Push not off from that isle, thou canst never return!" In the end, the enigmatic Ishmael is driven by the desire for knowledge and a peaceful life, and his constant wandering is geared toward attaining these goals. He is the foil for Ahab, who is overwhelmingly motivated by physical, psychological, and spiritual violence.

Ultimately, Ishmael's tale of Ahab's mad hunt for Moby Dick concludes in nearly complete destruction. Ishmael himself becomes infected with Ahab's magnetic hatred for Moby Dick, but Ishmael survives the violent hunt. He is the sole survivor picked up by another whaling vessel after Moby Dick destroys *Pequod* and its crew. The first and last chapters of the narrative ("Loomings" and "Epilogue") clearly indicate that Ishmael is still trying to process the trauma of his violent experiences. Perhaps in telling the tale, and remaining for so many years in the whaling industry after his experiences on *Pequod*, Ishmael is seeking the understanding that will bring a level of peace to a life riddled with traumatic violence.

Aaron Urbanczyk

MILLER, ARTHUR *The Crucible* (1953)

Based on the historical Salem Witch Trials, Arthur Miller's play *The Crucible* highlights the effects of juvenile hysteria on one Puritan town. At the onset, the town minister's daughter, Betty Parris, is suffering from a mysterious illness that overcame her after dancing in the forest with her friends and a slave known as Tituba.

Betty's friend Abigail arrives at her sickbed and is questioned about the events in the forest. Abigail claims the girls are innocent, and Tituba is ultimately accused of witchcraft. Pressured into confessing that she works for the devil, Tituba turns back to God and names other women in the town who cavort with the devil. Encouraged by her confession, the young girls do likewise, including Abigail and

Betty, who is mysteriously cured of her affliction. Several women are accused of witchcraft and hearings are set to begin.

The accusations are fueled by Abigail's jealousy of Elizabeth Proctor, a woman in the community for whom she used to work. When she was in the employ of the Proctors, Abigail had an affair with John Proctor. Now she wants nothing more than to take the place of Elizabeth as John's wife. Though Elizabeth knew of the relationship and ultimately fired the young girl, the town knows nothing of their adultery. As predicted, Elizabeth is accused of possessing a "poppet" (a symbol of devil-worship) and is arrested.

Upon the arrest of his wife, John Proctor realizes he must confess and expose Abigail as a fraud and sinner. John convinces Mary (the Proctors' current servant) to confess to the court that Abigail and her friends are lying. Abigail, however, accuses Mary of witchcraft, and Mary in turn accuses Proctor of witchcraft.

More are arrested, several are hanged for not confessing, and Abigail eventually runs away. Soon John Proctor, along with several godly women, is set to be hanged. The minister pleads with him to confess. Proctor, however, refuses to comply with the court's orders in naming other devil-worshipers. Ultimately, those who are hanged die with honor; though accused, they refuse to confess they are witches or charge others with the crime.

Erin Brescia

ALIENATION in *The Crucible*

In Puritan society, a good name was of the utmost importance. Without it, one could expect hostility and isolation from his or her peers. This harsh, rigid way of Puritan life kept the townspeople of Salem aware of the presence of good and evil, which they believed could not coexist. There was no middle ground of which to be spoken; one was either a sinner or a saint, and the two were not compatible. Therefore, obedience to God was a must for survival.

The Ten Commandments were central to life in Salem. If a townsperson were to disobey one of the commandments, he or she would be ostracized until a confession was made. Not being able to name the commandments was itself a cause for concern. In fact, Reverend Hale, unimpressed when John Proctor can name only nine of the 10, reminds Proctor, "Theology, sir, is a fortress; no crack in a fortress may be accounted small" (65).

Being a Christian in this society meant attending church regularly and never breaking the commandments. It meant maintaining a blameless life and avoiding even the suspicion of sin.

These rigid Puritan values are what kept John Proctor from originally confessing his adultery with Abigail. His wife was aware of the relationship, resulting in Abigail's dismissal as their servant, but Proctor never came forward and admitted their affair. As a result, the townspeople can only guess why Abigail was fired. To Proctor, sin is something that must be dealt with internally. Sin is personal—and no one's concern but the sinner. Society, however, feels differently; an individual's sin is everyone's business. The Proctors are keeping secrets and the rumors surfacing from Abigail's inappropriate behavior alone are enough to encourage the other women to avoid her.

John Proctor has also frequently missed church services in the past, and has even worked on the Sabbath. This is enough to bring the court to his doorstep, concerned that he is involved in devil-worship. When Proctor explains that his wife has been ill and that, when he is not in church, he is at home praying, Hale tells him, "Mr. Proctor, your house is not a church; your theology must tell you that" (65). According to Hale's Puritan values, one cannot consider himself a God-fearing Christian and not attend church.

Abigail, who has been alienated by the townspeople because of rumors of impurity, sets the stage for the trials by accusing Tituba of witchcraft. Tituba is forced by the ministers to confess her sins and turn her sights back to God. To prove her faithfulness, Tituba is asked to name others she knows who practice devil-worship. This leads her to name Goody Good.

When Abigail sees that Tituba is not punished, she realizes that a confession will be the perfect opportunity for her to clear her name among the townspeople and bring those who had ostracized her to shame. She realizes that under the Puritan code, as long as one is condemning others, her name is safe. If she confesses, it will appear that she has taken responsibility for her actions. Accusing her neighbors of sinful behavior serves to highlight Abigail's innocence.

As a result of this, the girls begin to pass their blame on to others, including some of the most upstanding, spiritual women in the community. No one is safe from their accusations. Even those with the most solid reputations are now considered out of favor with God and ostracized among the townspeople.

These sinners are alienated from the spiritual society simply because their good names are tainted. If one is seen with a sinner, he imposes the opportunity for others to speculate about his own good nature. In this society, one is guilty by association. No one wants to be involved with a sinner, for fear they will be accused of sinning as well.

When Proctor finally comes forward to confess his adultery, it is too late. The court believes that Abigail and her friends have been chosen by God to cleanse the town of evil and reestablish order in society. Abigail's plan to become John Proctor's wife backfires, however, when he is sentenced to be hanged for witchcraft. Unable to confess her wicked deeds, she steals her uncle's money and runs away. With no husband or means of support, it is rumored she becomes a prostitute, thus continuing her estrangement from society.

John Proctor is condemned for not confessing his sin of devil-worship—which would have been a lie—or accusing others of the crime. Therefore, along with those desperate to keep their good names, he is hanged. The trials are meant to purge evil from society, but the ultimate result is the unnecessary deaths of innocent people.

Erin Brescia

COMMUNITY in *The Crucible*

Salem, Massachusetts, a theocracy, was a rigid, Puritan community. Because church and state were connected and God was the ruler, sinners were condemned in the eyes of the law. Since everyone was expected to adhere to this moral, religious code, one would think that life in Salem would be near-utopian; however, this was far from the truth.

Before the witch trials are even set to begin, problems abound in this small community, the setting of *The Crucible*. First, there is resentment among the townspeople. Mr. Putnam has witnessed the deterioration of his family's good name, and his wife is angry because she believes supernatural forces have murdered seven of her children before they lived a day. She ultimately blames their deaths on a midwife who served her during several of the births. Abigail, a former servant of John and Elizabeth Proctor, is angry because Proctor had an affair with her, but refuses to leave his wife and marry Abigail. Elizabeth Proctor is resentful toward her husband, who cheated on her. Because he sees he cannot make her happy, Proctor tells her in anger, "I see now your spirit twists around the single error of my life, and I will never tear it free!" (62). No matter what he tries to do or how very careful he is, Elizabeth will refuse to believe or trust him, even though he is sorry for what he has done.

Second, there is a plethora of personal disputes among the citizens of the town. Because the church and state are one, more often than not these disputes are taken directly to court for a judge with religious authority to resolve. Giles Corey, who comes before the court in defense of his wife during the trials, attests that he has previously been in court 33 times and never once needed a lawyer to defend him. It is his belief that Mr. Putnam has accused another of witchcraft so that Putnam can buy the defendant's land.

Reverend Parris is also at odds with members of his congregation, and he is afraid of losing his post as minister. Several prominent members have left his church, and there are rumors that many are not pleased with Parris. When his daughter "falls ill" after dancing in the forest he is fearful that his good name will be called into question. He does not necessarily want to cry "witch," but it would be easier for him if the events could be attributed to supernatural forces rather than to his lack of control over his daughter.

When the witch trials begin, the town is pushed into further ruin. Reverend Parris is afraid to leave his house, and Hale confesses, "Excellency, there are orphans wandering from house to house; abandoned cattle bellow on the highroads, the stink of rotting crops hangs everywhere, and no man knows when the harlots' cry will end his life" (130). The typical, day-to-day operations of the town are no longer a concern—not when anyone can cry "devil-worship" and send another to jail.

The community itself has fallen apart, and Abigail and her friends are in control. They are responsible in the court for determining who is involved in witchcraft, and their dramatic antics serve to condemn the innocent. Unless those accused confess to witchcraft, repent, and name other devil-worshipers, they will be hanged. Fearing for their reputations and their lives, they lie to the court. The vicious cycle continues as new men and women are blamed.

No one in the town of Salem is safe. When Mary Warren comes forward and tries to tell the court that Abigail and her friends are lying, Abigail accuses Mary of witchcraft. Abigail controls her friends, the court, and ultimately the town. The trial becomes a power struggle. If the magistrates choose to believe John Proctor's confession of adultery and Abigail's motive to condemn his wife, it means admitting they have made an error—an error that will eventually cost townspeople their lives.

Salem is a town in distress. The problems plaguing the citizens are magnified when they find an outlet for their personal disagreements in the form of witch trials. When the dust settles on these disputes, innocent men and women are dead and trust and unity no longer exist.

Erin Brescia

SPIRITUALITY in *The Crucible*

One of the most pervasive themes in Arthur Miller's play *The Crucible* is the idea of spirituality. Based on the historical Salem Witch Trials, *The Crucible* is set in Puritan Massachusetts. Puritans were known for their strict interpretation of the Bible. At the time, Salem was a theocracy, meaning the church and the state were one and God was the ruler. Puritans lived by a harsh moral code; anyone who broke the Ten Commandments or sinned in the eyes of the church could expect severe punishment.

The stage for the trials is set by young girls who are caught dancing in the woods. One of the girls removes her clothes, and the slave who joins them, Tituba, is seen chanting over a fire and boiling pot.

Rumors of witchcraft spread through the town. Because of her disobedience, the reverend's daughter is now pretending to be ill in bed, hoping to avoid punishment for her sins.

When John and Elizabeth Proctor are questioned in act 2, the chief concern is that John Proctor has not attended church regularly. There is a rumor he has plowed on Sunday as well, directly disobeying the commandment to keep the Sabbath holy. He is told that one cannot attend church in his home; to please God he must attend church regularly.

This is the least of Proctor's concerns, however, for he previously had an affair with the family servant, Abigail, which resulted in her dismissal by Elizabeth Proctor. Abigail wants to marry John Proctor, which means eliminating his wife. Ultimately, her sins become the foundation for her accusations of "devil-worship."

Abigail sees the accusations and trials as a way to quell some of the rumors around town stemming from her dismissal. She ultimately confesses that she saw the devil when she and the other girls were with Tituba. She cries: "I want to open myself! I want the light of God, I want the sweet love of Jesus! I danced for the Devil; I saw him; I wrote in his book; I go back to Jesus; I kissed his hand" (48). The other girls join in, and, having been forgiven, begin to name others in the town they have witnessed worshiping the devil.

By making her "sins" known, Abigail can, according to Puritan doctrine, set her conscience free. In Puritan society, a confession clears one of all guilt. If you are not with God, you are with the devil. Because Abigail has forsaken the devil, she can turn to Jesus and all will be well. As soon as her name is cleared, she is free to pass her blame onto others.

At the trials, Abigail and her friends are put in charge of determining who among the townsfolk are involved in witchcraft. Their irrational antics—screaming, crying, and their chills—are led by Abigail and are seen as proof before the court that dark forces live among the people of Salem.

Uneducated and superstitious, the men and women of Salem often attribute the death of a child, or a farm animal, or a poor harvest to the supernatural. Mrs. Putnam believes someone murdered seven of her children, because each one died before they were one day old. When Goody Osburn is accused of witchcraft, Mrs. Putnam knows it must be true because three of her children died with Goody Osburn acting as her midwife: "I begged him not to call Osburn because I feared her. My babies always shriveled in her hands!" (47).

In addition, activities that are not considered "normal" by society were also cause for concern. This leads Mr. Giles to mention his wife, who enjoys reading books. He is unsure of what she's reading, but he knows it's not the Bible; therefore, he wonders if she could be involved in witchcraft. Many personal problems are considered related to supernatural forces, as well. In this way, there is no individual responsibility. One can admit "the devil made me do it" and be forgiven as long as they set their sights back on God.

The trials become a battle of personal sin. The men and women accused of witchcraft who confess are given a reprieve as long as they name other witches before the court. Those mentioned are brought in to confess, and the cycle continues. The irony is that those who do not confess devil-worship are the ones who are hanged for their sins. The repentant "devil-worshippers" (who are lying) are saved, and the honest condemned. In the end, John Proctor refuses to give a false confession so that he can keep his personal integrity.

In Salem, there is no such thing as hidden, or personal, sin. Every disobedience is noted and many times a confession is posted on the church door. The problem is that, while town members are hanging the innocent, they are blind to the accuser's true sin in that she is guilty of an affair.

Erin Brescia

MILLER, ARTHUR *Death of a Salesman* (1949)

Willy Loman is the tragic hero of today. Overworked, underpaid, and nearing the brink of insanity, the final days of this unsuccessful salesman are chronicled in Arthur Miller's classic play, *Death of a Salesman.* Through the Loman family, Miller portrays the idea of family, success, death, and, most prominently, the American dream.

As the play opens, Willy's behavior has become increasingly unsteady, and his wife, Linda, informs her sons, Biff and Happy, of his recurring suicide attempts. With the return of his sons, Willy again finds hope in their future successes. At Hap's urging, the boys decide to open their own business, and while Biff attempts to secure their loan through an old boss, Willy visits his own employer, requesting a weekly salary and a local position that would not require him to travel. Both meetings are unsuccessful: Biff realizes that his previous successes were delusions created by his father, and Willy finds himself unemployed.

With nowhere to turn, Willy determines that he is worth more dead than alive, and that his life insurance policy will ensure a bright future for his two boys. He desperately wants their respect and assumes that, when they see everyone who knew him attending his funeral, they will realize their father was "well liked." In reality, his family members are the only attendees. At the conclusion, Biff notes that his father had the wrong dreams and should have chosen a career he loved. Hap, however, vows to carry on the legacy of Willy Loman—proving to the world that one can succeed—so that his father will not have died in vain.

Erin Brescia

The AMERICAN DREAM in *Death of a Salesman*

One of the most pervasive themes in Arthur Miller's play *Death of a Salesman* is the American dream, and the happiness and success that it brings. The issue in this work is not the dream itself; the problem lies in the fact that Willy Loman's vision of the dream is skewed. To Willy, the dream is not achieved by hard work and determination, but by being "well liked."

In a flashback, Willy and his sons are conversing when a neighbor, Bernard, arrives to tutor Biff in math. Bernard reminds Biff that failing math will keep him from graduating. Biff is more concerned about football than academics, however, and Willy does nothing to deter the behavior. When Bernard leaves, Happy and Biff tell their father that Bernard is "liked" but not "well liked." Of course, according to Willy's vision of the American dream, his sons have a better chance to succeed in life than Bernard because they are both well liked. This is refuted toward the end of the play, when Willy discovers that Bernard has become a very successful attorney, while his own sons' lives are mediocre at best.

The chief problem in the Loman household is that Willy's ideas and fantasies have distorted family reality. Biff is a petty thief who cannot hold a steady job, and as an assistant to an assistant manager, Happy believes he is invaluable to the company for which he works. When the boys decide to start their own company, Biff agrees to contact a former employer for a loan. Willy assures him that the loan is guaranteed, because the boss liked Biff. The truth, however, is that his former boss does not even recognize Biff when he arrives. Biff had never worked as a salesman like his father said. In fact, he later remembers he was only a shipping clerk. Biff lets his father's delusions affect his personal reality—leading him to believe that because he was "well liked" he was successful in all of his endeavors, which was far from the truth.

It seems that everyone surrounding Willy has achieved the American dream. His older brother Ben discovered a diamond mine in Alaska; Willy had the opportunity to join him, but he refused on account of his pride. At this stage in his life, Willy is borrowing money from his neighbor and passing it off as his salary. The irony is that Willy was certain this particular man would never be successful because he was liked, but not well liked.

Willy is basing his idea of the American dream and personal success on one specific salesman's story. Of course, this man was well liked. He had connections in many states and was able to work from his hotel room. When he died, his funeral was attended by hundreds of buyers and sellers. He was respected and adored. "And when I saw that, I realized that selling was the greatest career a man could want," Willy says (81).

At this stage in his life Willy is hardly successful. His salary has been cut to commission only, and when he is fired, his quest to gain the American dream is over. His only hope lies in his sons. Unfortunately, the only money Willy has to give them is in a life insurance fund. If he dies, his sons will get the money. This will guarantee their success, he realizes, because they are already well liked.

Willy has an ulterior motive in dying. Not only does his family need the money, but also he knows that when they arrive at his funeral and see all the men he worked with in New England, they will realize that Willy was an important person. The number of attendees at his funeral is guaranteed to certify his status as someone well liked. As a result, his family will remember him fondly and respect his legacy as a salesman and a person.

In reality, Willy's suicide will more than likely negate the insurance policy and the family will receive nothing. Even more staggering is the day of the funeral, when only his immediate family and his next-door neighbor are present. Surprised, Linda asks, "But where are all the people he knew?" (137).

Willy Loman is not entirely successful as a salesman, yet during his lifetime he has secured a home in the city that is almost paid for and has raised two sons. For many, this is the American dream. Unfortunately, Willy is never able to realign his idea of success with reality. Because of this, he suffers psychologically and dies needlessly.

Erin Brescia

DEATH in *Death of a Salesman*

In order to fully understand *Death of a Salesman*, it is important to consider the idea of death and suicide within the framework of the play. The title itself hints at what is in store for Willy Loman, not only the physical act of taking his life, but also how he has been dying inside all along.

Willy had grand illusions and many misconceptions regarding death. Because he was a salesman, and a "New England man," he has come into contact with many buyers over the years. He considers himself "well-known" in the area and, depending on his frame of mind, "well liked." Willy wants to die the "death of a salesman." He bases this idea on the death of another great salesman, who was so well liked that the buyers came to him. He was wealthy, died in his hotel room, and hundreds of men and women came out to pay their respects at his funeral. Willy imagines this kind of procession for himself, and, in his own way, looks forward to the day he will die, when his sons will finally learn that he was liked by everyone who knew him.

Willy's chief desire is to be well liked. This alone is his American dream. If he is well liked, then he considers himself worthy. But this is not his reality, and from early in the play it is mentioned that he has reached a point where he has become suicidal. When he is at his highest, he feels he is loved and can accomplish anything. During his low points, however, he is aware that he is not as well liked as he hoped he would be; he travels around the New England area selling his wares, and yet still not making enough money to survive without his salary. Forced to borrow money from a friend, he pretends that this weekly loan is his paycheck. His delusions include the idea that he is "indispensable" to his company, and yet his manager still insists on letting him go.

At the beginning of the play, his family is worried that Willy has had another automobile accident. There is the idea that these "accidents" are reoccurring and are not accidents at all, but suicide attempts. "The insurance inspector came," Linda tells her sons. "He said that they have evidence. That all these accidents in the last year—weren't—weren't—accidents" (58). His wife has also discovered another one of Willy's secrets: a rubber hose attached to a gas pipe, which proves her suspicion that Willy is trying to kill himself.

Why are there so many failed attempts? One could wonder if Willy has the strength within himself to go through with the task. Perhaps, in some way, he still feels that there is hope, that he can make something great of himself. When his sons tell them of their plan to start their own business, Willy feels that there might be something to live for after all.

When their plans fail, Willy's hope is dashed. His only chance to provide anything for his family is to commit suicide and allow his sons to use his life insurance policy to become successful. In this way, Willy wants to leave a legacy. His opinion is that he is worth more dead than alive, yet through his mental ramblings with his brother Ben, he becomes aware of the possibility that the life insurance company might not honor his policy if they discover he has taken his own life. Still, there is the added hope that when his family attends his funeral and sees all of his friends and the buyers he has made contact with over the years, they will realize that their father

was a great, "well-liked" man. "Ben, that funeral will be massive! They'll come from Maine, Massachusetts, Vermont, New Hampshire! All the old timers with the strange license plates—that boy will be thunderstruck, Ben, because he never realized—I am known!" (126). These conditions finally give Willy the courage to go through with his suicide, which is disguised as another one of his "automobile accidents."

Willy's delusions ultimately lead to his destruction. His faith in his personal American dream (to be well liked) has skewed his idea of success, and his willingness to pursue this dream at any cost is what has caused him to choose a career that does not coincide with his interests and who he is as a person. It is because he cannot live up to his own expectations that he continually falls short. Had Willy altered his perception of the dream and found contentment in the life he created for himself, his needless death could have been avoided.

Erin Brescia

PRIDE in *Death of a Salesman*

The idea of "pride" in *Death of a Salesman* is a complex one. It cannot be said that Willy Loman was continually full of pride, but at the same time some of the biggest mistakes he makes center around the fact that he was too prideful to adjust his vision of success. This is most evident in his career choice. More than anything, Willy wants to prove to the world that he can achieve "the AMERICAN DREAM" by working as a salesman. Unfortunately, this goes against his true calling—working with his hands. This skewed vision also leads him to turn down two other, very important career opportunities.

The truth is that Willy Loman was not meant to be a salesman. At his funeral, his family comments on how much he enjoyed working outside and using his hands. Biff confesses to their neighbor, Charley, that "there is more of him in that front stoop than in all the sales he ever made" (138). His family remembers how skilled Willy was at construction, adding a bathroom to their house and building a garage. As his hobby, it is likely that Willy found more pleasure in his projects around the house than as a traveling salesman. Unfortunately, Willy's belief that there was no future for him in construction led him to work as a salesman. Even though planting, building, and working with his hands makes him happy, he goes against these natural inclinations and chooses a career that he believes will help him achieve success and notoriety.

Another example of Willy's pride is evidenced in his not going to work for his brother, a wealthy mine owner. Ben had prospects in Alaska, and, in a flashback, asks Willy why he does not want to help him. The offer is on the table, and it will make him rich. Willy, however, with his skewed vision of success, believes that he and his boys are on the precipice of something great. He chooses to stay in the city and continues to live out his miserable existence, hoping that a better future is just on the horizon.

When Willy is nearing his lowest point, he is offered a job working for Charley, his neighbor. Instead of accepting it, Willy assures him that he already has a job, and that he likes being a salesman. The truth is that Willy has just been fired. Charley does not understand why Willy will not work for him because it is a guaranteed salary. Willy never explains his reasoning, and refuses to work for Charley, even though he is no longer employed.

This is where Willy's pride problem becomes complicated. He will not take a job from Charley, but he has no problem taking his money. After refusing to work for him, Willy admits to his neighbor that he needs to pay his insurance bill, and that he does not have the money. "I'm keeping strict accounts," Willy tells Charley (98). It is learned through this encounter that Willy has sought Charley out every week for money. Charley does not know what Willy is doing with the money he gives him, or how Willy will survive without employment, but lends him the money just the same and urges him to take care of himself (98).

There is also nothing prideful in Willy's suicide at the end of the play. There have been many failed attempts, as Linda mentions to her sons that Willy's car accidents were not accidents at all, and that she found a rubber hose in the basement where Willy tried to asphyxiate himself. His final attempt, which is a success, comes with the realization that his sons will be better off if he is dead. He dreams of the wonderful things they will be able to do with the insurance money. His suicide, in fact, is a very self-less act, one of the few Willy manages during the course of his life.

Willy Loman is a very simple yet complicated character. He is unwilling to accept anything other than the life he has chosen for himself, even as it drives his family to ruin. He is, however, willing to throw his entire life away on the prospect that his death will bring success and a good name for his two sons. Willy should have chosen a different career, one he was more equipped for, and adjusted his perception of success. Ultimately, Willy's pride keeps him believing that his future depends on his being "well liked" as a salesman.

Erin Brescia

MILTON, JOHN *Paradise Lost* (1667)

Amid the volumes of Milton's poetry and prose, where can the average, modern reader begin to understand *Paradise Lost*? In a likely place: the beginning (1:1–26). John Milton establishes the poem's rhetorical situation by first identifying at least two characters who participate in the narration: the "Muse" and the "I" (Milton's poetic persona). The fall of humanity, or the story told in the Book of Genesis, is the subject of the poem, established by the opening line: "Of Man's First Disobedience" (1: 1). He further establishes the epic form that his poem is to follow, by echoing Homer's formal petition to the Muse, with the command to "Sing Heav'nly Muse" (1: 6). Fourth, when Milton's poet calls on the "Spirit" for illumination and support, we see the poet's audience and primary purpose: "That to the highth of this great Argument / I may assert Eternal Providence, / And justify the ways of God to men" (1:24–26). In other words, the poem will attempt to explain why and how man and woman "fell" in the Garden of Eden. But *Paradise Lost* seems to show the impossibility of such a justification; here we see that Milton's ends may differ from the speaker's in the poem. Similar to Milton's poem "Lycidas" (1638), *Paradise Lost* is an outstanding imitation of a poem written by a "hireling" (or bad) poet, who does not share the same perspective of the Fall as the author. Although designed to confront the tragedy of the fall (Gen. 3), the poem broaches its subject, as "Lycidas," often to satirically critique the fallacious view of its poet.

Jereme Wade Skinner

FREEDOM in *Paradise Lost*

John Milton exposes the tragic nature of *Paradise Lost* in part through freedom, a theme containing three distinct, yet interlocking, aspects: the spiritual, the domestic, and the political. The Archangel Michael provides a paradigm for understanding the entire poem's presentation of liberty, by juxtaposing these facets in his dialogue with Adam in book 12, using the concept of free will to emphasize the tragic nature of the Fall.

For Michael, the Fall marks the moment at which humans lose the liberty of free will enjoyed in a world without sin. When he speaks of Adam's descendant, who builds the tower of Babel (Gen. 11:4–9), Michael says that this action "subdue[s] / Rational libertie" (12:81–82). But, in order to distinguish this kind of freedom from pre-Fall liberty, Michael explains that, "Since thy original lapse, true Libertie / Is lost" (12:83–84). Thus, "true Libertie" is pre-Fall liberty, and subdued "rational libertie" pertains to post-Fall humanity. According to Michael, pre-Fall freedom is always interconnected with "right Reason" (12:84–85). Adam echoes Michael's description of "true Libertie" in his dialogue with Eve, where he says that "God left free the Will, for what obeyes / Reason, is free, and Reason he made right" (9:351–352). But, according to Adam, although "right," "Reason," if deceived, can "misinforme the Will / To do what God expresly hath forbid" (9:354–356). In book 5, the Angel Raphael warns Adam that "God made thee perfet, not immutable; / And good he made thee, but to persevere / He left it in thy power" (5:524–526). Thus, the power God gives Adam and Eve to persevere involves a right reason, but not a reason incapable of misdirecting the will. For Raphael, choosing rightly in the face of deception involves more than just reason; it also necessitates obedience.

Michael's phrase "thy original lapse" refers to what many theologians of Milton's era and beyond call "original sin" or "the Fall." This "lapse" is the moment Adam and Eve disobey God's command-

ment by eating the fruit of the tree of knowledge of good and evil (see book 9 and Genesis 3). According to Paul in the New Testament (KJV, 1611), "by one man sin entered into the world, and death by sin; and so death passed upon all men, for that all have sinned" (Romans 5:12). English Reformers of the 17th century, however, emphasized the all-pervasiveness of sin and death in humanity after the Fall, in the Calvinistic doctrine called "total depravity." According to this doctrine, sin affects even the human will and the ability to reason. Thus, the sinful will inclines toward disobedience rather than obedience. Michael reflects this perspective when he says that "Reason" in a sinful person is often "obscur'd, or not obeyd" (12:86). When this happens, he says desires and passions subsume reason. When sinful desires and passions govern the will, humans are reduced to what Michael calls "servitude" (12:89). Human servitude involves permitting "Within himself unworthie Powers to reign / Over free Reason" (12:91–92).

Michael melds together the internal and external elements of freedom with a discussion of the political aspect of liberty. For Michael, the person who allows "unworthie Powers to reign / Over free Reason, God in Judgement just / Subjects him from without to violent Lords" (12:91–93). These "Tyrant[s]" often, according to Michael, deprive the person of his/her "outward freedom" (12:95) through enslavement. Hence, the poet's previous reference to the "Government" controlled by sinful desires and passions and void of Reason also subtly refers to the political form of "Tyrannie." Tyranny, however, can manifest itself in the domestic sphere. Adam does not restrict Eve's movement in the face of Satan's "lurking" presence, because "force upon free Will hath here [in Paradise] no place" (9:11–74). External force can exist only in an imperfect environment, because it necessitates internal imprisonment. For Michael, as well as Adam, internal servitude leads to external enslavement. But internal servitude is not merely a moral problem. Michael's references to "desires" and "Passions" also allude to Paul's description of spiritual enslavement in the New Testament book of Ephesians. For Paul, all Christians, including himself, prior to experiencing the mercy and love of God, fulfilled sinful lusts and desires, because they walked "according to the prince of the power of the air" (Ephesians 2:1–2)—a reference to Satan and an echo of Michael's phrase, the "unworthie Powers."

Thus, for Milton, the loss of Paradise is the loss of "true Libertie." Although Satan and his "crew" of fallen angels do not possess any hope of real freedom, Adam and Eve, as well as their descendants, hope to possess what Michael calls "a Paradise within thee, happier farr" (12:586).

Jereme Wade Skinner

LOVE in *Paradise Lost*

For the poet of *Paradise Lost,* the fall profoundly impacts all subsequent human relationships, especially the most intimate of them—marriage. Although Adam and Eve's marriage suffers before God judges them, after this judgment they contemplate seriously the uncertainty of their future together. Ultimately, they agree to repent of their sin, rather than commit suicide. Eve wants to bear all of the punishment, but Adam quickly dismisses this option as impossible, since prayers, he says, cannot "alter high Decrees" (see 10:952–957). Alternatively, Adam proposes that the couple cease their contention and "strive / In offices of Love," (10:959–960). Thus, through Adam and Eve's marriage, the poet demonstrates that human love in all relationships after the Fall is not the same as before, because the love between Adam and Eve now requires work and obligation, whereas before it unfolded naturally and voluntarily.

The voluntary performance of love in Eden before the Fall is represented in part by the semantic duality of the term "offices." To the Eve who "at his feet / Fell humble, and imbracing them, besought / His peace" (10:911–913), Adam commands,

> But rise, let us no more contend, nor blame
> Each other, blam'd enough elsewhere, but
>   strive
> In offices of Love, how we may light'n
> Each other's burden in our share of woe.
>   (10:958–961)

The conjunction "But" marks a turn from Adam's hypothetical consideration of Eve's offer to bear his entire punishment to a threefold command: "rise," "let us no more contend, nor blame / Each other," and "strive / In offices of Love" (10:958–960). Adam's use of the term "offices" invokes the semantic range of the Latin term from which it derives, *officium.* According to Lewis and Short's *Latin Dictionary, officium* includes at least two primary meanings: It can be a "service" performed either willingly or "of necessity." That is, an *officium* may be a "voluntary service" performed on the basis of some "kindness" or "favor," or it may be an "obligatory service" rendered from a sense of "duty." Before the Fall, Adam and Eve's love reflects only the former connotation of *officium*: They love one another because they want to, not because they have to.

The entrance of sin and death into the world, however, disrupts this perfect love relationship. That Eve's relationship to Adam will no longer consist of "Unargu'd" obedience (4:636) manifests itself in the abundance of qualifying terms Adam uses in concert with the phrase "offices of Love," words that have negative connotations: "contend," "blame," "strive," "burden," and "woe." These qualities characterize in part the fallen marital relationship. Thus love, which was performed in a perfect world only from voluntary service, must now be enacted also out of an unwilling heart.

Therefore, even spousal love in a fallen world necessitates a divine command. The fallen narrator foreshadows the necessity of commanding even the most intimate part of a human love relationship—sex—when he refers to Adam and Eve's pre-Fall "wedded Love" as something "God declares / Pure, and *commands* to some, leaves free to all" (4:746–747, emphasis added). Sex between marriage partners must be commanded in a fallen world, because it follows from loving conversation and intimacy with God in prayer—things unnatural to sinful humans.

The poet draws a clear connection between conversation, prayer, and sex in Adam and Eve's pre-Fall marriage relationship. Immediately prior to the poet's chaste portrait of their pre-Fall sexual act, the poet says that Adam and Eve "Both turn'd, and under op'n Sky ador'd / The God that made both Sky, Air, Earth and Heav'n" (4:721–722). But this evening adoration occurs after they walk through the Garden "talking hand in hand alone" (4:689). In fact, Eve emphasizes the delight she takes in this "talking," whenever she says to Adam: "With thee conversing I forget all time, / All seasons and thir change, all please alike" (4:640). Thus, in the sequence from conversation to adoration to sex a progression of intimacy emerges through three types of human intercourse: verbal, spiritual, and physical. Adam and Eve's pre-Fall sex is a physical expression of the bond they share both verbally and spiritually.

But in an imperfect world, such intimacy necessitates commands, because love cannot be assumed. The tripartite division—verbal, spiritual, and physical—corresponds for the poet to the three most intimate levels of human relationships: friendship, Christian brotherhood, and marriage. The concept of love after the Fall in *Paradise Lost* calls all humans to "strive" against the selfish impulse of bearing one's own burden, and strive for lightening "Each other's burden in our share of woe" (10:959–961)—"offices" that require loving intercourse in varying degrees.

Jereme Wade Skinner

RELIGION in *Paradise Lost*

Although the term "religion" appears only three times in *Paradise Lost* (1:372; 11:667; 12:535), the theme of faithful devotion to an object or person is central to the entire poem. The poet uses the terms "faith," "devotion," "worship," "belief," and "adoration" in various forms to indicate a character's religious orientation. All characters in *Paradise Lost*, whether demonic, angelic, or human, have a religion, because they demonstrate varying levels of faithful devotion to something or someone.

Religion in *Paradise Lost* is not exclusive to the pious; even the demons share adoration for and faith in Satan. Satan laments his own internal "torments," while recognizing that the devils "adore me on the Throne of Hell, / With Diadem and Sceptre high advanc'd" (4:89–90). The words "adore," "Throne," "Diadem," and "Sceptre" suggest that Satan and his followers see him as a king or ruler. In one of his addresses as ruler of Hell, by addressing the demons as "our faithful friends / Th' associates and copartners of our loss" (1:264–265), Satan unknowingly highlights the fact that he and his "friends" are forever entrapped in the very thing they abandoned Heaven to escape—religion. Yet now their adoration

and faith are directed at a false "king," instead of the true King appointed by the Father in Heaven—the Son. Although there is a sense in which the demons willfully acknowledge Satan as their ruler in Hell, their confinement to and suffering in the Lake of Fire is a constant reminder that God, not Satan, is the ultimate ruler. Satan represents this truth when he calls God "our Conquerour" and in a parenthesis admits that God is the one "whom I now / Of force believe Almighty" (1:143–144).

Similar to the demons, the angels in Heaven express their religious devotion through acts and words of faithfulness and worship. But, unlike demonic religion, angelic religion lacks the chaos of the kingdom of Pandemonium and aims only at God. After the Father commands all the "Gods" in Heaven to "Adore the Son, and honour him as mee" (3: 343), the poet says that

> lowly reverent
> Towards either Throne they bow, and to the
> ground
> With Solemn adoration down they cast
> Thir Crowns inwove with Amarant and
> Gold. (3:349–352)

Unlike Satan's portrait of demonic adoration, the narrator's description here indicates that the angels interpret the Father's command to "honour" the Son "as mee," by responding with a "bow" that expresses their "lowly" or humble reverence. But their interpretation also elicits a debasing action of "Solemn adoration" that goes further than their bow: "down they cast / Thir Crowns inwove with Amarant and Gold" (3: 351–352). For the angels, properly adoring and honoring God means removing any symbol of their God-like stature. That the angels "cast" these "Crowns inwove with Amarant and Gold . . . to the ground" suggests one very important detail about their worship practice: It includes an immediate, unquestioning, and "Solemn" or sincere imitation of God the Son's voluntary offering of himself for the punishment of sinful humanity: "Behold mee then, mee for him, life for life / I offer, on mee let thine anger fall" (3:236–237). Thus, the angelic denial of place in Heaven reflects the Son's "offer" to bear the "anger" of the Father by casting off his full divinity and taking on the "lowly" identity of a human—even a reviled and a murdered one.

Before the Fall, human religion shares many similarities with angelic religion, because it is unencumbered by sin. The narrator's glimpse of unblemished human worship includes language reminiscent of the description of the angel's adoration of God in Heaven. Before Adam and Eve hasten to work in the "field," the poet observes that "Lowly they bow'd adoring, and began / Thir Orisons, each Morning duly paid / In various style" (5:144–146). Unlike the angels, Adam and Eve are not in the immediate presence of God's throne, so they must adore God through prayer. But the couple's posture is identical to the angels: It is both humble ("Lowly") and characterized by a bow. Further, the poet connects the types of worship offered to God by the angels and prelapsarian humanity with the term "adoration."

But after the Fall, human religion shares the divided nature of demonic religion, because it is encumbered by depravity. The Fall marks the point at which Satan redirects Adam and Eve's religious devotions away from God and toward himself. In a dream, God warns Adam not to eat "of the Tree whose operation brings / Knowledg of good and ill, which I have set / The Pledge of thy Obedience and thy Faith" (8:323–325). Thus, when he eats of this tree, Adam destroys the "Pledge" between himself and God, joining the ranks of the *dis*obedient and the faith*less*.

In the destruction of one "Pledge," however, Adam unknowingly sets up another, characterized by obedience and faith in a new "God": Satan. And though he

> learne[s], that to obey is best,
> And love with feare the onely God, to walk
> As in his presence, ever to observe
> His providence, and on him sole depend,
>   (12:561–564)

Adam and his progeny do not always do what "is best." Adam's loss of Paradise, his "fall" into sin, leads humanity, for the poet, into a struggle between doing what is "best" (obeying God) and doing what is worst (obeying Satan).

Jereme Wade Skinner

MISTRY, ROHINTON   *A Fine Balance* (1995)

Rohinton Mistry's third novel, *A Fine Balance*, surveys India's social landscape during the mid-1970s when Prime Minister Indira Gandhi instituted a state of emergency. In particular, Mistry illustrates how Gandhi's sweeping policies of discipline, forced sterilization, and beautification impacted the lives of ordinary Indians.

Throughout the novel, Mistry weaves together the life stories of four main characters: Dina Shroff Dalal, Maneck Kohlah, and Ishvar and Omprakesh Darji. Mistry portrays how, due to a combination of economic circumstances and fate, these four characters come together serendipitously to form an impromptu family. Dina, a widow of 42, needs money to pay rent, and so leases her room to Maneck, a young college student from the mountains. Because Dina's eyesight has grown poor, she can no longer sew and so decides to hire the two tailors, Ishvar and Omprakesh Darji. Following a straight narrative over the course of a year, Mistry spins a tale that develops relationships among these characters and delves sporadically into the past to develop their individual histories, blending in along the way a colorful cast of minor characters: Ashraf Chacha, Ibrahim, Monkey Man, Rajaram, Shankar, and Beggarmaster, among others.

A panoply of themes emerges as the novel progresses; foremost among these are IDENTITY, COMMUNITY, and OPPRESSION. As bleak as their circumstances are, Mistry depicts "a fine balance between hope and despair" (228–229) as his characters face social and economic vulnerabilities with personal fortitude and dignity. *A Fine Balance* won the Giller Prize (1995), was short-listed for the Booker Prize (1996), and was an Oprah's Book Club (2001) title.

H. Elizabeth Smith

COMMUNITY in *A Fine Balance*

Mistry creates and sustains multiple communities throughout the novel: the community of slum dwellers, the community of Chamaars in the rural villages, the community in the northern Indian mountain village where Maneck is from, the *jhopadpatti* (slum) communities in the City by the Sea, and the academic community at the college Maneck attends. In addition to communities defined by socioeconomic circumstances, Mistry also portrays a variety of religious communities: The Parsis, the Hindus, and the Muslims are key among communities in the novel. The people within each of the communities interact with each other, sometimes becoming friends and even family.

Regardless of the borders between and among the myriad communities, there is a sense that they are constantly operating in tandem with each other. In spite of the strict ethnic, caste, and socioeconomic boundaries in Mistry's portrayal of society in the City by the Sea, characters traverse multiple communities, creating unusual but nevertheless lasting personal relationships. Community, a prevailing theme throughout *A Fine Balance*, also presents a paradox: Mistry's characters' sense of community allegiance is juxtaposed with characters' desire to transcend and challenge the strict limits of the community boundaries that determine their socioeconomic lot. In addition, while the communities Mistry creates are distinct, they are also superimposed upon each other: Dina's household alone represents a variety of different religions, economic circumstances, and generational communities.

The most integral and closely examined community in the novel is the non-biological "family" that emerges from dire economic circumstance and, perhaps, fate; Dina, Maneck, Ishvar, and Omprakesh come together serendipitously for one year to forge an interdependent group of individuals from vastly diverse communities. Living together under one cramped apartment roof, Mistry brings together people from a variety of competing sectors in Indian society: Parsis and Hindus, well-off and very poor, educated and unschooled, young and middle-aged. Initially, these characters are wary of each other: Dina, a harsh taskmaster at first, watches over the tailors' every move, and she bosses Maneck around; the tailors, Ishvar and Omprakesh Darji, while desperate to find employment, worry that Dina is taking advantage of them, and Maneck often serves as a compassionate intermediary between Dina and the tailors. Ultimately, as the characters get to know each other, they appreciate, learn from, and depend upon one another. In fact, the family they forge

cannot exist without each other. The boundaries of caste, religion, and social class are eroded and a new, if unorthodox, community emerges and new, mutually sustaining relationships are formed. The happiness and fulfillment each character finds in this situation is short-lived, however, due to the usual terrible circumstances that force abrupt and often dramatic change in the lives of Mistry's characters.

In addition to the novel's seminal family, which brings together individuals from diverse communities, Mistry creates a variety of other communities in order to explore issues that emerge in the novel. In the rural villages, Mistry describes the "untouchable" Chamaar community and the senseless caste violence against them. Mistry examines three generations of men in Dukhi Mochi, Ishvar, and Omprakesh, who transcend traditional community boundaries. In the urban areas, Mistry brings to life a community of squatters who live in the slums at the edges of the City by the Sea. In spite of the material poverty, the characters Mistry develops are three-dimensional and rich in humanity. They are generous of spirit, helping each other with finding food, employment, and housing and to adjust to life in the slums. Maneck's college community is yet another kind of community Mistry develops in order to broaden his landscape. The hazing Maneck experiences at the hands of his peers and the cruel loss of his friend, Avinash, at the hands of government goondas (thugs) illustrate how Maneck is unwittingly caught up in a web of violence.

A Fine Balance is a compelling novel because Mistry challenges the perimeters of these various communities and forces their participants to meet each other, to interact, and even to get to know each other. Characters move fluidly from one community to the next, yet Mistry is unrelenting in illustrating how the hands of fate can sweep a character from one community to the next with relative ease. Ishvar, for example, goes from being a hardworking tailor with good job prospects and aspirations for his nephew at the beginning of the novel, to being a legless beggar on wheels by the end. Similarly, Dina goes from being an insouciant, independent, self-reliant young woman with a wonderful husband, to being a widow struggling desperately to make ends meet, and finally, to moving back in with her brother and his family at the end of the novel. All characters seem to transcend ethnic and religious allegiances in favor of personal loyalties that they come to depend upon.

H. Elizabeth Smith

IDENTITY in *A Fine Balance*

The four main protagonists in Rohinton Mistry's *A Fine Balance*—Dina Shroff Dalal, Maneck Kohlah, Ishvar Darji and Omprakesh Darji—provide useful lenses to explore both how society identifies them and how characters identify themselves according to ethnicity, caste, gender, economic status, and generation. Issues of identity also determine the social and financial limits placed on each character's life; moreover, each character's survival depends upon confronting these limits. Dina Shroff Dalal, a Parsi, is a middle-aged widow who is attempting to preserve her independence; Maneck Kohlah, also a Parsi, is a young student attending college in the "City by the Sea"; and Ishvar and Omprakesh Darji, both Hindus of the Chamaar caste (the tanning and leather working caste, considered by other Hindus to be "untouchable"). The tailors, uncle and nephew, have recently arrived from the countryside to search for employment and to escape the caste-related violence in their rural village.

Throughout the novel, Mistry explores how these four protagonists identify themselves beyond how they are constructed by society, especially as they have been identified by their religion, which almost always determines their economic status. None of Mistry's characters are satisfied with the lot assigned to them by their highly stratified society, and yet they each possess the ambition to be more than they have been "destined" to be. They desire economic independence and opportunities, and they have the will to pursue their professional ambitions. Mistry develops his characters' identities by illuminating their responses to particular situations. For example, Dina's position within her immediate family reflects the status of women in her middle-class Parsi culture, and she is constantly battling her older brother's hold on her desire for independence. Dina's happy but brief marriage was cut short by a traffic accident; as a widow, however, she refuses to move back in with her brother and instead chooses to struggle on her own to make ends meet. Dina's strong sense of self-reliance is always complicated by her ever-precarious economic situation; still, she resists succumbing to her brother's desire (with her extended family's support) that she move back with them.

Maneck, the only child of solidly middle-class Parsi parents, has been raised in the foothills of northern India. His sense of identity emerges in contrast to his family: First, as Maneck comes of age, he struggles against the decisions his father makes for him; and second, he struggles against his identity as a college student at a time when students are involved in demonstrations against the government over an immense crackdown against civil liberties. Over the course of the novel, for a brief time, Maneck also develops an identity as Dina's "son" and Omprakesh's "brother"—identities that cross the social boundaries of the caste system. The two tailors, Ishvar and Omprakesh Darji, are originally from the "untouchable" Chamaar caste; their ancestors were cobblers, which is considered to be an "unclean" trade. Ishvar's father and Omprakesh's grandfather, Dukhi Mochi, made a bold and unorthodox decision to have his sons serve as apprentices to a tailor, a decision that had wide reaching consequences. Mistry's representation of Ishvar and Omprakesh's struggle for social mobility is not hopeful.

Throughout the novel, the tension escalates between who the characters have been born to be and who they want to become. In addition to the main characters, Mistry vividly portrays the lives of the poorest in India's society, both in the rural villages and in the city slums. While Mistry does not typecast his characters, the myriad of minor characters we meet throughout the novel give the reader a glimpse into the lives of ordinary Indians during the state of emergency, people underrepresented in literature. Dina's brother, Nusswan Shroff, and her best friend, Zenobia, exemplify the comfortable lives of an emerging middle-class; Shankar, nicknamed "Worm," illustrates the cruelty of daily life for urban beggars; Beggarmaster symbolizes an endemic corruption within the system as he simultaneously controls, manipulates, and protects the beggars for whom he is responsible; Monkey Man's deep attachments to his monkeys and later to his niece and nephew cause him to take revenge upon those who took away all the family he possessed.

While Mistry identifies characters by their socioeconomic status and ethnicity or caste affiliation, it is the way in which they choose to deal with their circumstances that identifies them as individuals with an innately human desire not only to survive but also to contribute to their community and to enrich each other's lives. Keenly aware of the daily injustices against them and perpetually at the edge of disaster, characters rely upon each other to face the inevitable struggles of their quotidian lives. Ultimately, Mistry's characters emerge as individuals with strong individual identities and ambitions of their own.

H. Elizabeth Smith

OPPRESSION in *A Fine Balance*

Characters contend with a prevailing sense of oppression throughout *A Fine Balance*: Dina is oppressed both by her family and by her society's lack of economic opportunities for women; Maneck is oppressed by his parents, especially his father and later by classmates at college, and he is oppressed by witnessing his friends' desperate struggle for economic autonomy; Ishvar and Omprakesh are oppressed by their Chamaar (untouchable) caste, by their economic condition and lack of education, and by their family history. Other characters in the novel are more or less oppressed—and in myriad ways—than these central four. Indeed, oppression is a theme that resonates throughout *A Fine Balance,* as are related sub-themes: cruelty, fate, futility, oppression versus justice, violence, work. Within the larger sociopolitical context—India and the City by the Sea, in particular, under Indira Gandhi's state of emergency during the mid-1970s—that Mistry creates his numerous characters victimized by constant oppression: the poor, women, children, the public. And oppressors include the economy, the rich, fate, the government, the "goondas" (thugs), family members, middle-men, religion, and emergency policies.

Oppression because of religion is rampant in the novel; it has a psychological impact on the characters and especially upon the decisions they make and their sense of themselves. Mistry focuses on portraying caste violence, but he also illuminates how other minorities, including Muslims and Sikhs, become targets of violence at various points. Mistry's poignant discussion of Ishvar and Omprakesh's family history exemplifies the injustice of caste oppression in prior generations and at the time. For example, Mistry demonstrates the violent conflicts between Hindus and Muslims in Indian communities. What would have happened to Ashraf Chacha's family had he not taken in Dukhi Mochi's sons, Ishvara and Narayan? Surely they would all have been murdered.

In addition, Mistry critiques the government's oppression of the poor in countless situations where minor cruelties continue to add up to monumental disasters in individual lives: by wiping out the slums, by forcing young men to get vasectomies (sometimes more than once), by forcing beggars to work without pay, and by stealing and mutilating young children to serve as beggars who will generate a more lucrative yield because they are more pitiful. The government violently, and sometimes ridiculously, enforces a sterilization and birth control program that robs the poor of their dignity and their ability to reproduce. Corruption is rampant. The beggars are economically and socially oppressed, and their lives spiral into despair. In the stories Mistry tells of minor characters such as Monkey Man, Avinash, Shankar, Worm, Rajaram, Vasantrao, and Ibrahim, he illustrates the myriad ways ordinary Indians are oppressed, by the government, by their economic circumstances, by the choices they make. As the Sikh taxi driver informs Maneck when he returns to India after working in the Gulf for eight years, "'Of course, for ordinary people, nothing has changed. . . . Living each day is to face one emergency or another'": The government continues to raze poor people's homes and slums in the cities, and in the countryside the officials promise much needed wells and fertilizer only if their sterilization quotas are met.

Finally, while the government overtly oppresses its subjects, the social conditions of the times also serve as oppressors in the novel: the lack of adequate housing, food, water—let alone education and employment—destroys the lives of multitudes of the City by the Sea's poorest urban dwellers. Mistry does not refer directly to Indira Gandhi by name; instead his characters refer to the unnamed "Prime Minister." Dina yearns for independence but understands, especially later in the novel, that she also needs protection and that she is part of a larger political web that demands her allegiance. Dina's decision to remain independent costs her both financially and emotionally because she does not have the support and protection of her immediate family. While Dina struggles to maintain an income so she can be independent of her well-intentioned but nevertheless oppressive brother, the tailors, Ishvar and Omprakesh Darji, are often homeless and they succumb numerous times to circumstance. Ultimately, they pay enormous prices for attempting to move beyond the confines of what society allows them as Chamaars: Ishvar loses his legs and Omprakesh is castrated, a cruel and unjust punishment for standing up for his rights. By the end of the novel, Dina is reduced to living with her brother again, and the tailors have been reduced, physically as well as psychologically, to begging, and Maneck gives up completely, swallowed by the relentless oppression he witnesses—and lives vicariously through Dina, Ishvar, and Omprakesh.

H. Elizabeth Smith

MOLIÈRE   *The Misanthrope* (1666)

The Misanthrope is a play by Jean-Baptiste Poquelin—better known as Molière—and was first staged in Paris in 1666. Molière's masterpiece is often defined as a comedy of manners, because of its deep social critique; but it could be also seen as a comedy of character, because of the preeminence of the main character based on moral issues—the Misanthrope—Alceste. The reader will also find some farcical elements, borrowed from the Italian players of the commedia dell'arte, who at the time were working in the same theater in Paris as Molière.

The play aims to be a critical fresco of the 17th-century Sun King's court, with its hypocrisy, false appearances, and well-mannered aristocrats wholly dedicated to attending insignificant social events. Indeed, three main themes stand out in the play: a critique of contemporary ETHICS, the troubled relationship between the INDIVIDUAL AND SOCIETY,

and the Misanthrope's ISOLATION. Alceste is both a tragic and a comic character, since his statements on society and on the human condition can be really penetrating, while his excesses make him a comic masque or, as his confidant Philinte tells him, a ridiculous person, at least as compared to the rest of the aristocratic milieu to which he belongs.

On several occasions, the play shows some autobiographical features. Molière often uses Alceste's words to express his own doubts on humankind: The critique of the worthless poet Oronte reading his empty verses on LOVE, and the seclusion caused by Alceste's non-conformation to conventional models, mark the isolation of the man and the intellectual—incapable of negotiating his frank feelings.

Tania Collani

ETHICS in *The Misanthrope*

Molière's *Misanthrope* is above all a play based on criticism of contemporary society. Through the words and the behavior of its cynical and choleric hero, Alceste, readers can appreciate an ironic caricature of 17th-century aristocratic and Parisian habits and morality.

One can find two main complementary ethics within this play: the austere ideal Alceste pursues and the frivolous customs of the Sun King's court. Both are analyzed with humor and sharpness, with a special focus on their bad sides. Of course, since *The Misanthrope* is meant to be a comedy, exaggerations in both ideals occupy a larger space within the play than "normal."

In this perspective, Alceste is the excessive champion of sobriety and sincerity: He rallies against hypocrisy and empty accommodations of society's rituals, such as making "vows and promises" (4), or speaking with a "tone sweet and gentle as a maid's" (4). And from the beginning of the play, he stands up against the manners of his time: "No, all such modern manners I despise—Sheer affectation, sir, and downright lies" (4). Nonetheless, among all the Parisian salons' bows and vows, Alceste's morality is described with a tone of admiration by the author: his sincerity and his immunity to the blandishments of power make Alceste a modern hero. Unfortunately for him, all these virtues are only a source of misunderstanding for the other members of his upper class. Alceste's ethics is fast described: A man has to be sincere, "in every single word" (4). But this is rather incompatible with a society based exclusively on appearances.

The pompous lords and ladies' ethics showed in the play are even more caricatured than Alceste's austerity. The major representatives of this kind of morality are the two marquises, Acaste and Clitandre. The first thing Clitandre says, for example, as he enters the stage in act 2, is: "Goodness me! I've just come from His Majesty's levee" (30). And, at the very beginning of act 3, while speaking with Clitandre, Acaste confesses that the secret of his happiness is a life based on futile occupations. Acaste is in fact "graced with youth and fortune, and a family name of some distinction" (41). And he goes as far as saying: "intelligence and taste I have to spare; I need no erudition" (41); "I dress well, in the fashion of the times . . . my carriage is erect and manly; for my teeth—well, sir, neglect them at your peril! And my waist is trim" (42).

What makes the courtesan ethics of appearance incompatible with Alceste's ethics is ultimately esteem. Alceste often deals with the subject of esteem as crucial, because if all the social system lies on formalities, how can one recognize whether someone's esteem is true or false? The court ceremonial does not allow someone to say the truth to others, all the less so when a bad judgment is involved: "no man of principle would dream of falling for such cheaply-won esteem" (5), says Alceste about this milieu where everyone seems to love each other. There are no good opinions expressed toward the marquis's attitude, even though the wise Philinte tries to soothe the conflict between the two contrasting ethics of excessive austerity and excessive frivolity.

We could say that exaggeration is what prevents this play from turning into a tragedy. In this regard, Alceste's idea of ethics is both utopian and dictatorial, because he would like people to be true and talk beyond all appearance ("Let no disguise mask what you feel with flattery and lies!" (5); but, at the same time, he is not a democrat of feelings, since he wants everyone to behave like him. His wise confidant, Philinte, knows that the disproportion of Alceste's

rage makes him a comic character, not a tragic hero: "Your black moods simply make me want to laugh" (7). Alceste is a caricature of a man: He is a misanthrope and he hates the human race, "every man on earth" (7). This hate leaves him with little lucid judgment, and he doesn't understand that he cannot change the world with his bursts of anger. In the end, Molière is trying to say to his spectators that it is really difficult to be "normal," and that excesses characterize everyone's position, from the wisest to the silliest.

Tania Collani

INDIVIDUAL AND SOCIETY in *The Misanthrope*

The title of Molière's play speaks volumes about the relationship between individual and society: A "misanthrope" is a person who dislikes and avoids other people. Indeed, the main character of the play, Alceste, hates both the appearance and substance of the society he lives in, based as it is on empty and false ceremonies.

Since Alceste's values are sincerity and austerity, he cannot integrate himself properly into 17th-century Parisian and aristocratic society. Its salons full of women in pompous wigs and dresses chatting about fashion make him furious and willing to be alone—indeed, as he often says, he'd rather be in a desert. The individual's repulsion against society is made clear in act 1, when, speaking with his confidant and friend Philinte, Alceste cries: "For two pins I'd forsake the wretched human race entirely, make some wilderness my home" (8). Philinte tries uselessly to soothe Alceste's bad temper: "Good Lord, forget the modes and manners of the age and let frail human nature take its share of blame!" (8).

If Alceste hates society, the play makes clear that society returns the feeling, by isolating him and giving him the misfortunes he experiences in love (he will lose his beloved Célimène) as well as in everyday life (he will lose a case and have to pay a fine). Alceste is treated like a malcontent, incapable of enjoying life, although he is born into a wealthy environment. Philinte, a sincere and self-controlled man, repeatedly tells him not to waste his energy on such things, for the world cannot be changed: "It's utterly folly for one man to wage war on the world"

(9). From a dialogue among aristocrats in act 2, we also learn that two things cannot be forgiven within the microcosm of 17th-century mundane society: boredom and ridiculousness. For example, speaking of absent people, they say: "That stupid creature—she is *such* a bore! . . . She has no conversation, not a word" (32), and "His self-conceit exceeds all measure" (32). Although they are not referring to him—for he is present there—Alceste feels personally concerned, because he knows he is both boring and ridiculous to these people.

This difficult relation between individual and society is condensed in the complicated relationship of love and hate existing between Alceste, the cantankerous hermit, and Célimène, the obliging society woman. It is very difficult to explain why Alceste falls so helplessly in love with a woman whose behavior is so different from his. Moreover, he has an alternative to Célimène, the chaste Arsinoé, who openly shows her feelings for Alceste. Not even his wise friend Philinte can understand Alceste's love for Célimène, for he asks him: "This rigid moral stance you have taken up—have you by any chance observed the same in her whom you adore?" (11). Although the reader can perceive the mutual love between the two characters from their dialogues, Alceste hates that society so much that his own love is overshadowed. For example, he goes as far as telling Célimène: "You're constantly besieged by men, and really, that's too much for me" (24).

The perfect example of the falseness of society and the truth of the individual human being, almost tragic in his isolation, is the fact that everybody is described through indirect portraits. Human beings cannot entertain sincere relationships among themselves; Alceste is the only one who makes an effort at being sincere, but his uncompromising soul denies any constructive dialogue. For example, when asked to give a judgment on a very bad poem written by a lord, at first he tries not to say what he really thinks, but in the end he expresses his opinion so ardently, that he will eventually be sued. In any case, there are no chances for constructive dialogues between Célimène and Arsinoé. As Arsinoé says—"a free and frank exchange of views should be more common. We might disabuse ourselves, in that event, of such a wealth of self-deception, bad for moral health" (50)—the dialogue becomes a fervent quarrel.

The society described by Molière needs blind individuals, entertaining no real dialogue among them. That's probably the main reason why Alceste refuses Arsinoé's invitation to enter the court, that is to say, "the" society: "what would I do at court, Madame? You know I haven't got that sort of temperament" (55). Alceste's bad temper is indeed his greatest problem: He is a misanthrope from the beginning to the end of the play: "twenty thousand francs assure . . . my might to fulminate against human race, and nurse my hatred of its ugly face" (79).

Tania Collani

ISOLATION in *The Misanthrope*

A misanthrope is defined as a person who avoids other people and feels an intense desire for isolation. The play strongly confirms this meaning, since Alceste, the main character, does his best to be isolated from society, in particular from the friends and women around him. From the beginning of the play, Alceste wants to be left alone and refuses a constructive dialogue with his confident, Philinte: "Let me be! . . . Leave me, sir, I beg you—go away!" (3), he haughtily tells him. Alceste has a bad temper and he is aware of it. Nonetheless, he is unwilling to negotiate it: From his point of view, people have to accept him as is or leave him alone.

All or nothing: This is the basic rule of Alceste's character, which is applied to every field of his life, above all to relationships with other people. Either a sincere relationship based on esteem and mutual confidence exists, or any exchange becomes impossible. "I wish no further part / In friendship with a man so base at heart" (3), he says to the poor Philinte, who tries to make him understand the good side of being benevolent to the rest of mankind. Alceste's desperate search for transparency clashes with the aristocratic and well-mannered society of the Sun King's court: Not only does Alceste want to be left alone, but also others are not particularly fond of sharing their time with him. He has a peculiar power of embarrassing people, making them feel guilty. Even with his closest friends, he acts like a censor. Philinte is the first to feel guilty: "So then, Alceste, you think that I'm to blame?" (3). And then it is his beloved Célimène's turn: "Am I to blame because, it seems, I set some hearts aflame?" (24). In both cases Alceste's answer is categorical and doesn't leave any room for reply, nor negotiation of feelings and perspectives: "you should die of shame!" (3).

Alceste's nonnegotiable ideas bring him not only to a social isolation, but also to an intellectual seclusion. The episode of Oronte reading his sonnet to Alceste and Philinte (act 1) is quite illuminating: Considering the poem from an objective point of view, the reader as well would agree on its mediocrity. Philinte, who is very polite, makes Oronte immediately feel comfortable and pretends to like his composition; he also compliments him, as is customary among well-mannered people. On the contrary, Alceste first tries not to express his opinion on Oronte's literary skills but finally bursts and says what he actually thinks: "Frankly, I'd waste no more time upon it" (20). The fact of being "frank" makes Alceste feel released, and he states that pretending is "a skill I'm pleased to say I lack" (21). Needless to say, Oronte is deeply upset by that comment and cuts all relations with the unpleasant Alceste: "You think you're clever, sir, you're damn self-assured . . . " (22).

Alceste does everything he can to be disappointing also in his love affair with Célimène. She is a young widow and a frivolous courtesan, but Alceste's love is just as blind as his intolerance, and he would like to bring her within his isolation. Not even for a moment does he think of finding a compromise, an equilibrium that could possibly conciliate their different positions. He just expresses his hate for her choices and would like to convert her to his misanthropy: "Despite the passion Célimène arouses in me, I see and condemn [her faults] frankly" (12). The reader will notice that it is always his "frankness" that comes to be underlined when Alceste criticizes the others. But Célimène is not the kind of woman willing to abandon her freedom for a tyrant: "The way you show [your love] is some new creation, then, since you so ardently engage in quarrels. Passion, sir, with you means rage—I've never known a lover so irate!" (27).

Alceste, the misanthrope, seeks loneliness, and his bad temper and his bursts of rage help him to acquire it. The wise Philinte is aware of it from the beginning: "Your rage at everything and everyone exposes you to ridicule" (7). But, once more, Alceste's answer is categorical. He says, "So much, the better! Frankly, sir, to me that's such a comfort" (7). Alceste's choice to be alone discourages all faithful Philinte's attempts at making him aware of his condition. He is proud of his intolerance toward the entire "human race" (6), from the beginning to the end of the play, announcing, "Now leave me, sir, and climb the stairs alone. My sorrows at this time demand just a somber place as this" (80). Alceste proves undoubtedly to be the champion of misanthropy and isolation.

Tania Collani

MOLIÈRE *Tartuffe* (1664, 1667, 1669)

Actor and playwright Jean-Baptiste Poquelin, who used the pseudonym Molière, wrote several drafts of *Tartuffe*. An early version was performed for Louis XIV at Versailles in 1664 but was banned due to the influence of a powerful religious group. Finally allowed an extended run in 1669, *Tartuffe* became one of the most profitable plays produced by Molière's troupe. *Tartuffe* is a comedy in five acts, in rhyming alexandrine (12-syllable) verse. The best-known English translation is probably Richard Wilbur's version of 1963, in rhyming iambic pentameter.

Tartuffe is a con artist who has infiltrated the home of Orgon by pretending to be a devout Christian. As in many of Molière's plays, a comically flawed father (Orgon) arranges a marriage between his daughter (Mariane) and an inappropriate husband (Tartuffe). In their efforts to dissuade Orgon from this marriage, Mariane's saucy maid Dorine and Orgon's stoic brother-in-law Cléante use ridicule and logic, respectively. When Orgon's hot-headed son Damis denounces Tartuffe, Orgon disinherits Damis, taking Tartuffe as his heir. Orgon's wife, Elmire, finally unmasks Tartuffe by allowing him to flirt with her while Orgon hides under a table. After Tartuffe leaves with incriminating documents, the ironically named Monsieur Loyal arrives to evict the family. In the end, the king saves the day; Tartuffe is arrested because the king has seen through his fraudulent piety.

Themes developed in *Tartuffe* include FAMILY, RELIGION, JUSTICE, AMBITION, SEX, LOVE, PARENTHOOD, and RESPONSIBILITY. Because Molière's plays often include strong female characters, men behaving badly, and servants who outwit their masters, the themes of GENDER and SOCIAL CLASS are also relevant.

Dan Smith

FAMILY in *Tartuffe*

The importance of family in *Tartuffe* is apparent from a glance at the list of characters, for they are identified primarily in terms of their familial relationships. Household patriarch Orgon presides over his immediate family: his two children, Damis and Mariane, and his second wife, Elmire. Also living with the family are Orgon's mother, Madame Pernelle, and servants, including the outspoken Dorine. Orgon's brother-in-law Cléante is a regular visitor. As in many of Molière's plays, the flaws of the father figure cause a family crisis. In this case, Orgon's inability to distinguish between honest religious faith and the false performances of piety by the hypocritical Tartuffe have led him to invite Tartuffe into his home, upsetting the balance of his family's comfortable bourgeois life. Once installed as a guest, Tartuffe imposes his will on the family, gradually usurping Damis's place as Orgon's heir, with the ultimate goal of replacing Orgon as the property owner and head of household.

As the play begins, Madame Pernelle dramatically mobilizes the family crisis by moving out of the house. Like her gullible son, Madame Pernelle has been taken in by Tartuffe. She rails against the inhospitality the other family members have shown to Tartuffe, and against what she views as their lax morals. Her departure allows for much exposition, including important details about Tartuffe's character and about the future of the family. In act 1, scene 3, Damis explains his suspicion that Tartuffe wants to break off Mariane's marriage to Valère. Such an event would imperil his chances for a match with Valère's sister, because Orgon had already agreed to a marriage contract. Breaking the contract would be dishonorable, and would certainly cause a rift between the two families.

Orgon, however, demonstrates his skewed priorities from his first appearance on stage. When he asks for news of the household upon his return from a trip, Dorine informs him that his wife has been ill.

Orgon is unconcerned about Elmire's condition, and instead repeatedly asks about Tartuffe. This lack of concern for his wife is emblematic of Orgon's failure as a husband and father. An unhealthy obsession with Tartuffe has supplanted the protective instincts he should feel for his family.

As Damis feared, Orgon goes back on his word about Mariane's marriage to Valère. Upon hearing her father announce his intention of fully joining Tartuffe to his family by giving him his daughter's hand in marriage, Mariane is speechless. In the scene that follows, Dorine chides Mariane for not speaking up to her father. When Mariane explains that her father has absolute power over her, Dorine insinuates that Orgon's absurd proposition nullifies Mariane's duty to obey him.

Dorine enlists Elmire to save the family from this disastrous marriage by speaking with Tartuffe, who has displayed evidence of desire for Orgon's wife. After Tartuffe speaks frankly of his lust for Elmire, she rebuffs him and offers her silence on this delicate matter in exchange for his allowing Mariane to marry Valère. But Damis, who has overheard the incident, tries to use this information to turn his father against Tartuffe. Underestimating Orgon's devotion to Tartuffe at the expense of his family, Damis appeals to his father's sense of honor. Tartuffe saves himself with a discourse of repentance, and an enraged Orgon banishes Damis from the house. At the end of act 3, Orgon declares his intention to name Tartuffe his sole heir. In effect, Tartuffe would become both son-in-law and son, marrying Mariane and replacing the now-disgraced Damis.

Elmire, Mariane, Cléante, and Dorine make one last futile attempt to use reason to dissuade Orgon from marrying Mariane to Tartuffe. Finally, Elmire offers to show Orgon that Tartuffe is false. In perhaps the best-known scene of the play, Orgon hides under a table while Tartuffe tries to seduce his wife. Elmire's stratagem works, and Orgon finally sees Tartuffe for the hypocrite he really is. His family can throw out the interloper and begin to heal. But Orgon has already signed over his property to Tartuffe!

After Tartuffe leaves to set the legal proceedings into play, Madame Pernelle returns. Even she finally realizes Tartuffe's deceitful nature, thus uniting the entire family against the threat, albeit too late. His family unit repaired, Orgon must wait to see whether the family can be reintegrated into society. Fortunately for Orgon, his country is governed by a wise monarch who sees through Tartuffe's scheme. The family does not exist in isolation; state structures lend support even to flawed families.

Dan Smith

JUSTICE in *Tartuffe*

In *Tartuffe*, Molière presents a vision of justice that is connected to truth and regulated by the political system of an absolutist monarchy. The theme of justice becomes most prominent near the end of the play, when legal and political representatives arrive to sort out the conflict between Tartuffe and Orgon's family. While Tartuffe technically owns Orgon's house according to the letter of the law, the king's representative overrules him in favor of the spirit of the law because of Tartuffe's fraudulent manipulation of Orgon. Justice in the world of this play requires trust in the clemency of the king, who is able to see beyond the surface to a deeper level of truth in order to make effective judgments.

Early in the play, justice is closely tied to the theme of family, with Orgon functioning as an unjust father. Blinded by his loyalty to Tartuffe, Orgon behaves unjustly toward his daughter and son, ordering Mariane to marry Tartuffe and disowning Damis when he speaks against Tartuffe. When Orgon's wife, Elmire, finally manages to confront Orgon with the truth of Tartuffe's scheming ways, Orgon restores himself to the place of a just husband and father.

Unfortunately, Tartuffe has already managed to secure a deed of gift from Orgon. Based on this document, Tartuffe has become the rightful owner of Orgon's home. In act 5, scene 4, a bailiff named Monsieur Loyal comes on Tartuffe's behalf. He announces that his intentions toward the family are good and that his message from Tartuffe will make Orgon happy. But he actually wants to serve Orgon with a document that calls for the family's eviction from the house. Over the protestations of Damis, Monsieur Loyal argues that Orgon must accept this turn of events because of his belief in the rule of law. He appeals to Orgon as an upstanding man who submits to the authority of the state. Other characters deride Monsieur Loyal's call for justice as perverse, due to his initial misrepresentation of himself. Dorine makes a joke about the irony of the bailiff's name: Monsieur Loyal is loyal to no one, except perhaps himself. Loyal's jovial farewell underscores his hypocrisy and lack of commitment to true justice.

During the next scene Orgon's wife and brother-in-law urge him to seek justice by building a legal case against Tartuffe. They are interrupted by Mariane's faithful suitor Valère, who informs Orgon that Tartuffe has accused Orgon of treason before the king, based on the evidence of a strongbox containing documents belonging to a friend of Orgon who did conspire against the king. Valère offers to help Orgon escape, but Tartuffe arrives with a royal officer before Orgon can leave. Tartuffe claims that his sole purpose is to serve the king, but Cléante casts aspersions on his stated intentions by pointing out that Tartuffe's concern for the king began when he was caught trying to seduce Elmire. Cléante additionally suggests that Tartuffe should refuse to be Orgon's heir if he considers Orgon to be a traitor. Tartuffe cuts off the discussion, demanding that the officer arrest Orgon. In Tartuffe's twisted thinking, justice is constituted by the outcome that most benefits him personally.

The officer turns the tables on him, announcing that it is Tartuffe and not Orgon who will be going to prison. In a lengthy speech, the officer explains this surprising and fortuitous decision. First, he describes the king's sharp perception and measured judgment, in particular his ability to see through the charades of hypocrites. The king sees the malice in Tartuffe's soul, and his judgment stands in for the judgment of Heaven. The officer thus explicitly links royal justice to divine justice. He goes on to state that the king identified Tartuffe as a career criminal using an assumed name to flee from punishment. Finally, the officer nullifies Tartuffe's deed of gift and returns Orgon's documents to him. The king has pardoned Orgon for having subversive papers, thanks to Orgon's loyalty and devotion to the king in other matters. In the king's view, justice depends on a person's overall virtue. Minor transgressions can be forgiven; the spirit of the law is more important than the letter of the law.

When Orgon turns to chastise Tartuffe, Cléante cautions him not to gloat and urges him to go and thank the king for his mercy. With royal justice and divine justice having been dispensed by the monarch, the last lines of the play turn again to fatherly justice as Orgon announces that Mariane will marry Valère.

Dan Smith

RELIGION in *Tartuffe*

While it is impossible to discuss *Tartuffe* without considering religion, the play's primary engagement with this theme has to do with exposing religious hypocrisy. Tartuffe's phony performance of piety fools Orgon and his mother, Madame Pernelle, but most other characters see through him. The play sets up a conflict between excessive external displays of religiosity and true internal spiritual feeling. Indeed, the first scene sees Madame Pernelle praising Tartuffe's religious austerity in terms of how it will improve the family's reputation among the neighbors, while the outspoken maid Dorine and Orgon's rational brother-in-law Cléante argue that they should worry about their own consciences, not gossip. Dorine voices her suspicion that those who are most enthusiastic to condemn sin in others are secretly greater sinners themselves.

In act 1, scene 5, Orgon describes his relationship with Tartuffe. Having made a good first impression through his zealous prayers at church, Tartuffe went on to find favor with Orgon by fetching holy water for him and sharing gifts from Orgon with the poor. Orgon speaks with awe of Tartuffe's outward demonstration of piety. But Orgon's brother-in-law Cléante urges him to be skeptical. Cléante compares those who brag about their holiness with those who would brag about their courage; just as the truly courageous allow their actions on the battlefield to speak for them, so the truly pious do good works quietly, without boasting or proselytizing. When Orgon attempts to mock Cléante for claiming to be wise, Cléante replies with a lengthy speech that praises true faith and condemns hypocrisy. He defines hypocrites as those who use their religious reputation to make money or to curry social and political favor. Cléante goes on to offer several examples of model Christians, men who incorporate

their religious faith into their everyday actions without showing off or judging others.

Upon Tartuffe's first entrance in act 3, scene 2, he immediately speaks of two external symbols of worship involving self-abnegation: a hair-shirt and a whip. He then announces that he is going on an errand to give money to the poor. After Dorine comments directly to the audience on Tartuffe's hypocrisy, Tartuffe provides another striking example of it by asking her to cover her cleavage with a handkerchief so that her flesh will not tempt him. The conflict between Tartuffe's sexual appetite and his pious reputation is further developed in act 3, scene 3, when he attempts to seduce Orgon's wife, Elmire. In an effort to address this incompatibility, Tartuffe incorporates religious rhetoric to flatter Elmire. He argues, without much success, that it is natural for him to desire her because she was created in the image of God. When Elmire counters that such passion is unbecoming a man of his piety, Tartuffe says that his reputation can serve as a shield that allows them to engage in an affair without risk of scandal. He thus exposes himself as the fraud that Cléante and Dorine have accused him of being.

Act 4, scene 1, sees a confrontation between Cléante and Tartuffe. Cléante attempts to convince Tartuffe that Christian values of forgiveness and compassion should compel him to repair the rift between Orgon and his son Damis. Tartuffe cuts the conversation short, citing the need to perform some unspecified religious duty. Later, in a second scene with Elmire, Tartuffe elaborates on his prior discussion of how to maintain an outward appearance of piety while pursuing an adulterous affair. Hiding under the table, Orgon finally learns of Tartuffe's hypocrisy. Orgon sends Tartuffe away, with Tartuffe vowing that he will take over the house.

In act 5, scene 1, Orgon enumerates his woes, concluding that he will have no more dealings with religious men. Cléante criticizes Orgon's lack of moderation in drawing such a conclusion. The fact that Orgon was taken in by one charlatan whose piety was fake does not mean that the world is devoid of true Christians. According to Cléante, Orgon's new position is worse than his excessive trust of Tartuffe. Rather than rejecting everyone who appears pious, Orgon should attempt to learn how to distinguish between true Christians and those who are abusing a heavenly pose for earthly gain.

In effect, Orgon should emulate the king, who immediately sees through Tartuffe's posturing and restores order via a representative. Orgon's instinct is to berate Tartuffe, but Cléante interrupts and once again preaches forgiveness and tolerance. Cléante hopes that Tartuffe will experience a religious conversion, replacing his false performance of piety with a true interior spirituality.

Dan Smith

MOMADAY, N. SCOTT   *House Made of Dawn* (1966)

N. Scott Momaday's *House Made of Dawn* follows Abel as he tries to readjust to life in his Pueblo community and also tries to find his place in American society after World War II. Ill-equipped for war, when Abel returns he is alienated, detached from his community and tradition. Through the prologue and each of the novel's four sections, we follow only a few days in his life. However, these days stretch over a period of seven years as Abel struggles to find himself through a series of devastatingly wrong turns. His misdirection is revealed through his own thoughts as well as through flashbacks and other narrators. These narrative techniques provide insight into Native American identity and the importance of tradition, while also revealing the history of loss and displacement Native Americans have endured.

The short prologue that introduces the novel shows Abel running. While there is no date or scenario for this section, the tone and language indicate a transformation is occurring. The importance of this becomes apparent later. It is not until the first section, "The Longhair," that the reader is given a time and setting: the Jemez Pueblo in 1945. Arriving home from the war, Abel drunkenly stumbles off the bus into his grandfather Francisco's arms. His arrival portends the disaster that follows. Out of place, Abel finds he cannot reenter reservation life. Even when he does participate, entering a traditional rooster pull, his awkwardness on horseback is juxtaposed against the other participants' ease. The section culminates when he drunkenly murders an albino Native American, believing him to be an evil shapeshifter.

The last three sections are set in 1952 following Abel's release from prison. Relocated to Los Angeles, the sections entitled "The Priest of the Sun" and "The Night Chanter" show Abel's quick downward spiral as he tries to fit into the white world around him. The last section of the novel, "The Dawn Runner," comes full circle, picking up right before and shedding light on the prologue. He returns to the village to find his grandfather near death. After Francisco dies, Abel commemorates his grandfather, beginning a ceremonial, early morning run.

Lisa Wenger

ALIENATION in *House Made of Dawn*

From an early age, Abel feels alienated. This begins when his mother returns to her Pueblo village, bringing Abel and his brother. Since his father is not Pueblo, Abel thinks of him, and by extension himself, as an outsider. The deaths of his mother and brother while he is still a child make him feel even lonelier; suddenly Francisco is the only family he has. His sense of alienation deepens during his teenage years. Reaching an age where he can actively participate in important tribal ceremonies, Abel is allowed to aid the Eagle Watcher Society's eagle capture, an important ceremonial organization and tradition. Once the eagle is captured, though, Abel kills the bird rather than allowing his people to ceremonially cage it. No one, including his grandfather, understands his actions. Believing he has no place in the community, Abel enlists, leaving everything behind.

His alienation intensifies through his war experiences. Calling him "chief," his fellow soldiers' reactions to his weaponless and whooping charge at an enemy tank denote their stereotypical views of Native Americans. That is the sort of action they expect from an "Indian"—insane and idiotic. It is obvious, however, that the violence and destruction surrounding Abel has chipped away at him. Everything is foreign: the war, the violence, the battle-scarred countryside, the white soldiers around him. His charge at the tank represents his complete break, for he no longer understands or feels a part of anything. By the time he returns to his Pueblo community, he is numb, disconnected even from his own people, traditions, and way of life. Abel finds he "could not say the things he wanted; he tried to pray, to sing, to enter into the old rhythm of the tongue, but he was no longer attuned to it" (58), and he turns to alcohol as an escape. Later, his estrangement results in murder. Viewing an albino Pueblo man as an evil being capable of transforming into a snake, an intoxicated Abel kills the man, viciously disemboweling him. Abel's alienation is heightened further by the fact that other Native Americans deride his reasoning for the murder, while the white jury simply views him as insane.

After his release from prison, Abel's disconnection only worsens. As part of the Bureau of Indian Affairs relocation program, a program intent on moving and assimilating Native Americans into urban areas, he is sent to live in Los Angeles. It is soon apparent that this move further distances Abel. Once again an outsider, Abel has no understanding of modern urban life. He does befriend Ben Benally and acquires a job, but he cannot find his place in this society. Despite Milly's help and optimism that he can make it in Los Angeles, Abel quickly spirals into depression and alcoholism. He cannot resolve the new ways of this world with the traditions and ideas with which he was raised. Many of the Native Americans who have assimilated also ridicule Abel to his face for his ignorance, believing he is stuck in a past that offers nothing and is unable to take advantage of the opportunities, such as education, that he is offered. As Benally says of Abel, he "was unlucky. . . . He was a longhair. . . . You know, you have to change. That's the only way you can live in a place like this. You have to forget about the way it was, how you grew up and all. . . . Well, he didn't want to change, I guess, or he didn't know how." (148). As his anger over the ridicule heaped on him and his powerlessness grows, so does his use of alcohol. In a drunken rage, Abel confronts the corrupt police officer who had beaten him over the hands with his nightstick. He is severely beaten, his face a bloody pulp, hands broken and skin yellow from the loss of blood. Left vulnerable on the beach, Abel becomes one of the silversided fish whose depiction opens the section, a fish that helplessly hurls itself ashore during spawning season.

This sense of alienation also is echoed throughout the Los Angeles Native American population. Many, such as Benally and Tosamah, see themselves as outsiders. This stems from the realization that Native American culture and traditions do not belong to the modern world in which they live. Tosamah knows that to assimilate fully means abandoning these things, something he is not willing to do. For Benally, who unlike Tosamah comes from a reservation, this is compounded with the loss of place. While Benally longs to return, he knows that there is nothing left, "just empty land and a lot of old people, going nowhere and dying off." Their place is literally and figuratively eroded away, but what remains is history and heritage.

Momaday illustrates that alienation is a part of the Native American dilemma. Assimilation into the modern white world comes at a heavy price, the loss of culture, tradition, and even place. Estrangement also indicates the importance of place, as is seen through both Abel and Benally. Both men are displaced from their community and homeland. This displacement intensifies each character's sense of disconnection and loss, something for which Los Angeles offers no help. It is only by returning to his Pueblo home and embracing the people and culture that Abel finally finds himself again.

Lisa Wenger

IDENTITY in *House Made of Dawn*

Native Americans are caught between the white world and their own in *House Made of Dawn*. The white world has no understanding of Native American beliefs, traditions, history, of that which constitutes Native American identity. It also has no place for these things, viewing them as antiquated. As the modern world tries to strip away everything of importance to Native Americans, the search for and maintenance of identity become imperative.

Abel's search for identity begins at an early age. Not knowing his father's heritage, Abel feels "somehow foreign and strange" when his family returns to the Pueblo community. Given this, most of his youth is spent searching for identity and place, a search that culminates in his killing of the eagle and departure from the village. At first excited about leaving, Abel soon realizes his mistake. On the battlefield, he feels more out of place and lost than ever, the horror and violence a complete reversal of all he has ever known. In fact, "everything in advance of his going—he could remember whole and in detail. It was the recent past, the intervention of days and years without meaning, of awful calm and collision, time always immediate and confused, that he could not put together in his mind." His memory completely erased, Abel has even less of a sense of self than he did in the Pueblo community.

Finding neither himself nor his place in the white world, Abel returns home silenced. When he tries to sing or even speak, nothing comes out, and he realizes "[h]ad he been able to say it, anything of his own language—even the commonplace formula of greeting 'Where are you going'—which had no being beyond sound, no visible substance, would once again have shown him whole to himself." His experiences have stripped away what little sense of identity he had, disconnecting him from his own culture and traditions. Isolated, he transfers his anger onto the Native American albino. Representing the white world that has undermined Abel's sense of self, the albino is the "enemy" that must be eradicated.

His relocation to Los Angeles after his release from prison does little to rectify his identity problems. To make matters worse, the relocation department sends a barrage of useless questionnaires probing generalized, surface-level identity markers, such as age, sex, and even whether he prefers watching tennis or bullfighting. Abel quickly finds that he "had lost his place. He had been long ago at the center, had known where he was, had lost his way, had wandered to the end of the earth, was even now reeling on the edge of the void." This sense of loss is compounded with the way white words and language continue to silence him, as if he has no identity or existence whatsoever. Even at his trial, he is unable to speak, and "[w]ord by word by word these men [white] were disposing of him in language, their language, and they were making a bad job of it." Viewing the albino as an evil entity, Abel is stripped of words; what he can communicate in his own defense is something the white courtroom can never understand. Silencing Abel, their language

transforms him into a passive object rather than an active human being.

Words and language play a significant role in all Native American identity. First, there are the white words, words that silence, barring Native Americans from communicating. As Benally says, "[t]hey [whites] have a lot of *words,* and you know they mean something, but you don't know what, and your own words are no good because they're not the same; they're different, and they're the only words you've got." As the dominant culture, the whites do not understand the words and stories Native Americans speak and tell. Instead, as with Abel's trial, they see Native Americans as "primitive" peoples who have nothing relevant to say, which also diminishes their sense of self. Furthermore, Native Americans cannot understand the spiritually denuded words of the whites. Speaking of the Gospel of John, Tosamah preaches that "the white man deals in words, and he deals easily, with grace and sleight of hand. . . . He has diluted and multiplied the Word, and. . . . his regard for language—for the Word itself—as an instrument of creation has diminished nearly to the point of no return." White words are not creative but destructive and deceitful. They strip away at truths, denouncing those, such as Native Americans, who use them to find truth. In this way, they belittle and discredit the very words that constitutes Native American identity.

However, words become a powerful way of reclaiming identity. As many of the characters note, Native American words, language, and stories bring about a wholeness and understanding, something so easily lost in the modern world. In fact, words, in conjunction with tradition, help Abel reestablish his own sense of self. Unsure and lost, it is only when he begins the dawn run that his voice finally returns. The song that bursts out confirms that he finally knows and is happy with who he is.

Lisa Wenger

TRADITION in *House Made of Dawn*

Tradition as a way of retaining history and heritage as well as reaffirming Native American identity is crucial in *House Made of Dawn.* As the old ways of life die, ceremonial and oral tradition preserve Native American history and heritage. In turn, these aspects not only establish a basis for identity, but also provide a connection among the people. However, there is also a juxtaposition of the old and modern ways, as seen through Abel. Modern life has little use for tradition, often leading to tradition's abandonment. This often leads to a sense of loss and despair. Thus, a return to tradition also brings about healing and understanding.

Tradition's importance is illustrated through the Pueblo story of the Bahkyula people, a people whom murder and disease nearly eradicated. Less than 20 survived, joining the Pueblo community, yet they brought with them both ceremonial (it is from them the Eagle Watcher Society comes) and oral traditions. The survival of these traditions means the survival of the people. As Momaday writes, "after the intervening years and generations, the ancient blood of this forgotten tribe still ran in the veins of men." Without tradition, the people, their history and heritage would have disappeared long ago into the Pueblo community with whom they joined.

Through the oral tradition that permeates the novel, we also see the significance and fragility of history and heritage. As Native Americans are forced off the reservation and scattered, oral tradition becomes one of the few ways of retaining heritage. Describing his grandmother's stories, Tosamah says, "[s]he was asking me to go with her to the confrontation of something that was sacred and eternal. . . . her words were medicine; they were magic and invisible. They came from nothing into sound and meaning. They were beyond price; they could neither be bought nor sold." The stories, such as that of Tai-me, the Big Dipper's formation, and the Bear are permanent reminders of history, providing connection to the past. While words also cannot be taken away from the people, they are vulnerable, always on the verge of extinction, as both Tosamah and Francisco note. Therefore, the transmission of stories from generation to generation signifies the unbreakable bonds among the people.

On the other hand, disconnection from tradition leads to loss and despair, as Abel reveals. His participation in the Eagle Watcher Society's ceremonial hunt first shows his discomfort with the old ways. According to tradition, a sacred eagle is captured and kept in the village. While Abel willingly and gladly participates in the hunt for a new eagle, he soon finds that the thought of the captured bird, a creature so beautiful and graceful in the sky, yet ugly and ungainly caged, revolts him. Unable to understand the tradition, he kills the bird. This not only severs his ties to the community, but also initiates his self-destructive downward spiral; it is after this that Abel leaves, experiencing atrocities during war for which he is completely unprepared.

Upon his return to Walatowa, he is lost, estranged from his people and heritage. This is displayed through his awkward participation in the rooster ceremony during the Feast of Santiago. The other riders throw themselves into the event. They tumble from their horses, to the crowd's delight, as they reach for the rooster buried in the ground. Abel, on the other hand "made a poor showing, full of caution and gesture." Sitting clumsily in his saddle, the albino who grabs the rooster makes a mockery of Abel, beating him with it. Abel, incapable of escaping, is left cornered, hanging onto his horse until the rooster is dead and dismembered. From this point forward, violence, alcohol, and despair consume his life. He murders the albino, is sent to prison, then relocated after his release to Los Angeles. Even more ill-fitted for life in Los Angeles and detached from the old ways, Abel has nowhere to go. His inability to adapt leads to more drinking and violence, until he is beaten and left unconscious on the beach.

It is tradition, then, that also brings about healing. Understanding this, Benally sings a song of healing and recovery for Abel. Knowing that Abel cannot help himself, Benally invokes the prayer song's power. Returning home, it is only after his grandfather's death that Abel embraces tradition. In his sorrow, he ceremonially prepares his grandfather's body. It is at this point he undertakes the traditional dawn running. Emphasized throughout the novel, running reaffirms the connection between the people and the land, a spiritual connection that embodies their heritage. In fact, running shapes the novel, both the opening prologue and end showing Abel running and reconnecting with tradition and history. As exhaustion sets in, Abel finally "could see at last without having to think. He could see the canyon and the mountains and the sky. He could see the rain and the river and the fields beyond. He could see the dark hills at dawn" (21). Running not only opens Abel's eyes, but also helps him reclaim his voice. Unable to sing traditional songs and completely silent during his trial, Abel previously was voiceless. Turning to tradition, Abel begins singing as he runs. He also reconnects with all he had lost—his history, nature, his people, and even his voice.

As the novel exemplifies, losing touch with tradition leads to feelings of loss and confusion. Tradition keeps history and heritage alive, helping confirm identity and connection despite change and relocation. In this respect, it also is healing. Without tradition, Abel was adrift, living from one drink to the next with no real sense of self or purpose. Once he begins the dawn running, everything changes, and he finally becomes whole again.

Lisa Wenger

MOMADAY, N. SCOTT *The Way to Rainy Mountain* (1969)

An assortment of personal memories, stories, and legends of the Kiowa tribe taken from the very words of the author's grandmother, *The Way to Rainy Mountain* explores themes such as memory, tradition, family, and identity. After Momaday's grandmother, Aho, died in the spring, he decides to venture to Rainy Mountain that July to spend some time at her grave. An ancient and important landmark to the Kiowa, Rainy Mountain is described as merely a "single knoll" by Momaday. The knoll holds, however, a sacred position in his mind and heart. Not just a familiar and beautiful landscape, Rainy Mountain is full of myths and experiences that will last forever as they are passed from generation to generation.

After telling the history of the Kiowa people, Momaday introduces Aho with a great deal of admiration and respect. Possessing a great deal of Kiowa knowledge, Aho had maintained the ability to proudly tell stories from the very beginning of her heritage.

From learning of Tai-me, the sacred Sun Dance doll, to the importance of dogs, horses, and buffalo, *The Way to Rainy Mountain* also recounts how the Kiowa still wear war paint, beadwork, and bright colors in order to keep the special traditions of their ancestors alive. Momaday received a tremendous amount of information from his grandmother, which in turn he presents to the reader in written form.

Lauren Wasilewski

IDENTITY in *The Way to Rainy Mountain*

Aho, N. Scott Momaday's grandmother, was born into the very last stage of the North American Kiowa nation. In search of the background and identity of his ancestors that were once reflected from the stories of Aho, Momaday begins his journey to the setting of so many legendary Kiowa myths: Rainy Mountain. Just northwest of the Wichita Range, Momaday swears imagination comes to life upon viewing this single mound in Oklahoma. The members of the Kiowa tribe were warriors. Surprisingly, the specific language used by the tribe has never been classified into any language group; however, there is a symbol in sign language for Kiowa.

Aside from ruling the whole of the southern Great Plains in partnership with the Comanche for a long period of time, something the Kiowa will always be remembered for is their remarkable horsemanship. Legends say they were the finest horsemen the world has ever known. In fact, the Kiowa had more horses per man than any other tribe.

Momaday recognizes and feels that his people are visibly superior to those of the Comanche and Wichita. Tall, straight, relaxed, and graceful in appearance, the Kiowa looked more like tribes of the north than the south. In 1834, artist George Catlin recognized these dominant features in one of his classic portraits.

By making friends with the Crow during their migration to the south and east in the 17th century, the Kiowa learned of Tai-me, the Sun Dance doll, and gained a great deal of knowledge and respect for such sacredness. Aho participated in the last of the Sun Dances as a young girl, and after she had passed and Momaday had grown up, there were not many alive who still remembered those days. After their association with the Crow endowed the Kiowa with such a strong sense of religion, courage, and pride, the Kiowa advanced to the forefront of North American tribes.

Tracing back to the very beginning, the tribe was first named Kwuda, which means "coming out." Coming one by one through a hollow log into the world, one woman was pregnant and became stuck. No one after her made it to the other side of the log, which explains the small number of people in the tribe.

Before the tribe owned horses, dogs and sleds were the necessities; to the Kiowa, the dog is an extremely primitive animal. Momaday is able to identify with this by recalling how dogs were always roaming about his grandmother's house. Although the dogs were not named and were paid little attention by the old people, Momaday still felt they were sad to see the dogs pass away. The term "ownership" did not apply to the arrangement at Aho's house. In a sense, it seemed the dogs lived a life of their own.

The Kiowa have never been farmers or taken any part in agriculture. Hunting was what the tribe was passionate about. Momaday states that even to this day they are meat eaters. He states that his grandfather, Mammedaty, always worked hard to make wheat and cotton grow on his land, but to no avail. Momaday even remembers seeing a young boy holding a freshly slaughtered calf's liver in the palm of his hand, eating it ravenously. That particular memory of Momaday's identifies with the myth of how old hunters of the Plains placed the raw liver and tongue of the buffalo above anything else as a delicacy.

The policy of the Kiowa people is to never repeat a man's name after he dies. He takes his name out of the world with him when he goes, and to repeat it is a sign of disrespect. According to Momaday, Aho always chose to use the word *zei-dl-bei*, which means "frightful."

During his stay at Rainy Mountain, Momaday identifies spiritually with the 1872–73 burning of the once significant heraldic tipi, Do-giagya guat (tipi with battle pictures). This identification occurs when Momaday is walking around the Rainy Mountain Cemetery. For a few moments, there is a deep silence where nothing moves and there seems to be a subconscious rule to stay completely still. Only the jolting call of a bobwhite brings the world back to reality.

The Way to Rainy Mountain is written straightforwardly, with Momaday telling the reader the myths of the Kiowa, and then telling of his own personal identification with the past of his people. The pride Momaday possesses for the history of his family is not hard to see, and the stories of his grandmother's life have guided Momaday to identify that history with himself as well.

Lauren Wasilewski

MEMORY in *The Way to Rainy Mountain*

The theme of memory is crucial to *The Way to Rainy Mountain,* as the story is based on the stories told to Momaday by his grandmother, Aho. These stories help Momaday reminisce about growing up with a grandmother born into the last true generation of the Kiowa. The stories passed down to Momaday from Aho are memories from Aho's childhood. The very beginning of the prologue talks about how there are so many things upon which to reminisce and dwell.

Momaday speaks of his grandmother living in the shadow of Rainy Mountain, and how the specific landscape of the mountain was forever laid like memory in her blood. Most of the legends that Aho passed on to Momaday were from the very beginning of the Kiowa tribe's existence, although Aho would not be born for several more years. What impressed Momaday was how Aho had the ability to tell of the Crow whom she had never laid eyes upon and of the Black Hills where she had never set foot. This is precisely the motive for Momaday's traveling to Rainy Mountain, to experience in person what Aho had experienced in the mind's eye.

When Momaday seeks the Great Plains in late spring, he remembers the meadows full of blue and yellow wildflowers, and that moment will forever be planted in his memory, for that is when he realizes he will never see the world as he did the day before.

As a young boy, Momaday remembers a great deal of sound in Aho's house. From coming and going to eating and talking, Kiowa were always frequenting his grandmother's house. Since the Kiowa are known as being "summer people," summertime at Aho's was especially fun and made for plenty of reunions. Momaday remembers these visitors right down to their big black hats, and bright shirts that shook when the wind hit.

These particular visitors were using their memories as well. By rubbing fat on their hair and winding the braids in their hair with strips of cloth, the late Kiowa were reminding themselves of who they were and where they came from.

Always viewing his grandmother with admiration, Momaday talks of her usage of the word, *zei-dl-bei* (frightful). He liked her use of this word because her face would become distorted in an amusing look of displeasure, and she would click her tongue in disgust.

Keahdinekeah, Momaday's great-grandmother, had impressed Momaday's father, Al, just as Aho affected Momaday. As a boy, his father accompanied Keahdinekeah to the shrine of the talyi-da-i (a special tipi with holy medicine inside). Momaday's father was filled with wonder at the mere sight of this medicine, which would forever be a part of his human spirit. Touched by the remembrance of this experience, Al felt the need to pass this story from his youth on to his son. Upon meeting Keahdinekeah, Momaday clearly remembers the white hair and blind eyes of his great-grandmother. He recalls the touch of her skin as soft as that of a baby, and the sound of her happy tears.

As a young boy, Al Momaday recognized an older man in braids named Cheney coming to his house to pay his respects. An arrow maker, Cheney painted his face and would pray out loud into the rising sun. The Kiowa held their stories and memories in such a high regard that once the stories were passed on, recipients can see and feel the story as if they were there when it was taking place.

The earliest times Momaday can remember are the summers on Rainy Mountain Creek. He was living in the arbor with his family on the north side of his grandmother's house. The light, air, and sounds of the land are what he loved, and when the seasons changed and the time came to move back into the house, everyone felt depressed and confined.

Only once did Momaday come into contact with Tai-me, the holy Sun Dance doll. After making an offering of bright red cloth, Aho prayed out loud. This was such a sacred experience for Momaday that he remembers the very feeling of the room; he said it felt as if an old person had just died or a baby had been born.

After Aho died, all Momaday had left for comfort was the memory of his grandmother. He remembers her cooking meat in an iron skillet at the wood stove on a winter morning, but he especially remembers her praying. Although he never learned the Kiowa language, Momaday sensed a great deal of sorrow in her prayers. A Christian in her later years, Aho never forgot her heritage, and after his pilgrimage to Rainy Mountain, neither will Momaday.

Lauren Wasilewski

TRADITION in *The Way to Rainy Mountain*

Without tradition, the Kiowa people would never have been able to succeed in creating a legacy. In the tribe's heyday, their world revolved around Tai-me, the doll of the Sun Dance. The very reason for their existence and prayer, Tai-me would be stolen by the Osage. Even though Tai-me was later returned, the Kiowa were sent into a frenzy of devastation and panic, practically forcing the tribe to sign their first treaty with the United States in 1837.

Unfortunately, the passing down of verbal traditions from generation to generation has weakened over time. Although the myths and legends are no longer intact, the basic theory of Rainy Mountain is the history of man's idea of himself. Each and every Kiowa member partakes in his or her own historical, personal, and cultural journey toward their heritage. Because this is a time that is gone from the world forever, each reality must rely on imagination and the traditions of the Kiowa people, which may now have become blurry.

One tradition that stretched from the very beginning until the very end was the buffalo as animal representation of the sun. When the time came to sacrifice a victim for the Sun Dance, the buffalo was crucial. Spirits fell within the tribe when a herd of buffalo was destroyed, thus proving their importance.

Aho, N. Scott Momaday's grandmother, took part in the well known tradition of the sacred Sun Dance as a child. Performed annually by the Kiowa tribe, the tradition and rite was firmly planted in Aho's mind and soul. During a Sun Dance in 1861, held near the Arkansas River in Kansas, a spotted horse was left tied to a pole in the medicine lodge to starve to death as a sacrifice to Tai-me. When an epidemic of smallpox broke out within the tribe later that year, an old man sacrificed one of his best horses in order to save the lives of his family. Only seven when the last Sun Dance was held by the Kiowa in 1887 on the Washita River above Rainy Mountain Creek, Aho clearly remembers the absent buffalo. Trying to keep tradition alive, the Kiowa skewered the head of a buffalo bull upon the medicine tree and journeyed to Texas to beg for an animal from the Goodnight herd. Aho was only 10 years old when the Kiowa joined for the very last time as the Sun Dance culture. Buffalo was nowhere to be found, and an old hide from the sacred tree was forced to suffice as an offering. Appearance too was crucial to the continuation of Kiowa tradition. Rubbing fat in one's hair, wearing fringed and flowered shawls, bright beads, winding braids with strips of colored cloth, and carrying the scars of old and respected enmities helped the late Kiowa members keep their ancestors close at heart. Mammedaty, Momaday's grandfather, visibly characterized himself as a peyote man by wearing a necklace of beans and a beaded staff of feathers from a water bird.

At one time taking the name Gaigwu, which indicates how one-half will differ from the other in appearance, the Kiowa warriors used the custom of cutting their hair only on the right side of the head; on a line level with the lobe of the ear, their hair was kept long on the left side and braided in otter skin. Based solely on ancient custom, after antelope medicine was made, the men, women, and children of the Kiowa tribe would set out on foot and horseback after meat. Forming a large circle around the game and moving in on the center, antelope and other animals were trapped and killed with clubs and often times bare hands. This is yet another expression of how the Kiowa were reminded of the helpful ways of their ancestors. The pomme blanche, a plant eaten by most Indians and in some cases tried as a substitute for the potato, was never consumed by the Kiowa. Going against the tradition of agriculture, the Kiowa strictly stuck to hunting game.

The Kiowa owned the largest number of horses per person, far more than any other tribe, and Mammedaty kept this tradition alive by owning several. For Mammedaty, it was hard to be without horses; he felt it was essentially good to own them.

One personal and traditional opinion of this tribe regarding death was not speaking the name of any dead man. To speak the name of the deceased was downright disrespectful and dishonest. The Kiowa believed that when someone died, their name was to leave the world with their body.

Although the Kiowa thrived as an independent tribe only from 1740 to 1875, and there is very little material evidence to prove their customs, the spirit and traditions of the Kiowa people will be embedded in their memories forever.

Lauren Wasilewski

MORRISON, TONI   *Beloved* (1987)

Toni Morrison's Pulitzer Prize–winning novel is now regarded as one of the most important works of fiction of the late 20th century. The novel's plot is based loosely on the life of Margaret Garner, a woman who escaped from slavery with her children across the Ohio River and, when recaptured, killed her own daughter rather than allow her to be returned to slavery. Written in an experimental narrative style, *Beloved* explores the deep historical scars of slavery on American identity, motherhood, and the family; it also offers a promise of healing and a future beyond these traumas.

The main characters of *Beloved* are Sethe and her daughter Denver, who are living in Ohio after escaping Sweet Home, the plantation owned by Schoolmaster where they were slaves. Their new home, set apart and unvisited by neighbors, is haunted by the memory and physical presence of the unnamed two-year-old child—called only "Beloved" on her grave marker—whom Sethe killed under threat of recapture. Paul D., who has also escaped from Sweet Home, joins the pair, but when a strange young woman who calls herself Beloved appears at the home he is soon driven out by supernatural events.

The character of Beloved may be interpreted as the embodiment of Sethe's guilt and pain over the loss of her murdered child. Though she is physically mature, Beloved's emotional state is that of an insatiable two-year-old whose desires are coupled with uncontrollable anger and tantrums. Beloved's demands eventually overwhelm Sethe, who increasingly sacrifices herself to the girl's bottomless hungers. The novel's hopeful ending finds Denver, Sethe's shy daughter, leaving the home to ask her larger community for help. This healthful turn toward communal healing is powerful and effective; when people arrive at the home to exorcise Beloved, she disappears. Denver, we learn in the final pages of the work, will thrive and blossom into adulthood.

Noreen O'Connor

CHILDHOOD in *Beloved*

As many readers know, Sethe, the protagonist of *Beloved*, is based on Margaret Garner, who in 1856 murdered one of her children and tried to kill the others to keep them from being taken into slavery. The fact that in the true story and in the novel it is mothers who commit these murders is significant; because maternity is idealized in American culture, we are especially appalled to learn that a mother could kill her children. However, this is precisely Morrison's point: Slavery is so heinous that it can drive a mother to sacrifice her own children to escape it. As Morrison explains in her foreword to *Beloved*,

> thoughts led me to the different history of black women in this country—a history in which marriage was discouraged, impossible, or illegal; in which birthing children was required, but "having" them, being responsible for them—being, in other words, their parent—was as out of the question as freedom. Assertions of parenthood under conditions peculiar to the logic of institutional enslavement were criminal.

When *Beloved* opens, the reader is thrown into the center of Sethe's guilt. We don't know yet what her crime is, but we do know that Sethe, her daughter Denver, and her two sons, Howard and Buglar, are paying for it. Morrison purposefully delays the revelation of Sethe's murder of her baby girl, revealing only bits of Sethe's memory of the event and interweaving them with other memories of Sethe's own horrific sufferings as a slave, in order to secure the readers' sympathy for Sethe. Once

we hear Sethe's story, we cannot dismiss her as an unfeeling monster ("You got two feet, Sethe, not four," Paul D. tells her), as we may otherwise be inclined to do.

In fact, prior to the murder of "crawling-already?" baby, Sethe is foremost a mother. Consistently, the injustices that she laments the most are those intended to deny her the right to mother her children. For example, when Schoolteacher's nephews assault Sethe in the barn, she does not dwell on her own degradation but rather on the fact that they have taken her milk for "crawling-already?" baby. Similarly, when delivering Denver, Sethe is willing to die to escape her excruciating pain and exhaustion, except to do so would jeopardize the life of her child. The significance of this extraordinary act of love and selflessness is reflected in Denver's return to it again and again, a memory that reassures Denver of her mother's love for her.

Unfortunately, Sethe's love for her children is no match against the immorality of slavery. Indeed, one of the more insidious truths of slavery revealed in *Beloved* is that love is not only useless in a slave's world, it is also dangerous, a particularly perverse irony. As Paul D. notes, "For a used-to-be-slave woman to love anything that much was dangerous, especially if it was her children she had settled on to love" (54). Although at this point Paul D. does not know of Sethe's murder, his words explain well how the impotence of love and the rage that Sethe feels in light of that fact drive her to make her tragic decision.

Not only does Sethe take her child's life, the maternal love that once sustained Sethe now becomes grotesque. This is shown in Sethe's decision to remain at the house referred to only as 124 in order not to abandon "crawling-already?" baby's ghost (the missing "3" in the address). However, Sethe's choice exposes her other three children to constant fear and isolation. Ultimately Sethe's guilt is so great that she allows Beloved (and thus her guilt) nearly to consume her. Sethe, the mother, has lost her center; being a mother and loving her children has not been enough. That is the insidious power of slavery.

In the end, Sethe does survive, as does Paul D., but it is Denver, the baby whose miraculous birth sustains the hopes of so many of the characters—Sethe, Stamp Paid, Denver—whose future we're banking on. In contrast to her mother, who at the close of the novel has no plans, "no plans at all," and whose eyes have become "expressionless," Denver is working, learning "book stuff" from Miss Bodwin and Denver's face looks "like someone had turned up the gas jet." Christ-like, Denver has been sacrificed, but in the end she is resurrected, and her story of triumph becomes a promise of freedom for African Americans. It *is* a story to pass on.

Nancy Wilson

FREEDOM in *Beloved*

In slave narratives such as Harriet Jacobs's INCIDENTS IN THE LIFE OF A SLAVE GIRL and Frederick Douglass's NARRATIVE OF THE LIFE OF FREDERICK DOUGLASS, AN AMERICAN SLAVE, the authors bear witness to the sacrifices they endured in order to secure their freedom. In *Beloved*, too, we learn of the incredible lengths to which slaves had to go in their quest for freedom, such as Halle, who works "five years of Sundays" in order to purchase his mother's freedom, and Sethe, who chooses death over slavery. As W. E. B. DuBois in THE SOULS OF BLACK FOLK (1903) notes, "few men ever worshipped Freedom with half such unquestioning faith as did the American Negro for two centuries. . . . Emancipation was the key to a promised land of sweeter beauty than ever stretched before the eyes of wearied Israelites." However, DuBois questioned the naïveté of romanticizing freedom, asserting that freedom alone could not liberate the African-American people; they would need political power and EDUCATION, as well. Similarly, in *Beloved* Toni Morrison de-romanticizes Emancipation. She notes her intentions when creating the character of Sethe: "The heroine would represent the unapologetic acceptance of shame and terror; assume the consequences of choosing infanticide; claim her own freedom." One might wonder why Sethe has to "claim" her freedom. Wasn't freedom given? And why would Morrison list "shame," "terror," and "infanticide" alongside such a positive concept as "freedom?" The answer to both of these questions can be found in a recasting of what freedom really meant—it was an opportunity, not a gift,

an opportunity with a host of complications, coming too late for some, or with memories that could not be erased, or with new problems that would prove almost as insidious as slavery. Thus, *Beloved* is Morrison's attempt, as an African American, to recover her people's post-slavery history, the good and the bad, in order to help us understand and honor freed slaves' real-life experiences.

One of the ways in which Morrison de-romanticizes freedom is to show that, despite Emancipation, the damage slavery caused lasted well beyond 1863. For example, Paul D. tells of "a Negro about fourteen years old who lived by himself in the woods and said he couldn't remember living anywhere else. He saw a witless colored woman jailed and hanged for stealing ducks she believed were her own babies." Similarly, Paul D.'s rusted, tobacco box heart and Sethe's recurring flashbacks to her abuse by Schoolteacher's nephews exemplify the way that their slave days bled into their "free" lives. In fact, although free, Baby Suggs becomes so depressed by the continuing reminders of slavery, she comes to believe that God "gave her Halle who gave her freedom when it didn't mean a thing." Although this comment is difficult for a modern audience to hear, especially because Emancipation in particular and freedom in general is so exalted in the United States, Morrison's depiction of an old woman's bitterness at a life lost to slavery enhances our understanding of how individuals might have felt that there was nothing left in them to free.

The ways in which slavery continued to infiltrate freed slaves' lives is also evidenced in the haunting, literally, of not only the freed slaves but the African-American community at large. As Baby Suggs tells Sethe, "Not a house in the country ain't packed to its rafters with some dead Negro's GRIEF. We lucky this ghost is a baby." Similarly, Beloved relives her grandmother's experiences in the Middle Passage, recalling, "if I had the teeth of the man who died on my face I would bite the circle around her neck." This "circle," earlier referred to as a "circle of iron," is a slave collar in use during the time of the Middle Passage. The suggestion here is that slavery entered the racial memory of the African-American people, shaping African-American culture. Thus, although Emancipation is often taught as a date in a history book that demarcates the end of slavery, the legacy of slavery remains with us even now.

Although freedom is typically idealized and over-simplified, Morrison shows that freedom is instead contextual. For those freed slaves without resources, especially those unprepared due to a lack of education and experience to survive in the "free" world, Emancipation led to their own set of problems. Paul D. recalls the freed slaves he encountered on his travels who are "so stunned, or hungry, or tired or bereft it was a wonder they recalled or said anything." However, for Denver, who has never been enslaved, freedom is a given, and she cannot understand why her mother cannot let the past go. This range of experiences is Morrison's gift to us, helping us see slavery and freedom as individuals experienced it rather than as historians have retold it.

Nancy Wilson

GRIEF in *Beloved*

When Paul D. enters Sethe's house, "a wave of grief soaked him so thoroughly he wanted to cry. . . . [He] looked back at the spot where the grief had soaked him. The red was gone but a kind of weeping clung to the air where it had been." Although grief is a central theme in *Beloved*, nothing in a slave's life was ever simple. For example, although "crawling already?" baby was murdered by her own mother, Sethe was acting out of LOVE and desperation for a situation beyond her control. No wonder the reaction to the child's DEATH is so complicated—her FAMILY feels grief, of course, but that grief is often tinged with anger, resignation, GUILT, and denial.

For Sethe's children, the loss of "crawling already?" baby is less about grief for their sister and more about what they have lost personally. For instance, although she befriends the ghost at 124, Denver resents the fact that her sister's death has alienated her from friends and COMMUNITY: "All that leaving: first her brothers, then her grandmother—serious losses since there were no children willing to circle her in a game or hang by their knees from her porch railing." It is not surprising, then, that Denver describes the ghost as "rebuked. Lonely and rebuked." This is precisely how Denver feels.

Because she is a child, Denver cannot see beyond her own grief to forgive her mother or to recognize her mother's grief. On the other hand, compared to the adults around her, Denver's grief is manageable and survivable precisely because she does not fully recognize the endemic nature of grief among slaves.

In contrast, for Baby Suggs whose "past had been like her present—intolerable," grief for "crawling already?" baby is one grief too many. In response, Baby Suggs escapes into a dream world in which she can contemplate color as opposed to the sorrow that has followed her into freedom and indeed into her very home. Unfortunately, by retreating from family and community, Baby Suggs contributes to her own undoing. "Baby Suggs died shortly after the brothers left, with no interest whatsoever in their leave-taking or hers." She dies alone, of grief.

Like Baby Suggs, Paul D. has grieved intensely all of his life, and he also shuts down. His tale of grief reads like a litany: "It was some time before he could put Alfred, Georgia, Sixo, schoolteacher, Halle, his brothers, Sethe, Mister, the taste of iron, the sight of butter, the smell of hickory, notebook paper, one by one, into the tobacco tin lodged in his chest. By the time he got to 124 nothing in this world could pry it open." Given Paul D.'s survival strategy, it is not surprising that Paul D. literally drives the grief out of 124. Unfortunately, as the appearance of Beloved demonstrates, fighting one's grief will lead to its manifestation in another, potentially more hazardous form.

Sethe does grieve, but guilt prevents healing. Not only has she murdered her own child, she has also set into motion the grief that leads to Baby Suggs's death, the running away of Howard and Buglar, and the loneliness of Denver. "However many times Baby denied it, Sethe knew the grief at 124 started when she jumped down off the wagon, her newborn tied to her chest in the underwear of a whitegirl looking for Boston." Sethe's guilt blocks her MEMORY and feeds Beloved's vengeance, which nearly destroys Sethe. Although Sethe does survive, she takes to Baby Suggs's deathbed, suggesting that for Sethe, too, the grief is almost too much to bear. However, Sethe has Denver and Paul D., and in that sense the novel ends with HOPE.

Throughout *Beloved*, Morrison reveals the variety of ways in which individuals deal with an unspeakable tragedy. Interestingly, in the process she sheds light on why it has been difficult for the United States to grieve for the tragic victims of slavery. Like Sethe, the United States recognizes its complicity in the tragedy. However, the fact that *Beloved* has achieved such popularity, and films such as *Gone With the Wind* that deny the realities of slavery are no longer produced, suggests that the United States has finally conquered its feelings of guilt and can now remember the truth and sincerely and unselfishly grieve for its past. Morrison's effort in *Beloved* is a solid start.

Nancy Wilson

MORRISON, TONI   *The Bluest Eye* (1970)

The Bluest Eye tells the story of three little black girls whose lives are indelibly impacted by the racism of the 1940s. Nine-year-old Claudia MacTeer, who occasionally narrates the text, does not yet believe society's mandate that she is ugly and worthless because she is black. Yet her older sister Frieda and friend Pecola Breedlove have fully absorbed the message imparted by the adults' adoration of Shirley Temple and white baby dolls. Indeed, Pecola believes she would be loved if she only had blue eyes.

Claudia and Frieda passively witness the destruction of Pecola as she is tormented by her peers and shunned even by her family. Schoolmates Maureen Peal and Junior despise Pecola for her dark complexion, even though they also are black; even Pecola's mother, Pauline, thinks, "Lord she was ugly." Cholly, Pecola's alcoholic father, cannot comprehend PARENTHOOD after being abandoned at birth and traumatized by white men as a teenager. Ultimately, in what began as a misguided attempt to show her affection, Cholly rapes his daughter. Pregnant at 11 years, Pecola visits Soaphead Church, a fraudulent spiritualist, in the hope of receiving the life-changing blue eyes, as her prayers to God remain unanswered. He tricks her into believing her wish has been granted. Pecola's baby dies and she goes insane, finally happy from looking at her blue eyes in a mirror. An adult Claudia muses that the townspeople needed Pecola's destruction in order to feel better about themselves: "We were so beautiful when we stood astride her ugliness." *The Bluest Eye* is an impressive testament to the inveterate CRUELTY and destructiveness of racism in America. This novel addresses the themes of ISOLATION, RACE, and VIOLENCE.

Robin E. Field

ISOLATION in *The Bluest Eye*

Although the theme of isolation is one that transcends writer, place, and time, it has a special significance in African-American literature, considering that Jim Crow laws mandated racial segregation in all areas of American life. Even before the advent of Jim Crow laws, the institution of slavery featured an intentional separation of black family members from one another. Even though *The Bluest Eye* focuses on Pecola Breedlove's descent into madness and estrangement from everyone, it is vital to understand that her mother, Pauline Breedlove, shares much responsibility for Pecola's disconcerting conditions. Although Pauline contributes tremendously to Pecola's emotional and physical isolation, Pauline's own past impacts her ability to give her daughter the emotional support she needs.

In examining Pauline's past, the reader understands that Pauline's inability to help prevent Pecola's isolation is a result of Pauline's own mother, Ada's, emotional isolation from Pauline. When Pauline is a very young child, she accidentally suffers an injury that leaves " . . . her with a crooked, archless foot that flopped when she walked. . . . " Ada fails to protect Pauline from "the general feeling of separateness and unworthiness . . . " that her physical conditions create for her. With a full understanding of this aspect of Pauline's past, one can see that she has to battle internal demons of her own. Moreover, her mother's lack of response to her feeling of alienation suggests a reason why she might isolate herself from Pecola. Because Pauline never received the love she needed from Ada, she in turn feels no affection for Pecola. Ada's unwillingness to help Pauline confront her "feeling of separateness" has an impact on the type of love that Pauline is able to show Pecola. Without the love she wants to receive from Ada, Pauline has a void that she needs to satisfy before she can provide Pecola with the physical love that Pecola longs for.

Even though Pauline's past negatively impacts Pecola, understanding it is vital to understanding Pauline's effort to resist a descent into a state of isolation. Pauline seeks friendship as a means of filling the void of love that her mother does not provide. In Pauline's dreams, she longs for a companion who will fulfill her emptiness: " . . . the Presence would know what to do. She had only to lay her head on his chest and he would lead her away to the sea, to the city, to the woods . . . forever." Pauline's willingness to remain hopeful that this "Presence" will materialize enables her to embrace an opportunity for companionship when she meets Cholly Breedlove, her future husband. Although Pauline finds her "archless foot" to be a negative dimension of her body, Cholly embraces it: "Instead of ignoring her infirmity, pretending it was not there, he made it seem like something special and endearing." Pauline recognizes Cholly as her "Presence" because he recognizes that she matters. The attention that Cholly gives to her helps to fill some of the void. Pauline's inadequacy is a source of attraction for Cholly, which is a strong utopian suggestion that physical deformities cannot hinder true love. The emotional support Cholly shows Pauline suggests that love can be instrumental in helping vulnerable people from falling prey to the ravages of emotional and physical isolation.

Unfortunately, Pecola Breedlove does not receive enough love from Cholly Breedlove to overcome her emotional and physical isolation from society. Instead of assisting Pecola with the harsh realities of her social milieu, Cholly contributes to her tragic condition: He rapes Pecola. *The Bluest Eye* evinces the significance of parental involvement in helping children to avoid isolating themselves physically and emotionally from others. Although Pauline is able to gain some help with combating emotional isolation from Cholly, Pauline and Cholly do not seem to understand the need to help their daughter (Pecola) with her vexing descent into a disquieting emotional and physical isolation from others. It would seem natural that Pauline would want to return the support she receives from Cholly with the internal demons of her past, but she simply leaves her daughter to become the prey of a vicious and racist society.

Left without emotional support, Pecola attempts to find happiness in the false comforts of her physical and emotional isolation from her reality.

Antonio Maurice Daniels

RACE in *The Bluest Eye*

In *The Bluest Eye*, Toni Morrison's first novel, the reader encounters Pecola Breedlove—the protagonist of the novel who has to confront the dominant culture's oppressive standard of beauty. Morrison's narrative is situated in 1941, a time period that featured tremendous racial discrimination against African Americans on the basis of their skin color. Since the dominant culture's standard of beauty does not allow African Americans in 1941 to be considered as beautiful because of their dark (non-white) skin color, Pecola Breedlove experiences great racial shame because of this oppressive standard of beauty and desires to transcend the manacles of race. Pecola does not desire to be considered simply beautiful, but she has the strongest desire to be the most beautiful living human being. Therefore, in order to become the most beautiful living human being, Pecola aspires to have the bluest eye (a physical characteristic of the dominant culture's standard of beauty) to enable her to escape the oppressive bondage and limitations that her race places on her ability to see herself as the most beautiful human being. For Pecola, the only way that she will be able to be perceived as beautiful is to live imaginatively in a world where she does have the bluest eye—biologically impossible in the world in which she physically resides. In helping the reader to understand how Pecola Breedlove perceives how the dominant culture views her, Morrison writes: "She has seen it lurking in the eyes of all white people. So. The distaste must be for her, her blackness . . . But her blackness is static and dread. And it is the blackness that accounts for, that creates, the vacuum edged with distaste in white eyes." Although Pecola is able to see the "distaste" that the dominant culture has for her "blackness," Morrison is able to share with readers one of her most pervasive themes, permeating all eight of her novels, including *The Bluest Eye*: African Americans must seek alternatives to the oppressive reality that the social construction of race has caused them to experience. While Morrison's narrative interrogates salient issues surrounding the issue of race through Pecola, her focus on the racial shame of Claudia MacTeer, one of Pecola's closest friends and the novel's narrator, operates powerfully in illuminating her multifarious and nuanced ways of exploring the issue of race in *The Bluest Eye*.

One of the most important ways in which Morrison has Claudia MacTeer interface with the theme of race is through her interaction with Maureen Peal—a young African American with lighter skin than Claudia and Pecola. Claudia has internalized her racial shame and desires for Pecola not to voice her racial shame in the presence of Maureen. In a pivotal encounter where Claudia, Pecola, and Frieda (Claudia's sister) have an argument with Maureen about Maureen's claim that light-complexioned blacks are beautiful and dark-complexioned blacks are ugly, Pecola's silence, which endorses Maureen's claim about the relationship between skin color and beauty, accentuates and unveils Claudia's great internalized racial shame. In demonstrating her tremendous indignation for Pecola's conspicuous endorsement of Maureen's reprehensible claim, Claudia states, "She seemed to fold into herself, like a pleated wing. Her pain antagonized me. I wanted to open her up, crisp her edges, ram a stick down that hunched and curving spine, force her to stand erect and spit the misery out on the street." Claudia's internalized racial shame is vividly clear as she expresses her anger with Pecola for giving Maureen's disgraceful claim validity. While Claudia and Frieda attempt to conceal their racial shame through their incensed retorts to Maureen's claim, Claudia becomes increasingly angry with Pecola because she identifies with the conspicuous way in which Pecola sinks under "the wisdom, accuracy, and relevance" of Maureen's shameful and painful position.

Morrison's treatment of racial shame in the novel enables her readers not only to unearth the significant psychological impact of Pecola and Claudia perceiving themselves as racially inferior, but also to embrace the opportunity to understand the oppressive economic, social, and cultural milieu and problems that have plagued blacks historically. Pecola and Claudia are two of the most important vehicles Morrison employs for discussing salient issues about race. The novel is an instructive denunciation of the social construction of race.

Antonio Maurice Daniels

VIOLENCE in *The Bluest Eye*

The Bluest Eye is a novel filled with terrible violence. Toni Morrison's story revolves around an unthinkable crime: the rape of 11-year-old Pecola Breedlove by her father, Cholly. Yet Morrison demonstrates how this sexual violence derives from myriad personal and social circumstances, all of which must be acknowledged in order to understand the roots of Pecola's tragedy. Therefore, we learn about the psychological trauma Cholly suffered as a teenager at the hands of racist white men, information that does not condone his actions, but does explain their origins. In addition to Pecola's tragedy, the novel details the systematic psychological abuse of racism that in particular damages the young black girls in the story. *The Bluest Eye* chronicles the devastating effects of both physical and psychological violence in the black COMMUNITY.

Pecola's life is fraught with violence from the very first. Her parents' marriage has decayed into mutual loathing, punctuated by angry quarrels and physical brawls. Our first glimpse of the Breedlove household is a quarrel that occurs after Cholly comes home drunk. Morrison writes, "Because it had not taken place immediately, the oncoming fight would lack spontaneity; it would be calculated, uninspired, and deadly." What begins as a verbal exchange of insults soon escalates to blows: "He fought her the way a coward fights a man—with feet, the palms of his hands, and teeth. She, in turn, fought back in a purely feminine way—with frying pans and pokers, and occasionally a flatiron would sail toward his head." The children's reaction to this brawl differs. Pecola's older brother, Sammy, joins the fight against his father, screaming "Kill him!" But Pecola stays motionless in her bed, praying that God will make her disappear so she won't have to witness these events. Her desire to disappear eventually shifts to the wish for blue eyes; for she believes that being beautiful will bring LOVE and happiness into her life. And according to contemporary society, beauty means the big blue eyes of someone like Shirley Temple. Morrison uses Pecola's dream of having blue eyes to illustrate the psychological damage wrought by white beauty standards upon young black girls.

Psychological trauma is the genesis of Cholly's violent personality. Abandoned by his parents as an infant, Cholly grows up with few models for appropriate parenting. Yet more important to his warped psychological development is a terrifying encounter with armed white hunters when he is a teenager. Cholly is engaged in his first sexual experience with a neighbor girl in the woods when the two hunters happen upon them. The men order Cholly to continue having SEX with Darlene and to "make it good," reinforcing their power by ominously shifting their guns and running their lights over the couple's half-clothed bodies." Unable to refuse, Cholly and Darlene are transformed into a sexual spectacle for the voyeuristic gratitude of the hunters. Cholly lowers his pants and feigns intercourse, for he has been rendered impotent by fear. His concurrent anger he directs upon Darlene: "He hated her. He almost wished he could do it—hard, long, and painfully, he hated her so much." Cholly is unable to vent his frustration except upon the girl beneath him. For Cholly, sex is no longer an avenue for enjoyment, but a way to express anger and violence and to demonstrate power over another person. The metaphorical rape of Cholly by the white men—their stripping of his self-respect and agency through sexual humiliation—allows the reader to understand his warped understanding of sex. His subsequent rape of Pecola results from his feelings of anger, GUILT, and revulsion toward his child, all emotions he associates with sex.

The other two young black girls in the novel, Frieda and Claudia MacTeer, also suffer physical and psychological violence. In another example of the home as unsafe space, Frieda is sexually molested by the family's boarder, Mr. Henry. Frieda also joins the adult adoration of the "cu-ute" Shirley Temple, valorizing those blonde curls and blue eyes as superior to her own brown hair and eyes. The younger Claudia has not yet been brainwashed into believing whiteness is superior and destroys the white baby dolls she is given as Christmas gifts. Her observation is biting: "Adults, older girls, shops, magazines, newspapers, window signs—all the world had agreed that a blue-eyed, yellow-haired, pink-skinned doll was what every girl child treasured." Ultimately, however, Claudia is one of the many townspeople who passively witness Pecola's insanity and friendlessness after the death of her baby. The ultimate violence, Morrison intimates, is when the community turns upon one of its own: "when the land kills of its own volition, we acquiesce and say the victim had no right to live." *The Bluest Eye* beautifully documents the destructive effects of individual and societal violence.

Robin E. Field

MORRISON, TONI *Song of Solomon* (1977)

Toni Morrison's celebrated novel, *Song of Solomon,* is the story of Macon Dead, who seeks to make good in a world dominated by racial prejudice, and his son, Milkman Dead, whose quest for his real self and his struggle to discover his roots carries the burden of a major thematic strand of the novel. Guitar, Milkman's erstwhile best friend, tries to kill Milkman more than once after incorrectly suspecting he has been cheated of hidden gold. Ruth, Macon Dead's wife, Pilate, Macon's sister, her daughter Reba and her granddaughter Hagar are other characters who dominate the narrative. Their personal, familial, and social interactions are set against the backdrop of a world dominated by RACE and GENDER prejudice and a social fabric marred by a variegated pattern of VIOLENCE.

Hagar falls desperately in love with Milkman and is unable to cope with his rejection. Morrison's insights into distorted LOVE and its consequences are most intuitively apprehended and made credible and accessible to the reader.

Toni Morrison's work gives us a unique understanding of life and living in an African-American context. Also, as a remarkably skillful and perceptive author, she rises above her immediate concerns. Through the vividly delineated local color, she analyzes the universal and perennial human predicament. The ultimate impact of her work, especially *Song of Solomon,* is one of joy, HOPE and triumph of the human spirit.

Gulshan Taneja

GRIEF in *Song of Solomon*

After being reared for virtually her entire childhood by her devoted and elitist father, Ruth Foster Dead evolves into womanhood dependent on and loyal to her father for the great affection he showed her throughout her life. However, after her father's death, Ruth understands that her tremendous investment in her father's life contributed significantly to her lack of a personal IDENTITY. Since her father had great wealth and many of the finest material things, she developed a false consciousness that she would not need anything or anybody other than her father. Therefore, through convincing herself that her father is the only person or thing she needs in life, Ruth exposes herself to the possibility that she will have to experience the harmful impact of a lasting grief. In delineating her despondent condition, Ruth states, "I didn't think I'd ever need a friend because I had him. I was small, but he was big. The only person who ever really cared whether I lived or died . . . he cared . . . and there was, and is no one else in the world ever did." Ruth carries the burden of her self-inflicted grief by electing to alienate herself from establishing a meaningful camaraderie with someone other than her father. Therefore, the obsession that she develops for her father leads her to experience the significant grief that accompanies an excessive attachment to temporal beings or things that cannot transcend the ravages of time. As a means of attempting to satisfy constantly her fetish for her father, Ruth visits his grave each night to revitalize her connection to her father and restore that "cared-for-feeling." However, Ruth finds that her grief over her father's death only further complicates her relationships with her husband and son. The novel provides an interesting engagement with the theme of grief not only through its treatment of Ruth's response to her father's death, but also through its treatment of Macon Dead II's grief, which emerges in response to Ruth's uncanny fetish for her father.

Macon carries the grief of not being able to show his wife love and affection. He grieves the loss of their relationship after he finds her alone with her father's dead body. With disgust, he thinks, "In the bed. That's where she was when I opened the door. Laying next to him. Naked as a yard dog, kissing him. Him dead and white and puffy and skinny, and she had his fingers in her mouth." Therefore, the reader is able to see that the grief that Macon Dead II experiences results from his wife having such a strange fetish for her father that she places his dead fingers in her mouth. Ruth's eccentric sexual act with her dead father is so traumatic for Macon because it shocks his consciousness. He knows that he cannot ever kiss and show his wife affection without this unspeakable memory coming back to him. He becomes so psychologically disturbed that he "started thinking all sorts of things," including the possibility that he is not the father of his and Ruth's children.

Morrison's novel enables the reader to see how intricately complex and debilitating grief can be for individuals, especially individuals who already are situated in a historical moment that does not afford African Americans treatment and opportunities equal to those enjoyed by members of the dominant culture. Ruth and Macon are classic examples of how incommodious it can be to overcome the depredation of salient grief. Unfortunately, Ruth and Macon Dead II are unable to overcome their overwhelmingly challenging grief.

Antonio Maurice Daniels

RACE in *Song of Solomon*

In her novel, *Song of Solomon*, Toni Morrison does not attempt to provide a solution for racial conflict, but rather depicts the effects of racism on three generations of an African-American family and the communities in which they live. Morrison depicts racism as both a physical and mental barrier that exists not only between multiple races (interracial) but also within a single race (intraracial). For the Deads and the closely knit African-American community in *Song of Solomon*, race significantly affects every aspect of their lives.

The novel, set in the 1930s and 1940s in an unnamed Michigan town, opens with an introduction to race as a physical divider, which Morrison presents in terms of the socially and legally authorized, race-based segregation prevalent in American society up through the 20th century. Robert Smith, an African-American insurance agent, has determined to "take off from Mercy and fly away on [his] own wings." Smith's flight draws a crowd to Not Doctor Street, which is the unofficial name of the street where "the only colored doctor in the city had lived and died." As Morrison explains how the street came to be called Not Doctor Street, she also draws the physical line that separates the city's African-American population from the white population. When the doctor moved to the street in 1896, he was the only Negro on the street. His patients, who were predominantly Negroes, did not live on or near the street, which they began to call Doctor Street. As time progressed and the town's Negro population continued to refer to the street as Doctor Street, the city legislators attempted to force the black community to refer to the street as Mains Avenue.

> Some of the city legislators, whose concern for appropriate names and the maintenance of the city's landmarks was the principal part of their political life, saw to it that "Doctor Street" was never used in any official capacity. And since they knew that only Southside residents kept it up, they had notices posted in the stores, barbershops, and restaurants in that part of the city saying that the avenue . . . had always been and would always be known as Mains Avenue and not Doctor Street.

It was after this that the Southside residents began to refer it as Not Doctor Street. The idea that Negroes did not originally live on or near Doctor Street and were later confined to the "Southside," indicates the physical barriers of racial segregation between blacks and whites.

The physical segregation was not limited to where one lived, but extended to where people were able to obtain public services, including health care. In 1931, Robert Smith drew the crowd to Mercy Hospital on Not Doctor Street, and as a result "the first colored expectant mother was allowed to give birth inside its wards and not on its steps."

This incident was quite possibly a forced integration, being that the woman went into labor while standing outside the hospital witnessing Mr. Smith's flight. Until that time, neither the Negro doctor nor any of his patients, aside from two, both white, were granted privileges or admitted at Mercy.

Stories of interracial segregation are not uncommon; yet, Morrison moves beyond the external complications of race to the internal or intraracial effects of race and racism upon the African-American community. As a consequence of colonialism and interracial racism, many in the black community internalize this racism and inflict it upon one another. In *Song of Solomon,* the internalization of prejudice is expressed in terms of the internal thoughts of African-American characters and in their actions toward African-American characters.

Macon Dead II, the richest black man in town, is a materialistic, "colored man of property" whose chief interest is obtaining money and land. He is ashamed of his sister, Pilate, and her daughter and granddaughter, all of whom essentially reject the idea of materialism that he values. In a lone instance when Pilate visits Macon's house, his internalization of Eurocentric ideals is apparent by his thoughts. "He trembled with thought of the white men in the bank—the men who helped him buy and mortgage houses—discovering that this raggedy bootlegger was his sister." Rather than concern himself with his relationship with his sister, Macon Dead is more concerned with and even fearful of what "white men" might think. This is indicative of the mental barrier that is a consequence of racism.

Intraracial racism and internalized Eurocentrism is also presented in terms of how African Americans regard themselves and other African Americans. Mrs. Bains, one of Macon Dead II's tenants, says, "A nigger in business is a terrible thing to see. A terrible, terrible thing to see." Mrs. Bains says this after an encounter with Macon Dead II. She degrades an African American by referring to him as a "nigger," while implying that African Americans should not be business owners. This indicates her internalization of the notion of African-American inferiority.

Race is a prevalent theme throughout *Song of Solomon,* and there are several instances in which Morrison depicts the negative and lasting effects of racism on the African-American community. Racist notions uphold physical and mental barriers both externally and internally.

ShaShonda Porter

VIOLENCE in *Song of Solomon*

In the pattern of life and living that Toni Morrison weaves for her characters, violence appears as an unmistakable, insistent, and deliberately plotted component. Violence that marks the life of the characters in *Song of Solomon* is sometimes the result of a failure of self-restraint or of explosive emotional outbursts. Domestic violence in *Song of Solomon* falls in this category. The nature of the relationship that Macon Dead and his unloved wife Ruth share provides ample examples of this kind of violence.

Characters in *Song of Solomon* resort to extreme physical and emotional reaction in response to deep trauma. Hagar, who falls desperately in love with Milkman, is unable to cope with his rejection and, traumatized, hunts for him with a "Carlson skinning knife": " . . . Totally taken over by her anaconda love, she had no self left, no fears, no wants, no intelligence that was her own" (137). Ruth Dead addresses herself to Hagar: "'You are trying to kill him. . . . If you so much as bend a hair on his head, so help me Jesus, I will tear your throat out.'" Guitar's reaction to Milkman's betrayal in refusing to share the hidden gold leads to a ruthless manhunt in which he tries to kill Milkman more than once. Pilate threatens her daughter's current lover with a knife, "positioned . . . at the edge of his heart," when he beats her up.

There is street violence between Milkman and other Negroes in Shalimar town. In another dimension to the violence that casts a shadow over the lives of African Americans, there is the emotional violence that characters suffer in the context of racial discrimination when they are ill treated, or worse, when the humiliating treatment meted out to the blacks by the whites is assumed to be appropriate. Escalating the violence, both groups prey on each other. Macon Dead, Sr., is shot dead in front of his children. Every time a black American is killed, the members of the Seven Day Group kill a white man in the same manner.

The stories of killers fill the narrative. Winnie Ruth's doings are the talk of the town and staple gossip at the local barbershop where men regularly get together. The murder of Emmett Till receives much attention in the novel in order to remind the reader of the real history of racial violence in America. Milkman is supposed to have killed a white man in the cave. Pilate keeps a skeleton, eventually confirmed as that of her father, in a sack most of her life as her "inheritance."

It is significant that violence of all and any kind in *Song of Solomon* performs a deeply symbolic function in the total context of the novel, however essential it may appear to be to the basic narrative. By itself, the domestic violence in the Dead household seems to hold little significance to the characters, but it allows the reader to perceive a pattern of all-pervasive aggression that envelops the novel. The physical bloodshed resulting from racial hatred is orchestrated as a chorus-like, ritualistic and congruent occurrence, such as the reciprocal killings of the whites by the Seven Day Group. Milkman's clash with others in Shalimar town comes across more as a rite of passage than the angry outburst of young men having a go at each other. Morrison holds her prose in firm control and registers just the right nuance.

Violence is presented as the norm rather than as an exception in the variegated collage of human existence. An all-pervasive current of ferocity connects humanity to a state of raw, wild, and seemingly a pre-civilized existence. The violence and brutality that govern the life and times of black America reveal the nature and significance of black American experience. But this also allows Morrison to connect the postwar black American experience to human existence at its most elemental level, thus focusing on universal dimensions of humanity, much like ROBINSON CRUSOE, LORD OF THE FLIES, and Ayn Rand's ANTHEM, all of which show humanity shorn of the icings of civilization.

It is ironic that the African-American desire to achieve social equality is equated with the African-American ambition to achieve material gains, as Macon Dead's economic upward mobility, or the narrator's references to money, hidden gold, and poverty, is plainly designed to show. But Morrison's insights into deeper human urges raise her artistic endeavor to a finer level. Morrison's reliance on the myth as her essential artistic tool helps her achieve this goal. The essential core of *Song of Solomon*, in its deeper penetrations, therefore, projects a universal human dilemma rather than a limited and limiting black American experience.

Gulshan Taneja

MORRISON, TONI *Sula* (1973)

Sula (1973) is Nobel laureate Toni Morrison's second published novel. Spanning the years from 1919 to 1965, the story centers on the childhood friendship and later estrangement of two women living in a black community called the Bottom, near the town of Medallion, Ohio. Sula Peace, the only daughter of a young and attractive widow, Hannah Peace, lives in the labyrinthine house of her grandmother, Eva Peace, who is a fiercely protective but emotionally distant matriarch. Nel Wright is the only daughter of lakeman Wiley Wright and beautiful and morally impeccable Helene, whose mother, Rochelle Sabat, is a Creole prostitute in New Orleans. Meeting in 1920, when they are both around 10 years old, Sula and Nel become inseparable. After Nel marries a local man, Jude Greene, in 1927, Sula leaves town, presumably to attend college. Upon Sula's sudden return 10 years later, their friendship revives but quickly dies when Sula seduces Jude. Years later, in 1965, Nel realizes that she has actually been missing not her husband but Sula, who has been dead 25 years. The novel's other major characters include Shadrack, a World War I veteran who founds an enigmatic annual ritual called National Suicide Day; Plum, Sula's uncle and another traumatized war veteran; and Ajax, Sula's lover who is attracted to her fierce independence, which separates her from all other women of the community. The major themes of the novella include race, gender, sexuality, freedom, alienation, grief, individual and society, love, parenthood, community, oppression, violence, and religion.

Tomoko Kuribayashi

GENDER in *Sula*

In Toni Morrison's second novel, gender issues cannot be separated from issues of RACE and racism. The legacy of slavery has left its mark on Morrison's black characters, who live in a rural Ohio community called the Bottom. The many serious conflicts that exist between the black women and men, as well

as their traditional gender roles and expectations, need to be considered in light of this legacy and its aftereffects. All the male characters in *Sula*, for example, seem defeated, unable to become responsible adults in a society that will not grant them full manhood. Eva Peace's husband and the father of her three children is a prime example of stunted male growth, as his name, BoyBoy, clearly indicates. Nel Wright's husband, Jude Greene, also suffers from the sense that his masculinity is inadequate; he and other young black men of the Bottom are extremely disappointed and frustrated when, fully capable physically and eager to contribute hard labor, they are denied road construction jobs in favor of skinny white men. Even Ajax, a much admired local Lothario, yearns for a white man's job, the privilege of flying airplanes. The three Deweys, adopted by Eva as young boys, are healthy and active, but never grow beyond four feet and remain childish in behavior. Plum Peace and Shadrack, both traumatized World War I veterans, cannot function normally; though their major problems may stem from battle fatigue, arguably some of the trauma was caused by the army's racism and the black soldiers' treatment upon their homecoming.

The Bottom's black women are given the responsibility of caring for black men who suffer from the sense that they are not "man enough." While Eva wholeheartedly hates BoyBoy for deserting his family, she, and other Peace women, simply love maleness. Despite missing one leg, Eva has a steady flow of male visitors admiring her as if she were a goddess, even though they share no sexual intimacy. Her daughter Hannah, a young widow, has many lovers who appreciate her natural beauty and easy-going manners. Helene Wright, in contrast, suppresses any expression of female sexuality—or any spontaneous self-expression, for that matter—in herself and her daughter, Nel. Helene fears the blood of her prostitute mother, Rochelle Sabat, should be manifesting itself in them. Raised by her grandmother, a devout Catholic in New Orleans, Helene believes in women's spiritual and moral superiority. For the Wright women, as for the Peaces, taking care of men's various needs forms the core of a woman's life: Helene prides herself on her impeccable housekeeping and Nel devotes herself to meeting her husband's and, later, her children's needs; in fact, Jude's proposal to her is prompted by Nel's fierce desire to soothe his pain after his failure to get a more manly job. When Jude and Nel concur that the racist world humiliates black men at every possible juncture, Sula retorts that black women—and children—hang on every word black men say, making black men "the envy of the world."

Sula represents the opposite of what dictates the lives of the women in the Bottom. When she returns to the community after 10 years' absence, her grandmother Eva tells her to get married and have children. Sula replies that she would rather make herself than make babies. She takes numerous lovers, many of them other women's husbands, including her best friend Nel's, but she also discards them quickly afterward, unlike her mother Hannah who was generous with her sexual favors. Lovemaking, for Sula, is a means by which she can find herself and be alone with herself, despite the physical proximity to another person. Sula's radical independence, defying the black community's norm for female behavior, infuriates both men and women. When Nel tells Sula on her deathbed that a colored woman cannot act like a man or act independent, Sula replies that being a colored woman equals being a man, free to do as one likes. One man who is attracted to Sula's individualism is Ajax, who seeks in her the same quality he admires in his mother, an evil "conjure" woman worshipped by her seven sons. But Ajax's case may highlight another gender problem common in the black community: a too strong, often smothering bond between mother and son, also existent between Eva and Plum Peace. In admiring Sula for her resemblance to his mother, Ajax, like the other characters in the novel, reinforces traditional and troubling gender roles.

Tomoko Kuribayashi

PARENTHOOD in *Sula*

Like all other themes found in *Sula,* the issue of parenthood cannot be considered in separation from race and racism. Parent-child relationships in *Sula,* both for women and for men, are heavily influenced by the history of slavery and the racism that poisoned 20th-century American society.

Plainly put, Morrison's male characters fail to be responsible fathers. For example, after several years of womanizing, drinking, and spousal abuse, BoyBoy leaves Eva Peace with three young children and virtually nothing to her name, which forces Eva, as rumor goes, to have her leg severed so that she may collect insurance money with which to support her family. Jude Greene, Nel Wright's husband and also father to three young children, abandons his family after having a casual affair with Nel's best friend, Sula Peace. Both of these men, along with virtually all other male characters in the novella, seem to suffer from the sense that they are inferior to white men and therefore incapable of responsible adulthood and meaningful fatherhood; even BoyBoy, apparently successful and well-to-do upon his brief homecoming, seems to Eva to harbor defeat in his posture. Additionally, the practice of not granting slaves any paternal rights, or even recognition of biological fatherhood, has left black men unable to perform the duties of husbands and fathers. Significantly, the only responsible father figure in the novella, Nel's father Wiley Wright, is noticeable mainly as an absence. He is usually gone for his job on a lake ship, which is welcome to his wife, Helene, to whom sexual intimacy not for the purpose of procreation is anathema, having been raised by a devoutly Catholic grandmother.

The black men's failure to parent leaves the black women to raise their young single-handedly. Often that calls for extreme self-sacrifice, as in the case of Eva who reportedly mutilated herself physically to earn a living large enough for her family. Nel also takes on various cleaning jobs to support her children after Jude's desertion. A few black women, like Teapot's Mamma in the Bottom or Helene Wright's birth mother Rochelle Sabat, who is a New Orleans prostitute, are deemed guilty of neglecting—if not abusing—their children, emotionally or otherwise. Their failure as mothers seems to stem from their seemingly excessive sexual interest in men, which implies that black mothers cannot be sexual and maternal at the same time.

The novella, however, may suggest that even the most conscientious mother cannot respond to a child's every need. For example, Sula Peace overhears her young widowed mother, Hannah, comment that she loves Sula but does not like her, which sends the young girl on a self-destructive path while it also frees her from certain obligations of black womanhood, including motherhood. Devoted mothers like Eva and Helene can be labeled as domineering, suffocating, and/or manipulative, possibly doing what they do for their own satisfaction rather than for the well-being of their children. Helene focuses her energy on suppressing Nel's wilder inclinations to shape her in the mold of respectable black femininity. Eva provides for her children, both biological and adopted, but the children regard her with fear and anxiety. Asked by her daughter Hannah whether she ever loved her children when they were young, that is, whether she coddled and played with them, Eva angrily replies that she helped them survive amid extreme deprivation. Another question asked by Morrison's novella is how much control mothers should have over their children's lives. When her son Plum comes back from the World War a broken man and heroin addict, Eva chooses to burn him to death in his drug-induced stupor. The same Eva, however, almost kills herself trying to save Hannah from a fire.

Sula rebels against the sociocultural injunction that black women be good mothers, or at least be mothers. When Eva tells her that as a woman she needs to have babies, Sula replies that she wants to make herself, not babies. This refusal to give herself over to motherhood, coupled with her random sampling and callous dismissal of the community's men, leads to her ostracism in the Bottom. Paradoxically, Sula's selfish, unwomanly behavior ends up consolidating the parent-child bonds as well as marital relations in the black community.

Tomoko Kuribayashi

RACE in *Sula*

Toni Morrison's novel opens with the description of a linguistic manifestation of racism in the United States. A slave was promised freedom and a piece of bottom land—considered the best farm land—by a white farmer in exchange for several difficult feats. When the tasks were completed, the farmer made the slave believe that hilly land, less fertile and backbreaking to farm, was indeed the bottom land, being the bottom of heaven. Thus, the novel's first episode shows how racist society manipulates language to deprive and oppress black people while also pointing out that emancipated slaves were given little to no financial means to improve their lives. When *Sula* opens in 1920, the novel's main characters live in "the Bottom," near the town of Medallion, Ohio, in extreme poverty and in a state of general oppression. A drowned black child's body, dragged through the water by a white bargeman afraid that the corpse's smell might rub off on his gear, is unrecognizable by the time he is returned to his mother. Conflicts with the police are considered "the natural hazards of Negro life" by local young men. Even respectable black women like Helene Wright and her daughter Nel are subjected to racist treatment on their train ride south to Helene's grandmother's funeral. Accustomed to such mistreatment by fellow human beings, the residents of the Bottom accept evil as part of life. For them God has four faces, not the three of the Holy Trinity; the fourth face is the face of the devil.

Another major way race and racism affect Morrison's black characters' lives is through gender roles and expectations. The black men suffer from the sense that their masculinity is inferior to that of white men: For example, they are not given jobs for local road construction, which would allow them to prove their manhood. Much other desirable work, including the privilege of flying airplanes, is exclusively reserved for white men. Plum Peace and Shadrack both come home from World War I, never to become wholly functional again due to the racism experienced by black soldiers in the army and on their homecoming. The debilitating lack of confidence in their manhood, possibly coupled with the denial of paternal rights in slavery, leads to black men's failure to become husbands and fathers. BoyBoy, Eva Peace's husband, deserts her and their three young children, forcing Eva to make great sacrifices to feed her FAMILY. Nel Wright's husband, Jude Greene, also ends up abandoning his family after his affair with Sula Peace, Nel's best friend, is discovered. Given men's diffidence and inability to parent, black women must shoulder the double burden of nursing the men's hurt—or enduring their abuse—and raising their children single-handedly, as Eva Peace and Nel Greene are forced to do.

Because of race-specific gender expectations formed by a racist society, Sula Peace's insistence that she should retain her independence and individuality, and her refusal to cater to the needs of others, make her an outcast in the Bottom. The black community's suspicion and hatred of her are further fueled by the rumor that she has slept with white men. In light of the history of mass rape of black slave women by white men, it is an unforgivable sin for a black woman to have voluntary sexual relations with a white man. It is for the same reason that Helene Wright tries to suppress what she regards as the wild blood of her Creole mother, who as a prostitute had sex with white men, as Helene's own skin color proves.

Yet the color of their skin, a source of much suffering and sorrow, seems to be also what gives the characters their sense of self and of belonging. For one, Shadrack re-recognizes himself for the first time after the war when he sees his black face reflected in water; he then goes on to establish the annual ritual of National Suicide Day, which becomes an accepted part of the life of the Bottom and possibly is a celebration of slaves' defiance of the fear that permeated their lives. Sula sees Ajax's black skin and imagines alabaster bones and black loam underneath. Even Hannah Peace and Plum's death by fire may commemorate the death by burning experienced by many lynching victims. The three Deweys adopted by Eva continue to play chain-gang as adults. Thus, in 1965, Nel reflects that despite the much touted social progress made on behalf of black people, something important has been lost when the black community of the Bottom disintegrated.

Tomoko Kuribayashi

MORRISON, TONI *Tar Baby* (1982)

Toni Morrison's *Tar Baby* updates the classic Uncle Remus story about a doll made of tar used to trap Br'er Rabbit. Full of references to tar—in particular, the tar-like swamp into which Morrison's protagonist, Jadine (Jade), falls halfway through the novel—Morrison's text calls into question who is tricking whom and what is at stake when the trap is sprung. Most traditional readings of Morrison's novel interpret Jadine as trying desperately to escape

"the swamp" that is otherwise composed of aspects of her own origins. By "escaping" to Europe and modeling Eurocentric styles, Jadine feels as though she is above the swamp women who seem to call to her. However, in the end, it seems as though she has not been trapped, or even tricked, by the tar-like swamp at all, but by European standards of beauty that cause her to forget her roots and her identity as a woman of African-American descent.

Aimee Pozorski

LOVE in *Tar Baby*

Without exception, Toni Morrison's novels dramatize the effects of a love that is "too thick"—a mother's love or a lover's love that is so committed and intense that it threatens the lives of both lover and beloved. *Tar Baby* showcases this love through a mother and her child: the one, a former beauty queen and lonely wife of a candy-store owner; the other, a grown son who appears to resent his mother, although no one knows why, exactly, except for Ondine, the servant behind the scenes and running the lives of this family.

Although the novel more explicitly focuses on such themes as race, identity, and success, *Tar Baby* opens and closes with a discussion of whether Michael, the beloved son, will attend Christmas dinner with the Streets and their staff. As anticipation builds for the arrival of Michael, so too does it grow for the arrival of a camp footlocker, a locker that becomes a symbol for Michael: closed tight, not just to carry clothes, but also to carry secrets that he has kept locked inside since childhood.

In addition to the footlocker, several other details offered in the beginning of the novel suggest that something has gone awry between this mother, Margaret, and her son. Margaret's eyes, for example, are described as "blue-if-it's-a-boy blue"—not simply to emphasize Margaret's marks of beauty as valued by an Anglophilic world, but also to emphasize her role and ambivalence as a young mother: Her child was wrapped tight in a blue blanket upon birth, and the pressure seemed to mount from there." Morrison's novel seems to turn on this tension—both through flashbacks of a tormented past and through present-day conversations between the wealthy white Margaret, lady of the house, and

Ondine, the black servant who was as young as Margaret when she began working for the Streets.

Margaret and Ondine very nearly became friends. But, as we find out in one of the most intense conversations of the novel, only Ondine knows Michael and Margaret's secret—that Margaret cut and burned her baby because "she could," as she later confesses." "You white freak! You baby killer! I saw you! I saw you!" Ondine shrieks at the dinner table, to which Margaret responds, "Shut up! Shut up! You nigger! You nigger bitch! Shut your big mouth, I'll kill you! " After dinner, Jadine, Ondine's niece, says, "'That was awful, awful," which is the emotional response of the reader as well. What is interesting in this argument about a mother's inappropriate behavior is that, it, too, gets bound up with representations of race and the complicated relationships between women. Ondine calls Margaret a "white freak," to which Margaret retaliates with "you nigger." At no time during this argument is the experience of Michael mentioned. The argument is about these two women alone (women who once also loved each other, in their own way), with the accused, significantly, threatening murder—"I'll kill you"—instead of denying the charges.

It is not until later that it becomes clear that, from Morrison's point of view, this mother's abuse is the exemplary case, in this novel, of a mother's "too-thick" love: Margaret has decided to talk about it with her husband, to which he responds: "Why does he love you?" Margaret answers, her eyes again described as "blue-if-it's-a-boy," "Because I love him." Margaret and Valerian repeat this question and answer three times, to which Margaret finally—the third time—answers the question of why Michael could possibly love his mother with "I don't know."

Margaret's "I don't know" resonates not only within this scene, but also throughout the novel, in relation to nearly all of the love relationships: the romantic love between Jade and Son, one a privileged and successful, light-skinned mulatto, the other a dark African-American man who literally (as if to underscore the Streets' belief in primitivism) arrives naked on their boat; the familial bond between Ondine and Jade, the one a servant who worked her entire life for an abusive mother in order

to pay for the privilege of Jade; the marital bond between Ondine and her husband Sydney—working side by side all of those years for the "crazy, white" folks. The only relationship that so clearly lacks love is the relationship between Margaret and her husband Valerian, which seems to say something not only about wealth and beauty, but also about humanity generally: Money and beauty cannot buy love—and without adult love, the novel seems to suggest in the end, we are doomed to destroy our children.

Aimee Pozorski

RACE in *Tar Baby*

As *Tar Baby*'s epigraph—from 1 Corinthians—makes clear, "there are contentions among" the characters in the novel. These contentions arise from the characters' divergent experiences of themselves as black, and the way blackness has been constructed by white culture. This is a novel that pits the light-skinned Jadine Childs against the swampy, chronic blackness of Son, an African-American stowaway without a proper name. Through the characters of Jadine and Son, *Tar Baby* explores the way historically disadvantaged groups can frequently take on the oppressive categories of the dominant culture.

Tar Baby revolves around the family of a patriarchal white entrepreneur, Valerian Street, and his beauty-queen wife, Margaret; their black house servants, Sydney and Ondine, and the servants' niece, Jadine Childs. While the servants Sydney and Ondine do feel put upon by the Streets, the novel's real contention is in the younger generation, represented by Son and Jadine. Margaret finds Son hidden in a closet in the family's mansion, *L'Arbe de la Croix*. Playing upon the white racist fantasy that African-American men want to "sully" pure white women, Margaret assumes that Son fully intends to rape her. However, he is really in love with Jadine, a European sophisticate who admires the soft, black skin of baby seals wrapped around her when she first speaks with Son—a cloak symbolic of the potential of Son himself.

In fact, the novel begins and ends with the perspective of Son, who falls in love while watching the fair-skinned Jadine sleep. Immediately, Morrison contrasts the two characters based on their connections to racial heritage: Son appears to have come from a swamp, carrying with him an animal stench and unkempt hair. He is referred to by Jadine's uncle as a "stinking, ignorant swamp nigger" and "a wild-eyed pervert who hides in women's closets." By contrast, Jadine, with Valerian's help, is a European model in high demand; her fair complexion has earned her fame in Paris, as has her European education. While the elegant, beautiful, well-spoken Jadine seems to be the hero of the novel, it is actually Son who emerges as the most sympathetic character. As we see the city-raised Jadine lose touch with her ancestors, indicated by her haunting, guilt-provoking visions of the swamp women and African women who bare their breasts during their most private hours, Son remains faithful to his family and friends of African descent who continue to survive in the slow, southern town of Eloe, Florida.

Even at the end of the novel, when Son pursues Jade to the Isle of Chevaliers after a violent argument in New York City, Morrison does not clearly indicate whether Son and Jade will ever reunite. Led by Thérèse, a former employee of the Street family who is also aging and nearly blind, Son ends up figuratively blind himself, climbing out of a boat in the dark to take on the 10-mile walk to Jade's aunt and uncle with the intention of asking her whereabouts. When she leaves him, groping and in the dark, Thérèse says to Son, "The men. The men are waiting for you. . . . You can choose now. They are naked and they are blind too. . . . But they gallop; they race horses like angels all over the hills." While we do not get confirmation of Son's ultimate choice—Jade and her Eurocentric views, or "the men" as symbolized by the fraternity of Eloe and his experiences in the Vietnam War—the novel ends with a fairly strong indication that he chooses the men and their horses by mimicking the sound of blind men on horseback: "Lickety-split. Lickety-split. Lickety-lickety-lickety-split." After being celebrated for his trophy girlfriend and wealthy connections, in the end Son is reduced to blindness, surrounded by the onomatopoetic sounds of galloping horses. But in this reduction—to a primitive, more "pure" sense of self over and against the Eurocentric vision of Jadine that has caused her to lose all connection with her

African heritage, including her aunt and uncle—Son comes out on top.

Just as the rabbits in the African folktale are distracted from the white farmer's produce by a tar baby, Son is momentarily distracted by Jadine Childs. But, with the help of a blind old woman, Son himself becomes blind and, paradoxically, sees the light: The way home is not toward Jadine, but toward the men on horseback who represent his heritage. When the mist lifts, and he realizes the way "home," he runs toward them: "lickety-lickety-lickety-split," toward a racial origin that has maintained its identity despite the technology of the city and the values of a white, patriarchal economy.

Aimee Pozorski

SUCCESS in *Tar Baby*

Through the central figure of Jade, *Tar Baby* challenges key assumptions about what makes someone a success. Jade is an internationally known model whose face has graced the covers of *Vogue* and *Elle*; she has been educated in Europe and lived in France, and—when the novel opens—is being pursued by a wealthy businessman who sends her a seal-skin coat. Early in the novel, however, it becomes clear that even this kind of success has limitations. The signaled limitations take the form of a woman in yellow who emerges on a day when Jade goes to the market, knowing she is "intelligent and lucky." For Jade, "the vision itself was a woman much too tall. Under her long canary yellow dress Jadine knew there was too much hip, too much bust. The agency would laugh her out of the lobby, so why was she and everybody else in the store transfixed?" (45). The reference to tar later in this scene echoes the "tar baby" of the title, but also foreshadows a scene several chapters into the novel, when Jade gets stuck, alone, in a tar-like swamp, surrounded, apparently, by women who "looked down from the rafters of the trees [and] stopped murmuring. They were delighted when first they saw her, thinking a runaway child had been restored to them. But upon looking closer they saw differently. This girl was fighting to get away from them."

This swamp, surrounded by phantom women, is described as "slime," "moss-covered jelly," "oil," "mud," "shit," and "pitch." Ultimately, however, we understand that the color of the tar is like the color of the first nameless woman in the European market, and, as such, it is an important part of Jade's heritage from which she is trying to escape. The gaze of the women from the rafters of trees seems to suggest to Jade that, although she is successful by European standards, she has lost track of—even, perhaps, rejected—her African roots.

This rejection seems no more clear than in Jade's first meeting with Son, the descendant of Africans who hides in the home of Jade's benefactor, Valerian Street. Understood as primitive by the wealthy Americans on the island, and even, to an extent, Jadine, Son is the opposite of Jade: Whereas she chooses the city life of Paris or New York, Son values his home in Eloe, Florida; whereas Jade thinks of herself as an enlightened intellectual, Son embraces the communal life of a small southern town.

Son's connection to his past, however, suggests a different kind of success for Jade—one that she is able to entertain briefly by visiting Eloe with Son, but that she ultimately rejects for brighter lights and a bigger city. Son, in an attempt to make things work with Jade, in an attempt to foster the meeting of two different lives and perspectives on success, moves briefly with Jade to New York City, where he observes that black girls in New York City are perpetually unhappy and their husbands and boyfriends do not seem to notice. He thinks the men did not wish to see the "crying girls split into two parts by their tight jeans, screaming at the top of their high, high heels, straining against the pull of their braids and the fluorescent combs holding their hair." Even in New York, together, trying to make their relationship work, Son notices what Jadine does not: that "success" in New York causes women to cry and men to become oblivious; it requires the black girls, in particular, to suffer as they wear such unnatural styles as tight jeans, high heels, and dramatic hair.

In this way, Son appears in the novel as an unlikely doppelgänger for Jade's benefactor, Valerian. A wealthy, white, Philadelphia businessman, Valerian is the only nonplussed resident of L'Arbe de la Croix when Son appears before them, cramped in the closet of Valerian's wife. In fact, rather than turn Son in, Valerian and Son bond over plants struggling to thrive in Valerian's greenhouse. An important symbol for living things struggling to grow outside of their natural element, the plants represent the women both Son and Valerian love—women driven by success in innumerable ways, but who fall far short when it comes to personal happiness. Becoming the wife of Valerian and a mother at a young age, and taking over his impressive mansion in the Caribbean, Margaret is driven to abuse their only son and thus purge herself of his life in adulthood; becoming a successful model and European scholar at a young age, and escaping the visions of women who are trying to call her home, results in an equal sense of loss for Jade—loss not only of a particular kind of success, but also of identity, and, crucially, of the love that might save her.

Aimee Pozorski

MUKHERJEE, BHARATI *The Middleman and Other Stories* (1988)

Bharati Mukherjee offers new ways of examining East-West migration patterns in this complex collection of short stories. These stories unearth invisible spaces, silenced voices, and unknown borders from within the bowels of Western societies in Canada, Latin America, Europe, and largely America.

The reader is introduced to a variety of immigrant characters who have arrived at the homeland at different times. The eponymous middleman is the classic migrant persona of the wandering Jew exiled in a contemporary setting: Latin American guerrilla territory. In this story, Mukherjee's middleman embodies basic principles that guide all of her other migrant characters. Life in a new homeland is based on two things: provisional loyalty and/or the ability to remain consistently useful. Mukherjee's other migrants follow either one or both of these doctrines, which have interesting results, such as fluid identification and cultural patterns as well as the creation of new social and economic networks to facilitate both natives and other migrants.

However, Mukherjee also introduces another significant perspective in this collection: the citizens who have to deal with this influx of migrants through their borders. In this group Mukherjee represents a wide cross section of American society, hinting at its own variety and its older waves of migration. On both sides of the border, the reader discerns a similar range of responses toward others. Xenophobia, denial, grudging acceptance, sympathy, and, finally, integration are evident in both immigrants and citizenry. In this way, the reader is introduced to a more balanced perspective of both groups in diaspora and the text avoids becoming propaganda for either side.

This collection offers a raw, unflinching perspective about immigration, an outlook that is well supported by Mukherjee's clear, precise prose and the short story format. The open-ended nature of these stories attests to the immigrant's life as being in perpetual flux, subject to the whims of larger forces and learning to deal with their judgments. In the end, the reader is left dissatisfied, hungry for more immigrant vignettes and insights into an invisible world that lies just beneath the surface of mainstream society.

Saadiqa Khan

FREEDOM in *The Middleman and Other Stories*

In this collection of short stories, Mukherjee explores freedom from the migrant's perspective. The desire to leave the developing homeland constitutes the first freedom for the migrant. The opportunity of a better life in the developed society often motivates this departure. With money and connections with other successful migrants, Ro, Jasmine, Rosie, Alfred, Mr. Venkatesan, and Blanquita cross borders illegally. Marriage, education, and even adoption provide the legal options for Mrs. Bhave, Panna, Maya, and Eng in Canada and America respectively.

The manner of the migrant's entry determines his relationship with his new society. The illegal immigrant discovers that borders are paradoxically imaginary and real simultaneously. If he is successful, the illegal migrant has to deal with several changes. Because of his status, he is forced to become invisible, which limits his physical freedom and he is dependent on the goodwill of others to protect him. Mr. Venkatesan is instructed on "the most prudent conduct for undocumented transients" that turns out to be imprisonment in Queenie's flat until he can escape. Ro's roommates protest his invisibility over the phone. In the case of Jasmine, Rosie, and

Blanquita, they are often sexually exploited by their "protectors," which they endure in order to survive. The land they live in is " . . . America through the wrong end of the telescope." On the other hand, they believe they have gained freedom from their constricting pasts, a freedom that Mukherjee often reveals as illusory and half-realized. Jasmine leaves her home from "the middle of nowhere" thinking she can pursue her ambitions (which are never identified,) only to end up repeating those stereotypes of the exotic, promiscuous island girl that she disparages. Even when she thinks she has abandoned all the aspects of her old life, she keeps returning to them unconsciously, thus living within a state of ambivalence and uncertainty. What does the illegal gain? It is access to a new culture, new people, new relationships and the perspective of viewing their culture from outside its borders.

The legal immigrants also share this ambiguous freedom. They attempt to shape their futures in their new society. Maya and Panna free themselves from Hindu tradition as they pursue their goals of higher education; they break taboos of caste and religion in their new relationships while Mrs. Bhave is able to discover a new life after widowhood. However, they are never allowed to forget their past. Mrs. Chatterjee subtly informs Maya that her scandalous past is no secret to the Indian community. Panna confronts her own past when her husband visits her in New York and tries to assume his traditional role as her caretaker, only to grudgingly surrender because of his ignorance in the new land. Eng's nightmares of war-torn Vietnam migrate with her to her new home, denying her any chance of a new life. Whether legal or illegal, the migrant finds himself in limbo as he is suspended between two worlds, enjoying a tenuous relationship with both. Very few migrants ever achieve the freedom of the eponymous middleman. Alfred the Jew is a perpetual transient; he has no loyalties to any border or to anyone. He knows how to survive by keeping an emotional distance from his past and by deriving profit from the worst of circumstances.

The legal citizens have a diverse relationship with these new migrants. On one hand, there are xenophobes like Jeb who feels trapped and enraged by the fact that his country is overwhelmed with migrants but fails to realize that, ironically, he too is dependent on them to make a living. He attempts to "regain control" by raping the Indian girl, a throwback to his war days, a clue that he never really left Vietnam. Other characters like Rindy and Jason enter significant relationships with their migrants and learn of the real America that is brutal in its treatment of the Third World and its people. They also learn that the freedoms they enjoy have been created with the blood of such refugees. Other characters like the old migrants offer a mixture of support and exploitation, and this is seen between Jasmine and the Daboos, Ro and Mumtaz, Danny and his girls. Thus the freedom to move between and within borders can bring other losses and gains, which the migrant must be prepared to deal with if he is to survive in his new world.

Saadiqa Khan

SUCCESS in *The Middleman and Other Stories*

Bharati Mukherjee explores the theme of success in her collection of short stories through an examination of her immigrant characters, who attempt to renegotiate their lives in their new homelands. These immigrants belong to two groups that define and achieve success in different ways.

The first group includes immigrants who pursue different ambitions and goals that often involve the reshaping of cultural patterns and codes from the old homeland. Ro, Jasmine, Panna, Maya, and Mrs. Bhave are not afraid to surrender some of their cherished TRADITIONS and assimilate new ones in the quest for more rewarding lives. This cultural exchange challenges accepted patterns of identification as the immigrants demonstrate that there are new ways of being Afghan, Trinidadian, and Indian, respectively. Their attempts at integration, especially through relationships with Americans and other immigrants, also force them to confront stereotypes that seek to define and contain them. Ro, Panna, and Maya maneuver between superficial sympathy and racial insults while breaking sexual and social taboos and pursuing their educational careers. Mrs. Bhave and Jasmine fearlessly assume new roles through their labels of helpless Indian widow and exotic, naïve island girl. The movement from an inferior, backward, Third World victim to being equal to a Western individual is a rite of passage that the immigrants undergo; resilience and the willingness to adapt to new situations are two qualities that ensure success through this process.

In contrast, the other group of immigrants defines success through its manipulation in the host societies. Alfred Judah, Danny, Aunt Lini, Mumtaz, Mr. Chatterji, Eng, Blanquita, Mr. Venkatesan, Queenie, and the Patels are bent on material gain and social security at the expense of other vulnerable migrants and citizens or through the exploitation of the existing social and economic systems. Such immigrants are content to remain entrenched within their cultural norms. Devinder Chatterjee, the Patels, Blanquita, and Eng attempt to recreate the homelands they left behind in their new domestic spaces to the extent that it alienates others who enter the spaces and strains their relationships with others. On the other hand, Danny, Aunt Lini, Alfred, Mumtaz and Queenie, and even the Patels profitably conduct their legal and illegal businesses from their homes, which creates new economic spaces within the host society. Although they are socially isolated, their economic input cannot be ignored. Their economic success also introduces new power relations between their dependent migrant clients and themselves, which were nonexistent in the old homeland and which ignore traditional claims of class and gender on either side of this power binary. Aunt Lini as the female moneylender and brothel owner enjoys a power that would have been impossible back in the homeland, whereas Ro, the son of a wealthy landlord, is forced to do lowly jobs such as plucking chickens in Mumtaz's business to pay rent. The ability to transcend such praxes entails a limited social success.

Yet there is a final group that requires consideration. This is the "fringe citizenry": white Americans such as social misfits, corrupt exiles, and Vietnam veterans, who are considered outsiders in their own land. These outcasts are often intricately linked with both immigrant groups described earlier. Ironically, even though the American outcasts regard the migrants as outsiders, they are frequently dependent on them economically and socially. For Jeb, the Vietnam War never ended; he continues as a thug in Mr. Vee's pay, even though he hates immigrants. He despises the fact that he and his kind have become "coolie labor" in their own country. Maya's first landlord is dependent on her cash but he maintains a deliberate distance until he finds an excuse to evict her. The social and economic failures endured by this group serve as a unique contrast to the immigrant groups and reveal to the reader another face of American society: These people are a far cry from the white picket fence and suburban home. In fact, through this diasporic perspective, the reader is able to discern the emergence of another America: a society undergoing constant transformation through the activities taking place not through its mainstream life but rather on its peripheries and margins. In this society, it is the immigrant rather than the citizenry who enjoys economic and social success, often making more fruitful contributions to the larger society than the legal citizens; this is the invisible America that increasingly demands a voice, one that has been effectively provided through the short stories in this collection.

Saadiqa Khan

SURVIVAL in *The Middleman and Other Stories*

Bharati Mukherjee explores in her collection one of the oldest and most basic concerns in the study of ethnic literature: the business of survival. With the exception of "The Middleman" and "Buried Lives," the stories focus on the challenges of surviving in the new homeland of post-Vietnam America, depicted as an unforgiving and hostile landscape. The characters undertake these challenges in two ways that reflect their perceptions about living within these new borders. For those migrants who are forcibly uprooted from their old homes, the new homeland is viewed as an in-transit destination, and thus the acquisition of opportunities to remain economically viable remains central to their daily existence. For the lucky migrants who can return, being ready and prepared for such a border crossing is essential. In other cases where return remains elusive for the displaced person, provisionality remains the order of the day. For some migrants who voluntarily leave their old homes, life in the new host society goes beyond basic survival as they seek to recreate their lives and pursue goals and ambitions that

were unlikely or impossible in their old homes. Very often Mukherjee juxtaposes these two conflicting attitudes in her stories.

Alfred Judah, the displaced Jew, turns survival into an art form. Whether he is in New Jersey or in guerrilla territory, Alfred knows how to integrate himself into the best social networks and circles from which he can substantially profit. He also learns about the flexibility of borders and loyalties and the importance of being ready to depart at a moment's notice. For Alfred, self-preservation is the order of the day. He serves as an interesting contrast to the other characters, who have also reduced themselves to the business of survival. Mr. Venkatesan and Dr. Chatterji choose to alienate themselves from mainstream society while remaining immersed in memories of the old home, the only vestiges of the past to endure the border crossing. Such characters become the target of Mukherjee's irony as she portrays them greedily benefiting from the same social systems that they willingly berate and despise.

On another level, such characters are presented as foils to the other group of migrants, who approach survival differently. Maya, Panna, Mrs. Bhave, and Roashan free themselves from brutal and shattered pasts to recreate themselves in the American landscape. For them, migration is more than risk or resignation. It is rebirth and opportunity. These migrants brave the scorn of their diasporic communities to pursue spiritual and educational goals that would have been impossible to achieve at home. They manage with some difficulty to maintain a balance between two cultural systems. Even the liberated Maya cannot resist the lure of the Periodicals Room in the library where the foreign newspapers are located. It is in the Indian newspapers that she is confronted with a description of herself as the "new emancipated Indo-American woman." The irony of such a woman seeking LOVE in an Indian personals column emphasizes how strong the bonds of home can be, even for those who have supposedly left for good. When she meets Ashoke Mehta, her days of being a tenant are over; she has made the full circle and returned to her Indian roots once more, albeit in a new homeland.

For those who do not have the security of scholarships, EDUCATION, and family connections, the land of opportunity becomes one of manipulation. Jasmine, Blanquita, and Rosie become trapped in "contracts" that deprive them of economic independence and freedom. They allow themselves to be sexually exploited by their employers and/or lovers because their survival depends on it. They become mistresses, surrogate mothers, and unstable lovers who reinstate their males into traditional roles that had been lost or undermined in this post-Vietnam America. Paradoxically, even as they restore these GENDER power relations, they transform and reconstitute American family structures and relationship patterns.

Thus, survival for Indians abroad is more than a question of economics and finding a place to live. It entails complex psychological negotiations, brutality, and rebirth. It creates possibilities for both self-development and regression. It is a rite of passage for each of Mukherjee's migrant characters that determines his or her trajectory in the new land.

Saadiqa Khan